VISUAL QUICKSTART GUIDE

ACTIONSCRIPT 3.0

Derrick Ypenburg

Peachpit Press

Visual QuickStart Guide

ActionScript 3.0

Derrick Ypenburg

Peachpit Press

1249 Eighth Street
Berkeley, CA 94710
510/524-2178
510/524-2221 (fax)
Find us on the Web at: www.peachpit.com
To report errors, please send a note to errata@peachpit.com

Peachpit is a division of Pearson Education
Copyright © 2009 Derrick Ypenburg

Editor: Jill Marts Lodwig
Project Editor: Nancy Peterson
Technical Editor: Joseph Balderson
Production Coordinator: Becky Winter
Copy Editor: Elizabeth Welch
Compositor: Danielle Foster
Indexer: Valerie Perry
Cover Design: Peachpit

ISBN 13 978-0-321-56425-2
ISBN 10 0-321-56425-1

9 8 7 6 5 4 3 2 1

Printed and bound in the United States of America

Dedication:

For Bethany and Adrian. I'm a lucky man to have the both of you in my life.

Special Thanks to:

Bethany Lee, my beautiful wife who supported and assisted me greatly in getting this book out the door.

My son, who made me play and act like a kid when I needed a break. You're my best bud.

Joseph Balderson, for your encouragement and guidance, and for being a discriminating technical editor and holding me to the highest standards.

Nancy Peterson, for managing the team and making sure the book was completed.

Jill Marts Lodwig, for making my writing actually sound good.

Liz Welch, for her fine attention to detail.

Humber College, The CommunityMX team, and New Toronto Group, for moulding me into the writer, evangelist, and communicator I've become.

Sorenson Media (www.sorensonmedia.com) for use of their sample video.

Matt Halliday, for indulging me with my bad jokes and rants while I wrote at the office.

Carol Lee, my mother-in-law, who was always interested in how the book was coming along (no matter how boring the topic was to her).

The Mill Street Mall Crew, who always were on me to get the book done and gave me their full support.

Alexis on Fire, Alice in Chains, At the Drive-In, Bad Religion, Broken Social Scene, Catherine Wheel, City and Colour, The Cure, Curtis Mayfield, Death From Above 1979, Deftones, Dinosaur Junior, Feist, Filter, Foo Fighters, Interpol, Jeff Buckley, Joseph Arthur, Joy Division, K-OS, Klaxons, The Mars Volta, Moby, Neverending White Lights, New Order, Ours, Pearl Jam, A Perfect Circle, Photek, Portishead, Prodigy, Queens of the Stone Age, Radiohead, Red Hot Chili Peppers, Serj Tankian, The Smiths, Soundgarden, System of a Down, The Tea Party, Thom Yorke, Tool, A Tribe Called Quest, Underworld, The Verve, The White Stripes, Ambient Popsicle online radio, and all other creators of sonic soothing and mood companions that kept me sane, provided background noise that inspired me, and kept me company.

TABLE OF CONTENTS

Foreword   ix

Introduction   xiii

Chapter 1:   **Introduction to ActionScript 3**   **1**

The Language of ActionScript 2

ActionScript Syntax. 4

Punctuation 5

About Classes and Objects 8

Writing ActionScript. 12

Chapter 2:   **Working with Variables and Properties**   **17**

What Is a Variable? 18

Declaring and Assigning Values to Variables. 21

Data Typing Variables. 22

Working with Strings 24

Working with Numbers 27

Data Type Conversions 30

Instances and Properties. 31

About Booleans. 34

Chapter 3:   **Working with Functions and Methods**   **35**

Methods and Functions. 36

Returning Values from a Function 45

Function Scope 48

Chapter 4:   **Working with Classes and Objects**   **51**

Defining Classes and Objects. 52

Importing a Class 54

Instantiating Objects 56

Working with External Code 59

Chapter 5:   **Display Lists and Display Objects**   **63**

The Display List. 65

Display Classes and Objects. 67

Chapter 6:   **Working with Display Objects**   **83**

Display Object Properties 84

Managing Object Depths......................... 91

Removing Display Objects from the
    Display List 94

Chapter 7:   **Communication and Events**   **95**

The ActionScript 3 Event Model................. 96

Working with Event Listeners.................. 100

Event Flow 107

Subclasses of the Event Class.................. 110

Chapter 8:   **Controlling the Timeline**   **111**

Controlling Timelines.......................... 112

Navigating Timelines with Target Paths 119

Declaring the Frame Rate at Runtime 123

Chapter 9:   **Working with Strings**   **125**

The String Class................................ 126

Combining Strings............................. 128

Manipulating Strings 131

Chapter 10:   **Working with Text Fields**   **135**

Working with Text Fields....................... 136

Formatting Text Fields 142

Embedding Fonts.............................. 148

Chapter 11:   **Working with the Math and Date Classes**   **151**

The Math Class 152

The Date Class................................. 158

Time Zones and UTC Time 164

Chapter 12:   **Working with Data Using Arrays and Objects**   **165**

Working with the Array Class 166

Manipulating Arrays 170

The Object Class and Associative Arrays........ 175

Chapter 13:   **Creating Conditional Statements**   **179**

Conditional Statements........................ 180

Checking for Conditions Using the
    Switch Statement 188

Chapter 14: **Iteration and Repetition** **189**

The for Loop Statement........................190

Building a Dynamic Menu Using an
    Associative Array.........................192

Iterating Object Properties 197

The while and do...while Loop Statements......200

Chapter 15: **HTTP Requests and External Communications** **203**

URL Navigation with HTTP Requests 204

Loading External Text Content................208

Error Handling...............................216

Chapter 16: **Loading External Assets** **221**

Using the Loader Class to Load
    External Data 222

Monitoring Load Progress.....................227

Controlling Externally Loaded SWFs 230

Chapter 17: **Using Shapes, Masks, Blends, and Filters** **233**

The Shape Class 234

Applying Dynamic Masking to Objects 238

Creating Visual Effects with ActionScript.......242

Chapter 18: **Dynamic Animation** **247**

The Timer Class 248

The ENTER_FRAME Event.....................253

The Tween and Easing Classes 255

Transitions 262

Caching Display Objects 264

Chapter 19: **Working with Sound** **265**

Working with Embedded Sound................266

Controlling Playback with SoundChannel 269

Loading External Sounds 270

Monitoring Loading with Sound Events 272

Using ID3 Data in MP3 Files....................275

Controlling a Sound's Volume 276

Monitoring Playback Progress..................278

Chapter 20: **Working with Video** **283**

Using the FLVPlayback Component............284

FLVPlayback Events 290

Advanced Video Applications..................301

Index **303**

FOREWORD

It can be easy to feel overwhelmed by the range of options and possibilities that Adobe Flash ActionScript 3.0 presents to developers. Where to start? What can Flash and ActionScript do? How has the technology changed? All of these questions are answered in this book, through the step by step exercises and the insightful writings of the Derrick Ypenburg.

Flash has in recent years become a term to describe a whole ecosystem of technologies with vast capabilities. But how did Adobe Flash ActionScript become the programming powerhouse of today? Like most Internet-based technologies, Flash came from humble beginnings just over a decade ago, primarily as a quirky alternative to GIF animations.

Flash acquired its first noteworthy programming capabilities with Macromedia Flash 4 at the end of the 1990s, which was a step up from Flash 3, which had only a handful of "commands." The Flash 4 language was perhaps too simple to call a scripting language. But designers and animators still managed to use it to push the boundaries of this technology, creating interactive animations never before seen on the Internet, simulating mature programming constructs, and even hacking their way into putting video on the timeline before Flash had video publishing capabilities. Countless creative people in the print and Web industries—artists, graphic designers, Web developers—became intrigued with the exciting, creative capabilities of this technology, and made the switch to Flash.

In its next evolution, Flash acquired a true prototype-based scripting language, loosely based on the same ECMAScript specification as JavaScript, with the launch of Flash 5 in 2000. ActionScript 1.0 was born. Flash's scripting language employed the concepts of object-oriented programming: almost everything could be described in dot syntax. The MovieClip in its current incarnation was also born. The Flash Player, and by extension its programming language, gained a boatload of new capabilities. Flash could now outperform JavaScript in many respects. One of the most impressive results of this first version of ActionScript was the ability to programmatically control and animate graphical assets and sound to create dynamic, interactive animations. This may be old hat to some Flash creatives, but in its day this was nothing short of a revolution. Pioneers in the field created incredible-looking (and sounding) animations. Publishers began producing books showcasing Flash's new "Technicolor interactivity."

But it wasn't until the introduction of Flash MX and Flash Player 6 in 2002 that the technology really began to take off. ActionScript as a language stayed pretty much the same, but the capabilities of the Flash Player received two major facelifts. First, what is known as the Drawing API was born, enabling Flash designers to create vector graphics completely with code without any imported assets of any kind. This kicked Flash's creative capabilities into high gear and liberated designers and programmers from the limitations of Flash 5's fixed asset–based programming to the delight and amazement of "Flashers" everywhere.

At that time, Macromedia also acquired the Sorenson Spark video codec, and the beginnings of the Flash video revolution began. The Flash Player could now record video through a Webcam, stream it to a dedicated video server called the Flash Media Server (FMS), and play back that video in real time. The FLV video format was also created, which has since become the de facto standard for Internet video. FMS also opened up chat application capabilities and Server-Side ActionScript (SSAS), further pushing the boundaries of what is possible in Flash. YouTube would later launch in 2005, and because it made Flash the focus of its delivery platform, it ushered in the Flash Video revolution.

All of this new capability in the Flash Player necessitated an increased emphasis on larger and more complex applications in ActionScript. This demand set the stage for the next version of the Flash language. ActionScript 2.0 came about in 2004 with the advent of the Flash MX 2004 authoring environment and Flash Player 7. Now Flash creators had a tool to focus on building complex applications, where code could be externalized in ActionScript class files in a much more object-oriented fashion, opening the door for third-party ActionScript code editing tools.

Macromedia also released Flex 1.5, a component-based enterprise development environment that relied on component-based, server-compiled ActionScript code edited in Flex Builder. Although this development of the technology was still in its early days, for the first time in Flash history you didn't necessarily need the Flash authoring application to create a SWF file. So to say that the progression of ActionScript has paralleled, even pushed the evolution of Flash, is an understatement.

Flash 8, released in 2005, was a unique development in a few ways. The Flash Player, and ActionScript, added dynamic bitmap rendering and Adobe Photoshop-like filters. This propelled the creative aspects of the technology once again.

The next version of the Flash programming language, ActionScript 3.0, and in its cousin Flash Player 9, arrived in 2006 like a searing lightning bolt from the heavens. The changes in this new version swept away all contenders vying to be *the* Web 2.0 Rich Internet Applications platform of the new millennium. This new version of the language, formerly created by Macromedia, and now Adobe, is so powerful that engineers needed to split the Flash Player into two separate "runtimes" to give this new language the power it truly deserved. ActionScript 3.0 is now a full compiler-based, object-oriented language capable of holding its own with the likes of C++ and Java—no small achievement. Tools and technologies such as Flex and AIR have extended ActionScript's reach into Web and desktop-enabled "Web 2.0" Rich Internet Applications.

And ActionScript 3's capabilities in the new Flash runtime now enable calculations up to 100 times faster than what was possible in ActionScript 2, facilitating the Holy Grail of Flash interactivity: real-time 3D animation, courtesy of third-party libraries such as Papervision3D.

In recalling the early days of Flash, and of ActionScript, as a graphic designer at the time, the first book I used to teach myself Flash was the *Flash 4 for Windows and Macintosh: Visual QuickStart Guide*. Through the years I eagerly followed this series, and now, as an ActionScript programmer, it is my great honor to contribute to Derrick Ypenburg's book on ActionScript 3.

Joseph Balderson
Technical Editor
Flash Platform Developer
www.joeflash.ca

INTRODUCTION

Welcome to *ActionScript 3 Visual QuickStart Guide*. The pages that follow introduce various ActionScript 3 concepts that will guide you in developing for Flash CS3. After you've finished reading this book, your knowledge of ActionScript will help you create rich applications for the Flash platform.

ActionScript is an exciting scripting language for creating applications for the Web, desktop, and personal devices. It's unique compared to many languages in that it is not strictly a data exchange language. It is capable of generating interactive, rich media–driven applications, complete with design, animations, sound, and video.

ActionScript 3 is a full-fledged object-oriented programming language. Compared to the previous version, it offers improved event handling, a new display list, and a drawing API. In addition, overall performance has drastically increased, making the latest version definitely worth a try.

Is ActionScript 3 for you?

If you're reading this right now, you are obviously interested in learning ActionScript 3 or updating your ActionScript 2 skill set. This book is for those who have a basic skill level in Flash and want to learn how to create ActionScript-driven Flash applications, or for Flash designers who want to take their applications to the next level.

ActionScript 3 is the latest incarnation of the Flash platform's scripting language. If you have no previous ActionScript coding experience, now is a perfect time to learn ActionScript. Version 3 is easier to learn than previous versions of the language.

If you are a designer or developer who uses Flash, you may be one of the many who are responding to the notion of ActionScript 3 with some trepidation. That's because to make the leap from ActionScript 2 to ActionScript 3 in some respects requires learning the language all over again. But the endeavor is well worth the effort for several reasons.

First, in addition to its more significant improvements—object-oriented programming, better event handling, and optimized performance—other improvements in ActionScript 3, such as the new, single event model, actually make learning or relearning the language easier than learning ActionScript 2 from scratch.

Another benefit is that version 3 broadens the program's horizons—it isn't just for programming in Flash anymore. You can now use ActionScript 3 in a variety of tools for the Flash platform, including Flash CS3, Flex 2 and 3, and Adobe AIR.

Finally, keep in mind that working with the timeline and sticking with basic ActionScript commands has its limitations. Interfaces, menus, and interactivity often come up short when it comes to enhanced user interactivity and updating. The only way to make an intelligent, dynamic, easy-to-update application is to learn ActionScript.

If you do choose to go with ActionScript 3, you'll find that as you enter into a more advanced level of ActionScript programming, your ActionScript 2 skills will transfer over naturally, making the time you invest in learning well worth it.

What's in this book?

Because ActionScript 3 is a vast improvement over ActionScript 2, I have decided to teach it to you from the ground up. If you have experience in ActionScript 2, the fundamentals in this book should be a good refresher as you learn the structure and logic behind this latest language version.

This book guides you through the core programming concepts you need to get up-to-speed with ActionScript programming. Some of those concepts include the following:

- ◆ **Introduction to ActionScript 3.** Everything ActionScript, including the language syntax and how to write using it, as well as working with variables, methods and functions, and classes and objects.

- ◆ **Display objects.** Working with display objects such as MovieClips, text fields, buttons, and so on. Display objects can be added to an application and controlled entirely using ActionScript.

continues on next page

◆ **Creating interactivity.** Working with the event model to create communications throughout an entire application, including mouse events, timed events, and so on. Navigating the timeline is also covered.

◆ **Working with information and data structure.** Storing, retrieving, and manipulating data and objects using variables, arrays, and objects.

◆ **Looping and decision making.** Using the different types of looping and logical repetition to create intelligence and decision making in an application.

◆ **Loading external assets and information.** Loading external images and SWF files and controlling and manipulating them. Loading external text and HTML/CSS content and working with math is also covered.

◆ **Programmatic visualizations.** Drawing shapes with ActionScript and manipulating images with programmatic filters and blend modes. Programmatic animation is also explored.

◆ **Sound and video.** Loading and playing back internal and external sound and videos. Creating playback mechanisms for video.

I explain all of these concepts first, and then I combine them with complementary concepts to demonstrate more advanced applications. These demonstrations are illustrated with step-by-step, hands-on tasks that you can use to build your skills. By the end of this book, you should confidently be able to merge the concepts into rich media applications for the Flash platform.

Resources

The companion Web site for this book provides downloads of all the source files used in the step-by-step tasks presented in this book. Updates and embellishments to the book will also be posted on the companion Web site:

www.focusonmedia.com/vqs/as3

There are also many valuable resources on the Web. Flash has more online resources dedicated to the software than any other rich media application that I've worked with. The following Web sites can get you started with learning more about Flash and help you grow into a more advanced developer:

◆ **Abobe Labs (http://labs.adobe.com/).** Get the latest updates and developments for ActionScript and the Flash platform (among other Adobe software developments).

◆ **Adobe Flash Product Page (www.adobe.com/products/flash/).** Trial downloads, updates, and announcements for Flash CS3

◆ **CommunityMX (www.communitymx. com).** An online resource full of articles and tutorials for Adobe products, Web development and Flash, Flex and ActionScript, written by industry experts.

In addition, you can search the Web for Flash and ActionScript to find a world of online resources, communities, and showcase sites for everything Flash and ActionScript.

INTRODUCTION

What's next?

Covering all of the concepts of the ActionScript API would fill at least four Visual QuickStart Guides, and possibly more. After you learn the concepts presented in this book, the best way to become an expert is to experiment! Flash and ActionScript development skills and the ability to learn new techniques come only with practice.

Of course, all of your projects may not be ideal projects for hashing out ideas you may want to try. But practicing and growing through a series of experimental projects when you can will beef up your portfolio as well as your experience and knowledge. And when you find that you feel comfortable with a concept, expand on it.

In addition, get in the habit of reading about ActionScript and the Flash platform as much as you can. Attend one of the many fine Flash conferences around the world. And join ActionScript and Flash user groups.

Happy reading!

Introduction to ActionScript 3

The key word for interactive applications for the Flash platform is "experience." The ability to add sound, video, animation, and a "touch-and-feel" experience are powerful tools for creating a rich Internet experience. Programming with ActionScript takes your application beyond simple animated logos and "Click here to skip intro or play movie" applications. Users expect a lot more out of a Flash application nowadays; they expect a full-on interactive experience. ActionScript is the tool that will help you accomplish this.

ActionScript is the programming language understood by the Flash platform. Much like traveling around the world, each country or region you visit has a native language or dialect that is understood locally. You speak the language of ActionScript when you travel through the "Nations of Flash" (Flash Player, Flash Lite, Adobe AIR, Tamarin) in order to be understood.

In this chapter, you will be introduced to ActionScript and learn what object-oriented programming is. How and where ActionScript is written will also be covered, including topics such as working in the Actions panel, customizing the ActionScript environment, testing your code, and leaving notes to describe what your code is doing in a script.

At the end of this chapter, you should be ready to start writing your own code.

The Language of ActionScript

Before we explore learning how to "speak" (or program with) ActionScript, you need to learn the basic structure, format, and aspects of the language. The terms that follow will be referenced throughout this chapter.

Classes and objects

ActionScript 3 is based on the principle of object-oriented programming (OOP).

Objects

OOP revolves around visual and programmatic objects that all have a particular job to perform in the grand scheme of an application. Let's consider an analogy of objects in ActionScript: a construction site. The site is busy with cranes, bulldozers, cement trucks, dump trucks, blueprints, and construction workers. They are all individual objects with specific jobs to do to help achieve the overall goal of constructing a building. Some objects do the heavy lifting and can be seen doing the work on the site, such as operating a crane or bulldozer. Other objects, such as blueprints, are behind the scenes, storing and serving up information that is needed for other objects to perform their jobs to a certain specification.

Classes

A class is the DNA makeup of an object. Classes are ActionScript files that contain instructions for how objects are built, what their function is, what they look like, and how they communicate. Without a class to define an object, objects would be lifeless, nondescript entities floating around without a purpose.

Throughout this book, we will use classes to define the objects we create, and those objects will do specific jobs in the grand scheme of our application development.

Elements of a class that define an object are:

◆ **Properties**—Properties define visible attributes and functional descriptions of an object. For example, a MovieClip is 200 pixels wide and 300 pixels high. You can click the MovieClip with the mouse.

◆ **Methods**—Methods are tasks that an object can perform. By calling the method of an object, you are asking the object to do something. Methods are the equivalent of verbs in ActionScript. For example, a MovieClip can play and stop its time-line. Methods of objects can be private or public. Public methods can be called from outside the class (you can call these methods to control the object). Private methods are used inside the class for its own functional purposes. These methods cannot be called from outside the class.

◆ **Events**—Interactivity and communication in Flash is entirely event based. Events occur when something happens. To listen for, and respond to events, a listener is set up to listen for events that are dispatched from an object. When an event is dispatched and "heard" by a listener function, code within the function is executed in response to the event. Events are dispatched and handled in many ways in ActionScript—for example, a button has been clicked, a certain amount of time has passed, or a value has changed.

Classes, objects, properties, methods, and events will all be extensively covered throughout the rest of the book. You will become more familiar with these terms as we move through the rest of this chapter.

ActionScript Syntax

Every programming language has its own *syntax*. With spoken language, there are rules for grammar and structure that make a language understood by all. Languages work with nouns, verbs, conjunctions, and punctuation, stringing words together into logical messages. This is no different in ActionScript. The ActionScript syntax does, however, string messages together differently and uses punctuation for different purposes than our spoken languages.

Dot syntax

ActionScript statements are structured using the convention of *dot syntax*. The *dots* in dot syntax are the conjunctions that put objects, properties, and methods together into logical ActionScript statements. To set or get the appearance and/or behavior of an object, begin the statement with the name of the object, and then follow the name with its methods or properties, all separated by dots.

The following code sets the `type` and `color` properties of an object called `Truck` and tells it to `start`:

```
Truck.manufacturer = "Mack";

Truck.color = "yellow";

Truck.start();
```

Here's the plain language equivalent of the preceding code:

◆ The `manufacturer` of the Truck is `Mack` (property).

◆ The `color` of the Truck is `yellow` (property).

◆ `start` the Truck (method).

Punctuation

Punctuation plays a big role in the syntax of ActionScript. Although used differently compared to the rules of spoken language, punctuation in ActionScript helps structure messages into understandable and individual statements.

As you've already learned, *dots* (periods) are the conjunctions of the ActionScript language. Let's look at other common usages of punctuation.

Semicolon

The semicolon is used to terminate an ActionScript statement. It is the ActionScript equivalent of a period ending a sentence:

```
Truck.start();
```

```
Truck.drive();
```

This code (in order from top to bottom) starts the truck and then tells it to drive. Each line is a unique statement as specified by terminating each statement with a semicolon.

✔ Tip

■ Although ActionScript sometimes allows you without mishap to get away with not using the semicolon to terminate a statement, it is good practice to do so for visual reference as well as to avoid situations where the Flash platform may be picky when it encounters an instance where a semicolon was needed.

PUNCTUATION

Parentheses

Parentheses can be used for several purposes in ActionScript. One common use is to specify the order of *mathematical operations*. With math operations, the order of operations performed affects the outcome of the equation.

For example, the expression

$1 + (2 * 3)$

equals 7 as the 2 * 3 in the parentheses is multiplied first and then 1 is added to the product.

The following formula would produce 9:

$(1 + 2) * 3$

1 and 2 are added first and then the sum (3) is multiplied by 3.

Another common use of parentheses is to *pass values to methods*.

An example of passing information (a parameter) to a method within the parentheses would be:

```
Truck.accelerate(50);
```

If the `accelerate` method was programmed to accept speed values, the above method would accelerate the `Truck` to 50 Km/hr.

We will get into more detail with methods in Chapter 3.

✔ Tip

- Even if a method doesn't require that a parameter be passed to it, it must still include parentheses: `truck.stop();`

Curly braces

Curly braces group multiple statements and commands into blocks. When the block is triggered, all the statements and commands in the block are executed:

```
function driveTruck():void {

    Truck.start();

    Truck.drive();

    Truck.accelerate(50);

}
```

The start, drive, and accelerate statements are grouped together inside the curly braces of the driveTruck function. These statements will only execute when the driveTruck function is called.

Commas

Most commonly, commas are used to separate multiple parameters that are passed to a method:

```
addNumbers(5, 3);
```

Commas are also used to separate values in an array and properties of generic objects (we will cover this topic in a later chapter).

About Classes and Objects

In object-oriented programming, classes and objects are the basis of all functionality. Objects on their own, however, are useless unless they are defined by a class. A class is the "blueprint" for an object's behavior, functionality, and characteristics.

Think of a real-life object such as a crane. Before you construct a crane, you need a blueprint. The blueprint describes:

◆ How the crane is constructed

◆ How it looks and appears (properties)

◆ What it's capable of doing and how to control it (methods)

◆ How it responds (events)

In the context of ActionScript, a class is the equivalent of a blueprint. A class defines how an object is constructed (how it is introduced to the application); an object's properties; an object's methods; and how an object communicates (its events).

Classes are not stored in the Flash document itself, but in separate ActionScript files that live in the Flash installation folder. They are imported into a script either automatically when a movie is compiled or by using an import directive in your code. This need varies from class to class, and I will make it clear when an import statement is needed throughout this book.

You can also create your own classes, as well as extending built-in classes that are already part of Flash API (Flash class library). This is a more advanced topic, however, and is not within the scope of this book.

What is an object?

An object is a copy of a class either in code or physically on the stage, or an *instance* of a class. If you construct more than one object

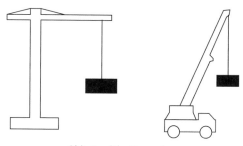

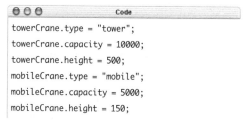

Objects of the Crane class

Tower Crane
type: tower
capacity: 10000 lbs
height: 500 ft.

Mobile Crane
type: mobile
capacity: 5000 lbs
height: 150 ft.

Figure 1.1 Two object instances of the Crane class with different properties.

Code 1.1 Setting the properties for towerCrane and mobileCrane.

```
● ● ●                    Code
towerCrane.type = "tower";
towerCrane.capacity = 10000;
towerCrane.height = 500;
mobileCrane.type = "mobile";
mobileCrane.capacity = 5000;
mobileCrane.height = 150;
```

of a class, you have multiple *instances* of a class. Multiple objects of a single class can run autonomously from one another. Once an object of a class is instantiated (*instantiate* means to copy or create an instance of), you can set its properties, call its methods, and listen and respond to its events.

Objects appear everywhere in everyday life. Let's take a look at the crane analogy again. All the cranes on the site have a specific job in common: lifting and moving heavy items. There are different types of cranes on the site: tower cranes and mobile cranes are two examples. What makes these two cranes different from each other, though?

Think about all cranes at their core being defined by a master Crane class. The Crane class defines that all objects of the Crane class can raise and lower items and can turn either to the left or to the right. All types of cranes differ beyond those basic similarities (**Figure 1.1**). These differences would be reflected in their properties.

To add the two cranes from Figure 1.1 to an application with ActionScript, the constructor method of the Crane class is used:

```
var mobileCrane:Crane = new Crane();
```

```
var towerCrane:Crane = new Crane();
```

Next specify the behavior of each each Crane object. This can be done by setting each object's instance properties (**Code 1.1**).

There also has to be a way to tell each Crane what to do. Real cranes have different controls to operate them. The ActionScript equivalent is to call methods of the Crane class to operate a Crane object instance:

```
towerCrane.lift();
```

```
mobileCrane.lower();
```

Finally, we need a way to listen for feedback from the Crane and act upon it. To do this, we'll define an event listener to "listen" for the Crane object's events. An eventListener function is registered to listen for an event that is dispatched by the Crane object (**Code 1.2**).

The first two lines of code register an event listener with the Crane objects to "listen" for when their LIFT_FINISHED and LIFT_LOWERED events are dispatched. The event listener functions will be called when the event is dispatched from the crane object, and "heard" by the listeners.

Objects are everywhere in Flash. MovieClips and Buttons on the stage are objects. They are defined by their own MovieClip and SimpleButton classes, respectively. They can be instantiated just by dragging them from the library to the stage instead of using ActionScript. Setting MovieClips' or Buttons' properties using the Properties panel is not much different than setting an object's properties with ActionScript, except that the Properties panel lets you define an object's properties at authortime, and using ActionScript defines an object's properties at runtime and can be changed on the fly.

Instantiating an object of the MovieClip class

To construct a MovieClip object using ActionScript, write the following code:

```
var myMC:MovieClip = new MovieClip();
```

To set the object's x and y properties (its position on the stage) add the following:

```
myMC.x = 100;
```

```
myMc.y = 100;
```

Code 1.2 Registering an event listener to listen for events of the Crane object.

```
towerCrane.addEventListener
  (CraneEvent.LIFT_FINISHED,
  eventListener);
mobileCrane.addEventListener
  (CraneEvent.LOWER_FINISHED,
  eventListener);
funtion eventListener
  (evt:CraneEvent):void {
  // execute code here in response
  to event
}
```

Authortime vs. Runtime

Throughout this book, I refer to the terms *authortime* and *runtime*. The term *authortime* is used to describe something that happens while you are working in the FLA file, such as dragging a MovieClip from the library to the stage and applying a DropShadow filter to it from the Properties panel. The drop shadow is applied and viewable at authortime. The term *runtime*, on the other hand, is involved in a different process. For instance, if you apply a DropShadow to the same MovieClip with ActionScript, you can only see the results of Action-Script when a movie is previewed, or at runtime. Another term you will come across is *compiletime*. When a Flash movie is previewed or published, it is compiled. When a movie is compiled, errors and warnings can occur. They will be referred to as compiletime errors or warnings.

After a MovieClip (or any visible object for that matter) has been constructed and its properties have been set, it needs to be added to the display of the movie (it is not visible yet). This is done using the `addChild()` method:

```
addChild(myMC);
```

Calling one of the `MovieClip` class methods such as the `gotoAndStop()` method (go to a particular frame and stop) looks like this:

```
myMC.gotoAndStop(5);
```

Listening for one of the many events dispatched from the `MovieClip` class looks like this:

```
myMC.addEventListener(Event.ENTER_FRAME,
eventHandlerFunction);
```

No doubt at this point you are beginning to grasp the concepts of classes and objects (see **Figure 1.2**). The explanations you have just read are just scratching the surface of all the classes and objects that you will use in ActionScript. As this book progresses, you will gain an even clearer understanding of ActionScript and its OOP structure.

ABOUT CLASSES AND OBJECTS

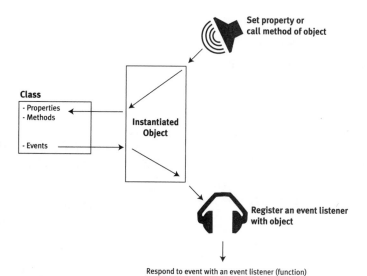

Figure 1.2 You can call an object to set its properties; call its methods; and listen to an object for its events and respond accordingly.

Writing ActionScript

In Flash CS3, you use the Actions panel to write and edit ActionScript (**Figure 1.3**).

The Actions panel consists of three panes for working with ActionScript:

◆ **Actions toolbox**—Lets you access a list of available ActionScript classes, objects, events, methods, and properties categorically and/or alphabetically.

◆ **Script Navigator**—Allows you to navigate to different scripts throughout a Flash file.

◆ **Script pane**—Lets you write and edit ActionScript. This is where you earn your money!

You can also determine how the script is displayed in the panel by choosing items from the Actions panel menu. Displaying line numbers (to help make finding code easier), using word wrapping (returning a long line of code to the next line to display long lines of code without horizontally scrolling), and printing are all tasks that can be done using the Actions panel menu.

To open and set up the Actions panel:

1. With Flash open, create a new Flash file.

2. Select the first keyframe on Layer 1 (the only layer and keyframe in the new file).

3. Open the Actions panel (F9 or Windows > Actions).

4. Click the down-pointing triangle in the upper-right corner of the Actions panel to open the panel menu (**Figure 1.4**).

Actions toolbox   *Script pane*

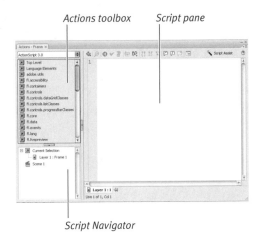

Script Navigator

Figure 1.3 The Actions panel.

Figure 1.4 Actions panel menu.

Writing Your Own Code from This Book

The Actions toolbox is a great reference and can help you add code to the Script pane, especially if you forget the exact syntax for a bit of code. In this book, however, we will not be using it. The focus of this book is learning to write ActionScript ourselves instead of having Flash do it for us.

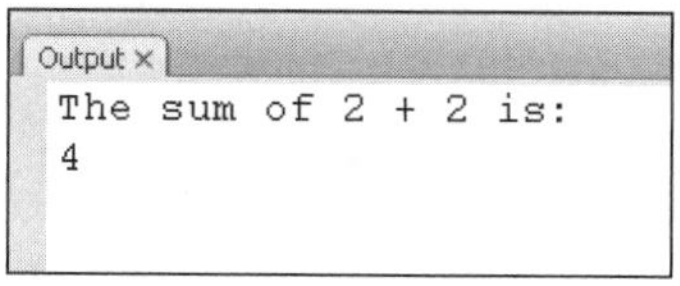

Figure 1.5 The Output panel can display values from the `trace()` statement.

5. To display line numbers in the Script pane, ensure Line Numbers is checked.

6. To wrap lines of ActionScript, ensure Word Wrap is checked.

7. To print a script, choose Print.

8. To close the Actions panel, press F9 or choose Window > Actions.

Using the trace() statement

The `trace()` statement will become your best friend in ActionScript development. Much of the ActionScript functionality you will create does not have a visual result on the stage, so it can be difficult to tell if your ActionScript is doing its job properly in the background. The `trace()` statement displays the results of your ActionScript as messages in the Output panel at runtime. The Output panel is also used to display loading errors and other non-ActionScript errors at runtime. You can also use the `trace()` statement to alert you when a task has begun and when it has completed.

To trace a value to the Output panel:

1. Create a new Flash file.

2. Select the first keyframe on Layer 1 and launch the Actions panel (F9).

3. Add the following ActionScript:
   ```
   trace("The sum of 2 + 2 is:");
   trace(2 + 2);
   ```

4. Press Ctrl+Enter (Win) or Cmd+Enter (Mac) to preview the results of your script.

5. The results of the script will be displayed in the Output panel (**Figure 1.5**).

We will be using the `trace()` statement extensively in the examples throughout this book.

Using comments

Commenting code is like leaving a trail of breadcrumbs so you can find your way back out of a dark cave.

You can add comments to a script to describe the particular functionality of a block of code, explain a problematic section of code, indicate where to start and end if editing the code at future dates, and so on. Because ActionScript does not exactly read like a book of instructions with straightforward wording and points, you need to leave comments to help yourself, and others, navigate and understand your code. If someone had a patent on the syntax for comments, they would be as wealthy as the inventor of Post-it™ notes!

There are two ways of commenting in ActionScript:

- **Single line**—Inserting two forward slashes (//) before a bit of code, will comment out the code for the rest of that line (but that line only).

- **Multiline**—Inserting a forward slash followed by an asterisk (/*) at the start of a block of code, and terminated by an asterisk and a forward slash (*/) at the end of the block of code, will comment out an entire block of code.

Code 1.3 This code contains two trace statements. The one that is commented out will produce no results in the Output panel.

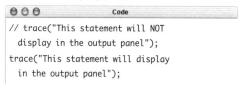

```
// trace("This statement will NOT
   display in the output panel");
trace("This statement will display
   in the output panel");
```

Code 1.4 The entire code will not execute or display as it is wrapped in a multiline comment block.

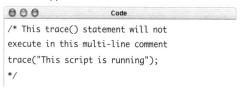

```
/* This trace() statement will not
execute in this multi-line comment
trace("This script is running");
*/
```

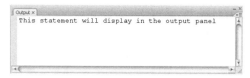

Figure 1.6 The Output panel displays the results of running the script.

To add comments to your script:

1. Do one of the following:
   - ▲ To add a single-line comment, begin the line with two forward slashes (//) (**Code 1.3**).
   - ▲ To add a multiline comment, type a forward slash and an asterisk (/*) at the start of the comment, then type an asterisk and forward slash (*/) at the end of the comment (**Code 1.4**).

2. Choose Control > Test Movie to preview the movie (Ctrl+Enter/Cmd+Enter).

3. The Output panel shows the results of running the script (**Figure 1.6**).

✔ Tip

- ■ Using a multiline comment is also useful for commenting out code that you may want to use later without having to delete it from the script.

WRITING ACTIONSCRIPT

Setting ActionScript preferences

Everybody has different preferences when it comes to reading and writing code. Programmers indent blocks of code, shrink or enlarge code font sizes, and customize code elements with unique colors. Why? This makes code easier to read and identify. Think about looking at tens or hundreds of lines of code and having to identify what blocks of code are and what they do. Setting ActionScript preferences helps you achieve a comfortable coding environment to work in.

To set ActionScript preferences:

1. Open the Actions panel and choose Preferences from the Actions panel menu (Ctrl+U/Cmd+U). The Flash Preferences dialog box opens, showing the ActionScript pane (**Figure 1.7**).

2. Do any of the following:

   ▲ To have nested commands indented automatically, select Automatic Indentation. Enter the number of spaces you want the code to be indented in the Tab Size field.

   ▲ Flash can show code hints when it recognizes code being typed. Use the Delay Slider to set how fast (if at all) code hinting appears.

   ▲ To apply different colors to different types of syntax in your code, select Syntax Colors: Code Coloring. To customize code coloring, choose colors from the individual menus next to each code component.

3. Click OK when done to dismiss the dialog box and save your preferences.

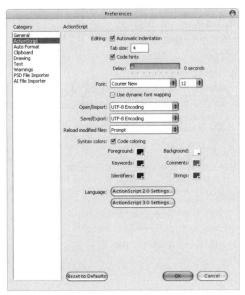

Figure 1.7 Open the ActionScript Preferences panel to set your own preferences for displaying and working with ActionScript.

WORKING WITH VARIABLES AND PROPERTIES

2

Variables and properties are the foundation of all Flash applications. Without *variables* (buckets of data), nothing can have a value or property (a property is a data bucket specifically associated with a class). Object instances could not exist, since instances of objects are referenced by variables. Objects also would not have properties to define them. Without instances and variables, properties would have no meaning or just simply not exist. In other words, ActionScript would be a useless language.

This chapter defines what variables are and how to work with them. Working with variables involves working with text and numbers and manipulating them and performing math operations.

This chapter also discusses object instances of classes and explains how to add them to ActionScript. After an object is created with ActionScript, its properties can be set. All variables and objects in ActionScript have their own distinct data types as well.

Finally, this chapter shows you how to define the data type of variables and objects. When you have finished, you should find that you're comfortable with variables, properties, and object instances and their data types.

What Is a Variable?

A variable is a "container" for storing data. Variables store information such as numbers, text, or references to an object or another variable (**Figure 2.1**). In order to work with any type of data or object instance in ActionScript, the information is stored in, or referenced by, a variable. Every object or piece of information in ActionScript is a variable at its core.

Naming variables

To make variables unique, they must be assigned unique names when they are created. Without unique names, it would be impossible to retrieve information from a particular variable.

ActionScript is very considerate and addresses objects and variables only by their proper, unique names. Think about working on a construction site where everyone's name is Joe. You want to ask Joe the crane operator a question. When you call out "Hey Joe!" everyone turns around to see what you want. Worse yet, what if no one had names at all? Not being able to call out unique names for individuals makes it impossible to communicate. A variable's name is also referred to as its *identifier*.

When naming variables, ActionScript only permits the use of letters and numbers (however, variables cannot *begin* with a number). No spaces or special characters are allowed, with the exception of underscores (_) and dollar signs ($). Not adhering to these rules of naming will result in errors in your code and broken variable references.

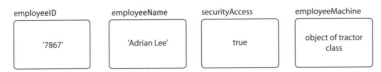

Figure 2.1 Variables are containers for storing information and instances of objects.

The following variable names are acceptable:

◆ `employee`

◆ `employee01`

◆ `_employee`

◆ `$employee`

The following variable names are *not* acceptable:

◆ `1employee`

◆ `employee 01`

◆ `#employee`

◆ `employee.name`

Naming conventions

Having a standard naming convention and descriptive names for variables is very important. It is common for many programmers to begin constructing a variable name by assigning it a general name, followed by a description of what the variable does or stores:

◆ `employeeID`

◆ `employeeName`

◆ `employeeTitle`

The above variable names also follow another common naming convention. The descriptive variable name starts with a lowercase letter and then each subsequent descriptive word starts with an uppercase letter.

Another common naming convention is to use underscores to string descriptive words together:

◆ `employee_id`

◆ `employee_name`

◆ `employee_title`

When naming instances of objects, a common convention (and a convention that will be used in this book) is to begin the variable (or instance) name with an abbreviation of the class to which the object belongs, followed by a description or name for the object:

◆ `mcMovieExample` (in which `mc` represents an instance of the MovieClip class)

◆ `btnButtonExample` (in which `btn` represents an instance of a button)

◆ `tfTextTitle` (in which `tf` represents an instance of `TextField`)

Working with a common convention not only makes it easy for you to set up a system of writing and recognizing variables, but also makes it easy for other developers to work with your code once they understand the naming patterns in your code.

Figure 2.2 The variable values `Adrian Lee` and `40` should be displayed in the Output panel.

Code 2.1 Changing a variable's value after it has been initially set.

```
Code
var employeeName = "Adrian Lee";
var employeeHours = 40;
trace(employeeName); //Adrian Lee
trace(employeeHours); //40
employeeHours = 60;
trace(employeeHours); //60
```

Figure 2.3 The value of a variable can be changed at any time after it has been declared.

Declaring and Assigning Values to Variables

To create a new variable, or *declare* a variable, begin with the `var` keyword, followed by the name of the variable:

```
var nameOfVariable
```

To assign a variable a value, the equals symbol (=) is used after the variable name, followed by the value for the variable:

```
var employeeName = "Adrian Lee";
var employeeHours = 40;
var securityStatus = true;
```

To declare a variable, and assign and display its value:

1. To declare variables and assign them values, add the following ActionScript to the Actions panel:
   ```
   var employeeName = "Adrian Lee";
   var employeeHours = 40;
   trace(employeeName);
   trace(employeeHours);
   ```

2. To preview the file, select Control > Test Movie, or press Ctrl+Enter (Win) or Cmd+Enter (Mac) (**Figure 2.2**).

3. To change the value of a variable after it has been declared, add the ActionScript code in **Code 2.1**.

4. Preview your file and note that the value of the `employeeHours` variable has changed (**Figure 2.3**).

DECLARING AND ASSIGNING VALUES TO VARIABLES

Data Typing Variables

ActionScript supports strict data typing of variables. Declaring a data type defines what kind of data can go in a container (variable). If a variable is data typed as a `Number`, that variable can store only numbers; if a variable is data typed as a `String`, it can store only string values, and so on.

A data type is any data that is typed after the variable is named and is separated from the variable name by a colon (`:`):

```
var employeeName      = "Adrian Lee";
var employeeHours     = 40;
```

Data typing is not enforced in ActionScript 3, but it is good practice to always be in the habit of doing it. Data typing makes variables easy to identify because you can easily determine what the variable stores based on its data type.

Data typing can cause compile errors when a variable has been assigned a value that does not match its data type. These errors are displayed in the Compile Errors panel.

Data typing helps avoid "silent" errors that can occur in code. For example, if a variable is assigned the wrong type of value, it will cause errors with whatever tries to utilize the variable, since the type of value does not match how it should be used. Without compile errors, you would not be able to determine where these errors are occurring. Instead, you would simply notice that things aren't working as planned, and then the long search begins to find the problem.

The following code would create a compiler error since a `String` variable is being assigned a `Number` and a `Number` variable is being assigned a `String`:

```
var employeeName      = 40;
var employeeHours     = "Adrian Lee";
```

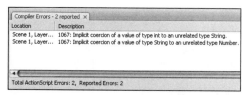

Figure 2.4 Setting a variable's value with data that does not match its data type causes a compile error.

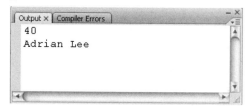

Figure 2.5 The ActionScript in Step 4 does not create an error since the variables were not data typed and can store any type of value.

To data type variables:

1. Add the following code to the Actions panel to data type `employeeName` and `employeeHours` as `String` and `Number` variables:

```
var employeeName:String =
    "Adrian Lee";
var employeeHours:Number = 40;
trace(employeeName);
trace(employeeHours);
```

2. Preview your file. The values should display in the Output panel.

3. Modify the code as shown to create a data type mismatch and cause a compile error (**Figure 2.4**).

```
var employeeName:String =   ;
var employeeHours:Number =
    "          "; trace(employeeName);
trace(employeeHours);
```

4. Remove the `String` and `Number` data types from Step 3:

```
var employeeName = 40;
var employeeHours = "Adrian Lee";
trace(employeeName);
trace(employeeHours);
```

5. Preview your movie. Note that there is no compile error this time as the data types have been removed (**Figure 2.5**).

Although a compile error did not occur in Step 5 after the data types were removed, the data used in the code was still erroneous. An employee name would most likely not be 40, and `"Adrian Lee"` is not the number of hours that employee 40 worked.

Make sure you get into the habit of data typing so that you can avoid assigning variables values that will cause problems in the logic of your code.

Working with Strings

Strings and numbers are the basis of all logic in ActionScript. Without strings and numbers, the two most important data types in the ActionScript language, you'd be hard-pressed to create an application.

Strings

Strings can be any combination of characters: single words, sentences, paragraphs. Even numbers can be a string.

What all strings have in common is that they are surrounded by quotations (**Code 2.2**).

String variables are used to store and display text. They can also be used for literal comparisons when validating data such as passwords and to check for certain conditions.

Combining strings

In many cases when using ActionScript, you will need to combine strings. For example, say a user enters his or her first and last name in separate text fields that get sent to a database, but the first and last names need to be combined for display purposes in the application. Combining values with ActionScript is known as *concatenation*.

Our next example combines the string values of firstName and lastName together, separated by a blank space character. The values are concatenated together using the plus (+) symbol. The + sign works the same way in ActionScript as it does in math; it can add string values together (**Code 2.3**).

✔ Tip

■ To make adding strings together a bit easier to read in your code, store the values in separate variables first, and then add the values together using their variable identifiers.

Code 2.2 String variables.

```
var employeeName:String = "Adrian Lee";
var employeeJobDesc:String = "Adrian
  crunches numbers in finance";
var employeePassword:String =
  "5employ04";
var employeeID:String = "1023";
```

Code 2.3 Combining strings.

```
var firstName:String = "Bob";
var lastName:String = "Jones";
var fullName:String =
  firstName + " " + lastName;
trace(fullName);
```

Code 2.4 Concatenating `firstName` and `lastName` variables.

```
                    Code
var firstName:String = "Bob";
var lastName:String = "Jones";
var fullName:String =
  firstName + " " + lastName;
trace("Employee name is: " +
  fullName);
```

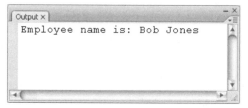

```
Output ×
   Employee name is: Bob Jones
```

Figure 2.6 The concatenated variables stored in `fullName` are then added to the "`Employee name is: `" string in the `trace()` statement.

Table 2.1

Common Escape Sequences	
ESCAPE SEQUENCE	DESCRIPTION
\n	New line; adds a new line in a string.
\r	Carriage return; same as new line.
\t	Tab; adds a tab indent.
\' and \"	Single and double quotes; since quotes are also part of ActionScript syntax, an escape sequence is needed to add a single quote as a string and not be read as code.
\\	Backslash.

To combine strings together:

1. In the Actions panel, add the code in **Code 2.4**, which concatenates the values of `firstName` and `lastName` together into a full name.

2. Preview your file. The concatenated value should display in the Output panel (**Figure 2.6**).

Appending a value to a string

To append a value to a variable, you can use the + and = operators together.

To append a value to a string:

1. Add the following code to the Actions panel to append a value to a string variable:

   ```
   var employeeFullName:String = "Bob";
   employeeFullName += " Jones";
   trace(employeeFullName);
   ```

2. Preview your file. `Bob Jones` should display in the Output panel.

Escape sequences

To add tab spaces, line breaks, and special characters that are not to be confused with the same characters that are part of ActionScript syntax, you must use an escape sequence (see **Table 2.1**). An escape sequence begins with a backslash (\). When the Flash platform reads the backslash character, it treats the character immediately after it as a string character or a command.

To add commands in strings using escape sequences:

1. Add the code in **Code 2.5** to the Actions panel to add tab indents and new lines in String variable.

2. Preview your file. The string and results of the escape sequences will display in the Output panel (**Figure 2.7**).

Code 2.5 Adding tab indents and new lines in String variable using escape sequences.

```
var employeeInfo:String =
  "Employee name: \t Bob Jones \n";
employeeInfo += "Employee age: \t 24 \n";
employeeInfo += "Employee id: \t 1234";
trace(employeeInfo);
```

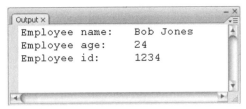

Output ×

Employee	name:	Bob Jones
Employee	age:	24
Employee	id:	1234

Figure 2.7 Include the tab (\t) and newline (\n) escape sequences to format employeeInfo.

Working with Numbers

Numbers are, well, numeric values in ActionScript. Numbers are used for performing mathematical operations and comparisons. ActionScript works with whole numbers, numbers with decimal points, positive and negative numbers, as well as hexadecimal values (used for colors):

```
var hoursRegular:Number = 40;
var hoursOvertime:Number = 10.5;
var hoursDeducted:Number = -2.5;
var employeeHairColor:Number = 0xFFCC00;
```

Working with math

Working with numbers in ActionScript is all about the math. Math can actually be fun in ActionScript. If ActionScript was around when I took math in high school, I would have done much better.

Performing math equations in ActionScript is the same as working with math on a calculator, on paper, or in Microsoft Excel.

To perform math with ActionScript, the ActionScript API uses the Math class. The Math class has methods that can be called to perform math functions such as sine, tan, PI, random numbers, and rounding of numbers. Its methods can also perform basic addition, subtraction, division, and multiplication.

To perform basic arithmetic:

1. To add and subtract numbers, add the following code to the Actions panel:

```
var num1:Number = 4;
var num2:Number = 2;
trace(num1 + num2); // 6
trace(num1 - num2); // 2
```

continues on next page

2. Preview your file and the answers will display in the Output panel.

3. To divide and multiply numbers, add the following code to the Actions panel:

```
var num1:Number = 4;
var num2:Number = 2;
trace(num1 * num2); // 8
trace(num1 / num2); // 2
```

4. Preview your file; the answers will again display in the Output panel.

5. To perform multiple operations, add the following code to the Actions panel:

```
var num1:Number = 4;
var num2:Number = 2;
trace(num1 + num2 * 3); // 10
trace((num1 + num2) * 3); // 18
```

6. Save a preview of your file. The answers will display in the Output panel. Notice that the brackets around the addition in the second `trace()` statement are completed first, and then the sum is multiplied by 3 (18). The math in the first `trace()` statement is executed in a different order, so it produces a different result (10).

Using compound operators

For short and simple math functions, ActionScript has compound operators (**Table 2.2**).

To perform math using compound operators:

1. Add the code in **Code 2.6** to the Actions panel.

2. Preview your file. The changing values will display in the Output panel.

Table 2.2

Compound Operators	
COMPOUND OPERATOR	**DESCRIPTION**
++	Adds 1 to current value
--	Subtracts 1 from current value
+=	Adds specified value to a variable
-=	Subtracts a specified value from current value of a variable
/=	Divides the current value of a variable by a specified value
*=	Multiplies the current value of a variable by a specified value

Code 2.6 Using addition, multiplication, and subtraction compound operators.

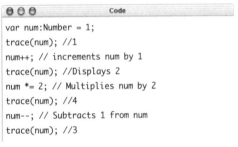

```
var num:Number = 1;
trace(num); //1
num++; // increments num by 1
trace(num); //Displays 2
num *= 2; // Multiplies num by 2
trace(num); //4
num--; // Subtracts 1 from num
trace(num); //3
```

Number data types

As discussed earlier in this chapter, all variables should be data typed, including numbers. For numerical values, however, there are three different data types for numbers, and two of them are new to ActionScript 3:

◆ **int (integer)**—The int class works with values representing a 32-bit signed integer. The range of values of the int class is −2,147,483,648 to 2,147,483,647. int is new to ActionScript 3.

```
var integer:int = -20;
```

◆ **uint (unsigned integer)**—The uint class works with values representing a 32-bit unsigned integer. Unsigned integers can only be positive. The range of the uint class is 0 to 4,294,967,295. uint is new to ActionScript 3.

```
var uinteger:uint = 13;
```

◆ **Number (appeared in previous versions of ActionScript)**—The Number data type is needed for working with numbers with floating-point values or when values will exceed the range of the int and uint data types. The Number data type can use up to 53 bits to represent integer values. This uses more CPU resources and could affect the overall processing performance of the application.

```
var decimal:Number = 4.152;
```

✔ Tip

■ Use the int and uint data types for whole numbers such as counting products, tracking scores in a game, and so on. Use the Number data type for any type of math equation that could possibly result in a floating decimal and numbers that will exceed 4,294,967,295.

Data Type Conversions

In many cases in ActionScript development, a value needs to be used in a way that its data type will not permit. For example, numbers that are typed into an input field are recognized as strings. To perform math with a number that is considered a String, you have to *retype* it, or convert it to a Number.

In ActionScript there are String and Number classes, which allow you to work with strings and numbers. These classes have a few built-in methods for recasting and converting data types. String() and toString() are methods of the Number class. Number() is a method of the String class.

To convert a variable data type:

1. Add the following code to the Actions panel, which will recast the String in value1 as a Number using the Number() method:

   ```
   var value1:String = "5";
   var value2:uint = 3;
   trace(value1 + value2); //53
   trace(Number(value1) + value2); //8
   ```

2. Preview your file and note the values displayed in the Output panel (the values can be found in the comments in Step 1).

3. Data type conversion will also take place automatically if a number is added to a string. Add the code in **Code 2.7** to the Actions panel.

4. Preview your file and note the value displayed in the Output panel.

Code 2.7 Combining String and Number data types.

```
var employeeString:String =
  "Employee hours for week: ";
var employeeHours:Number = 40;
var hoursWorked:String =
  employeeString + employeeHours;
trace(hoursWorked);
```

Instances and Properties

Instances are an object of a class on the stage or in ActionScript. Instances are defined by their properties. Once an object has been constructed on the stage or in ActionScript, it can be defined by setting its properties. This section will cover adding instances of a class to the stage in ActionScript and defining them by setting their properties.

Instances

An *instance* is an object of a class that exists in code or on the stage. Instances are unique. If you are using the same MovieClip five separate times in an application, you are using five unique instances of the MovieClip class. As mentioned earlier, *instantiate* is a programming term for when an object is constructed.

To reference an instance of a class, you first create a variable using the var keyword, followed by a name for the object and the data type of the object:

```
var myMovieClip:MovieClip;
```

To create the instance as an object of the MovieClip class, call the new MovieClip() constructor method of the MovieClip class:

```
var myMovieClip:MovieClip;
myMovieClip = new MovieClip();
```

We will be constructing instances extensively throughout this book so we'll go into further detail later in this book.

Properties

Properties are variables of an instance (object). You set properties to define the attributes of an object or to enable the object to manipulate external information. Properties of an instance are set like any other variable, with the exception of calling the instance of the object first, and then the property name.

When you look at an object's *x* and *y* position on the stage in the Properties panel, you are viewing its x and y properties. `width` and `height` are other properties you may be familiar with. To set a MovieClip's x, y, `width`, and `height` properties using ActionScript, first access the `MovieClip` object by calling its instance name and then calling and setting the property.

To set a MovieClip's properties with ActionScript:

1. Select a drawing tool of your choice from the Tool palette and draw a shape on the stage.

2. Select the shape and convert it to a MovieClip symbol by pressing F8 (Win) or Ctrl+F8 (Mac), or by choosing Modify > Convert to Symbol. In the Convert to Symbol dialog box, assign the MovieClip whatever name you want and click OK (**Figure 2.8**).

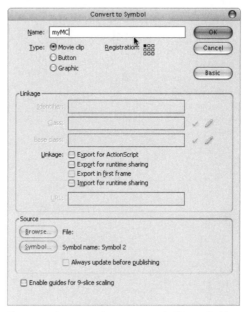

Figure 2.8 Convert a shape to a MovieClip symbol by selecting it and choosing Modify > Convert to Symbol.

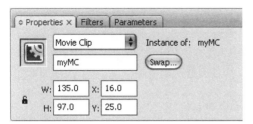

Figure 2.9 Assigning a MovieClip instance name of myMC.

3. Select the MovieClip on the stage and launch the Properties panel by pressing Ctrl+F3, or by choosing Window > Properties > Properties. Assign the MovieClip an instance name of myMC in the Instance Name input field of the Properties panel (**Figure 2.9**).

4. Create a new layer and name it Actions. Select the first keyframe on the Actions layer and launch the Actions panel.

5. Add the code in the ActionScript that will position myMC and change its width and height:

```
myMC.x = 50;
myMC.y = 50;
myMC.width = 200;
myMC.height = 75;
```

6. Preview your file and note the property changes applied to myMC using ActionScript.

✔ Tips

- It's good practice to put all of your ActionScript on a keyframe on its own layer named Actions (or something that says ActionScript on that layer). This makes locating ActionScript throughout an application much easier.

- Different classes define different properties for objects in ActionScript. Because many objects are code only and are not visible on the stage, there are many properties at work that we cannot see. You will have lots of opportunities to get and set object properties, both visible and invisible, throughout this book, so let's move on.

About Booleans

Booleans are variables that can only have a `true` or `false` value (1 or 0). A `Boolean` is used for logical operations. In the case of a `Boolean`, a logical operation is a question that has a yes or no answer.

The following `Boolean` variable (`employeeSecurityClearance`) tells us that an employee has security clearance (`true`):

```
var employeeSecurityClearance:Boolean =
    true;
```

You will work more with Booleans later in this book.

WORKING WITH FUNCTIONS AND METHODS

3

Functions and methods in ActionScript, for the most part, are one and the same. They are containers of functionality that execute only when called. Functions and methods can calculate, process, and return data, or they can perform certain tasks. Just like a variable, a function can be written (or *invoked*) once and can be called (or reused) many times. A single function or method can perform the same tasks but with different values (or *arguments*) that are passed to it, yielding different results each time.

This chapter addresses the key differences between methods and functions. It begins by discussing methods of classes and providing you with an opportunity to work with them. You'll then have the chance to create your own user-defined functions so that you can customize functionality. To accomplish this, you'll create reusable functions using parameters and arguments that return values for setting properties and variables. You'll also learn how to check for function errors that return incorrect values, and what types of scoping issues can arise when working with variables in the timeline versus within the functions.

At the end of this chapter, you should be comfortable with the fundamentals of methods and functions, which will be used throughout the rest of this book.

Methods and Functions

The difference between a method and a function is that a method is associated with a specific class (a task that an object of the class can perform), and a function is a user-defined block of code that is declared in code on the timeline or as part of a custom class (which in turn would be a method of that class).

Methods

Methods are functions written within a class. They are ready to be called when an object is required to perform a calculation, change a property, return a value, or perform any type of predefined action.

Common methods of a class that most developers are familiar with in ActionScript include the public methods of the `MovieClip` class. Public methods of a class are methods that are available for an object outside the class (that can be called from outside the class). Private methods are those that are used only internally by the class for its own functionality.

Table 3.1 lists the most common public methods of the `MovieClip` class that are ready to be called when an object of the class is instantiated.

✔ Tip

- Table 3.1 covers the most common public methods of the `MovieClip` class—it is not intended to be exhaustive. For more information on all the methods of the `MovieClip` class, search the Flash Help menu using the keywords "MovieClip class."

Table 3.1

Public Methods of the `MovieClip` Class

Method	Description
MovieClip()	The constructor method of the MovieClip class. Creates a new MovieClip instance.
gotoAndPlay()	Tells the MovieClip to move the playhead and play from a specific frame number or label on its timeline: gotoAndPlay(5); gotoAndPlay('labelName');
gotoAndStop()	Tells the MovieClip to move the playhead to a specific frame number or label on its timeline and stop: gotoAndStop(5); gotoAndStop('labelName');
nextFrame()	Tells the playhead to advance to the next frame and stop in a MovieClip's timeline.
play()	Tells the playhead to play a MovieClip's timeline from its current frame location.
stop()	Tells the playhead to stop at a frame in a MovieClip's timeline.

Constructor Methods

In Table 3.1, the `MovieClip()` method of the `MovieClip` class is referred to as the constructor method of the class. Many classes of the ActionScript API have a constructor method. The constructor method is used to construct a new object of the class. All constructor methods start with a variable of the class, followed by the equals sign and the new operative, followed by the name of the class. This code is an example of the constructor method for the `Sprite` class:

```
var s:Sprite = new Sprite();
```

The following code is an example of the constructor method for the `TextField` class:

```
var tf:TextField = new TextField();
```

Figure 3.1 Convert the circle shape to a MovieClip named mcCircle.

Figure 3.2 Assign the circle an instance name of mcCircle.

Inherited Methods

Classes inherit methods from other classes to create a logical chain of relationships between classes so there is a minimum of duplication of functionality. Cutting down on file size and code duplication is a side effect of this practice. (There are other reasons that involve a discussion of abstraction and composition as the sister pillars of OOP to inheritance, but that's outside the scope of this book.)

Each external ActionScript (AS) file that defines a class consumes file size and CPU resources. If the same methods were being written over and over in every class, file sizes would be unnecessarily large and the Flash compiler would have to do more thinking.

If a method of common functionality is written once and reused (in other words, inherited by other classes), the class files become more lightweight. In addition, if you have to update the method's functionality, you have to do it in only one place—"Create once, use many times."

The MovieClip class also has what are called *inherited* methods. These are methods that are imported into the MovieClip class from other classes to extend the functionality of the MovieClip class. The addEventListener() method of the EventDispatcher class is one example. We will be working with inherited methods extensively throughout this book, so we'll stop with this brief definition. Just be aware that most classes you'll be working with have their own public methods, as well as methods they inherit from other classes to extend their functionality.

To call methods of the MovieClip class:

1. Begin a new Flash file.

2. Rename Layer 1 to Circle.

3. Draw a circle that is roughly 50 × 50 pixels at the top-left corner of the stage using the Oval tool from the Tool palette.

4. Select the circle and convert it to a MovieClip symbol named mcCircle (**Figure 3.1**).

5. Select the mcCircle symbol on the stage and give it an instance name of mcCircle in the Properties panel (**Figure 3.2**).

6. Double-click mcCircle on the stage to enter its timeline.

7. Select the circle shape and convert it to a Graphic symbol called Circle.

8. Insert a new keyframe at frame 10 and drag the Circle graphic instance to the right side of the stage.

9. Insert a keyframe at frame 20 and drag the Circle graphic instance back to the left side of the stage (x 0, y 0).

continues on next page

METHODS AND FUNCTIONS

10. Select the keyframe at frame 1 and select Motion from the Tween type drop-down menu in the Properties panel (**Figure 3.3**). Repeat this step for frame 10.

11. Preview your movie; you should see the Circle moving back and forth across the stage.

12. To stop the timeline of `mcCircle` on the first frame, add a new layer named Actions. Select the first keyframe on the Actions layer and open the Actions panel (by choosing Window > Actions).

13. Add the following `stop()` method to stop the timeline of `mcCircle` at frame 1:
```
stop();
```

14. Return to the main timeline by clicking Scene 1 at the top left of the stage.

15. Create a new layer named Actions on the main timeline. Select the first keyframe on the Actions layer and open the Actions panel.

16. Call the instance name `mcCircle` followed by its `gotoAndPlay()` method to tell the timeline of `mcCircle` to play from frame 2:
```
mcCircle.gotoAndPlay(2);
```

17. Preview your movie. You should see `mcCircle` begin to play from frame 2 and then stop once it returns to frame 1 in its timeline, where it has been commanded to stop again by the `stop()` method.

18. Call the `gotoAndStop()` method to tell `mcCircle` to go to and stop at a particular frame. The following code tells `mcCircle` to go to and stop at frame number 10:
```
mcCircle.gotoAndStop(10);
```

19. Preview your movie. You should see the Circle stopped at the right side of the stage.

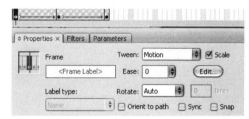

Figure 3.3 Select the Motion tween type for the keyframe to tween the circle from frame 1 to frame 10 and from frame 10 to frame 20.

✔ Tips

■ In Flash, when a timeline animation reaches its last frame, the playhead will return to frame 1 and continue looping unless ActionScript tells it otherwise.

■ We will continue to work with methods of different classes as we move through this book. Although there are all sorts of different methods, the dot syntax we just used to call methods of the `MovieClip` class is the same for calling all methods of all objects of classes.

METHODS AND FUNCTIONS

Functions

Functions are user-defined containers of code that help "stitch" together the overall functionality of an application.

Object-oriented programming (OOP) involves working with a bunch of objects that are already predefined to take care of themselves. All you have to do is pass instructions to them and ask them to perform certain tasks when you need them to.

The script that is programmed in an application basically manages various objects to achieve the overall functionality of the application. Just like a foreman on a construction site has specific instructions for how each piece of equipment should be used and how each worker should apply his or her skills and knowledge to complete a final product, OOP programmers use objects that utilize the needed skill sets they have at their disposal to help create the final product. These sets of instructions are handled by functions.

In other words, a function is a canned set of instructions that address certain needs.

METHODS AND FUNCTIONS

Defining a function

Creating your own function begins with entering the function declaration keyword, followed by the name of the function and ending with left and right parentheses ( ). The code that is executed when the function is called sits inside left and right curly braces { } that follow the function invocation.

A function is invoked like this:

```
function functionName() {
  // actions function will perform
  go here inside curly braces

}
```

✔ Tip

■ Be descriptive with your function names and follow the same naming rules that were discussed regarding variables in Chapter 2. Do not use any of the allowed special characters in your function names. Stick with letters only.

To write and call your own function:

1. Add the following ActionScript to invoke a function called traceName():

   ```
   function traceName() {
   }
   ```

2. Add a trace() statement within the curly braces of the function:

   ```
   function traceName() {
     trace("traceName() function has
     been called.");
   }
   ```

3. Preview your movie. Notice the code block within the traceName() function does not execute. This is because it has not been called yet.

4. To call the function, add the following function call after the `traceName()` function:

```
function traceName() {
  trace("traceName() function has
  been called.");
}
traceName();
```

5. Preview your movie. You should now notice this message in the Output panel:

```
traceName() function has been called
```

Using arguments and parameters with functions

Functions and methods can accept values when those values are called for the function or method to process.

In many cases, functions do not require any parameters for them to function. For example, they can do something like play or stop the timeline. As demonstrated earlier in this chapter, when calling the `gotoAndStop(10)` method of the `MovieClip` class, frame `10` is the required parameter that is passed to the method for the MovieClip to `gotoAndStop()`.

When writing your own functions, you are constructing a set of instructions to be executed when the function is called. Sometimes your instructions require information for them to execute.

For example, if you ask a person something rather generic like "Open the window, please," there are no variables in that task. They either open the window or they don't. But what if you ask someone to get you a cup of coffee? What do you take in your coffee? Getting a coffee is a common task in life, but there are unknown variables for the person who is making the coffee. Do you take cream? Sugar? If so, how much? These are values (or arguments) that need to be passed with the command.

"I want a coffee with two creams and one sugar." How would this statement be written as a function in ActionScript?

The first thing you need to do is create a function that will handle the making of the coffee:

```
function getCoffee() {
}
```

Next you need the function to accept values for how many creams and sugars you want in your coffee. The values are passed to the parameters of the function (pCream and pSugar):

```
function getCoffee(pCream, pSugar) {
}
```

The pCream and pSugar parameters are both variables that will be used in the function to make the coffee. These values will be numbers. To avoid a data type error, parameters should be data typed according to the kind of values they will handle.

```
function getCoffee(pCream:Number,
  pSugar:Number) {
}
```

pCream and pSugar are both variables of the Number class. If any other kind of data type is passed to these parameters, it will cause an error when the movie is compiled.

The last thing that needs to happen is to call the getCoffee() function and pass how many creams and sugars you want in your coffee as arguments:

```
getCoffee(2, 1);
```

This function call says the ordered coffee will have two creams and one sugar. The arguments need to be in the same order as the parameters that are in the function setup:

```
function getCoffee(pCream:Number,
pSugar:Number) {
}
getCoffee(2, 1);
```

Now let's actually try it.

✔ Tip

■ The Number data type was used since someone may want 1.5 spoons of sugar. The only data type of the Number class that can handle decimals is Number.

METHODS AND FUNCTIONS

Code 3.1 Displaying the value of the pCream and pSugar parameters passed to the function in the Output panel.

```
Code
function getCoffee(pCream:Number,
  pSugar:Number) {
    trace("Cream:  " + pCream);
    trace("Sugar: " + pSugar);
}
getCoffee(1, 2);
```

```
Output ×
Cream: 1
Sugar: 2
```

Figure 3.4 Results of the trace() statement in the getCoffee() function.

Code 3.2 Adding the coffee's size as a third parameter to the getCoffee() function. "large" is passed as a String to the function call, and the pSize parameter is added to a new trace() statement in the code block.

```
Code
function getCoffee(pCream:Number,
  pSugar:Number, pSize:String) {
    trace("Cream:  " + pCream);
    trace("Sugar: " + pSugar);
    trace("Size: " + pSize);
}

getCoffee(1, 2, "large");
```

```
Output ×
Cream: 1
Sugar: 2
Size: large
```

Figure 3.5 The new pSize:String parameter is added to the getCoffee() function. The "large" parameter passed to the function is traced to the Output panel.

To use arguments and parameters in a function:

1. Create a new movie and launch it in the Actions panel.

2. Invoke a function called getCoffee() and add two Number parameters that will "catch" how many creams (pCream) and sugars (pSugar) will go into the coffee:

   ```
   function getCoffee(pCream:Number,
     pSugar:Number) {
   }
   ```

3. Call the getCoffee() function and pass how many creams and sugars will go into the coffee as arguments:

   ```
   getCoffee(1, 2);
   ```

4. Add a trace() statement within the getCoffee() function code block (curly braces) to display the values of the pCream and pSugar parameters in the Output panel (**Code 3.1**).

5. Preview your movie. You should see the trace() statement display in the Output panel (**Figure 3.4**).

6. Add a third parameter to the getCoffee() function called pSize:String and pass the value "large" as an argument from the function call (**Code 3.2**).

7. trace() the new parameter value within the code block of the getCoffee() function.

8. Preview your movie; you should see the new value traced to the Output panel (**Figure 3.5**).

To pass variables as arguments to a function:

1. Start a new script by declaring the following variables that will be passed to a function:

```
var number1:Number = 5;
var number2:Number = 2;
```

2. Create a function below the variable declarations called addNumbers() that has two parameters called pNum1:Number and pNum2:Number:

```
function addNumbers(pNum1:Number,
   pNum2:Number) {
}
```

3. Declare a variable called sum in the addNumbers() code block that adds the values of pNum1 and pNum2 together. Then trace() the value of sum (**Code 3.3**).

4. Call the addNumbers() function and pass the number1 and number2 variables as arguments to the function (**Code 3.4**).

5. Preview your movie. You should see the sum of the variables display in the Output panel (**Figure 3.6**).

Code 3.3 Adding the values of pNum1 and pNum2 together to make a value for sum.

```
● ● ●                    Code
function addNumbers(pNum1:Number,
  pNum2:Number) {
    var sum:Number = pNum1 +
      pNum2;
    trace('The sum of number1 and
      number2 is: ' + sum);
}
```

Code 3.4 Final code with the addNumbers() function call that passes the number1 and number2 variables as arguments to the function.

```
● ● ●                    Code
function addNumbers(pNum1:Number,
  pNum2:Number) {
    var sum:Number = pNum1 +
      pNum2;
    trace('The sum of number1 and
      number2 is: ' + sum);
}
addNumbers(number1, number2);
```

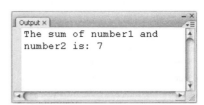

Figure 3.6 Displaying the value of sum in the Output panel.

Code 3.5 The value of the variable numberSum is set by the return value from addNumbers().

```
Code
var number1:Number = 5;
var number2:Number = 2;
var numberSum:Number;
function addNumbers(pNum1:Number,
  pNum2:Number) {
    var sum:Number = pNum1 + pNum2;
    return sum;
}
numberSum = addNumbers(number1, number2);
trace('The sum of number1 and
  number2 is: ' + numberSum);
```

Returning Values from a Function

Functions can give back as well as accept values. One of the real powers of functions is to reuse code that performs a common bit of functionality. For example, the previous walk-through that added the two number parameters together could return that value back to the caller as a value. This is similar to calling a variable to get its value. The code to return the value of sum is shown in **Code 3.5**.

Setting a function's return type

When creating a function that returns a value, ActionScript allows strict return typing of functions. Just like data typing a variable to hold only a certain value type such as a String or Number, return typing a function will display an error when compiling if a variable returns a data type different from what is specified in the function's return type.

In Code 3.3, numberSum has a data type of Number. In turn, the addNumbers() function should only be able to return a Number. A return type is added to a function at the end of the parameter brackets separated by a colon:

```
function addNumbers(pNum1:Number,
  pNum2:Number):Number
```

To return type a function:

1. Add the ActionScript in **Code 3.6**, which gives the addNumbers() function a return type of Number.

2. Preview your movie and note the statement "The sum of number1 and number2 is: 7" displays in the Output panel.

3. Change the return type from Number to String for the addNumbers() function:

   ```
   function addNumbers(pNum1:Number,
     pNum2:Number):String
   ```

4. Preview your movie and note the two compile errors that display in the Errors panel (**Figure 3.7**). One error is for the Number being returned when the function's return type was supposed to be a String, and the other error results from trying to set a Number variable with a String.

5. Change the return type back to Number; everything should compile fine again.

Code 3.6 Return typing the addNumbers() function with Number to specify that it can only return a Number.

```
var number1:Number = 5;
var number2:Number = 2;
var numberSum:Number;
function addNumbers(pNum1:Number,
  pNum2:Number):Number {
    var sum:Number =
      pNum1 + pNum2;
    return sum;
}
numberSum = addNumbers(number1, number2);
trace('The sum of number1 and number2 is: '
  + numberSum);
```

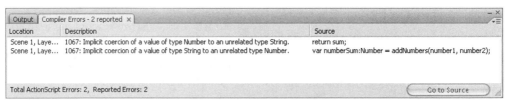

Figure 3.7 A compile error for an improper return type in which a Number was found when a String was supposed to be returned from the function.

Figure 3.8 A compile error for a function that returns a value but has a `void` return type.

Return typing functions that do not return values

It is good practice to return type functions (also known as strict typing) that do not return anything. This is done by `void` return typing a function:

```
function getCoffee(pCream:Number,
  pSugar:Number, pSize:String):void
```

If the previous function tries to return a value, the compiler will create an error, since the function was return typed `void`, or not supposed to return anything.

If the `addNumbers()` function from the previous walkthrough had a `void` return type, a compile error would display in the error panel (**Figure 3.8**):

```
function addNumbers(pNum1:Number,
  pNum2:Number):void
```

It is considered best practice to always specify a return type for your functions whether or not they return a value.

Function Scope

Scope is an important term in programming. It refers to the placement and ownership of variables and objects in ActionScript. Depending on where a variable or object is created, its scope, or the location that it is accessed within, varies. A variable that is declared in the main part of your code (on the timeline) has a scope of the timeline that the code is on. A local variable that is created within a function on the timeline has a scope within that function only:

```
var sum:Number = 5;
function addNumbers():void {
  var sum:Number = 2 + 2;
}
```

The two variables named sum have two different scopes. They can both have the same name, with unique values, without causing any errors or confusion. This is because the first instance of sum is within the global (timeline) scope of the code, and the second instance of sum has a scope within the addNumbers() function.

With functions, what happens in the function stays in the function (no relation to "What happens in Vegas, stays in Vegas!"). The "lifespan" of sum within the addNumbers() function is only as long as the execution of the function. When addNumbers() is called, sum is declared. When the function has finished executing, sum no longer exists.

Code 3.7 Two variables named sum with different scopes.

```
Code
var sum:Number = 50;
function addNumbers(pNum1:Number,
  pNum2:Number):Number {
    var sum:Number = pNum1 + pNum2;
    return sum;
}
```

Code 3.8 Demonstrating the different values of sum, which have different scopes.

```
Code
trace('Global scope of sum: ' + sum);
trace('Scope of sum in function: ' +
  addNumbers(10, 10));
trace('Notice Global scoped sum has
  not changed: ' + sum);
```

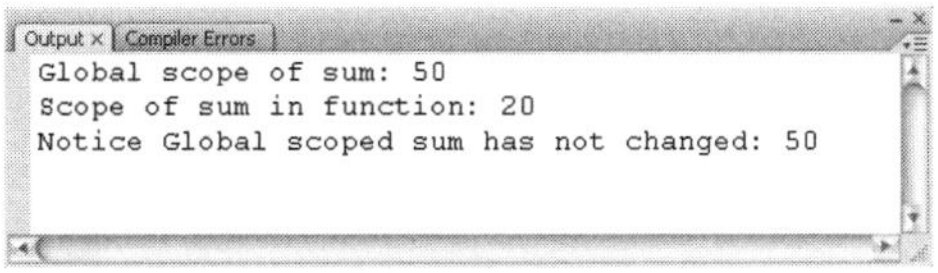

```
Output ×   Compiler Errors
Global scope of sum: 50
Scope of sum in function: 20
Notice Global scoped sum has not changed: 50
```

Figure 3.9 The values of sum retain their own values within their own scopes.

Always be aware of where you are putting things in ActionScript. After typos, scoping problems are the biggest reason for compile errors and things not functioning properly in your code. I cannot tell you how much this aggravated me when I was learning ActionScript on my own back in the day and how much time I spent debugging what turned out to be simple scoping errors.

To practice using function scope:

1. Add the code in **Code 3.7**, which creates two variables named sum: one in the global (timeline) scope of the code and the other within the scope of a function called *addNumbers()*.

2. To make sure that the scope of the sum variables indeed makes them unique, add the trace() statements of **Code 3.8** after the addNumbers() function.

3. Preview your file. The Output panel should display the message shown in **Figure 3.9**.

To access and change the value of sum in the global scope, sum can be referenced from the function by simply calling it and assigning it a new value, provided a variable with the same name is not created within the function.

continues on next page

FUNCTION SCOPE

4. Modify your code as shown in **Code 3.9** to change the value of sum within the global scope of the code from the addNumbers() function.

5. Preview your movie. You should see the timeline variable of sum has been set to a new value from the addNumbers() function call (**Figure 3.10**).

Scoping goes beyond just where a variable is set; it can also refer to where a MovieClip instance sits and where other objects are instantiated. We'll look more at those scoping issues and how to prevent them later on in the book.

Code 3.9 Changing the value of sum in the global scope from the addNumbers() function.

```
var sum:Number = 50;
function addNumbers(pNum1:Number,
  pNum2:Number):void {
    sum = pNum1 + pNum2;
}
trace('sum is: ' + sum);
addNumbers(10, 10);
trace('sum has been changed: ' +
  sum);
```

```
sum is: 50
sum has been changed: 20
```

Figure 3.10 Changing the value of sum from the addNumbers() function scope.

WORKING WITH CLASSES AND OBJECTS

The most important knowledge about ActionScript and object-oriented programming that you can possess is knowing how to work with objects and classes. You may remember from reading Chapter 1 that everything in ActionScript is an object. A MovieClip is an instance of the MovieClip class; a Sprite is an instance of the Sprite class, and so on.

Because objects and classes are so central to working with ActionScript, nearly every chapter of this book delves into working with classes and objects. You will have gained plenty of experience with them by the time you've finished reading and working through the step-by-step instructions. But before you move on, you must understand the basic concepts, terminology, and definitions of classes and objects.

This chapter provides a high-level overview, beginning with the definition of classes, objects, and class hierarchy and inheritance (the "family tree" of how classes are stored and referenced). It also provides opportunities for you to practice importing classes and instantiating objects using ActionScript so that you can call their methods and set their properties. Finally, this chapter shows you how to work with external ActionScript files, which enables you to work with different ActionScript editors and to separate programming from design.

Defining Classes and Objects

A *class* is the blueprint for an object. It defines everything about the object: how it looks, how it acts, what it does, what data it processes, and how it is built.

An *object* is an instance of a class, or a copy of the class's blueprint. Once an object of a class is instantiated, you have access to the public properties, events, and methods of that class to manipulate the object for your programming and display purposes.

Class hierarchy involves the way in which classes are categorized. Classes are external ActionScript files that define objects; they are stored and organized in a specific directory structure in the Flash CS3 program directory (**Figure 4.1**). To use them in your code, you have to import them.

To import the ActionScript class files into your code, you don't need to know the full computer path to the files (the compiler will do that for you), but you *do* need to know how the classes are categorized. To import a particular class, you need to know what directory, or *class package*, they are stored in. For example, the MovieClip class is located in the flash.display package. The full import path to the package would thus be import flash.display.MovieClip;.

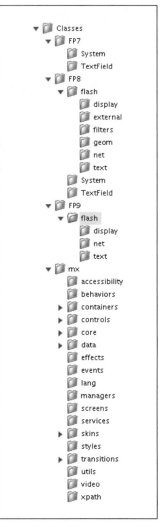

Figure 4.1 Class package locations of class files in the Flash program directory.

The last concept that it's important to be familiar with is *class inheritance*. As a general rule, the deeper into a package a class gets, the more it inherits from the parent classes for its core functionality. As discussed in Chapter 3, the `MovieClip` class has inherited methods from other classes to help extend its functionality. Classes share, or inherit, methods, properties, and events from one another, so functionality has to be defined only once and shared throughout the class structure. This is not an entirely new concept for ActionScript 3, but it has been universally implemented in this version. This helps improve code performance, reduces the file size of imported classes, and makes future updates and additions to the ActionScript API easier to implement.

We'll be seeing more of classes and subclasses throughout the rest of this book, since many classes we'll work with are subclasses of different class packages.

DEFINING CLASSES AND OBJECTS

Importing a Class

You must import classes in ActionScript before you can construct objects and utilize methods, properties, and events of a class. Classes are imported at the beginning of the code, so unqualified class names can be used throughout the code. If a class is not imported, all references to a class need to be qualified. An example of using a qualified class name for constructing a `MovieClip` object would be as follows:

```
var mc:MovieClip = new
  flash.display.MovieClip();
```

The import directive for a class allows the use of unqualified (or shortened) class names in the code without indicating the package each and every time, thus saving lots of typing.

However, because the approach of this book is tailored to users who are new to ActionScript, all of the ActionScript code that you will construct is timeline based, which means you don't have to import many of the classes that we use (Flash will automatically do this for us).

If you were to take a class-based approach to ActionScript, or if you were a developer using Flex, then you would need to import all of the classes used in your code.

So that you can become aware of what a more advanced ActionScript developer would do, and to help you see the big picture, I will include `import` statements whenever possible in the timeline, even though you don't need to construct them.

If you do need to import a class, you would use the `import` statement followed by the class package path and the subclass that you wish to import.

To import classes:

◆ To import the DisplayObject, Graphics, and Shape subclasses of the flash.display class package, add the following ActionScript:

```
import flash.display.DisplayObject;
import flash.display.Graphics;
import flash.display.Shape;
```

These classes are required to construct a Shape object, draw the shape on the stage, fill and stroke it with methods of the Graphics class, and add it to the display list on the stage using methods of the DisplayObject class.

Instantiating Objects

Instantiating an object involves constructing an instance of a class as an object using ActionScript. Whether the object will be used for display purposes or for managing data, objects are always instantiated the same way:

```
var objectName:ClassType =
  new ClassType();
```

To instantiate an object:

◆ Add the following ActionScript after the import statements from the previous example to construct an object of the Shape class called square:

```
var square:Shape = new Shape();
```

Leave this file open for the next set of instructions.

Object methods

As discussed in Chapter 3, methods are functions that are defined in or written inside a class. Methods of a class are actions that an object can perform. They can accept arguments and return values if required. Methods of an object of a class can be called after the object has been instantiated.

To call methods of an object:

1. Return to the file from the previous set of instructions.

2. Add the following code, which will draw and fill the rectangle using methods of the Graphics class (which are inherited in the Shape object) after the square constructor method:

```
square.graphics.beginFill(0xffcc00);
square.graphics.lineStyle
  (2, 0x000000);
square.graphics.drawRect
  (0, 0, 200, 200);
square.graphics.endFill();
```

3. Add the instance of `square` to the display list (make it viewable on the stage) using the `addChild()` method of the `DisplayObject` class at the end of the script:

```
addChild(square);
```

4. Preview your movie; you should see a 200 × 200 orange square drawn on the stage.

Leave this file open for the next task.

Object properties

Properties are variables of an instance. They store physical and logical attributes of the object such as location (x and y position), size (width, height, `scaleX`, `scaleY`), and various values for behind-the-scenes use.

To set properties of an object:

1. Return to the file from the previous task.

2. Add the following ActionScript to the end of the code to set the x and y properties of the square to x 200 and y 50:

```
square.x = 200;
square.y = 50;
```

3. Set the `alpha` property of square to .5 (50 percent of its full opacity):

```
square.alpha = .5;
```

4. Set the `scaleX` (horizontal) and `scaleY` (vertical) properties of square:

```
square.scaleX = 1.5;
square.scaleY = .5;
```

As with the `alpha` property, the values for setting the scale properties are decimal based. 1 equals 100 percent, 1.5 equals 150 percent, .50 equals 50 percent, and so on.

5. Set the `rotation` property of square to 45 (%):

```
square.rotation = 45;
```

continues on next page

INSTANTIATING OBJECTS

6. Preview your file. The position (x, y), transparency (alpha), scale (scaleX, scaleY), and rotation of square should all be changed from the original property values.

Data-typing object instances

Just like variables, object instance variables need to be data typed. This practice prevents unintentionally instantiating a variable as a wrong object type, which produces a compile error.

To data-type an object instance:

1. Add the following code to import the MovieClip class and create a variable named myMC. myMC is data-typed as an object of the MovieClip class:

   ```
   import flash.display.MovieClip;
   var myMC:MovieClip;
   ```

2. To instantiate the object, use the new MovieClip() constructor method of myMC:

   ```
   myMC = new MovieClip();
   ```

3. Preview your movie; you won't see anything, but you should not get a compile error either.

4. To create a compile error, try using the new Shape() constructor method:

   ```
   myMC = new Shape();
   ```

   Because myMC is data-typed as a MovieClip, using this constructor method should cause a compile error (**Figure 4.2**).

✔ Tip

- When data-typing object instances, the data type is always the same as the class name.

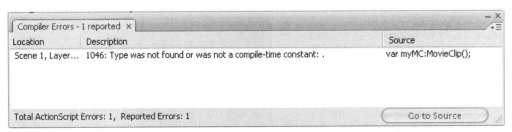

Figure 4.2 A compile error is produced when the instance data type and its class constructor method are mismatched.

INSTANTIATING OBJECTS

Working with External Code

Working with ActionScript in an external file and including or importing it in your application has many advantages:

◆ It allows you to have some separation in your workflow between Flash and the stage on one monitor (if you are using a stand-alone ActionScript editor), and have all of your code displayed at the same time on another monitor.

◆ It is a good choice when multiple developers are all coding different aspects of the same application.

continues on next page

Third-Party ActionScript 3 Editors

There are many third-party ActionScript editors on the market today. External editors provide more features to assist you in your programming than the built-in Actions panel in Flash. Some external editors are capable of managing other programming languages as well. This allows all programming for a single project to happen in a single editor. The following is a list of my preferred editors that have made the upgrade to ActionScript 3 and the new Flash API:

◆ **FlashDevelop** (www.flashdevelop.org). My most recent favorite. And did I mention it's free?

◆ **PrimalScript** (www.primalscript.com). Sapien Technologies' multilanguage editor.

◆ **TextMate** (www.macromates.com). MacroMates' TextMate is for the Mac only.

◆ **Eclipse** (www.eclipse.org). An open source development platform.

We will be using Flash CS3 to create external ActionScript files in this book, but feel free to work along with an external editor if you wish.

When working with an external ActionScript file, you write your code exactly the same as you would directly in Flash in frame-based ActionScript. The only difference is that the ActionScript is, well, in an external .as file. The external .as file is included in the timeline of the Flash file when compiled. Including an external .as file into a Flash application is not the same as creating an external class.

- It is the start of getting into and appreciating class-based programming using ActionScript.

- Many developers are not that fond of the ActionScript panel in Flash and prefer third-party ActionScript editors.

To create an external .as file:

1. Choose File > New > ActionScript File from the menu bar to open the New Document dialog shown in **Figure 4.3**. The new .as file displays and you will see only the ActionScript panel interface.

2. Add the following ActionScript to the .as file to add numbers in a function, return the sum, and display it in the Output panel:

```
function addValues
  (val1:Number, val2:Number):Number {
  var sum:Number = val1 + val2;
  return sum;
}
var sum:Number = addValues(6, 8);
trace(sum);
```

3. Save the file to a directory of your choice and name it chapter4_include.as.

Next you need to add this .as file to the timeline of a Flash movie.

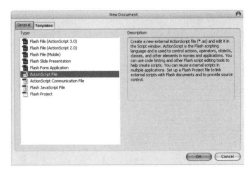

Figure 4.3 Creating a new ActionScript file.

To include an ActionScript file:

1. Create a new Flash file and save it as chapter4_main.fla in the same directory as the chapter4_include.as file.

2. Rename Layer 1 to Actions and open the Actions panel.

3. Add the following ActionScript to include chapter4_include.as in the timeline:

```
include "chapter4_include.as";
```

4. Preview your movie; you should see the result 14 display in the Output panel. This was the result of the ActionScript from the external .as file compiling in the Flash movie.

DISPLAY LISTS AND DISPLAY OBJECTS

Applications for the Flash Platform are primarily oriented around displaying graphics and information. The underlying ActionScript functionality addresses how these graphics and bits of information function and how they are displayed. New to ActionScript 3 is the way Flash renders visual objects. Visual objects, or *display objects*, are added to the stage (and are visible) through the *display list*. The display list manages the hierarchy of display objects, and the display objects themselves are the visible elements. This methodology is referred to as *display programming* in the programming world.

Understanding how the display list works and how to add display objects to the display list programmatically is fundamental to programming visual objects in ActionScript. In this chapter, you will become familiar with the display list and the different types of display object classes and their subclasses. You will also learn how to instantiate and add display objects to the display list (in other words, make them viewable) and position them with ActionScript.

continues on next page

This chapter represents a point in ActionScript programming where you as a programmer have to become both left- and right-brained at the same time. On the left side of the brain, you are tasked with programming logic and data; on the right side, you are adding and creating visuals with ActionScript. Being able to juggle the placement and behavior of the visuals in your head before you see the output on the screen as you are programming them is a skill that you will acquire over time. It is important to try to begin thinking like this from the get-go to become proficient in display programming.

The Display List

The DisplayList is a treelike hierarchy that determines how display objects are placed and traversed on the stage. The DisplayList could be likened to a screen facing the viewer where visual objects are "projected" onto it in a certain order. If you drag a MovieClip or other symbols (DisplayObjects) from the library to the stage at authortime, you are adding it to the DisplayList, of which the stage is the "root," or main element. If you drag a graphic or a button into the timeline of a MovieClip at authortime, you are adding those objects to the display list whose MovieClip is the "container," or timeline, of the display object. Display objects can be added to the display list at runtime as well with ActionScript. When first creating an application, the Stage is the main container in which all display objects are displayed. Subsequently, any objects displayed on the stage that are capable of acting as containers for other objects have their own display list for managing their child display objects.

Figure 5.1 illustrates the Stage of an application, the children of its display list, and the children of the display list objects.

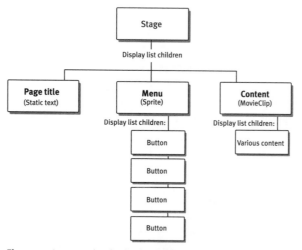

Figure 5.1 An example of a display list hierarchy of display objects.

When you map out an application like the one in Figure 5.1, a treelike hierarchy begins to take form that illustrates the relationship among display objects and shows how the display list can be traversed to communicate and control objects throughout the application.

Depending on the position in which the display objects are located in the display list, display objects follow a stacking order based on the hierarchy in which they were added. The stacking order, or depth, of a display object defines whether they appear on top or below one another visually when display objects overlap.

Changing the stacking order of display objects created at authortime is accomplished by reordering layers in the timeline panel, thus changing their depth order on the stage, or using the Modify > Arrange menu. You can also change the stacking order using ActionScript, which we'll explore at the end of this chapter.

Adding objects to the display list

Display objects can be added to the display list at authortime in one of several ways:

◆ By adding graphics using the shape and drawing tools

◆ By dragging an object to the stage from the library

◆ At runtime with ActionScript using the addChild() method of the DisplayObject class

These approaches will be performed throughout this chapter after the section on display objects.

✔ Tip

■ For a comprehensive overview of the display list approach in ActionScript, view Adobe LiveDocs: http://livedocs.adobe.com/flash/9.0/main/00000144.html.

Display Classes and Objects

Display objects can be created at runtime with ActionScript, or they can be added to the stage at authortime. Whichever way they are added to the stage (or display list), they are all objects derived from the `DisplayObject`, `InteractiveObject`, or `DisplayObjectContainer` classes.

Figure 5.2 illustrates the different display object classes in ActionScript 3 and their relationships to one another. With the exception of the `MorphShape` and `StaticText` classes, all display objects can be created and added to the display list at runtime and managed with ActionScript. All display classes reside in the `display` class package.

The display classes in Figure 5.2 are listed in the hierarchy that defines their core functionality. There are three core display classes: `DisplayObject`, `InteractiveObject`, and `DisplayObjectContainer`.

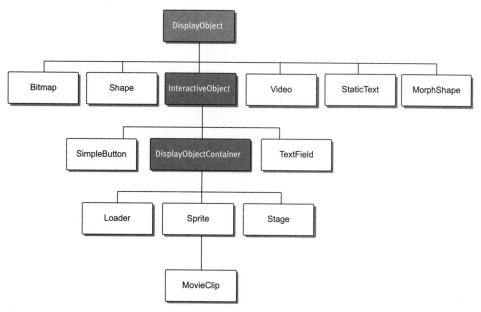

Figure 5.2 Display class hierarchy

Display objects

The DisplayObject class is used to define display objects that are used only for display purposes (no interaction or timeline). The DisplayObject class defines the core functionality of all other display objects as well. This class can also be referred to as a *superclass*. In programming terms, a superclass is a class from which other classes are derived.

The DisplayObject class defines core properties, methods, and events for the display object. **Table 5.1** lists some of the properties, methods, and events of the DisplayObject class.

✔ Tip

■ For a comprehensive list of properties, methods, events, and subclasses of the DisplayObject class, view Adobe LiveDocs: http://livedocs.adobe.com/flash/9.0/ActionScriptLangRefV3/flash/display/DisplayObject.html.

Table 5.1

Properties, Methods, and Events of the DisplayObject **Class**

TYPE	DESCRIPTION
Properties	x, y, width, height, scaleX, scaleY, alpha, filters, mask
Methods	hitTestObject(), globalToLocal(), getBounds(), getRect()
Events	addedToStage, enterFrame, removedFromStage

Table 5.2

Subclasses of the `DisplayObject` **Class**	
SUBCLASS	**DESCRIPTION**
`Bitmap`	Handles loaded bitmap images or bitmap images created with ActionScript.
`Shape`	Creates vector graphics such as circles, lines, rectangles, and complex shapes using math and ActionScript.
`InteractiveObject`	Defines interactive functionality for an object. This will be described in detail in the next section.
`Video`	For displaying video files.
`StaticText`	Handles text creation using the Text tool at authortime only. Cannot be created or manipulated with ActionScript, but still is driven by a class.
`MorphShape`	Used for creating transitions when creating a shape tween at runtime only.

All visual objects at their core are `DisplayObjects`, as shown in Figure 5.2. The `DisplayObject` class can be thought of as first "DNA link" of the display object evolution chain.

All subclasses (or objects) of the `DisplayObject` class "extend" the functionality defined in the `DisplayObject` class. Extending a class means a class uses the superclass for its core functionality and then adds on to that functionality to customize the class for a specific purpose.

The subclasses of the `DisplayObject` class listed in **Table 5.2** all inherit the core functionality from the superclass shown in Table 5.1, and extend the class to serve their own purposes.

In **Figure 5.3**, the Page title in the Flash movie page wireframe is displayed via static text created using the Text tool at authortime. This piece of static text is an object of the `StaticText` class, which extends the `DisplayObject` superclass.

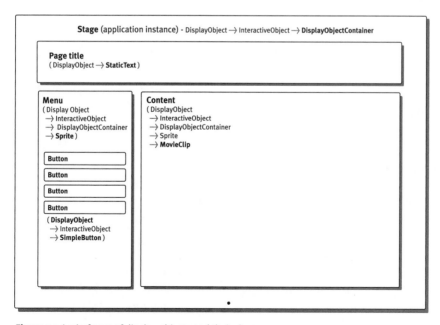

Figure 5.3 A wireframe of display objects and their classes.

DISPLAY CLASSES AND OBJECTS

To add a StaticText display object to the display list at authortime:

1. Create a new Flash file and save it as "Chapter 5 – display objects.fla." Leave its width and height at the default 550 × 400 pixels.

2. Rename Layer 1 to "Page title."

3. Add static text to the display list by selecting the Text tool and typing "Website of bouncing shape" at the top-left corner of the stage.

4. Save and preview the movie (**Figure 5.4**).

5. Save the file and leave it open for the next task.

Interactive objects

The InteractiveObject class extends the DisplayObject superclass (Figure 5.2).

*DisplayObject → **InteractiveObject***

The InteractiveObject class is the core class for all objects that enable user interaction, including keyboard input and mouse interaction. The InteractiveObject class has its own set of properties, methods, and events as well as the ones it has inherited from the DisplayObject class. **Table 5.3** lists some of the more common properties, methods, and events of the InteractiveObject class.

Subclasses of the InteractiveObject class extend the functionality of the InteractiveObject class. **Table 5.4** lists the subclasses that extend the InteractiveObject class to serve their own functional purposes.

In Figure 5.3 the SimpleButton objects within the Menu container in particular are subclasses of the InteractiveObject class since they need to accept mouse interactivity in order to navigate the movie.

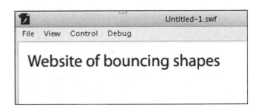

Figure 5.4 A preview of static text added to the display list at runtime.

Table 5.3

Properties, Methods, and Events of the InteractiveObject Class

TYPE	DESCRIPTION
Properties	contentextMenu, mouseEnabled, doubleClickEnabled
Methods	InteractiveObject()
Events	click, keyDown, keyUp, mouseDown, mouseOver, mouseOut, mouseUp, mouseWheel, rollOver

Table 5.4

Subclasses of the InteractiveObject Class

SUBCLASS	DESCRIPTION
DisplayObjectContainer	Defines an object that has a display list for nested object. Described in detail in the next section.
SimpleButton	Controls all instances of buttons in an application.
TextField	Controls all input and output text that is controlled and manipulated with ActionScript.

✔ Tip

■ For a comprehensive list of properties, methods, events, and subclasses of the InteractiveObject, view Adobe LiveDocs: http://livedocs.adobe.com/ flash/9.0/ActionScriptLangRefV3/flash/ display/InteractiveObject.html.

Figure 5.5 Converting the rectangle shape to a Button symbol named `MenuItem`.

Open library options menu here

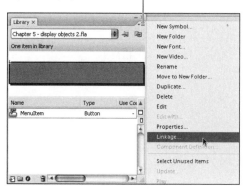

Figure 5.6 The Linkage option in the Library options menu.

Figure 5.7 Making `MenuItem` an object of the `SimpleButton` class from the Linkage panel.

To add an interactive object to the display list from the library at runtime:

1. Return to the Chapter 5 – display objects.fla file that you left open in the previous task.

2. Using the Rectangle tool, draw a rectangle that is 145 pixels wide and 25 pixels high. (I've specified these dimensions so that you can follow the directions when placing the buttons with ActionScript and you won't have to deal with overlaps and erroneous display results.)

3. Select the rectangle shape and convert it to a button symbol (Modify > Convert to Symbol); name it `MenuItem` (**Figure 5.5**).

4. Delete the `MenuItem` instance from the stage since it will be added to the stage at runtime with ActionScript.

5. Select `MenuItem` in the library and from the Library options menu choose Linkage (**Figure 5.6**). The Linkage Properties panel opens.

6. To make the `MenuItem` symbol an object of the `SimpleButton` class, check the Export for ActionScript Linkage option in the Linkage Properties panel. The class field should automatically display the symbol name (`MenuItem`), and `flash.display.SimpleButton` will be defined as the base class for the symbol automatically (**Figure 5.7**).

continues on next page

7. Click OK to close the panel. A warning message appears (**Figure 5.8**). This is Flash's way of saying "You did not create this class file, so I will create one for you." Just ignore this warning by clicking OK. Remember this, since I won't mention this warning in subsequent tasks in this book.

Now we'll write the ActionScript that will add an object instance of the new `MenuItem` class to the display list (of the stage).

8. Create a new layer on the main timeline and name it Actions.

9. Launch the Actions panel and instantiate an instance of `MenuItem`:

```
var miChapterOne:MenuItem =
  new MenuItem();
```

10. Preview the movie. You will not see the instance of `miChapterOne` on the stage as it has not been added to the display list yet. It only exists as an unseen object right now.

11. Add the `miChapterOne` instance to the display list:

```
var miChapterOne:MenuItem =
  new MenuItem();

addChild(miChapterOne);
```

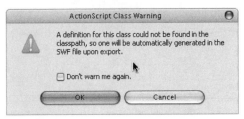

Figure 5.8 The ActionScript Class Warning window appears once you close the Linkage panel. Click OK to ignore this warning.

Figure 5.9 Preview of miChapterOne instance added to the display list.

12. Save and preview the file. You should now see the miChapterOne instance at the top left of the stage (**Figure 5.9**).

13. Roll over the button and you should see the mouse cursor change as you roll over it. This occurs because the SimpleButton class is a subclass of InteractiveObject.

14. Set the x and y positions of miChapter-One:

```
var miChapterOne:MenuItem =
  new MenuItem();
miChapterOne.x = 15;
miChapterOne.y = 60;
addChild(miChapterOne);
```

15. Save and preview your file. The button should now appear below the page title and have a bit of a left margin between it and the left side of the preview window. Keep this file open for use later in this chapter.

✔ Tips

■ It is good practice to use the same name for both the Linkage Identifier and the Library symbol. This makes it easy to reference the name of the object in the library just by looking at its display name in the Library panel when using it with ActionScript.

■ The stage object is a subclass of the DisplayObject class (which will be explained further in the next section). Because it is a subclass of DisplayObject, it inherits the method addChild(), which is used to add objects to the display list.

■ It is good practice to set the properties of an object before it is added to the display list. This ensures the object is ready before it is displayed in the application.

To instantiate and add an interactive object to the display list at runtime:

1. Create a new Flash file.

2. Add an object of the TextField class (a subclass of the InteractiveObject class) to the display list at runtime:

   ```
   var tfText:TextField =
     new TextField();
   ```

3. Set the properties of tfText (**Code 5.1**).

4. Add the instance of tfText to the display list (**Code 5.2**).

5. Preview your file. You should see the text field display the text property in the Output panel.

6. Highlight the text and type a new message into the input text field.

Display object containers

The DisplayObjectContainer class extends the InteractiveObject class and the DisplayObject superclass (Figure 5.2):

DisplayObject InteractiveObject
DisplayObjectContainer

The DisplayObjectContainer class defines objects that serve as containers for other objects. These objects form the containers, or "grandfathers," for all objects contained within their display list hierarchy.

Code 5.1 Set the x, y, width, and text properties of tfText. Make it an interactive text field by setting its type property to input.

```
Code
var tfText:TextField = new TextField();
tfText.x = 10;
tfText.y = 10;
tfText.width = 400;
tfText.text = "This text field was
  created with ActionScript";
tfText.type = TextFieldType.INPUT;
```

Code 5.2 Add the instance tfText to the display list.

```
Code
var tfText:TextField = new TextField();
tfText.x = 10;
tfText.y = 10;
tfText.width = 400;
tfText.text = "This text field was
  created with ActionScript";
tfText.type = TextFieldType.INPUT;
addChild(tfText);
```

DISPLAY CLASSES AND OBJECTS

Table 5.5

Properties, Methods and Events of the DisplayObjectContainer Class

Type	Description
Properties	mouseChildren, numChildren, tabChildren, textSnapshot
Methods	addChild(), getChildAt(), removeChild(), swapChildren()
Events	added, addedToStage, enterFrame, removed, removedFromStage, render

Table 5.6

Subclasses of the DisplayObjectContainer Class

Subclass	Description
Loader	Loads external SWFs and images (JPG, PNG, or GIF)
Sprite	Can contain graphics as well as children
Stage	The entire canvas where all display objects appear

The DisplayObjectContainer class has numerous properties, methods, and events that aid in displaying and controlling multiple display objects. **Table 5.5** lists some of the properties and methods of the DisplayObjectContainer class.

The subclasses that extend the DisplayObjectContainer class are listed and described briefly in **Table 5.6**.

The MovieClip class

The MovieClip class extends the Sprite and DisplayObjectContainer classes (Figure 5.2):

DisplayObject InteractiveObject
DisplayObjectContainer Sprite MovieClip

There is one more class that could be considered a subclass of the DisplayObjectContainer class: the MovieClip class. The MovieClip class is the same as the Sprite class except that it can have a timeline (or a playhead) for frame-by-frame effects and functionality.

All subclasses of the DisplayObjectContainer have their own display lists, just like the stage.

In Figure 5.3, the Stage, Menu, and Content areas of the wireframe are all objects of the DisplayObject class and the Sprite class since they all contain child objects.

✔ Tip

- For a comprehensive list of properties, methods, events, and subclasses of the DisplayObjectContainer class, see the Adobe LiveDocs: http://livedocs.adobe.com/flash/9.0/ActionScriptLangRefV3/flash/display/DisplayObjectContainer.html.

To add a display object container from the library with ActionScript at runtime:

1. Return to the Chapter 5 – display objects. fla file.

2. Using the Rectangle tool, select No Fill Color and a stroke color of your liking. Draw a rectangle that is 350 pixels wide and 310 pixels high.

3. Select the rectangle and convert it to a MovieClip symbol called ShapeContainer.

4. Leave the Convert to Symbol dialog window open after naming the symbol and click the Advanced button at the lower right. This reveals the Linkage properties for the symbol (**Figure 5.10**).

5. Check the Export for ActionScript option and click OK.

6. Delete the ShapeContainer instance from the stage (it will be added to the display list with ActionScript).

7. Select the Actions layer and instantiate, position, and add an instance of the ShapeContainer object to the display list (**Code 5.3**).

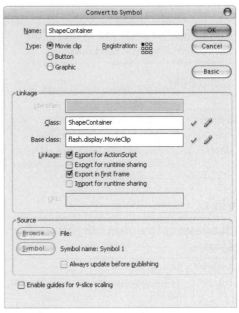

Figure 5.10 Check the Export for ActionScript option in the advanced symbol settings to create a ShapeContainer.

Code 5.3 Instantiate an object of the ShapeContainer class called scShapeContainer and position it at x:15 and y:60. Add the instance to the display list using the addChild() method.

```
var miChapterOne:MenuItem =
  new MenuItem();
var scShapeContainer:ShapeContainer =
  new ShapeContainer();
miChapterOne.x = 15;
miChapterOne.y = 60;
scShapeContainer.x = 180;
scShapeContainer.y = 60;
addChild(miChapterOne);
addChild(scShapeContainer);
```

scShapeContainer instance on display list

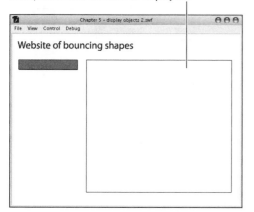

Figure 5.11 The scShapeContainer should be located below the page title and to the right of the menu item button.

8. Save and preview your file. The added instance of scShapeContainer should appear in the preview (**Figure 5.11**).

Because scShapeContainer is a display object container, it should be used as one. Eventually, we'll be using scShapeContainer as a container for changing content within the application.

To add a child object to a MovieClip display object container:

1. Return to the Chapter 5 – display objects. fla file.

2. Double-click the ShapeContainer symbol in the library to edit its timeline.

3. Add a new temporary layer.

4. Draw a small circle on this layer that is roughly 30 pixels × 30 pixels using the Oval tool (**Figure 5.12**).

continues on next page

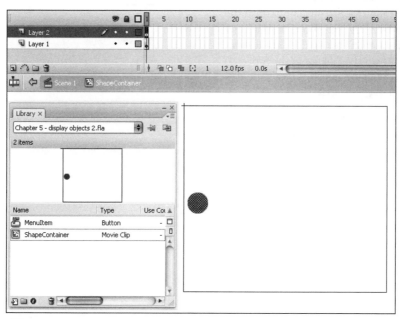

Figure 5.12 Using the Oval tool, draw a circle located just to the right of the left side of the rectangle outline.

5. Select the circle shape and convert it to a MovieClip symbol called `CircleContent`. Check the Advanced option in the Convert to Symbol dialog (if it's not already expanded) and check the Export for ActionScript option. Ensure that the Class entry reads `CircleContent` (**Figure 5.13**). Click OK when you're finished.

6. Double-click the `CircleContent` instance on the stage to enter its timeline.

7. Select the circle shape and convert it to a Graphic symbol called `Circle` so that it can be tweened on the timeline (**Figure 5.14**).

8. Select frame 10 on the timeline of `CircleContent`, and from the main menu, choose Insert > Timeline > Keyframe.

9. Repeat Step 8 for frame 20.

✔ Tip

■ Now that we're beginning to dig deeper into timelines of display objects, it's always a good idea to ensure you're in the right timeline. At this point, you should be in the timeline of `CircleContent`. You can locate this by looking at the top left of the stage. The timeline location should be displayed (**Figure 5.15**).

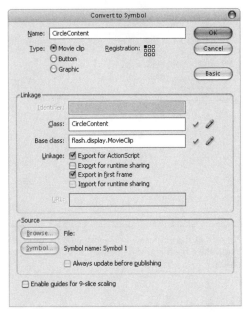

Figure 5.13 Converting the circle shape to a MovieClip symbol called `CircleContent`.

Figure 5.14 Preparing to tween the circle shape on the timeline of `CircleContent`.

Figure 5.15 Current timeline location at the top left of the stage.

10. Return to frame 10 and drag the `Graphic` instance of `Circle` to the right, but still within the left side of the right border of the box outline of the parent timeline of `CircleContent` (**Figure 5.16**).

11. To tween the circle back and forth across the stage, select frame 1, and then from the Tween option drop-down menu in the Properties panel for the frame, choose Motion.

12. Repeat Step 11 for frame 10.

13. Return to the timeline of `ShapeContainer` and remove the instance of `CircleContent` by deleting the layer that was originally added to create the symbol.

14. Return to the main timeline and select the Actions layer.

continues on next page

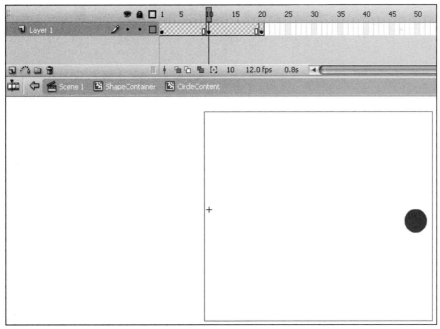

Figure 5.16 Positioning the Circle graphic just inside `CircleContent`. The Circle in frames 1 and 20 should be located on the left in the default position. The circle in frame 10 should be on the right.

15. Open the Actions panel and add an instance of `CircleContent` to the display list of `ShapeContainer` (**Code 5.4**).

16. Save and preview your file (**Figure 5.17**). It should show the instance of `ccCircle` tweening its Circle graphic, with the confines of the square shape inside `scShapeContainer`.

Although it is not obvious during preview, `ccCircle` is a child of the display list of `scShapeContainer` because it displays in the same position of the `ShapeContainer` and not the default `x:0` and `y:0` of the main stage when a child is added.

Code 5.4 Instantiate and add an instance of `CircleContent` to the display list of `scShapeContainer` by calling the `addChild()` method of `scShapeContainer`.

```
                    Code
var miChapterOne:MenuItem =
  new MenuItem();
var scShapeContainer:ShapeContainer =
  new ShapeContainer();
var ccCircle:CircleContent =
  new CircleContent();

miChapterOne.x = 15;
miChapterOne.y = 60;
scShapeContainer.x = 180;
scShapeContainer.y = 60;

addChild(miChapterOne);
addChild(scShapeContainer);
scShapeContainer.addChild(ccCircle);
```

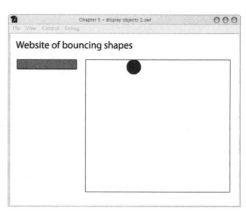

Figure 5.17 The preview should show `ccCircle` tweening its `Circle` graphic.

Code 5.5 Instantiating spMenuContainer using the new Sprite() constructor method.

```
● ○ ●              Code
var miChapterOne:MenuItem =
  new MenuItem();
var scShapeContainer:ShapeContainer =
  new ShapeContainer();
var ccCircle:CircleContent =
  new CircleContent();
var spMenuContainer:Sprite =
  new Sprite();

spMenuContainer.x = 15;
spMenuContainer.y = 60;
scShapeContainer.x = 180;
scShapeContainer.y = 60;

addChild(scShapeContainer);
scShapeContainer.addChild(ccCircle);
addChild(spMenuContainer);
spMenuContainer.addChild(miChapterOne);
```

To instantiate and add a display object container with ActionScript at runtime:

1. Return to the Chapter 5 – display objects. fla file.

2. Select the Actions layer and construct an object of the Sprite class called spMenuContainer using the new Sprite() constructor method (**Code 5.5**).

   spMenuContainer will be a display object container for the miChapterOne object. It will display miChapterOne in its original position but as a result of the position of spMenuContainer. Refer to Code 5.5 for Steps 3 and 4, too.

3. Modify the code that positions miChapterOne so that it positions spMenuContainer with the same properties instead.

4. Modify and add the code that will add miChapterOne to the display list of spMenuContainer.

continues on next page

5. Add another instance of MenuItem to the display list of spMenuContainer directly below the instance of miChapterOne (**Code 5.6**).

6. Save and preview your file. You should now see a second MenuItem instance directly below miChapterOne (**Figure 5.18**). Notice that the y property values are relative to the spMenuContainer object because the child objects are in its display list. As spMenuContainer gets moved around, the child objects will move with it.

Code 5.6 Adding another MenuItem instance to spMenuContainer.

```
var miChapterOne:MenuItem =
  new MenuItem();
var miChapterTwo:MenuItem =
  new MenuItem();
var scShapeContainer:ShapeContainer =
  new ShapeContainer();
var ccCircle:CircleContent =
  new CircleContent();
var spMenuContainer:Sprite =
  new Sprite();

spMenuContainer.x = 15;
spMenuContainer.y = 60;
/* Position the instance of miChapterTwo
   below miChapterOne inside of
   spMenuContainer */
miChapterTwo.y = 30;
scShapeContainer.x = 180;
scShapeContainer.y = 60;

addChild(scShapeContainer);
scShapeContainer.addChild(ccCircle);
addChild(spMenuContainer);
spMenuContainer.addChild(miChapterOne);
spMenuContainer.addChild(miChapterTwo);
```

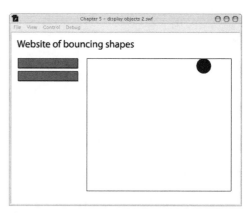

Figure 5.18 Add a second instance of MenuItem to the display list of spMenuContainer and set its y position to just below the first instance.

WORKING WITH DISPLAY OBJECTS

Display objects are all the visible assets of a Flash application. You can both add and manipulate them at authortime, or at runtime using ActionScript. Determining whether to add an object to the stage at authortime or runtime depends on the dynamics of your application. Basic interface graphics that are consistent throughout an application are easier to add and lay out at authortime. If you need to build a menu based on external information, you must add the buttons at runtime. Regardless of which method you choose, you must control those display objects using ActionScript.

You control display objects with ActionScript by setting their properties, calling their methods, and listening for their events (events will be covered in Chapter 7). Display objects are also controlled by methods of the `DisplayObjectContainer` class.

This chapter shows you how to add display objects to the display list and set their properties. You can also set properties of display objects dynamically based on the properties of other display objects. Depth management (the stacking order) of display objects is handled using methods of the `DisplayObjectContainer` class. You'll also learn how to group display objects in containers and remove display objects from the display list.

Display Object Properties

Properties represent the visual and nonvisual attributes of an object. A nonvisual attribute is a value that an object requires to calculate or work with data. A visual attribute is the color, position, or size of an object. Without properties, objects wouldn't look like much or have much to do. ActionScript development would be rather boring.

Table 6.1 lists the most common properties of a display object. You can use ActionScript to set and read all of these public properties.

Even if you have not yet worked with properties in ActionScript, you are most likely still familiar with display object properties. Any display object that is selected on the stage at authortime has properties that can be read and set in the Properties panel (**Figure 6.1**).

All the properties that you have set in Flash at authortime have an ActionScript equivalent.

Table 6.1

Properties of the `DisplayObject` Class	
METHOD	**DESCRIPTION**
`alpha`	Current opacity level of the `DisplayObject`
`blendMode`	Applies a value from the `BlendMode` class to the `DisplayObject`
`filters`	Indexed array of filter objects applied to the `DisplayObject`
`mask`	Specifies a `DisplayObject` to be applied as a mask to the current `DisplayObject`
`mouseX`	Current x coordinate (in pixels) of the mouse in the `DisplayObject`
`mouseY`	Current y coordinate (in pixels) of the mouse in the `DisplayObject`
`name`	Instance name of the `DisplayObject`
`parent`	The `DisplayObjectContainer` that contains the `DisplayObject`
`root`	Topmost `DisplayObject` container of the application
`rotation`	Rotation of the `DisplayObject` (in degrees) from its original orientation
`scaleX`	Horizontal scale percentage applied to the `DisplayObject`
`scaleY`	Vertical scale percentage applied to the `DisplayObject`
`stage`	Stage of the `DisplayObject`
`visible`	Sets the visibility of object (visible or not)
`width`	Width of the `DisplayObject` (in pixels)
`x`	x coordinate (or horizontal position) of `DisplayObject` relative to the coordinates of the `DisplayObjectContainer` that holds the `DisplayObject`
`y`	The y coordinate (or vertical position) of the `DisplayObject` relative to the coordinates of the `DisplayObjectContainer` that holds the `DisplayObject`

Instance name

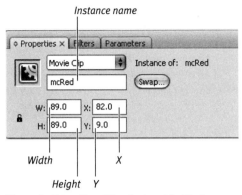

Width

Height   Y

X

Figure 6.1 Properties of the display object in the Properties panel and the corresponding property values in ActionScript that can be referred to in Table 6.1.

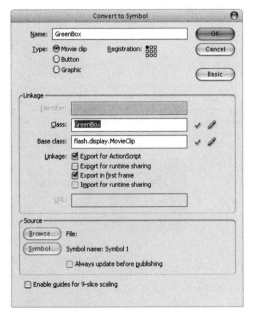

Figure 6.2 Checking the Export for ActionScript option in the Advanced symbol settings assigns the GreenBox symbol a class name of GreenBox.

To set the properties of MovieClip display objects with ActionScript:

1. Draw a red and green rectangle (roughly 90 × 90 pixels each) using the Rectangle tool from the Tool palette.

2. Select the red rectangle and convert it to a MovieClip symbol called RedBox.

3. Select the mcRed instance on the stage and give it an instance name of mcRed in the Properties panel.

4. Select the green rectangle and convert it to a MovieClip symbol named GreenBox.

5. In the Convert to Symbol dialog, click the Advanced button.

6. Check the Export for ActionScript option in the Linkage properties (**Figure 6.2**).

7. Click OK. (Click OK again to ignore the ActionScript warning that appears.)

8. Delete the instance of GreenBox from the stage.

9. Create a new layer called Actions.

continues on next page

10. Open the Actions panel and add the following ActionScript, which sets the x, y, and scaleX properties of mcRed:

```
mcRed.x = 100;
mcRed.y = 50;
mcRed.scaleX = 1.5;
```

11. Preview your file. The position and scaled width of mcRed has been changed with ActionScript regardless of its original properties at authortime.

12. Add an instance of GreenBox at runtime with ActionScript by adding the highlighted code in **Code 6.1**.

13. Preview your file. mcGreen should be displayed on the stage at the top-left corner of the stage. By default, when a display object is added to the display list, its position is x 0 and y 0, unless set otherwise with ActionScript.

14. Add the ActionScript in **Code 6.2** to position and set the transparency of mcGreen.

15. Preview your file. mcGreen should be in a new position and have 50% transparency (**Figure 6.3**).

16. Create a blue rectangle of the stage using the Rectangle tool.

17. Convert the rectangle to a MovieClip symbol called BlueBox and check the Export for ActionScript option in the Advanced symbol settings. The symbol should have a class name of BlueBox. Click OK.

Code 6.1 Adding the GreenBox MovieClip to the display list at runtime.

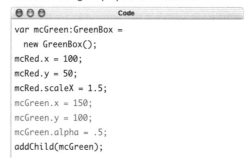

```
var mcGreen:GreenBox =
  new GreenBox();
mcRed.x = 100;
mcRed.y = 50;
mcRed.scaleX = 1.5;
addChild(mcGreen);
```

Code 6.2 Setting the properties of mcGreen.

```
var mcGreen:GreenBox =
  new GreenBox();
mcRed.x = 100;
mcRed.y = 50;
mcRed.scaleX = 1.5;
mcGreen.x = 150;
mcGreen.y = 100;
mcGreen.alpha = .5;
addChild(mcGreen);
```

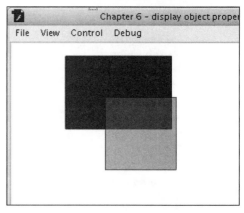

Figure 6.3 The position of mcGreen overlaps the bottom-right corner of mcRed. The alpha setting of .5 (50%) for mcGreen shows a portion of mcRed where the two display objects overlap.

Code 6.3 An instance of mcBlue is added to the display list and is rotated 45 degrees.

```
⬤ ⬤ ⬤          Code
var mcGreen:GreenBox =
  new GreenBox();
var mcBlue:BlueBox =
  new BlueBox();
mcRed.x = 100;
mcRed.y = 50;
mcRed.scaleX = 1.5;
mcGreen.x = 150;
mcGreen.y = 100;
mcGreen.alpha = .5;
mcBlue.x = 200;
mcBlue.y = 150;
mcBlue.rotation = 45;
addChild(mcGreen);
addChild(mcBlue);
```

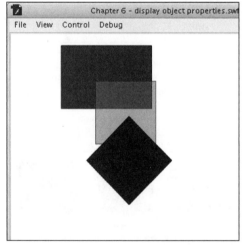

Figure 6.4 mcBlue is positioned over the bottom of mcGreen and rotated 45 degrees.

18. Delete the instance of BlueBox from the stage.

19. Add the following ActionScript to add an instance of BlueBox to the stage and set its x, y, and rotation properties (**Code 6.3**).

20. Preview your file. mcBlue should be added to the display list with its set properties (**Figure 6.4**).

Keep this file open for the next task.

Positioning display objects dynamically

A powerful function of display object properties is the ability to get a property from one display object and have it affect the property of another. This is a big step toward having your applications think for you and build themselves based on information you provide them. The code becomes streamlined and reusable when you build an application "dynamically."

In the previous task, we used a specified value to position the rectangle display objects. Those display objects can also be positioned by getting property information from them to help position the next object added to the display list.

To dynamically position display objects:

1. Save the file from the previous task as a new file.

2. Delete the mcRed instance from the stage.

3. Delete all the ActionScript from the Actions layer.

continues on next page

4. Add an instance of GreenBox to the stage by adding the following ActionScript:

```
var mcGreen1:GreenBox =
  new GreenBox();
addChild(mcGreen1);
```

5. Add a second instance of GreenBox to the stage and position it horizontally beside mcGreen1 by using the width, x position of mcGreen1 and a margin value of 5 (**Code 6.4**).

6. Preview your file. mcGreen2 should be positioned 5 pixels to the right of mcGreen1 (**Figure 6.5**).

7. Repeat Step 5 to create a new instance named mcGreen3 and use the x and width properties of mcGreen2 to position the new instance.

We will cover a self-building menu using dynamic property placement in Chapter 12.

Positioning and registration points

x, y, scaleX, scaleY, and rotation properties are all dependent on the registration point of a display object. The registration point is the x 0 and y 0 coordinates of a display object. Think of the registration point as the point where a display objects is "pinned" to the stage. Wherever the registration point for an object is, that's where it will be positioned for its x and y coordinates. The registration point is also the origin for where an object is scaled from and what an object is rotated around (**Figure 6.6**).

Code 6.4 Adding a second instance of GreenBox to the display list and setting its properties.

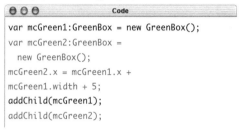

```
var mcGreen1:GreenBox = new GreenBox();
var mcGreen2:GreenBox =
  new GreenBox();
mcGreen2.x = mcGreen1.x +
mcGreen1.width + 5;
addChild(mcGreen1);
addChild(mcGreen2);
```

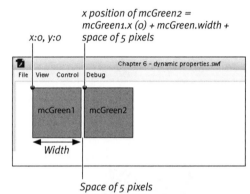

Figure 6.5 The position of mcGreen2 is determined based on the x and width properties on mcGreen1.

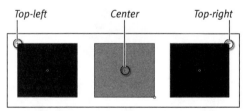

Figure 6.6 The registration point of a display object acts as its center for positioning, scaling, and rotating.

Center registration point

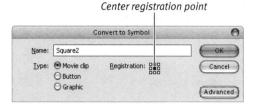

Figure 6.7 The center registration point of Square2.

Bottom-right registration point

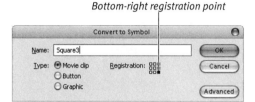

Figure 6.8 Bottom-right registration point of Square3.

Code 6.5 Setting the scaleX and rotation properties of each MovieClip instance.

```
mcSquare1.rotation = 45;
mcSquare1.scaleX = 1.5;
mcSquare2.rotation = 45;
mcSquare2.scaleX = 1.5;
mcSquare3.rotation = 45;
mcSquare3.scaleX = 1.5;
```

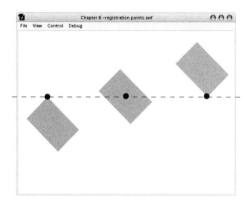

Figure 6.9 Each display object rotates around a different axis and scale from a different origin based on the different registration points.

To experiment with display object properties using different registration points:

1. Create a new file and draw three squares on the stage using the Rectangle tool. Space the squares and horizontally align them across the stage.

2. Select the first square and convert it to a MovieClip symbol called Square1. Keep its registration point top-left (the default registration point).

3. Select the second square and convert it to a MovieClip symbol called Square2. Set its registration point to center (**Figure 6.7**).

4. Select the third square and convert it to a MovieClip symbol called Square3. Set its registration point to the bottom-right registration point (**Figure 6.8**).

5. Give the Square1, Square2, and Square3 instance names of mcSquare1, mcSquare2, and mcSquare3, respectively.

6. Create a new layer called Actions and add the ActionScript in **Code 6.5** to set the rotation and scaleX properties of each instance.

7. Preview your file. Note the differences in the scaleX origin and the axis point for the rotation property of each (**Figure 6.9**).

Using display object containers to position groups of display objects

Using display object containers is perfect for grouping objects that can be positioned as a single group of objects. For instance, you can add all the buttons for a menu to the display list of a single display object container so that you can move the menu around the stage.

To group display objects in a display object container:

1. Open the file you created from the "To dynamically position display objects" task earlier in this chapter.

2. Modify the ActionScript on the Actions layer to add the MovieClips to a `DisplayObjectContainer` called `mcBoxContainer` (**Code 6.6**).

3. Add the following code at the end of the ActionScript to move `mcBoxContainer` and the `DisplayObjects` within it as a group:

   ```
   mcBoxContainer.x = 150;
   mcBoxContainer.y = 200;
   ```

4. Preview your file. Note that `mcBoxContainer` and the display objects within it have all moved as one.

Code 6.6 Adding the MovieClip instances to `mcBoxContainer`'s display list.

```
var mcBoxContainer:MovieClip =
  new MovieClip();
var mcGreen1:GreenBox =
  new GreenBox();
var mcGreen2:GreenBox =
  new GreenBox();
mcGreen2.x =
  mcGreen1.x + mcGreen1.width + 5;
addChild(mcBoxContainer);
mcBoxContainer.addChild(mcGreen1);
mcBoxContainer.addChild(mcGreen2);
```

Table 6.2

Depth-Management Methods of the `DisplayObjectContainer` Class

METHOD	DESCRIPTION
`addChildAt()`	Adds a `DisplayObject` to a display list at a specific depth index
`getChildAt()`	Returns a `DisplayObject` instance at a specified index
`getChildIndex()`	Returns the index position of a specified child `DisplayObject`
`removeChildAt()`	Removes the child `DisplayObject` from the specific index position
`setChildIndex()`	Changes the index position of the specified child `DisplayObject`
`swapChildren()`	Swaps the index positions of two specified child `DisplayObjects`
`swapChildrenAt()`	Swaps the position of two child `DisplayObjects` at specified index positions

Code 6.7 Adding `SquareA` and `SquareB` MovieClip objects to the display list.

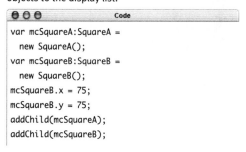

```
var mcSquareA:SquareA =
  new SquareA();
var mcSquareB:SquareB =
  new SquareB();
mcSquareB.x = 75;
mcSquareB.y = 75;
addChild(mcSquareA);
addChild(mcSquareB);
```

Managing Object Depths

In applications for the Flash platform, all display objects reside on their own *depth* on the display list. If two display objects overlap each other, the display object with the higher depth sits in front of the object(s) on the lower depth(s).

Depths are like a z-index in Cascading Style Sheets (CSS)-driven Web pages. As display objects are added to the display list, the newest one to be added is assigned the next highest available depth. You sometimes have to shuffle object depths in an application when you need a display object to sit underneath or on top of other display objects. This is where depth management comes in to play.

Depth management can be achieved in many different ways. In addition to automatic depth assignment when a display object is added to the display list, you can use methods of the `DisplayObjectContainer` class to shuffle and change depths of objects (**Table 6.2**).

To manage DisplayObject depths:

1. Draw two different-colored square shapes on the stage roughly 100 × 100 pixels and convert them to MovieClips named SquareA and SquareB, respectively. Check the Export for ActionScript option in the Advanced symbol settings. This will give the MovieClips class names of SquareA and SquareB.

2. Delete the instances of SquareA and SquareB from the stage.

3. Add the ActionScript in **Code 6.7** to the timeline to add SquareA and SquareB to the display list.

4. Preview your movie. mcSquareB should be overlapping and sitting on top of mcSquareA.

continues on next page

5. Change the order in which mcSquareA and mcSquareB are added:

   ```
   addChild(mcSquareB);
   addChild(mcSquareA);
   ```

6. Preview your movie. mcSquareA should now be sitting on top of mcSquareB as it was added to the display list last.

7. Add the following code at the end of the ActionScript, which will swap the depths of mcSquareA and mcSquareB using the swapChildren() method:

   ```
   swapChildren(mcSquareB, mcSquareA);
   ```

8. Preview your file. mcSquareB should now be sitting back on top of mcSquareA. It does not matter which order the display objects are passed in the swapChildren() method.

9. Add the following ActionScript at the bottom of the code to display the depths that mcSquareA and mcSquareB are sitting on by using the getChildIndex() method:

   ```
   trace("mcSquareA depth: " +
     getChildIndex(mcSquareA));
   trace("mcSquareB depth: " +
     getChildIndex(mcSquareB));
   ```

10. Preview your file (**Figure 6.10**).

11. Comment out the swapChildren() method and preview your file (**Figure 6.11**).

mcSquareA

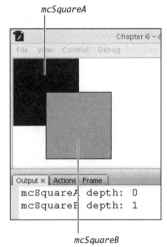

mcSquareB

Figure 6.10 The depths for mcSquareA and mcSquareB are determined by the order they were added to the display list.

mcSquareA

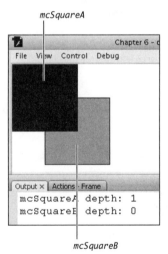

mcSquareB

Figure 6.11 The depths for mcSquareA (index 1) and mcSquareB (index 0) have changed to the order in which they were added to the display list.

MANAGING OBJECT DEPTHS

Code 6.8 Add a new instance of SquareB to the stage and name it mcSquareC. Get the index depth of mcSquareA and add mcSquareC as a child at that depth. mcSquareA will automatically get bumped up an index position.

```
var mcSquareA:SquareA =
  new SquareA();
var mcSquareB:SquareB =
  new SquareB();
var mcSquareC:SquareB =
  new SquareB();
mcSquareB.x = 50;
mcSquareB.y = 50;
mcSquareC.x = 25;
mcSquareC.y = 25;

addChild(mcSquareB);
addChild(mcSquareA);
addChildAt(mcSquareC,
getChildIndex(mcSquareA));

trace('mcSquareA depth: ' +
  getChildIndex(mcSquareA));
trace('mcSquareB depth: ' +
  getChildIndex(mcSquareB));
trace('mcSquareC depth: ' +
  getChildIndex(mcSquareC));
```

12. Add code that will add another instance of SquareB to the display list and place it between mcSquareA and mcSquareB (**Code 6.8**).

It may seem like a lot of work to put mcSquareC between the two MovieClips. It could have been added between in the order of addChild() methods. The purpose of this step is primarily to show an example of using the getChildIndex() and addChildAt() methods when needed in more complicated instances.

13. Preview your file. mcSquareC should lie between mcSquareB and mcSquareA (**Figure 6.12**).

Managing DisplayObject depths is needed in many scenarios in application development. Hopefully, this has been a good introduction to depth management. Subsequent chapters of the book revisit this topic, since it can present many problems as well as solutions.

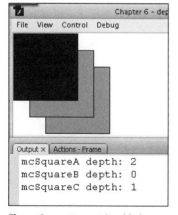

Figure 6.12 mcSquareC is added as a child at the depth of mcSquareA. mcSquareA automatically bumps up an index position.

Removing Display Objects from the Display List

Removing display objects from the display list is an important part of managing a Flash application. I've seen many developers simply turn off the visibility of a display object, or move it out of the viewable area of the stage. This is effective in hiding the object from the application's viewable area, but the object is still in memory and possibly executing code that consumes valuable CPU resources. Whether a display object was added at authortime or at runtime, it can be removed by calling the `removeChild()` method of the `DisplayObjectContainer` class and specifying the instance name of the object to be removed.

✔ Tip

■ Just as important as removing the object from the display list is removing any listeners and code that is running for the object being removed. Removing ActionScript associated with an object will be covered in future chapters in this book.

To remove a DisplayObject from the display list:

1. Draw a shape on the stage and convert it to a MovieClip symbol.

2. Give the MovieClip an instance name of `mcRemoveMe`.

3. Add the following ActionScript to the first keyframe that will remove `mcRemoveMe` from the display list:

   ```
   removeChild(mcRemoveMe);
   ```

4. Preview your movie. The `mcRemoveMe` instance should be gone from the display list at runtime.

COMMUNICATION AND EVENTS

Communications in ActionScript is completely event driven. The ActionScript 3 event model allows class objects to be completely encapsulated. *Encapsulation* means that class objects take care of themselves internally and are not concerned with how any other class objects function. They do their job and keep their heads down. When objects do need to communicate with the outside world, they dispatch events. Listeners are registered with objects to listen for dispatched events, and they act accordingly.

Events are triggered in many ways depending on the class. The process of handling them, however, is standardized throughout the ActionScript API. In this chapter, you will become familiarized with the ActionScript 3 event model by defining its phases and working with events of the `Event`, `MouseEvent`, and `KeyboardEvent` classes. You will also learn to utilize the information within the dispatched event object to simplify and streamline ActionScript development. Finally, we'll examine how event flow functions with user interaction.

When you've finished reading this chapter, you should be comfortable with the event model and using the event classes.

The ActionScript 3 Event Model

The ActionScript 3 event model makes communication between objects straightforward and consistent. In previous versions of ActionScript, the event models were much murkier; there were a few different event models you had to use depending on what class you were working with. In ActionScript 3, there is only one event model.

Event process details

The three processes of handling events are as follows:

◆ **Event listener declaration**—The declaration registers a function to listen for an event.

◆ **Event dispatchers**—When an event happens within a class, it is dispatched from the object. *Event objects* are passed with the event. Event objects contain information about the event (**Figure 7.1**).

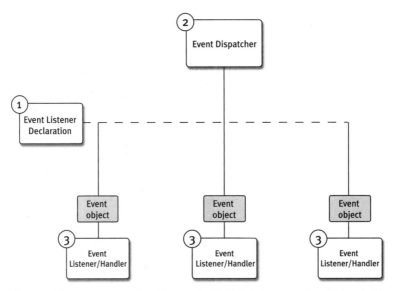

Figure 7.1 Three processes of handling events. Multiple listeners can be registered with a single object as the object can dispatch different types of events.

Table 7.1

Event Class Properties

PROPERTY	DESCRIPTION
bubbles	Boolean value (true/false) that indicates whether the event is a bubbling event
cancelable	Boolean value that specifies whether the behavior associated with an event can be stopped
currentTarget	The object and event listener processing the event object
phase	Current phase of the event flow
target	The target object of the event
type	The type of event dispatched

◆ **Event listener, or handler**—An event listener, or handler, is a function that has a list of instructions (code) called in response to the function "hearing" an event.

The *event listener* and *event handler* are one and the same—a function that listens for an event as well as handling it. I'll refer to this function as either a listener or a handler from this point on, but keep in mind they are the same.

Event dispatchers

All classes that dispatch events use the dispatchEvent() method inherited from the EventDispatcher class or implement the IEventDispatcher interface. The dispatchEvent() method is called when something happens within the class that it wants to broadcast to the rest of the application to let it know something is happening. Pertinent information about the event and other parameters that may need to be sent are passed in an event object to the listener. The event dispatcher is the start of the event process.

The Event class is the base class for event objects. When an event is triggered by an EventDispatcher method (such as addEventListener), an event object is passed to the parameter in the listener method. The event object contains pertinent data for the event that is being dispatched. The Event class has standard properties, methods, and constants that are utilized by most classes. **Table 7.1** lists properties of the Event class that are passed in an event object. These properties can be accessed through the event listener.

This book focuses mainly on the fundamental type, target, and currentTarget properties of event objects.

✔ **Tip**

■ You can also program custom events for your own custom classes; however, this topic is outside the scope of the book. You can learn more by searching the Flash Help menu using the keywords "EventDispatcher class."

Registering event listeners

Event listeners are registered with objects to listen for dispatched events. An object will always dispatch its events when they occur, regardless of whether a listener is registered to "receive," or "listen to," that event.

Listeners just need to be "wired-up" with an object to "hear" them.

Listeners are registered with an object when a particular event that has been dispatched from an object is important to the functionality of an application, such as when a user clicks a button (the mouseDown event is dispatched), or when an image has finished loading (when the complete event is dispatched).

Each listener registered with an object is listening for a specific *event type*. The type of event being dispatched is represented by a string, which is stored in a *static class constant*. Constants are read-only properties that do not change and are, by convention, written in uppercase. As we covered earlier, static properties can be referenced by the class name directly. The event class associated with the event object also stores these event constants. For example, the type of MouseEvent event dispatched could be of the "mouseDown," or MouseEvent.MOUSE_DOWN type. The reason we use an event constant (i.e., MOUSE_DOWN) instead of a string (i.e., "mouseDown") for the event type is to enable code completion in the ActionScript editor, and to have the compiler catch any possible spelling mistakes we might make in typing the event type.

Table 7.2 shows some common event types of the Event class and their constants.

Table 7.2

Event Types of the Event Class	
Constant	**Event Type**
ADDED_TO_STAGE	"addedToStage" event object
CHANGE	"change" event object
COMPLETE	"complete" event object
ENTER_FRAME	"enterFrame" event object
FULL_SCREEN	"fullScreen" event object
INIT	"init" event object
REMOVED	"removed" event object
REMOVED_FROM_STAGE	"removedFromStage" event object
RESIZE	"resize" event object
SOUND_COMPLETE	"soundComplete" event object
UNLOAD	"unload" event object

THE ACTIONSCRIPT 3 EVENT MODEL

The syntax for adding an event listener to an object begins with the object and then the `addEventListener()` method:

```
objectName.addEventListener();
```

You must pass two mandatory arguments to the `addEventListener()` method:

◆ The event type to listen for

◆ The function that will be the event listener for the event

Here's an example:

```
objectName.addEventListener
  (EventClass.EVENT_TYPE,
  EventHandlerFunction);
```

Here's an example of registering a `MouseEvent` with a button:

```
buttonName.addEventListener
  (MouseEvent.MOUSE_UP, mouseUp);
```

Event listeners

The event listener (otherwise known as an event handler) is a function or method that is registered with an object to "listen for" a specific event type. This function is declared just like any other function. You must, however, type the event object of the event as a parameter of the function:

```
function eventHandler(evt:Event):void {

}
```

The properties of the event object can be accessed from the handler function parameter.

✔ Tip

■ Using a string ("mouseDown") instead of an event constant (`MOUSE_DOWN`) is legal, but not recommended.

Working with Event Listeners

Event listeners are the conduit for all communications in ActionScript. An event is dispatched; a listener "hears" it and handles the event.

When we say "handles the event," we mean that the listener function has received the event object as a value for its event parameter, and proceeds to execute the code contained within.

The Event class

The `flash.events.Event` class handles the most common events used in the ActionScript API. For example, the `addedToStage` event is dispatched from every display object that is added to the stage at runtime.

To listen for an event of the Event class:

1. Add the following ActionScript to the first keyframe in a new file, which instantiates a new object of the `Sprite` class and registers an event listener for the `addedToStage` event of the `Event` class:

```
var s:Sprite = new Sprite();
s.addEventListener
  (Event.ADDED_TO_STAGE,
  spriteAddedHandler);
```

2. Add the following code, which creates the event listener for the `ADDED_TO_STAGE` event:

```
function
  spriteAddedHandler(evt:Event):void {
    trace("s has been added to the
    stage.");
}
```

Figure 7.2 The spriteAddedHandler() listener executes when the Event. ADDED_TO_STAGE event is dispatched from Sprite once it has been added to the stage.

Code 7.1 Registering an event listener for the REMOVED_FROM_STAGE event.

```
var s:Sprite = new Sprite();
s.addEventListener
  (Event.ADDED_TO_STAGE, spriteAddedHandler);
s.addEventListener
  (Event.REMOVED_FROM_STAGE,
  spriteRemovedHandler);
```

Code 7.2 Adding the spriteRemovedHandler() event listener and removing the sprite from the display list.

```
function spriteAddedHandler(evt:Event):void {
  trace("s has been added to the stage.");
}
function
  spriteRemovedHandler(evt:Event):void {
    trace("s has been removed from the
      stage.");
}
addChild(s);
removeChild(s);
```

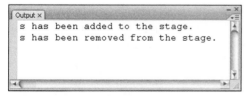

Figure 7.3 The spriteRemovedHandler() event listener is called when the Sprite is removed from the stage and dispatches the REMOVED_FROM_STAGE event type.

3. Add the following code, which adds the Sprite as a child to the stage:

addChild(s);

4. Preview your file. The message in the trace() statement should display in the Output panel (**Figure 7.2**).

Multiple event listeners can be added to an object (i.e., the same object dispatching different event types to different listeners). Multiple objects can also be associated with the same event listener (i.e., a generic listener that identifies which event type was dispatched, and from which object).

To listen for multiple event types of the Event class:

1. Add the highlighted code in **Code 7.1**, which will register a listener for the REMOVED_FROM_STAGE event type of the Event class.

2. Add the highlighted code in **Code 7.2**, which creates the spriteRemovedHandler event listener and removes the Sprite from the stage.

3. Preview your file. The message from the spriteRemovedHandler() listener should display in the Output panel (**Figure 7.3**).

As these steps demonstrate, multiple event listeners can be registered with a single object—one for each event type dispatched.

Working with event objects

Event objects are referenced by calling the Event object parameter passed to the event listener. Refer back to Table 7.1 for the properties passed in an Event object.

To access the properties of an event object:

1. Return to the file from the previous task.

2. Modify the ActionScript code to display the event type and the event target (**Code 7.3**).

3. Preview your movie. The Event object properties should display in the Output panel (**Figure 7.4**).

✔ Tip

- One good use of properties of an Event object is to check multiple event types in a single event handler rather than creating an event handler for each listener individually. We'll discuss this in the next section.

The MouseEvent class

Some class objects need extra event types to be dispatched from an object that the Event class alone does not cover, so we use an "enhanced" event object. These "enhanced" event classes extend the Event class to include more event types and properties. The flash.events.MouseEvent class is an example.

The MouseEvent class is one of the most commonly used event classes in ActionScript. Without mouse events, user interaction would be rather limited. **Table 7.3** is a list of all the MouseEvent types in the ActionScript API.

Code 7.3 Calling the Event object's properties and displaying them in the Output panel.

```
function spriteAddedHandler(evt:Event):void {
  // trace("s has been added to the
  // stage.");
  trace("Event object: " + evt);
  trace("Event type: " + evt.type);
  trace("Event target: " + evt.target);
}
function spriteRemovedHandler(evt:Event):void {
  //trace("s has been removed from the
  // stage.");
}
addChild(s);
removeChild(s);
```

```
Output ×
Event object: [Event type="addedToStage" bubbles=
false cancelable=false eventPhase=2]
Event type: addedToStage
Event target: [object Sprite]
```

Figure 7.4 Displaying properties of the Event object.

Table 7.3

Event Types of the MouseEvent Class	
CONSTANT	**EVENT TYPE**
CLICK	"click" event object
DOUBLE_CLICK	"doubleClick" event object
MOUSE_DOWN	"mouseDown" event object
MOUSE_MOVE	"mouseMove" event object
MOUSE_OUT	"mouseOut" event object
MOUSE_OVER	"mouseOver" event object
MOUSE_UP	"mouseUp" event object
MOUSE_WHEEL	"mouseWheel" event object
ROLL_OUT	"rollOut" event object
ROLL_OVER	"rollOver" event object

Code 7.4 Adding an event listener for the MOUSE_DOWN event type.

```
●  ●  ●            Code
btnButton1.addEventListener
  (MouseEvent.MOUSE_DOWN, mousePressedHandler);
function mousePressedHandler
  (evt:MouseEvent):void {
    trace("btnButton1 was pressed");
}
```

Code 7.5 All objects dispatch a MouseEvent to the same listener/event handler function.

```
●  ●  ●            Code
btnButton1.addEventListener
  (MouseEvent.MOUSE_DOWN, mouseEventHandler);
btnButton1.addEventListener
  (MouseEvent.MOUSE_UP, mouseEventHandler);
btnButton1.addEventListener
  (MouseEvent.MOUSE_OVER, mouseEventHandler);

function
  mouseEventHandler(evt:MouseEvent):void {
      trace("Event type: " + evt.type);
}
```

```
Output ×                                    _ ×
Event type: mouseOver
Event type: mouseDown
Event type: mouseUp
```

Figure 7.5 The single event handler uses the type property from the MouseEvent object to display the different mouse events to the Output panel.

To listen for mouse events:

1. Draw a rectangle shape on the stage.

2. Select the rectangle shape and convert it to a Button symbol.

3. Give the Button instance on the stage an instance name of btnButton1.

4. Create a new layer named Actions.

5. Add the ActionScript code from **Code 7.4**, which adds an event listener to btnButton1 to listen for the MOUSE_DOWN event of the MouseEvent class.

6. Preview your file. The trace() message should appear in the Output panel when the button is clicked.

7. Modify and add the ActionScript to register the same event listener for the MOUSE_OVER and MOUSE_UP events and the MouseEvent class (**Code 7.5**).

8. Preview your file. The three different event types should display in the Output panel (**Figure 7.5**).

WORKING WITH EVENT LISTENERS

Checking for multiple event types in the same event handler

A common practice for any experienced programmer is to write as little code as possible. This allows applications to perform better and makes updating and managing code easier. A good opportunity to streamline your code is in the event handlers. By referencing the type property of an event object, the event type can be determined and the appropriate actions can be taken in the event handler.

To check for multiple event types in an event listener:

1. Return to the file from the previous task.

2. Add the ActionScript in **Code 7.6** just below the trace() statement in the mouseEventHandler event handler function.

Conditional statements will be covered in Chapter 12.

The KeyboardEvent class

The flash.events.KeyboardEvent class is another class that extends the Event class. The KeyboardEvent has two new events that add keyboard functionality in an application: the keyDown and keyUp events. Their constant values are KEY_DOWN and KEY_UP, respectively.

To listen for keyboard events globally within an application, a listener can be registered on the stage: stage.addEventListener();. The listener can then listen for the KEY_DOWN or KEY_UP events and call their corresponding event handlers.

To detect and to react to a keypress, a KeyboardEvent event listener must be declared. Combinations of keypresses, such as the Ctrl, Alt, and Shift keys and any other key, can also be detected. These properties are listed in **Table 7.4**.

Code 7.6 Using an if conditional statement to match the MouseEvent types in a single event handler. When the literal value of an event type is matched in the if statement, the code block in the if statement is executed.

```
function
  mouseEventHandler(evt:MouseEvent):void {
    trace("Event type: " + evt.type);
  if (evt.type == "mouseDown") {
    trace("mouseDown event.
      Do something.");
  } else if (evt.type == "mouseUp")
    trace("mouseUp event.
      Do something.");
  } else if (evt.type == "mouseUp")
    trace("mouseOver event.
      Do something.");
  }
}
```

Table 7.4

KeyboardEvent **Properties**	
PROPERTY	DESCRIPTION
charCode	The character code of key pressed or released
keyCode	The key code value of key pressed or released
keyLocation	Location of key pressed or released on keyboard
ctrlKey	True if key is pressed; false if not
altKey	True if key is pressed; false if not
shiftKey	True if key is pressed; false if not

Code 7.7 Displaying key code values to the Output panel.

```
Code
stage.addEventListener
  (KeyboardEvent.KEY_DOWN, keyDownHandler);
function keyDownHandler
  (evt:KeyboardEvent):void {
    trace("keyCode value is: " + evt.keyCode);
}
```

Code 7.8 Listening if the W key is pressed.

```
Code
function
  keyDownHandler(evt:KeyboardEvent):void {
    if (evt.keyCode == 87) {
      trace("keyCode value is: " + evt.keyCode);
    }
}
```

Key detection is achieved by comparing the keyCode value of the key that's currently pressed and matching it with the standard keyboard values that are used to identify keys in ActionScript.

To detect keyboard events and key values:

1. Add **Code 7.7** to the stage to listen for a KEY_DOWN event and use trace() to display the keyCode value in the Output panel.

2. Preview your file. Press W on your keyboard and the message "keyCode value is: 87" should display in the Output panel.

3. Wrap the trace() statement in the downEvent() function with an if conditional statement, which executes only when a user presses the W key (**Code 7.8**).

4. Preview your file. The trace() statement will only execute if the W keyCode of 87 is matched in the if statement.

A full list of key codes can be found at Adobe LiveDocs: http://livedocs.adobe.com/flash/9.0/main/00001136.html.

✔ Tip

■ Previewing the file straight from the Flash IDE may not allow all keypresses to be registered in the player, because the Flash IDE itself may capture them as keyboard shortcuts and interfere with the Flash Player.

WORKING WITH EVENT LISTENERS

Removing event listeners

Just as important as adding event listeners to objects is deleting them when you either remove an object from the stage or no longer need to listen to object events. Even though an object may no longer be needed, its event listeners still consume resources if not removed.

To remove an event listener, you'll use code syntax similar to adding an event listener, except you'll use the `removeEventListener()` method call. The first step in deleting an event listener is calling the object with which the event listener is registered. The next step is calling the `removeEventListener()` method, and, finally, specifying the event type and event listener as arguments:

```
objectName.removeEventListener
  (EventClass.EVENT_TYPE,
    eventHandler);
```

To remove an event listener:

1. Add **Code 7.9**, which declares an event listener for the `MOUSE_DOWN` `MouseEvent` to the stage.

2. Add the `removeEventListener()` call after the `trace()` statement to disassociate the `MouseEvent.MOUSE_DOWN` event from the stage (**Code 7.10**).

3. Preview your file. Click the stage and a message that says "stage clicked." appears in the Output panel. Click the stage again. You won't see the message this time because the listener for the `MOUSE_DOWN` event has been removed.

Code 7.9 Listening for a `MOUSE_DOWN` event on the stage.

```
stage.addEventListener
  (MouseEvent.MOUSE_DOWN, stageClickHandler);

function
  stageClickHandler(evt:MouseEvent):void {
    trace("stage clicked.");
}
```

Code 7.10 Removing the `MOUSE_DOWN` event listener.

```
function stageClickHandler
  (evt:MouseEvent):void {
    trace("stage clicked.");
    stage.removeEventListener
    (MouseEvent.MOUSE_DOWN, stageClickHandler);
}
```

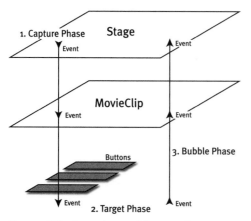

Figure 7.6 The three phases of the event flow.

Event Flow

The event flow concept is a new concept in ActionScript 3 and is primarily used with MouseEvent and KeyboardEvent objects. An event such as a MouseEvent dispatched from a button is not just an event dispatched from the button itself, but an event is also dispatched from the parent display object containers in which the button object sits (**Figure 7.6**).

This is helpful if you have a MovieClip container object that contains a series of buttons. Rather than creating an event listener for all the buttons in the MovieClip container, you can register a single event listener with the container itself. You can verify whether a button within the MovieClip container was clicked in the process by referencing the target and currentTarget properties of the MouseEvent object.

The event flow takes place in three phases:

◆ **Capture phase**—The event begins at the stage and works its way through all display objects until it reaches the object from which the event is originating.

◆ **Target phase**—The event is dispatched from the target object.

◆ **Bubble phase**—If the bubble event is set when the event object is created; the event process bubbles back up through all parent display object containers until the stage is reached again.

The difference between the capture and bubble phases reflects whether you want the event to work on the way down in the capture phase and/or on the way back up after the target phase. If you want to use the capture phase only, an additional parameter of useCapture is set to true after the event object in the event-handler function:

```
function eventHandler
  (evt:EventObject, useCapture=true)
```

By default, useCapture is set to false, and events are handled in the target and bubble phases.

To work with event flow, use the target and currentTarget properties of the event object.

The currentTarget property is always the object with which the event listener is registered. The target property is the object currently targeted in the event flow.

For example, a button named button1 is in the display list of a MovieClip called buttonContainer, and a MOUSE_DOWN event listener method named clickHandler is registered with buttonContainer. If the mouse pointer is hovering over button1 when buttonContainer is clicked, the currentTarget property of the MouseEvent object will return buttonContainer, and the target property will return button1.

To work with the event flow:

1. Draw a rectangle button on the stage.

2. Convert the rectangle shape to a Button symbol named Button.

3. Drag two more instances of the Button symbol to the stage.

4. Assign the three Button symbols instance names of button1, button2, and button3.

5. Select all the Button instances on the stage and convert them to a MovieClip symbol called ButtonContainer. All three button instances now sit in the ButtonContainer instance.

6. Assign the ButtonContainer an instance name of buttonContainer.

7. Create a new layer called Actions.

EVENT FLOW

Code 7.11 Displaying the `target` and `currentTarget` properties of the `MouseEvent` object.

```
                    Code
function
  buttonEventHandler(evt:MouseEvent):void {
    trace("Target is: " +
    DisplayObject(evt.target).name);
    trace("Current target is: " +
    DisplayObject(evt.currentTarget).name);
}
```

```
Output ×
Target is: button1
Current target is: buttonContainer
Target is: button2
Current target is: buttonContainer
Target is: button3
Current target is: buttonContainer
```

Figure 7.7 The `currentTarget` property value is `buttonContainer` because the event listener is registered with this object. The target properties, however, change from button to button because they are the `target` object under the mouse click when the `mouseDown` event occurs.

8. Add the following code to the Actions layer, which adds an event listener to `buttonContainer` and registers `buttonEventHandler` as the listener:

   ```
   buttonContainer.addEventListener
       (MouseEvent.MOUSE_DOWN,
       buttonEventHandler);
   ```

9. Add **Code 7.11** to create the `buttonEventHandler` event listener and display the `target` and `currentTarget` properties from the `MouseEvent` object to the Output panel.

   Notice that in the `trace()` statements, the `evt.target` and `evt.currentTarget` properties are recast as `DisplayObjects` before their `name` properties are called. We do this because the `target` and `currentTarget` properties are string references to a `DisplayObject`'s name and not the objects themselves. Casting prevents them from being called directly as `DisplayObjects`. The `DisplayObject()` method tells Flash to treat the `target` and `currentTarget` properties as display objects so that they can be called and controlled with ActionScript.

10. Preview your file. Click the buttons and notice the `trace()` statement messages that appear in the Output panel (**Figure 7.7**).

✔ Tip

- Using capturing versus bubbling phases is useful in the case of complex component interactions where certain events need to be intercepted before reaching other objects, or code needs to be executed specifically on the bubbling phase. You don't need to worry about the event flow phase at this point, although it may be useful if you are trying to troubleshoot mouse interactivity or another bug that you might suspect is the result of event flow issues.

EVENT FLOW

Subclasses of the Event Class

In this chapter, we have covered the Event, MouseEvent, and KeyboardEvent classes. We will work with many more subclasses of the Event class in later chapters. **Table 7.5** lists common Event subclasses for your reference. To get a full list and explanation of each subclass, search the Flash help menu using the phrase "Event class."

Table 7.5

Event Class Subclasses	
CLASS	DESCRIPTION
ColorPickerEvent	Event object associated with the ColorPicker component
FocusEvent	Event object used when focus is changed from one object to another
KeyboardEvent	Event object used for key input through keyboard
MetadataEvent	Event object used when FLV video file's metadata information packet is received
MotionEvent	Event object dispatched by fl.motion.Animator class
MouseEvent	Event object dispatched when mouse events occur
NetStatusEvent	Event object dispatched by NetConnection, NetStream, and SharedObject class status updates
ProgressEvent	Event object dispatched by loader objects at regular intervals when a load operation has started
SoundEvent	Event object dispatched by a Sound object when settings have been changed
TextEvent	Event object dispatched when a TextField is interacted with or changed
TimerEvent	Event object dispatched by Timer object when intervals are reached
TweenEvent	Event object dispatched by the fl.transitions.Tween class
VideoEvent	Event object passed when status of a video changes

CONTROLLING THE TIMELINE

Developers making the leap from timeline-driven applications to ActionScript-driven applications will use a combination of frame-based functionality with ActionScript control. In some cases, it just makes sense to create visual states of a display object on separate frames and toggle between the visual states using ActionScript. In many cases, pure ActionScript is overkill. Some experienced coders snub their noses at timeline-based functionality, but there's nothing wrong with using the timeline. Just keep it short and simple.

This chapter introduces you to controlling the timeline using ActionScript. We discuss starting and stopping animations and targeting specific frames on the timeline using `MovieClip` class methods. We also cover traversing the hierarchy of display objects to target different timelines using absolute and relative target paths, and changing a movie's frame rate using the `frameRate` property of the `Stage` class, which is new to ActionScript 3.

By the end of this chapter, you should be comfortable navigating multiple timelines, using target paths, changing a movie's frame rate at runtime, and using the timeline and ActionScript together.

Controlling Timelines

The timeline can be used for all sorts of effects, animations, and visual states of display objects. To use the timeline effectively, you ultimately need control of it. The MovieClip class has many methods for controlling the timeline (**Table 8.1**).

To stop the timeline:

1. Draw a circle shape on the stage roughly 50 × 50 pixels.

2. Select the shape and convert it to a Graphic symbol called Circle.

3. Convert the Circle symbol to a MovieClip named TweenContainer. Assign the TweenContainer symbol an instance name of mcTweenCont.

4. Double-click mcTweenCont to enter its timeline.

5. Insert new keyframes at frame 10 and frame 20 on the timeline (**Figure 8.1**).

6. Return to frame 10 and drag the Circle instance to the right side of the stage.

7. Add frame tweens to frame 1 and frame 10 by selecting each keyframe and choosing Motion from the Tween type menu in the Properties panel (Figure 8.1).

8. Preview your movie. Your shape graphic should be tweening back and forth across the stage.

9. Return to mcTweenCont's timeline. Create a new layer named Actions.

Table 8.1

MovieClip Methods That Control the Timeline	
METHOD	**DESCRIPTION**
gotoAndPlay()	Moves the playhead to, and plays the timeline at, a specific frame
gotoAndStop()	Moves the playhead to a specific frame and stops there
nextFrame()	Moves the playhead to the next frame
play()	Plays the timeline from its current frame
prevFrame()	Moves the playhead to the previous frame
stop()	Stops the playhead at its current position

stop() method on frame 1 of the Actions layer

Frame tweens are added to frames 1 and 10

Figure 8.1 The timeline is set up so that the Circle graphic tweens back and forth but is stopped on the first frame until told to do otherwise.

CONTROLLING TIMELINES

Code 8.1 mcTweenCont's timeline plays when btnPlay is clicked.

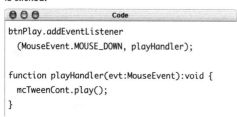

```
btnPlay.addEventListener
  (MouseEvent.MOUSE_DOWN, playHandler);


function playHandler(evt:MouseEvent):void {
  mcTweenCont.play();
}
```

10. Add the following code to the first frame on the Actions layer to stop mcTweenCont's timeline (Figure 8.1):

    stop();

11. Preview your movie. mcTweenCont's timeline should be stopped on the first frame.

To play the timeline:

1. Return to the main timeline.

2. Draw a shape on the stage that would make a good button.

3. Convert the shape to a Button symbol named Button.

4. Give the Button symbol an instance name of btnPlay.

5. Ensure that the btnPlay is not placed in the way of the path that the Circle graphic tweens on in mcTweenCont.

6. Add a new layer named Actions to the timeline.

7. Add the code from **Code 8.1**, which will play mcTweenCont's timeline when a user clicks btnPlay.

8. Preview your file. The Circle graphic symbol will be stopped on the first frame in mcTweenCont. Click btnPlay, and mcTweenCont will play its timeline and stop once it returns the first frame and the stop() method is called again.

To navigate to frames on the timeline:

1. Double-click mcTweenCont on the stage to enter its timeline.

2. Add a keyframe at frame 20 on the Actions layer (it should be aligned with the last keyframe on the Circle layer).

3. Add gotoAndPlay(2); to the last keyframe on the Actions layer that will tell the playhead to go to and play frame 2 to bypass frame 1, thus skipping the stop() method. This will loop the playhead (**Figure 8.2**).

4. Preview your file. The Circle should now tween back and forth indefinitely as the stop() method on frame 1 is being skipped by the gotoAndPlay(2) method.

5. Return to the main timeline.

6. Add a new instance of the Button symbol from the library to the stage and just below btnPlay. Give it an instance name of btnStop.

7. Add **Code 8.2** to tell the playhead in mcTweenCont to go to and stop at frame 1 on its timeline. This will stop and reset the tween sequence.

8. Preview your file. Clicking btnPlay will start the Circle tweening back and forth. Clicking btnStop will return the playhead to frame 1, where the timeline is stopped.

gotoAndPlay(2) method on last frame of Actions layer

Figure 8.2 The gotoAndPlay() method on the last frame of the Actions layer will tell the playhead to play from frame 2 and skip frame 1. The result is the Circle tween will loop on the timeline until instructed to do otherwise.

Code 8.2 Returning the playhead to frame 1 and stopping it.

```
btnPlay.addEventListener
  (MouseEvent.MOUSE_DOWN, playHandler);
btnStop.addEventListener
  (MouseEvent.MOUSE_DOWN, stopHandler);
function
  playHandler(evt:MouseEvent):void {
    mcTweenCont.play();
}
stopHandler(evt:MouseEvent):void {
  mcTweenCont.gotoAndStop(1);
}
```

Enter frame label name in Frame field

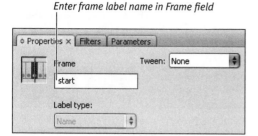

Figure 8.3 Assign a keyframe a frame label by entering a label name in the Frame field in the Properties panel.

Using frame labels

In the previous task, we navigated to frames on the timeline using the `gotoAndStop()` and `gotoAndPlay()` methods. Navigating to frame numbers does the trick as long as you know that the frames will always remain in the same spot. If you're building an application that has a timeline that may grow and/or be edited over time, it's hard to ensure navigating to frame numbers will always be accurate since frames may be moved. Frame labels, on the other hand, are always accurate as you are instructing the playhead to find a frame with a particular label name, not a particular location. This allows your applications to scale as timelines are edited.

Frame labels can be assigned only to keyframes. You can add labels to a keyframe by selecting the keyframe on the timeline and adding a frame label in the Properties panel (**Figure 8.3**). Frame label names should not have spaces in them or begin with numbers.

To make buttons with MovieClips and frame labels:

1. Draw a shape that would make a nice button on the stage.

2. Select the shape and convert it to a MovieClip symbol named Button.

3. Double-click the `Button` symbol to enter its timeline.

4. Insert a keyframe at frame 5 on the timeline.

5. Select the shape on frame 5 and change its fill color to a new color.

continues on next page

6. Insert a frame (not a keyframe) at frame 10 to extend the timeline (**Figure 8.4**). This enables the keyframes to be extended with regular frames and leave room for the frame labels to be readable on the timeline, thus making them easier to read and identify.

7. Add a new layer in Button's timeline called Labels.

8. Select the first keyframe on the Labels layer and give it a frame label of off in the Properties panel (**Figure 8.5**).

9. Insert a keyframe at frame 5 on the labels layer and give it a frame label name of over (**Figure 8.6**).

Figure 8.4 Two keyframes were created for different display states of the MovieClip that will be a button.

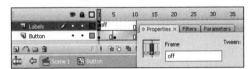

Figure 8.5 Name the first keyframe on the Labels layer off.

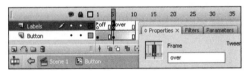

Figure 8.6 The over frame label at frame 5 on the Labels layer.

Code 8.3 Adding the mouseOver and mouseOut events to the Button MovieClip's timeline toggles between the over and off frames by using the gotoAndStop() method.

```
● ● ●              Code
this.addEventListener
  (MouseEvent.MOUSE_OVER, overHandler);
this.addEventListener
  (MouseEvent.MOUSE_OUT, outHandler);
function overHandler
  (evt:MouseEvent):void {
    this.gotoAndStop('over');
}
function outHandler(evt:MouseEvent):void {
  this.gotoAndStop('off');
}
stop();
```

10. Create a new layer called Actions in Button's timeline.

11. Add the following code, which listens for MOUSE_OUT and MOUSE_OVER events on the MovieClip and toggles between the off and over frames accordingly (**Code 8.3**).

12. Return to the main timeline and preview your file. The MovieClip should have over and off states like a regular button when you roll over it.

13. Drag multiple instances of Button from the library to the stage.

14. Preview your file. All the buttons should be working independently but in the same fashion.

15. Activate the hand cursor for the MovieClip by adding the following code on the Actions layer in Button's timeline:

```
this.buttonMode = true;
```

16. Preview your file. You will see that the hand cursor is activated for all of the instances.

While this section is primarily about navigating to frame labels, the task we have just completed is also a technique in advanced button creation.

The MovieClip button we had created is similar to the Button symbol, but it's the foundation for creating buttons that:

◆ Are fully animated

◆ Are reusable (you simply add dynamic labels from an external resource)

◆ Contain other display objects

The Button symbol on its own is not capable of much beyond basic mouse events. A MovieClip acting as a button has a full timeline and can be fully ActionScript-driven from within its timeline for advanced interactivity and effects.

This technique will be revisited later in this book when we cover iteration and looping.

✔ Tips

■ A frame was inserted at frame 10 in Step 6 so that the timeline could be extended for the next step. A keyframe was not required as no change is taking place on the timeline. Keyframes should only be used to introduce changes to the timeline as they take up more resources than regular frames, even if there is nothing in them. Regular frames should be used if you need to make space on the timeline.

■ Using a single MovieClip with ActionScript nested within it encapsulates functionality for the MovieClip within its own timeline. This allows you to reuse a MovieClip throughout an application without writing extra code.

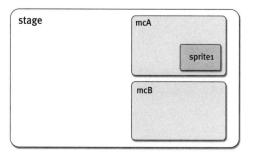

Figure 8.7 Wireframe of nested display objects in a basic application.

Navigating Timelines with Target Paths

Nested display objects in display object containers are common in Flash development. Menu buttons can be grouped in a menu container; items for certain sections can be grouped together in MovieClips so that they can be moved and added or deleted all at once, and so on.

It's a good idea to draw a wireframe of your display objects and nested display objects and their hierarchy within an application. This will give you a clear roadmap of how to target the display objects with ActionScript and tell them what to do.

Figure 8.7 is a simple wireframe of an application. It comprises the following:

◆ `stage`—The main `DisplayObjectContainer` of the application. The stage is the root of the application.

◆ `mcA`—The child MovieClip of the `stage`.

◆ `sprite`—The child Sprite of `mcA`.

◆ `mcB`—The child object of the `stage`.

To call `mcA` from the stage and set its `rotation` property to 45 degrees, you simply enter this code:

```
this.mcA.rotation = 45;
```

To set the alpha of `sprite1` in `mcA`, you need to access it through `mcA` by entering this code:

```
this.mcA.sprite1.alpha = .5;
```

Going the other way is a bit trickier. You can communicate back out of an object with ActionScript by using relative or absolute target paths.

Absolute and relative target paths

If you wanted to call the stage from the timeline of mcA, you could call it in two ways: with an absolute path or a relative path.

Calling the stage from the timeline via an absolute path involves calling the root timeline (the stage itself) using the root identifier. To declare the root as a display object and call it from inside of the timeline of mcA (or any other display object for that matter), you would write the following code:

```
var myRoot:MovieClip = root as MovieClip;
myRoot.doSomething();
```

ActionScript 3 is not a trusting language. It needs to be explicitly told what type of object an instance or object reference is. In order to have ActionScript call the root timeline, you need to explicitly tell Flash that the root timeline is a MovieClip and to reference it through a MovieClip variable. Basically, root returns an object cast as a display object, which does not have MovieClip properties, so we need to recast it as MovieClip for it to be useful. This is done by casting root as a MovieClip (as shown in the previous code). You can then call the reference to the root and call whatever objects or script you want.

As Figure 8.1 shows, the stage (or root) is also the parent timeline of mcA. This is also known as a relative path. To call the stage by a relative path from the timeline of mcA, enter this code:

```
var myParent:MovieClip =
  this.parent as MovieClip;
myParent.doSomething();
```

Here's a shorthand version:

```
MovieClip(this.parent).doSomething();
```

Either way, to call the parent of mcA with a relative path, you need to tell Flash that mcA's parent is indeed a MovieClip object.

To call the alpha property of mcB from sprite1's timeline, the absolute path would be:

```
var myRoot:MovieClip = root as MovieClip;
myRoot.mcB.alpha = .5
```

The relative path would be:

```
var myStage:MovieClip =
  this.parent.parent as MovieClip;
myStage.mcB.alpha = .5
```

To control timelines with target paths:

1. Draw a small rectangle on the stage using the Rectangle tool.

2. Convert it to a MovieClip symbol called nestedMC.

3. Give nestedMC an instance name of nestedMC.

4. Draw another rectangle on the stage that is larger than nestedMC and place it behind nestedMC.

5. Select the rectangle shape and nestedMC and convert both of them to a MovieClip symbol called mcA.

6. Give the mcA symbol an instance name of mcA.

7. Draw another rectangle on the main timeline and convert it to a MovieClip symbol called mcB. Give it an instance name of mcB.

8. Create a new layer called Actions.

9. Add the following code, which will set the alpha property of mcA:

```
this.mcA.alpha = .5;
```

continues on next page

NAVIGATING TIMELINES WITH TARGET PATHS

10. Add the following code, which will change the `rotation` property of `nestMC` in `mcA`:

```
this.mcA.nestedMC.rotation = 45;
```

11. Preview your file. `mcA` should be 50 percent of its original opacity, and `nestedMC` should be rotated 45 degrees.

12. Double-click `mcA` on the stage to enter its timeline.

13. Double-click `nestedMC` to enter its timeline.

14. Create a new layer called Actions.

15. Add the following code, which will set the `scaleX` property of `mcB` in the main timeline:

```
var myStage:MovieClip =
  this.parent.parent as MovieClip;
myStage.mcB.scaleX = 1.5;
```

16. Preview your file. The width of `mcB` should be stretched 1.5 times its original width (**Figure 8.8**).

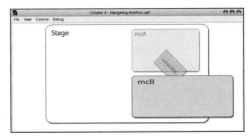

Figure 8.8 Setting the properties of `mcA`, `nestedMC`, and `mcB` from different timelines using relative target paths.

Declaring the Frame Rate at Runtime

Changing the frame rate at runtime is new to ActionScript 3. This is a great feature because it gives you the ability to "throttle" an application. Slow frame rates perform well in regard to processing but look clunky visually when it comes to smooth animations. Faster frame rates have smooth animations and visuals but can cause processing slowdowns, and the visual items on the stage may render slowly, resulting in clunky performance.

Say, for example, that you have an application that runs smoothly at 12 fps, but there is one sequence in a section that could run smoother at a higher frame rate. When the application needs to perform normally, it can run at the normal frame rate, and then using the `frameRate` property of the `Stage` class, you can increase the frame rate to accommodate the animation sequence in need of the higher frame rate. You can set the `frameRate` property again to return the stage to the lower frame rate when the animation is complete.

By default, the frame rate of an application is whatever value is set in the Properties panel for the document (usually 12 fps).

To change the frame rate with ActionScript:

1. Draw a circle on the left of the stage.

2. Convert the circle shape to a Graphic symbol called Circle.

3. Add new keyframes at frame 10 and frame 20.

4. Select the Circle in frame 10 and drag it to the right side of the stage.

5. Add a motion tween to frames 1 and 10.

6. Preview your file. The Circle should be tweening back and forth across the stage.

7. Create a new layer called Buttons.

8. Draw a shape that would make a nice button.

9. Select the shape and convert it to a Button symbol named Button.

10. Drag two more instances of Button to the Buttons layer on the stage so that there are three in total.

11. Assign the three Button instances instance names of btnSlow, btnMed, and btnFast.

12. Add the ActionScript from **Code 8.4** to add MOUSE_DOWN event listeners to each button, some of which can change the frameRate of the stage.

13. Save and preview your file. The Circle should be tweening at the default frameRate of 12 fps. Watch the speed of the tween change as the frameRate changes to 6, 24, and 36 fps when each button is clicked.

Code 8.4 The slowPace, medPace, and fastPace event handlers set the frame rate of the stage to 6, 24, and 36 frames per second, respectively.

```
btnSlow.addEventListener
  (MouseEvent.MOUSE_DOWN, slowPaceHandler);
btnMed.addEventListener
  (MouseEvent.MOUSE_DOWN, medPaceHandler);
btnFast.addEventListener
  (MouseEvent.MOUSE_DOWN, fastPaceHandler);

function slowPaceHandler(evt:MouseEvent):void {
  stage.frameRate = 6;
}
function medPaceHandler(evt:MouseEvent):void {
  stage.frameRate = 24;
}
function fastPaceHandler(evt:MouseEvent):void {
  stage.frameRate = 36;
}
```

Working with Strings

Strings are pieces of literal information or text that are used for display text and literal references, such as passwords, usernames, or any content that needs to be displayed or utilized in its literal form. Strings can be stored in variables, concatenated from different variables and values, or derived from external resources. Strings can also come from user input, such as input text field entries. Text, numbers, special characters, and punctuation can all be part of a string. String variables are objects of the String class.

This chapter discusses the following:

◆ The methods and properties of the String class that enable you to control and manipulate String objects

◆ How to use simple operators to combine different strings for the purpose of concatenating new strings

◆ How to format strings using tab spacing, line breaks, and special characters

By the time you've finished reading this chapter, you should understand how to combine, manipulate, and use special characters and escape sequences, as well as know how to search and splice strings into substrings.

The String Class

The String class in ActionScript is used to display and interpret text as literal values. All strings are objects of the String class. String values (also known as String literals) are defined by wrapping the string value in double or single quotes. Text, numbers, and punctuation can all be string values.

Here's an example:

```
var sampleString:String = 'This is
  Chapter 9 of this book!';
```

The String class has a single property. You can use several methods to work with and manipulate strings.

The single property of the String class is length. This property is used to return the length of a string in characters:

```
var myString:String = "This string is 36
  characters long.";
```

This string is 36 characters long, including the spaces and period.

Table 9.1 lists the more commonly used methods (but not all) of the String class.

Methods of the String class will be demonstrated throughout this chapter.

✔ Tip

- For a complete list of all the methods of the String class, search the Flash help menu using the keywords "String."

Table 9.1

Methods of the String Class	
METHOD	**DESCRIPTION**
String()	Creates a String object
charAt()	Returns a character from a specified index position
concat()	Adds supplied argument values to the end of a String object
slice()	Returns a String object based on a range of index positions passed as arguments to return from the current String object
split()	Splits a String object into an array of substrings based on a specified delimiter passed as an argument to the method
substring()	Returns a string consisting of characters specified by a start and end index position
toLowerCase()	Returns a string with all uppercase characters converted to lowercase
toUpperCase()	Returns a string with all lowercase characters converted to uppercase

Code 9.1 Using the \t escape sequence to add tab indents.

```
var software:String =
   "Software:\t Flash";
var version:String =
   "Version:\t CS3";
var company:String =
   "Company:\t Adobe";
trace(software);
trace(version);
trace(company);
```

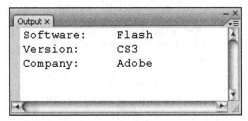

```
Output ×
  Software:      Flash
  Version:       CS3
  Company:       Adobe
```

Figure 9.1 The three variables in the Output panel have equal tab spaces based on the \t escape character.

Code 9.2 Using the \n escape sequence to add line spaces.

```
var softwareInfo:String =
   "Software: \tFlash \n";
softwareInfo += "Version:\tCS3 \n";
softwareInfo += "Company:\tAdobe";
trace(softwareInfo);
```

Code 9.3 Using the \" escape sequence to add double quotation marks.

```
var softwareInfo:String =
   "Software: \t\"Flash\" \n";
softwareInfo +=
   "Version: \t\"CS3\" \n";
softwareInfo +=
   "Company: \t"\Adobe\"";
trace(softwareInfo);
```

Escaped characters

Some punctuation and characters in strings are also part of the ActionScript syntax. To ensure that these characters can be used in strings without confusing the compiler, escape characters are employed by the String class. When creating an escape character, place a backslash character (\) before it. The String class also recognizes escape sequences for adding spacing, line breaks, tabs, and so on in a string.

See Chapter 2, Table 2.1, for common escape sequences that can be used in strings.

To use escape sequences in strings:

1. Add the code in **Code 9.1** to the Actions panel to incorporate tab indents in String variables.

2. Preview your file. The strings and results of the escape sequences will display in the Output panel (**Figure 9.1**).

3. Modify the code from Step 1 to combine the three string values into a single variable with line spaces using the newline (\n) escape sequence (**Code 9.2**).

4. Preview your file. The Output panel should look the same as Figure 9.1.

5. Add the code in **Code 9.3** to use an escaped character for adding double quotation marks to the software information.

6. Preview your file. The message in the Output panel should now display double quotes.

Combining Strings

Combining strings, also known as *concatenation*, is a common practice in any programming language. Values for strings can change at any time, and their display values can come from different sources.

Concatenation can be achieved by using the + and += operators or by using the concat() method of the String class.

To combine strings:

1. Add the code in **Code 9.4** to the script you've written thus far to introduce two variables that will be concatenated together to create a string value for fullName.

2. Preview your file. Theodore Cleaver should display as a single name in the Output panel. Note the space is present in the name because the empty space was added between the two variables during concatenation.

3. Modify the code from Step 1 to achieve the same result, this time using the concat() method of the String class (**Code 9.5**).

4. Preview your file. The result in the Output panel should be the same as in Step 2.

Using the + and += operators or the concat() method are all acceptable methods of concatenating strings. However, you may get an occasional compiler warning that says using the concat() method is required when publishing a file that uses the + and += operators.

Code 9.4 Concatenating the values of firstName and lastName as a single string in fullName.

```
Code
var firstName:String = "Theodore";
var lastName:String = "Cleaver";
var fullName:String =
  firstName + " " + lastName;
trace(fullName);
```

Code 9.5 Using the concat() method to concatenate the lastName variable to firstName variable.

```
Code
var firstName:String = "Theodore";
var lastName:String = "Cleaver";
var fullName:String =
  firstName.concat(" " + lastName);
trace(fullName);
```

Converting nonstrings to strings

In many instances in ActionScript development, you have a need to use numbers and display them as strings. The String() method of the String class helps you do just that. This method accepts nonstring values as arguments and returns the value as a string.

To recast values as strings:

1. Add the following code to the script you were working with in the previous task. This code creates two number variables and attempts to combine their values in a string:

   ```
   var num1:Number = 2;
   var num2:Number = 3;
   var sum:String = num1 + num2;
   trace(sum);
   ```

2. Preview your file. You will get a compile error (**Figure 9.2**) because the + symbol used in this instance is adding two numbers. The result of the addition is a number and not a string.

3. Modify the code that recasts the sum of num1 + num2 as a string in sum.

   ```
   var num1:Number = 2;
   var num2:Number = 3;
   var sum:String = String(num1 + num2);
   trace(sum);
   ```

continues on next page

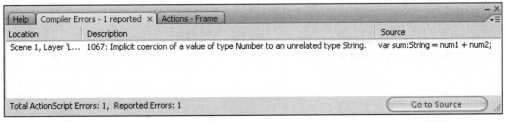

Figure 9.2 Adding numbers together to set a string triggers a compile error, since the result of the addition is a number and not a string.

COMBINING STRINGS

4. Preview your file. The sum 5 will now display as a string in the Output panel. This is because the addition of the numbers happens in the `String()` conversion method and the sum is then output as a string.

   There's one exception to the rule for recasting numbers to strings: when a number is concatenated with a string in the same statement or when using the `concat()` method. When a number is added to a string using the + operator, the number is automatically recast as a string to concatenate the number with the string. The `concat()` method automatically recasts numbers as well.

5. Modify your code to concatenate the number variables with a string value (**Code 9.6**).

6. Preview your file. The result of `The value of sum is: 23` in the Output panel is not quite what we want. This is because when numbers are concatenated with strings, they are automatically recast as strings, and the + symbol combines the two numbers as strings rather than adding them as numbers.

7. Modify your code to add the two number variables first, and then concatenate the sum with a string (**Code 9.7**).

8. Preview your file. The message `The value of sum is: 5` should now display in the Output panel. This is because the numbers were added before they were automatically recast as strings.

Code 9.6 Concatenating a number with a string automatically converts the number to a string.

```
var num1:Number = 2;
var num2:Number = 3;
var sum:String =
  "The value of sum is: " + num1 + num2;
trace(sum);
```

Code 9.7 Adding the numbers together first and then adding to a string ensures the addition of the numbers is performed before adding to the string.

```
var num1:Number = 2;
var num2:Number = 3;
var sum:Number = num1 + num2;
var answer:String =
  "The value of sum is: " + sum;
trace(answer);
```

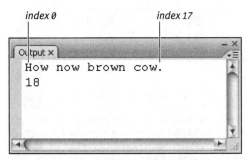

index 0   *index 17*

Figure 9.3 The first index position of `sampleString` is 0, and the last position is 17. The total `length` of the string is still 18 characters, but the index count starts from 0.

Manipulating Strings

ActionScript provides many ways to manipulate strings. You may need to extract from a string a particular value, word, text pattern, or list of words that are separated by common delineators. String manipulation is achieved using different methods of the `String` class.

To obtain a substring of a string variable:

1. Add the following ActionScript to create a `String` variable and trace the length of the string to the Output window:

   ```
   var sampleString:String =
      "How now brown cow.";
   trace(sampleString);
   trace(sampleString.length);
   ```

2. Preview your file. Note that the string is 18 characters long.

3. Add the following code to return a substring that begins at index position 0 and returns three positions from the start point:

   ```
   trace(sampleString.substr(0, 3));
   ```

   The `substr()` method accepts two arguments. The first argument is the starting index position in the string (index positions start at 0, as shown in **Figure 9.3**). The second argument reflects how many indexed values to return, counting from the start position. The argument of 3 in the previous code sample means to start at index position 0 and return 3 index positions starting from 0 (0, 1 and 2, or, H, o, w).

   continues on next page

MANIPULATING STRINGS

4. Preview your file. Note that How is displayed as the return value from the substr() method in the Output panel.

5. Change the index positions in the substr() method to the following:

```
trace(sampleString.substr(4, 9));
```

6. Preview your file. now brown should display in the Output panel.

The substring() method of the String class works similarly to the substr() method, but the arguments retrieve the values differently.

7. Add the following code below the substr() method call:

```
trace(sampleString.substring(4, 9));
```

The arguments passed to the substring() method are the same as the ones in the substr() method. However, the difference between using these two methods is that with the substring() method, the first argument is the start index position and the second argument is the end index position. The substr() method returns a substring comprising the characters that start at the specified startIndex (first parameter) and with a length (second parameter).

8. Preview your file. You should see now brown display as a result of the substr() method and now b display as a result of the substring() method in the Output panel (**Figure 9.4**).

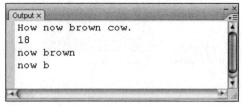

Figure 9.4 The substr() method returns a substring from a start index position and a specified amount of subsequent characters. The substring() method returns a substring from a range between a start and end index position.

Separating delineated values in a string

In some cases of communication involving external data resources such as a text file or URL-encoded string, the information is returned as a string with a common delineator separating the values in the string. (Common delineators are the same character used in a string to indicate separation of values such as a comma or pipe (|).) The following is a long string of names that are separated by the pipe character (|) to delineate each name value:

```
var names:String =
    "Derrick|Bethany|Adrian|Matt|Goergia|";
```

Using the `split()` method of the `String` class, you can strip out the names as separate values in an array using the pipe symbol as the delineator.

To split a string of values using a common delineator:

1. Add the following code to create a string variable of name values:

   ```
   var names:String =
       "Derrick|Bethany|Adrian|Matt|
       Georgia";
   ```

2. Add the following code to separate the names in the `names` string as separate indexes of an array using the `split()` method and to specify the pipe symbol as the delineator:

   ```
   var aNames:Array = names.split("|");
   trace(aNames.toString());
   ```

   The `trace()` statement displays the values of the array as a string in the Output panel.

3. Preview your file. `Derrick,Bethany, Adrian,Matt,Georgia` should appear in the Output panel.

WORKING WITH TEXT FIELDS

Any text that needs to be displayed in an application using ActionScript is done using `TextField` objects. This chapter shows you how to create dynamic and input text fields at authortime and at runtime.

Next, you'll learn how to control those fields using properties and methods of the `TextField` class. You'll also see how to use events of the `TextField` class to listen for and react to events dispatched from a `TextField`. And you'll get the chance to practice formatting text field properties (using the `TextFormat` class) and embedding fonts (so that you can display them on computers that do not have the fonts installed).

By the end of this chapter, you should be comfortable working with text fields using ActionScript and setting their text properties using the skills you learned in the previous chapter.

Working with Text Fields

Text fields in Flash display all text and content that is created dynamically from external resources, variable values, and/ or concatenated values in ActionScript. Text fields can be added to the stage at authortime or with ActionScript at runtime. However they are added, they can be controlled with ActionScript at runtime. Text fields are objects of the TextField class.

The TextField class

The TextField class has properties, methods, and events that control the TextField object type, display properties, and control how they are interacted with. The TextField class has two types of text fields that can be used to display dynamic information and that a user can interact with. They are dynamic and input text fields.

Dynamic text fields

Dynamic text fields are used to display what is known as "dynamic data." Dynamic data can come from external resources or from variable values generated by ActionScript. Dynamic text fields can be created at authortime using the Text tool or at runtime with ActionScript. Regardless of when they were created, the text property dynamic text fields are set at runtime.

To create a dynamic text field at authortime and set its text properties at runtime:

1. Select the Text tool from the Tool palette and choose Dynamic Text from the text options menu in the Properties panel (**Figure 10.1**).

2. Select a font face, size, and so on for the dynamic text field in the Properties panel (**Figure 10.2**).

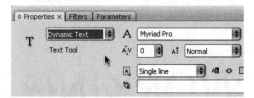

Figure 10.1 Choose the Dynamic Text option from the Properties panel.

Single line or Multiline option   *Text field is selectable when button is active*

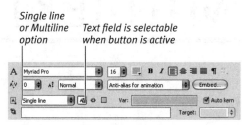

Figure 10.2 Font and dynamic text field properties.

Code 10.1 This code allows you to dynamically add a `TextField` object to the display list and set its properties. By default, a dynamically created text field has a DYNAMIC text field type.

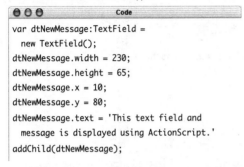

```
var dtNewMessage:TextField =
  new TextField();
dtNewMessage.width = 230;
dtNewMessage.height = 65;
dtNewMessage.x = 10;
dtNewMessage.y = 80;
dtNewMessage.text = 'This text field and
  message is displayed using ActionScript.'
addChild(dtNewMessage);
```

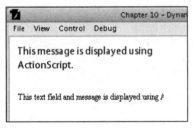

Figure 10.3 The text message displayed in dtNewMessage gets cut off because the wordWrap property is not set to true.

3. In the Properties panel, select Single line or Multiline (depending on the length and reason for display of your text) and specify whether or not you want the text to be selectable (Figure 10.2).

4. Draw a dynamic text field on the stage using the Text tool. The size of the text field is up to you—just make sure it can display your text the way you want it to.

5. Select the dynamic text field on the stage and give it an instance name of dtMessage.

6. Create a new layer and name it Actions.

7. Add the following code to set the `text` property of dtMessage with the value from sMessage:

   ```
   var sMessage:String = 'This message
     is displayed using ActionScript.';
   dtMessage.text = sMessage;
   ```

8. Preview your file. The value of sMessage should be displayed in dtMessage.

To create a dynamic text field and set its text properties at runtime:

1. Note the x and y coordinates of dtMessage on the stage so that the text field you create in this next set of steps does not display over the top of it.

2. Add **Code 10.1**, which adds a dynamic TextField object of the TextField class that is 230 px x 65 px and is placed at x 10 and y 80.

3. Preview your file. It should have the same result as **Figure 10.3** if your text message is too long for the new text field.

continues on next page

4. Add the following code just before the text property of `dtNewMessage` is set to enable word wrapping in the text field:

```
dtNewMessage.wordWrap = true;
```

5. Preview your file. The text should now wrap to the next line(s) in the text field.

✔ Tip

■ For an extensive list of the various properties of the `TextField` class, search the Flash Help menu using the keywords "TextField class."

Input text fields

Input text fields allow user input. Users can enter information required by the application to log in, interact with an interface, and submit information. Again, an input text field can be created at authortime as well as at runtime. You can set its properties the same as you would for a dynamic text field: by using the Properties panel or by setting the properties at runtime.

To create an input text field at authortime and set its text properties at runtime:

1. Select the Text tool from the Tool palette and choose Input Text from the text options menu in the Properties panel (**Figure 10.4**).

2. Set the Input Text properties.

3. Draw an input text field on the stage using the Text tool. Make sure it's wide and high enough to display your font and a desired length of characters. Select Show Border Around Text in the Properties panel so that you can locate the text field on the stage (**Figure 10.5**).

4. Give the input text field an instance name of `itMessage`.

5. Preview your file. Click in `itMessage` and start typing a message.

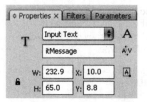

Figure 10.4 Choose the Input Text option in the Properties panel.

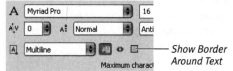

Show Border Around Text

Figure 10.5 The Show Border Around Text option in the Properties panel of Input Text field.

Code 10.2 Adding a `TextField` object to the display list.

```
○ ○ ○              Code
var itNewMessage:TextField =
  new TextField();
itNewMessage.type = TextFieldType.INPUT
itNewMessage.wordWrap = false;
itNewMessage.width = 232;
itNewMessage.height = 23;
itNewMessage.x = 10;
itNewMessage.y = 44;
itNewMessage.background = true;
itNewMessage.backgroundColor = 0xffffff;
itNewMessage.border = true;
itNewMessage.borderColor = 0x000000;


addChild(itNewMessage);
```

To create an input text field and set its text properties at runtime:

1. Note the x and y coordinates on the stage so that the text field you add during this set of steps does not display over the top of the `itMessage` you created in the previous task.

2. Add the code in **Code 10.2**, which adds a `TextField` object with an INPUT type to the display list and sets its properties.

   By carefully examining this code, you'll notice that the `type` property of the `TextField` object is set to a constant of `INPUT` of the `TextFieldType` property. Its `wordWrap` is set to `false` so that the added text stays on one line. The `background`, `backgroundColor`, `border`, and `borderColor` properties are also set so that the input field is visible and blocks out any underlying graphics or objects.

3. Preview your file. The `itNewMessage` `TextField` object should be displayed underneath the `itMessage` `TextField` object that you added at authortime. Type a message into `itNewMessage` to ensure it is indeed an input text field type.

4. Add the following code just before the `addChild(itNewMessage)` method, which will set both input text fields with a default value:
   ```
   itMessage.text = "Type message
     here.";
   itNewMessage.text = "Type message
     here.";
   ```

5. Preview your file. Both text fields should now have a default `text` value of `Type message here`.

   Note that you have to highlight the text to type over it.

Text field events

The TextField class has its own set of events, as well as inherited events such as MouseEvents that extend the functionality of a TextField object.

Table 10.1 lists the events of the TextField class.

Using the events of the TextField class in combination with inherited events of the class, TextField objects can react and respond to user input, interaction, and change.

To work with text field events:

1. Return to the file you created in the previous task.

2. Place the code in **Code 10.3** just before the addChild(itNewMessage) method call that you added in the previous task. This code instructs ActionScript to listen for the FOCUS_IN event of the flash.events.FocusEvent class for itMessage and itNewMessage.

   The same textFocus event handler is used for both text field events, because we can use object (evt) as the target property of the event to reference the text field that currently has focus. The text property of the target is set to no characters so the user does not have to highlight the default text to type over it.

Table 10.1

Events of the TextField Class	
Event	**Description**
change	Dispatched after the text field's value is changed.
link	Dispatched when a link in an HTML-enabled text field is clicked. The URL must begin with event:.
scroll	Dispatched after a text field has been scrolled.
textInput	Dispatched when one or more characters of text have been entered in the field.

Code 10.3

```
itNewMessage.addEventListener(
  FocusEvent.FOCUS_IN, textFocus);
itMessage.addEventListener(
  FocusEvent.FOCUS_IN, textFocus);
function textFocus
  (evt:MouseEvent):void {
    evt.target.text = "";
}
```

Code 10.4 Returning the text field backgounrds back to normal once the text field loses focus (FOCUS_OUT).

```
⚫ ⚫ ⚫                    Code
itNewMessage.addEventListener
  (FocusEvent.FOCUS_OUT, textFocusOut);
itMessage.addEventListener
  (FocusEvent.FOCUS_OUT, textFocusOut);
function
  textFocusOut(evt:FocusEvent):void {
    evt.target.backgroundColor = 0xffffff;
}
```

3. Add the following code in the `textFocus` event handler to change the background color of a `TextField` object when the text field is in focus:

   ```
   itNewMessage.backgroundColor =
     0xffcc00;
   ```

4. Preview your file. Note that the background color changes to yellow only when each text field is selected.

5. Add the code in **Code 10.4** just after the `textFocus` event listener. This adds an event listener for the FOCUS_OUT event of the `flash.events.FocusEvent` class to both text fields. It returns the fields to their original background color when the text field is deselected.

6. Preview your file. Each text field should turn yellow when it is selected and return to white when it is not selected.

7. Add the following code inside the `textFocusOut` event listener to display the `text` property of the `target` text field in the Output panel:

   ```
   trace(evt.target.text);
   ```

8. Preview your file. When a text field is not selected, the message typed in it displays in the Output panel.

Formatting Text Fields

Formatting text fields with ActionScript can be a complex task. Each text field created with ActionScript must be formatted to address font face, font size, alignment, kerning, and so on. Having to do this for multiple text fields that will be styled the same way creates a lot of repetitive code. The TextFormat class helps you format text fields without all the redundant code.

The TextFormat class has one method (the TextFormat() constructor) and a list of properties specifically for formatting text fields. Once a TextFormat object has been created and its properties are set, the object can be applied to the defaultTextFormat and/or setTextFormat property of a text field(s). TextFormat objects are the ActionScript equivalent of style sheets to a certain degree.

Table 10.2 lists the properties of the TextFormat class that can be applied to a text field.

Table 10.2

Properties of the TextFormat Class	
PROPERTY	DESCRIPTION
align	Specifies the paragraph alignment of the text field.
blockIndent	Specifies the block indent of the text field in pixels.
bold	Indicates whether text is bold.
bullet	Specifies the text part of a bulleted list.
color	Specifies the color of text.
font	Contains the name of the font for the text field.
indent	Specifies indentation of the first line in each paragraph from the left margin.
italic	Specifies whether the font is italicized.
kerning	Indicates if kerning is enabled or disabled.
leading	Contains the integer value that represents the vertical space between lines of text.
leftMargin	Indicates the left margin of paragraphs (in pixels).
letterSpacing	Contains the value that represents the spacing between characters.
rightMargin	Indicates the right margin of paragraphs in pixels.
size	Contains the size of text in points.
target	The target window link is displayed when the link is clicked in the text field.
underline	Specifies whether the text in the text field is underlined.

Code 10.5 Here, we're creating a new `TextFormat` object and setting the `defaultTextFormat` property of `dtValueA` with `tfFormatter`. Other properties of `dtValueA` are also set before adding it to the display list.

```
● ● ●                Code
var tfFormatter:TextFormat =
  new TextFormat();
var dtValueA:TextField = new TextField();


tfFormatter.font = "Arial";
tfFormatter.color = 0xff0000;
tfFormatter.size = 14;


dtValueA.type = TextFieldType.INPUT
dtValueA.wordWrap = false;
dtValueA.width = 250;
dtValueA.height = 25;
dtValueA.x = 10;
dtValueA.y = 10;
dtValueA.background = true;
dtValueA.backgroundColor = 0xffffff;
dtValueA.border = true;
dtValueA.borderColor = 0x000000;
dtValueA.defaultTextFormat = tfFormatter;
dtValueA.text = "Type message here.";


addChild(dtValueA);
```

To format a text field using a TextFormat object:

1. Add the code in **Code 10.5** to create a new `TextFormat` object and apply it to a dynamic `TextField` object named `dtValueA`.

2. Preview your file. An input `TextField` object should display on the stage with a black border and in a red Arial font.

continues on next page

3. Modify your code to place the property settings of dtValueA inside a function that is called as an event handler when a TextField object is added to the display list.

The properties in the event handler are applied to the target of the event and not a particular TextField object itself. The event handler is called from the addedToStage (ADDED_TO_STAGE) event of a text field (inherited from the DisplayObject class) (**Code 10.6**).

Code 10.6 Formatting the TextField object when it is added to the stage using the target property of the event object allows many text fields to be formatted using the same function.

```
Code
var tfFormatter:TextFormat =
  new TextFormat();
var itValueA:TextField = new TextField();

dtValueA.y = 10;
dtValueA.addEventListener(
  Event.ADDED_TO_STAGE, itAdded);

tfFormatter.font = "Arial";
tfFormatter.color = 0xff0000;
tfFormatter.size = 14;

function itAdded(evt:Event):void {
  evt.target.wordWrap = false;
  evt.target.width = 250;
  evt.target.height = 25;
  evt.target.x = 10;
  evt.target.background = true;
  evt.target.backgroundColor = 0xffffff;
  evt.target.border = true;
  evt.target.borderColor = 0x000000;
  evt.target.defaultTextFormat =
    tfFormatter;
  evt.target.text = evt.target.type;
}


addChild(dtValueA);
```

Code 10.7 Reuse the itAdded event handler to format new instances of a TextField object when they are added to the stage.

```
Code
var tfFormatter:TextFormat =
  new TextFormat();
var dtValueA:TextField =
  new TextField();
var itValueB:TextField =
  new TextField();

dtValueA.y = 10;
itValueB.type = TextFieldType.INPUT;
itValueB.y = 40;

tfFormatter.font = "Arial";
tfFormatter.color = 0xff0000;
tfFormatter.size = 14;

dtValueA.addEventListener
  (Event.ADDED_TO_STAGE, itAdded);
itValueB.addEventListener
  (Event.ADDED_TO_STAGE, itAdded);

function itAdded(evt:Event):void {
  evt.target.wordWrap = false;
  evt.target.width = 250;
  evt.target.height = 25;
  evt.target.x = 10;
  evt.target.background = true;
  evt.target.backgroundColor = 0xffffff;
  evt.target.border = true;
  evt.target.borderColor = 0x000000;
  evt.target.defaultTextFormat =
    tfFormatter;
  evt.target.text = evt.target.type;
}
addChild(dtValueA);
addChild(itValueB);
```

4. Preview your file. It should look the same as it did earlier, except that it is now formatted with a flexible function that can be applied to other TextField objects.

5. Add an instance of an input TextField object by adding the highlighted portion of the final code in **Code 10.7**.

6. Preview your file. You should see a second, formatted TextField instance below the first one (**Figure 10.6**).

continues on next page

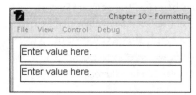

Figure 10.6 Both TextField objects have been added and formatted using ActionScript.

7. After previewing the file, set the `text` property of the added event handler before the `TextFormat` object is applied to the target object.

8. Preview the file and note that the formatting no longer works. There is a specific order in which code needs to be placed, and in this instance, the `text` property needs to be applied after the default `TextFormat` object is set as a property of the `TextField` object.

If the `text` property of a `TextField` object is set to a new value after the initial text value has been set, the `setTextFormat()` method of the `TextField` class needs to be called to reapply the `TextFormat` object:

```
textFieldName.setTextFormat
   (textFormatObjectName);
```

✔ Tip

■ This is a great example of using a single function to affect multiple objects that require the same functionality. Another advantage of using this function is that it is an event listener, so it is automatically called when needed using the `ADDED_TO_STAGE` event. It should be your goal to always think in this manner so that you're using the simplest code that's easy to update.

HTML text formatting

`TextField` objects are able to display HTML text formatting tags. They do this by setting the `htmlText` property of a `TextField` object with HTML-formatted text. Cascading Style Sheet (CSS) styles, such as the `<span>` tag, can also be applied as class IDs and names in HTML tags.

Table 10.3 lists the accepted HTML tags of the `TextField` class.

Table 10.3

HTML Tags of the TextField Class	
TAG	**DESCRIPTION**
`<a>`	Creates a hyperlink. The `href` and `target` attributes are supported.
`<b>`	Bold tag.
` `	Line break tag.
`<font>`	Specifies font for text. `color`, `face`, and `size` attributes are supported.
`<img>`	Embeds external images (JPEG, GIF, and PNG). The following attributes are supported: `src`, `width`, `height`, `align`, `hspace`, `vspace`, `id`, and `checkPolicyFile`.
`<i>`	Italic tag.
`<p>`	Paragraph tag.
`<span>`	Span tag for CSS styling.
`<textformat>`	Inserts paragraph properties of a TextFormat object.
`<u>`	Underline tag.
SUPPORTED ENTITIES	
`&lt;`	< (less than).
`&gt;`	> (greater than).
`&amp;`	& (ampersand).
`&quot;`	" (double quotes).
`&apos;`	' (apostrophe, single quote).

Code 10.8 The `htmlText` property of a `TextField` object allows HTML-formatted text to be displayed in the text field.

```
                    Code
var dtMessage:TextField =
  new TextField();
dtMessage.width = 250;
dtMessage.multiline = true;
dtMessage.wordWrap = true;
dtMessage.autoSize =
  TextFieldAutoSize.LEFT;

dtMessage.htmlText = '<p><b>This text
  field</b> and message is displayed
  using ActionScript.<p>';
dtMessage.htmlText += '<p><i>This italic
  text</i> was formatted with
  HTML.<p>';
dtMessage.htmlText += '<a href="#"><font
  color="#ff0000"><b>This is a
  link</b></font></a> Links need to be
  formatted with a color and such as
  they do not change appearance with
  just an <a> tag.';

addChild(dtMessage);
```

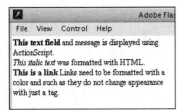

Figure 10.7 HTML-formatted text displayed in text field.

To format a TextField with HTML:

1. Add the code in **Code 10.8**, which creates a dynamic text field and sets its `htmlText` property with HTML-formatted text.

2. Preview your file and note the appearance of the HTML-formatted text in the `TextField` object (**Figure 10.7**).

   Notice that the <p> tags do not double-space paragraphs. Also, links do not automatically change colors, which means you need to change the font within the <a> tag. Experiment with the other accepted tags from Table 10.3.

Embedding Fonts

When you're working with dynamic text, font issues are bound to arise. If you do not type a font face directly in a dynamic or input text field at runtime, and/or do not embed it using the Embed Font option in the Text tool's Properties panel, the font will not display on a user's computer if that font is not installed. To embed a font and dynamically apply it to a text field at runtime using ActionScript, you need to create the font as a font symbol in the library and add it to the timeline as an object.

To create a font symbol and apply it to a TextField object with ActionScript:

1. Select New Font from the library's Options menu (**Figure 10.8**).

2. Enter a name for the font symbol (I am embedding the font Myriad, so my symbol is named Myriad). Then select a font to embed. If you want outlines for bold and italic versions of the font to be included, select the bold and italic options.

   Note that if you want to apply the regular font, you must leave the options deselected. Checking the bold and italic options will make all the text bold and italic. If you want the text to be displayed as bitmap text (no anti-aliasing), you must select the Bitmap text check box and specify the Size option (**Figure 10.9**). Click OK when you finish.

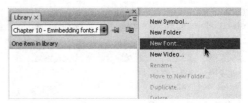

Figure 10.8 Creating a new font symbol using the library's Options menu.

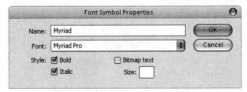

Figure 10.9 Selecting the Myriad font along with the Bold and Italic options.

Figure 10.10 Checking the Export for ActionScript option applies a class name to the font symbol.

Code 10.9 Instantiating new TextField, TextFormat and Myriad objects.

```
● ● ●              Code
var myriad:Myriad = new Myriad();
var dtFormatter:TextFormat = new TextFormat();
var dtText:TextField = new TextField();
```

Code 10.10 Setting the font property of dtFormatter and applying it to the defaultTextFormat property of dtText.

```
● ● ●              Code
dtFormatter.font = myriad.fontName;
dtFormatter.size = 18;

dtText.autoSize =
  TextFieldAutoSize.LEFT;
dtText.defaultTextFormat = dtFormatter;
dtText.embedFonts = true;
dtText.text = "This font is Myriad."
addChild(dtText);
```

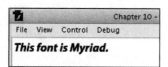

Figure 10.11 A final preview of the text field with the Myriad font (with bold and italic) embedded.

3. Select your font symbol in the library and choose Linkage from the library's Options menu. Check the Export for ActionScript option to give the symbol a class name (mine is Myriad) (**Figure 10.10**).

4. Add the code in **Code 10.9** to the timeline to create new TextField, TextFormat, and Font (the same name as the class name of Text symbol in the library) objects.

5. Add the code in **Code 10.10** just after the constructor's dtText declaration. This sets the properties of dtFormatter. The font property is set to the fontName of the myriad Font object, and dtFormatter applies it to the defaultTextFormat of dtText. dtText is then added to the display list.

6. Preview your file. The text field and the embedded font should be displayed (**Figure 10.11**).

WORKING WITH THE MATH AND DATE CLASSES

11

Math in programming is used for calculating commerce-driven applications, dynamic display layout, random activity for gaming interfaces and functionality, as well as in applications that need algebra and trigonometry to govern their functionality. Advanced math requires functions and constant values for equations. The Math class includes functions and constants to assist in math operations. After reading this chapter, you should be comfortable with the Math class methods.

The Date class offers an extensive list of properties and methods for working with the local date and time of a user, as well as time zone and Coordinated Universal Time (UTC) for international users. The class also includes properties and methods for working with date and time comparisons (past, present, and future). This chapter covers getting and displaying the local time of a user and setting a custom date and time. You will also be briefly introduced to UTC and how it can assist you in working with time zones.

The Math Class

Working with math in ActionScript goes beyond the common addition, subtraction, multiplication, and division operators. The Math class has methods and constants that enable you to perform arithmetic and trigonometry, and generate random numbers. These methods and constants are similar to function keys on a calculator, such as sin, tan, and PI (π).

The Math class is a static class, so you don't have to construct an object of the Math class to access its methods and constants. Instead of using the new keyword to create a class instance to access class members, you simply call methods or properties on the class itself, such as Math.method(); or Math.CONSTANT;.

Table 11.1 lists the methods of the Math class that perform arithmetic and trigonometry.

Table 11.1

METHOD	DESCRIPTION
abs(val)	Calculates and returns an absolute value specified in the parameter
acos(val)	Returns the arc cosine of the specified parameter in radians
asin(val)	Returns the arc sine of the specified parameter in radians
atan(val)	Returns the value of an angle (in radians) of the tangent specified in the parameter
atan2(y, x)	Returns the value of the angle when a line drawn from the point of origin intersects the y and x parameters
ceil(val)	Rounds a number to the next highest integer
cos(angle)	Returns the cosine of angle in radians
floor(val)	Rounds a number to the next lowest integer
max(val1, val2, …)	Returns the highest value of two or more specified parameters
min(val1, val2, …)	Returns the lowest value of two or more specified parameters
pow(val1, val2)	Returns val1 to the power of val2
random()	Returns a random pseudonumber between 0 and .9999999999999999
round(val)	Returns a specified value rounded off to the nearest integer
sin(angle)	Returns the sine of angle in radians
sqrt(val)	Returns the square root of a specified number
tan(angle)	Returns the tangent of a specified angle

Methods of the Math Class

The Math class also includes constant values that do not change, such as PI (3.141592653589793) and E (2.71828182845905). You can look up these values by searching the Flash Help menu using the keywords "Math class."

How much and what type of math you need depends on the complexity of the application you are creating. This section focuses on using the random() method and the rounding methods of the Math class.

Obtaining random numbers

You can obtain random numbers with ActionScript by using the Math class's random() method and specifying a value or range from which the random number should derive. The random() method returns a random value between 0 and .9999999999999999. The random value never goes as high as 1 and could be 0. Random numbers are used to simulate realistic patterns that are chaotic and unpredictable by nature. You'll find this method valuable when developing games, designing interfaces, and dealing with ever-changing, organic environments.

Static Class

Static classes are used to create data and functions that can be accessed without creating an instance of the class. Static classes can be used when there is no data or behavior in the class that depends on object identity. The methods and properties of a static class never change. The Math class is a static class as its properties and methods never change and always perform the same way.

THE MATH CLASS

To generate random numbers:

1. Add the following code, which returns a random number and assigns it to a variable named pseudoRandomNumber:

```
var pseudoRandomNumber:Number =
  Math.random();
trace('pseudoRandomNumber: " +
  randomNumber);
```

2. Preview your movie. A random number between 0 and .9999999999999999 should display in the Output panel.

3. Add the following code, which generates a random number between 0 and 20:

```
var randomNumber:Number =
  Math.random() * 20;
trace('randomNumber: ' +
  randomNumber);
```

4. Preview your file. A random number between 0 and 19.999999999999999 should display in the Output panel. Keep previewing the file, and you will get a different value each time.

5. Add the code in **Code 11.1** to round the randomNumber variable to make it a random integer after the randomNumber variable is set.

6. Preview your file. You should get a number from the full range of 0 to 20 since the round() method rounds a random number greater than 19.5 up to 20.

Code 11.1 Generating a random number between 0 and 20.

```
var randomNumber:Number =
  Math.random() * 20;
var randomInt:int =
  Math.round(randomNumber);
trace('randomNumber: ' + randomNumber);
trace('randomInt: ' + randomInt);
```

Code 11.2 Generating a random number between the range of 5 and 25.

```
⊖ ⊖ ⊖                    Code
var randomNumber:Number = Math.random() * 20;
var randomInt:int = Math.round(randomNumber);
var randomRange:Number = randomInt + 5;
trace('randomNumber: ' + randomNumber);
trace('randomInt: ' + randomInt);
trace('randomRange: ' + randomRange);
```

Code 11.3 Generating a random value between -5 and 15.

```
⊖ ⊖ ⊖                    Code
var randomNumber:Number = Math.random() * 20;
var randomInt:int = Math.round(randomNumber);
var randomRange:Number = randomInt - 5;
trace('randomNumber: ' + randomNumber);
trace('randomInt: ' + randomInt);
trace('randomRange: ' + randomRange);
```

```
Output ×
randomPseudoNumber: 0.887598040048033
randomNumber: 2.106975642964244
randomInt: 2
randomRange: -3
randomPseudoNumber: 0.21437173755839467
randomNumber: 13.323069894686341
randomInt: 13
randomRange: 8
```

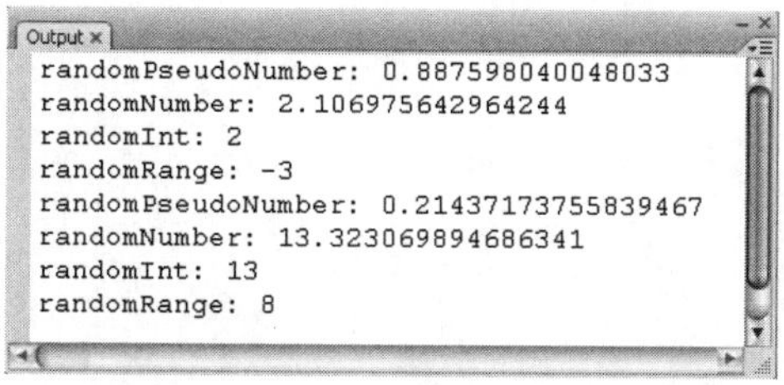

Figure 11.1 Subtracting a value from the `randomInt` variable results in a range between a negative and positive number.

7. Add the ActionScript in **Code 11.2** to get a random number from a range between 5 and 25. Adding a value of 5 to `randomInt` increments the lowest value (0) by 5 and the target value by 5 (25), resulting in a random number in the range of 5 to 25.

8. Preview your file; you should see a random value between 5 and 25 in the Output panel.

9. Modify the code to get a random value between a negative and positive number range (**Code 11.3**).

10. Preview your file. You should see a range of numbers display in the Output panel between -5 and 15 after previewing a number of times (**Figure 11.1**).

THE MATH CLASS

155

Rounding numbers

The ability to round numbers is used for all sorts of mathematical purposes. For example, using rounded numerical data types such as int or uint allow for better performance. Rounding off numbers is also useful for values that determine pixel placement and sizing of display objects on whole pixels to avoid antialiasing or pixel blurring.

Here are the methods of the Math class used for rounding off numbers:

◆ **round(val)**—Returns a specified value rounded off to the nearest integer

◆ **ceil(val)**—Rounds a number to the next highest integer

◆ **floor(val)**—Rounds a number to the next lowest integer

To round numbers:

1. Add the code in **Code 11.4** to create a random number and round it to the nearest integer.

2. Preview your file. The random number in randomNumber should display, and the rounded integer in roundedNumber should trace after in the Output panel.

3. Add the code in **Code 11.5** to use the floor() method to round a number to the next lowest integer value.

Code 11.4 Rounding off a random number.

```
var randomNumber:Number = Math.random() * 20;
var roundedNumber:int =
  Math.round(randomNumber);
trace('randomNumber: ' + randomNumber);
trace('roundedNumber: ' + roundedNumber);
```

Code 11.5 Rounding a number to the next lowest integer value.

```
var randomNumber:Number = Math.random() * 20;
var roundedNumber:int =
  Math.round(randomNumber);
var flooredNumber:int =
  Math.floor(randomNumber);
trace('randomNumber: ' + randomNumber);
trace('roundedNumber: ' + roundedNumber);
trace('flooredNumber: ' + flooredNumber);
```

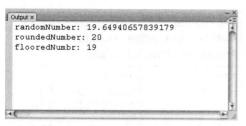

```
Output ×
randomNumber: 19.64940657839179
roundedNumber: 20
flooredNumbr: 19
```

Figure 11.2 Rounded values of randomNumber differ between the round() and floor() methods depending on the decimal value.

Code 11.6 Rounding off a random number to the next highest integer.

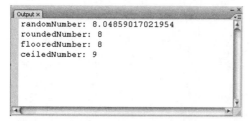

```
Code
var randomNumber:Number = Math.random() * 20;
var roundedNumber:int =
  Math.round(randomNumber);
var flooredNumber:int =
  Math.floor(randomNumber);
var ceiledNumber:int =
  Math.ceil(randomNumber);
trace('randomNumber: ' + randomNumber);
trace('roundedNumber: ' + roundedNumber);
trace('flooredNumber: ' + flooredNumber);
trace('ceiledNumber: ' + ceiledNumber);
```

```
Output ×
randomNumber: 8.04859017021954
roundedNumber: 8
flooredNumber: 8
ceiledNumber: 9
```

Figure 11.3 The rounded values of randomNumber using the round(), floor(), and ceil() methods of the Math class.

4. Preview your file. Note that the rounded and floored values may different depending on the decimal value of randomNumber (**Figure 11.2**).

5. Add the code in **Code 11.6** to use the ceil() method to round randomNumber to the next highest decimal point.

6. Preview your file. Note the differences between the rounded, floored, and ceiled values of randomNumber (**Figure 11.3**).

THE MATH CLASS

The Date Class

The Flash platform allows you to check the current date and time on a user's computer using the Date class. By calling methods and setting properties of the Date class, you can get the local time and date from a user's computer as well as set a date and time to compare a past or future time and date with the current date and time of the user's machine. You'll find this valuable when you want to count down to event dates, flight times, and so forth. To work with the Date class, you must instantiate a Date object:

```
var myDate:Date = new Date();
trace(myDate);
```

Getting the date and time

After a Date object has been constructed, you can call methods of, or get properties of, the Date class to get date and time values:

```
var myDate:Date = new Date();
trace(myDate.getDate());
```

The getDate() method obtains the current day of the month.

The getMonth() method returns the month of the year as an integer. Numeric references to the current month are not the normal month numbers we are used to working with. For instance, the count for months starts at 0 (January) and ends at 11 (December). Always add 1 to the returned month number to get the true calendar month value (adding 1 to January (0) would result in 1, which is the more common reference to the calendar position of January).

Table 11.2 lists some methods used to get time and date properties from the Date class.

For a full list of the methods of the Date class, search the Flash Help menu using the keywords "Date class."

Table 11.2

Methods for Getting Time and Date Properties of the Date Class	
METHOD	**DESCRIPTION**
getDate()	Returns the number of the day of the month (from 1 to 31), local time
getDay()	Returns the number of the day of the week (Sunday (0) to Saturday (6)), local time
getFullYear()	Returns the four-digit, full-year local time as a number
getHours()	Returns the number of the current hour (0 to 23), local time
getMilliseconds()	Returns the number of the current millisecond (0 to 999), local time
getMinutes()	Returns the number of the current minute (0 to 59), local time
getMonth()	Returns the number of the current month (January (0) to December (11)), local time
getSeconds()	Returns the number of the current second (0 to 59), local time

Code 11.7 Declaring date and time variables.

```
⊙ ⊙ ⊙              Code
var localDate:Date = new Date();
var day:int;
var date:int;
var month:int;
var year:int;
var hour:int;
var minute:int;
var second:int;
```

Code 11.8 Displaying the date and time values in the Output panel.

```
⊙ ⊙ ⊙              Code
day = localDate.getDay();
month = localDate.getMonth();
year = localDate.getFullYear();
hour = localDate.getHours();
minute = localDate.getMinutes();
second = localDate.getSeconds();
trace(month + '/' + day + '/' + year);
trace(hour + ':' + minute + ':' + second);
```

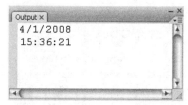

Figure 11.4 Local date and time properties displayed in the Output panel.

To get and display the date and time:

1. Start a new file and re-name Layer 1 to Actions.

2. Add the code in **Code 11.7** to construct a new Date object and declare variables that will store date and time properties returned from the Date object.

3. Add the ActionScript code in **Code 11.8** after Code 11.7 to set the variables with date properties using methods of the Date class and display them in the Output panel.

4. Preview your file. The current date and time should display in the Output panel. Note that the number of the month is incorrect; again, this is because the count for months starts at 0 (**Figure 11.4**).

5. Modify the following line of code to set the month to the correct calendar numbered position:

   ```
   month = localDate.getMonth() + 1;
   ```

6. Preview your file. The correct month value should now be displayed.

THE DATE CLASS

159

Building a simple clock application

Building a live clock application involves using a couple of techniques using the Date class. The Date class returns the current date and time when its corresponding methods are called and only once per object instantiation. The previous set of instructions performed this once.

To have a clock that continually rolls through the time and date, a new Date object must be instantiated and the methods of the Date class that return the date and time properties must be called at regular intervals to display the changing time. To create a simple clock application, we will use the Timer class and verify that certain returned values are using a conditional statement (more about conditional statements in Chapter 13).

To build a simple clock application:

1. Add the ActionScript from **Code 11.9** to instantiate a TextField object to display the time and a Timer object that updates the time every 1/10th (100) of second in the updateTime() event handler for the TIMER event of the Timer class.

   When the updateTime() event handler is called on each TIMER event, a new Date object and new variables for the time are instantiated, concatenated, and set as the text property for clockDisplay. A new Date object needs to be created each time because the Date class stores only the time and date values for the time in which the object was instantiated.

Code 11.9 The clockTimer Timer object is created and a listener is registered to listen for the TIMER event, which is dispatched every 1/10th of a second (100).

```
var clockDisplay:TextField = new TextField();
var clockTimer:Timer = new Timer(100);
clockTimer.addEventListener
  (TimerEvent.TIMER, updateTime);


function updateTime(evt:TimerEvent):void {
  var localDate:Date = new Date();
  var hour:int = localDate.getHours();
  var minute:int = localDate.getMinutes();
  var second:int = localDate.getSeconds();
  clockDisplay.text =
      hour + ':' + minute + ':' + second;
}


clockTimer.start();
addChild(clockDisplay);
```

Using Date Class Methods vs. Properties

In ActionScript 3, the new API also has properties of the Date class that can be called directly. Previous to ActionScript 3, the methods in Table 11.2 were used to get date and time properties from the Date class. The method calls for getting the date and time simply by returning their associated property.

I believe that just because something is new, it doesn't make it right or better. The methods used in the previous set of instructions are as acceptable as any other means of getting date and time properties. It is a matter of personal preference. For a full listing of properties of the Date class, search the Flash Help menu using the keywords "Date class."

Code 11.10 Using a conditional statement to insert a
0 before the second and minute values if the current
second is less than 10.

```
Code
var clockDisplay:TextField = new TextField();
var clockTimer:Timer = new Timer(100);
clockTimer.addEventListener
  (TimerEvent.TIMER, updateTime);


function updateTime(evt:TimerEvent):void {
  var localDate:Date = new Date();
  var hour:int = localDate.getHours();
  var minute:String;
  var second:String;

  if (localDate.getMinutes() < 10) {
    minute = String(0) +
    localDate.getMinutes();
  } else {
    minute =
    String(localDate.getMinutes())
  }

  if (localDate.getSeconds() < 10) {
    second = String(0) +
    localDate.getSeconds();
  } else {
    second =
    String(localDate.getSeconds());
  }

  clockDisplay.text = hour + ':' +
    minute + ':' + second;
}

clockTimer.start();
addChild(clockDisplay);
```

2. Preview your file. The time should constantly update to the local time of your computer at the regular interval of 1/10th of a second. Note that if the second and minute values are less than 10, they display as single digits with no preceding 0.

3. Modify your code to add the following conditional statements that display a 0 before minute and second values less than 10 (**Code 11.10**).

   Using an if conditional statement that checks to see if the minute and second variables are less than 10 results in adding a 0 before each if the condition is true; therefore, the minute and second values are always displayed as double digits, as with "regular" clocks.

4. Preview your file. The minutes and seconds should now display in a double-digit format even if the second and minute values are less than 10.

✔ Tips

- The hour, minute, and second variables did not need to be cast as strings before they were displayed in the text field. This is because numbers are automatically cast to strings when concatenated with other strings (:).

- To go a step further and display the hours from 0 to 12 rather than the 24-hour display, use a conditional statement to verify whether the hours are greater than 12. If they are, subtract the current hour from 24, which should be the current PM time in the 12-hour format:

  ```
  var hour:int = 24 -
    locateDate.getHours();
  ```

Setting a custom date and time

The Date class has a set of methods that allow you to set an exact date in time. The date you set can be from the past or present, or in the future. You'd use a Date object to set a date to make a countdown clock to an event, for example. First you set a date for the event to compare to the local date and time on the user's computer, and then compare the two dates to make a countdown clock. You specify a date for a Date object by using the Date class methods shown in **Table 11.3**.

For a full list and descriptions of the setter methods of the Date class, search the Flash Help menu using the keywords "Date class."

To set a custom date and time:

1. Add the code in **Code 11.11** to set a custom date of September 24, 2008.

2. Preview your file. The full date should appear in the Output panel (**Figure 11.5**).

Table 11.3

Methods for Setting Date Properties of the Date Class

Method	Description
setDate(day)	Sets the number of the day of the month, local time
setFullYear(y, m, d)	Sets the full-year, local time as a number
setHours(h,m,s,ms)	Sets the current hour, local time
setMilliseconds(ms)	Sets the current millisecond, local time
setMinutes(m, s, ms)	Sets the current minute, local time
setMonth(m, d)	Sets the current month and day of month, local time
setSeconds(s, ms)	Sets the current second, local time
setDate(ms)	Sets the date in milliseconds since January 1, 1970

Code 11.11 Setting a custom date.

```
var newDate:Date = new Date();
newDate.setDate(24);
newDate.setMonth(08);
newDate.setFullYear(2008);
trace(newDate);
```

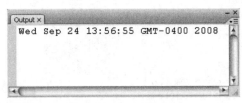

Figure 11.5 Display of set date of September 24, 2008.

THE DATE CLASS

Code 11.12 Setting a custom time.

```
Code
var newDate:Date = new Date();
newDate.setDate(24);
newDate.setMonth(08);
newDate.setFullYear(2008);
newDate.setHours(4);
newDate.setMinutes(20);
newDate.setSeconds(20);
trace(newDate);
```

Set time

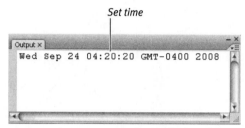

```
Output ×
Wed Sep 24 04:20:20 GMT-0400 2008
```

Figure 11.6 The date is displayed with the set time properties.

3. Add the code in **Code 11.12** to set the time of day to 04:20:20.

4. Preview your file. The date should appear in the Output panel with the set time displayed, too (**Figure 11.6**).

THE DATE CLASS

Time Zones and UTC Time

Coordinated Universal Time (UTC) is an international time with leap seconds added at irregular intervals for a precise measurement of time. (UTC is nearly the same as Greenwich Mean Time.)

Time zones around the world are values of positive or negative offsets from UTC. Local time is UTC plus the time zone offset for that location, plus an offset (typically +1) for daylight saving time, if in effect.

So what does this mean to you? To accurately calculate the difference between local time and a different time zone, the Date class has UTC methods that help figure out the difference for you.

Working with UTC time is beyond the scope of this book, but it does warrant this introduction. For more information on UTC time, search the Date class in the Flash Help menu and read the descriptions for the UTC getter and setter methods.

WORKING WITH DATA USING ARRAYS AND OBJECTS

If you are creating any kind of logic or data storage and retrieval with ActionScript, you most likely will accomplish this using arrays. Arrays are the most common and basic data structure, other than variables, in any programming language. Arrays are one of the first data structures most programmers learn. Using arrays, you can store a series of one or more values in a list-like data structure.

Basic objects of the Object class are another type of data structure. A custom object can be created, and properties for the object can be created and set to store custom values for different pieces of information for an item. Using arrays and objects together to create *associative arrays* makes the array data structure even more powerful.

This chapter addresses data storage and retrieval using arrays and objects and introduces you to the powerful concept of associative arrays for advanced data storage and retrieval.

Working with the Array Class

All arrays are objects of the Array class. Once you create an Array object, you can use the class methods to create, sort, add, retrieve, and remove elements stored in an array.

Creating an array

An array needs to first be declared as a variable and then instantiated as an object of the Array class. The Array() constructor method is used to create a new Array() object:

```
var sampleArray:Array = new Array();
```

Adding elements to an array

After an array has been instantiated, values can be stored in the array as indexed elements. Indexed elements (or *indices*) of an array are an integer-ordered list of values. You store and retrieve these indexed elements by specifying an index position for the value in the array. The following list of cars can be stored in an array:

0. Honda

1. Nissan

2. Ford

3. Chrysler

Each item from this list would have a unique index position in the array, beginning with position 0. Array-index positions always start at 0, so the first position of the array is 0, the second index position is 1, and so on.

Code 12.1 Creating an array and adding a list of car manufacturers as elements.

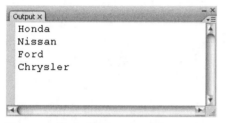

```
000                    Code
var carList:Array = new Array();
carList[0] = 'Honda';
carList[1] = 'Nissan';
carList[2] = 'Ford';
carList[3] = 'Chrysler';
```

```
Output ×
 Honda
 Nissan
 Ford
 Chrysler
```

Figure 12.1 Displaying the car manufacturers in the Output panel by calling each indexed element of the carList array.

To set an element of an index of an array, call the name of the Array object, followed by the index position in square ([ ]) brackets, followed by a value that the array element will contain by way of the equality (=) operator:

```
carList[0] = 'Honda';
```

To retrieve a value of an indexed element of an array, call the name of the array followed by the index position:

```
trace(carList[0]); // Returns Honda
```

To create and add elements to an array:

◆ Create a new file and rename Layer 1 to Actions. Add **Code 12.1**, which constructs an array named carList and adds various car manufacturers as indexed elements of the array.

To retrieve elements from an array:

1. Add the following code at the bottom of the script from the previous task to retrieve and display the indexed elements to the Output panel:

```
trace(carList[0]);
trace(carList[1]);
trace(carList[2]);
trace(carList[3]);
```

2. Preview your file. The list of car manufacturers should display in the Output panel (**Figure 12.1**).

continues on next page

3. Add the following code to display all the indices of the array as comma-separated values using the `toString()` method of the `Array` class:

```
trace(carList.toString());
```

4. Preview your file. The list of car manufacturers should appear in the Output panel as a comma-separated list of values:

```
Honda,Nissan,Ford,Chrysler
```

✔ Tip

- Most programming languages only allow a single data type to be stored in an array. ActionScript allows an array to store multiple objects of any data type. You'll find this useful if you need to store multiple objects of different classes as a list.

Array constructor shorthand

The `Array` class provides shorthand code for creating an `Array` object and passing the indexed elements directly to the constructor method. This eliminates the lengthy number of lines required when listing each indexed element separately. ActionScript will assign the index positions automatically when the elements are passed to the constructor method:

```
var carList:Array = new Array('Honda',
    'Nissan', 'Ford', 'Chrysler');
```

You can avoid explicitly calling the constructor method of the `Array` class by using square brackets. This technique is called an *array literal*:

```
var carList:Array = ['Honda', 'Nissan',
    'Ford', 'Chrysler'];
```

WORKING WITH THE ARRAY CLASS

To pass indexed elements in the Array constructor method:

1. Create a new file and rename Layer 1 to Actions. Add the following code to pass the indexed elements of the array through the constructor method:

```
var carList:Array =
  new Array('Honda', 'Nissan',
  'Ford', 'Chrysler');
trace(carList.toString());
```

2. Preview your file. The list of car manufacturers should display in the Output panel as a comma-separated list.

To create an array with an array literal:

1. Add the following code to replace the array constructor from Step 1 of the previous task with an array literal:

```
var carList:Array = ['Honda',
  'Nissan', 'Ford', 'Chrysler'];
trace(carList.toString());
```

2. Preview your file. The list of car manufacturers should display in the Output panel as a comma-separated list.

Using the array constructor and adding elements, or using an array literal, is all a matter of preference.

Manipulating Arrays

The Array class has a number of methods used for manipulating arrays. Class methods can be used to add and remove elements at specific locations, return values, and concatenate elements.

Adding or removing elements to and from an array

In the previous section, you learned how to add index elements after the constructor method, through the constructor method, or with an array literal. You can also add values to an array at any time, not just at time of instantiation. In addition, you can remove elements from an array when they are no longer needed.

Adding elements to an array

The Array class has three methods for adding elements to an array:

◆ push() adds an element to the end of an array.

◆ unshift() adds an element at the start of an array (at index position 0).

◆ splice() deletes or inserts a value at a specified index of an array. The splice() method requires three parameters: the index position where you wish to add the new element, how many elements should remain after the specified elements are replaced or deleted (0 means none), and the element(s) you want to add.

Code 12.2 Adding elements to the end of an array using the push() method.

```
● ● ●              Code
var carList:Array = ['Honda',
  'Nissan', 'Ford', 'Chrysler'];
trace(carList.toString());
// Displays Honda, Nissan, Ford,
  Chrysler
carList.push('BMW');
trace(carList.toString());
// Displays Honda, Nissan, Ford,
  Chrysler, BMW
```

Code 12.3 Adding multiple elements to an array using the splice() method.

```
● ● ●              Code
carList.splice(1, 0, 'Volvo',
  'Volkswagen');
trace(carList.toString());
// Displays Honda, Volvo, Volkswagen,
  Nissan, Ford, Chrysler
```

To add elements to an array:

1. Create a new file and rename Layer 1 to Actions. Add the code in **Code 12.2** to use the push() method to add a new car manufacturer to the end of the array.

2. Preview your file. BMW should be displayed at the end of the second trace() statement.

3. Edit your code to replace the push() method with the unshift() method and to add BMW to the start of the array:

   ```
   carList.unshift('BMW');
   trace(carList.toString());
   // Displays BMW, Honda, Nissan, Ford,
     Chrysler
   ```

4. Preview your file. BMW should now display at the start of the array in the Output panel.

5. Add the following code to replace the unshift() method with the splice() method and add Volvo at index position 1 within the array:

   ```
   carList.splice(1, 0, 'Volvo');
   trace(carList.toString());
   // Displays Honda, Volvo, Nissan,
     Ford, Chrysler
   ```

6. Preview your file. Volvo should display as the second value in the string from the array.

7. Modify your code to add multiple elements to the array using the splice() method (**Code 12.3**).

8. Preview your file. Volvo and Volkswagen should display within the array string beginning at index position 1 in the Output panel.

MANIPULATING ARRAYS

Removing or returning elements from an array

The `Array` class has three methods for removing or returning elements from an array. Each method for removing an element also returns the element's value if it is needed before discarding the element:

◆ `pop()` removes and returns the last element from an array.

◆ `shift()` removes and returns the first element of an array.

◆ `slice()` removes and returns an array of element(s) from a specified index position. The `slice()` method has two parameters: the index position at which to start returning elements, and the position at which to stop returning elements.

If you do not specify a second parameter in the `slice()` method, all the elements after the start parameter will be returned.

Specifying the first parameter as a negative integer means values will begin slicing from the end of the array minus that value forward. For example:

```
var aNames:Array =
  ['Derrick', 'Bob', 'Bill', 'Duke'];

trace(aNames.slice(-2));
// Displays Bill, Duke
```

Note that the `slice()` method, unlike `splice()`, does not remove elements from the array.

To remove elements from an array:

1. Create a new file and rename Layer 1 to Actions. Add the code in **Code 12.4**, which uses the `pop()` method to remove an element from the end of the array and sets the value of `popElement` with the returned value from the `pop()` method.

Code 12.4 Removing an element from the end of an array using the `pop()` method.

```
var carList:Array = ['Honda',
  'Nissan', 'Ford', 'Chrysler'];
trace(carList.toString());
var returnedElement:String =
  carList.pop();
trace(returnedElement);
trace(carList.toString());
```

MANIPULATING ARRAYS

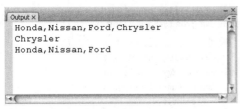

Figure 12.2 Displaying the array, the returned value from the pop() method, and the revised array with the removed element.

Code 12.5 Removing and returning the first element of the array using the shift() method.

```
var carList:Array = ['Honda',
  'Nissan', 'Ford', 'Chrysler'];
trace(carList.toString());
var returnedElement:String =
  carList.shift();
trace(returnedElement);
trace(carList.toString());
```

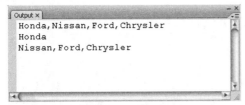

Figure 12.3 Returning and removing the first element of the array using the shift() method.

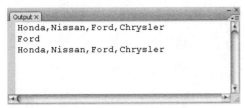

Figure 12.4 Returning an element from within the array using the slice() method.

2. Preview your file. The original array should display in the Output panel, followed by the returned element from the pop() method, followed by the revised array, with one less element (**Figure 12.2**).

3. Modify your code so that the pop() method is replaced by the shift() method to return and remove the first element from the array (**Code 12.5**).

4. Preview your file. The first element of the array (Honda) should be returned and removed from the array and appear in the Output panel (**Figure 12.3**).

5. Modify your code so that it uses the slice() method to return indexed value 2 from within the array. 3, the second parameter, tells the method to stop returning values at the element before index position 3:

```
var returnedElement:Array =
  carList.slice(2, 3);
trace(returnedElement.toString());
trace(carList.toString());
```

6. Preview your file. Ford should be the value that is sliced from the array and displayed to the Output panel. Notice that Ford is still an element of the array since the slice() method does not remove elements from an array (**Figure 12.4**).

MANIPULATING ARRAYS

Iterating through arrays

In many cases, arrays are used to store a list of values that will be used all at once. All the car manufacturers in the sample array used so far can be used to create a list of buttons for the different manufacturers. To retrieve all the elements from an array, the `for..each` loop of the class is used. The `for..each` loop loops through all the elements of an array. Each time an element is found by the `for..each` loop a function is called for each element found in each iteration.

The function called by the `forEach()` method receives three parameters from the method call:

◆ `element:*`—The element value of the current index position in the loop

◆ `index:int`—The index position of the current element in the loop

◆ `array:Array`—The array of the `forEach()` method

The `forEach()` method call and its handler function look like this:

```
arrayName.forEach(arrayLoopFunction);

function arrayLoopFunction(element:*,
  index:int, array:Array):void {
  // do something
}
```

To loop through an array:

1. Create a new file and rename Layer 1 to Actions. Add the code in **Code 12.6**, which uses the `forEach()` method to loop through the `carList` array and displays all its individual elements to the Output panel.

2. Preview your file. Each element of the array should be individually handled by the function, and their values and index positions should appear in the Output panel (**Figure 12.5**).

Code 12.6 Iterating through all the elements of the array using the forEach() loop.

```
function displayCars(element:*,
  index:int, arr:Array):void {
    trace("Current element value is: "
    + element);
    trace("Current index is: " + index);
}
carList.forEach(displayCars);
```

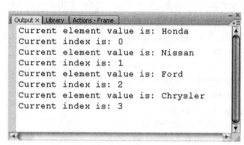

Figure 12.5 Display the elements of the array in the Output panel for each iteration of the forEach() loop.

The Object Class and Associative Arrays

Arrays are one of the most common data structures in ActionScript (and most programming languages). They are great for storing lists of values, which generally should be the same category or type for each array for consistency of information as far as best practice goes, such as names and numbers. However, when you're storing data with a complex information structure for each item, basic arrays fall short. Using basic objects of the Object class and associative arrays allows you to create more advanced data structures for categorizing and storing large amounts of information for each item of data you are working with.

The Object class

The Object class is the foundation for all objects. It lets you create and define objects from scratch. The reason for creating objects in regard to data structures is so that you can set the properties of a custom object, which can be used as data buckets of information.

To create an object of the Object class, use the new Object() constructor method:

```
var obj:Object = new Object();
```

Once you've created the object, you can define and set custom properties:

```
obj.firstName = 'Tony';
obj.lastName = 'Alva';
```

You can avoid explicitly calling the constructor method of the Object class by using square brackets. This technique is called an *object literal*:

```
var obj:Object = { firstName:'Tony',
  lastName:'Alva' };
```

To retrieve a property from the object, simply call the object name followed by the property name:

```
trace(obj.firstName);
// Display 'Tony'
```

Array Accessor

You can use the array access operator to dynamically set and retrieve values for a property of an object. Using an array accessor, you can reference a value stored within a variable that is equal to a property of an object:

```
var newSkater:String = 'firstName';

var obj:Object = { firstName:'Tony' }

trace(obj[newSkater]);
```

You can also use the array accesor to dynamically set or retrieve a property of an object:

```
var obj:Object = new Object();

obj['skater' + 1] = 'Tony';

trace(obj['skater1']);
```

Finally, array accessors allow you to add properties to an array object and use the object as an associative array:

```
var arr:Array = new Array();

arr['skater1'] = 'Tony';

trace(arr['skater1']);
```

To create a custom object and its properties:

1. Add the code in **Code 12.7** to create an object about skateboarder Tony Alva.

2. Preview your file. All the property information from the object should display in the Output panel (**Figure 12.6**).

3. Add the code in **Code 12.8**, which uses an object literal to create an object with shorthand code.

Code 12.7 Creating an object with properties that store information about Tony Alva.

```
var obj:Object = new Object();
obj.firstName = 'Tony';
obj.['lastName'] = 'Alva';
obj.originalTeam = 'Zephyr';
obj.company = 'Alva Skates';
trace(obj.firstName);
trace(obj.lastName);
trace(obj.originalTeam);
trace(obj.company);
```

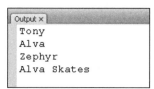

```
Output ×
Tony
Alva
Zephyr
Alva Skates
```

Figure 12.6 Displaying the properties of the custom object in the Output panel.

Code 12.8 Creating an object using an object literal.

```
var obj:Object = {
  firstName:'Tony',
  lastName:'Alva',
  originalTeam:'Zephyr',
  company:'Alva Skates'
}
trace(obj.firstName);
trace(obj.lastName);
trace(obj.originalTeam);
trace(obj.company);
```

The Object Class and Associative Arrays

Code 12.9 Info about skateboarder stored in an array.

```
⊝ ⊝ ⊝                Code
var namesList:Array = new Array();
namesList[0] = 'Tony';
namesList[1] = 'Alva';
namesList[2] = '41';
namesList[3] = 'male';
```

Code 12.10 Storing an object in an associative array.

```
⊝ ⊝ ⊝                Code
var namesList:Object = new Object();
namesList.skater1 =
  {firstName:'Tony', lastName:'Alva',
  age:'41', gender:'male' };
trace(namesList.firstName);
// Tony should appear in the Output panel
```

Original Zephyr Skateboard Team Members

◆ **person0**
   firstName:'Tony'
   lastName:'Alva'
   age:'41'
   gender:'male'

◆ **person1**
   firstName:'Nathan'
   lastName:'Pratt'
   age:'46'
   gender:'male'

◆ **person2**
   firstName:'Stacey'
   lastName:'Peralta'
   age:'51'
   gender:'male'

◆ **person3**
   firstName:'Jay'
   lastName:'Adams'
   age:'47'
   gender:'male'

Associative arrays

Arrays allow storage of a series of one or more values in a single data structure. Arrays in their most basic form ideally work with lists of like values, such as a list of names and numbers. Arrays aren't powerful tools when you're storing multiple details of items in a list. Associative arrays, using the `Object` class, however, can be used to store a list of like values, with each value storing its own details as properties.

For example, when storing information about people in a list, you most likely would be storing more than just their first name. The sidebar titled "Original Zephyr Skateboard Team Members" shows an example of storing multiple pieces of information about some legendary skateboarders.

The first skateboarder from the list would look like **Code 12.9**.

As you can see, the array indices for storing the information about only Tony Alva is a long list. You can imagine looping through the array to get information about each person from the list. The logic to loop through four indices for each person to obtain his or her information is an awkward and inefficient process. Ideally, an array that stores this type of information should be stored in an associative array using the `Object` class.

To store an information object in an associative, the code would look like **Code 12.10**.

Notice that when passing a properties object to an associative array object, an object instance does not even have to be created. Setting the index with a properties object can take place in the curly braces, and no other objects are needed.

To create an associative array:

◆ Create a new file and rename Layer 1 to Actions. Add the code from **Code 12.11**, which creates an associative array for the list of skateboarders.

To loop through an associative array:

1. Add the code from **Code 12.12**, which loops through all the properties of each associative array object property and displays them in the Output panel.

2. Preview your file. Each time the for each..in loop iterates (loops), the firstName, lastName, age, and gender properties are referenced from the current associative array object property and displayed in the Output panel (**Figure 12.7**).

Code 12.11 Storing personal information as objects and properties in array indices.

```
var namesList:Object = new Object();
namesList.skater1 =
  {firstName:'Tony', lastName:'Alva',
  age:'41', gender:'male' };
namesList.skater2 =
  {firstName:'Nathan', lastName:'Pratt',
  age:'46', gender:'male' };
namesList.skater3 =
  {firstName:'TStacey', lastName:'Peralta',
  age:'51', gender:'male' };
namesList.skater4 =
  {firstName:'Jay', lastName:'Adams',
  age:'47', gender:'male' };
```

Code 12.12 Looping through associative array using the for each..in loop (the for each..in loop will be discussed in Chapter 14).

```
var namesList:Object = new Object();
namesList.skater1 =
  {firstName:'Tony', lastName:'Alva',
  age:'41', gender:'male' };
namesList.skater2 =
  {firstName:'Nathan', lastName:'Pratt',
  age:'46', gender:'male' };
namesList.skater3 =
  {firstName:'TStacey', lastName:'Peralta',
  age:'51', gender:'male' };
namesList.skater4 =
  {firstName:'Jay', lastName:'Adams',
  age:'47', gender:'male' };

for each (var prop in namesList) {
  trace("First name: " + prop.firstName);
  trace("Last name: " + prop.lastName);
  trace("Age: " + prop.age)
  trace("Gender: " + prop.gender)
}
```

```
Output ×
First name: Tony
Last name: Alva
Age:  41
Gender: male
First name: Nathan
Last name: Pratt
Age:  46
Gender: male
First name: Stacey
Last name: Peralta
Age:  51
Gender: male
First name: Jay
Last name: Adams
Age:  47
Gender: male
```

Figure 12.7 Properties of associative array object displayed in the Output panel.

CREATING CONDITIONAL STATEMENTS

All of our decisions in life are based on conditional logic. Is the traffic light red or green? Did I leave the iron on? Am I tired or not? These everyday decisions are based on conditions. For some of these questions, the answers are either `true` or `false`. To react to a condition, we assess the condition, get a `true` or `false` response, and act accordingly. If the condition is `true`, we react one way; if the answer is `false`, we react in a different way.

To create "decision forks" in ActionScript, you must implement conditional logic. You set a condition, and if the condition is `true`, the code will respond; if it is `false`, the code will move on and check another condition, if one exists.

Many different kinds of conditions can be used with ActionScript. You can compare variable values, evaluate object properties, assess types of objects, compare strings, and so on.

This chapter shows you how to create conditional statements that automate decisions based on conditions in an application. You achieve this decision-making capability by using `if`, `else if`, `else`, and `switch` statements.

Conditional Statements

The most elementary conditional statements in ActionScript are the if [...else if] [...else] statements: if a condition is true, react; else if another condition is true, react to that; else if none of the conditions are true, do something else. The ActionScript syntax for this kind of thinking would be:

```
if (check for a condition) {
  if condition is met, respond here, if
  not, move on
} else if (check for another condition) {
  if condition is met, respond here, if
  not, move on
} else {
  if none of the previous conditions are
  met, this is the default response
}
```

The if, else if, and else statements can be used in different combinations. If you want to check for a single condition and nothing else, you can just use a single condition:

```
if (check for condition) {
  do something here
}
```

If the condition is not met, nothing happens.

If you want something to always happen when checking for a condition, the else statement can be used as a default response if no conditions have been met previously:

```
if (check for condition) {
  do something here
} else {
  do something by default
}
```

Relational and equality operators

Relational and *equality operators* are used to check for *conditional expressions* (**Table 13.1**). Conditional expressions are tested in various ways but they always return a true or false response.

Table 13.1

Relational and Equality Operators	
OPERATOR	DESCRIPTION
>	Checks if an expression is greater than another
<	Checks if an expression is less than another
==	Checks if an expression is equal to another
>=	Checks if an expression is equal to or greater than another
<=	Checks if an expression is equal to or less than another
!=	Checks if an expression is not equal to another

Code 13.1 Checking whether a parameter is less than 1.

```
⊖ ⊙ ⊖                    Code
function evalCondition(val:int):void {
  if (val < 1) {
    trace(val + ' is less than 1')
  }
}
evalCondition(0);
```

Code 13.2 Adding a second condition to the statement.

```
⊖ ⊙ ⊖                    Code
function evalCondition(val:int):void {
  if (val < 1) {
    trace(val + ' is less than 1');
  } else if (val > 1) { trace(val + ' is
    greater than 1') }
  }
evalCondition(2);
```

Code 13.3 Adding a third condition to the statement.

```
⊖ ⊙ ⊖                    Code
function evalCondition(val:int):void {
  if (val < 1) {
    trace(val + ' is less than 1');
  } else if (val > 1) {
    trace(val + ' is greater than 1')
  } else if (val == 1) {
    trace(val + ' is equal to 1')
  }
}
evalCondition(1);
```

To check for true conditions using relational and equality operators:

1. Create a new file and rename Layer 1 to Actions. Add the code from **Code 13.1** to verify whether a parameter passed to a function is less than 1.

2. Preview your file. 0 is less than 1 should display in the Output panel, because the val < 1 condition is true.

3. Add the code from **Code 13.2** to verify whether another condition of val is greater than 1.

4. Preview your file. 2 is greater than 1 should display in the Output panel, because the first condition is false and the second condition in the statement is true.

5. Add the code from **Code 13.3** to verify whether val is equal to 1.

6. Preview your file. 1 is equal to 1 should display in the Output panel, because the last condition is true.

   Another way to verify whether val is equal to 1 is to use a default else statement instead of the else if (val == 1) condition. If val is not greater than 1 and is not less than 1, it must be equal to 1.

   continues on next page

CONDITIONAL STATEMENTS

7. Modify your code as shown in **Code 13.4** to use a default else statement to display that val is equal to 1.

8. Preview your file. 1 is equal to 1 should still be displayed in the Output panel.

String expressions can also be checked in a conditional statement.

9. Add the code in **Code 13.5**, which matches a string expression in a new conditional statement.

10. Preview your file. Flash is equal to Flash should display in the Output panel.

Note that String expressions are case sensitive.

To check for false conditions using relational and equality operators:

1. Create a new file and rename Layer 1 to Actions. Add the code from **Code 13.6**, which checks to see if a string expression comparison is false.

2. Preview your file. Illustrator is not equal to Flash should display in the Output panel.

Verifying the value of a Boolean with a conditional statement

Booleans either have true or false values. Shorthand can be used to check the state of a Boolean.

If a variable has only a true or false value, simply using the variable name on its own in the condition will verify a true value. To verify a false value, use the logical NOT operator (!) in front of the variable name.

Code 13.4 Adding a default else statement.

```
function evalCondition(val:int):void {
  if (val < 1) {
    trace(val + ' is less than 1');
  } else if (val > 1) {
    trace(val + ' is greater than
    1')
  } else {
    trace(val + ' is equal to 1')
  }
}
evalCondition(1);
```

Code 13.5 Checking a string expression.

```
function evalString(val:String):void {
  if (val == 'Flash') {
    trace(val + ' is equal to Flash');
  } else {
    trace(val + ' is not equal to Flash');
  }
}
evalString('Flash');
```

Code 13.6 Checking for a false condition.

```
function evalString(val:String):void {
  if (val != 'Flash') {
    trace(val + ' is not equal to Flash');
  } else {
    trace(val + ' is equal to Flash');
  }
}
evalString('Illustrator');
```

Code 13.7 Verifying the `alpha` property of a MovieClip.

```
 ⊖ ⊙ ⊖                Code
mcClick.addEventListener(MouseEvent.
  MOUSE_DOWN, toggleAlphaHandler);
function
  toggleAlphaHandler(evt:MouseEvent):void {
    if (evt.target.alpha == 1) {
      evt.target.alpha = .5;
    } else {
      evt.target.alpha = 1;
    }
}
```

To verify whether a `Boolean` is `true`, use the following conditional statement:

```
var boo:Boolean = true;

if (boo) {
  trace('boo is true.');
} else {
  trace('boo is false.');
}
```

To verify whether a `Boolean` is `false`, the conditional statement would look like this:

```
var boo:Boolean = false;

if (!boo) {
  trace('boo is false.'');
} else {
  trace('boo is true.');
}
```

To verify properties of a MovieClip using a conditional statement:

1. Draw a shape on the stage and convert it to a MovieClip symbol.

2. Give the MovieClip symbol on the stage an instance name of `mcClick`.

3. Create a new layer called Actions.

4. Add the code from **Code 13.7** to add a `MOUSE_DOWN` event listener to `mcClick` and toggle its `alpha` property depending on the current `alpha` property of the MovieClip.

5. Preview your movie. Click `mcClick`, and the `alpha` of the MovieClip should toggle between `.5` and `1` with each click.

CONDITIONAL STATEMENTS

Verifying for multiple conditions

In many cases, when creating conditional logic you may need to meet more than one condition in the same statement. To verify multiple conditions in the same statement, two or more conditions have to be met, or one condition or another needs to be met. You do this using the and (&&) and or (||) logical operators.

If two or more conditions are required to return true, use the && operator. To verify whether a number is within a certain range, use the following code:

```
var eval:int = 6;
if (eval > 5 && eval <10) {
  trace(eval + 'is between 5 and ten.');
}
```

Both conditions have to be met for the condition to be true and the message to display in the Output panel.

To verify whether one condition or another is true, use this code:

```
var eval:int = 4;
if (eval < 5 || eval > 10) {
  trace(eval + 'is less than 5 or
  greater than 10.');
}
```

If eval is less than 5 or if it is greater than 10, the condition is true and the statement appears in the Output panel.

Code 13.8 Checking an object's type.

```
var mcClip:MovieClip =
  new MovieClip();
  if (mcClip is MovieClip) {
    trace('Object is a MovieClip
    instance.');
  } else {
    trace('Object is not a MovieClip
    instance.');
}
```

Object-based relational operators

Conditional logic also extends to verifying a variable type or object class. This is achieved using the typeof operator for variable types and the is operator for class instances. There are many situations in which you might want to verify a variable's data type or an object's instance type. Just remember this section for the time when you need this type of logic for your application.

To verify an object type:

1. Create a new file and rename Layer 1 to Actions. Add the code from **Code 13.8** to verify whether an object is an instance of the MovieClip class.

2. Preview your file. Object is a MovieClip instance should display in the Output panel because the condition returned true.

3. Modify your code to retype the object as a Sprite:

   `var mcClip:Sprite = new Sprite();`

4. Preview your file. Object is not a MovieClip instance should display in the Output panel because mcClip is not a MovieClip object.

5. Add the following code to verify whether a variable is a String variable:

   ```
   var string:String = 'hello';
   if (typeof(string) == 'string') {
     trace('Variable is a string.');
   }
   ```

6. Preview your file. Variable is a string should display in the Output panel.

CONDITIONAL STATEMENTS

Checking for multiple event types in a single event handler

Chapter 7 discussed the event system in ActionScript. Many different kinds of events and event classes can be dispatched from a single object, and multiple objects can dispatch the same event.

If you use conditional logic within a single event handler, that event handler can handle multiple event classes and event types dispatched from one or many objects. Every event handler has an incoming event object that is passed by the event dispatcher. One of the properties of all event objects is its type. Using conditional logic, it is possible to differentiate between event types, and handle them separately and within a single event handler. This can really streamline your code by encapsulating all of the event-handling functionality for an object in a single method.

As covered in Chapter 7, an event type is represented by a string (such as "mouseOver") stored in an event constant (such as MouseEvent.MOUSE_OVER), dispatched to the event-handler method as an event class object (such as MouseEvent).

To check for multiple MouseEvent types in a single event handler:

1. Draw a shape on the stage and convert it to a Button symbol.

2. Give the Button symbol an instance name of btnButton.

3. Create a new layer named Actions and add the code from **Code 13.9** to add four event listeners to btnButton that call a single event handler and display the event type to the Output panel.

Code 13.9 Adding the event listeners and event handler for btnButton.

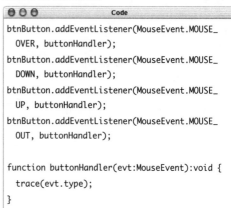

```
btnButton.addEventListener(MouseEvent.MOUSE_
  OVER, buttonHandler);

btnButton.addEventListener(MouseEvent.MOUSE_
  DOWN, buttonHandler);

btnButton.addEventListener(MouseEvent.MOUSE_
  UP, buttonHandler);

btnButton.addEventListener(MouseEvent.MOUSE_
  OUT, buttonHandler);

function buttonHandler(evt:MouseEvent):void {
  trace(evt.type);
}
```

CONDITIONAL STATEMENTS

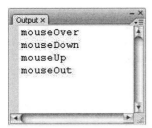

Figure 13.1 Displaying the MouseEvent event types in the Output panel.

Code 13.10 Checking for multiple mouse event types.

```
function buttonHandler(evt:MouseEvent):void {
  if (evt.type == MouseEvent.MOUSE_OVER) {
    trace('Button has been rolled over.');
  } else if (evt.type == MouseEvent.MOUSE_DOWN)
  {
    trace('Button has been pressed.');
  } else if (evt.type == MouseEvent.MOUSE_UP) {
    trace('Button has been released.');
  } else if (evt.type == MouseEvent.MOUSE_OUT)
  {
    trace('Button has been rolled off of.');
  }
}
```

4. Preview your file. You should see the different event types display in the Output panel as you roll over, out, click, and release btnButton (**Figure 13.1**).

5. Add the code from **Code 13.10** in the buttonHandler() function to differentiate among the event types using conditional logic.

6. Preview your file. The different messages from each mouse event type should display in the Output panel according to the logic in the if statement.

To customize this code, add functionality that is required for each mouse event in place of the trace() statements.

Checking for Conditions Using the Switch Statement

The switch statement also performs conditional logic. It takes up a bit more space as far as the number of lines it occupies, but switch statements are less verbose in their syntax and are easier to read when creating long lists of conditions.

The switch statement is a function call that is passed an expression, which is then used to check against different values in case comparisons. If a case clause resolves to true, code within the case statement is executed. The break statement at the end of each case breaks out of the switch statement if a case resolves to true. If a case clause resolves to false, the statement moves on to the next case statement in the switch block. If no case statements return true, a default clause can handle any resulting action, much like an else statement.

A basic switch statement that matches a string expression would look like this:

```
switch('Bob') {
  case 'Bob':
    // Do something here
      break;
}
```

To check for conditions using the switch statement:

1. Add the code from **Code 13.11** to employ a switch statement that displays the literal conversion for the day of the week, depending on the indexed value returned from the Date object.

2. Preview your file. The current day of the week should display in the Output panel.

Code 13.11 Checking for the day of the week using a switch statement.

```
var date:Date = new Date();

function convertDay(day:int):void {
  switch(day) {
    case 0:
      trace('Sunday');
      break;
    case 1:
      trace('Monday');
      break;
    case 2:
      trace('Tuesday');
      break;
    case 3:
      trace('Wednesday');
      break;
    case 4:
      trace('Thursday');
      break;
    case 5:
      trace('Friday');
      break;
    case 6:
      trace('Saturday');
      break;
    default:
      //add default action if required
  }
}

convertDay(date.getDay());
```

ITERATION AND REPETITION

Looping logic consists of iteration and repetition. Loops are control structures used to count (iterate) through a data structure. With loops, we can write code once and use it many times to repeat a set of actions. Loops allow us to accommodate for variations in data that we simply cannot plan for ahead of time. For instance, an array in an application may begin with three elements. After certain events take place in the application, the array length grows to five elements.

We do not know what scenarios might take place ahead of time, so it's hard for us to program the number of elements to get from an array if we do not know the array's length. Loops handle those types of scenarios for us, so we do not have to do the guessing. Loops are intelligent control structures that execute defined actions based on conditions that are set by the programmer as well as the events that occur in the executing of an application.

There are many uses for loops in ActionScript. They can be used to assess all the pixel data of an image, count through an array that has 75 elements, find all of the `MovieClip` objects in an application, and more.

By the end of this chapter, you should be familiar with loops and be able to decide what looping control structure to use in a particular scenario.

The for Loop Statement

The for loop statement is one of the most common loop statements used in ActionScript. The for loop executes a block of code while it iterates through a specific range of values. To iterate through a range of values, you must supply three expressions to the loop:

◆ An integer variable

◆ A condition that checks value of the integer

◆ An expression that changes the integer value

The code for a for loop looks like this:

```
var val:int = 10;
for (var i:int = 0; i < val; i++)
```

The preceding for loop begins with the i variable at 0 and ends when i reaches 9. Each time the for loop executes, the value of i is incremented by 1 (i++). After the for loop has looped 10 times (0 through 9), i will no longer be less than 10 and the for loop is finished. Each time the for loop repeats, a block of code is executed.

To create a for loop:

1. Add the following ActionScript code to the Actions panel to trace the incrementing value of i to the Output panel:

```
var value:int = 10;
for (var i:int = 0; i < value; i++) {
  trace('Current value of i = ' + i);
}
```

2. Preview your file. The incrementing value of i should display as 0 through 9 until the loop conditional is false, which means that i is no longer less than 10 (**Figure 14.1**).

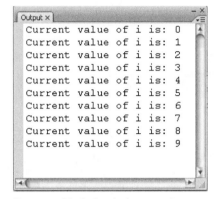

Figure 14.1 Displaying the incrementing value of i to the Output value.

THE FOR LOOP STATEMENT

Code 14.1 Iterating through array elements using a for loop.

```
                                    Code
var numbers:Array = ['zero', 'one', 'two'];
var arrayLength:int = numbers.length;


for (var i:int = 0; i < arrayLength; i++) {
  trace(numbers[i]);
}
```

Code 14.2 Creating an array of the days of the week and storing its length property in weekdaysLength.

```
                                    Code
var weekdays:Array =
  ['Sunday', 'Monday','Tuesday',
  'Wednesday', 'Thursday', 'Friday',
  'Saturday'];
var weekdaysLength:int = weekdays.length;
```

Code 14.3 Iterating through the elements of weekdays.

```
                                    Code
var weekdays:Array =
  ['Sunday', 'Monday', 'Tuesday',
  'Wednesday', 'Thursday', 'Friday',
  'Saturday'];
var weekdaysLength:int = weekdays.length;

for
  (var i:int = 0; i < weekdaysLength; i++) {
    trace(weekdays[i]);
}
```

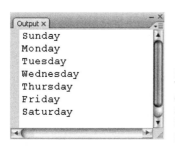

Figure 14.2
The elements of the weekdays array displayed in the Output panel.

Iterating through array elements using the for loop

The key to using a for loop for looping logic is to utilize the changing value of i. For example, you can use the changing value of i to iterate through the numbered elements of an array (**Code 14.1**).

The numbers array in Code 14.1 has three elements and has a length of 3, which is the value of arrayLength. arrayLength is used in the condition of the for loop so that the for loop will only loop as many times as the numbers array is long. Each time the loop executes its code block, the value of i is used to get the respective indexed element value from the numbers array.

To iterate through an indexed array using the for loop:

1. Add the ActionScript code from **Code 14.2** in the Actions panel to create an indexed array called weekdays and set the value of an integer called weekdaysLength to the length of the array.

2. Add the highlighted code from **Code 14.3** to employ a for loop that iterates through the values of weekdays using the changing value of i.

3. Preview your file. The elements from weekdays should display in the Output panel as separate values (**Figure 14.2**).

The "loop of death"

Be very careful when writing a for loop—or any type of conditional loop for that matter. If the conditions for the loop are never met (maybe as a result of a typo or a reference to a variable that does not exist), your application may be stuck in a "loop of death" and will crash or dramatically slow down. ActionScript 3 is a lot better at policing variable references and incorrectly used data types, but there's always a chance you may become a victim of the "loop of death."

THE FOR LOOP STATEMENT

Building a Dynamic Menu Using an Associative Array

Once you know how to iterate through the elements of an array using the for loop, you can move up to using an associative array (covered in Chapter 12). In this chapter, we'll use an associative array to store multiple pieces of information for buttons that we'll then use to create a menu with dynamic menu items. Using associative arrays, as well as the MovieClip, TextField, and MouseEvent classes, we will create a menu button that will be used repeatedly to add to a menu dynamically that has its own text label and properties.

To build a reusable menu button class:

1. Draw a rectangle on the stage that would make a reasonably sized button for a menu list.

2. Select this rectangle shape and convert it to a MovieClip symbol called MenuItem.

3. Double-click on the MenuItem symbol to enter its timeline.

4. Create a new layer in MenuItem's timeline called Label.

5. Draw a dynamic text field on the Label layer that fits within the boundaries (in other words, displays as a nice label for the button) of the rectangle for the button. Ensure that the Selectable property is turned off in the Properties panel for the text field, as shown in **Figure 14.3**.

6. Select Anti-alias as the font rendering method (for readability) for the text field in the Properties panel.

7. Give the dynamic text field an instance name of tLabel.

8. Create a new layer called actions on MenuItem's timeline.

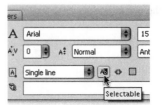

Figure 14.3 Ensure that the Selectable property for the text field is disabled so that it does not interfere with the button click.

Code 14.4 Declaring a string variable called `url` and adding a `MOUSE_DOWN` event listener to `MenuItem`.

```
●●●                    Code
var url:String;
this.addEventListener
  (MouseEvent.MOUSE_UP, gotoURLHandler);
function gotoURLHandler(evt:MouseEvent):void {


}
```

Code 14.5 Navigate to a URL that is specified by the `url` variable.

```
●●●                    Code
var url:String;
this.addEventListener
  (MouseEvent.MOUSE_UP, gotoURLHandler);

function gotoURLHandler(evt:MouseEvent):void {
  navigateToURL(new URLRequest(url));
}
```

Code 14.6 The completed code for the button.

```
●●●                    Code
var url:String;
this.addEventListener
  (MouseEvent.MOUSE_UP, gotoURLHandler);
function gotoURLHandler(evt:MouseEvent):void {
  navigateToURL(new URLRequest(url));
}
this.buttonMode = true;
tLabel.mouseEnabled = false;
```

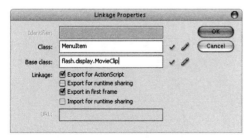

Figure 14.4 Setting the Linkage properties for MenuItem.

9. Add the ActionScript code from **Code 14.4** to declare a variable called `url` and register an event listener for a `MOUSE_UP` MouseEvent for MenuItem.

10. Add the highlighted ActionScript from **Code 14.5** to use the `navigateToURL` method to open a browser window and navigate to a URL that will be specified by the `url` string variable's value (this variable will be set when we construct the menu).

11. Add the following ActionScript code at the end of your code. This code sets the `buttonMode` property of the MenuItem MovieClip to `true` (it shows a hand cursor when it's rolled over) and sets the `mouseEnabled` property of the `tLabel` text field to `false` (so it does not interfere with mouse interactivity for the button):

    ```
    this.buttonMode = true;
    tLabel.mouseEnabled = false;
    ```

    The complete code is shown in **Code 14.6**.

12. Preview your file. The cursor should turn into a hand when you roll over the MenuItem instance. You will get an error when you click the button, because the `url` variable has no URL value.

13. Return to the main timeline and delete the MenuItem instance from the stage.

14. Select MenuItem in the library and select Linkage from the Library options menu.

15. Check the Export for ActionScript option in the Linkage Properties panel and ensure the class name is MenuItem (**Figure 14.4**). Click OK when you have finished.

16. Save your file as "Chapter14_dynamic menu.fla" and keep this file open for the next task.

BUILDING A DYNAMIC MENU

193

To build a dynamic menu:

1. Rename Layer 1 in the main timeline to Actions.

2. Add the ActionScript code from **Code 14.7** to the Actions layer to create an associative array object of my favorite Formula 1 racing teams and the links to their Web sites.

3. Add the ActionScript code from **Code 14.8** after the f1Teams object. This code uses a for each..in loop to trace out the properties from the f1Teams object to the Output panel.

4. Preview your file. The properties of the array elements should display in the Output panel as shown in **Figure 14.5**.

Code 14.7 An associative array object of Formula 1 teams and their website addresses.

```
var f1Teams:Object = new Object();

f1Teams.team1 = {team:'BMW Sauber',
  url:'http://www.bmw-sauber-f1.com'};

f1Teams.team2 = {team:'McLaren F1',
  url:'http://www.mclaren.com/'};

f1Teams.team3 = {team:'Ferrari',
  url:'http://www.ferrariworld.com/'};

f1Teams.team4 = {team:'ING Renault',
  url:'http://www.ing-renaultf1.com/'};
```

Code 14.8 Looping through the properties of the associative array object.

```
for each (var prop in f1Teams) {
    trace('team: \t' + prop.team);
    trace('url: \t' + prop.url);
}
```

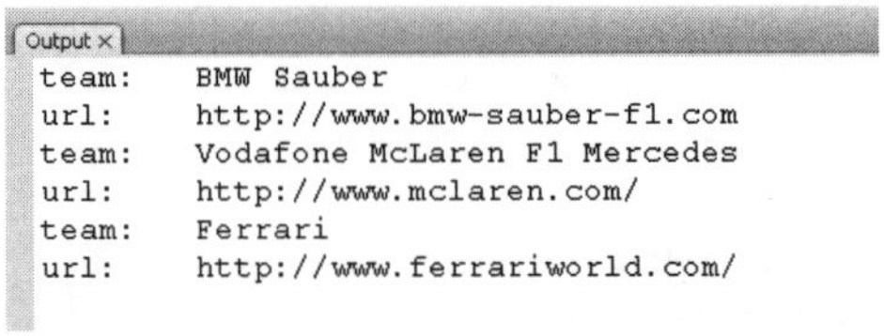

```
Output ×
team:     BMW Sauber
url:      http://www.bmw-sauber-f1.com
team:     Vodafone McLaren F1 Mercedes
url:      http://www.mclaren.com/
team:     Ferrari
url:      http://www.ferrariworld.com/
```

Figure 14.5 Properties of array elements displayed in Output panel.

Code 14.9 Add instances of MenuItem to menuContainer and set each instance's tLabel.text and url properties.

```
○○○                    Code
var menuContainer:Sprite = new Sprite();


var f1Teams:Object = new Object();


f1Teams.team1 = {team:'BMW Sauber',
  url:'http://www.bmw-sauber-f1.com'};


f1Teams.team2 = {team:'McLaren F1',
  url:'http://www.mclaren.com/'};


f1Teams.team3 = {team:'Ferrari',
  url:'http://www.ferrariworld.com/'};


for each (var prop in f1Teams) {
    var miItem:MenuItem = new MenuItem();
    miItem.tLabel.text = prop.team;
    miItem.url = prop.url;
    miItem.y =
      (miItem.height * buttonCount);
    menuContainer.addChild(miItem);
}
addChild(MenuContainer);
```

Code 14.10 Stacking the menu items at incrementing y positions.

```
○○○                    Code
var buttonCount:int = 0;
for each (var prop in f1Teams) {
    var miItem:MenuItem = new MenuItem();
    miItem.tLabel.text = prop.team;
    miItem.url = prop.url;
    miItem.y =
      (miItem.height * buttonCount);
    menuContainer.addChild(miItem);
    buttonCount++;
}
```

5. Modify the ActionScript code highlighted in **Code 14.9**. This code creates a menuContainer Sprite to store the menu items, adds MenuItem instances to menuContainer, and sets the text property of tLabel to the team property and the url String properties of MenuItem to the url property of each object property of the associative array object.

6. Preview your file. All the instances of MenuItem are added to the display list of menuContainer. However, only the Ferrari button (the last in the array list) is shown, since it was added last and sits on top of the other MenuItem objects.

7. Add the highlighted code from **Code 14.10**. This code uses the height property of each MenuItem and the value of the variable buttonCount (which keeps tracks of how many buttons are added) to position each MenuItem object at an incrementing y position of the height of each MenuItem instance multiplied by buttonCount within menuContainer (buttonCount is incremented by 1 in each loop iteration).

continues on next page

8. Preview your file. The menu items should now display as a vertical list (**Figure 14.6**). Clicking a button will open each URL in your browser.

9. Return to the Actions layer and add another team in the f1Teams object (**Code 14.11**).

10. Preview your file. The new team button should appear on the menu.

This technique of using an associative array object for creating scaling menu systems is a valuable skill in developing applications for the Flash platform. Associative arrays can be built from external data such as XML files and scripts that return database values.

Once external information has been parsed and stored in an associative array, this information can be passed all around an application for building menus and other sections of the application that require the same data. Further, you no longer have to add menu items manually, since it is code driven and scalable.

Figure 14.6
Menu items displayed as a list of buttons.

Code 14.11 Adding another team to the f1Teams associative array object.

```
var f1Teams:Object = new Object();

f1Teams.team1 = {team:'BMW Sauber',
  url:'http://www.bmw-sauber-f1.com'};

f1Teams.team2 = {team:'McLaren F1',
  url:'http://www.mclaren.com/'};

f1Teams.team3 = {team:'Ferrari',
  url:'http://www.ferrariworld.com/'};

f1Teams.team4 = {team:'ING Renault',
  url:'http://www.ing-renaultf1.com/'};
```

Iterating Object Properties

ActionScript provides other looping options that iterate through array elements or object properties. Much like the for loop or statement, each cycle through the loop executes a block of code. The block of code utilizes the current information from the loop to perform a set of actions. These loops are the for..in and for each..in statements.

Retrieving properties of an object using the for..in loop

The for..in loop iterates through array elements and object properties by retrieving a reference to the element or property.

To iterate through array elements using the for..in loop:

1. Add the following ActionScript code in the Actions panel to construct an array and its elements:

   ```
   var carsList:Array = ['Honda',
     'Nissan', 'Ford'];
   ```

2. Add the following ActionScript code, which iterates through the elements of the carsList array using the for..in loop:

   ```
   for (var i:String in carsList) {
     trace(carsList[i]);
   }
   ```

3. Preview your file. The string values of each element should display in the Output panel.

✔ Tip

- The for and the for..in loops are equally acceptable methods of iteration, although the for..in loop does more of the work for you.

To iterate through object properties using the for..in loop:

1. Add the following code to the Actions panel to create an object that stores employee information:

```
var employeeInfo:Object =
  new Object();

employeeInfo.name = 'Bob Smith';

employeeInfo.age = '36';

employeeInfo.id = 90210;
```

2. Add the highlighted code from **Code 14.12** to use the for..in loop to iterate through the properties on employeeInfo.

The value of i in the for..in loop is equal to the name of the current property that is referenced by the loop. Each value of i (the property name) is used to reference the property of the employeeName object.

3. Preview your file. Each property from the employeeInfo object should be displayed in the Output panel as shown in **Figure 14.7**.

Retrieving properties of an object using the for each..in loop

The for each..in loop iterates through a collection much like the for..in loop; however, the loop stores the actual value of the property or elements being referenced rather than a reference to the element or property.

Code 14.12 Iterating through the properties of the employeeInfo object.

```
var employeeInfo:Object = new Object();
employeeInfo.name = 'Bob Smith';
employeeInfo.age = '36';
employeeInfo.id = 90210;

for (var i:String in employeeInfo) {
  trace(i + ": " + employeeInfo[i]);
}
```

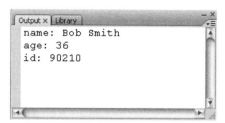

```
name: Bob Smith
age: 36
id: 90210
```

Figure 14.7 Iterating through the employeeInfo object using the for..in loop and displaying each property in the Output panel.

Code 14.13 Iterating through the properties of the employeeInfo object using the for each..in loop.

```
● ○ ●            Code
var employeeInfo:Object = new Object();
employeeInfo.name = 'Bob Smith';
employeeInfo.age = '36';
employeeInfo.id = 90210;

for each(var prop in employeeInfo) {
   trace(prop);
}
```

To iterate through array elements using the for each..in loop:

1. Add the following ActionScript code to the Actions panel, which constructs an array and its elements:

   ```
   var carsList:Array = ['Honda',
      'Nissan', 'Ford'];
   ```

2. Add the following ActionScript code after the array constructor, which iterates through the elements of the carsList array using the for each..in loop:

   ```
   for each (var element in carsList) {
      trace(element);
   }
   ```

   The element variable in the loop is used to store the current value of the element currently being referenced by the loop.

3. Preview your file. The values of each element should display in the Output panel.

To iterate through object properties using the for each..in loop:

1. Add the following code to create an object that stores employee information:

   ```
   var employeeInfo:Object =
      new Object();
   employeeInfo.name = 'Bob Smith';
   employeeInfo.age = '36';
   employeeInfo.id = 90210;
   ```

2. Add the highlighted code from **Code 14.13** to use the for each..in loop to iterate through the properties on employeeInfo.

   The prop variable in the loop is used to store the value of each property being referenced by the loop.

3. Preview your file. Each property value from the employeeInfo object should be displayed in the Output panel.

ITERATING OBJECT PROPERTIES

The while and do...while Loop Statements

The while and do...while loops work much like the for loop, with the exception that the iteration variable is declared outside of the loop.

The value of i in the following for loop is set within the parameters of the loop:

```
for (var 1:int = 0; i < 5; i++){
  trace(i);
}
```

The value of i for the following while loop is set outside the loop and incremented from within the code block of the loop:

```
var i:int = 0;
while (i < 5) {
  i++;
}
```

The do...while loop is the same as the while loop, except that a do...while loop executes at least once. The following do...while loop loops at least once, even though the condition is false. This is because the condition is verified at the end of the loop and not at the beginning:

```
var i:int = 1;
do {
  trace(i);
  i++;
} while (i < 1);
```

Code 14.14 A while loop.

```
var i:int = 0;
while (i < 5) {
    trace(i);
    i++;
}
```

```
the default timeout period of
15 seconds.
    at Chapter14_fla::
MainTimeline/frame1()
```

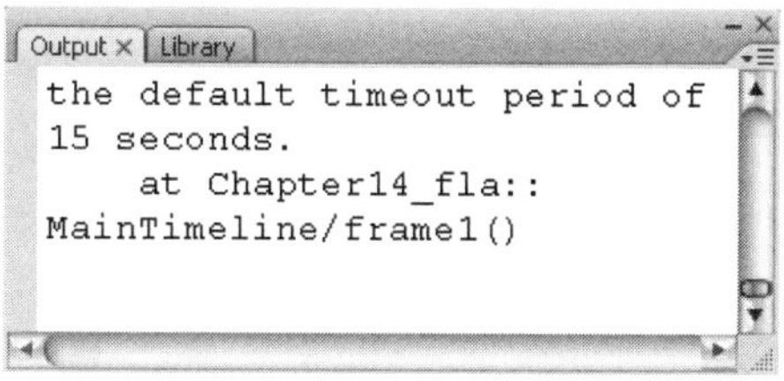

Figure 14.8 The compiler times out after 15 seconds because of an infinite loop.

The danger of using `while` and `do...while` loops is that it's easy to leave the expression out of the code block (for example, `i++`) and your application will be stuck in an infinite loop because the condition for the loop is always `true`. The following code will run infinitely and always trace the same value because the expression is missing from the code block that increments the value of `i`:

```
var i:int = 0;
while (i < 5) {
    trace(i);
}
```

If a loop runs infinitely, your application will dramatically slow down and possibly crash, as explained previously in the section "The 'Loop of Death.'"

To use the while loop:

1. Add the ActionScript code to the Actions panel from **Code 14.14** to create a `while` loop that loops as long as `i` is less than or equal (`<=`) to 5.

2. Preview your file. The values `0` through `5` should display in the Output panel.

3. Remove the `i++` expression from the `while` loop (just for fun) so that you get caught in an infinite loop.

4. Preview your file at you own risk. Flash may crash or you will get a message after 15 seconds saying the application timed out (**Figure 14.8**).

To use the do...while loop:

1. Add the code from **Code 14.15** to the Actions panel to trace the value of i to the Output panel when i is less than or equal to (<=) 5.

2. Preview your file. The values should display in the Output panel exactly the same as the while loop in the previous task.

3. Modify the condition in the while statement at the end of the loop as shown:

```
do {
   trace(i);
   i++;
} while (i < 0);
```

4. Preview your file. Although the condition is false even the first time around, the condition is not verified until after the loop has executed its code block, ensuring that a do..while loop runs at least once under any condition.

Code 14.15 The do..while loop runs while i <= 5.

```
var i:int = 0;
do {
   trace(i);
   i++;
} while (i <= 5);
```

HTTP REQUESTS AND EXTERNAL COMMUNICATIONS

15

Nearly all applications for the Flash platform support some type of external communication. Most external requests and communication take place via HTTP requests. Flash applications use HTTP requests to communicate with the browser and navigate to URLs; load external text, HTML, and XML files; send and get data using GET and POST methods; and pass other information required for external communications.

Beyond simply navigating to URLs, external communications are the start of making a Flash application truly dynamic. An application can have all of its text content, information for functional purposes, and images come from external locations, so an application can be updated via external tools and methods. This allows updating of an application from other sources.

This chapter discusses the basics of issuing HTTP requests, navigating to URLs, and loading external text content. When you're working with external resources, there is a greater chance of errors, since external files are never guaranteed to load properly (due to network and bandwidth issues). These problems can affect the functionality of an application. Therefore, we also tackle the subject of error handling.

URL Navigation with HTTP Requests

Most applications for the Flash platform make some kind of HTTP request. An HTTP request may involve specifying a URL to navigate to or communicate with, and variables that may be passed using GET or POST methods. The most common HTTP request in Flash applications is navigating to a URL. This is done using the URLRequest class and the navigateToURL() function.

Making an HTTP request

The URLRequest class handles all communication involved in making an HTTP request. The URLRequest class used by other class methods of the ActionScript API requires an HTTP request, such as the navigateToURL and Loader classes.

To make an HTTP request, you must create a URLRequest object:

```
var urlRequest:URLRequest =
  new URLRequest();
```

The URLRequest class also has an optional parameter in the constructor method for the URL in the HTTP request:

```
var urlRequest:URLRequest =
  new URLRequest
  ('http://www.website.com/');
```

Once you've created a URLRequest object, you can pass it to any method that requires an HTTP request object.

Navigating to a URL

Navigating to a URL requires the `navigateToURL()` method with a `URLRequest` object as a parameter.

Navigating to a URL using the `navigateToURL()` function looks like this:

```
var urlRequest:URLRequest =
  new URLRequest
  ('http://www.website.com/');

navigateToURL(urlRequest);
```

This `navigateToURL()` call will browse to a new URL in the same browser window. To browse to a URL in a new tab or window (or frameset), you can specify a second parameter in the function. The following code displays the URL in a new window by specifying `'_blank'` as the second parameter:

```
var urlRequest:URLRequest =
  new URLRequest
  ('http://www.website.com/');

navigateToURL(urlRequest, '_blank');
```

There is a shortcut to creating a `URLRequest` as a parameter for another method. You can create a `URLRequest` directly in the parameter for the `navigateToURL()` function:

```
navigateToURL
  (new URLRequest
  ('http://www.website.com/'));
```

This technique works fine for a single HTTP request, but if an HTTP request is required for the same URL throughout an application, having a single `URLRequest` object is the better choice.

To browse to URLs using the navigateToURL() function:

1. Draw a shape on the stage that would make a nice button.

2. Select the shape and convert it to a Button symbol.

3. Give the button an instance name of `btnLink`.

4. Create a new layer named Actions and add the ActionScript code from **Code 15.1**. This code creates a `URLRequest` object that specifies the Adobe Web site as the URL for the `navigateToURL()` method when a user clicks `btnLink`.

5. Select File > Publish Settings. In the Publish Settings dialog box, ensure that the HTML check box is selected under Type (**Figure 15.1**). Click OK.

6. Press the F12 key to preview your file in a browser. Click the `btnLink` button. Your browser may open the Adobe Web site in the same window, or you may get the warning shown in **Figure 15.2**. If you see the warning, proceed to the next step; if not, proceed to Step 11.

Code 15.1 Navigating to www.adobe.com when `btnLink` is clicked.

```
var urlRequest:URLRequest =
  new URLRequest('http://www.adobe.com/');
btnLink.addEventListener
  (MouseEvent.MOUSE_UP, gotoLinkHandler);
function gotoLinkHandler(evt:MouseEvent):void {
  navigateToURL(urlRequest);
}
```

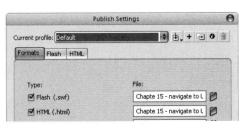

Figure 15.1 Make sure HTML is selected.

Figure 15.2 An Adobe Flash Player Security warning.

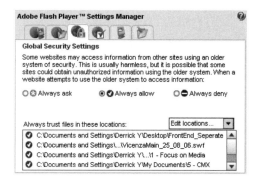

Figure 15.3 The Adobe Flash Player Settings Manager.

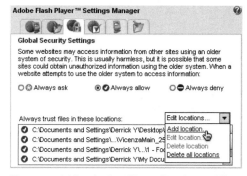

Figure 15.4 Adding the SWF file to a list of trusted files.

7. Click the Settings button; you'll be directed to the Adobe Flash Player Settings Manager Web page (**Figure 15.3**).

   Because the SWF is being run locally from your computer, the Flash Player considers this a security threat. The SWF on your computer must be added to a list of trusted locations for the Flash Player. This is because SWF files from nontrusted sources on your computer are capable of doing damage to your system.

8. Click the Edit Locations drop-down menu in the Settings Manager and select the Add Location option (**Figure 15.4**).

9. Browse to and select the saved SWF file created by the preview (saved in the same directory as your FLA file by default), and click Open. The SWF file has now been added to the list of trusted file locations by the Flash Settings Manager.

10. Restart your browser and preview your file again. The browser should now navigate to Adobe's Web site without the security warning.

11. Return to your Flash application and add the '_blank' window parameter to the navigateToURL() function:

    navigateToURL(urlRequest, '_blank');

12. Press F12 to preview your file in a browser. Click the btnLink button, and the Adobe Web site should open in a new window or tab.

✔ Tip

- For more information on security issues for the Flash Player and the Settings Manager, visit the Flash Player Help page at http://www.macromedia.com/support/documentation/en/flashplayer/help/index.html.

Loading External Text Content

The ActionScript API allows you to obtain external data from external resources. You do this using the URLLoader class. Using a URLRequest object with the URLLoader class, you can download text files, XML, and other sources to create a dynamic application.

To create a URLLoader object, use the following ActionScript code:

```
var ulLoader:URLLoader =
  new URLLoader();
```

To load an external file into the URLLoader object, create a URLRequest object for the HTTP request, and use the load method of the class to load the file:

```
var urRequest:URLRequest = new
  URLRequest('http://www.website.com/');
var ulLoader:URLLoader =
  new URLLoader();
ulLoader.load(urRequest);
```

The URLLoader class requires that the entire file be loaded into the URLLoader object before it makes the data available to ActionScript. The URLLoader class also dispatches events that enable monitoring of loading progress, completion and errors. **Table 15.1** lists some common events of the URLLoader class.

Code 15.2 listens for the data to be fully loaded in the URLLoader object.

When the file from http://www.focusonmedia.com/vqs/as3/externaltext.txt has fully loaded, its HTML code will display in the Output panel. The HTML data is stored in the data property of the event object (**evt**) passed from the URLLoader object to the listener.

Table 15.1

Events of the URLLoader Class	
EVENT	DESCRIPTION
COMPLETE	flash.events.Event.COMPLETE Dispatched once all the data is loaded and decoded and placed in the data property of the URLLoader object.
IO_ERROR	flash.events.IOErrorEvent Dispatched if a fatal error occurs during downloading and the download is terminated.
OPEN	flash.events.Event.OPEN Dispatched when downloading starts after the load method is called.
PROGRESS	flash.events.ProgressEvent.PROGRESS The event is dispatched while data is received during the downloading operation.

Code 15.2 Listening for the COMPLETE event of the URLLoader object.

```
var urRequest:URLRequest = new URLRequest
  (http://www.focusonmedia.com/vqs/as3/
  externaltext.txt');
var ulLoader:URLLoader = new URLLoader();
ulLoader.addEventListener
  (Event.COMPLETE, loaderCompleteHandler);
function loaderCompleteHandler(evt:Event):void {
  trace(evt.target.data);
}
ulLoader.load(urRequest);
```

Code 15.3 Monitoring the load progress of ulLoader.

```
var urRequest:URLRequest = new URLRequest
  (http://www.focusonmedia.com/vqs/as3/
externaltext.txt');
var ulLoader:URLLoader = new URLLoader();
ulLoader.addEventListener
  (ProgressEvent.PROGRESS,
  loaderProgressHandler);
ulLoader.addEventListener
  (Event.COMPLETE, loaderCompleteHandler);
function loaderProgressHandler
  (evt:ProgressEvent):void {
    var bLoaded:Number =
      evt.target.bytesLoaded;
    var bTotal:Number = evt.target.bytesTotal
    trace(bLoaded + ' / ' + bTotal +
      ' has loaded');
}
function loaderCompleteHandler(evt:Event):void {
  trace(evt.target.data);
}
```

bytesLoaded   bytesTotal

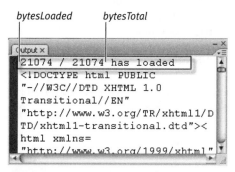

Figure 15.5 bytesLoaded and bytesTotal of ProgressEvent object properties displayed in the Output panel.

To load and track the loading progress of a URLLoader object:

1. Start a new Flash file and rename Layer 1 to Actions. Add the ActionScript code from Code 15.2 to load the home page HTML file from http://www.focusonmedia. com/vqs/as3/externaltext.txt into the data property of the ulLoader object and trace the data to the Output panel when the load is complete.

2. Preview your file. Depending on the bandwidth, a certain amount of time will pass before the data is traced to the Output panel as the HTML is being loaded by the URLLoader object.

3. Add the highlighted ActionScript code from **Code 15.3** to display the load progress of the URLLoader object.

4. Preview your file. Depending on how fast the file loads, you should see at least one progress event is dispatched (**Figure 15.5**). Because the file will be cached after the first preview, try a different Web page to see the progress event dispatch a few times to show download progress.

continues on next page

5. Add the ActionScript code from **Code 15.4**. This code adds an IOErrorEvent for the URLLoader object that will display a message if an error occurs in the loading of the data. Remove the "m" from .com in the URL www.focusonmedia.com in the URLRequest object to create a loading error.

6. Preview your file. The URLLoader object will try to load the file from the erroneous URL and display the type of error in the Output panel (**Figure 15.6**) from the text property of the IOErrorEvent object passed to the listener (dispatching the error event may take 5 seconds or so).

Handling error events will be discussed later in this chapter in the "Error Handling" section.

Leave this file open; we'll use it in the next section.

Code 15.4 Adding an IOErrorEvent to the URLLoader object and catching and displaying a load error that results from using the wrong URL in the URLRequest object.

```
var urRequest:URLRequest = new URLRequest
  (http://www.focusonmedia.co/vqs/as3/
  externaltext.txt');
var ulLoader:URLLoader = new URLLoader();
ulLoader.addEventListener
  (IOErrorEvent.IO_ERROR, loaderErrorHandler);
ulLoader.addEventListener
  (ProgressEvent.PROGRESS,
  loaderProgressHandler);
ulLoader.addEventListener(Event.COMPLETE,
  loaderCompleteHandler);
ulLoader.load(urRequest);
function
  loaderErrorHandler(evt:IOErrorEvent):void {
    trace(evt.text);
}
function loaderProgressHandler
  (evt:ProgressEvent):void {
    var bLoaded:Number =
      evt.target.bytesLoaded;
    var bTotal:Number =
  evt.target.bytesTotal;
    trace(bLoaded + ' / ' + bTotal +
      ' has loaded');
}
function loaderCompleteHandler(evt:Event):void {
  trace(evt.target.data);
}
```

Figure 15.6 Error opening URL message displayed by the IO_ERROR event.

Code 15.5 Creating a new `TextField` object and setting its `htmlText` property with the `target.data` property of the event object.

```
● ● ●                    Code
var urRequest:URLRequest = new URLRequest
  ('http://www.focusonmedia.com/vqs/as3/
  externaltext.txt');
var ulLoader:URLLoader = new URLLoader();

var tfDisplay:TextField = new TextField();
tfDisplay.width = stage.stageWidth;
tfDisplay.height = stage.stageHeight;
tfDisplay.wordWrap = true;
tfDisplay.border = true;

ulLoader.addEventListener
  (IOErrorEvent.IO_ERROR, loaderErrorHandler);
ulLoader.addEventListener
  (ProgressEvent.PROGRESS,
  loaderProgressHandler);
ulLoader.addEventListener
  (Event.COMPLETE, loaderCompleteHandler);

ulLoader.load(urRequest);
addChild(tfDisplay);

function
  loaderErrorHandler(evt:IOErrorEvent):void {
    tfDisplay.htmlText = 'Content has failed
      to load. Please try again.';
}

function loaderProgressHandler
  (evt:ProgressEvent):void {
    var bLoaded:Number =
      evt.target.bytesLoaded;
    var bTotal:Number =
      evt.target.bytesTotal
    trace(bLoaded + ' / ' + bTotal +
      ' has loaded');
}

function
  loaderCompleteHandler(evt:Event):void {
    tfDisplay.htmlText = evt.target.data;
}
```

Loading external text and formatting with HTML

Creating external text or HTML files for the text content of an application is a great way to update an application dynamically and in real time. The text can be a hard-coded page that is updated occasionally or a dynamically generated page from a server-side script such as PHP. This enables you to update the content of a well-designed application without having to open the source file, edit, recompile, and upload.

You load external text into an application by using the `URLRequest`, `URLLoader`, and `TextField` classes. You can format external text files with basic HTML tags that the `TextField` class can display. Text fields can even display images in the HTML—just use the `<img>` tag.

To load external text into a text field:

1. Return to the file from the previous task and add the highlighted code from **Code 15.5**.

continues on next page

2. Preview your file. The text content of the text file should now display as rendered HTML in the text field, including the image (**Figure 15.7**).

The HTML-formatted text in the text file is shown in **Code 15.6**.

Table 15.2 lists the supported HTML tags of the TextField class.

The TextField class also supports HTML entities for special characters (**Table 15.3**).

Figure 15.7 HTML-formatted text displayed in text field.

Code 15.6 First paragraph of HTML-formatted text file.

```
<p><strong><img src="http://www.focusonmedia.
com/vqs/as3/danda.jpg" alt="d and a" width="111"
height="150" hspace="5" align="left">Lorem ipsum
dolor sit amet</strong>, consectetuer adipiscing
elit. Aliquam dapibus. Quisque eleifend odio
sed tortor. Phasellus nisl. Ut eget massa
consectetuer ipsum varius congue. Pellentesque
elit odio, laoreet non, fringilla eu, tincidunt
interdum, risus. Aliquam erat volutpat.
Praesent id dolor. Cum sociis natoque penatibus
et magnis dis parturient montes, nascetur
ridiculus mus. In ultricies nunc sit amet quam.
Aliquam tempus. Morbi blandit dolor ut nisl.</p>
```

Table 15.2

Supported HTML Tags of TextField Class	
TAG	**DESCRIPTION**
<a>	Anchor tag; creates a hypertext link. Supports the href and target attributes.
<b>	Bold tag; bolds text within opening and closing tag.
 	Break tag; inserts a single line break at the insertion point.
<font>	Font tag; specifies a font for text. Supports the face, size, and color attributes.
<img>	Image tag; embeds external JPEG, GIF, and PNG files in the text flow. Supports the src, width, height, align, hspace, vspace, id, and checkPolicyFile attributes.
<i>	Italic tag; italicizes text within opening and closing tags.
<li>	List item tag; places a bullet beside all spans of text within <li> tags. The TextField class does not support <ul> or <ol> tags so they are unnecessary. All lists are treated as unordered, bulleted lists.
<p>	Paragraph tag; creates a new paragraph. Supports the align and class attributes.
<textformat>	TextFormat tag; allows you to use paragraph-formatting properties of the TextFormat class. For a full description and list of these properties, view Adobe LiveDocs: http://livedocs.adobe.com/flash/8/main/00001469.html.
<u>	Underline tag; underlines text within opening and closing <u> tags.

Table 15.3

Supported HTML Entities	
ENTITY	DESCRIPTION
&lt;	< (less than)
&gt;	> (greater than)
&amp;	& (ampersand)
&quot;	" (double quotes)
&apos	' (apostrophe or single quote)

Loading an external CSS file

The StyleSheet class handles formatting rules of Cascading Style Sheets (CSS). Once you've created an object of the StyleSheet class, an external style sheet loaded using the URLLoader class can be parsed by the StyleSheet object and applied to an HTML/CSS-formatted text field. This allows HTML-formatted text fields to be formatted beyond the basic HTML tags that are available and supported by the TextField class.

Use the following code to create a StyleSheet object:

```
var cssStyles:StyleSheet =
  new StyleSheet();
```

An external style sheet is loaded into an application using the URLLoader class. Once the style sheet has been loaded, the StyleSheet object parses it by using the parseCSS method of the StyleSheet class. Parsing a loaded CSS file looks like this:

```
cssStyles.parseCSS(loadedCSSData);
```

Once an external style sheet has been loaded and parsed into the StyleSheet object, you can apply the StyleSheet object to a TextField by setting the styleSheet property of the text field to the StyleSheet object:

```
textField.styleSheet = styleSheetObject;
```

Not all CSS properties are supported by the StyleSheet class. For a complete list of supported properties, view the StyleSheet documentation at Adobe LiveDocs: http://livedocs.adobe.com/flash/9.0/main/00002174.html.

To style a text field with CSS:

1. Preview the CSS code in **Code 15.7** and note the style names and properties.

2. Add the ActionScript code from **Code 15.8**. This code creates URLRequest and URLLoader objects that load an external CSS file to be parsed by the cssSheet StyleSheet object using the parseCSS method of the StyleSheet class.

3. Add the highlighted code from **Code 15.9** to set a String variable with HTML-formatted text, create a text field, and apply the cssStyles object as a styleSheet property for the tfDisplay text field after the style sheet has loaded.

   Note that the text field's text property can also display an error message in case an IO_ERROR occurs when you're trying to load the CSS file.

4. Preview your file. The embedded image should display with a 5-pixel margin all around and the text should display with the Geneva font at 18 pixels and bolded (as specified in the style sheet and shown in **Figure 15.8**).

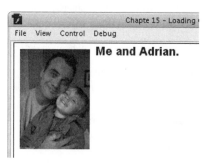

Figure 15.8 A CSS-formatted text field.

Code 15.7 We're using the .georgia style for text and the .image style for image margins.

```
.georgia {
    font-family: Geneva, Arial, Helvetica,
    sans-serif;
    font-size: 18px;
    font-weight: bold;
    color: #333333;
}


.image {
    margin: 5px;
}
```

Code 15.8 Loading an external style sheet and parsing it with the StyleSheet object.

```
var cssRequest:URLRequest = new URLRequest
    ('http://www.focusonmedia.com/vqs/as3/style.
    css');
var cssLoader:URLLoader = new URLLoader();
var cssSheet:StyleSheet = new StyleSheet();

cssLoader.addEventListener
    (Event.COMPLETE, styleTextHandler);
cssLoader.addEventListener
    (IOErrorEvent.IO_ERROR, loadErrorHandler);

function styleTextHandler(evt:Event):void {
    cssSheet.parseCSS(evt.target.data);
}

function
    loadErrorHandler(evt:IOErrorEvent):void {
}

cssLoader.load(cssRequest);
```

Code 15.9 Creating a text field and styling its HTML text with a StyleSheet object.

```
var cssRequest:URLRequest = new URLRequest ('http://www.focusonmedia.com/vqs/as3/style.css');
var cssLoader:URLLoader = new URLLoader();
var cssSheet:StyleSheet = new StyleSheet();


var textSample:String = '<p><img src="http://www.focusonmedia.com/vqs/as3/danda.jpg" alt="d and a"
  width="111" height="150" class="image"><span class="georgia">Me and Adrian.</span></p>'


var tfDisplay:TextField = new TextField();
tfDisplay.width = stage.stageWidth;
tfDisplay.height = stage.stageHeight;
tfDisplay.wordWrap = true;
tfDisplay.border = true;


cssLoader.addEventListener(Event.COMPLETE, styleTextHandler);
cssLoader.addEventListener(IOErrorEvent.IO_ERROR, loadErrorHandler);


function styleTextHandler(evt:Event):void {
  cssSheet.parseCSS(evt.target.data);
  tfDisplay.styleSheet = cssSheet;
  tfDisplay.htmlText = textSample;
  addChild(tfDisplay);
}


function loadErrorHandler(evt:IOErrorEvent):void {
  tfDisplay.htmlText = 'There was a problem while loading the content styles. Please try again.';
}


cssLoader.load(cssRequest);
```

Error Handling

Error handling is one of the most overlooked aspects of application development. In all of the tasks in this chapter that have used the URLLoader class, I've addressed error handling (at a basic level) by displaying an error message in the text field used in each example.

You are now at a point where you are dealing with external factors that can cause runtime errors in your applications. If you're working with an application that relies on externally loaded data and the data doesn't load, the application will not function as intended. The user needs to be informed.

As a developer of user-friendly applications, you must create listener methods for handling potential errors in an application. As demonstrated in the URLLoader example, loading errors are dispatched through the IOErrorEvent class. If such an event does occur, an IO_ERROR event type is dispatched and information about the error is passed to the listener as an event object.

The text property of the event object contains information about the error. It's important to determine the different types of errors that may occur, and to make sure users are informed when a particular error has occurred and what action they should take. Catching errors and responding to them ensures that users aren't left staring at a blank screen.

Classes such as the URLLoader and Loader classes provide an error event if there is a problem loading the external content. Always build in handling of error events to make your application more user-friendly. Planning for errors is not too difficult; it just takes time. You must set up a listener for an error event, determine the type of error in the event listener, and perform a set of actions to let users know what is going on and how the application will try to fix the erroneous state.

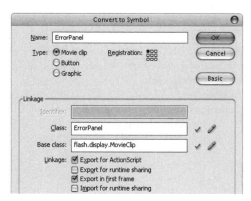

Figure 15.9 Advanced symbol options for creating an ErrorPanel class.

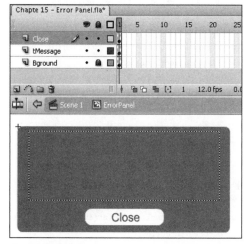

Figure 15.10 Clicking btnClose removes the ErrorPanel from the display list.

Always plan to handle errors in an application the same way you would plan to handle events in any other section of your application. Displaying and interacting with error messages is the same as creating any other interactive section of your application.

To create an error panel:

1. Draw a rectangle shape that will act as the background for your error panel. Ensure that the rectangle is large enough to hold a few lines of text as well as a button that will close the panel when clicked.

2. Select the rectangle and convert it to a MovieClip symbol called ErrorPanel. Click the Advanced option in the Convert to Symbol panel and check the Export for ActionScript option. Ensure that the class name field reads ErrorPanel (**Figure 15.9**).

3. Enter the timeline of ErrorPanel and rename the first layer to Background.

4. Create a new layer named tMessage. Draw a dynamic text field on the tMessage layer that fits within the area of the background rectangle, leaving room for a button at the bottom of the rectangle (**Figure 15.10**). Ensure that the multiline property for tMessage is selected.

5. Give the dynamic text field an instance name of tMessage.

6. Draw a small rectangle below tMessage and give it a text label of Close.

7. Select the rectangle and Close text and convert them to a Button symbol.

8. Give the Button symbol an instance name of btnClose.

   The layout of ErrorPanel should look similar to Figure 15.10.

continues on next page

ERROR HANDLING

9. Create a new layer called Actions.

10. Add the ActionScript code from **Code 15.10** to make a reference to the ErrorPanel's parent timeline so that it removes itself from its parent's display list.

11. Return to the main timeline and remove the instance of ErrorPanel from the timeline.

12. Rename Layer 1 to Actions.

13. Add the ActionScript from **Code 15.11**, which loads an external text file.

14. Preview your file. There should be a loading error that displays a message to the Output panel, as shown in **Figure 15.11**. This error happens because the last "t" is missing from the .txt extension at the end of the file path in the URLRequest object.

Code 15.10 Removing the ErrorPanel instance from the display list.

```
btnClose.addEventListener(MouseEvent.MOUSE_UP,
  closePanelHandler);
function
  closePanelHandler(evt:MouseEvent):void {
    var target:MovieClip =
    MovieClip(this.parent);
    target.removeChild(this);
}
```

Code 15.11 Loading an external text file.

```
var urRequest:URLRequest = new URLRequest
  ('http://www.focusonmedia.com/vqs/as3/
  externaltext.tx');
var ulLoader:URLLoader = new URLLoader();
ulLoader.addEventListener
  (IOErrorEvent.IO_ERROR, loaderErrorHandler);
ulLoader.addEventListener
  (Event.COMPLETE, loaderCompleteHandler);

function
  loaderErrorHandler(evt:IOErrorEvent):void {
    trace(evt.text);
}

function loaderCompleteHandler(evt:Event):void {
    trace(evt.target.data);
}
ulLoader.load(urRequest);
```

```
Output ×
Error opening URL
'http://www.focusonmedia.com/vqs/as3/externaltext.tx'
Error #2032: Stream Error. URL: http:
//www.focusonmedia.com/vqs/as3/externaltext.tx
```

Figure 15.11 A loading error occurs because of a wrong file name.

Code 15.12 Display a message in the error panel when the IO_ERROR event is dispatched.

```
                        Code
var urRequest:URLRequest = new URLRequest
  ('http://www.focusonmedia.com/vqs/as3/
  externaltext.tx');
var ulLoader:URLLoader = new URLLoader();
ulLoader.addEventListener
  (IOErrorEvent.IO_ERROR, loaderErrorHandler);
ulLoader.addEventListener
  (Event.COMPLETE, loaderCompleteHandler);

function
  loaderErrorHandler(evt:IOErrorEvent):void {
    var epPanel:ErrorPanel = new ErrorPanel();
    epPanel.tMessage.text = 'Text has failed
    to load. Please close this panel and try
    reloading the application';
    addChild(epPanel);
}

function loaderCompleteHandler(evt:Event):void {
  trace(evt.target.data);
}
ulLoader.load(urRequest);
```

15. Add the highlighted code from **Code 15.12**. This code responds to the error event by adding the error panel to the display list and setting the text property of tMessage with a message for the end user to respond to.

16. Preview your file. The ErrorPanel object should appear (**Figure 15.12**). Click the Close button to remove the ErrorPanel from the display list.

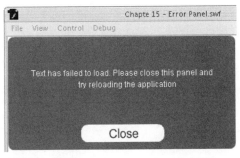

Figure 15.12 ErrorPanel appears when a loading error occurs.

LOADING EXTERNAL ASSETS

16

The ActionScript API allows you to load assets such as GIF, JPEG, PNG, and SWF files into an application. By loading external assets, as well as loading in support images for content on-demand, the appearance of an application can be changed and updated dynamically.

The ability to load external SWF files allows you to create an application consisting of a series of interactive modules rather than one giant application. Since each SWF module is compiled from a separate FLA document, this enables multiple developers to work on separate aspects of a single project at the same time. Modularizing the source into separate SWFs enables the application as a whole to load faster, since only the main assets of a file are initially loaded; other content is then loaded only when users navigate to a section where that content is needed.

This chapter shows you how to load external assets into an application using the Loader class. You'll also learn how to monitor this activity using events dispatched from the Loader class. Finally, I'll show you how to communicate with externally loaded SWF files, call their methods, and set their properties.

Using the Loader Class to Load External Data

One technique of loading external data is using the Loader class. It's similar to the URLLoader class we discussed in Chapter 15, but the Loader class loads and displays loaded images and SWF content. The Loader class is a part of the DisplayObject class; it is capable of displaying content as well as loading it.

To load external assets using the Loader class, you need to create an object of the Loader class as shown here:

```
var assetLoader:Loader = new Loader();
```

To load an asset into the Loader object, the load method of the Loader class is used, along with a URLRequest, as highlighted in the following code:

```
var assetLoader:Loader = new Loader();
assetLoader.load
  (new URLRequest('img_src.jpg'));
```

The LoaderInfo class also has events and event types that dispatch information about the progress of the load through the Loader class. This is done by listening for events of the contentLoaderInfo property of the Loader class. **Code 16.1** traces a loaded message after the Loader object has completed loading the image.

Code 16.1 Listening for the COMPLETE event type of the contentLoaderInfo property of assetLoader.

```
var assetLoader:Loader = new Loader();
assetLoader.contentLoaderInfo.
  addEventListener(Event.COMPLETE,
  loaderCompleteHandler);

function
  loaderCompleteHandler(evt:Event):void {
    trace('Image has loaded.');
}
assetLoader.load(new URLRequest
  ('http://www.focusonmedia.com/vqs/as3/
  cheese_and_crackers.jpg'));
```

Code 16.2 Adding the Loader object to the display list after the image has completed loading.

```
var assetLoader:Loader = new Loader();
assetLoader.contentLoaderInfo.
  addEventListener(Event.COMPLETE,
  loaderCompleteHandler);

function
  loaderCompleteHandler(evt:Event):void {
  trace('Image has loaded.');
  addChild(assetLoader);
}
assetLoader.load(new URLRequest
  ('http://www.focusonmedia.com/vqs/as3/
  cheese_and_crackers.jpg'));
```

Code 16.3 Clicking the stage unloads the asset from assetLoader using the unload() method and removes the event listener.

```
●●●                    Code
var assetLoader:Loader = new Loader();
assetLoader.contentLoaderInfo.
  addEventListener(Event.COMPLETE,
  loaderCompleteHandler);
function
  loaderCompleteHandler(evt:Event):void {
    addChild(assetLoader);
    stage.addEventListener
      (MouseEvent.MOUSE_UP,
      unloadAssetHandler);
}

function
  unloadAssetHandler(evt:MouseEvent):void {
    assetLoader.unload();
    stage.removeEventListener
      (MouseEvent.MOUSE_UP,
      unloadAssetHandler);
}
assetLoader.load(new URLRequest
  ('http://www.focusonmedia.com/vqs/as3/
  cheese_and_crackers.jpg'));
```

Because the Loader class is a DisplayObject, you must add the Loader object to the display list for it to be viewable. To do this, you use the addChild() method of the DisplayObject class:

addChild(assetLoader);

When do you add the Loader object to the display list? It depends on how your application functions. **Code 16.2** adds the assetLoader object to the display list only after the asset has successfully loaded (in the loaderCompleteHandler() event listener).

You can choose to load the Loader object to the display list after it has been created:

var assetLoader:Loader = new Loader();

assetLoader.load
  (new URLRequest('image.jpg'));

addChild(assetLoader);

An asset can also be unloaded from the Loader object if it's no longer needed. To unload an asset from a Loader object, call the unload method of the Loader class (**Code 16.3**).

As you learned in Chapter 15, it's extremely important for an application to check for loading errors. The `contentLoaderInfo` property of the `Loader` class has an `IOErrorEvent` event. If there is a problem loading the external asset or an HTTP error occurs, an `IO_ERROR` event type will be dispatched, and the error should be handled in the listener. **Code 16.4** traces an error message when an error occurs during the download of the `Loader` object.

To load an external graphic with a Loader object:

1. Create a new Flash file and rename Layer 1 to Actions.

2. Add the ActionScript from **Code 16.5** to the Actions layer to create a `Loader` object called `imageLoader` and load an external JPEG using the `load` method.

Code 16.4 Listening for and responding to an IOErrorEvent.

```
var assetLoader:Loader = new Loader();
assetLoader.contentLoaderInfo.
  addEventListener(Event.COMPLETE,
  loaderCompleteHandler);
assetLoader.contentLoaderInfo.
  addEventListener(IOErrorEvent.IO_ERROR,
  loaderErrorHandler);

function
  loaderCompleteHandler(evt:Event):void {
    addChild(assetLoader);
}

function loaderErrorHandler
  (evt:IOErrorEvent):void {
    trace('An error has occurred while
    loading the image.');
}
assetLoader.load(new URLRequest
  ('http://www.focusonmedia.com/vqs/as3/
  cheese_and_crackers.jp'));
```

Code 16.5 Creating a Loader object and calling its load method.

```
var imageLoader:Loader = new Loader();
imageLoader.load(new URLRequest
  ('http://www.focusonmedia.com/
  vqs/as3/cheese_and_crackers.jpg'));
```

Code 16.6 Adding `imageLoader` to the display list when it has completed loading.

```
●●●                    Code
var imageLoader:Loader = new Loader();
imageLoader.contentLoaderInfo.
  addEventListener(Event.COMPLETE,
  loaderCompleteHandler);


function loaderCompleteHandler(evt:Event):void {
    addChild(imageLoader);
}
imageLoader.load(new URLRequest
  ('http://www.focusonmedia.com/vqs/as3/
  cheese_and_crackers.jpg'));
```

Code 16.7 Listening for a loading error for `imageLoader`.

```
●●●                    Code
var imageLoader:Loader = new Loader();
imageLoader.contentLoaderInfo.
  addEventListener(Event.COMPLETE,
  loaderCompleteHandler);
imageLoader.contentLoaderInfo.
  addEventListener(IOErrorEvent.IO_ERROR,
  loaderErrorHandler);


function
  loaderCompleteHandler(evt:Event):void {
    addChild(imageLoader);
}


function loaderErrorHandler
  (evt:MouseEvent):void {
    trace('An error has occurred while
    loading the image.');
}
imageLoader.load(new URLRequest
  ('http://www.focusonmedia.com/vqs/as3/
  cheese_and_crackers.jpg'));
```

3. Add the code from **Code 16.6** to register an event listener for the COMPLETE event type for the `contentLoaderInfo` property of the `imageLoader` object and add the `Loader` object to the display list.

4. Preview your file. The `cheese_and_crackers.jpg` image should display when `imageLoader` has finished loading the image (**Figure 16.1**).

5. Add the highlighted code from **Code 16.7** to listen for an IOErrorEvent in case a problem occurs loading the image.

6. Remove the `.jpg` extension from the image link in the `load` method for `imageLoader` to create a loading error. Preview your file. The error message from the `loadErrorHandler()` event listener should display in the Output panel.

   Leave this file open for the next task.

Figure 16.1 Loaded image is displayed.

Loading an external SWF file

Loading an external SWF file works the same as loading an external image. The advantage is that an external SWF can have full interactivity and animation. Controlling externally loaded SWFs involves more specific details, which are discussed later in this chapter.

To load an external SWF with a Loader object:

1. Replace the URL in the URLRequest in the load method of imageLoader:

   imageLoader.load(new URLRequest
   ('http://www.focusonmedia.com/vqs
   /as3/external_movie.swf'));

2. Preview your file. The external SWF should load into the imageLoader object (as in Figure 16.1).

The LoaderInfo object

The LoaderInfo object is a package of information about the load that is passed to the event listener of a contentLoaderInfo property of the Loader object. The properties of the LoaderInfo class passed with the event object provide all the information needed for working with and handling the external object once it has been loaded into the application. **Table 16.1** lists some of the more commonly used properties of the LoaderInfo class.

The LoaderInfo event object references the Loader object by means of the event.target.loader property. Some common event types of the LoaderInfo class are listed in **Table 16.2**.

By listening for one of these event types and utilizing the property information passed with the LoaderInfo object, it's possible to monitor loading progress and managing of externally loaded assets.

Table 16.1

Properties of LoaderInfo Class	
PROPERTY	DESCRIPTION
bytesLoaded	The number of bytes of the asset that are currently loaded
bytesTotal	The size of the loaded asset in total in bytes
content	The display object content loaded within the Loader object
frameRate	The frame rate of the loaded SWF
height	The height of the loaded asset
loader	The Loader object associated with the LoaderInfo object
width	The width of the loaded asset

Table 16.2

Event Types of the LoaderInfo Class	
TYPE	DESCRIPTION
COMPLETE	Dispatched when the asset has completely loaded
INIT	Dispatched when methods and properties of a loaded SWF become available
PROGRESS	Dispatched frequently as data is loading into the Loader object to update the loading progress
UNLOAD	Dispatched when a Loader object's content is unloaded

Code 16.8 Listening for the PROGRESS event to track the loading progress of a Loader object.

```
 ●  ●  ●              Code
var imageLoader:Loader = new Loader();
imageLoader.contentLoaderInfo.
  addEventListener(ProgressEvent.PROGRESS,
  loaderProgressHandler);

function loaderProgressHandler
  (evt:ProgressEvent):void {
    trace('bytesLoaded: ' + evt.bytesLoaded);
    trace('bytesTotal:' + evt.bytesTotal);
}

imageLoader.load(new URLRequest
  ('http://www.focusonmedia.com/vqs/as3/
  cheese_and_crackers.jpg'));
addChild(imageLoader);
```

Monitoring Load Progress

Use the PROGRESS event type of the flash.events.ProgressEvent class to monitor the loading progress of an external asset such as an image or SWF. ProgressEvent events dispatched from a Loader object are accessed through the contentLoaderInfo property of the Loader class. The PROGRESS event is dispatched as data is received during the download of an asset. To monitor the progress of a Loader object, the bytesLoaded and bytesTotal properties of the ProgressEvent object passed to the event listener are utilized to calculate how much has been downloaded. Use **Code 16.8** to listen for a PROGRESS event type from a Loader object.

Why would you want to track the progress of the download of a Loader object? The answer is to meet functional requirements for your application. Perhaps you want to display the percentage of what's been downloaded to users while they wait, or you want to set other actions into motion after a certain amount of data has been downloaded.

The most common use of the PROGRESS event is to display the percentage of the load progress to the user. To show the percentage of what's been downloaded during the loading progress, a simple piece of math is required. Dividing the number of bytes that have been loaded by the asset's size (in total bytes) will result in a percentage of what's been loaded:

bytesLoaded / bytesTotal = percentage of load

To display the percentage of a load:

1. Create a new Flash file and rename layer 1 to Actions.

2. Add the code from **Code 16.9** to the Actions layer to load an external asset and display the percentage of the bytes downloaded.

3. Preview your file. If the image hasn't been loaded to your computer yet, the PROGRESS event should dispatch a few times before the load is complete (**Figure 16.2**).

   If the image loads too fast, choose another image online that is larger in size by changing the URL string.

Code 16.9 Dividing the bytesLoaded by the bytesTotal of the download results in a percentage of the download.

```
var imageLoader:Loader = new Loader();
imageLoader.contentLoaderInfo.
  addEventListener(ProgressEvent.PROGRESS,
  loaderProgressHandler);

function loaderProgressHandler
  (evt:ProgressEvent):void {
    var percentage:Number =
    evt.bytesLoaded / evt.bytesTotal;
    trace('Percentage: ' + percentage);
}

imageLoader.load(new URLRequest
  ('http://www.focusonmedia.com/vqs/as3/
  cheese_and_crackers.jpg'));
addChild(imageLoader);
```

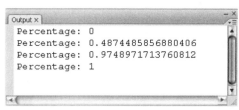

Figure 16.2 The percentage of the load displays in the Output panel.

Code 16.10 Displaying a value between 0 and 100 in the text field as the asset loads.

```
                    Code

function loaderProgressHandler
  (evt:ProgressEvent):void {
    var percentage:Number =
      Math.round((evt.bytesLoaded /
      evt.bytesTotal) * 100);
    loadDisplay.text = percentage + '%';
}
```

Code 16.11 Removing the text field from the display list after the load has completed.

```
                    Code

var imageLoader:Loader = new Loader();
imageLoader.contentLoaderInfo.
  addEventListener(ProgressEvent.PROGRESS,
  loaderProgressHandler);
imageLoader.contentLoaderInfo.
  addEventListener(Event.COMPLETE,
  loaderCompleteHandler);

function loaderProgressHandler
  (evt:ProgressEvent):void {
    var percentage:Number =
    evt.bytesLoaded / evt.bytesTotal;
    trace('Percentage: ' + percentage);
}
function loaderCompleteHandler
  (evt:Event):void {
    removeChild(loadDisplay);
}

imageLoader.load(new URLRequest
  ('http://www.focusonmedia.com/vqs/as3/
  cheese_and_crackers.jpg'));
addChild(imageLoader);
```

4. Create a new layer called Text Display and add a dynamic text field instance to the layer.

5. Give the text field an instance name of `loadDisplay`.

6. Modify the code in the `loaderProgressHandler` event listener to convert the percentage of the load to a value between 0 and 100 and display it in the text field, as shown in **Code 16.10**.

7. Add a `COMPLETE` event listener to remove the text field from the display list after the load has completed (**Code 16.11**).

MONITORING LOAD PROGRESS

Controlling Externally Loaded SWFs

Loading external SWF files into an application allows other interactive Flash applications to extend another Flash application. It also enables multiple developers to work on multiple aspects of a project that will all be loaded into a single, final application. Communicating with loaded SWFs is important so that multiple SWF files can work together as a single application.

The first thing you do with a loaded SWF is create a `MovieClip` object and cast the loaded SWF as the `MovieClip`. You have to do this because the `Loader` object that a SWF is loaded into is a `DisplayObject` and not a `MovieClip` object. The SWF needs to be cast as a `MovieClip` in order to call methods and properties and listen for events of the loaded SWF.

To load a SWF and cast it as a MovieClip:

1. Create a new Flash file and rename Layer 1 to Actions.

2. Add the code from **Code 16.12** to the Actions layer. This code loads an external SWF file into a `Loader` object named `swfLoader` and casts `swfLoader`'s content as a `MovieClip` object called `swfContainer` (which holds the contents of the loaded SWF).

3. Preview your file. The external SWF should load and display in the movie. Now let's move to the next task.

Code 16.12 Loading an external SWF and casting it as a `MovieClip` object.

```
var swfContainer:MovieClip;
var swfLoader:Loader = new Loader();
swfLoader.contentLoaderInfo.
  addEventListener(Event.COMPLETE,
  loaderCompleteHandler);

function loaderCompleteHandler
  (evt:Event):void {
    swfContainer = swfLoader.content as
      MovieClip;
    addChild(swfContainer);
}

swfLoader.load(new URLRequest
  ('http://www.focusonmedia.com/vqs/as3/
  external_movie.swf'));
```

Code 16.13 Calling the setText() method of the loaded SWF.

```
Code
var swfContainer:MovieClip;
var swfLoader:Loader = new Loader();
swfLoader.contentLoaderInfo.
  addEventListener(Event.COMPLETE,
  loaderCompleteHandler);

function loaderCompleteHandler
  (evt:Event):void {
    swfContainer = swfLoader.content as
      MovieClip;
    addChild(swfContainer);
    swfContainer.setText('Loaded SWF');
}

swfLoader.load(new URLRequest
  ('http://www.focusonmedia.com/vqs/as3/
  external_movie.swf'));
```

Figure 16.3 Setting the text property in the loaded SWF by calling its setText() method.

To set properties of a loaded SWF:

1. Add the following code after the addChild() method in the loaderCompleteHandler event listener to position the x and y properties of swfContainer at x 10, y 20:

   ```
   swfContainer.x = 10;
   swfContainer.y = 20;
   ```

2. Preview your file. The loaded SWF content in swfContainer is positioned at x 10, y 20.

Now it's time to call methods of the loaded SWF. The external SWF file (http://www.focusonmedia.com/vqs/as3/external_movie.swf) we'll use for this task has a method built into it that sets the text property of a dynamic text field called tLabel:

```
function setText(pLabel:String):void {
  tLabel.text = pLabel;
}
```

To call methods of a loaded SWF:

1. Return to the file from the previous task and add the highlighted code from **Code 16.13**, which calls the setText() method of the loaded SWF file.

2. Preview your file. The text field in the loaded SWF should display "Loaded SWF" (**Figure 16.3**).

USING SHAPES, MASKS, BLENDS, AND FILTERS

17

ActionScript has the ability to draw shapes at runtime. When you need a simple shape to act as a background, button, or mask, using the Shape class of the ActionScript Drawing API to draw the shape is usually advantageous as shapes can be drawn in specific locations of an application at will. Once a shape has been drawn with ActionScript, it can also dynamically mask other display objects.

Dynamically drawn shapes (and loaded or embedded images) in an application can be visually merged by applying blend modes with ActionScript. Blend modes are algorithms that affect the color difference between two overlapping display objects. In addition, you can apply drop shadows, blurs, beveling, and embossing to display objects with ActionScript using various filter classes.

By the end of this chapter, you will be able to draw basic shapes and apply dynamic masks using ActionScript. You will also know how to apply blend modes and filters with ActionScript to achieve dynamic image effects.

The Shape Class

The Shape class is used for drawing vector shapes such as rectangles and circles. The Shape class is the most basic class of all DisplayObject classes.

The Shape class has a single property: graphics. This property specifies a flash.display.Graphics class object, which you use to draw a shape. The Graphics class also has methods you can use to draw vector shapes.

The Shape class has a single noninherited method: the constructor method. The constructor method is called when creating a new Shape object:

```
var square:Shape = new Shape();
```

After creating a Shape object, you call its graphics property to get access to the methods of the Graphics class that will draw the shape.

Table 17.1 lists the basic methods used for creating basic shapes.

Table 17.1

Basic Methods of the Graphics Class for Drawing Simple Shapes	
METHOD	**DESCRIPTION**
beginFill()	Specifies the fill color and alpha of a shape
clear()	Clears graphics drawn in a Graphics object
drawCircle()	Draws a circle at a specified position and with a specified radius
drawEllipse()	Draws an ellipse at a specified position and with a specific width and height
drawRect()	Draws a rectangle at a specified position with a specified width and height
drawRoundRect()	Draws a rectangle with rounded corners at a specified position with a specified width, height, and corner radius width and height
endFill()	Applies a fill to shapes drawn since the last call to the beginFill() method (closes the fill of the shape)
lineStyle()	Specifies a border thickness (in pixels) and color (this is not a full list of arguments that can be passed to the method but are the required ones for creating basic strokes for a shape)

Code 17.1 Drawing a rectangle with the Shape class.

```
var rectangle:Shape = new Shape();
rectangle.graphics.beginFill(0xff0000);
rectangle.graphics.lineStyle(1, 0x000000);
rectangle.graphics.drawRect(0, 0, 100, 200);
rectangle.graphics.endFill();
addChild(rectangle);
```

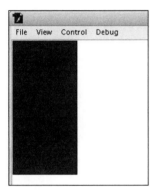

Figure 17.1
A rectangle drawn with the Shape class.

There are many more methods of the Graphics class that can be used for creating more advanced shapes and fills (such as gradient and bitmap fills), but they are beyond the scope of this book.

Drawing a simple shape using the Shape class requires the following:

◆ A new Shape object.

◆ The fill color (beginFill())—which is specified as a hexadecimal number (0xRRGGBB). An example of a black-and-white fill is 0xffffff.

◆ The line style (lineStyle()). A border thickness is specified in pixels and a color is specified as a hexadecimal number. An example of a black stroke (line) is 0x000000.

◆ The shape type (drawRect(), drawCircle(), drawEllipse(), drawRoundRect()).

◆ The end fill (which ends the fill of the shape). Fills will not be rendered unless the endFill() method is called after the creation of the shape).

◆ Addition of the shape to the display list (addChild()).

To draw a rectangle using the Shape class:

1. Create a new Flash file and rename Layer 1 to Actions.

2. Add the code from **Code 17.1** to the Actions panel. This code draws a rectangle with a red fill (0xff0000) and a black (0x000000), one-pixel border that is 100 pixels wide and 200 pixels high.

3. Preview your file. You should see a rectangle drawn from the top left of the stage (x 0, y 0) (**Figure 17.1**).

continues on next page

THE SHAPE CLASS

4. Modify the drawRect() method as shown to draw the rectangle at x 100 and y 50:

```
rectangle.graphics.drawRect
    (100, 50, 100, 200);
```

5. Preview your file. The rectangle should now display 100 pixels from the left and 50 pixels from the top of the stage.

Leave this file open for the next task.

To draw a rounded rectangle using the Shape class:

1. Change the drawRect() method as shown to alter the rectangle you created in the previous task so that it has rounded corners with a corner radius of 20 pixels:

```
rectangle.graphics.drawRect(100, 50,
    100, 200, 20);
```

2. Preview your file. The rectangle should now display with rounded corners with a 20-pixel radius.

To draw a circle using the Shape class:

1. Add the code from **Code 17.2**, which draws a circle using the drawCircle() method so that the circle sits at x 0 and y 0 and has a 75-pixel radius.

Code 17.2 Drawing a circle using the drawCircle() method.

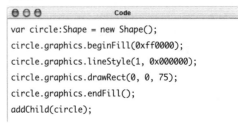

```
var circle:Shape = new Shape();
circle.graphics.beginFill(0xff0000);
circle.graphics.lineStyle(1, 0x000000);
circle.graphics.drawRect(0, 0, 75);
circle.graphics.endFill();
addChild(circle);
```

Code 17.3 Using an offset value to display the circle at an x and a y point near its top-left corner.

```
                    Code
var radius:uint = 75;

var circle:Shape = new Shape();
circle.graphics.beginFill(0xff0000);
circle.graphics.lineStyle(1, 0x000000);
circle.graphics.drawCircle
  (0 + radius, 0 + radius, radius);
circle.graphics.endFill();
addChild(circle);
```

Figure 17.2
Only the bottom right of the circle is showing at the top-left corner of the stage.

2. Preview your file. Notice how you only see the bottom-right portion of the circle. This is because the registration point of the circle is in the center of the circle. In order for the circle to sit at a specific coordinate in full view, we need to perform some calculations.

3. Modify your code as shown in **Code 17.3** to use a variable called radius. This variable not only sets the radius of the circle but also acts as an offset of the x and y coordinates of the circle's position. That way, the circle is truly placed at specified coordinates at the top-left corner (of the square area it occupies), as shown in **Figure 17.2**.

(For the record, there is a reason I'm adding a value to 0. It is to illustrate that you need to add an offset to the x and y position of a circle that has been drawn using the Shape class.)

To move any shape object after it has been drawn, simply set its x and y properties to a new value as shown:

```
circle.x = 300;
circle.y = 100;
```

THE SHAPE CLASS

Applying Dynamic Masking to Objects

The masking of objects can be displayed dynamically using ActionScript. This is accomplished by designating:

◆ The display object that is to be masked (or the "maskee")

◆ The display object that will act as a mask

◆ The mask property of the maskee display object that needs to be set to the masking display object

A MovieClip can be created at authortime, added to the stage, and set to mask an object using ActionScript.

To create a dynamic mask using a MovieClip created at authortime:

1. Create a new Flash File.

2. Draw a square shape of the stage that is 200px × 200px and is positioned at x 0 and y 0.

3. Select the square and convert it to a MovieClip symbol called Square.

4. Assign the Square symbol an instance name of mcSquare.

5. Draw a circle on the stage that is 200px × 200px.

6. Select the circle shape and convert it to a MovieClip symbol named SqMask.

7. Delete the SqMask symbol from the stage.

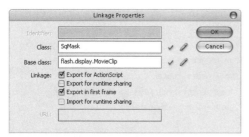

Figure 17.3 Linkage properties for Circle MovieClip symbol.

Figure 17.4 Masking `mcSquare` with `mcSqMask` by setting the `mask` property of `mcSquare`.

8. Select the SqMask symbol in the Library and select Linkage from the Library's properties panel.

9. Select the Export for ActionScript option in the Linkage Properties panel so the MovieClip has a class name of `SqMask` and its base class is `flash.display.MovieClip` (**Figure 17.3**).

10. Click OK and return to the main timeline.

11. Create a new layer called Actions and add the following ActionScript code to it that adds an instance of `SqMask` to the stage and is set as the `mask` property of `mcSquare`:

    ```
    var mcSqMask:SqMask = new SqMask();
    mcSquare.mask = mcSqMask;
    addChild(mcSqMask);
    ```

12. Preview your file. `mcSquare` should appear as a circle because of the circle mask shape of `mcSqMask` (**Figure 17.4**).

A shape can also be drawn at runtime using ActionScript and then set as a mask of an object.

In order for an object to act as a mask, it simply has to be a solid (i.e., filled-in) shape. Note that lines (strokes) do not act as masks; only fills can act as masks.

The code for masking a display object looks like this:

```
maskee.mask = maskingObject;
```

To create a dynamic mask using the Shape class:

1. Create a new Flash file and rename Layer 1 to Actions.

2. Add the code from **Code 17.4** to the Actions layer to load an external image.

3. Add the highlighted code from **Code 17.5** to mask the Loader object with a Shape object.

4. Preview your file. You should see the rectangle shape masking the imageLoader object and its image contents (**Figure 17.5**).

   Leave this file open for the next task.

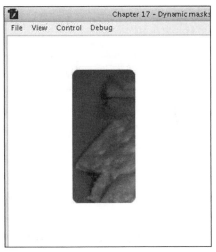

Figure 17.5 The Loader object is dynamically masked by the Shape object.

Code 17.4 Loading an external image into a Loader object.

```
var imageLoader:Loader = new Loader();
imageLoader.contentLoaderInfo.
  addEventListener(Event.COMPLETE,
  loaderCompleteHandler);


function loaderCompleteHandler(evt:Event):void {
  addChild(imageLoader);
}


imageLoader.load(new URLRequest
  ('http://www.focusonmedia.com/vqs/as3/
  cheese_and_crackers.jpg'));
```

Code 17.5 Creating a Shape object and setting it to mask the Loader object.

```
var rectangle:Shape = new Shape();
rectangle.graphics.beginFill(0xff0000);
rectangle.graphics.lineStyle(0, 0x000000);
rectangle.graphics.drawRoundRect
  (100, 50, 100, 200, 20);
rectangle.graphics.endFill();


var imageLoader:Loader = new Loader();
imageLoader.contentLoaderInfo.
  addEventListener(Event.COMPLETE,
  loaderCompleteHandler);


function loaderCompleteHandler(evt:Event):void {
  addChild(imageLoader);
  addChild(rectangle);
  imageLoader.mask = rectangle;
}


imageLoader.load(new URLRequest
  ('http://www.focusonmedia.com/vqs/as3/
  cheese_and_crackers.jpg'));
```

Code 17.6 Drawing a Shape object the same width and height as the Loader object.

```
Code
var imageLoader:Loader = new Loader();
imageLoader.contentLoaderInfo.
  addEventListener(Event.COMPLETE,
  loaderCompleteHandler);


function
  loaderCompleteHandler(evt:Event):void {
    var rectangle:Shape = new Shape();
    rectangle.graphics.beginFill(0xff0000);
    rectangle.graphics.lineStyle(0,
      0x000000);
    rectangle.graphics.drawRoundRect
      (imageLoader.x, imageLoader.y,
      imageLoader.width, imageLoader.height,
      20);
    rectangle.graphics.endFill();
    addChild(imageLoader);
    addChild(rectangle);
    imageLoader.mask = rectangle;
}
imageLoader.load(new URLRequest
  ('http://www.focusonmedia.com/vqs/as3/
  cheese_and_crackers.jpg'));
```

To create a mask that rounds the corner of an image:

1. Add the highlighted code in **Code 17.6** to the Actions layer to create a Shape object that is the same width and height and that is positioned in the same location as the Loader object. The corner radius of the shape will give the appearance that the image has rounded corners when it is set as the mask of the Loader object.

2. Preview your file. The image should appear to have rounded corners because of the rounded corners of the rectangle shape (**Figure 17.6**).

   Leave this file open for the next task.

Figure 17.6 Masking the Loader object with a rectangle that has rounded corners.

APPLYING DYNAMIC MASKING TO OBJECTS

Creating Visual Effects with ActionScript

All of the blend modes and filter effects that are available in the Property inspector for a display object can be applied to a display object at runtime using ActionScript. You do this by setting the `blendMode` and `filters` properties of a display object.

Blend modes

Blend modes are applied to a display object using the `BlendMode` class. Blend mode types are specified through the `blendMode` property of a display object, which returns a `BlendMode` class object, which you can then apply to a display object. Applying a blend mode to a display object would look like this:

```
displayObject.blendMode =
  BlendMode.SUBTRACT;
```

Blend modes generally work by using different algorithms that display the differences in color between two overlying objects as a blended image. Blend modes are always applied to the top image in an overlay sequence. The list of blend modes is extensive; check the Flash Help documentation by searching for the phrase "BlendMode class."

To apply a blend mode:

1. Return to the code from the previous task and replace the line that masks the `imageLoader` object (`imageLoader.mask = rectangle;`) with the following:

```
rectangle.blendMode =
  BlendMode.MULTIPLY;
```

Table 17.2

Filter Classes

FILTER	DESCRIPTION
GradientGlowFilter	Applies a realistic glow of color with a gradient that can be controlled
BlurFilter	Applies a visual blur to a display object
GradientBevelFilter	Bevels the edges of a display object to create a 3-D look
GlowFilter	Applies an inner, outer or knockout glow effect to a display object
ColorMatrixFilter	Manipulates color values of a display object that affect the saturation, hue, luminance, and other color effects
ConvolutionFilter	Combines pixels of an image with neighboring pixels to produce a convoluted image or multiple effects
BevelFilter	Adds a beveled effect to display objects
DisplacementMapFilter	Uses pixels values from image object to perform displacement effects
DropShadowFilter	Applies a drop shadow to display objects

2. Preview your file. You should see the image change to a red, monochromatic color scheme.

3. Experiment using the various blend modes from the following list:

   ▲ ADD
   ▲ ALPHA
   ▲ DARKEN
   ▲ DIFFERENCE
   ▲ ERASE
   ▲ HARDLIGHT
   ▲ INVERT
   ▲ LAYER
   ▲ LIGHTEN
   ▲ OVERLAY
   ▲ SCREEN
   ▲ SUBTRACT

4. To remove a blend mode from a display object, set its blendMode property to NORMAL as shown:

```
rectangle.blendMode =
    BlendMode.NORMAL;
```

Dynamic filters

The filters that can be applied to a display object using ActionScript are the same ones that are applied from the Filters panel at authortime. Using ActionScript, you can also apply more complicated filters than those found in the Filters panel as well.

Each filter applied to a display object has its own class, which is defined in the flash.filters class package. **Table 17.2** lists the filters you'll find in the flash.filters package.

CREATING VISUAL EFFECTS WITH ACTIONSCRIPT

You apply a filter to a display object through the object's `filters` property. The `filters` property accepts an array of preconstructed filter objects and applies the filter(s) to the display object. Each filter object can have an extensive list of arguments that are passed in the constructor method for the object. For example, the arguments for a new `DropShadowFilter` object look like **Code 17.7**.

A `BlurFilter` object has properties that need to be set by arguments in the constructor method:

```
var bfObject:BlurFilter = new
  BlurFilter(blurX, blurY, blurQuality);

displayObject.filters = [ bfObject ];
```

Besides the `BlurFilter` and `DropShadow` filter classes, the other filter classes of the Flash API require complicated matrices of information, which fall outside the scope of this book.

For more information on all the filters of the `flash.filters` class package, search the Flash Help menu using the keywords "Filters class."

Code 17.7 Creating a `DropShadowFilter` object.

```
var dsObject:DropShowFilter =
  new DropShadowFilter (distance, angle,
  color, alpha, blurX, blurY, quality,
  inner, knockout);
displayObject.filters = [ dsObject ];
```

Code 17.8 Applying a BlurFilter object to a Loader object.

```
Code
var imageLoader:Loader = new Loader();
imageLoader.contentLoaderInfo.
  addEventListener(Event.COMPLETE,
  loaderCompleteHandler);


function loaderCompleteHandler(evt:Event):void {
  var bfFilter:BlurFilter =
    new BlurFilter(20, 0, 3);
  imageLoader.filters = [ bfFilter ];
  addChild(imageLoader);
}

imageLoader.load(new URLRequest
  ('http://www.focusonmedia.com/vqs/as3/
  cheese_and_crackers.jpg'));
```

Figure 17.7 A loaded image with a BlurFilter object applied to its filters property.

To apply a blur filter to a display object:

1. Add the ActionScript from **Code 17.8** to load an external image and apply a blur filter to it with a blurX setting of 20, a blurY setting of 0, and a quality blur setting of 3 (1 = low, 2 = medium, 3 = high).

2. Preview your file. The loaded image should appear to have a horizontal motion blur effect (**Figure 17.7**).

3. Change the blurQuality setting to 1 and note the difference in the blur quality. It should appear less blurry and of lower quality.

4. Experiment with different blurX and blurY values.

5. To remove filters from a display object, specify an empty array for the filters property:

   ```
   imageLoader.filters = [  ];
   ```

✔ Tip

- A higher-quality blurQuality of a BlurFilter may require higher CPU resources to render the effect at runtime. As long as things don't get too complicated, your filters effects should run smoothly. But remember to keep an eye on things as you progress.

To apply a drop shadow filter to a display object:

1. Add the ActionScript from **Code 17.9** to draw a rounded rectangle shape and apply a DropShadowFilter to it that has the following properties:
   ▲ depth: 7
   ▲ angle: 45%
   ▲ color: 0x000000
   ▲ alpha: .25
   ▲ blurX: 10
   ▲ blurY: 10
   ▲ quality: 3

2. Preview your file. You should see a rectangle with a drop shadow like the one in **Figure 17.8**.

3. Experiment with various property settings for the DropShadowFilter object.

Code 17.9 Applying a DropShadowFilter filter to a Shape object.

```
var dsObject:DropShadowFilter =
  new DropShadowFilter
  (7, 45, 0x000000, .25, 10, 10, 3);

var rectangle:Shape = new Shape();
rectangle.graphics.beginFill(0xff0000);
rectangle.graphics.lineStyle(0, 0x000000);
rectangle.graphics.
  drawRoundRect(50, 50, 200, 75, 10);
rectangle.graphics.endFill();

rectangle.filters = [ dsObject ];
addChild(rectangle);
```

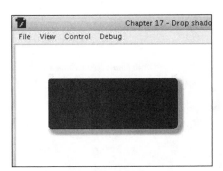

Figure 17.8 A rectangle shape with a DropShadowFilter object applied to it.

DYNAMIC ANIMATION

Dynamic animation can be one of the most rewarding uses of ActionScript, and it's what makes ActionScript, Flash, and Flex applications so unique. The ability to animate (or *tween*) display objects at runtime using various classes, events, and methods is a must for game development and for creating random, always-changing animations in an application. In addition, creating transitions that introduce or remove display objects and content in a unique and interesting way within an application is another key ability.

By the end of this chapter, you should feel quite comfortable animating display objects with ActionScript using the Timer class, the ENTER_FRAME event, and the Tween class, along with various effects from the transition classes. You will also know how to improve performance during tweens using bitmap caching.

The Timer Class

The Timer class makes a connection to Flash Player timers. The Timer class dispatches an event at specified time intervals based on a timer running in the Flash Player. Timer objects can run once after a specified amount of time has passed or repeatedly with every increment of time that has passed. The Timer class can be used for many purposes, but is best used for programmatic animation due to its lack of precision at the millisecond level in the Flash Player.

The Timer class has four methods, as outlined in **Table 18.1**.

To track the time that has passed from a Timer object, you need to listen for events of the TimerEvent class. **Table 18.2** lists the two events that are dispatched from the Timer class using the TimerEvent class.

To create a Timer object, which will listen for TimerEvent events, use the code shown in **Code 18.1**.

The interval argument passed in the new Timer() constructor method is the number of seconds for the interval in milliseconds. A value of 1000 would be one second, 500 would be a half a second, 3000 would be three seconds, and so on. The second parameter, repeat, is optional. If the repeat parameter is not defined, the Timer object will continue to repeat infinitely until its stop() method is called. If a repeat parameter of 5 is passed, the Timer object will repeat 5 times at the specified interval and then stop on its own. Regardless, every time the specified interval is hit, the TimerEvent.TIMER event type is dispatched. The TIMER_COMPLETE is dispatched only if the repeat property has been specified and reached.

Table 18.1

Methods of the Timer Class

METHOD	DESCRIPTION
Timer()	Constructs a new Timer object with specified delay and repeat states
reset()	Stops and resets the Timer object if running
start()	Starts the Timer object if it's not running
stop()	Stops the Timer object

Table 18.2

Event types of the TimerEvent Class

EVENT CONSTANT	DESCRIPTION
TIMER	Dispatched every time the Timer object reaches a specified interval set in the delay property in the constructor method
TIMER_COMPLETE	Dispatched when the specified number of repeat states has been reached

Code 18.1 Creating a Timer object and listening for TimerEvent event.

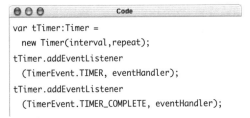

```
var tTimer:Timer =
  new Timer(interval,repeat);
tTimer.addEventListener
  (TimerEvent.TIMER, eventHandler);
tTimer.addEventListener
  (TimerEvent.TIMER_COMPLETE, eventHandler);
```

✔ Tip

- Depending on the frame rate of a movie, the TimerEvent.TIMER event type may vary slightly as memory and other factors alter the precision of the time that has passed in the Flash Player.

Code 18.2 Listening for the `TimerEvent.TIMER` event of the `Timer` object.

```
● ● ●              Code
var tTimer:Timer = new Timer(500);
tTimer.addEventListener
  (TimerEvent.TIMER, timerEventHandler);


function
  timerEventHandler(evt:TimerEvent):void {
    trace('timerEvent listener has been
    called with timer event');
}


tTimer.start();
```

Code 18.3 Handling the `TIMER_COMPLETE` event.

```
● ● ●              Code
var tTimer:Timer = new Timer(500, 5);
tTimer.addEventListener
  (TimerEvent.TIMER, timerEventHandler);
tTimer.addEventListener
  (TimerEvent.TIMER_COMPLETE,
  completeEventHandler);


function
  timerEventHandler(evt:TimerEvent):void {
    trace('timerEvent listener has been
    called with timer event');

}


function
  completeEventHandler(evt:TimerEvent):void {
    trace('timerComplete event has been
    dispatched');
}


tTimer.start();
```

To listen for events of the Timer class:

1. Create a new Flash file and rename Layer 1 to Actions.

2. Add the ActionScript from **Code 18.2** to the Actions panel. This code creates a `Timer` object that dispatches a TIMER event every 0.5 seconds and traces a message to the Output panel.

3. Preview your file. Note that the first trace statement only happens after the first 0.5 seconds have passed.

4. Add the highlighted code from **Code 18.3** to specify the `Timer` object to repeat 5 times and call the `completeEventHandler` event listener when the `TIMER_COMPLETE` event is dispatched.

5. Preview your file. The `timerEventHandler` listener has been called with TIMER event message should repeat five times in the Output panel and then the `TIMER_COMPLETE` event has been dispatched message should appear after the `Timer` object has repeated five times (**Figure 18.1**).

   Leave this file open for the next task.

Figure 18.1 The `Timer` object counts five times and then dispatches a `TIMER_COMPLETE` event.

THE TIMER CLASS

To animate a display object using the Timer class, you need to change a property or properties of the object each time the TIMER event is dispatched.

Figure 18.2 demonstrates the x property of a MovieClip instance called mcCircle that is incremented by 5 pixels every 10/100th of a second as specified in a Timer object. Every time the TIMER event is dispatched (every 10/1000th of a second), mcCircle moves over to the right by 5 more pixels. As time goes on, this gives the effect of an animation as mcCircle moves across the stage.

To animate a display object with the Timer class:

1. Create a new Flash file and rename Layer 1 to Actions.

2. Create a new Layer called Circle.

3. Draw a circle shape on the Circle and convert it to a MovieClip symbol called Circle.

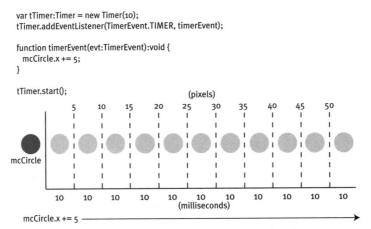

```
var tTimer:Timer = new Timer(10);
tTimer.addEventListener(TimerEvent.TIMER, timerEvent);

function timerEvent(evt:TimerEvent):void {
  mcCircle.x += 5;
}

tTimer.start();
```

Figure 18.2 mcCircle is moved to the right by 5 pixels every time the TIMER event is dispatched from the Timer object.

Code 18.4 Moving `mcCircle` to the right by 5 pixels for each interval of the `Timer` object.

```
● ● ●                    Code
var tTimer:Timer = new Timer(10);

tTimer.addEventListener
  (TimerEvent.TIMER, timerEventHandler);


function
  timerEventHandler(evt:TimerEvent):void {
    mcCircle.x += 5;
    trace(mcCircle.x);
}


tTimer.start();
```

4. Select the `Circle` MovieClip symbol on the stage and give it an instance name of `mcCircle` in the Property inspector.

5. Drag the instance of `mcCircle` just off the left-hand side of the stage.

6. Remove the repeat parameter in the `new Timer()` constructor method and set the interval to 10/1000 of a second. Increment the x position of `mcCircle` by 5 every time the TIMER event is dispatched, as highlighted in **Code 18.4**. Trace the current x position of `mcCircle` for each interval.

7. Preview your file. Notice that `mcCircle` keeps on moving to the right even after it moves off the right side of the stage.

Leave your file open for the next task.

If you want the circle to continue appearing that it is constantly moving across the stage from left-to-right, you must write a conditional statement that verifies whether the circle has moved outside the viewable area of the stage (`stage.stageWidth`). If it has, return the circle back to the left of the stage and continue to move it to the right until the condition is true again, as illustrated in **Figure 18.3**.

Figure 18.3 `mcCircle` is moved back to the left of the stage if its x position exceeds the width of the stage.

To loop the circle animation in the viewable area of the stage:

1. Add the conditional statement from **Code 18.5**, which returns mcCircle to the left side of the stage if it animates off the right side of the stage.

2. Preview your file. If the x position of mcCircle is greater than the width of the stage, it is returned to the left side of the stage to continue looping across the stage.

3. Modify your code as shown in **Code 18.6**. This code stops the Timer object after mcCircle has moved across the stage once, removes its event listener, and removes it from the display list.

✔ Tip

■ It is extremely important to stop all Timer objects and remove their event listeners when they are not needed any more. If a Timer object is left running, it is using resources that are not needed and can thus affect the performance of an application. Further, all display objects that are not needed are best removed from the display list so they are not consuming resources unnecessarily as well.

Code 18.5 Resetting mcCircle's x position to the left side of the stage if its x position is greater than the width of the stage.

```
var tTimer:Timer = new Timer(10);
tTimer.addEventListener
  (TimerEvent.TIMER, timerEventHandler);


function
  timerEventHandler(evt:TimerEvent):void {
  if (mcCircle.x > stage.stageWidth) {
    mcCircle.x = 0 - mcCircle.width;
  } else {
    mcCircle.x += 5;
  }
}


tTimer.start();
```

Code 18.6 Stopping the Timer object, removing its event listener, and removing mcCircle from the display.

```
function
  timerEventHandler(evt:TimerEvent):void {
  tTimer.stop();
  tTimer.removeEventListener
    (TimerEvent.TIMER, timerEventHandler);
  removeChild(mcCircle);
}
```

Code 18.7 Fading `mcCircle` out with each loop of the ENTER_FRAME event.

```
● ● ●                  Code
this.addEventListener
  (Event.ENTER_FRAME, fadeCircleHandler);


function fadeCircleHandler(evt:Event):void {
  mcCircle.alpha -= .1;
}
```

The ENTER_FRAME Event

The ENTER_FRAME event is an event dispatched from the DisplayObject class at the same frequency as the frame rate of a movie. If a movie has a frame rate of 12 frames per second, the ENTER_FRAME event is dispatched 12 times per second. To listen for the ENTER_FRAME event, register an event listener either with the stage of a movie or a DisplayObject in an application. The code that listens for an ENTER_FRAME event looks like this:

```
DisplayObject.addEventListener
  (Event.ENTER_FRAME, eventHandler);
```

The ENTER_FRAME event is always dispatched from a DisplayObject object. All you have to do is write the code that listens for it.

The ENTER_FRAME event is inherited by the stage and MovieClip class.

Animating a display object every time an ENTER_FRAME event is dispatched is the same as using the Timer class. Only the method of repetition is different.

To animate using the ENTER_FRAME event:

1. Draw a circle shape on the stage and convert it to a MovieClip symbol named Circle.

2. Select the Circle instance on the stage and give it an instance name of mcCircle.

3. Create new layer called Actions and add the ActionScript from **Code 18.7**, which uses the ENTER_FRAME event of the stage to fade out mcCircle by fading its alpha property each loop by .1 (or 10%).

4. Preview your file. mcCircle should fade out by a value of .1 every time the ENTER_FRAME event dispatches.

continues on next page

5. Modify the code as shown here to listen for the ENTER_FRAME event of mcCircle rather than the event of the stage:

```
mcCircle.addEventListener
  (Event.ENTER_FRAME,
   fadeCircleHandler);
```

6. Modify the code using the highlighted code in **Code 18.8** to remove the event listener from mcCircle and remove mcCircle from the display list after its alpha property has reached 0.

7. Preview your file. mcCircle should fade out as it did before, but it is now removed from the display list after it has faded out.

8. Select Debug > List Objects from the Flash Player preview (**Figure 18.4**). mcCircle should not appear in the Output panel as it has been removed from the display list (**Figure 18.5**).

If mcCircle was not removed from the display list, it will still be listed as an object in the Output panel, as shown in **Figure 18.6**.

✔ Tips

■ It is always handy to use the Debug > List Objects menu to verify whether objects that are not visible are listed in a movie. Sometimes nonvisible display objects are still required in a movie, so it's a good idea to use Debug > List Objects to verify, in case the event objects are not functioning correctly behind the scenes.

■ If an object is no longer needed after it has faded out (0 alpha), always check to ensure that it is removed from the display list so it is not using unnecessary resources.

Code 18.8 Cleaning up object listeners and the display list.

```
mcCircle.addEventListener
  (Event.ENTER_FRAME, fadeCircleHandler);

function fadeCircleHandler(evt:Event):void {
  if (mcCircle.alpha <= 0) {
    mcCircle.removeEventListener
    (Event.ENTER_FRAME, fadeCircleHandler);
    removeChild(mcCircle);
  } else {
    mcCircle.alpha -= .1;
  }
}
```

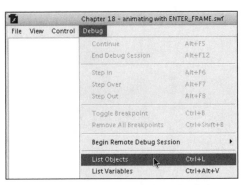

Figure 18.4 Selecting List Objects from the Flash Player Debug menu.

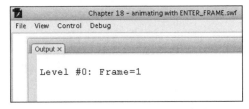

Figure 18.5 mcCircle does not appear in the Output panel as an object since it was removed from the display list.

Figure 18.6 mcCircle listed as an object in the Output panel.

THE ENTER_FRAME EVENT

The Tween and Easing Classes

The Tween class enables you to move, resize, rotate, or fade display objects using ActionScript. Any property of a display object can be programmatically tweened, such as x, y, rotation, scaleX, scaleY, and alpha properties. You can also specify how long the animation will last in either seconds or frames using the Tween class.

There's an advantage to using the Tween class to animate with ActionScript: it automatically detects when a specified tween is completed and the tween is done (unlike the tweens using the Timer class or ENTER_FRAME event where we had to do the detection ourselves). The Tween class and its methods also take care of what otherwise is a tricky lesson in math and trigonometry to make certain tween effects occur.

To create a Tween object and set its required parameters, use the following code:

```
var twTween:Tween =
  new Tween(object, property, easing,
    start, finish, duration, useSeconds);
```

Let's look at each of these parameters:

- `object`—The instance name of the MovieClip that you want to animate.

- `property`—The property of the display object that will be tweened.

- `easing`—The type of easing that is applied to the tween to affect its acceleration and deceleration.

- `start`—The starting value of the property being tweened.

- `finish`—The ending value of the property being tweened.

- `duration`—How long the animation will take, either in frames or seconds.

- `useSeconds`—If you want the duration in seconds, set this optional parameter to `true`. If your duration is in frames, set this to `false` (or do not set it at all).

To utilize the `Tween` class in ActionScript, it must be imported:

```
import fl.transitions.Tween;
```

To apply a tween to a display object, the `Tween` class *must* be imported and a `Tween` object must be created and applied to a display object.

To tween a display object called `mcCircle` and tween its x property from x `0` to x `300` over a duration of 2 seconds and no easing (`null`), use this code:

```
import fl.transitions.Tween;
var twTween:Tween =
  new Tween(mcCircle, "x", null, 0,
  300,2, true);
```

Code 18.9 Tweening `mcShape` from x 0 to x 500 over a period of 2 seconds.

```
● ● ●                    Code
import fl.transitions.Tween;
var twTween:Tween =
  new Tween(mcShape, 'x', null, 0, 500,
  2, true);
```

Code 18.10 Tweening multiple properties.

```
● ● ●                    Code
import fl.transitions.Tween;
var twXTween:Tween =
  new Tween(mcShape, 'scaleX', null, 1, 0,
  2, true);
var twYTween:Tween =
  new Tween(mcShape, 'scaleY', null, 1, 0,
  2, true);
```

To tween a display object using the Tween class:

1. Create a shape on the stage and convert it to a MovieClip symbol called MCShape.

2. Select the MCShape symbol on the stage and give it an instance name of `mcShape`.

3. Create a new layer called Actions and add the ActionScript from **Code 18.9** to tween `mcShape` from x 0 to x 500 over a duration of 2 seconds with no easing.

4. Preview your file. `mcShape` should tween from the left to the right of the stage at a consistent pace.

5. Experiment with tweening various properties of `mcShape` such as y, `alpha`, `scaleX`, and `scaleY` properties and their respective values.

   Leave this file open for the next task.

✔ Tip

■ The examples in this section specify seconds rather than frames for tween durations because seconds are more accurate. Frames are acceptable practice as well, however.

To tween multiple properties using the Tween class:

1. Modify the ActionScript as highlighted in **Code 18.10** to tween both the `scaleX` and `scaleY` properties of `mcCircle`.

   Note that unique `Tween` objects need to be created for each property.

2. Preview your file. The `scaleX` and `scaleY` properties should scale down in unison.

   Leave this file open for the next task.

The Easing class

You may have noticed in the previous tasks that mcCircle tweens at a consistent rate of movement. Specifying the easing of a tween is paramount for any good motion effect. Easing equations allow us to specify how and when a tween accelerates, decelerates, or accelerates and decelerates. These equations are encapsulated in easing methods such as easeIn, easeOut, and easeInOut.

Beyond acceleration and deceleration, tweens can also bounce, act like an elastic, back up, or exhibit logarithmic progression.

To accomplish realistic physics in a tween, use the easeIn, easeOut, and easeInOut methods and one of the classes of the fl.motion.easing classes.

Table 18.3 lists the various classes of the easing class package.

An easing class is paired with an easing function to control which end of the tween (beginning, end, or both) is affected. **Table 18.4** describes the easing methods.

To apply an easing class and method to a Tween object, you must import an easing class from the fl.transitions.easing class package for the Strong class:

import fl.transitions.easing.Strong;

To apply an easing class and method to a Tween object, use the code from **Code 18.11**.

Table 18.3

Easing Classes	
CLASS	DESCRIPTION
Back	Causes the animation to overshoot and return to its position
Bounce	Causes the animation to reverse direction, like a ball bouncing on a floor
Elastic	Causes the animation to overshoot and reverse, like at the end of a rubber band
Regular	Accelerates along a steady curve
Strong	Accelerates along a exponential curve, more aggressively than Regular
null	Results in no acceleration; a steady speed

Table 18.4

Easing Methods of Easing Classes	
METHODS	DESCRIPTION
easeIn	Applied to the beginning of the tween
easeInOut	Applied to the beginning and end of a tween
easeOut	Applied to the end of a tween

Code 18.11 Applying an easing method.

```
import fl.transitions.Tween;
import fl.transitions.easing.*;
var twTween:Tween =
  new Tween(mcShape, 'x', Strong.easeOut,
  0, 500, 2, true);
```

Code 18.12 Using the `Elastic` easing method.

```
⊖ ⊙ ⊙                    Code
import fl.transitions.Tween;
import fl.transitions.easing.*;
var twTween:Tween =
  new Tween(mcShape, 'x', Elastic.easeOut,
  0, 500, 2, true);
```

Table 18.5

Methods for Controlling the Tween Class

METHODS	DESCRIPTION
continueTo	Tells the Tween object to continue tweening from its current tween point to a new finish and duration point
fforward()	Fast-forwards to the end of a tween
nextFrame()	Forwards a stopped tween to the next frame
prevFrame()	Rewinds a stopped tween to its previous frame
resume()	Plays a tween that has been stopped
start()	Plays a tween from its start value
stop()	Stops a tween
yoyo()	Plays a tween in reverse

Code 18.13 Stopping the tween using the `stop()` method.

```
⊖ ⊙ ⊙                    Code
import fl.transitions.Tween;
import fl.transitions.easing.*;
var twTween:Tween = new Tween(mcShape, 'x',
  Strong.easeOut, 0, 500, 8, true);

stage.addEventListener
  (MouseEvent.MOUSE_UP, stopTweenHandler);

function
  stopTweenHandler(evt:MouseEvent):void {
    twTween.stop();
}
```

To tween a display object with an easing method:

1. Modify the ActionScript from the previous task using the highlighted code in **Code 18.12**, which uses the `Elastic` easing class and the `easeOut` method.

2. Preview your file. `mcCircle` should look like it's bouncing at the end of the tween.

3. Experiment with the various easing classes and methods outlined in Tables 18.3 and 18.4.

4. Leave this file open for the next task.

Controlling tween playback

A `Tween` object's playback can be controlled by using methods of the `Tween` class.

Table 18.5 lists the various methods for controlling the playback of a `Tween` object.

To control a Tween object's playback:

1. Modify your code as highlighted in **Code 18.13** to increase the duration of the tween to 8 seconds so that it gives you time to click the stage and stop the tween by calling the `stop()` method of the Tween class.

2. Preview your file and click the stage. The tween should stop at whichever point you clicked the stage.

continues on next page

THE TWEEN AND EASING CLASSES

3. Add and modify the code as highlighted in **Code 18.14** to stop the tween immediately and start it when the stage is clicked.

4. Preview your file. The tween should start when you click the stage.

5. Keep this file open for the next task.

TweenEvents

The Tween class dispatches events of the TweenEvent class that tell you what is happening with a tween. **Table 18.6** lists the events of the TweenEvent class that are dispatched from a Tween object.

To listen for events from a Tween object, you must import the TweenEvent class from the fl.transitions class package:

```
import fl.transitions.TweenEvent;
```

Code 18.14 Restarting the stopped tween using the start() method.

```
function
  stopTweenHandler(evt:MouseEvent):void {
    twTween.start();
}
twTween.stop();
```

Table 18.6

TweenEvent Class Event Types	
EVENT	DESCRIPTION
MOTION_CHANGE	Indicates when the animation has changed
MOTION_FINISH	Indicates that the animation is complete
MOTION_LOOP	Indicates that the animation has started again in looping mode
MOTION_RESUME	Indicates that the animation has been resumed after being paused
MOTION_START	Indicates that the animation has started
MOTION_STOP	Indicates that the animation has stopped

Code 18.15 Calling the yoyo() method of the Tween class each time the tween dispatches the MOITON_FINISH event type.

```
import fl.transitions.Tween;
import fl.transitions.easing.*;
import fl.transitions.TweenEvent;

var twTween:Tween = new Tween(mcShape, 'x',
  Strong.easeOut, 0, 500, 5, true);

twTween.addEventListener
  (TweenEvent.MOTION_FINISH,
  tweenFinishedHandler);
stage.addEventListener
  (MouseEvent.MOUSE_UP, stopTweenHandler);

function
  tweenFinishedHandler(evt:TweenEvent):void {
    twTween.yoyo();
}

function
  stopTweenHandler(evt:MouseEvent):void {
    twTween.start();
}

twTween.stop();
```

To listen for events from a Tween object:

1. Modify your code from the previous task as shown in **Code 18.15** to add a MOTION_FINISH TweenEvent listener to twTween that calls the yoyo() method of the Tween class each time the tween completes.

2. Preview your file. mcCircle should move back and forth across the stage each time the MOTION_FINISH event is dispatched and the yoyo() method is called.

THE TWEEN AND EASING CLASSES

Transitions

The fl.transitions package contains classes that let you use ActionScript to create animation effects. Transition classes (apart from the Tween and easing classes of the transitions class package we previously covered) create transitional effects much like the dissolves and transitions you see in film and television.

Transitions can be used effectively to introduce content to (or remove content from) an application. As long as you don't get too carried away with them, transitions can produce an attractive effect for showing and removing display objects.

To use transitions, you must import the TransitionManager class and the type of transition class that you want to use. You have to import the easing class used from the fl.transitions.easing class package as well.

You apply a transition to a display object by creating a new DisplayManager object and passing the display object in the constructor method as shown here:

```
import fl.transitions.*;

import fl.transitions.easing.*;

var tmManager:TransitionManager =
  new TransitionManager(displayObject);
```

You specify a transition class when the startTransition method of the TransitionManager class is called. The type of transition and the required parameters for each transition type are specified in the startTransition method, as shown in **Code 18.16**.

Table 18.7 lists the various transition classes.

Code 18.16 Applying a Zoom transition to a display object with a TransitionManager object.

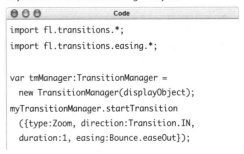

```
import fl.transitions.*;
import fl.transitions.easing.*;

var tmManager:TransitionManager =
  new TransitionManager(displayObject);
myTransitionManager.startTransition
  ({type:Zoom, direction:Transition.IN,
  duration:1, easing:Bounce.easeOut});
```

Table 18.7

Transition Classes	
TRANSITION	DESCRIPTION
Blinds	Reveals the display object with appearing or disappearing rectangles
Fade	Fades a display object in or out
Fly	Slides a display object in from a specified direction
Iris	Reveals a display object by using an animated mask of a square shape or a circle shape that zooms in or out
Photo	Makes a display object appear or disappear like a camera flash
PixelDissolve	Reveals a display object by using randomly appearing or disappearing rectangles in a checkerboard pattern
Rotate	Rotates the display object
Squeeze	Scales display object horizontally or vertically
Wipe	Reveals or hides a display object by using an animated mask of a shape that moves horizontally
Zoom	Zooms a display object in or out by scaling it in proportion

TRANSITIONS

Code 18.17 Applying a `PixelDissolve` transition to `mcShape`.

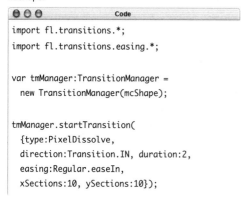

```
import fl.transitions.*;
import fl.transitions.easing.*;

var tmManager:TransitionManager =
  new TransitionManager(mcShape);

tmManager.startTransition(
  {type:PixelDissolve,
  direction:Transition.IN, duration:2,
  easing:Regular.easeIn,
  xSections:10, ySections:10});
```

To use the TransitionManager with transitions:

1. Draw a nice large shape on the stage using one of the drawing tools.

2. Select the shape and convert it to a MovieClip symbol called mcShape.

3. Select the mcShape instance on the stage and give it an instance name of `mcShape`.

4. Create a new layer called Actions and add the code from **Code 18.17**, which applies a `PixelDissolve` transition to `mcShape` through the `tmManager` TransitionManager object. The `xSections:10` and `ySections:10` properties represent the number of pixel blocks used on each axis to create the dissolve.

5. Preview your file. You should see `mcShape` dissolve in pixel by pixel over a duration of 2 seconds.

6. Experiment with other transitions and change their properties for different results. Leave this file open for the next task.

The transition classes are too numerous to explain in detail in this chapter. For an overview, visit Adobe LiveDocs and experiment with the transition classes listed on the topic page:

http://livedocs.adobe.com/flash/9.0/
ActionScriptLangRefV3/fl/transitions/
package-detail.html

TRANSITIONS

Caching Display Objects

Setting a display object's `cacheAsBitmap` property to `true` makes a vector-based display object cache a bitmap representation of itself. This results in better performance and quality when animating vector data because the vector data does not need to be redrawn and display as a complex image of anchor points and lines. The code is simple for enabling a display object to be cached as a bitmap:

```
displayObject.cacheAsBitmap = true;
```

To enable bitmap caching:

◆ Add the following code after the import statements in the file from the previous task to enable bitmap caching for `mcShape`:

```
mcShape.cacheAsBitmap = true;
```

The reasons for using bitmap caching are extensive and fall outside of the realm of ActionScript. For more information about bitmap caching, you can view the following article on Adobe's Web site: http://www.adobe.com/devnet/flash/articles/bitmap_caching.html.

Working
with Sound

The Sound class provides us with programmatic control over sounds embedded or loaded into Flash applications. Other classes, such as SoundTransform and SoundChannel, also assist the Sound class in controlling and setting the properties of sounds.

Flash allows developers to embed a sound on the timeline, but you have limited options for controlling sound when you're working with the timeline. Instantiating and controlling a sound using ActionScript, on the other hand, gives you full control over the playback, volume, and channels (left and right speakers). You can also load external sounds into an application using ActionScript and the Loader and Sound classes. Once a sound is loaded into a Sound object, you have full control over its start and stop functionality, loading and playback progress, volume, and so on.

This chapter will show you how to control sounds with ActionScript using both embedded sounds and loaded sounds at runtime. It also covers how to track the loading and playback progress of a sound.

Working with Embedded Sound

Working with an internal sound file requires that you import the sound into the library using the File > Import > Import to Library option (**Figure 19.1**).

Once you select a sound in the Import dialog, click Open, and the file appears as a symbol in the library.

Flash allows importing of the file formats listed in **Table 19.1**.

Once you've imported a sound into the library, set the sound symbol's linkage properties to Export for ActionScript and specify a class name.

To play a sound with ActionScript, it must first be instantiated as an object of the custom sound class created in the Library, as shown:

```
var mySound:CustomSoundClass =
  new CustomSoundClass();
```

After the sound is instantiated, it can be played using the play() method of the Sound class:

```
var mySound:CustomSoundClass =
  new CustomSoundClass();

mySound.play();
```

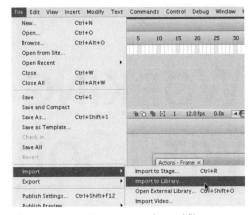

Figure 19.1 Importing an external sound file.

Table 19.1

Accepted Sound Formats for Import	
FORMAT	PLATFORM
AIFF	Windows and Mac OS
MP3	Windows and Mac OS
Sound Designer 2	Mac OS only
SunAU	Windows and Mac OS
QuickTime (sound only)	Windows and Mac OS

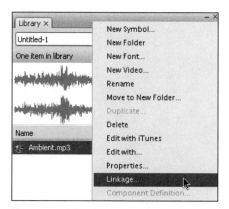

Figure 19.2 Linkage properties for Ambient.mp3.

The `play()` method accepts three arguments:

◆ `startTime`—The starting position of the sound (in milliseconds)

◆ `loops`—The number of times the sound loops from the `startTime`

◆ `soundTransform`—Assigns a `SoundTransform` object to the sound channel of an object

If no arguments are specified, the sound will play from its start time and play once (no looping). Sound and pan properties of the sound object are not available at this time, since there is no `SoundTransform` object assigned to the `Sound` object's sound channel.

The following code plays a sound object beginning at 2 seconds and loops five times:

```
mySound.play(2000, 5);
```

To instantiate and play an embedded sound:

1. Download the Ambient MP3 sound file from http://www.focusonmedia.com /vqs/as3/Ambient.zip.

2. Unzip the Ambient.zip file.

3. Start a new Flash file.

4. Import the Ambient.mp3 file to the library by selecting File > Import > Import to Library (Figure 19.1).

5. Select the Ambient.mp3 symbol in the library and open its Linkage properties panel from the Library options menu (**Figure 19.2**).

continues on next page

6. Select the first keyframe on the timeline and open the Actions panel.

7. Add the following ActionScript, which instantiates and plays the `Ambient` sound object:

```
var ambientSound:Ambient =
  new Ambient();
ambientSound.play();
```

8. Preview your file. The sound should play once from its beginning.

9. Add the arguments in the following highlighted code to the play method to play the sound from 2 seconds (`2000` ms) and loop it four times:

```
var ambientSound:Ambient =
  new Ambient();
ambientSound.play(2000, 4);
```

10. Preview your file. The sound should loop four times beginning at 2 seconds into the sound each time.

Leave this file open for the next task.

Code 19.1 Stopping the SoundChannel object.

```
● ● ●                    Code
var ambientSound:Ambient = new Ambient();
var scChannel:SoundChannel = new SoundChannel();

scChannel = ambientSound.play();
scChannel.stop();
```

Code 19.2 Stopping the sound channel.

```
● ● ●                    Code
var ambientSound:Ambient = new Ambient();
var scChannel:SoundChannel = new SoundChannel();

stage.addEventListener
  (MouseEvent.MOUSE_UP, stopSoundHandler);

function stopSoundHandler(evt:MouseEvent):void {
  scChannel.stop();
}

scChannel = ambientSound.play();
```

Controlling Playback with SoundChannel

Every sound played in the Flash platform is played through a unique sound channel. You control sound channels by using the SoundChannel class. By instantiating a uniquely named SoundChannel object, you have the ability to stop a sound, get the current position of a sound, and listen for an event signifying when a sound has finished playing. All SoundChannel objects are managed by the SoundMixer class.

To control a Sound through a SoundChannel object, the Sound object is set to play through the SoundChannel object as highlighted in the following code:

```
var ambientSound:Ambient =
  new Ambient();

var scChannel:SoundChannel =
  new SoundChannel();

scChannel = ambientSound.play();
```

Once the sound is playing through the SoundChannel object, you stop the sound by stopping the sound channel (not the sound object), as highlighted in **Code 19.1**.

To stop the playback of a sound:

1. Return to the file from the previous task.

2. Add the ActionScript from **Code 19.2** to stop the sound channel when a user clicks on the stage.

3. Preview your file. The sound should play automatically and stop when the stage is clicked.

✔ Tip

■ Always give viewers the option to stop sounds. Sound in a SWF file can be bothersome to users, and they may stop viewing the SWF if they cannot turn it off.

Loading External Sounds

Loading sounds as external files can decrease the size of SWF files and make SWF applications faster to download and perform better. Working with external sounds also gives you the ability to create MP3 players, podcast players, and other types of audio playback applications that can be embedded directly into a Web page or even as a stand-alone application that runs on a user's computer.

Controlling externally loaded sounds is the same as controlling internal sounds. The difference is that an external sound file needs to be loaded into a sound object in order for it to be controlled.

You call the load method of the Sound class to load an external file set in a URLRequest object. **Code 19.3** creates a new Sound object and loads an external sound file into the object.

Now that you know how to load an external file into a Sound object, you need a way to detect when the file has loaded so that it can be played once the file has downloaded. The Event.COMPLETE event that is dispatched by the Sound object lets you do just that (**Code 19.4**).

To load and play an external sound:

1. Start a new file and add the ActionScript from **Code 19.5**. This code loads an external MP3 file into a Sound object and plays it once the file has completely loaded.

Code 19.3 Loading an external sound file into a Sound object called song.

```
var songURL:String = "pathToFile";
var songRequest:URLRequest =
  new URLRequest(songURL);
var song:Sound = new Sound();
song.load(songRequest);
```

Code 19.4 Playing the Sound object after the sound file has completely loaded.

```
song.addEventListener
  (Event.COMPLETE, loadingCompleteHandler);

function
  loadingCompleteHandler(evt:Event):void {
    trace('Song has loaded.');
    song.play();
}
```

Code 19.5 Loading an external sound file and playing it once it has fully loaded into the Sound object.

```
var songURL:String =
  "http://www.focusonmedia.com/vqs/as3
  /Ambient.mp3";
var songRequest:URLRequest =
  new URLRequest(songURL);
var song:Sound = new Sound();

song.addEventListener
  (Event.COMPLETE, loadingCompleteHandler);

function
  loadingCompleteHandler(evt:Event):void {
    trace('Song has loaded.');
    song.play();
}

song.load(songRequest);
```

Code 19.6 Playing the Sound object through a SoundChannel object so that it can be stopped when a user clicks on the stage.

```
● ● ●                   Code
var songURL:String =
  "http://www.focusonmedia.com/vqs/as3
  /Ambient.mp3";
var songRequest:URLRequest =
  new URLRequest(songURL);
var song:Sound = new Sound();
var scChannel:SoundChannel =
  new SoundChannel();

song.addEventListener
  (Event.COMPLETE, loadingCompleteHandler);
stage.addEventListener
  (MouseEvent.MOUSE_UP, stopSoundHandler);

function
  loadingCompleteHandler(evt:Event):void {
    trace('Song has loaded.');
    scChannel = song.play();
}

function
  stopSoundHandler(evt:MouseEvent):void {
    scChannel.stop();
}

song.load(songRequest);
```

2. Preview your file. The sound should start playing after it has loaded.

3. Add the ActionScript highlighted in **Code 19.6** to play a SoundChannel object so that it can be stopped when a user clicks on the stage.

4. Preview your file. The song should start playing when the sound has loaded and stop when the stage is clicked. Leave this file open for the next task.

Monitoring Loading with Sound Events

In Chapter 16, we used events dispatched from a Loader object to monitor the loading progress of an external asset. The same events are also dispatched from a Sound object so that we can monitor an external sound's loading progress. The dispatched events used to monitor loading progress are:

◆ Event.COMPLETE

◆ IOErrorEvent.IO_ERROR

◆ ProgressEvent.PROGRESS

◆ ErrorEvent.SecurityErrorEvent (not covered as it falls outside the scope of the book)

These event classes and event types are explained in detail in Chapter 16. **Code 19.7** shows how to register an event listener for each event type to a Sound object.

As with loading any external asset, it is extremely important to notify the user of loading progress and any loading errors.

To track the loading progress of a sound file:

1. Add the ActionScript from **Code 19.8**, which tracks the loading progress.

Code 19.7 Registering event listeners with a Sound object.

```
var song:Sound = new Sound();
song.addEventListener
  (Event.COMPLETE, completeHandler);
song.addEventListener
  (IOErrorEvent.IO_ERROR, ioErrorHandler);
song.addEventListener
  (ProgressEvent.PROGRESS, progressHandler);
```

Code 19.8 Tracking the loading progress of an external sound by listening for the ProgressEvent. PROGRESS event type dispatched by the Sound object.

```
var songURL:String =
  "http://www.focusonmedia.com/vqs/as3/
  Ambient.mp3";
var songRequest:URLRequest =
  new URLRequest(songURL);
var song:Sound = new Sound();

song.addEventListener
  (ProgressEvent.PROGRESS,
  loadingProgressHandler);

function
  loadingProgressHandler(evt:Event):void {
    trace(song.bytesLoaded + ' : '
    + song.bytesTotal);
}

song.load(songRequest);
```

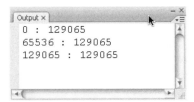

Figure 19.3 The number of bytes that have loaded compared to the size of the file in total bytes.

Code 19.9 Play the Sound object when the sound has completed loading.

```
                    Code
var songURL:String =
  "http://www.focusonmedia.com/vqs/as3/
  Ambient.mp3";
var songRequest:URLRequest =
  new URLRequest(songURL);
var song:Sound =
  new Sound();
var scChannel:SoundChannel =
  new SoundChannel();

song.addEventListener
  (ProgressEvent.PROGRESS,
  loadingProgressHandler);
song.addEventListener
  (Event.COMPLETE, loadingCompleteHandler);

function
  loadingProgressHandler(evt:Event):void {
    trace(song.bytesLoaded + ' : ' +
    song.bytesTotal);
}

function
  loadingCompleteHandler(evt:Event):void {
    trace('Song has loaded.');
    scChannel = song.play();
}

song.load(songRequest);
```

2. Preview your file. The Output panel displays the number of bytes that have loaded in relation to the total size of the file (**Figure 19.3**).

3. Add the highlighted ActionScript from **Code 19.9** to play the Sound object when the sound has completed loading.

4. Preview your file. The sound should start playing when the sound has completely loaded and the message Song has loaded displays in the Output panel.

continues on next page

MONITORING LOADING WITH SOUND EVENTS

5. Modify the ActionScript highlighted in **Code 19.10**, which listens for an IOErrorEvent.IO_ERROR event type if a loading error occurs. The code removes the 3 from the end of the .mp3 file extension specified in the songURL variable. This creates a loading error, since a file with the extension .mp does not exist.

6. Preview your file. The Output panel should display a loading error and message, as shown in **Figure 19.4**.

Leave this file open for the next task.

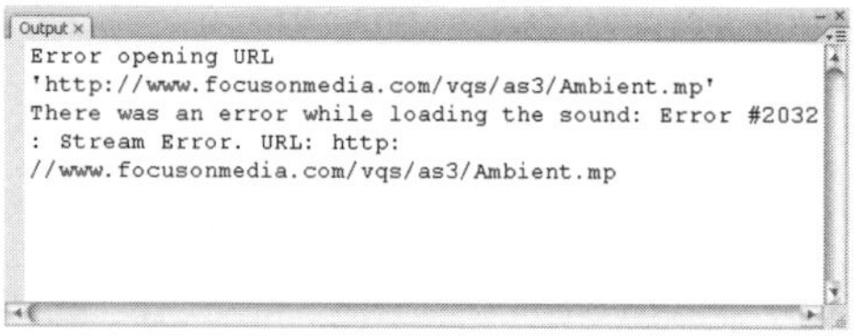

Figure 19.4 The IO_ERROR error event type that is dispatched from the Sound object is displayed in the Output panel.

Code 19.10 Creating and listening for a loading error.

```
var songURL:String =
  "http://www.focusonmedia.com/vqs/as3/
  Ambient.mp";
var songRequest:URLRequest =
  new URLRequest(songURL);
var song:Sound = new Sound();
var scChannel:SoundChannel =
  new SoundChannel();

song.addEventListener
  (ProgressEvent.PROGRESS,
  loadingProgressHandler);
song.addEventListener
  (IOErrorEvent.IO_ERROR,
  loadingErrorHandler);
song.addEventListener
  (Event.COMPLETE, loadingCompleteHandler);

function
  loadingProgressHandler(evt:Event):void {
    trace(song.bytesLoaded + ' : ' +
    song.bytesTotal);
}

function loadingErrorHandler
  (evt:IOErrorEvent):void {
    trace('There was an error while loading
    the sound: ' + evt.text);
}

function
  loadingCompleteHandler(evt:Event):void {
    trace('Song has loaded.');
    scChannel = song.play();
}

song.load(songRequest);
```

Code 19.11 Getting ID3 data from the Sound object.

```
var songURL:String =
  "http://www.focusonmedia.com/vqs/as3/
  Ambient.mp3";
var songRequest:URLRequest =
  new URLRequest(songURL);
var song:Sound = new Sound();
var scChannel:SoundChannel =
  new SoundChannel();

song.addEventListener
  (ProgressEvent.PROGRESS,
  loadingProgressHandler);
song.addEventListener
  (IOErrorEvent.IO_ERROR, loadingErrorHandler);
song.addEventListener
  (Event.COMPLETE, loadingCompleteHandler);
song.addEventListener(Event.ID3,
  songInfoHandler);

function
  loadingProgressHandler(evt:Event):void {
    trace(song.bytesLoaded + ' : ' +
    song.bytesTotal);
}

function
  loadingErrorHandler(evt:IOErrorEvent):void {
    trace('There was an error while loading
    the sound: ' + evt.text);
}

function
  loadingCompleteHandler(evt:Event):void {
    trace('Song has loaded.');
    scChannel = song.play();
}

function songInfoHandler(evt:Event):void {
  trace(song.id3.songName);
}

song.load(songRequest);
```

Using ID3 Data in MP3 Files

ID3 data stored as properties within an MP3 file contains information about a sound or song, such as the artist's name, track name, album title, and so on. If the ID3 data exists in an MP3 file, related information, such as its duration, can be displayed in a text field.

You access ID3 data from an MP3 file that is loaded into a Sound object using the id3 property of the Sound class. Here are the properties of the id3 property of a Sound object:

◆ comment

◆ album

◆ genre

◆ songName

◆ artist

◆ track

◆ year

To get ID3 data from an MP3 file:

1. Return to the file from the previous task.

2. Add the highlighted ActionScript from **Code 19.11** to listen for the Event.ID3 event type of the Sound object and display the song's name to the Output panel once the ID3 data has loaded.

3. Preview your file. The song name "Ambient" should display in the Output panel.
   Leave this file open for the next task.

Controlling a Sound's Volume

You set the volume of a Sound object using the SoundTransform class. The SoundTransform class lets you control the volume and panning (left and right channels) of a sound. A SoundTransform object is instantiated and you can then set its properties to control a sound. Once you do that, you can apply to the soundTransform property of a SoundChannel object as shown:

```
var stTransform:SoundTransform =
  new SoundTransform();

stTransform.volume = .5

scChannel.soundTransform = stTransform;
```

This code sets the volume of the SoundTransform object to .5 (50 percent of the current system volume) and applies it to the SoundChannel object.

To control the volume of a Sound object

1. Add the highlighted ActionScript from **Code 19.12**. This sets the volume of a SoundTransform object to .5 (50 percent of the current system volume) and sets a SoundChannel object's soundTransform property to the SoundTransform object when a user clicks the stage.

2. Preview your file. The volume of the sound should be reduced to 50 percent of the current system volume when a user clicks the stage.

Code 19.12 Setting the volume of a sound.

```
var songURL:String =
  "http://www.focusonmedia.com/vqs/as3/
  Ambient.mp3";
var songRequest:URLRequest =
  new URLRequest(songURL);
var song:Sound = new Sound();
var scChannel:SoundChannel =
  new SoundChannel();
var stTransform:SoundTransform =
  new SoundTransform();

song.addEventListener
  (ProgressEvent.PROGRESS,
  loadingProgressHandler);
song.addEventListener
  (IOErrorEvent.IO_ERROR, loadingErrorHandler);
song.addEventListener
  (Event.COMPLETE, loadingCompleteHandler);
song.addEventListener
  (Event.ID3, songInfoHandler);
stage.addEventListener
  (MouseEvent.CLICK, setVolumeHandler);

function
  loadingProgressHandler(evt:Event):void {
    trace(song.bytesLoaded + ' : ' +
    song.bytesTotal);
}

function
  loadingErrorHandler(evt:IOErrorEvent):void {
    trace('There was an error while loading
    the sound: ' + evt.text);
}

function
  loadingCompleteHandler(evt:Event):void {
    trace('Song has loaded.');
    scChannel = song.play();
}
```

(code continues on next page)

Script 19.12 *continued*

```
●○○            Code
function songInfoHandler(evt:Event):void {
  trace(song.id3.songName);
}

function
  setVolumeHandler(evt:MouseEvent):void {
    stTransform.volume = .5;
    scChannel.soundTransform = stTransform;
}

song.load(songRequest);
```

3. Modify the volume property of the SoundTransform object as shown to "mute" the sound:

   ```
   stTransform.volume = 0;
   scChannel.soundTransform =
       stTransform;
   ```

4. Preview your file. The sound should now "mute" when a user clicks the stage.

   Leave this file open for the next task.

Experiment with creating different buttons or other mechanisms, such as a slider or dial, for ideas on how to adjust the volume of sound.

Monitoring Playback Progress

Monitoring the progress of a sound as it plays back requires a few techniques:

◆ The SoundChannel.position property, which returns the current position of a sound (in milliseconds)

◆ The length property of the Sound class (in milliseconds)

◆ A Timer object that checks the current position of a sound using the SoundChannel.position property at regular intervals

To display the playback progress of a sound in a text field:

1. Return to the file from the previous task.

2. Add the highlighted ActionScript from **Code 19.13**. This code instantiates a Timer object that displays the current position of the sound (in milliseconds) to the Output panel at an interval of 50/1000th of a second.

Code 19.13 Tracking the current position of sound playback.

```
var songURL:String =
  "http://www.focusonmedia.com/vqs/as3/
  Ambient.mp3";
var songRequest:URLRequest =
  new URLRequest(songURL);
var song:Sound = new Sound();
var scChannel:SoundChannel =
  new SoundChannel();
var stTransform:SoundTransform =
  new SoundTransform();
var soundTimer:Timer = new Timer(50);

song.addEventListener
  (ProgressEvent.PROGRESS,
  loadingProgressHandler);
song.addEventListener
  (IOErrorEvent.IO_ERROR, loadingErrorHandler);
song.addEventListener
  (Event.COMPLETE, loadingCompleteHandler);
song.addEventListener(Event.ID3,
  songInfoHandler);
stage.addEventListener
  (MouseEvent.CLICK, setVolumeHandler);
soundTimer.addEventListener
  (TimerEvent.TIMER, trackTimeHandler);

function
  loadingProgressHandler(evt:Event):void {
    trace(song.bytesLoaded + ' : '
    + song.bytesTotal);
}

function
  loadingErrorHandler(evt:IOErrorEvent):void {
    trace('There was an error while loading
    the sound: ' + evt.text);
}
```

(code continues on next page)

Code 19.13 *continued*

```
function
  loadingCompleteHandler(evt:Event):void {
    trace('Song has loaded.');
    scChannel = song.play();
    soundTimer.start();
}


function
  songInfoHandler(evt:Event):void {
    trace(song.id3.songName);
}


function
  setVolumeHandler(evt:MouseEvent):void {
    stTransform.volume = .5;
    scChannel.soundTransform = stTransform;
}


function
  trackTimeHandler(evt:TimerEvent):void {
    trace('Current position: ' +
    scChannel.position);
}


song.load(songRequest);
```

Code 19.14 Converting milliseconds to seconds.

```
function
  trackTimeHandler(evt:TimerEvent):void {
  var currentSeconds:int =
    Math.round(scChannel.position / 1000);
  trace('Current position: ' +
  currentSeconds);
}
```

3. Preview your file. The current position of the sound should display as milliseconds at each interval (**Figure 19.5**).

4. Modify the ActionScript highlighted in the `TimerEvent.TIMER` event handler in **Code 19.14**. This converts the `position` property to seconds and rounds the seconds to an even number.

5. Preview your file. The milliseconds should now be converted to seconds. Notice that the `Timer` object does not stop after the sound has stopped playing.

continues on next page

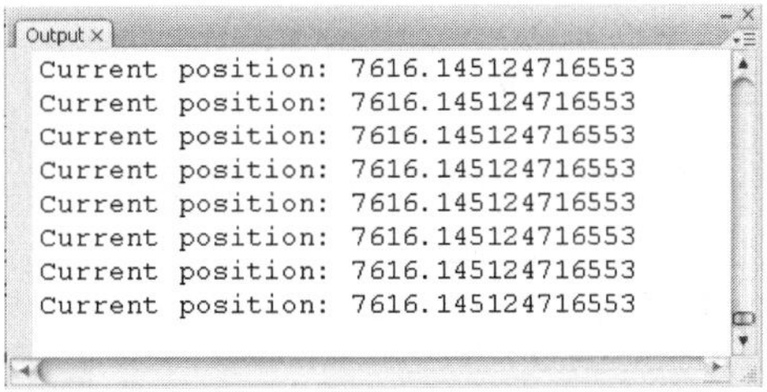

Figure 19.5 Current position of sound (in milliseconds) at frequent intervals of the `Timer` object.

MONITORING PLAYBACK PROGRESS

6. Add the highlighted ActionScript from **Code 19.15**. This stops the Timer object after the Event.SOUND_COMPLETE event is dispatched from the Sound object.

7. Rename the current layer to Actions and create a new layer called "Time display."

8. Using the Text tool, create a dynamic text field on the Time display layer.

9. Assign the dynamic text field an instance name of tTimeDisplay.

Code 19.15 Stopping the Timer object after the sound has completed playing.

```
var songURL:String =
  "http://www.focusonmedia.com/vqs/as3/
  Ambient.mp3";
var songRequest:URLRequest =
  new URLRequest(songURL);
var song:Sound = new Sound();
var scChannel:SoundChannel =
  new SoundChannel();
var stTransform:SoundTransform =
  new SoundTransform();
var soundTimer:Timer = new Timer(50);

song.addEventListener
  (ProgressEvent.PROGRESS,
  loadingProgressHandler);
song.addEventListener
  (IOErrorEvent.IO_ERROR, loadingErrorHandler);
song.addEventListener
  (Event.COMPLETE, loadingCompleteHandler);
song.addEventListener(Event.ID3,
  songInfoHandler);
stage.addEventListener
  (MouseEvent.CLICK, setVolumeHandler);
soundTimer.addEventListener
  (TimerEvent.TIMER, trackTimeHandler);

function
  loadingProgressHandler(evt:Event):void {
    trace(song.bytesLoaded + ' : ' +
    song.bytesTotal);
}

function
  loadingErrorHandler(evt:IOErrorEvent):void {
    trace('There was an error while loading
    the sound: ' + evt.text);
}

function
  loadingCompleteHandler(evt:Event):void {
    trace('Song has loaded.');
    scChannel = song.play();
```

(code continues on next page)

Code 19.15 *continued*

```
● ○ ●              Code
  scChannel.addEventListener
    (Event.SOUND_COMPLETE,
    songCompleteHandler);
  soundTimer.start();
}


function songInfoHandler(evt:Event):void {
  trace(song.id3.songName);
}


function songCompleteHandler(evt:Event):void {
  trace('song complete');
  soundTimer.stop();
}


function setVolumeHandler(evt:MouseEvent):void {
  stTransform.volume = .5;
  scChannel.soundTransform = stTransform;
}


function trackTimeHandler(evt:TimerEvent):void {
  var currentSeconds:int =
    Math.round(scChannel.position / 1000);
  trace('Current position: ' + currentSeconds);
}


song.load(songRequest);
```

Code 19.16 Display the current position and the total length of the sound in a text field.

```
● ○ ●              Code
function
  trackTimeHandler (evt:TimerEvent):void {
    var currentSeconds:int =
      Math.round(scChannel.position / 1000);
    var totalLength:int =
      Math.round(song.length / 1000);
    tTimeDisplay.text = currentSeconds + " / "
      + totalLength;
}
```

10. Return to the Actions layer and add the highlighted ActionScript from **Code 19.16**. This code gets the total length of the sound using the `length` property of the Sound class, converts it to milliseconds, and displays it in the text field by concatenating it with the current position of the song.

11. Preview your file. The current position compared to the total length of the sound should display in the text field.

Working with Video

Flash video has quickly become the most preferred delivery method of video on the Internet. Compared with other video delivery plug-ins, Flash video offers ease of customization and development as well as cross-browser and cross-platform integration.

This chapter focuses on ActionScript development for the FLVPlayback class. You will become well versed in developing ActionScript-driven video playback applications using the FLVPlayback component (and the classes it extends). You can listen and respond to events, as well as monitor the playback state of the FLVPlayback component and listen for loading errors, metadata, and cuepoints. Taking all of this into consideration will result in a high-end rich media experience for the end user.

This chapter also explores classes designed to help you create advanced video applications, such as an application that publishes a video stream from a Webcam.

Using the FLVPlayback Component

The quickest and easiest way to get video up on the Web with Flash is to use the FLVPlayback component. You can add the FLVPlayback component to the stage at authortime or configure it via the Parameters panel. As with most objects in Flash, however, its true potential comes to light when you use ActionScript to control it.

The FLVPlayback component is an object of the flash.video.FLVPlayback class. Using the class's properties, methods, and events, you can create the simplest or the most complex online video delivery applications. The properties, methods, and events of the FLVPlayback class are far too numerous to fully list in this chapter. For a comprehensive list, search the Flash Help menu using the keywords "FLVPlayback."

This section covers the core properties, methods, and events for creating an ActionScript-driven video playback application.

To work with the FLVPlayback component using ActionScript, you must first import the FLVPlayback class:

```
import flash.video.FLVPlayback;
```

Any subsequent classes required by the FLVPlayback class for certain functionality must be imported as well. For example, if you plan to use the VideoScaleMode class, you must first import it:

```
import fl.video.VideoScaleMode;
```

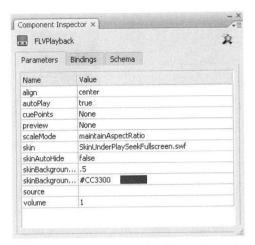

Figure 20.1 Setting the properties of an FLVPlayback component in the Component Inspector's Parameters panel.

Setting properties of an FLVPlayback component

To set the properties of an FLVPlayback component at authortime, drag an instance to the stage and set the properties in the Parameters panel (**Figure 20.1**).

Each of the parameters in Figure 20.1 has an ActionScript equivalent. **Table 20.1** lists the ActionScript syntax for each of the parameters set at authortime.

To set the properties of an FLVPlayback component:

1. Create a new file and rename Layer 1 to FLVPlayback.

2. Open the Components panel and drag an instance of the FLVPlayback component from the Video category to the stage.

3. Select the FLVPlayback component on the stage and open the Component Inspector (Window > Component Inspector).

continues on next page

Table 20.1

ActionScript Property Equivalent of FLVPlayback Parameters	

PROPERTY	DESCRIPTION
align	Aligns the layout of the video display within the player to coincide with the component's scaleMode property.
autoPlay	Boolean value. If true, video will automatically play; if false, the user needs to click play manually in the component's playback controls.
cuePoints	An array that specifies ActionScript cuepoints. Embedded cuepoints in the video will be disabled.
preview	Specifies a PNG file or time code for displaying a live preview.
scaleMode	Specifies how video will be resized using constant properties of the VideoScaleMode class.
skin	Specifies a path to a runtime-loaded skin SWF file to be used as the skin UI for the player.
skinAutoHide	Boolean value. If true, skin controls will hide when the mouse is not over the video and will display when the mouse is over the video. A false setting leaves controls always visible.
skinAlphaBackground	Sets the transparency of the skin overlay.
skinBackgroundColor	Sets the background color of the skin (0xRRGGBB).
source	Specifies the URL of the FLV to stream through the component.
volume	A value between 0 and 1 that sets the initial volume level of the component.

USING THE FLVPLAYBACK COMPONENT

4. Select the Parameters tab and click the magnifying glass icon in the Skin field (**Figure 20.2**).

5. Select a skin of your choice and click OK when done.

6. Assign the `FLVPlayback` component an instance name of `flvDisplay` in the Properties panel.

7. Create a new layer called Actions.

8. Add the ActionScript from **Code 20.1**, which sets the properties of `flvDisplay` listed in **Table 20.2** to the Actions layer.

9. Preview your file. The video should play within the specified 320 x 240 width and height. You must click the component's play button to play the video. The controls should also appear and disappear as you roll over and off the component.

10. Experiment with various property settings and preview the results.

    Leave this file open for the next task.

Figure 20.2 Selecting a component skin.

Code 20.1 Setting properties of `flvDisplay`.

```
import fl.video.FLVPlayback;
import fl.video.VideoScaleMode;

var videoSrc:String =
  'http://www.focusonmedia.com/vqs/as3/
  SkySurfing_384K.flv';

flvDisplay.width = 320;
flvDisplay.height = 240;
flvDisplay.autoPlay = false;
flvDisplay.scaleMode =
  VideoScaleMode.MAINTAIN_ASPECT_RATIO;
flvDisplay.skinAutoHide = true;
flvDisplay.skinBackgroundAlpha = .5;
flvDisplay.skinBackgroundColor = 0xff0000;
flvDisplay.source = videoSrc;
flvDisplay.volume = .5;
```

Table 20.2

Properties of `flvDisplay`

PROPERTY	VALUE
width	320
height	240
autoPlay	`false` (the user will have to click the play button to start the video)
scaleMode	`MAINTAIN_ASPECT_RATIO` (a constant property of the imported `VideoScaleMode` class)
skinAutoHide	`true` (the skin will appear and disappear as the user rolls over and off the component)
skinBackgroundAlpha	.5 (the skin's background and controls will be 50% alpha)
skinBackgroundColor	0xff0000 (the skin will be the color red)
source	The video path is specified in the `videoSrc` variable. The source for a video can be a relative or absolute path.
volume	The volume is initially set to .5 (50% of the current system volume).

USING THE FLVPLAYBACK COMPONENT

Figure 20.3 List of custom UI components in the Components panel.

Customizing the FLVPlayback component

The FLVPlayback component class allows the addition of custom UI components. These components let you create your own set of controls and arrange them however you wish with an FLVPlayback component. You can therefore create a unique-looking video player based on your own design that doesn't appear as if the FLVPlayback component was even used. The custom UI components are listed in the Components panel (**Figure 20.3**).

Although the custom UI components are listed as components in the Components panel, their assets (the symbols that compose each component) appear as MovieClips in the library when they are dragged to the library or stage. This means you can customize these components by editing them just as you would MovieClips. To edit the custom UI components, however, you need to become familiar with their setup, as they are constructed in a specific way.

To control an FLVPlayback component with custom UI controls, set the skin property of the FLVPlayback component to null:

```
flvPlayback.skin = null;
```

To set custom UI components to control an FLVPlayback component, assign the UI components instance names (i.e., btnPlay is a best practice for the PlayButton component). Then set the corresponding property of the FLVPlayback class to the UI component as shown here:

```
flvPlayback.playButton = btnPlay;
```

USING THE FLVPLAYBACK COMPONENT

287

The full set of custom UI control properties of the FLVPlayback class are listed next:

◆ FLVPlayback.playButton

◆ FLVPlayback.pauseButton

◆ FLVPlayback.playPauseButton

◆ FLVPlayback.stopButton

◆ FLVPlayback.muteButton

◆ FLVPlayback.backButton

◆ FLVPlayback.volumeBar

◆ FLVPlayback.seekBar

◆ FLVPlayback.bufferingBar

◆ FLVPlayback.fullScreenButton

To attach custom UI controls to the FLVPlayback component:

1. Modify your code as shown in **Code 20.2**. This sets the skin property to null, since the component will be controlled by custom UI components.

2. Select the FLVPlayback layer and drag instances of the following custom UI components from the Components panel to the stage (**Figure 20.4**): PlayPauseButton, MuteButton, VolumeBar, and SeekBar.

Code 20.2 Editing the code so the skin property is set to null.

```
import fl.video.FLVPlayback;

var videoSrc:String =
  'http://www.focusonmedia.com/vqs/as3/
  SkySurfing_384K.flv';

flvDisplay.width = 320;
flvDisplay.height = 240;
flvDisplay.autoPlay = false;
flvDisplay.skin = null;
flvDisplay.source = videoSrc;
flvDisplay.volume = .5;
```

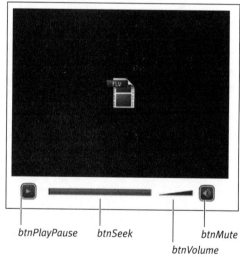

btnPlayPause   btnSeek   btnMute
                           btnVolume

Figure 20.4 Layout and instance names of custom UI controls.

Code 20.3 Setting the properties of flvDisplay to be controlled by the custom UI components.

```
Code
import fl.video.FLVPlayback;
var videoSrc:String =
  'http://www.focusonmedia.com/vqs/as3/
  SkySurfing_384K.flv';
flvDisplay.width = 320;
flvDisplay.height = 240;
flvDisplay.autoPlay = false;
flvDisplay.skin = null;
flvDisplay.source = videoSrc;
flvDisplay.volume = .5;

flvDisplay.playPauseButton = btnPlayPause;
flvDisplay.seekBar = btnSeek;
flvDisplay.volumeBar = btnVolume;
flvDisplay.muteButton = btnMute;
```

3. Select each UI component and assign the corresponding instance names listed in Figure 20.4.

4. Select the Actions layer and add the highlighted code from **Code 20.3**. This code sets the properties of flvDisplay so it can be controlled by the custom UI components.

5. Preview your file. The controls should be activated once the video has loaded. Control the video using the custom UI controls (**Figure 20.5**).

6. Experiment with various controls and combinations to make your own custom video application.

Leave this file open for the next task.

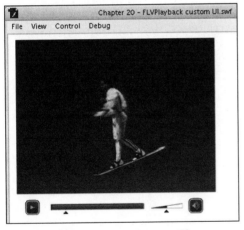

Figure 20.5 This FLVPlayback component is controlled by custom UI components.

FLVPlayback Events

The FLVPlayback class dispatches events of the VideoEvent class that allows for monitoring of the playback and state of an FLVPlayback component instance. **Table 20.3** lists some commonly used event types for basic monitoring of playback and player states.

For a comprehensive list of the events dispatched by the FLVPlayback class, search the Flash Help menu using the keywords "FLVPlayback class."

To use the events of the VideoEvent class, you must import the VideoEvent class:

```
import fl.video.VideoEvent;
```

Table 20.3

Common Events Dispatched by the VideoEvent Class	
EVENT	DESCRIPTION
COMPLETE	Dispatched when the video has reached the end of the file.
CUE_POINT	Dispatched when a cuepoint is reached.
METADATA_RECEIVED	Dispatched when FLV file metadata is received.
PROGRESS	Dispatched when a progressive video is downloaded from an HTTP server. Specifies bytes downloaded.
READY	Dispatched when the FLV has fully loaded and is ready to play.
SCRUB_FINISH	Dispatched when scrubbing an FLV with the seek bar has stopped.
SCRUB_START	Dispatched when scrubbing an FLV with the seek bar has started.
STATE_CHANGE	Dispatched when the playback state changes.

Code 20.4 Listening for dispatched VideoEvent types from the FLVPlayback component instance.

```
● ● ●                Code
import fl.video.FLVPlayback;
import fl.video.VideoEvent;

var videoSrc:String =
  'http://www.focusonmedia.com/vqs/as3/
  SkySurfing_384K.flv';

flvDisplay.addEventListener
  (VideoEvent.READY, playerReadyHandler);
flvDisplay.addEventListener
  (VideoEvent.STATE_CHANGE,
  playerChangeHandler);
flvDisplay.addEventListener
  (VideoEvent.COMPLETE,
  playerCompleteHandlerr);

function
  playerReadyHandler(evt:VideoEvent):void {
     trace('Video has loaded and is ready
     to play.');
}

function
  playerChangeHandler(evt:VideoEvent):void {
     trace('State of video: ' + evt.state);
}

function
  playerCompleteHandler(evt:VideoEvent):void {
     trace('Video has reached the end.');
}
```

```
 Output ×                         - X
                                   ≡
 State of video: loading
 State of video: stopped
 Video has loaded and is ready to play.
 State of video: buffering
 State of video: playing
 State of video: seeking
 State of video: paused
 State of video: playing
 State of video: stopped
 Video has reached the end.
```

Figure 20.6 Displaying the events and event types of flvDisplay in the Output panel.

To monitor the playback of an FLVPlayback component:

1. Return to the file from the previous task.

2. Add the highlighted code from **Code 20.4**. This code adds event listeners for the READY, STATE_CHANGE, and COMPLETE events of flvDisplay.

3. Preview your file. You should see the loading state and playback states of flvDisplay displayed in the Output panel, similar to **Figure 20.6**.

Leave this file open for the next task.

Displaying video status

Informing the user of the loading and playback status of a video is very important. Sometimes users continue waiting for the video to start when they actually have to click the play button first. The video may be paused or buffering, and users need to be informed of those states as well. Most importantly, users should be notified if a video could not be loaded so that they are not left watching a blank display. All of these status messages can be read from the type property of the VideoEvent.STATE_CHANGE event object. These states can be assessed and displayed to the user through a text field, alert panel, or whatever method of messaging you come up with.

To display the status of video playback in a text field:

1. Select the FLVPlayback layer and insert a new layer. Name the layer statusText.

2. Draw a gray rectangle at the bottom and over top of the FLVPlayback component using the Rectangle tool (**Figure 20.7**).

3. Draw a dynamic text field over top of the gray rectangle and type "statusText" as its initial value; set its properties so that it displays well over top of the gray rectangle (Figure 20.7).

4. Assign the test field an instance name of statusText.

5. Modify the code in the Actions layer as shown in **Code 20.5**. This code displays the various event statuses in the statusText text field.

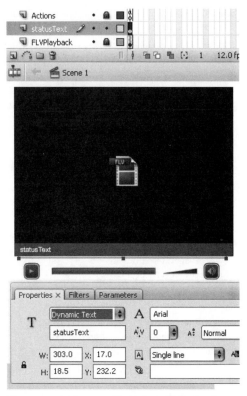

Figure 20.7 Adding a text field that will display the playback status of the video and a background to make it stand out on top of the video display.

Code 20.5 Display the playback status of the video in the text field depending on event type.

```
function
  playerReadyHandler(evt:VideoEvent):void {
     statusText.text = 'Player is ready.
       Press play to start video.';
}

function
  playerChangeHandler(evt:VideoEvent):void {
     statusText.text = 'Video is ' + evt.state;
}

function
  playerCompleteHandler(evt:VideoEvent):void {
     statusText.text = 'Video is completed.';
}
```

Figure 20.8 Playback status of video displayed in statusText.

Code 20.6 Using a conditional statement to check whether an error occurred loading the video.

```
function
  playerChangeHandler(evt:VideoEvent):void {
    if (evt.state == 'connectionError') {
      statusText.text = 'Video cannot load.
      Please try again at a later time';
    } else {
      statusText.text = 'Video is '
      + evt.state;
    }
}
```

6. Preview your file. The status of the video should display in the text field (**Figure 20.8**).

7. Modify the code in the playerChange function highlighted in **Code 20.6**. This code checks to see if the player could load the video file. If there was a problem, the code informs the user that the video could not load; otherwise, it displays the playback status.

8. Remove the v from the end of the .flv extension in the video URL set in videoSrc. This will cause a loading error:

   var videoSrc:String =
     'http://www.focusonmedia.com/
     vqs/as3/SkySurfing_384K.fl';

9. Preview your file. The message Video cannot load. Please try again at a later time should display in statusText.

Return the code to its error-free state and leave this file open for the next task.

✔ Tip

■ It's important to listen for and respond to errors of any object of a class that loads external data. Video is no different. Informing the user of playback status is always a good thing. The video may buffer, stop, or disconnect, and the user may not know exactly what is happening, or why. Take the time to build mechanisms like status messages and alert panels that respond to and handle errors, check playback states, and so forth to create robust, intelligent applications that take the end user's experience into consideration.

FLVPLAYBACK EVENTS

FLV metadata

Metadata is usually automatically embedded in an FLV file by the encoder software. The embedded metadata includes information about the video such as duration, frame rate, and bitrate, as well as cuepoint information. When the metadata of an FLV file has been loaded, the FLVPlayback class dispatches a MetadataEvent.METADATA_RECEIVED event. The metadata information can be retrieved as properties of the MetadataEvent object passed to the event listener.

Table 20.4 lists the properties of the MetadataEvent event object.

Table 20.4

Properties of the MetadataEvent Event Object	
PROPERTY	DESCRIPTION
canSeekToEnd	A Boolean value that specifies whether a keyframe is encoded on the last frame of the video. If true, a progressive download video is able to seek to the end. If false, no keyframe is encoded on the last frame.
cuePoints	An array of objects that contain cuepoint data.
audiocodecid	A number that indicates the audio codec that was used during encoding.
audiodelay	A number that indicates what time in the FLV file "time 0" of the original FLV file exists to delay video in order to keep audio synchronized.
audiodatarate	Audio data rate in kilobytes per second.
videocodecid	A number that is the codec version that was used during video encoding.
framerate	The frame rate of the FLV file.
videodatarate	The video data rate of the FLV file in kilobytes.
height	The height of the FLV file.
width	The width of the FLV file.
duration	The duration of the FLV file in seconds.

Code 20.7 Registering an event listener for the MetadataEvent.METADATA_RECEIVED event type.

```
import fl.video.FLVPlayback;
import fl.video.VideoEvent;
import fl.video.MetadataEvent;

var videoSrc:String =
  'http://www.focusonmedia.com/vqs/as3/
  SkySurfing_384K.flv';

flvDisplay.addEventListener
  (VideoEvent.READY, playerReadyHandler);
flvDisplay.addEventListener
  (VideoEvent.STATE_CHANGE,
  playerChangeHandler);
flvDisplay.addEventListener
  (VideoEvent.COMPLETE, playerCompleteHandler);
flvDisplay.addEventListener
  (MetadataEvent.METADATA_RECEIVED,
  metaDataHandler);

function
  playerReadyHandler(evt:VideoEvent):void {
    statusText.text = 'Player is ready.
      Press play to start video.';


function
  playerChangeHandler(evt:VideoEvent):void {
    if (evt.state == 'connectionError') {
      statusText.text = 'Video cannot load.
      Please try again at a later time';
  } else {
    statusText.text = 'Video is ' +
      evt.state;
  }
}

function
  playerCompleteHandler(evt:VideoEvent):void {
    statusText.text = 'Video is completed.';
}

function
  metaDataHandler(evt:MetadataEvent):void {

}
```

To get FLV metadata information:

1. Return to the file from the previous task.

2. Add the code highlighted in **Code 20.7**, which imports the MetadataEvent class and registers an event listener for the MetadataEvent.METADATA_RECEIVED event.

continues on next page

FLVPlayback Events

3. Add the highlighted code from **Code 20.8** to the `metaDataHandler` event listener; this code displays the metadata properties from the `MetadataEvent` object to the Output panel.

Leave this file open for the next task.

Adding and listening for cuepoints

Cuepoints can be used for synchronizing support data at certain times in a video, closed-captioning titles, and any other information that requires video synchronization. Cuepoints can be added to a video during encoding as well as with ActionScript.

There are three types of cuepoints in Flash:

◆ **Navigation**—Allows seeking to a particular frame in the FLV file because it creates a keyframe within the FLV file as near as possible to the specified time (a keyframe is only inserted in the video encoder and not with ActionScript).

◆ **Event**—Enables synchronization of a point in time within the FLV file with an external event in the application.

◆ **ActionScript**—An external cuepoint that is added either through the component's Flash Video Cue Points dialog box or through the `addASCuePoint()` method. The component stores and tracks ActionScript cuepoints separately from the FLV file.

Code 20.8 Displaying the `MetadataEvent` event object properties to the Output panel.

```
function
  metaDataHandler(evt:MetadataEvent):void {
    trace('canSeekToEnd: ' +
      evt.info.canSeekToEnd);
    trace('cuePoints: ' + evt.info.cuePoints);
    trace('audiocodecid : ' +
      evt.info.audiocodecid );
    trace('audiodelay: ' + evt.info.audiodelay);
    trace('audiodatarate: ' +
      evt.info.audiodatarate);
    trace('videocodecid: ' +
      evt.info.videocodecid);
    trace('framerate: ' + evt.info.framerate);
    trace('videodatarate: ' +
      evt.info.videodatarate);
    trace('height: ' + evt.info.height);
    trace('width: ' + evt.info.width);
    trace('duration: ' + evt.info.duration);
}
```

Code 20.9 Adding cuepoints using a cuepoint object or as arguments directly in the addASCuePoint() method call.

```
● ● ●                    Code
// Using cue point object
var cuePoint:Object = new Object();
cuePoint.time = 2;
cuePoint.name = "cuePoint1";
cuePoint.parameters =
  {text:"Cue point 1 added with ActionScript"};
FLVPlayback.addASCuePoint(cuePoint);


// By passing as parameters
FLVPlayback.addASCuePoint
  (2, 'cuePoint1',
  {text:"Cue point 1 added with ActionScript"} );
```

ActionScript cuepoints

You can add a cuepoint to a video using the addASCuePoint() method in one of two ways: with a cuepoint object, or as separate arguments passed to the addASCuePoint() method (**Code 20.9**).

The addASCuePoint() method requires the following three parameters:

◆ time—The time location of the cuepoint (in seconds)

◆ name—The name of the cuepoint

◆ parameters—The object of properties for extra information to be passed with cuepoint

Embedded vs. ActionScript Cuepoints

There is a difference between cuepoints embedded in a video in the encoder and those added with ActionScript. When a cuepoint is embedded in the video encoder, a keyframe is placed at the time of the cuepoint. This enables precise pausing at, and seeking to, a cuepoint. Flash video can only be paused at, and seek to, keyframes. Frames in between are skipped until a new keyframe is hit. Adding cuepoints with ActionScript may have an effect on the precision of pausing at, and seeking to, cuepoints, since your cuepoint time may not be able to be seeked because of a mismatch in keyframes in the video and the actual cuepoint time.

This chapter focuses on using cuepoints added with ActionScript. Listening for cuepoints uses the same syntax, whether the cuepoints are embedded in the FLV or added at runtime with ActionScript.

To add and listen for cuepoints with ActionScript:

1. Return to the file from the previous task.

2. Select the Actions layer and add the ActionScript from **Code 20.10**, which adds three cuepoints to flvDisplay.

Code 20.10 Creating three ActionScript cuepoints.

```
import fl.video.FLVPlayback;
import fl.video.VideoEvent;
import fl.video.MetadataEvent;

var videoSrc:String =
  'http://www.focusonmedia.com/vqs/as3/
  SkySurfing_384K.flv';

flvDisplay.autoPlay = false;
flvDisplay.skin = null;
flvDisplay.source = videoSrc;
flvDisplay.playPauseButton = btnPlayPause;
flvDisplay.seekBar = btnSeek;
flvDisplay.volumeBar = btnVolume;
flvDisplay.muteButton = btnMute;

flvDisplay.addASCuePoint(1, 'cuePoint1',
  {text:"The parachute was invented
  in 1873."} );

flvDisplay.addASCuePoint(10, 'cuePoint2',
  {text:"Tom Simms made the first
  snowboard in 1963."} );

flvDisplay.addASCuePoint(20, 'cuePoint3',
  {text:"Skysurfing was tried for the first
  time in the late 1980's."} );
```

Code 20.11 Registering an event listener for the MetadataEvent.CUE_POINT event type.

```
import fl.video.FLVPlayback;
import fl.video.VideoEvent;
import fl.video.MetadataEvent;

var videoSrc:String =
  'http://www.focusonmedia.com/vqs/as3/
  SkySurfing_384K.flv';

flvDisplay.addEventListener
  (MetadataEvent.CUE_POINT,
  readCuepointHandler);

function readCuepointHandler
  (evt:MetadataEvent):void {
    trace('-- ' + evt.info.name);
    trace('-- ' + evt.info.time);
    trace('-- ' + evt.info.parameters.text);
}

flvDisplay.autoPlay = false;
flvDisplay.skin = null;
flvDisplay.source = videoSrc;
flvDisplay.playPauseButton = btnPlayPause;
flvDisplay.seekBar = btnSeek;
flvDisplay.volumeBar = btnVolume;
flvDisplay.muteButton = btnMute;

flvDisplay.addASCuePoint(1, 'cuePoint1',
  {text:"The parachute was invented
  in 1873."} );

flvDisplay.addASCuePoint(10, 'cuePoint2',
  {text:"Tom Simms made the first
  snowboard in 1963."} );

flvDisplay.addASCuePoint(20, 'cuePoint3',
  {text:"Skysurfing was tried for the first
  time in the late 1980's."} );
```

3. Add the ActionScript from **Code 20.11**, which registers an event listener for the MetadataEvent.CUE_POINT event type of flvDisplay and traces each text property of the parameters object of the MetadataEvent event object passed to the event listener.

continues on next page

FLVPLAYBACK EVENTS

4. Preview your file. The text property of the parameters object should display each time a CUE_POINT event type is dispatched (**Figure 20.9**).

5. Modify the code in the readCuePoint-Handler() event listener highlighted in **Code 20.12**. This code displays each text property in the statusText text field for each event.

6. Preview your file. The text properties should display in statusText as closed captions (**Figure 20.10**).

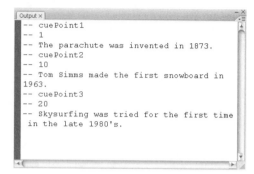

```
Output ×
-- cuePoint1
-- 1
-- The parachute was invented in 1873.
-- cuePoint2
-- 10
-- Tom Simms made the first snowboard in
1963.
-- cuePoint3
-- 20
-- Skysurfing was tried for the first time
   in the late 1980's.
```

Figure 20.9 The text property of the parameters object traces to the Output panel each time a CUE_POINT event is dispatched.

Code 20.12 Displaying the text property of each cuepoint in statusText.

```
Code
function
  readCuepointHandler(evt:MetadataEvent):void {
    statusText.text = evt.info.parameters.text;
}
```

Figure 20.10 Closed captioning using the text properties of an event object.

Advanced Video Applications

The ActionScript API and Flash offer classes that allow you to create more advanced video applications such as live streaming, Webcam streaming, and multiuser communication applications. The details of these classes fall outside the scope of this book, but once you are comfortable with working with the `FLVPlayback` class and feel a need to create more advanced applications, the following classes are what you'll be working with:

◆ `Video`—A `Video` object is used to display video from a camera, from a Real-Time Messaging Protocol (RTMP) server, or from an HTTP server. The `Video` class itself is basic. It inherits from the `DisplayObject` class and has properties that specify its size, scale, filters, and so on. Its sole purpose is for displaying video.

To play video through a `Video` object, you must attach the `Video` object to a `NetStream` object, which handles the streaming and playback of FLV files.

Figure 20.11 shows the single-directional (HTTP) and bidirectional (Flash Media Server) communications between NetStream and NetConnection objects. The Video object only displays FLV files streamed through a NetStream object.

continues on next page

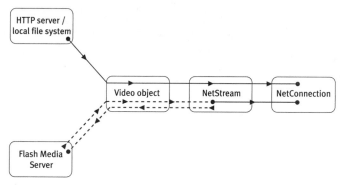

Figure 20.11 Communication between `NetStream` and `NetConnection` objects.

ADVANCED VIDEO APPLICATIONS

- NetStream—The NetStream class manages a one-way connection between the Flash platform and an RTMP server, HTTP server, or local file system. The NetStream object can subscribe to a stream or progressive download as well as publish a video stream from a Webcam (NetStream objects can only publish to the Flash Media Server). The NetStream class can also be used for live messaging. In order for a NetStream object to connect with a server or local file system, it must channel through a NetConnection object. The NetStream class has a set of properties, methods, and events for handling and managing streams and connections (Figure 20.11).

- NetConnection—A NetConnection object acts as an open pipe between the Flash platform and a server for a bidirectional connection. Using a NetStream object (or multiple NetStream objects), communication can flow in and out of an application (an HTTP server is only capable of loading FLV files through a NetConnection object). The NetConnection class has a set of properties, methods, and events for handling and managing connections (Figure 20.11).

- Camera—Allows a camera to capture and broadcast video from a camera attached to a computer running the Flash Player. The video from the camera can be run locally or transmitted through the NetStream and NetConnection classes to a Flash Media Server for live publishing and communications.

- Microphone—Allows you to capture and listen to, and publish audio from a microphone attached to a computer running the Flash Player. The audio can be played back locally on the user's computer within the application, or published through a NetStream or NetConnection object to a Flash Media Server for live publishing and communications.

INDEX

Symbols

-- compound operator, using, 28
!= (not equal to) operator, using, 180
&& logical operator, using, 184
<&;> tag, using with TextField class, 146
<'> tag, using with TextField class, 146
<>> tag, using with TextField class, 146
<<> tag, using with TextField class, 146
<"> tag, using with TextField class, 146
() (parentheses)
    uses of, 6
    using with functions, 40
*= compound operator, using, 28
// comments, using, 14–15
/* and */ comments, using, 14–15
/= compound operator, using, 28
: (colon)
    using with time variables, 161
    using with variables, 22
; (semicolon), using in statements, 5
[] (square brackets), using with arrays, 167–169
\ (escape sequences), using, 25–26, 127
\" escape sequence, using, 127
_ (underscores), using with variables, 19–20
{} (curly braces)
    grouping statements with, 7
    using with functions, 40
| (pipe), delineating values with, 133
|| logical operator, using, 184
+ (plus) symbol, using with strings, 25
+ operator
    using with numbers, 130
    using with strings, 128
++ compound operator, using, 28
+= compound operator, using, 28
+= operator, using with strings, 128
< (less than) operator, using, 180–181
<= (less than or equal to) operator, using, 180

= (equals) symbol
    using with constructor methods, 36
    using with variables, 21
-= compound operator, using, 28
== (equal to) operator, using, 180
> (greater than) operator, using, 180
>= (greater than or equal to) operator, using, 180
" (quotations)
    escape sequence for, 127
    using with strings, 24
, (comma), separating parameters with, 7

A

<a> HTML anchor tag
    description of, 212
    using with TextField class, 146
absolute versus relative target paths, 120–122
abs(val) method, using with Math class, 152
acos(val) method, using with Math class, 152
Actions panel
    closing, 13
    keyboard shortcut for, 12
    opening and setting up, 12–13
    panes in, 12
Actions toolbox pane, description of, 12
ActionScript
    classes, 2–3
    objects, 2
    placing on keyframe, 33
    setting properties of display objects with, 85–87
    using in external files, 59
ActionScript 3 editors, using, 59–60
ActionScript 3 event model, event process, 96–97
ActionScript Class Warning window, displaying, 72
ActionScript cuepoints, explanation of, 296
ActionScript files
    adding to timeline for Flash, 61
    creating externally, 60

ActionScript results, displaying, 13
addASCuePoint() method, using, 297
addChild() method
    using with Loader class, 223
    using with MovieClip class, 76, 80
addChildAt() method, description of, 91
ADDED_TO_STAGE event type
    creating event listener for, 100
    using, 98, 146
addedToStage() event, using with text fields, 144
addEventListener() method, using, 99
adding numbers, 27–28
addNumbers() function
    creating, 44
    setting return type for, 46
    sum variables in, 49–50
Adobe LiveDocks resources. *See also* Web sites
    display lists, 66
    DisplayObject class, 68
    DisplayObjectContainer class, 75
    InteractiveObjects, 70
    key codes, 105
    StyleSheet documentation, 213
AIFF sound format, platforms for, 266
align property
    using with TextFormat class, 142
    using with video, 285
alpha method of DisplayObject class, description of, 84
alpha property
    of mcB, 121
    setting for mcA, 121–122
    verifying for MovieClip, 183
altKey property, using with KeyboardEvent, 104
Ambient MP3 sound file, downloading, 267
& HTML entity, description of, 213
animating. *See also* tweens
    using ENTER_FRAME event, 253–254
    using Tween class, 255–257
animation effects, creating with transitions,
        262–263
' HTML entity, description of, 213
arguments
    passing variables as, 44–45
    using with functions, 41–43
arithmetic, performing, 27–28
array access operator, using, 176
Array class, methods for, 170, 172
Array constructor method, using, 168–169
array elements, iterating through, 191, 199
array indices, storing info in, 178
array literal technique, using, 168–169
array values, using trace() statement with, 133
arrays
    adding elements to, 166–167, 170–171
    assigning index positions for, 168

contents of, 177
creating, 166
for days of week, 191
indices of, 166–168
iterating through, 174
looping through, 174
removing elements from, 172–173
retrieving elements from, 167–168
returning elements from, 172, 174
using for...each loop with, 174
.as files
    adding to timeline for Flash, 61
    creating externally, 60
asin(val) method, using with Math class, 152
asset loads, displaying values for, 229
assetLoader, unloading assets from, 223
assets
    loading into Loader objects, 222
    unloading from Loader objects, 223
associative array objects, looping through, 194
associative arrays
    creating, 178
    looping through, 178
    using for each...in loops with, 178
    using Object class with, 175–178
atan2(y, x) method, using with Math class, 152
atan(val) method, using with Math class, 152
attributes of objects, representing, 84
audio* properties, using with MetadataEvent, 294.
        See also sounds
authortime versus runtime, 10
Automatic Indentation, using, 16
autoPlay property
    of flvDisplay, 286
    using with video, 285

B

<b> HTML bold tag
    description of, 212
    using with TextField class, 146
Back easing class, description of, 258
background color, changing for TextField objects, 141
beginFill() method, using with shapes, 234
BevelFilter, description of, 243
bitmap caching, enabling, 264
Bitmap subclass, using with DisplayObject, 69
blend modes
    applying, 242–243
    specifying types of, 242
    types of, 243
blendMode method, description of, 84
Blinds Transition class, description of, 262
blockIndent property, using with TextFormat class, 142

BlurFilter
    description of, 243
    using, 244–245
bold property, using with TextFormat class, 142
Booleans. *See also* variables
    checking true status of, 183
    using, 34
Bounce easing class, description of, 258

 HTML break tag
    description of, 212
    using with TextField class, 146
break statement, using with case clause, 188
btnButton, adding event listeners for, 186
btnStop, clicking, 114
bubble phase of event flow
    versus capture phase, 109
    explanation of, 107
bubbles event class property, description of, 97
bullet property, using with TextFormat class, 142
Button symbol
    converting rectangle shape to, 71
    limitations of, 118
buttonContainer, adding event listener to, 109
buttons
    creating, 118
    displaying menu items as list of, 195
    making with MovieClips, 115–118
bytesLoaded property
    displaying, 209
    using with LoaderInfo class, 226
bytesTotal object property, displaying, 209
bytesTotal property, using with LoaderInfo class, 226

C

cacheAsBitmap property, setting for display
        objects, 264
call methods, using with MovieClip class, 37–38
Camera class, description of, 302
cancelable event class property, description of, 97
canSeekToEnd property, using with
        MetadataEvent, 294
capture phase of event flow
    versus bubble phase, 109
    explanation of, 107
Cascading Style Sheets (CSS), styling text fields
        with, 214–215
case clause, using break statement with, 188
ceil(val) method, using with Math class, 152,
        156–157
CHANGE constant, event type of, 98
change event, using with TextField class, 140
charAt( ) method of String class, description of, 126
charCode property, using with KeyboardEvent, 104

child objects, adding to MovieClip display object
        container, 77–80
circle
    converting to MovieClip symbol, 37
    drawing with Shape class, 236–237
circle animation, looping in stage, 252
Circle graphic
    positioning, 79
    setting default frame rate for, 124
    tweening, 114
Circle MovieClip symbol
    creating, 250–251
    linkage properties for, 239
CircleContent
    adding instance of, 80
    creating, 78
    removing instance of, 79
class hierarchy, defined, 52
class inheritance, defined, 53
class names, qualification of, 54
class packages, locations in Flash, 52
classes. *See also* instances; static classes
    events for, 3
    import directives for, 54
    importing, 55
    instances of, 8–9
    methods of, 3
    versus objects, 8, 52
    properties of, 3
    storage of, 8
clear( ) method, using with shapes, 234
CLICK constant, event type for, 102
clock application, building, 160–161
Cmd key. *See* keyboard shortcuts
code. *See also* scripts
    adding to Script pane, 12
    commenting, 14
code coloring, customizing, 16
code hints, showing, 16
colon (:)
    using with time variables, 161
    using with variables, 22
color property, using with TextFormat class, 142
ColorMatrixFilter, description of, 243
ColorPickerEvent subclass, description of, 110
colors, applying to syntax, 16
comma (,), separating parameters with, 7
commands
    adding in strings, 26
    indenting automatically, 16
comments, using, 14
compile errors
    creating, 58
    occurrence of, 22–23, 49
    for return type, 46–47

compiletime, defined, 10
COMPLETE constant, event type of, 98
COMPLETE event
    listening for, 222
    of LoaderInfo class, 226
    using for load progress, 229
    using with URLLoader class, 208
    of VideoEvent class, 290
component skin, setting, 286
Components panel, UI components in, 287
compound operators, using, 28
concat() method of String class
    description of, 126
    using, 128, 130
concatenating strings, 24–25, 128
conditional expressions, checking for, 180–181
conditional logic
    using with event types, 186
    using with object classes, 186
    using with variable types, 186
conditional statements
    syntax for, 180
    using with MovieClips, 183
    using with video, 293
conditions
    adding to statements, 181
    checking with switch statement, 188
    verifying for, 184
constant, defined, 98
constructor methods
    for arrays, 168–169
    creating compile errors with, 58
    for Shape class, 234
    using, 36
    using with Crane class, 9
containers, registering event listeners with, 107
content property, using with LoaderInfo class, 226
continueTo() method, using with Tween class, 259
Convert to Symbol option, choosing, 32
ConvolutionFilter, description of, 243
Coordinated Universal Time (UTC), 164
cos(angle) method, using with Math class, 152
Crane class, objects of, 9
Crane object instance, operating, 9
CSS (Cascading Style Sheets), styling text fields
        with, 214–215
Ctrl key. See keyboard shortcuts
ctrlKey property, using with KeyboardEvent, 104
CUE_POINT event, using with VideoEvent class, 290
cuepoints
    adding and listening for, 296–300
    embedded versus ActionScript, 297
cuePoints property
    using with MetadataEvent, 294
    using with video, 285

curly braces ({})
    grouping statements with, 7
    using with functions, 40
currentTarget property
    description of, 97
    using with event flow, 108–109

D

data types
    conversions, 30
    defined, 22
    numbers, 29
data-typing object instances, 58
date and time
    customizing, 162–163
    getting and displaying, 159
    values, 159
    variables, 159
Date class
    methods of, 158–163
    using, 158–163
Date class properties, calling directly, 160
Date object, instantiating, 158
Date properties, methods for, 162
day of month, returning, 158
Debug feature, using with nonvisible display
        objects, 254
decimals, data type for, 42
declaring variables, 21
default clause, using case statement, 188
Delay Slider, using with code hints, 16
delineated values, separating in strings, 133
depth of display objects, defined, 91
depths, swapping and displaying, 92
dispatchEvent() method, use of, 97
DisplacementMapFilter, description of, 243
display classes, hierarchy and location of, 67
display lists
    adding imageLoader to, 225
    adding interactive objects to, 71–73
    adding Loader objects to, 222–223
    adding miChapterOne instance to, 72–73
    adding objects to, 66, 73, 91
    adding StaticText subclass to, 70
    adding TextField objects to, 139
    concept of, 65
    removing display objects from, 94
    removing objects from, 254
    removing text fields from, 229
display object containers
    adding at runtime, 81–82
    using, 90

display objects. *See also* objects
  adding to display lists, 65
  animating with Timer class, 250–251
  applying blur filters to, 245
  applying DropShadowFilter to, 246
  applying filters to, 243–245
  applying transitions to, 262
  defined, 83
  drawing wireframes for, 119
  masking, 239
  nesting, 119
  positioning dynamically, 87–88
  positioning groups of, 90
  properties of, 84, 87–88
  relationships between, 66
  removing form display lists, 94
  rotation of, 88
  setting cacheAsBitmap property for, 264
  stacking order of, 66
  tweening, 257, 259
  using Debug feature with, 254
  using with registration points, 89
  using Tween class with, 255–257
  wireframe of, 69
display programming, defined, 63
DisplayManager object, creating for transitions, 262
DisplayObject class
  properties, methods, and events of, 68
  properties of, 84–85
  subclasses of, 69
DisplayObject depths, managing, 91–93
DisplayObjectContainer class
  depth-management methods of, 91
  description of, 74
  properties, methods, and events of, 75
  subclasses of, 75
dividing numbers, 28
do...while loop versus while loop, 200–202
dot syntax, 4
DOUBLE_CLICK constant, event type for, 102
download percentage, calculating, 228
draw*() methods, using with shapes, 234, 236
DropShadowFilter
  applying to display objects, 246
  description of, 243
  using, 244
dtFormatter, setting properties of, 149
dtMessage, setting text property of, 137
duration parameter, using with Tween object, 256
duration property, using with MetadataEvent, 294
dynamic animation. *See* animating
dynamic filters, using, 243–245
dynamic masking, applying to objects, 238–241
dynamic menus, building, 194–196
dynamic text fields, using, 136–138

E

easing classes
  applying to Tween objects, 258
  easing methods of, 258
editors, using, 59–60
Elastic easing class
  description of, 258
  using, 259
element:* parameter, using with arrays, 174
else if statements, using, 180
else statements
  adding default for, 182
  using, 180
embedded sounds, instantiating and playing,
    267–268. *See also* sounds
encapsulation, defined, 95
endFill() method, using with shapes, 234
ENTER_FRAME constant, event type of, 98
ENTER_FRAME event, animating with, 253–254
equal to (==) operator, using, 180
equality operators
  checking for false conditions with, 182
  checking for true conditions with, 181–182
  using, 180–181
equals (=) symbol
  using with constructor methods, 36
  using with variables, 21
error handling, 216–217
error panel, creating, 217–219
errors
  avoiding via data typing, 22–23
  listening for and responding to, 293
escape sequences (\)
  using, 25–26
  using in strings, 127
Event class
  description of, 97
  extending, 102, 104
  listening for events of, 100–101
  subclasses of, 110
event constants versus strings, 99
event cuepoints, explanation of, 296
event dispatchers, overview of, 96–97
event flow
  phases of, 107
  using, 108–109
event handlers
  adding for btnButton, 186
  reusing itAdded, 145
event listeners
  adding for btnButton, 186
  adding for FOCUS_OUT events, 141
  adding for MOUSE_DOWN event type, 103
  adding to buttonContainer, 109
  adding to objects, 99

event listeners (*continued*)
  checking event types in, 104
  creating for ADDED_TO_STAGE event, 100
  versus event handler, 97
  for mouseOut and mouseOver, 117
  registering, 98–99
  registering for FLV metadata, 295
  registering for MetadataEvent.CUE_POINT, 299
  registering for REMOVE_FROM_STAGE event, 101
  registering in ActionScript 3, 96
  registering with containers, 107
  registering with Sound objects, 272
  removing, 106
  removing from assetLoader, 223
  for Timer class, 249–250
  for TIMER event, 160
  using, 99
  using with Crane, 10
event objects
  accessing properties of, 102
  base class for, 97
  properties of, 97
  referencing, 102
  using target.data property with, 211
event types
  checking in event handlers, 104, 186
  defined, 98
  of Event class, 98
  listening for, 101
  of LoaderInfo class, 226
  of MouseEvent class, 102
  of TimerEvent class, 248
  of TweenEvent class, 260
EventDispatcher method, events triggered by, 97
events
  defined, 3
  of DisplayObject class, 68
  handling in ActionScript 3, 96–97
  listening for, 11
  for TextField class, 140–141
  triggering, 97
  of URLLoader class, 208
  of VideoEvent class, 290
expressions
  operators for, 180
  using parentheses (()) with, 6
external .as file, creating, 60
external CSS files, loading, 213–215
external data, loading with Loader class, 222
external editors, using, 59–60
external graphics, loading with Loader objects,
    224–225
external sounds, loading and playing, 270–271.
    See also sounds

external SWF files
  controlling, 230–231
  loading, 226
external text file, loading, 218
external text, loading into text fields, 211–212

F

F keys. *See* keyboard shortcuts
Fade Transition class, description of, 262
false conditions, checking for, 182
fastPace event handler, setting frame rate with, 124
fforward() method, using with Tween class, 259
filter classes, 243
filters, applying to display objects, 243–245
filters method of DisplayObject class, description of, 84
finish parameter, using with Tween object, 256
Flash
  class packages in, 52
  "Nations of," 1
Flash CS3, Actions panel in, 12
Flash timeline, adding .as file to, 61
FlashDevelop editor, downloading, 59
floor(val) method, using with Math class, 152, 156–157
FLV files, metadata embedded in, 294
FLV metadata information, getting, 295–296
flvDisplay, setting properties of, 286, 289
FLVPlayback class
  events of, 290
  importing, 284
FLVPlayback components. *See also* video
  attaching custom UI controls to, 288–289
  customizing, 287–288
  monitoring playback of, 291
  setting properties of, 285–286
Fly Transition class, description of, 262
FOCUS_IN event, listening for, 140
FOCUS_OUT events
  adding event listeners for, 141
  listening for, 141
FocusEvent subclass, description of, 110
font property, using with TextFormat class, 142
font symbols, creating, 148–149
<font> HTML tag
  description of, 212
  using with TextField class, 146
fonts, embedding, 148–149
for each...in loop, using with associative arrays, 178
for each...in statement, using, 198–199
for loop statement. *See also* loops
  code for, 190
  creating, 190–191
  expressions required by, 190
  using with indexed arrays, 191

for...each loop, using with arrays, 174
for...in statement, using, 196–198
forEach() method, using with arrays, 174
frame 1, returning playhead to, 114
frame labels, using, 115–118
frame numbers, navigating to, 115
frame rate, declaring at runtime, 123–124
frame tweens, adding, 112
frameRate property, using with LoaderInfo class, 226
framerate property, using with MetadataEvent, 294
FULL_SCREEN constant, event type of, 98
functions
    defined, 39
    defining, 40
    invoking, 40
    versus methods, 35, 56
    naming, 40
    passing variables as arguments to, 44–45
    returning values from, 45–47
    scope of, 48–50
    setting return types for, 45–47
    specifying return types for, 47
    using arguments with, 41–43
    using parameters with, 41–43
    void return typing, 47
    writing and calling, 40–41

G

get*() methods, using with Date class, 158
getChildAt() method, description of, 91
getChildIndex() method, description of, 91
getCoffee() function, calling, 42–43
GlowFilter, description of, 243
gotoAndPlay() method
    adding to keyframe, 114
    description of, 36, 112
    using, 38
gotoAndStop() method
    description of, 36, 112
    using, 38
GradientBevelFilter, description of, 243
GradientGlowFilter, description of, 243
graphics, loading with Loader objects, 224–225
graphics property, using with Shape class, 234
greater than (>) operator, using, 180
greater than or equal to (>=) operator, using, 180
> HTML entity, description of, 213

H

height property
    of flvDisplay, 286
    using with LoaderInfo class, 226
    using with MetadataEvent, 294

hints, showing, 16
hours, returning number of, 158
HTML, formatting TextFields with, 147
HTML entities, 213
HTML tags for TextField class, 212
htmlText property, setting, 146, 211
HTTP requests, making, 204

I

<i> HTML italic tag
    description of, 212
    using with TextField class, 146
ID3 data, accessing from MP3 files, 275
identifiers, using with variables, 18–19
if statements
    using, 180
    using with MouseEvent types, 104
imageLoader
    adding to display list, 225
    listening for loading error for, 225
images, rounding corners of, 241
<img> HTML image tag
    description of, 212
    using with TextField class, 146
import directives, using with classes, 54
include, using with external .as file, 61
indent property, using with TextFormat class, 142
index depth, getting, 93
index positions
    assigning for arrays, 168
    returning substrings from, 131–132
indexed arrays, iterating through, 191
indexed elements, using with arrays, 166–168
index:int parameter, using with arrays, 174
inheritance, defined, 53
inherited methods, using, 37
INIT constant, event type of, 98
INIT event type, of LoaderInfo class, 226
input text fields, creating at authortime, 138–139
instance name, assigning, 33
instances. *See also* classes
    creating as objects, 31
    defined, 8–9, 31
    naming, 20
    versus properties, 32
    properties of, 57
    storing, 18
instantiating objects, 9, 31, 56, 58
int (integer) data type, using, 29
interactive objects. *See also* objects
    adding to display lists, 71–73
    instantiating at runtime, 74

IOErrorEvent
    adding, 210
    dispatching from Sound object, 274
    displaying message for, 219
    listening for and responding to, 224
    using with URLLoader class, 208
Iris Transition class, description of, 262
itAdded event handler, reusing, 145
italic property, using with TextFormat class, 142
iterating
    through array elements, 191
    through object properties, 197–199

K

kerning property, using with TextFormat class, 142
key code values, displaying in Output panel, 105
key detection, achieving, 105
key values, detecting, 105
KEY_DOWN events, listening for, 105
keyboard events
    detecting, 105
    listening for, 104
keyboard shortcuts
    Actions panel, 12–13
    convert shape to MovieClip symbol, 32
    Preferences, 16
    previewing files, 206–207
    previewing movies, 15
    previewing results of scripts, 13
    Properties panel, 33
KeyboardEvent class, events of, 104, 107, 110
keyCode property, using with KeyboardEvent, 104
keyframes
    assigning frame labels to, 115
    extending, 116
    placing ActionScript on, 33
    using, 118
keypresses, detecting and reacting to, 104

L

layers, reordering in timeline panel, 66
leading property, using with TextFormat class, 142
leftMargin property, using with TextFormat class, 142
length property
    using with sounds, 278, 281
    using with String class, 126, 131
less than (<) operator, using, 180–181
less than or equal to (<=) operator, using, 180
letterSpacing property, using with TextFormat
    class, 142
<li> HTML list-item tag, description of, 212
Library options menu, Linkage option in, 71

Library symbol, naming, 73
line breaks, adding, 25–26
line numbers, displaying in Script pane, 13
line spaces, escape sequence for, 127
lineStyle() method, using with shapes, 234
link event, using with TextField class, 140
Linkage Identifier, naming, 73
Linkage option, using in Library options, 71
List Objects, selecting from Debug menu, 254
listeners. *See* event listeners
load method, calling for Loader object, 224
load percentage, displaying, 228–229
load progress, monitoring, 227–229
Loader class, using with external data, 222
Loader objects
    adding to display lists, 222–223
    applying BlurFilter objects to, 245
    loading assets into, 222
    loading external graphics with, 224–225
    loading external images into, 240
    masking, 241
    tracking progress of, 227
    unloading assets from, 223
loader property, using with LoaderInfo class, 226
LoaderInfo class
    event types of, 226
    properties of, 226
loading errors
    creating and listening for, 274
    generating, 218
    listening for, 225
loading progress, tracking for sound files, 272
"loop of death," avoiding, 191
loop statements, while and do...while, 200–202
loops, using with associative arrays, 174, 178. *See
    also* for loop statement
loops argument, using with play() method, 267
< HTML entity, description of, 213

M

Mac OS, sound formats for, 266
mask method of DisplayObject class, description of, 84
masking, applying to objects, 238–241
masks, creating to round image corners, 241
math, performing with compound operators, 28
Math class
    constant values for, 153
    methods for rounding numbers, 156–157
    methods of, 152
    random() method of, 153–155
    as static class, 153
    using, 27–28

math equations, performing, 27–28. *See also* numbers

mathematical operations, ordering, 6

max (val...) method, using with Math class, 152

medPace event handler, setting frame rate with, 124

menu button class, reusing, 192–193

menuContainer Sprite, creating, 195

MenuItem Button symbol
creating, 71
instantiating instance of, 72

MenuItem instance, adding to display lists, 82

menus, building, 194–196

METADATA_RECEIVED event, using with VideoEvent class, 290

MetadataEvent class, importing, 295

MetadataEvent subclass, description of, 110

methods
defined, 3, 36
versus functions, 35–36, 56
inherited, 37
passing values to, 6
public versus private, 36

Microphone class, description of, 302

milliseconds
converting to seconds, 279
returning number of, 158

min (val...) method, using with Math class, 152

minute value, using conditional statement with, 161

minutes, returning number of, 158

mobileCrane class, properties of, 9

month of year, returning, 158

MorphShape subclass, using with DisplayObject, 67, 69

MOTION_* events, using with TweenEvent class, 260

MotionEvent subclass, description of, 110

mouse events, listening for, 103

MOUSE_DOWN event type, event listener for, 103, 106

MouseEvent class
dispatching, 103
event types of, 102

MouseEvent objects
currentTarget property of, 109
event flow of, 107
target property of, 109

MouseEvent subclass, description of, 110

MouseEvent types
checking in event handlers, 186–187
using if statements with, 104

mouseOut and mouseOver events, listening for, 117

mouseX method of DisplayObject class, description of, 84

mouseY method of DisplayObject class, description of, 84

movie display, adding MovieClip to, 11

MovieClip button, using, 118

MovieClip class
call methods of, 37–38
description of, 75
instantiating object of, 10–11
methods for controlling timeline, 112
public methods of, 36
versus Sprite class, 75

MovieClip display objects, setting properties of, 85–87

MovieClip() method, description of, 36

MovieClip objects
loading SWFs as, 230–231
setting properties for, 32

MovieClip symbols, converting shapes to, 32

MovieClips
casting root as, 120
reusing, 118
verifying properties of, 183

movies, previewing, 15

MP3 files, accessing ID3 data from, 275

MP3 sound format, platforms for, 266

multiline comments, using, 14–15

multiplying numbers, 28

N

\n (newline) escape sequence, using, 26, 127

name method of DisplayObject class, description of, 84

name parameter, using with addASCuePoint() method, 297

"Nations of Flash," 1

navigateToURL() method, using, 205–207

navigation cuepoints, explanation of, 296

nestedMC MovieClip symbol, creating, 121

nesting display objects, 119

NetConnection class, description of, 301–302

NetStatusEvent subclass, description of, 110

NetStream class, description of, 301–302

new operative, using with constructor methods, 36

newline (\n) escape sequence, using, 26, 127

nextFrame() method
description of, 36, 112
using with Tween class, 259

nonvisual attribute, defined, 84

not equal to (!=) operator, using, 180

null easing class, description of, 258

Number class, using, 30

Number data types
int (integer), 29
Number, 29
uint (unsigned integer), 29
using, 29
using with functions, 42

numbers. *See also* math equations; random
    numbers
    adding, 129–130
    adding and subtracting, 27
    converting to strings, 130
    multiplying and dividing, 28
    rounding, 156–157
    verifying in ranges, 184
numberSum variable, value of, 45

O

Object class, using with associative arrays, 175–178
Object() constructor method, using with arrays, 175
object depths, managing, 91–93
object instances, data-typing, 58
object listeners, cleaning up, 254
object literal technique, using, 175–176
object methods, calling, 56–57
object parameter, using with Tween object, 256
object properties, iterating through, 197–199. *See
    also* properties
object type, verifying, 185
object-oriented programming (OOP), 2
objects. *See also* display objects; interactive objects
    adding event listeners to, 99
    adding to display lists, 66, 73, 91
    applying dynamic masking to, 238–241
    calling to set properties, 11
    versus classes, 8, 52
    concept of, 2
    creating instances as, 31
    customizing with properties, 176–177
    defining as containers, 74
    examples, 9–10
    instantiating, 10–11, 56, 58
    listening to, 11
    naming instances of, 20
    overview, 8–10
    removing from display lists, 254
    setting properties of, 57–58, 73
    storing in associative arrays, 177
    storing instances of, 18
off and over frames, toggling between, 117
OOP (object-oriented programming), 2
OPEN event, using with URLLoader class, 208
operations, ordering, 6
Output panel
    displaying key code values in, 105
    displaying results in, 13
    tracing values to, 13
over and off frames, toggling between, 117

P

<p> HTML paragraph tag
    description of, 212
    using with TextField class, 146
parameter, using with addASCuePoint() method, 297
parameters
    separating, 7
    using with functions, 41–43
parent method of DisplayObject class, description
    of, 84
parentheses (())
    uses of, 6
    using with functions, 40
phase event class property, description of, 97
Photo Transition class, description of, 262
pipe (|), delineating values with, 133
PixelDissolve Transition class
    applying to mcShape, 263
    description of, 262
play() method
    arguments for, 267
    description of, 36, 112
    using with sounds, 266
playback, controlling with SoundChannel, 269
playback progress, monitoring for sounds, 278–281
playhead, returning to frame 1, 114
plus (+) symbol, using with strings, 25
pNum1 and pNum2, adding values of, 44
pop() method, using with arrays, 172–173
pow (val...) method, using with Math class, 152
preferences, setting, 16
prevFrame() method
    description of, 112
    using with Tween class, 259
preview property, using with video, 285
PrimalScript editor, description of, 59
printing scripts, 13
private methods, defined, 36
PROGRESS event
    listening for loading error for, 227
    of LoaderInfo class, 226
    using, 227
    using with Sound objects, 272
    using with URLLoader class, 208
    of VideoEvent class, 290
ProgressEvent object properties, displaying, 209
ProgressEvent subclass, description of, 110
properties. *See also* object properties
    defined, 3, 57
    versus instances, 32
    setting, 11
    tweening, 257
Properties panel, launching, 33
property parameter, using with Tween object, 256
pseudoRandomNumber variable, creating, 154

public methods, defined, 36
punctuation of syntax
    commas (,), 7
    curly braces ({}), 7
    parentheses (()), 6
    semicolon (;), 5
push() method, using with arrays, 170–171

Q

QuickTime sound format, platforms for, 266
" HTML entity, description of, 213
quotations (")
    escape sequence for, 127
    using with strings, 24

R

radius variable, using with circle, 237
random() method, using with Math class, 153–155
random numbers. *See also* numbers
    generating, 154–155
    rounding off, 156–157
READY event, using with VideoEvent class, 290
rectangles
    applying DropShadowFilter to, 246
    converting to Button symbol, 71
    drawing with Shape class, 235–236
registration points
    positions of, 88–89
    using with display object properties, 89
Regular easing class, description of, 258
relational operators
    checking for false conditions with, 182
    checking for true conditions with, 181–182
    using, 180–181
relative versus absolute target paths, 120–122
REMOVE_FROM_STAGE event, registering event
    listener for, 101
removeChildAt() method, description of, 91
REMOVED constant, event type of, 98
REMOVED_FROM_STAGE constant, event type of, 98
removeEventListener() method call, using, 106
reset() method, using with Timer class, 248
RESIZE constant, event type of, 98
resume() method, using with Tween class, 259
return types
    compile error for, 46–47
    setting for functions, 45–47
rightMargin property, using with TextFormat class, 142
ROLL_OUT constant, event type for, 102
ROLL_OVER constant, event type for, 102
root method of DisplayObject class, description of, 84
root timeline, calling, 120
Rotate Transition class, description of, 262

rotation method of DisplayObject class, description
    of, 84
rotation property
    changing for nestMC in mcA, 122
    relationship to registration point, 88
round(val) method, using with Math class, 152,
    156–157
runtime
    adding display object container at, 76–77
    adding interactive objects at, 71–74
    versus authortime, 10
    creating dynamic text fields at, 137–138
    creating input text fields at, 139
    declaring frame rate at, 123–124
    drawing shapes at, 239
    instantiating display object container at, 81–82
    instantiating interactive objects at, 74

S

scaleMode property
    of flvDisplay, 286
    using with video, 285
scaleX method of DisplayObject class, description
    of, 84
scaleX property
    relationship to registration point, 88
    setting for mcB, 122
scaleY method of DisplayObject class, description
    of, 84
scaleY property, relationship to registration point, 88
scope of functions, 48–50. *See also* variables
Script Navigator pane, description of, 12
Script pane
    adding code to, 12
    description of, 12
    displaying line numbers in, 13
scripts. *See also* code
    adding comments to, 14
    determining display of, 12
    displaying results of, 13
    previewing results of, 13
    printing, 13
scroll event, using with TextField class, 140
SCRUB_* events, using with VideoEvent class, 290
scShapeContainer, location of, 77
second value, using conditional statement with, 161
seconds
    converting milliseconds to, 279
    returning number of, 158
security issues, resource for, 207
Selectable property, disabling, 192
semicolon (;), using in statements, 5
set*() properties, using with Date class, 162
setChildIndex() method, description of, 91

setText() method, calling for loaded SWF, 231
setTextFormat() method, calling, 146
Settings Manager, resource for, 207
Shape class
    creating dynamic masks with, 240–241
    graphics property of, 234
    method of, 234
    requirements of, 235
    using, 234–237
Shape() constructor method, using, 58
Shape objects
    applying DropShadowFilter to, 246
    moving, 237
    setting to mask Loader objects, 240
Shape subclass, using with DisplayObject, 69
ShapeContainer
    creating, 76
    editing timeline for, 77
shapes
    converting to MovieClip symbols, 32
    drawing at runtime, 239
shift() method, using with arrays, 172–173
shiftKey property, using with KeyboardEvent, 104
SimpleButton class, adding MenuItem symbol to, 71
sin(angle) method, using with Math class, 152
single-line comments, using, 14–15
size property, using with TextFormat class, 142
skateboarder info, storing in array, 177
skin* properties
    of flvDisplay, 286
    setting to null, 288
    using with video, 285–286
slice() method
    of String class, 126
    using with arrays, 172–173
slowPace event handler, setting frame rate with, 124
sound events, monitoring loading with, 272–274
sound files, tracking loading progress of, 272–275
sound formats, 266
Sound objects
    controlling volume of, 276–277
    dispatching IO_ERROR events from, 274
    getting ID3 data from, 275
    id3 properties of, 275
    playing, 267, 273
sound playback, tracking current position of,
        278–279
SOUND_COMPLETE constant, event type of, 98
SoundChannel, controlling playback with, 269
SoundChannel.position property, using, 278
SoundDesigner 2 format, platform for, 266
SoundEvent subclass, description of, 110
sounds. See also embedded sounds; external sounds
    importing into library, 266
    monitoring playback progress of, 278–281

    playing, 266
    stopping playback of, 269
soundTransform argument, using with play()
        method, 267
SoundTransform class, controlling volume with,
        276–277
source property
    of flvDisplay, 286
    using with video, 285
<span> tag, using with TextField class, 146
special characters, adding, 25–26
splice() method, using with arrays, 170–171
split() method
    of String class, 126
    using with strings, 133
spMenuContainer
    adding MenuItem instance to, 82
    instantiating, 81
Sprite class
    constructor method for, 36
    versus MovieClip class, 75
Sprite() constructor method, using, 81
spriteAdded() listener, executing, 101
spriteRemovedHandler() event listener, adding, 101
sqrt(val) method, using with Math class, 152
square brackets ([]), using with arrays, 167–169
squares
    constructing, 56
    drawing, 89
    setting properties of, 57–58
Squeeze Transition class, description of, 262
stacking order, changing for display objects, 66
stage
    calling by absolute path, 120
    calling by relative path, 120
    calling from timeline, 120
    as root of DisplayList, 65
    setting frame rate for, 124
stage method of DisplayObject class, description
        of, 84
Stage of application, example of, 65
start() method
using with Timer class, 248
using with Tween class, 259
start parameter, using with Tween object, 256
startTime argument, using with play() method, 267
STATE_CHANGE event, using with VideoEvent
        class, 290
statements
    adding conditions to, 181
    dot syntax of, 4
    grouping, 7
    punctuation in, 5–7
    terminating, 5

static class constants, event types for, 98
static classes, using, 153. *See also* classes
StaticText subclass
    adding to display list, 70
    using with DisplayObject, 67, 69
stop() method
    adding, 38
    description of, 36, 112
    using with Timer class, 248
    using with Tween class, 259
strict typing, defined, 47
String class, using, 30, 126–127
String expressions
    case sensitivity of, 182
    checking, 182
String() method
    description of, 126
    using, 129–130
string variables, obtaining substrings of, 131–132
strings
    adding commands in, 26
    combining, 24–25, 128
    converting nonstrings to, 129–130
    converting numbers to, 130
    defined, 125
    versus event constants, 99
    manipulating, 131–132
    recasting values as, 129–130
    separating delineated values in, 133
    splitting, 133
    using escape sequences in, 127
    using quotations (") with, 24
Strong easing class, description of, 258
StyleSheet object
    creating, 213
    parsing style sheet with, 214
    styling HTML text with, 215
substr() method, using, 131–132
substring() method, description of, 126
subtracting numbers, 27–28
sum variable
    creating, 44
    scope of, 48–49
SunAU sound format, platforms for, 266
superclass, DisplayObject class as, 68
swapChildren() method, description of, 91
swapChildrenAt() method, description of, 91
SWF files
    adding to list of trusted files, 207
    calling setText() method of, 231
    decreasing size of, 270
    loading, 226
    loading and casting as MovieClips, 230–231
    setting properties of, 231

switch statement, checking conditions with, 188
syntax
    applying colors to, 16
    dot, 4
    punctuation in, 5–7

T

\t (tab) escape sequence, using, 26, 127
tab indents, escape sequence for, 127
tab spaces, adding, 25–26
tan(angle) method, using with Math class, 152
target event class property, description of, 97
target paths, absolute and relative, 120–122
target phase of event flow, explanation of, 107
target property
    using with event flow, 108
    using with event object, 211
    using with TextFormat class, 142
tasks, using trace() statement with, 13
text fields
    displaying HTML-formatted text in, 147
    displaying playback progress in, 278–281
    displaying status of video playback in, 292–293
    enabling word wrapping in, 138
    formatting, 143–146
    loading external text into, 211–212
    removing from display lists, 229
    styling with CSS (Cascading Style Sheets),
        214–215
text properties, displaying for cuepoints, 299
TextEvent subclass, description of, 110
TextField class
    constructor method for, 36
    dynamic text fields, 136–138
    events of, 140–141
    HTML tags for, 212
    HTML tags of, 146
    input text fields, 138–139
TextField objects
    adding to display lists, 139
    applying font symbols to, 148–149
    changing background color of, 141
    creating, 211
    formatting, 144
    formatting with HTML, 147
    formatting instances of, 145
textFocus event handler, using, 140
TextFormat class
    method of, 142
    properties of, 142
TextFormat objects, creating, 143–146
<textformat> HTML tag
    description of, 212
    using with TextField class, 146

textInput event, using with TextField class, 140
TextMate editor, description of, 60
time and date
    customizing, 162–163
    getting and displaying, 159
    values, 159
    variables, 159
time parameter, using with addASCuePoint()
    method, 297
Time properties, methods for, 158
time zones, values of, 164
timeline location, displaying, 78
timeline panel, reordering layers in, 66
timelines
    adding .as file to, 61
    calling stage from, 120
    controlling with target paths, 121–122
    navigating to frames on, 114
    navigating with target paths, 119–122
    playing, 113
    stopping, 112–113
Timer class
    animating display objects with, 250–251
    listening for events of, 249–250
    methods of, 248
TIMER event, listening for, 160
Timer() method, description of, 248
Timer objects
    creating, 248
    stopping and removing, 252
    using with sounds, 278–279
TIMER* event constants, description of, 248–249
TimerEvent class, event types of, 248
TimerEvent subclass, description of, 110
toLowerCase() method of String class, description
    of, 126
toUpperCase() method of String class, description
    of, 126
towerCrane class, properties of, 9
trace() statement
    adding, 40
    using, 13
    using comments with, 15
    using with function scope, 49
    using with getCoffee() function, 43
    using with keyboard events, 105
    using with values of arrays, 133
traceName() function, invoking, 40–41
TransitionManager, using with transitions, 263
transitions, applying to display objects, 262
true conditions
    checking for, 181–183
    verifying, 184

Tween class
    importing, 256
    methods for, 259
    using, 255–257
    using with multiple properties, 257
Tween objects
    applying easing classes to, 258
    creating, 255–256
    listening for events from, 260
Tween option, using with MovieClips, 79
tween playback, controlling, 259–260
TweenEvent class, event types of, 260
TweenEvent subclass, description of, 110
tweening display objects, 259
tweens. *See also* animating
    defined, 247
    restarting, 260
    stopping, 259
type event class property, description of, 97

U

<u> HTML underline tag
    description of, 212
    using with TextField class, 146
UI components, customizing for FLVPlayback,
    287–288
UI controls, customizing for FLVPlayback
    component, 288–289
uint (unsigned integer) data type, using, 29
underline property, using with TextFormat class,
    142
underscores (_), using with variables, 19–20
UNLOAD constant, event type of, 98
UNLOAD event type, of LoaderInfo class, 226
unLoad() method, using with assets, 223
unshift() method, using with arrays, 170–171
url variable, declaring, 193
URLLoader class, events of, 208
URLLoader object
    adding IOErrorEvent to, 210
    creating, 208
    loading progress of, 209–211
    monitoring progress of, 209
    tracking progress of, 209–211
URLRequest object, creating, 204, 206
URLs
    browsing to, 205–207
    navigating to, 205
useCapture, setting, 107–108
useSeconds parameter, using with Tween object, 256
UTC (Coordinated Universal Time), 164

V

values
    appending to strings, 25
    appending values to, 25
    assigning to variables, 21
    changing for variables, 21
    passing to methods, 6
    recasting as strings, 129–130
    returning from functions, 45–47
    tracing to Output panel, 13
var keyword, using, 31
variable data types, converting, 30
variable references, breaking, 18
variable type, verifying, 185
variables. *See also* Booleans; scope of functions
    assigning values to, 21
    changing values of, 21
    creating, 31
    data typing, 22–23
    declaring, 21
    defined, 18
    making unique, 18–19
    naming, 18–19
    naming conventions for, 19–20
    passing as arguments to functions, 44–45
vector shapes, drawing with Shape class, 234–237
video, adding cuepoints to, 297–300. *See also* FLVPlayback components
Video class, description of, 301
video status, displaying, 291–293
Video subclass, using with DisplayObject, 69
videocodecid property, using with MetadataEvent, 294
videodatarate property, using with MetadataEvent, 294
VideoEvent class, events of, 290
VideoEvent subclass, description of, 110
VideoEvent types, listening for, 291
visible method of DisplayObject class, description of, 84
visual attribute, defined, 84
visual effects
    blend modes, 242–243
    dynamic filters, 243–246
void return typing, 47
volume of sounds, controlling, 276–277
volume property
    of flvDisplay, 286
    using with video, 285

W

Web sites. *See also* Adobe LiveDocks resources
    Ambient MP3 sound file, 267
    bitmap caching, 264
    Eclipse editor, 59
    FlashDevelop editor, 59
    PrimalScript editor, 59
    security issues, 207
    Settings Manager, 207
    TextMate editor, 60
weekdays, iterating through elements of, 191
while loop versus do...while loop, 200–202
width method of DisplayObject class, description of, 84
width property
    of flvDisplay, 286
    of LoaderInfo class, 226
    of MetadataEvent, 294
Windows, sound formats for, 266
Wipe Transition class, description of, 262
wireframes, drawing for display objects, 119
Word Wrap, using, 13
word wrapping, enabling in text fields, 138

X

x and y properties
    setting for miChapterOne, 73
    setting for MovieClip, 10
    setting for shape objects, 237
x method of DisplayObject class, description of, 84
x property, relationship to registration point, 88

Y

y method of DisplayObject class, description of, 84
y property, relationship to registration point, 88
year local time, returning, 158
yoyo() method, using with Tween class, 259, 261

Z

Zephyr skateboard team, 177
z-index versus depth, 91
Zoom Transition class, description of, 262

Adventures in Virtual Reality

Tom Hayward

que

AA3 9809

Adventures in Virtual Reality

©1993 by Que® Corporation

Library of Congress Catalog No.: 93-83388

ISBN: 1-56529-208-1

96 95 94 93   8 7 6 5 4 3 2 1

Interpretation of the printing code: the rightmost double-digit number is the year of the book's printing; the rightmost single-digit number, the number of the book's printing. For example, a printing code of 93-1 shows that the first printing of the book occurred in 1993.

Publisher: Lloyd J. Short

Associate Publisher: Rick Ranucci

Operations Manager: Sheila Cunningham

Publishing Plan Manager: Thomas H. Bennett

Book Designer: Scott Cook

Production Team: Jeff Baker, Claudia Bell, Julie Brown, Jodie Cantwell, Brook Farling, Heather Kaufman, Bob LaRoche, Linda Seifert, Sandra Shay

Credits

Publishing Manager
Joseph Wikert

Production Editor
Bryan Gambrel

Editor
Lori Cates

Technical Editor
Jerry Isdale

Editorial Assistant
Elizabeth D. Brown

Figure Specialist
Wilfred R. Thebodeau

Illustrations
Jodie Cantwell

Indexer
Johnna VanHoose

Composed in Cheltenham and MCPdigital by
Prentice Hall Computer Publishing

This book is dedicated to my wife, Caren Hayward, who is a virtual angel but who firmly does not want to be put on a pedestal, and our four children, Tanya, Lara, Johnna, and Andrew, for being such a great family, and just for being.

About the Author

Tom Hayward

Tom Hayward received a B.A. in English Education from Northern Illinois University in DeKalb, Illinois in 1971, and has collaborated with schools studying the impact of Virtual Reality on education. In addition, as a free-lance programmer since 1980, he has written other computer applications for a number of industries, including accounting, insurance, and manufacturing.

Born in India of American missionary parents, Tom grew up in South Africa with four brothers. The father of three girls and a boy, he currently resides in Stoughton, Wisconsin, where he cofounded and edits a virtual reality newsletter with his nine-year-old son, Andrew. In addition, he is Director of Programming for VRontier worlds of Stoughton, Inc., a manufacturer of virtual reality equipment.

Acknowledgments

Writing a book is an endeavor that, like oil and water, doesn't mix well with having a family. I want to thank my wife and children for their support even though they had to live, in effect, without much of a father for several weeks. The encouragement from my parents and four brothers has been very helpful and much appreciated.

Many other people have given of themselves and their time to help this effort, and I thank them all, including the writers who contributed to this book and the programmers who wrote the software. I owe a special thank you to Joe Wikert of Que Publishing, who bravely agreed to give me this chance, to Bryan Gambrel, my editor at Que, and to Ed La Hood, the founder of VREAM, Inc., who went out of his way to make the VREAM demo possible.

I also want to thank many people in the virtual reality industry for their influence and generous help, including Howard Rheingold for his inspiring book, *Virtual Reality,* for helping Andrew's VEE-AR Club get started, and for agreeing to write the Foreword for this book. I would also like to thank the many other people who struggle to get out the newsletters (information is the key), such as Steve Aukstakalnis, Mike Bevan, Ben Delaney, Sandra Heisel, and Brian Lareau. In addition, I would like to thank Jerry Clark, Marge Clark, Brad Burnett, and Dana Burnett, for their willingness to gamble on me and each other in starting a company to produce virtual reality equipment—and for making it possible to write this book.

I especially want to thank New Dimensions, Incorporated for the use of images from its Superscape program that appear throughout this book and on the cover.

Trademarks

All terms mentioned in this book that are known to be trademarks or service marks have been appropriately capitalized. Que cannot attest to the accuracy of this information. Use of a term in this book should not be regarded as affecting the validity of any trademark or service mark.

Overview

Foreword xi

Introduction 1

   1. Introduction to Virtual Reality 9

   2. The Evolution of Virtual Reality 25

   3. The State of Virtual Reality 51

   4. 3-D Applications 97

   5. Virtual Reality Systems 135

   6. Authoring a VR Environment 169

   7. Virtual Reality Arcade 193

Appendix A 227

Appendix B 239

Index 251

Table of Contents

Introduction   **1**

1 Introduction to Virtual Reality   **9**
The Goal of Virtual Reality 11
    The Human Side of Things 12
    Basic Concepts of Virtual Reality 12
Summary 21

2 The Evolution of Virtual Reality   **25**
The Dream Is Primal and Prehistoric 25
The Invention that Made It Possible 27
Improving Communication with the Computer 31
People with Early Visions of Virtual Reality 35
The Role of the Military and NASA in Developing
    Virtual Reality 41
    The Role of Telepresence 44
    NASA Meets "The Guru of Virtual Reality" 46
Where Does the Path Lead Next? 48

3 The State of Virtual Reality   **51**
What's Happening Now? 52
The Sense of Sound 55
    The Convolvotron 57
The Sense of Touch 58
    The Feedback Loop 61
    Interacting with Pressure and Texture 63
    Interacting with Weight, Shape, and Size 65
    Putting Haptic Clues to Work in Virtual Reality Systems 67
    Other Examples of Haptic Interaction 69
The Other Senses 74
Current VR-Related Software 75
    Defining VR-Related Software 77
    Flight Simulator Software 80
    3-D Animation Software 82
    Computer-Aided Design (CAD) Software 83
    Rendering Software 85
    Simulation Software 88

World-Creating Tools Using Virtual Reality Principles 89
    Superscape Development System 89
    Virtual Reality Studio. 91
    Swivel 92
    WorldToolKit 92
    VREAM Virtual Reality Development System 93
    Where and How Is the Software Used? 94

4 3-D Applications   97

What's Important about 3-D? 98
3-D Modeling 99
    Building Models 100
    Virtual Models 100
    Models of the Atmosphere 101
    Object Modeling 101
    Form Changes 103
3-D Architecture 104
3-D Training 107
3-D Science 110
    3-D Chemistry 110
    3-D Physics 111
    3-D Medicine 116
3-D Education 122
3-D Shopping 124
3-D Sports 125
3-D Tools for the Physically Challenged 127
Putting It All Together 130

5 Virtual Reality Systems   135

Exploring Human Factor Issues 135
Exploring Display Issues. 137
    The Divergence Problem 139
    The Immersion Problem 141
    VRon Lenses 148
    Stereoscopic Mode 153
    Boom Display 155
    Retinal Display 156
Exploring Tracking Issues. 156
Exploring Manipulation Issues 158
Exploring Application Issues 160

Exploring Navigation Issues 164
    Bio-Navigation 165
From Exploring to Discovery 166

6 Authoring a VR Environment   169
Introduction to Building Virtual Worlds 169
    A Student's Perspective 171
    An Ethical Perspective 173
Talking Terminology 176
    Three-Dimensional Coordinates 177
    Creating Objects 178
    Grouping Objects 179
    Attributes 180
Types of World-Building Tools 181
    Building Worlds with a World-Editing System 182
Creating Advanced Worlds 186
    Large-Scale Advanced Worlds 187
    Virtual World Development Project Phases 188
Time for the Fun! 190

7 Virtual Reality Arcade   193
Installing and Operating the Software on the Enclosed Disk . . . 193
    Understanding More about Installing the Program Files 194
Instructions for the Programs Requiring 3-D Glasses 196
Description and Instructions for FLY the Grand
    Canyon Demo 197
Description and Instructions for ANAGLYPH 200
Description and Instructions for MOVER 203
Description and Instructions for MINO-DINO Demo 208
Description and Instructions for CASTLE 212
Description and Instructions for Adventure in VREAM 213
Have Fun! 223

A Virtual Reality and Technology   227

B Virtual Reality Resource Information   239

Index   251

Foreword

by Howard Rheingold

Virtual reality is a topic that seems to fascinate people, no matter where they are in the world, or what they know or don't know about computer technology. I learned that the words "virtual reality" have an almost magical attraction to people after I wrote my book on the subject and was invited to speak about virtual reality all over America, Japan, and Europe. In many ways, people are fascinated more with a certain idea than they are genuinely interested in the nuts and bolts of computer simulations—the idea that our increasingly technological and mass-media-oriented world is leading toward a day when *everything* can be simulated by a computer.

People are both fearful and fascinated. Fearful because they understand how technology takes things away from people even as it bestows gifts. Fearful because their own lives seem less meaningful as machines become more meaningful. Fearful because technology triggers change, and we are all suffering from the effects of too much change—the phrase "future shock" is decades old. People are fascinated because they know that science and technology routinely accomplish things that were, until recently, considered impossible. If we can build supersonic jetliners, portable color televisions, and space ships, it isn't out of the realm of possibility that some near-future technology will make it possible to manufacture illusions at will. And isn't control of illusion part of our history of art and drama? Certainly, it is something that humans have been striving for for a long time.

I like Thomas Hayward's approach to the subject. Precisely because VR is so fearful and fascinating, it is a perfect way to talk with people about our fears and hopes for technology. And we need to talk about technology—especially those of us who aren't technical experts. If we are to conduct informed debates and make decisions about the technologies that are going to shape our lives, we must

understand what the technologies are all about. I watched with fascination as Thomas and his young son Andrew started writing a newsletter about virtual reality from a young person's point of view.

The more we talk about VR, the better. It has positive potential as a scientific tool and medical technology, and negative potential as yet another form of addictive electronic escapism and as a tool for warfare. We need to understand the full potential of this technology while we still have a chance to influence the way it is shaped.

Thomas Hayward's book not only takes a light approach—and takes the care to explain the meaning of all the technical jargon—but offers the tools for doing your own hands-on experiences of virtual reality.

Howard Rheingold
January, 1993

Howard Rheingold is the author of several books, including Virtual Reality *and* Tools for Thought, *and the editor of "Whole Earth Review." As a veteran observer of the developments in cyberspace technologies, he has met most of the people in the virtual reality industry. While writing* Virtual Reality, *he travelled for two years trying out VR systems in research labs and meeting VR pioneers around the world. Reingold's descriptions of what he saw and experienced ignited the imaginations of thousands of readers.*

Introduction

Virtual reality. Has there ever been such a confusing phrase?

Virtual reality. VR. Is it possible to understand it?

Virtual... Almost like... Something like... Virtual reality. Something like reality. Almost like reality. But who can say what reality is? Reality for me is one thing. For my neighbor it's quite another. And isn't reality affected by my emotions? (Scratch my head.) I'm not sure I can figure this out.

Wait a minute. The TV show I watched last night said virtual reality has something to do with computers. So... maybe the computer can create something close to reality. What would that be like? It might be too confusing. Sometimes regular reality is confusing enough. I can't handle this. Virtual reality on the computer? Bah. Sounds stupid. What is this world coming to—now they'll probably go and spend a lot of money making reality on the computer. What a joke. You won't catch me fooling around with computers trying to make computer realities. I have enough trouble as it is. And they better not raise my taxes (any more) to pay for this silliness.

Growl, growl, grumble, mumble. I'm not going to think about that stuff anymore. I have a real problem to deal with. The boss wants me to meet with the sales staff next month and present the plans for the new expansion wing of the office. I just know what's coming. Everyone will discuss all the ways we could do this and do that. Randy will ask a thousand questions about the blueprints. I'll have to reassure Sue that I have included her concerns about the size of the reception room and whether the secretary will be able see her all the time. Solidifying all the details will take a long time. Then we'll have to start making all the changes. What a lot of work!

It's so hard to get everyone to understand what we're getting at. Blueprints aren't easy to read. Conceptual drawings are better—but I'll have to order so many. Then I'll have to make sure the artist gets it just right. And they're so expensive—especially if I have to have them done over again.... What a pain. And I only have one month to get this all done. I better get started. Where's that phone book? I wish I could just take everyone for a walk through the pictures in my mind. Then they'd know exactly what I'm talking about.

Oh, here's the artist's phone number. "Steve, this is Tom. Got another project for you, but it's gonna be a tight time frame. The department is planning another expansion wing, and I need to get together with you soon to get you started on the drawings. Tomorrow afternoon? Sure. I'll bring the prints."

Good old Steve. Glad we have him around. Can't find many renderers like him, that's for sure. "Hey, Steve, how're you doing? Been busy? Thanks for fitting me in so fast. Here are the prints." I see some new faces. Construction must be picking up. "What do you mean—you have a new tool for conceptualizing? You do it on the computer? A walk-through—what's that? Oh, you make pictures on the computer that make everyone feel like they're inside the building. Three-dimensional? Okay. So, how does it work?"

While Steve shows me an innovative application of virtual reality—an artificial or synthetic environment—and points to unusual equipment I haven't seen before, questions flood my mind. What is this all about? Why is this better than looking at drawings or photographs? How can he show me what the architect created in his mind? Can I grasp the nature and origin of this new visual medium? How did we get here from there?

If you are a person who is intrigued by new ideas, this book has been written for you. If you are also an individual who does not like to wade knee-deep in formulas, this book will make you happy. If, in addition, you prefer not to struggle with fifty-dollar words, or if you haven't had much contact with computers, these pages were designed with you in mind. If you have also heard of a new technology called virtual reality, and if you've been wondering what some of it is all about and what it is supposed to mean, then this is the book you've been looking for.

There are a number of recently published books on the subject of virtual reality. Many of them are carefully executed, include high-quality information, and deserve outstanding achievement awards. In 1991, Howard Rheingold wrote the first definitive book that covered the history and larger implications of this fascinating new technology, *Virtual Reality,* and sparked the interest of many readers. Others, like Steven Aukstakalnis and David Blatner, Ken Pimental and Kevin Teixeira, have widened our perspectives even further with more recent books packed with interesting and helpful details.

It is not the goal of this book to strive to attain the authoritative voice or expertise of writers, such as the ones listed above, who have illuminated the virtual reality landscape so eminently. Instead, the purpose of this book is to help you scramble up to the first branch of the tree, where you can see farther down the path ahead. With the media focusing more on the panorama of virtual reality, this book will be your guide to some of the major landmarks in VR. This is intended as an overview of the directions, concepts, and trends in virtual reality.

Now that movies are weaving virtual reality plot devices into their scripts, TV commercials are increasingly using virtual reality components to attract attention, and news stories are more frequently mentioning events related to virtual reality companies and advancements, a need to know and understand this topic has been created in the public mind. The objective of this book is to fulfill this need in ways that are accessible to most individuals. At the same time, the software on the disk included with this book presents some of the latest and hottest—and at the same time most affordable—PC-based 3-D programs available in the industry. Remarkably, one of

3

the programs on this disk is a sneak preview of what can be achieved with a virtual reality development system that, at the time of writing, has not yet reached the market.

What you are about to read and experience offers a broad range of information and perspectives that can contribute to your understanding of the concepts no matter what your background or vocation is. And you might be pleasantly surprised at the applications you may begin to envision for your own life, your lifestyle, and your business. That is part of the process of grasping the implications of this technology—especially in relation to potential future developments—and it merits encouragement. After all, applying imaginative and practical solutions to broader problems in the real world will be the force that leads to more advancements in the technology. And the field is wide open for you to contribute new ideas.

As you read the descriptions and explanations in the following pages, focus your attention on grasping the underlying notions, and remember that this book attempts to communicate concepts. The technically trained reader may find some of the discussion overly simplistic and perhaps, at times, omitting some details for the sake of clarity. But, this discussion should be perceived as an introductory tutorial, not a reference manual. The hope is that, once you understand the foundation and structure of the fundamental concepts and relationships, you will examine the details more closely in related readings. The books listed above plus the reference material in Appendix B provide further materials for any person who wants to extend his or her study on the subject.

As far as the particular computer technology included in this book, the discussion has been limited, with a few exceptions, to the PC platform—partly because the programs on the disk are all for the PC (IBM compatible).

Here's a brief summary of each of the chapters of *Adventures in Virtual Reality*:

In Chapter 1 you will be introduced to the basic concepts of virtual reality, and find out how they will work on the computer. Then, in Chapter 2, some of the milestones in the history of the technology are described; the contributions of major figures are explained in context.

Chapter 3 lays out details of the current capabilities of VR software and hardware, and examines what is achievable now in trying to simulate human senses. After this preparation, Chapter 4 reviews the existing and possible ways to put three-dimensional technology to practical use in several fields. Chapter 5 explores issues, problems, and solutions involved with virtual reality systems on the market today.

By the time you reach Chapter 6, you will be ready to consider some of the perspectives that need to be considered when constructing your own virtual worlds. Chapter 7 describes the software on the disk at the end of the book, and how to install and operate the programs. There are two appendixes at the back of this book. Appendix A relates the story of Bradley Burnett's head-mounted display. Appendix B lists sources for the software on the disk and other information related to virtual reality organizations, literature, and events. Instructions for installing the disk software can be found on the last page.

With that preparation, you are invited to participate, in more ways than one, in the rapidly developing and expanding field called virtual reality. Join the pioneers who have journeyed into the frontier looking for challenge, action, and adventure!

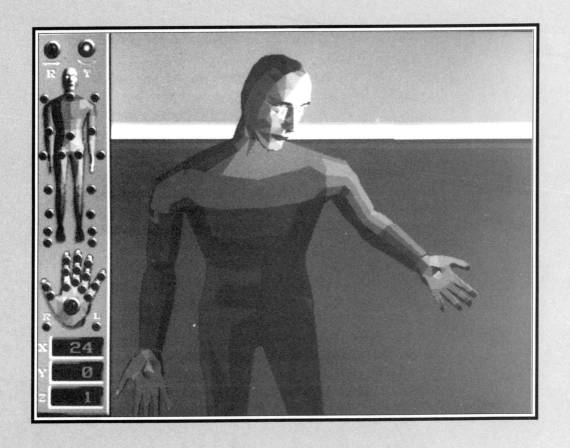

Chapter 1

Introduction to Virtual Reality

On the rear surface of your right eye is a *virtual television screen*. There's another one in the back of your left eye (unless it's glass—pardon me). It's usually called the retina, and it's one of the most complex components of the eye. Various features of the retina do share some characteristics of a television.

If your experience with your eyes is similar to most people's, you haven't spent a great deal of time pondering the "incomprehensible mysteries of the retina." You might even admit that you have allowed entire months to fritter away without one passing thought about your retinae, left or right.

To grasp the interrelated concepts involved in virtual reality, you need to think slowly and carefully about your eyes. What do you see right now? Instead of thinking about what's in front of you, think about the picture forming on the retina screen in the back of your eye. Think about the entire picture, not just one or two objects.

Pretend you can make a tiny copy of yourself—a clone of you, the size of the head of a pin. Imagine you can let your tiny clone walk around on the back of your retina screen and look at the colors being received by the rods and cones. Since we're pretending, we can imagine whatever we want. What would your clone see? Little dots of different colors that are part of the complete picture formed by the rays of light shining through the front window of the eye. What's important here is to think of the whole picture. Hold your head still. Move your eyes all around and look at each part of the scene that you can see. Figure 1.1 shows the dot image that forms on the back of your eyeball.

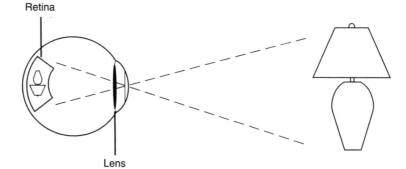

Retina

Lens

Figure 1.1.

An illustration of how the eye perceives a scene.

While you are moving your eyes all around, think about the picture on your retina screen. (Forget about that technician waving his hand in the air saying it's not a real screen—we know the brain has to interpret the light signals—we're pretending, remember?) Just be aware of the "photograph" your brain is creating as you look at the scene in front of you. Think about the little picture on your retina screen that is a copy of what you're looking at. (Ignore the eye doctor who is saying the picture is backwards—she's seeing the picture from the wrong direction.) You know which picture we're talking about: the one your clone is looking at from behind the retina. Got it? Okay. That's the picture we'll use while we learn more about "virtual reality." We'll call it the *clone picture*.

The Goal of Virtual Reality

At this time there is no single definition of virtual reality (also nicknamed "VR") that finds total agreement among all participants. The name "virtual reality" itself causes controversy. The term "artificial reality" is preferred by some proponents. Others support the phrases *synthetic environments* (man-made), *artificial environments, cyberspace,* or *information design.*

Because the most popular name is virtual reality, that's the one we're using here. Nevertheless, the selection of a name doesn't change the direction of the technology. The basic concepts are still the same; the goal is still the same.

The goal, the dream, the passionate search for the Grail, is simply stated: Everyone who is working with virtual reality is trying to do the same thing—*Create better ways to communicate.*

It is a simple statement of five words, yet it is the boiled down essence of years of hard work and incremental problem-solving of many people all over the world. It is the result of the creative development of complex equipment and machinery, and the infusion of special talents, skills, and knowledge from persons and institutions involved in practically every field of human endeavor. Just as a bottle of maple syrup only hints at the hard work and long hours that went into it, the goal of virtual reality merely hints at the multitudes of facets that require examination and understanding. This book not only examines these layers and facets, but enables you to "test-drive" the concepts discussed by trying out the programs on the disk at the end of this book.

The search for better means of communication between computers and humans requires a step-by-step analysis of why humans do what they do so well, and why computers do what they do so inflexibly—and finding methods to make the computer simulate what humans do. Let's look at what humans do and what computers do and see if we can understand some of the fundamental problems and solutions.

The Human Side of Things

Here we are. Humans. Sitting, standing, riding. Looking, seeing, taking it all in. Grasping, touching, feeling. We are what we are: struggling to understand other humans, and valiantly trying to make ourselves understood.

It can be said that much of the conflict between humans is due to misunderstandings and miscommunications. How frequently do we raise our voices in argument over a misconception or an unknown mistake? Sometimes it's minor and blows over. Other times it's tragic and causes great harm; we react with horror: "What a terrible misunderstanding. And they didn't speak to each other for eight years." How many lawsuits have been brought to court because of misinterpreted verbal or written agreements? How many battles, skirmishes, and great wars have been fought as the result of mis-communication? Achieving accurate and timely communication is often the biggest problem of all.

So here we are, and here's what we do. The idea is to simulate the way we perceive the world, the way we manipulate the world, and the way we are a part of the world. Harness the power and flexibil-ity of the computer to create a new way of "talking"—to ourselves, to the computer, and to each other.

Basic Concepts of Virtual Reality

When you analyze in detail what humans can do with the aim of simulating human capabilities on the computer, you can identify four fundamental areas that have to be included and dealt with.

Figure 1.2 shows the four human characteristics that define the basic concepts in virtual reality: *viewpoint, navigation, manipulation,* and *immersion.*

Your viewpoint is the point from which you view a scene. Naviga-tion is your ability to move your viewpoint around. Manipulation is your ability to act upon objects in your vicinity. Immersion is the condition of being inside the world.

Again, think of the clone picture previously formed on your retina (and now in your memory). There you were, holding your head

still, looking around the scene in front of you very slowly and carefully taking in each part of the "picture." Your physical location and the direction you were looking defined your viewpoint—the point in space where you were viewing the scene. The concept of viewpoint is where we have to start.

Figure 1.2.

The four basic concepts of virtual reality.

Viewpoint

To visually communicate with you, I have to know where your point of view is located in physical space, and I have to know what direction it is facing. A baseball umpire knows that when he signals "safe" with his hands, all the viewpoints of the people in the stadium, or those watching the game on TV, are located where he can be seen, and faced in his direction. On the computer, with virtual reality, the location and direction of the viewpoint is the basis for everything that is shown on the computer screen. When you try the programs on the disk at the end of this book, notice that the pictures, or graphics, change with the location and direction of your virtual viewpoint. Before the computer can do anything in virtual reality, it must locate your viewpoint—both the position of the point and the direction of the view (see Figure 1.3). The computer must either be told the position of your point of view, or be able to calculate where it moves as you navigate.

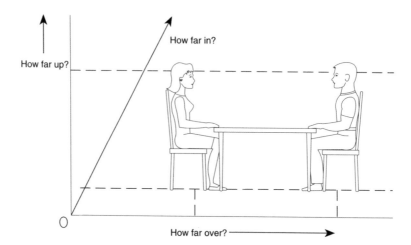

How far in?

How far up?

How far over?

O

Figure 1.3.

How your viewpoint is calculated.

You change the viewpoint in a virtual world by using a device, such as a joystick, to tell the computer from what point of view, or perspective, you want to see the object. By placing your virtual viewpoint in a certain location (by specifying the desired coordinates) and with a certain direction (by specifying the desired orientation), you are communicating to the computer your desire to look at the picture or object from the chosen coordinates and with your chosen orientation. You could use these pictures to illustrate your ideas to your friend or client by saying "Look at this. See what I mean?" Your client can communicate to you by saying "I like where you put the door, but don't you think it should be wider?"

Using the technology of VR to convey messages really isn't that different in principle from using any other tool to communicate. Hand signals and smoke signals require knowing the location of the receiver of the message. If you write a message, the location of the reader is less important, but you still have to know other information about the viewpoint of the receiver—do the intended readers know the language in which you're writing? Do they understand the words you use?

All communication requires knowing the viewpoint of the receiver. If the receiver does not understand the message, the desired communication does not take place. When thought of as a communication tool, virtual reality is really no different. Being a visual medium, the visible viewpoint is more crucial to virtual reality than

radio. Radio communication depends on description of the viewpoint. If the umpire signals the runner "safe," the radio announcer must verbally describe what is happening. The announcer conveys his viewpoint to the listeners, who use these sounds to create the viewpoint in their minds. But knowledge of the viewpoint is still required for communication involving radio and other nonvisual media.

So, virtual reality is constructed around your visual viewpoint. But that's just the beginning. A photograph and a TV screen both have a visual viewpoint, and although both incorporate some aspects of being "almost like reality," neither is qualified to be called virtual reality.

Let's return to the clone picture (Figure 1.1) and identify another factor that can help us move closer to virtual reality and better communication. Fortunately, most humans don't have to stare at one scene forever. We usually have a way to change our scenery. We can change our perspective by moving our eyes or our heads. We can even relocate ourselves over to another point in space by walking, running, driving, or telling the chauffeur where to drive.

Yes, we can move our viewpoint. How we change or move our viewpoint to a different position and orientation defines the way we *navigate* through the world. The concept of navigation, or moving your viewpoint, is what we'll look at next.

Navigation

To communicate better, we need to be able to move around. If a bat just flew into the living room, and we want to tell each other how to locate it, it will save a lot of time if we can both look up, down, and sideways. Then, if you say "It's hanging from the ceiling," I can look up and see what part of the ceiling it is hanging from. If I say, "Look out, it's flying towards the couch," you can look sideways and move towards the door at the same time. We communicate more efficiently if we can move the position and the direction of our viewpoints.

With computerized virtual reality, the pictures change as your viewpoint moves around. If you move your viewpoint towards a chair, the computer calculates how far you've moved, and redraws

the graphics in relation to your new location. By navigating your viewpoint backwards, you can look at the chair from a distance. Moving around in the pictures is often called a *walk-through* if you follow a predetermined path. All the objects created together in a continuum are referred to as a *world,* or *environment.*

If you change the coordinates of your viewpoint, the computer understands that you desire to look at the pictures and objects from a new angle. The computer shows you what the scene looks like from your new position in the world. If you had designed the pictures in the virtual world, you could communicate your ideas to your friend or client by saying "Let's go through the doorway of this room and I'll show you the other room." Your friend can say "I like where you put the door, but don't you think it should be taller?" And you can say, "Why should it be taller? This is a zoo. Aardvarks don't need tall doors."

Now we're starting to see the real benefit of virtual reality. Many communication tools are static like a photograph; once you take the snapshot, it never changes. After you've written your idea on paper, it doesn't change. But in virtual reality, you can look at the ideas from many angles simply by moving to new positions. As a communication tool, virtual reality is quite powerful. Seeing is believing, but navigating in a synthetic environment is seeing, believing, communicating, and having fun, too. As you navigate the programs on the disk with this book, try moving your viewpoint to unusual angles and positions; focus your awareness on the unique abilities under your control.

There's an even more powerful feature in virtual reality that contributes to an enjoyable experience and adds to effective communication. This is what really separates virtual reality from photographs and television. Think of your clone picture: While you were looking at the scene in front of you, your hands were holding this book and turning the pages. You were manipulating the book. You might also have been sipping a beverage and manipulating the container. You can control and activate at least some of the objects around you. Let's now look now at this third basic concept of virtual reality— manipulation.

Manipulation

We can communicate more effectively when we have the power to manipulate the objects around us. A farmer can teach his city-raised granddaughter how to milk a cow much faster by showing her how to do it. He can say "Here, I'll show you," and squeeze the teat just right so the milk squirts into the pail. She will probably understand the method and be able to milk a cow herself more quickly and without too much frustration—and the visiting family can have breakfast before everyone becomes famished. Communication is much more efficient if we can manipulate objects.

You can market your invention of an improved design for bicycle brake calipers much more easily using a model than using blue-prints or photographs. As you squeeze the brake handles, your client can quickly understand the effect on the calipers of your improved design. You can create this effect with computer-generated software, known as *virtual prototype design*. These computer-generated prototypes provide substantial cost benefits compared to designing real prototypes. The time, effort, and expense involved in building a real prototype is frequently quite substantial. Ask any inventor.

As an inventor, you also face unknown risks in each phase of development. Perhaps the design you've envisioned will be unwork-able or physically incompatible with another component. Another danger is the unpleasant prospect that the client absolutely insists on a feature that you overlooked. Or, just when you have finished three months of intensive problem-solving, a new material or technology is announced that promptly relegates your hard work to the obsolescent shelf. These are only a few of the unknown dangers that can force the inventor back to the drawing board.

Using a computer-generated prototype design in virtual reality, or a synthetic environment, cannot eliminate these risks, of course, but they are lessened. Because the computer can draw three-dimensional pictures quickly, you might develop a design concept in three hours instead of three months. Then, if you find that the design is unworkable or that you overlooked a feature, you can redesign changes quickly.

By now you should be starting to realize the extraordinary power we can unleash by using the computer and synthetic environments as tools to improve communication. As you explore the programs on the disk included with this book, think about the implications of being able to manipulate objects in the worlds provided.

Immersion

If you have tried scuba diving, you have experienced the shocking difference between looking down into the water while standing in a boat or on land, and looking around you while you are actually immersed in the water. Immersion is the quintessential ingredient of virtual reality.

We certainly take immersion for granted during our day-to-day lives. Think of the difference between watching a parade live and watching a parade on a TV screen. Because you are not at the parade, you can only see and hear the bands and floats at a distance; you are clearly not part of the picture. Watching the parade live is quite different. You can look in any direction you desire—you are actually immersed in the atmosphere and "world" of the parade, not merely watching it out a window.

To experience what may be called "true" virtual reality requires each and every one of the four basic concepts, but the feeling of being "inside" the pictures, or immersion, is the one that gets most of the popular attention. Immersion is often thought of as almost equivalent to the concept of virtual reality, because immersion is so fundamental to our existence.

To achieve an illusion of immersion in the computer-generated environment requires some method of putting pictures in front of your eyes so that your total view, no matter which direction you turn, encompasses only the virtual world. Your brain will do the rest of the work by creating the desired feeling that you are immersed.

The most common attempt to put pictures in front of your eyes is to rig up some sort of holder, like a helmet or goggles (see Figure 1.4 and Figure 1.5), with small screens in front of your eyes so the pictures are the only view you can see. A larger challenge is to actually surround your body with pictures—like being in a room

where the walls, ceiling, and floor are just pictures. Other methods are being considered, but the principle and the goal will remain the same: to provide a complete immersion experience for the virtual reality user.

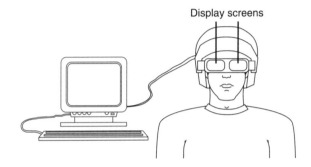

Display screens

Figure 1.4.

An illustration of a head-mounted display system.

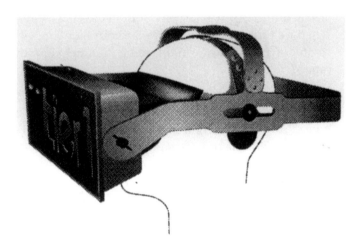

Figure 1.5.

A visor type of head-mounted display (the tier 1 visor).

But there is another dimension to immersion besides merely seeing the pictures displayed in front of your eyes. If you're walking down the sidewalk looking at the budding leaves on the trees in front of you and your neighbor calls out "Hi!" from behind you, you naturally turn around and wave—and you see a completely different scene. This is called rotating your viewpoint. As we all know, our perception of the world would be quite limited if we couldn't rotate our viewpoint.

19

When using a synthetic environment, signals must be sent to the computer's processor informing it of the position and orientation of your head. The most common device that accomplishes this is a *head-tracker*, which is attached to your head in some manner and transmits signals to the computer with every motion of your head. If you turn your head to the right, the head-tracker calculates the degrees of rotation and tells the computer how far your head has turned; the computer then calculates the required changes in the pictures it sends to your *head-mounted display* so that your eyes can see the appropriate view. Sounds complicated, doesn't it? It certainly is quite complicated—and we need to applaud the efforts of the developers of the equipment for their crucial role in helping to solve the knotty problems involved in this virtual reality technology.

While wearing the helmets and head-trackers, we become completely immersed. We have the illusion of being inside the pictures. When we turn our heads, we see the corresponding view of the environment. But how can this immersion help improve communication?

Right now, at this early stage in the development of virtual reality, the most impacted channel of communication is that between the human user and the computer. The head-tracker and head-mounted display are not the only means of communication between yourself and your virtual environment, but the other methods of indicating what you would like to see are slower and take more effort than turning your head. Typing instructions on the keyboard or clicking and dragging with the mouse are time-consuming and training-intensive actions. You have to learn what actions provide the desired results—and it can be quite irritating to wait for the results. Turning your head, however, is a natural and well-perfected motion for most people over the age of three months; it is almost instantaneous. Communication with the computer (and with ourselves) can be much more efficient with an immersive head-mounted display (HMD) and head-tracker.

NOTE: Displaying a VR program on the monitor, without an HMD, is called *desktop VR* or *window-on-world VR (WOW)*. WOW applications, like the ones on the disk with this book, are less encumbering, have better resolution, and are less expensive. WOW immersion refers to the location of the virtual viewer inside the world.

Virtual reality technology may soon provide us with improved communication between humans as well. Psychological research is starting to examine the potential benefits of immersive virtual reality experiences. If therapists can more effectively understand their patients by mutually entering an immersive environment that allows for better communication, or if people with disabilities can experience immersive activities that are physically impossible for them in the real world, then they will have a new tool to use for deeper understanding. It is actually difficult to think of a human activity that might not be impacted and influenced by virtual reality technology: training and development, sports, architecture, entertainment, science, medicine. What would you add to the list?

Summary

When you test the programs on the disk, keep in mind that you are not experiencing the full immersive effect. Full immersion requires appropriate software and access to an HMD and a head-tracker. But if you try and imagine what it would be like to be fully immersed, you may become inspired to help develop better immersive equipment. If you did, you would be joining quite a unique and exclusive group: the determined and persistent developers of VR technology, the subject of the next chapter.

Chapter 2

The Evolution of Virtual Reality

Now that we've looked at the key components underlying virtual reality, let's follow through the stages of its development. In this chapter, we look behind the flashy equipment and images usually associated with virtual reality and try to find out where VR came from. We also make acquaintances with a few of the visionaries and innovators who helped bring us this elusive and enigmatic ideal.

The Dream Is Primal and Prehistoric

There are at least two passionate dreams that probably have been shared by all members of the human species since the first cavemen (cavepeople? cavepersons?): the desire to fly like the birds, and the ability to transmit clear and accurate information.

If you were a caveman standing at the mouth of your cave, and you looked up and glimpsed the shape of a mountain lioness on the prowl headed towards your sister's family in the cave over in the next hill, you might get a little excited. While you are running along the path toward Sissy's cave, your adrenaline is pumping, your hands are waving, you're using every holler and whoop you've ever learned—and a couple you just invented. You are doing everything you can think of to gain the attention of Sissy and her family. But getting their attention is the easy part. What you really want to do is show them the picture in your mind of the shadowy shape you saw so they will realize the danger they are in. They've already realized that you are acting even more strangely than usual, but they're standing at the mouth of the cave looking bewildered.

You wish there was a better way to transmit the warning, but you can't flip open your skull, grab the picture in your mind, and display it in front of their noses. You can't run into their immaculate cave living room, seize the 'M' volume of the encyclopedia, and flip to the page with pictures of mountain lions. And it's certainly not possible to stop at the library and check out a mountain lion videotape to play for them on the VCR. There is only one avenue for you: all the grunting, yipping, shrieking, screeching, jumping up and down, and pointing that you are already performing so flawlessly.

And when the mountain lioness, irritated by the noise, pounces on your sister's male protector and drags him into the bushes while the rest of you throw stones and grunt "bad kitty" in cave language, it finally dawns on you that you need a new grunt to warn everyone of the approaching cat. The next time you see a dangerous mountain lioness in your sub-division, you can immediately turn towards each hill in the area and yell the new warning to everyone.

The burning wish for effective, speedy communication must have begun way back in the mists of time, before written records, before speech—even before the first cave dweller drew a line in the dirt to show the direction of the coming hunt. Many methods have been

invented and developed to better transmit information and meaning, including language, writing, and art.

But it was the advent of the computer that made virtual reality slowly become more and more feasible, although no one knew it until much later. Progress was slow because computers started out clunky, bulky, and blind. Many years often passed while the next step forward was being sought, shaped, and developed.

The Invention that Made It Possible

Imagine what it must have been like when the first room-sized computer, called ENIAC, was being painstakingly pieced together. If you are visualizing it as similar to the computers you're familiar with now, you have the wrong picture. There were no desktop monitors to display information. There were no keyboards to type instructions. There were no disk drives with blinking lights.

If you had been standing there in 1946, you would have seen a spectacularly large machine, but you would not have seen any monitors, drives, or keyboards. If you asked "Where's the keyboard?," the technicians would have stared at you, baffled by your question. They simply had never heard of a keyboard, because no keyboards had been invented yet. If you had said "You know, it's like the keys of a typewriter," the engineers would have laughed and scooted you out of the room, saying "You don't know what you're talking about; we have to plug these wires in."

As you were being escorted from the room swarming with intense technicians, you might have glimpsed the thousands of black wires and cables snaking around on the back wall of the ENIAC computer (see Figure 2.1). You might have even wondered how long it took to figure out where the wires should be plugged in—and what kind of genius could follow such a spaghetti trail. You probably would not have imagined, however, that the wires had to be changed frequently—but they did. Every single time they wanted the computer to do a different job, the engineers had to rearrange the wires.

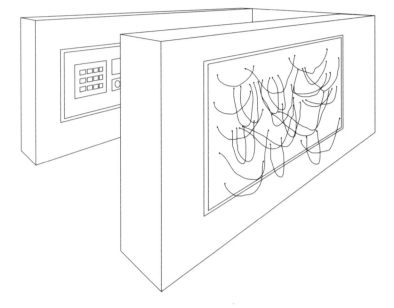

Figure 2.1.

*An illustration
of wires and
cables behind
the early
computers.*

Half a century later, it is difficult to realize how long it took the early computer developers to change the computer's instructions. It sometimes required many days to figure out which outlet each wire was supposed to be plugged into. Then they had to instruct dozens of technicians with diagrams: "Take Wire A from Outlet B and plug it into Outlet C, then take Wire B and...." Can you imagine the frustration of expending that amount of effort, only to have to start all over again when it didn't work—day after day?

The reason they kept doing it day after day is that they had no choice. Besides, there was another very important consideration. Even after spending all those hours and days programming the computer wire-by-wire, they still saved hours, weeks, and months of time. How? Because the computer, when hooked up correctly, calculated numbers much faster than humans. In fact, it could accomplish in one second what might have taken years for humans to complete.

It was incredible and exciting what the big dinosaur computer could do—and the time it could save. Sure, it was expensive—and it certainly required a lot of people and effort to make it work—but the return on the investment was awesome. You could start planning projects that were previously impossible. Many months might pass before you saw the results, and you would have to dig deep into your bank account, but the computer made it possible to make your idea bear fruit. It was a glorious new tool that happened to have a few serious drawbacks.

Looking back almost fifty years, it is tempting to believe at least a few people started planning small desk-size computers that show pictures, but such an idea was more ludicrous and unthinkable than baking a cake in the refrigerator. First, just the thought of "small" computers was silly. You might as well have asked if the ocean could be designed smaller so that it would fit into your bathtub. The computer had to be a big box so that the thousands of vacuum tubes, light bulbs, and electric switches would fit inside it. If there ever was a "dumb" question, "Can the computer be smaller?" would have taken top prize.

Second, suggesting that the computer show pictures would have resulted in a discussion of how to design a computer that can turn on a movie projector, and a bewildered question, "Why do you want this complicated and expensive computer to show movies?" Although the television had been invented before 1946, it was tiny and only in black and white (although color was "in the works")—it could only receive pictures taken by a camera. Computer technology was not yet ready to be small or show pictures. The concept of virtual reality was still about forty years in the future.

The fascinating story of those forty years includes the work of brilliant visionaries such as John von Neumann (see the related sidebar in this chapter) and Ivan Sutherland, and the progressive march of technology (and input and output devices) such as the teletype, keypunch machine, punchcards, tape recorder, television, computer monitor, keyboards, joysticks, and the mouse. Captivating though it may be, that story is the history of the computer. Our focus is the evolution of virtual reality, which, although born of the computer, is the story of a different family.

Although there were important people who earned their place in history for their work in the development of virtual reality, the driving force behind these VR pioneers was similar to, and branching from, the thrust propelling the advances in the development of the computer itself. For lack of a better name, we might refer to it as *the communication force*. It is the motivation that all sociable humans share: The desire to hear and be heard; the yearning to understand and be understood; the longing to transmit clear, accurate information and meaning.

The communication force does not restrict its impulse to humans, it is at work in all living creatures and in all life. The wolf lifting his howling praises to the moon is hoping to communicate certain meanings to all who are within earshot. The blinking firefly is transmitting a message to all receivers in the neighborhood. The pancreatic cell is busily cranking out enzymes to inform the body to produce insulin. Even the honeysuckle bush creates a few announcements of its own for the bees flying by.

But remember, communication has many facets. The wolf may be communicating to other wolves as well as other creatures with trembling ears, but it is also "talking" or communicating with itself. If we could translate the howl to English, it might sound like "I'm a strong, healthy wolf, and I feel good about myself." This message falls on the wolf's own ears and makes it feel stronger and healthier. In the recording industry, this is called *feedback*—caused by a microphone too close to its own speaker, resulting in a screech louder than the wolf can produce. But, for the wolf, receiving the feedback from its own howl helps make it more confident.

It is important to establish these manifestations of communication in order to achieve a better understanding of virtual reality. VR is not a mysterious psychic experience. Although the term "virtual reality" has generated frequent philosophical ramblings such as "What's real, what's virtual, and isn't all reality virtual?", its actual meaning is specific and concrete: using the computer and accessories to create simulations of human experience. And the purpose of virtual reality is to improve the effectiveness of all forms of communication: with the computer, with ourselves, and with other beings.

Improving Communication with the Computer

The progress of improving communication with the computer is a subplot of the story of the development of the computer for forty years (from 1946 to 1986). This is the part of the story that sheds the most light on the evolution of virtual reality. Communicating with ENIAC in the beginning was as inconvenient and laborious as speaking a sentence while waiting an hour between words. It was even worse at first, though, because, in a sense, the computer had to be re-taught the sentence each time it was started up. How much conversation could you endure with your two-year-old if you were forced to spend several hours each day teaching her the same single sentence she had been taught the day before? The situation was absolutely intolerable, and the only sane response was, of course, "There must be a better way!" But sanity was not of sufficient strength to overcome this inflexibility, or to find a better way. The battering-ram to crumble this wall was going to have to be a radically new idea from a crackerjack mind. A person with a brain so powerful that it could solve this problem would have to come along.

And, come along he did. A man whose reputation for mathematical ability was almost as well established as Albert Einstein's, and whose sharp mind worked so fast almost no one could keep up with his ideas, turned his attention to the computer problem. John von Neumann hit upon a solution that forever changed the computer industry: create a storage device in the computer's memory (not at all an easy task by itself, at the time) that holds the start-up instructions for the computer (the "sentence"). Wire the computer in such a way that it looks for the start-up instructions before it does anything else. Sure, it sounds simple now, but it was an enormous insight back then. This procedure of finding the start-up instructions when the power is turned on was nicknamed *bootstrapping* because of the analogy to "pulling yourself up by your bootstraps," which was quickly shortened to *booting*—as in "I'm booting the computer now." (And you thought it meant kicking the poor thing.)

John von Neumann

ohn von Neumann, a twentieth-century Hungarian-born mathematician, was responsible for the development of the stored-program (Read-Only Memory) concept. An architect of the first computer, von Neumann also impacted several other fields of research as far ranging as game theory and quantum mechanics.

Von Neumann, who earned his bachelor's degree in chemical engineering, is considered one of the last "generalists" among modern scientists. He did not begin his computer-related work until his last ten years of life, during which time he also served on the US Atomic Energy Commission.

John von Neumann brought about the first major improvement in communicating with the computer. After the "bootstrap" solution was implemented, it became considerably easier to "tell" the computer to do something different by simply changing the start-up instructions. The computer had no trouble finding the new instructions because it always looked in the same place. And, since the storage memory (now known as ROM—Read-Only Memory) had now been invented, copies of different instructions could be kept and quickly selected when needed. The large team of technicians was no longer needed to reprogram the computer each day. Communication with the computer is much more efficient when the computer has a memory that remembers start-up instructions.

Although no one knew it at the time, each successive advancement in communicating with the computer after the development of the storage memory became another stepping stone towards virtual reality.

Imagine the excitement and relief exhibited when a teletype was hooked up to the shrinking computer—and the plug-in wires and cables were no longer necessary. This excitement and relief must have only grown with another advancement: the famous punch cards—which warned "Do Not Fold, Spindle, or Mutilate." Although the punch cards seem terribly old-fashioned and antiquated now, the improvement in communicating with the computer was great; the punch cards allowed quick and flexible data entry into the computer. But it was the next step, the television, that finally gave the computer a visual component—moving the computer within reach of virtual reality.

By connecting the computer (which by now was only the size of several cabinets) to a monitor, it became possible to show pictures on the surface of the flat, two-dimensional screen. Although it required much time and effort to actually make a picture appear, the television made possible what was previously impossible. Using the monitor and the keyboard together made it feasible to type instructions and read the instructions while typing them. Communicating became much more efficient when you could "talk" to the computer at the same time you "talked" to yourself.

But, the grumbling and complaining started once more. Computer users started criticizing the "slowness" and "difficulty" of typing instructions to the computer. "There must be a better way" came to be heard frequently, again. Knowing that the customer is always right, an invention was introduced that was so natural and easy to use that it made communicating with the computer almost instantaneous. Because it had a wire attached to it that looked like a tail, it was quickly dubbed a mouse. By using it in conjunction with new software programs that made the mouse function, a user could simply point to a selected area of the screen and "click" the mouse button; the instructions were immediately transmitted to the computer. Ah, the ease of "talking" with the computer now. Who could want more? Communication with the computer is very efficient when you have a mouse (except when you want to do something that isn't listed on the screen—then you have to type again).

The User-Friendly GUI

There's a fancy term that refers to special programs, or software, that have mouse control options. Because the software usually has pictures, or graphics, on-screen, such a mouse-driven application is called a *Graphical User Interface,* or *GUI* ("gooey") for short (see Figure 2.2). The choice of the word "interface" is interesting. In geometry, an interface (a "face between") is a surface that forms the common boundary between two solids or spaces. You could call a wall between two rooms an interface, because it faces both rooms. A user's interface on the computer, then, is a device or method that permits communication in two ways—to the computer, and back to

the user. The computer "tells," or shows, the pertinent information to the user, and the user "tells" the computer what to do by selecting the desired activity with the mouse.

The word "interface" is effective due to its connotation of "two-way" (no, not two-faced). Thus, a Graphical User Interface is an interface that incorporates graphics, or pictures, to help communicate in both directions. See how close we are to approaching virtual reality?

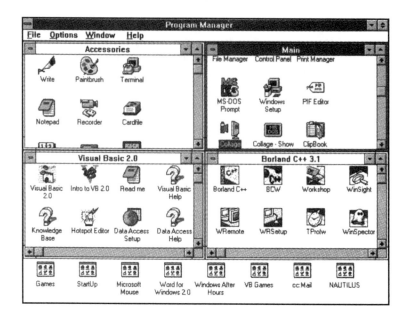

Figure 2.2.

A GUI—the Microsoft Windows Program Manager.

A GUI uses pictures to make communication between the computer and the user more efficient. By moving the mouse with normal human movements, the user controls the on-screen pointer. When you move the mouse to the right, for example, the on-screen pointer moves in the same direction.

Consequently, a GUI begins to empower three of the basic concepts of VR: a limited means of natural navigation (in two dimensions), a form of manipulating (activating) objects, and the utilization of pictures (2-D). Of course, the viewpoint is present because it is always associated with the user, or viewer. It is becoming clearer that the functional foundation for virtual reality evolved step-by-step, and should not be perceived as a technology that suddenly sprang up overnight.

People with Early Visions of Virtual Reality

The people involved in the evolution of virtual reality would certainly agree that the technology did not spontaneously appear any more than did the Pyramids of Egypt. But let's recognize our perspective—we can't look back through time and pinpoint weavers who knowingly developed a pattern in the way that the builders of the pyramids planned their undertaking. The early builders of VR did not think "I want to develop virtual reality." They had never even heard the expression. It's hard to pin down the first use of the term VR, but most sources concur that it was in the late 1980s. Even the term "artificial reality" wasn't used in the beginning.

But where is the beginning? Do we start with the cave-painters who transmitted information with pictures instead of words and hand gestures? Should we describe the early ideas from authors like Aldous Huxley, with his descriptions of "feelies" in *Brave New World,* or from Ray Bradbury, with his vivid description of children communicating directly with machines in *The Veldt*?

Should we include everyone who has awakened with wispy memories of dreams and nightmares that seem so *real* and are so emotionally moving and provoking? And who isn't caught up in the wonder and fascination of listening to another person's strange dreams and nightmares? The evolution of the human brain is assuredly the foundation of the evolution of virtual reality. Human nature has driven our rapid advancements in technology: The more we know about something, the more curious we become.

Perhaps we should start in the 1880s with Charles Babbage who envisioned what can be called the world's first computer, although it was never built because the materials did not exist that could accomplish what his mind dreamed up. He tried to build his "Difference Engine" out of wood and metal. Can you imagine a wooden calculating machine?

But why not start with the abacus or the slide rule? In fact, what is so important about a calculating apparatus in the first place? Why doesn't the camera or the stereoscope mark the starting line for the changes that led to virtual reality? After all, the essence of VR is the visual effect, isn't it?

These questions and others like them are actually impossible to answer. We may as well philosophize about the essence and nature of humanness. Is it our heart, our brain, or our speech that comprises the significance of being "human"? Of course, the arguments could rage without conclusion. But, if we agree on one thing, it might be that the brain, being the control center, is one of the most crucial components. That's why the computer, being a fast calculating machine and a superlative control center, is central to our discussion of virtual reality. Therefore, the people who contributed to making a computer work deserve our study of their contributions and our awareness of the effort they expended and the breakthroughs they achieved.

But let's swing our binoculars around, away from the computer, and focus on some of the people who, although they might not have foreseen virtual reality, conceived and contemplated new ways of using emerging technologies.

Douglas Engelbart might have been the first person who, in 1950, actually pictured in his mind a scenario that, when described, sounds eerily similar to what we now see all around us—computers helping people solve problems and creating more effective communication. An earlier alert to coming changes was flagged by Vannevar Bush in 1945. To understand the significance of Engelbart's vision, you must realize that he wrote of small computers that displayed output on monitors and made it possible for people to learn and communicate in new ways. He wrote this in 1950—before computers even had monitors. This idea was so radical and so strange he might as well have suggested that holding the sun in your hand would add two hundred years to your life. It's difficult, now, to realize how crazy he must have sounded. No one paid any attention to his ideas because computers were those huge boxes that had wires falling out all over. People weren't ready for such a large paradigm shift. They couldn't understand the computer as it existed, much less the computer as it might be.

About seven years later, another person started to think similar thoughts. J.C.R. Licklider, a scientist who studied human hearing, began to wonder how he could save time in his work and deal with all the information and numbers he was required to handle. His work involved taking a great number of measurements, and plotting

and analyzing the results. He graphed the results of his measurements and then compared the shape of the line with other lines calculated by mathematics in an attempt to figure out which formula best matched his measurements. This is called *modeling*. Licklider did an enormous amount of measuring, graphing, and modeling. You can imagine how long it took to do all these steps.

Licklider wanted to spend less time graphing and more time finding ways to understand the graphs. He started to think about whether computers could allow him to do interactive modeling, where the computer would use the numbers from his measurements and quickly draw the lines and the mathematical models. By this time, computers had improved quite a bit: they were smaller and easier to work with, although they were still the size of a big refrigerator, and you "talked" to them with punched tape.

By 1960, Licklider had written an essay titled "Man-Computer Symbiosis," in which he reached a prediction parallel to Englebart: Computers and people would work together in new ways and communicate more effectively. He even hypothesized that the human brain and the computer would be connected in new ways, or "coupled together very tightly," to accomplish far greater results.

Licklider was a prophet who was in a position to get people to listen to him, unlike Englebart. He was able to convince an agency in the military that finding better ways to communicate with the computer would lead to improved control and management of information. He described the possible use of keyboards and television screens in communicating information. He was put in charge of an office that funded the development of interactive computing—and led to the desktop computers we have today.

While this office, the Information Processing Techniques Office (IPTO), was funding many of the technological advances that made interactive computing possible, it was also the breeding-ground for the work of an ingenious young man by the name of Ivan Sutherland, who has been called "the father of computer graphics." By 1965, Sutherland had built the first piece of equipment that sparked the beginnings of the concept of immersion: the head-mounted display that put pictures in front of the eyes. But even before that, he had built the first interactive computer screen that showed visual images, called "Sketchpad." The concepts

derived from Sketchpad eventually led to the development of Computer Aided Design (CAD) programs on later computers.

Licklider was also responsible for bringing another visionary into the development of interactive computing, the person whom no-one would listen to fourteen years earlier: Douglas Englebart. Licklider and IPTO endowed Engelbart with the money and equipment necessary to put his ideas, written on paper for so many years, into reality. By 1968, Engelbart and his team of scientists were able to demonstrate a version of a computer system that showed how word-processing could work—and he even used a mouse. This system showed how it was possible to control information and communication in new ways, just as he had imagined eighteen years earlier in 1950.

There was another person who tried to look far into the future at a very early time. In 1955 he wrote a description of an idea he called an "Experience Theater." He even received a patent for a head-mounted display in 1960 that was based on television technology. But Morton Heilig's thoughts were involved with video and movie technology, not computers. He wanted to provide an experience that surrounded you with sensory simulations so you would feel like you were there. In 1962, Heilig built a cubicle called *Sensorama* that created a virtual reality based on driving a motor-cycle through city streets. You could hear the sounds of the engine, feel vibrations, and experience the ride. He even included smells that would emanate from vents at just the right moment. But the Sensorama concept was not successful. Potential investors could not be convinced in the 1960s that Heilig's creation could be a winner—primarily because the cubicle couldn't stand the abusive environment of the Times Square pinball arcade in which it was installed. So the inventive genius of Morton Heilig did not result in video virtual reality, which, if it had, might have changed the direction of technology in ways we can't know.

Myron Krueger, who invented the term "Artificial Reality" in 1970, had a larger vision about virtual reality than the head-mounted display. His new ways of hooking up video technology with computer technology gained more success than Heilig's Sensorama. He wanted to immerse a person in a virtual reality room that displayed pictures on the walls, ceiling, and floor. The video equipment

projected the pictures, and the computer equipment activated responses to what the person did in the room. In 1969, the year after Englebart demonstrated the interactive information system, Krueger demonstrated a responsive environment to the public in Madison, Wisconsin. It was called GLOWFLOW, and it set up an artificial reality that reacted to the weight of people standing on the floor by changing the pictures on the walls all around. The interesting part of the puzzle was that the people did not know that their own weight was causing the reactions on the walls. So, as they walked around, the pictures and lights in the environment changed, but they did not realize that they were controlling the changes. It was exciting and different from any other experience. As the participants began to figure out that they were controlling the changes, Krueger monitored their reactions and interactions.

Since then, Krueger developed several other responsive environments, such as METAPLAY, PSYCHIC SPACE, VIDEO PLACE, and CRITTER PLACE. By watching the reactions of the human players and the interactions that resulted, Krueger was able to discover, examine, and experiment with the psychological implications of responsive artificial reality crucial to the continuing progress of improving communication between humans and computers. Krueger has played a key role in exploring many VR issues during the last twenty-five years.

While some of the early VR visionaries, like Engelbart and Heilig, were isolated pioneers and poorly funded at times, other leaders, like Licklider, had the necessary funding, equipment, and personnel. One of the most important leaders was Frederick Brooks, who / worked for IBM before taking a position at the University of North Carolina at Chapel Hill that allowed him to start building an exceptional and renowned team of VR pioneers in the late 1960s. Brooks was a confidence-building leader who created an atmosphere that cultivated and challenged the best in people. His researchers have been involved in some of the most advanced VR research in the medical and chemistry fields.

One of the most important contributors to the development of head-mounted displays and associated computer graphics in the last fifteen years is Henry Fuchs, another UNC team member, who studied under Alan Kay—who was inspired by Ivan Sutherland's

original work. Henry Fuchs has tackled some of the most difficult problems involved in making the pictures in head-mounted displays respond quick enough to a person's head motions, such as improving the lag-time and the calculation speed. *Lag-time* refers to the phenomenon in which you move your head and there is a delay while the pictures in your display "catch-up" to where your head is oriented. A great number of factors affect the amount of lag-time, such as how sharp and clear the pictures are, the speed of the computer that is drawing the pictures, and the number of objects within the virtual environment.

Another team member at UNC, Warren Robinett, was previously with NASA. Robinett started programming in the late 1970s and wrote one of Atari's best-selling game programs when the total amount of computer memory available was only four thousand (4K) bytes. That's about the amount of information in a one-page letter. It takes extraordinary programming skill to squeeze an entire game into such a small space.

Together with Fuchs, Robinett, and dozens of other people with expertise in various areas, Brooks led the attack on medical-imaging applications that allow doctors to use VR to train other doctors in learning procedures for operating on the three-dimensional human patient with more precision and understanding. One of the ways to do this was to make the display transparent, so the doctors could see the patient and the computer pictures at the same time. This type of transparent display is called an *overlay,* in which you lay one kind of information over another. The communication efficiency of this virtual reality application is rather obvious.

Another major application with far-reaching consequences is the work done by Brooks' team regarding chemical molecules. Using virtual reality, they were able to generate "pictures" of atoms as if they were as big as balloons, and then you can design entire molecules containing these big atoms, and display the molecules on the headset. As you navigate your viewpoint, you can see the relationships between the atoms and the connections, or bonds, between them. Brooks' team has been able to add another feature to this capability. They have hooked up a manipulating arm allowing them to move the atoms around in the virtual environment—and the atoms are programmed to respond like real atoms. Then, when an

atom meets a force-field from another atom in the environment, the manipulating arm is programmed to resist the motion. This is called *force feedback;* it really helps when the scientist seems to "feel" the forces between the atoms. For chemical companies and drug companies that need to modify molecules, this is a very useful way of communicating. With force feedback, a scientist can move an atom around until he finds a place where it "docks" in the molecule correctly, and thus design new drugs and chemicals more quickly and more precisely.

The Role of the Military and NASA in Developing Virtual Reality

When computers cost millions of dollars, research budgets are substantial, and you want to build a technology as broad-ranging as virtual reality, who are you going to call? Not the Ghostbusters. You have to call on a source with enough money to pay for it all, as well as a need for the potential application that results. One source with the money and the need would be a government that is building a sophisticated military and a complex space program, like the United States government.

Sometimes a well-timed event will ignite an explosion of activity more quickly than otherwise. In the evolution of virtual reality, the instigating event didn't happen in America. It happened in Russia, where an announcement was made in October, 1957, that shocked the United States and brought about many changes in our perceptions of the world—big changes in American education and science, and blockbuster changes in the military and space programs. The announcement was that Sputnik 1, a Soviet satellite, had been launched and was successfully orbiting earth. The galvanizing impact of this statement on the population and leaders of the Western world is hard for us to grasp thirty-five years later if we didn't live through it. But it's very clear what was spawned in response: The struggle to catch up with Russia was started. One massive program that directly affected the future of virtual reality was the Advanced Research Projects Agency, called ARPA.

Earlier, we mentioned J.C.R. Licklider's military funding. That funding came from ARPA—and we have seen how that funding led to the kind of interactive computing that has revolutionized lifestyles, careers, business functions, and many other fields and interests all over the world. In addition, the technology of virtual reality has uses in the military itself. The army, for instance, employs sophisticated VR in tank simulators to train soldiers for combat (see Figure 2.3). The "tanks" are actually rooms designed to look like the interior of a tank, often times miles apart connected by computer networks, and the soldiers follow procedures that simulate actual combat. Instead of windows, the tank simulator has window-sized monitors that project computer-generated pictures duplicating the view of the terrain that would normally be seen during fighting. The sounds of firing and tank engines are reproduced, and the perception is quite similar to real combat experience—with all the pressure of sergeants barking orders in your earphones, penalties being assigned for mistakes, and shells exploding all around. It is almost as grueling and nerve-racking as real combat. But, valuable soldiers and personnel are unharmed, and no expensive tanks are damaged.

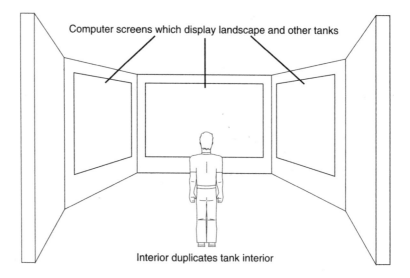

Computer screens which display landscape and other tanks

Interior duplicates tank interior

Figure 2.3.

Illustration of a Tank Simulator.

If you are a pilot in the Air Force, you can expect to use VR in equally realistic ways. After you return from a sortie in which you shot down enemy aircraft, you might be asked to put on a VR

headset and "fly" back to where the mission occurred and repeat the incident in VR. Your VR flight would be monitored by your superior who would gain a more accurate understanding of exactly what took place.

Because of the military's ability to pay large amounts of money to get what it needed, the first person to actually try out the first complete, fully operational virtual reality system was in the military: Thomas Furness III, the director of the United States Air Force's center for research on VR. Furness later became director of the Human Interface Technology Laboratory (HIT Lab) at the University of Washington, which is funded by a consortium of large companies, such as the Boeing Company and Microsoft Corporation.

One of the projects at HIT Lab is a VR simulation environment of the Port of Seattle that is used to develop plans for changing the harbor and the docks. The management of the Port of Seattle came to HIT Lab with a problem: the difficulty of communicating between people from different countries with varied languages regarding such decisions as where to put the docks, how big to make them for the ships, and so on.

In the VR environment, you can simply point to a forty-foot wide dock, and the other person, who might speak in Japanese, can immediately shake his head and gesture with his hands further apart, and then nod happily when the virtual dock is expanded to sixty feet in width. Compared to using blueprints and drawing tools, the VR tool is much easier to communicate with and simulate concepts with. Dr. Furness' experience in the military certainly was helpful in establishing the important role of the HIT Lab in VR development.

In addition to military uses of VR, personnel in the space exploration program at the National Aeronautics and Space Administration (NASA) realized they could use the benefits of VR as well, which was the driving force for some of the cost breakthroughs in VR research. Because NASA didn't have access to as much money as the military, they had to choose lower cost components. Plus, because they are more open to the public than the military, a wider range of visitors came to try out the new virtual reality equipment.

The crucial role that NASA has performed in revealing a path towards more affordable VR, and in showing that path to larger numbers of people, should not be underestimated. Remember, the military developments in VR were extremely expensive, and the university research laboratory VR equipment was accessible to few people. This is yet another example of the technological advances originated by the United States space program that have impacted our everyday lives.

The Role of Telepresence

Beyond the contributions of NASA in improving the accessibility of VR to more people, there is also a fascinating idea in which the space researchers at NASA are very interested. The concept is *telepresence* (see Figure 2.4), and it represents a remarkable offshoot from virtual reality capabilities. Telepresence refers to the ability to "be present from a distance" (the Greek word "tele" means "far," so television, telephone, and telegraph mean to have vision, sounds, and "writing" from afar—communication from a distance). Even though telepresence sounds like you're "having an out-of-body experience," it does not mean that. The goal of telepresence is to find ways to connect your senses to a machine in a different place and perceive the other place as if you were there. Another "virtual" existence, you might say.

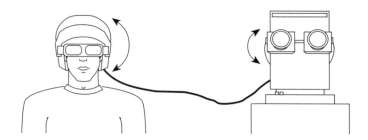

Figure 2.4.

An illustration of a telepresence machine.

Telepresence might sound a little confusing to you now, but it is really fairly straightforward once it is described. Imagine creating a machine that has two video cameras placed side-by-side, the same distance apart that your eyes are. Let's visualize a beach scene where the machine is placed on the sand facing the ocean waves. On the

left is the lifeguard's chair, and on the right is the cabin you've rented for the week. You'd have to make sure the cameras on the machine can swivel back and forth like your eyes do when you look left and right, and also have the ability to move up and down, like you can.

You then connect the cameras so the pictures taken with the cameras are sent to the head-mounted display you would place on your head, so that the images from the left-hand camera would show on the display screen in front of your left eye, and the images from the right-hand camera would be displayed in front of your right eye. If you do it right, you would see everything the cameras are pointed at. If you told your friend to move the cameras to the left, you would see the lifeguard suddenly standing up and blowing his whistle at a swimmer moving out too far from shore. As your friend pointed the cameras forward, you would see the fool sputtering as a big wave hit him. Finally, as the cameras were pushed further to the right, you would see the ocean waves splash on the rocks in front of your resort cabin, where your wife is waving at— you? or the lifeguard?

You then remember: you're not there. You have just experienced the power of telepresence. Your dear wife merely saw a machine with two video cameras, and, of course, waved at the lifeguard. It doesn't matter where you are—you could be in the kitchen or living room of the cabin, or you could have been hundreds of miles away in Alaska. With telepresence, you can be anywhere you want and be anywhere else you want—at the same time. We won't ask why you're in Alaska while your wife is at the beach waving at the lifeguard.

But making arrangements with your friend to accompany the machine and turn the cameras for you could become a burden after awhile. Let's go back to the beach and improve your telepresence experience. We've checked out the cameras and they work fine. Now, let's hook up another connection.

Let's design a sensor that attaches to your head-mounted display. The sensor detects any motion you make with your head—and transmits the movement information to the cameras. If you rotate your head to the left, the sensor will compare that rotation with the

original orientation and "tell" the cameras the number of degrees they should rotate. The cameras will then rotate to the left the appropriate number of degrees, and you will see the lifeguard again. Your friend will no longer have to turn the cameras, and can go visit your wife in the cabin and celebrate. But you can turn your head to the right and watch your friend walk towards the cabin.

This is the point where you will suddenly invent a telepresence machine, or robot, with speakers on it, so you can say "Where are you going, Bart?" And Bart can jump with surprise and stutter "Uh, I'm going to get those pliers we need in the car. Be right back."

Of course, as far as we know, NASA is not interested in telepresence to look up and down a beach. The people at NASA want to have telepresence technology to do things that are difficult or expensive for astronauts and scientists to accomplish. For instance, if a person at Houston Control could wear an HMD and gloves that were connected to a robot in a space station, then the control engineer could see what the robot "sees." If the gloves were hooked up, or "coupled," to the robot's mechanical arms and grasping devices to allow the control engineer to "steer" the robot's arms and hands, then the engineer might be able to repair the space station without actually being on the space station. Because it costs about fifty thousand dollars per hour while a real live astronaut is doing EVA (extra-vehicular activity) work, the development of telepresence technology is likely to be a cost effective investment.

If you think telepresence capability is far off in the future, you'll be interested to learn that, in November 1992, NASA placed a small submarine with two video cameras into the ocean near Antarctica with the purpose of letting the submarine explore under the ice. One of the control engineers was actually in Houston, Texas wearing a head-mounted display.

NASA Meets "The Guru of Virtual Reality"

The beginning of the VR effort at NASA that eventually led to this submarine expedition was in the mid-1980s when Walter McGreevy and Scott Fisher, of NASA, contacted VPL Research, Inc. This was the beginning of a long and fruitful relationship between VPL and NASA. See the sidebar on VPL's co-founders Jaron Lanier and

Thomas Zimmerman for more information on these VR pioneers.

VPL Research's first product, the DataGlove, was improved through its work with NASA. VPL also developed a head-mounted display, called EyePhones, that used special optical lenses (described in detail in Chapter 5), called the LEEP system. The lenses for EyePhones were invented by a brilliant optics engineer named Eric Howlett.

VPL Research's virtual reality equipment—the EyePhones, the DataGlove, and the corresponding Body Electric software—became the dominant market leader for NASA and many other research laboratories.

It would be more satisfying if this chapter could end here, with the giant figure of Jaron Lanier intoning "virtual reality" for the first time, but there is a historical footnote that, sadly, must be mentioned. In December 1992, VPL Research was restructured due to a management crisis, and most of the employees—including Lanier—were forced out. Unfortunately, according to the *Wall Street Journal*, VPL had borrowed a large amount of money by using the value of about 20 patents as collateral. When a cash shortage resulted in a default on the loans, the lender ended up with the patents, and, shocking though it was

Jaron Lanier and Thomas Zimmerman

aron Lanier is often the first person people think of when they hear the term "Virtual Reality." Lanier and his friend Thomas Zimmerman co-founded VPL Research, the market leader in research and production of VR technology.

Inspired by his desire to play music on a guitar without an actual guitar, Zimmerman had figured out a way to make a wired glove interact with his computer. He accomplished this by making the computer play the guitar notes while he moved his fingers in a guitar-playing fashion. Lanier, an accomplished musician as well as a successful computer programmer, was excited and intrigued by the possibilities of controlling the computer with natural gestures.

Lanier and Zimmerman started VPL Research together, but Zimmerman later left and assigned his glove patent to Lanier. VPL Research was the first company to sell VR equipment, and its DataGlove underwent improvements—most notably through VPL's teamwork with NASA.

Lanier is unconventional in many ways, and it is Lanier who is credited, by Myron Krueger (the one who coined the phrase "artificial reality" in 1970) and others, with coining the term "virtual reality" in 1989. Lanier attracted a great deal of attention since starting VPL, and a large number of articles have been written about him.

to the VR industry, VPL Research was no longer Lanier's company. As of this writing, it is not known how the patent issue will be resolved.

Where Does the Path Lead Next?

As the English say when a monarch passes away, "The King is dead, long live the King." The previously dominant company, VPL, will naturally be replaced with another leading company in the industry, unless VPL resuscitates itself and regains its position. There are fresh faces in younger start-up companies with vigor and creativity who will vie for the top spot as they roll out new and improved advancements. Some of these candidates make the products and programs we will investigate in the next chapter, in which we take an in-depth look at what is available now and how these products relate to our senses.

Chapter 3

The State of Virtual Reality

The art and science of virtual reality is now moving into a different and excitingly new phase. Perhaps historians will call this period "VR—Phase II." The beginning of the first phase could be marked by the appearance of Ivan Sutherland's Sketch-Pad in 1965. The sign of the end of phase one might be the disappearance of Jaron Lanier from VPL Research, Inc., at the end of 1992. These twenty-seven years can be described as the infancy of VR; the time when the equipment was first prototyped, tested, and experimented with. The newborn concept of virtual reality was taking its first struggling breaths and opening its eyes. It needed nourishment and tender care from committed "parents." No one knew if it would live, how long it would live, or what it would "do" when it grew up. It was a time when equipment was bulky, primitive, and feeble in its capacity to simulate the real world.

Phase II will be the time when VR begins to show signs of purposeful development, when some muscles begin to show, and when the toddler takes several steps. VR is now at the point where it begins to walk on its own; people all over the world are trying to influence the direction it will take as it enters its adolescent years.

What's Happening Now?

This new technology of communication and interaction is starting to develop a clear identity. VR equipment developed in Phase II is expected to become smaller, more affordable, and render more realistic simulations. The software is becoming more accessible, easier to use, and more realistic. Many new people will probably become familiar with virtual reality during its second phase.

Just think how much the costs of VR equipment have already spiralled downwards. From the multi-million dollar military VR systems, to the hundred thousand dollar VPL systems, to the ten thousand dollar Sense8 systems (described later), to the eighty-nine dollar authoring program (called Virtual Reality Studio, which can be operated on a five-hundred dollar standard personal computer), we have seen the cost curve plummet over the last decade. Of course, VR Studio (see Figure 3.1), for $89.00, does not include an immersive experience with a head-mounted display and the manipulations of objects with gloves, but it clearly shows what direction VR is headed towards: lower cost and WOW usage.

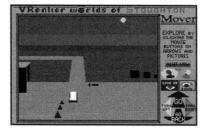

Figure 3.1.

Screen capture of a program created with VR Studio.

Another example is the glove. The DataGlove, invented by Thomas Zimmerman, was first sold by VPL Research for about ten thousand dollars. In 1989, Abrams Gentile Entertainment and Mattel created the PowerGlove, which was designed for the Nintendo game

machine and retailed for $99.00. About one million gloves were sold the first three years. Although it is no longer manufactured, the PowerGlove was the first VR toy. Some PowerGloves are still found now and then on toy store shelves for about twenty or thirty dollars, so if you search diligently you might still find one. These gloves can be connected to other computers such as the Amiga and the Macintosh, as well as the PC.

As faster and more powerful computers and software tools have become more affordable, the accessibility to virtual reality tools has grown beyond the research labs to include a wider audience and greater numbers of designers and developers. This increasing accessibility is resulting in an explosion of new ideas, inventions, and challenging issues that must be addressed. Because VR is an ✓ interactive communication technology that generates, modifies, responds to, and affects the perceptions of human senses, it requires the collective expertise of people trained in almost every field of human endeavor. Artists, scientists, psychologists, educators, technicians, engineers, and people in many other fields are grappling with the implications, problems, and challenges of virtual reality.

Interacting with the Senses

Let's focus on the subject of human senses and perceptions, and look at the current approaches to the thorny problems encountered when attempting to simulate sensory perceptions. Our discussion to this point has been mostly limited to the visual sense: the eyes. Of course, the visual display—whether in a head-mount, projected on the walls, or in a future method not yet invented—is crucial in an immersive, full-featured virtual reality experience. But the human body has several other senses. A full-fledged system that immersively simulates reality must include as many senses as possible, to fully create the illusion that we're "there." Because the intended scope of this book does not include a philosophical treatise on the meaning of "reality," our discussion on simulating reality is limited to the intricacies of simulating our senses.

David Mitchell, operator of the Diaspar VR Network (see Appendix B), has pointed out that there are actually eight senses we can identify—not just the five we normally think of. The eight senses

on Mitchell's list are sight, sound, touch, balance, smell, taste, pheromonal, and immunological. The three senses added to the common five are balance, pheromonal, and immunological. Pheromones are chemical messages we transmit through means similar to smell; immune sensors and transmitters seem to be located in the skin and other tissues. On what basis can we talk about eight senses, rather than five? Mitchell addresses this question in the related sidebar.

An Excerpt From...

Diaspar VR Network

... overwhelming scientific evidence supports specific organs and neural nets around these [balance, pheromonal, and immunological] organs. Any real long term virtual reality endeavors must take into account all human senses.... In summary: balance is both sensed by portions of the ear and by relative muscle tension for neural position extrapolation; pheromonal communications occur using various scent glands for transmission and olfactory lobes (physically separate from those used for common smell) for reception; and tonsils, lymph nodes and hemorrhoidal tissue all seem to act as immunological sensors with histamine reactions in the skin and mucous linings as transmitters. Full exploration of virtual reality for advanced social and biomedical study, therapy and treatment must take these communications systems into account.*

As if the challenge of simulating the obvious five senses isn't difficult enough, Mitchell suggests the need for three more, and goes even further by pointing out another potential feature in a VR system: "In emergency aid telepresence, for example, infrared vision for spotting hot spots in a fire might aid fire-fighters." A face mask display system that uses ultrasonic techniques to produce a visual display has already been developed and patented. It is used by firefighters in heavy smoke and scuba divers in murky waters.

As you can see, the description of telepresence in Chapter 2 (the story about a person coupled with a machine or robot that

---

*Diaspar VR Network, September 3, 1992.
Excerpted with permission by David Mitchell.
(See listing of BBS number in Appendix B)

transmits images of a scene far away) can be broadened to include perceptions that are not normally accessible to us, like infrared frequencies in the electromagnetic spectrum. In other words, suppose you were a firefighter with an infrared-capable telepresence robot designed to enter the blazing building. You could don your head-mount display and safely search for trapped workers by controlling the robot. The robot would transmit pictures to your display through video cameras, and the infrared sensors would "overlay" on the display the "shapes" of the heat emitted from the building. You would "see" where the hot spots were by simply turning your head left and right, while the robot propelled itself, under your control, through the building. The military has used sophisticated night-vision goggles, which enable soldiers to "see" during nighttime excursions, for several years.

The Sense of Sound

Let's return to the five human senses with which we are commonly familiar. Sound, for example, involves intricate relationships that become increasingly formidable as research and analysis are carried out to find ways to simulate the human perception of sound in virtual reality systems.

Consider what happens when you are eating breakfast in the kitchen (in the real world) and you hear a distressed "Meow." At first, your brain signals an alert as you turn your head in response to the unusual sound in the environment. As your head starts to swivel around, and your eyes move in the direction of the sound, you think "What's going on? We don't have a cat!" As several moments pass, and the memory of the sound fades, your brain tries to determine from what direction and distance the sound came from. "Did I really hear a meow? Yes, I really think I did. Was the sound from the living room, or from the basement? Is there a cat stuck in the cabinet?" Then, another anguished but weak "Meeeooowww" reaches your ear canals and agitates your eardrums. Thus armed with additional information, your brain constructs a hypothesis and prompts you to look out the window where your eyes locate a kitten stuck on a branch high upon a nearby tree.

The key concept in the above scenario was determining the direction of the sound. Our ears receive sound in such a way that the brain can then obtain enough information from the sound to ascertain the direction of the source of the sound in the three-dimensional space all around us. Part of this is due to the fact that we have not just one eardrum, but two, and another major reason is the shape of the outside ears (the "pinnae") themselves.

The information received by the brain from two eardrums (actually, the inner ear), instead of just one, is necessary for the determination of direction. See the diagram in Figure 3.2. The brain calculates the time difference between when the sound wave hits the first eardrum and when it hits the second eardrum. That is probably one reason why ears evolved on opposite sides of the head: If both ears were on one side of your head, sound waves would hit both ears at the same time and your brain wouldn't be able to figure out the calculation needed for direction. With your ears located at the maximum possible distance from one another, your brain doesn't have to work quite as hard to get its bearings. In addition, more assistance is provided to your brain by the particular shape of your ears.

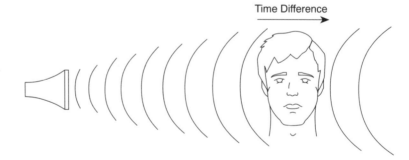

Figure 3.2.

Illustration of sound wave acoustics.

Now, if your goal was to simulate this three-dimensional sound capability that's built into your body, what would you do? If you gathered together all of your electronic sound equipment and fashioned a pair of headphones, you would discover an annoying, even frustrating, problem as soon as you started testing. Once you've placed the sound sources on each ear, you notice that the brain perceives the sound as coming from inside your head. If you lower the sound volume in your right ear, your mind perceives the

sound as being located in the left side of your head. If you play tones at equal volume in both ears, your mind perceives the sounds as if they were situated in the middle of your head.

When Elizabeth Wenzel, a perceptual psychologist, Scott Foster, president of Crystal River Engineering, and Dr. Frederick Wightman, a sound researcher at the University of Wisconsin, began to look for ways to make 3-D sound for virtual reality systems at NASA, they knew they were facing the difficulties outlined above—but they had an idea for a solution. They fabricated tiny microphones that were placed inside the ear canals near the eardrums of research subjects. They then set up dozens of speakers all around the subjects and meticulously recorded the sounds from one speaker at a time.

This procedure provided a recording of what the ear actually hears from different locations. They then had to calculate the complex math functions necessary for the computer to reproduce the sounds matching what the ear hears. They discovered that each person's ear shape changes what that person hears. If you listen to a recording made from microphones in your own ears, you will perceive the direction of each sound exactly the same as when it was recording, but if you listen to a recording made from the microphones in another person's ears, you will make varying mistakes in determining the location of the sounds. Because a fast computer is able to quickly calculate complicated math, the sounds in a virtual reality system can be adjusted to approximate the shape of a person's ears.

The Convolvotron

The result of this sound research is a device called the *Convolvotron* (*convolve* means to coil, spin, or twist). The Convolvotron—invented by Wenzel, Foster, and Wightman—is a large collection of computer chips, located on a board inside the computer, that process the sound signals transmitted to the headset accompanying a virtual reality system.

When I first phoned Dr. Wightman after discovering he worked nearby, he informed me that, after trying to develop 3-D sound capability for about twenty-five years, he had just received his

Convolvotron. I accepted his invitation to test the Convolvotron, and found that it truly does represent 3-D sounds—but you have to get used to it.

Dr. Wightman does not use his Convolvotron in a virtual reality system. He uses it to do research on the technical aspects of the psychological perception of sounds. His subjects sit in a completely dark cubicle, listen to carefully measured tones in headphones, and indicate where they perceive the location of the sound. The setup reminded me of taking a hearing test.

Dr. Wightman is full of interesting information. He explained that the owl has the best perception of "up and down" directions because the shape of its two outer ears are different from one another. I suppose if you had to find mice and moles in the middle of the night while you were flying, you would also need some way of precisely identifying the "down" direction.

He also described the dolphin's method of locating direction: It uses sonar for general navigation by swinging its head from side to side, but for pin-pointing direction it relies on its jaw, which has an extremely sensitive sound wave sensor. Imagine pointing your jaw towards your boss' face to hear his words better!

Achieving a realistic simulation of 3-D sound in a VR system results in a more immersive aural experience, and creates a more effective communication tool. Solutions like the Convolvotron are expensive—about fifteen thousand dollars as of this writing—but, as usual, pricing should become more affordable with time, and with other suppliers of 3-D sound joining in the competition, such as Virtual Audio Systems, Focal Point 3-D Audio, and the new Gravis 3-D sound card.

The Sense of Touch

Is there a stronger desire burning in our brains and hearts than the urge to touch? We want to see and we like to hear, but we long to touch. As you meander through the aisles of a store, searching for the perfect carpet texture, don't your fingers reach out to handle the fabric? Don't you find your hands stroking the texture of the rug automatically? Imagine how frustrated you would be if the store

strictly enforced its "NO TOUCHING OF SAMPLES ALLOWED" policy? How many seconds would it take for you to vote with your feet and find another carpet store? Perhaps a store is a store is a store, but not that store. It would have FOR SALE signs plastered up in a hurry, and be turned into a doughnut shop.

Trying to build a virtual reality system without including a method to simulate the sense of touch would not result in a fully satisfying experience. But the problems facing inventors brave enough to attempt a solution are immensely difficult. Let's define the situation first in order to clearly understand what's involved in this challenge.

We have described the visual aspects in detail already, and have portrayed the visually immersive nature of a combined head-mounted display and head-tracker. We have also mentioned manipulation devices such as the VPL DataGlove and the Mattel PowerGlove that provide the capability to "hold" virtual objects with your real hand.

There are other versions of the glove, like the CyberGlove by James Kramer, or even the non-glove solutions, like the EXOS Dextrous Hand Master made by Exos, Inc., that also provide input signals to the computer about your hand and finger positions. Unlike the DataGlove or the CyberGlove, which use sensing channels (fiber-optic cables and strain gauges, respectively) inside or on the glove material, the Hand Master straps metal sensing arms on each finger and hand joint—this is called an "exo-skeleton" (outside the skeleton) arrangement. Figure 3.3 compares a fiber optics glove and an exo-skeleton glove.

But gloves that are designed to hold and move—and even throw or drop—virtual objects are not always designed to provide a sense of touch. For the sake of clearer identification, let's refer to such a glove as a "non-touching" glove. If you get the opportunity to test a non-touching glove, like the DataGlove, you'll notice that it is difficult to tell if you are close enough to an object to grasp it. You don't even have to wait until you put your hand into a non-touching glove to find out how perplexing the experience is—you can try it out right now by running the demonstration program called "Adventure in VREAM" located on the disk enclosed with this book. Chapter 7 provides instructions on how to install the

program and how to control the "virtual hand" with a mouse. It won't take long before you discover the slightly awkward maneuvering that is necessary to put the hand into the correct position to grip or push an object, although there are some helpful tips in Chapter 7 on how to make it easier.

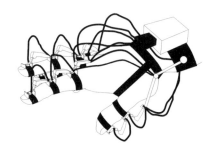

The non-touching glove duplicates this scenario, and for the same reason—there simply is no sense of touch. When we use our hands in the real world to touch real objects, we receive sensations, or clues, that our brains use to make decisions. For example, as you reach your hand forward to stroke a real kitten's soft fur, the nerves in your fingertips "tell" your brain when the moment of touching has occurred. That's a fairly strong clue that the brain uses to make a decision to signal the muscles in your arm to stop pushing your hand forward.

With the VREAM program, as well as with a non-touching glove, there is no similar clue, or sensation, to notify your brain when the moment of touching a virtual object has happened. You can visually perceive that your viewpoint is approaching the virtual object, and you can see the moment when the hand has disappeared behind the surface of the object, but you can't tell exactly when the moment of "touching" takes place.

It is precisely this sort of gap that makes it so difficult to achieve full immersion simulations for all human senses in virtual reality. Our senses are built-in detectives that gather nerve-signal clues to send

to our brain, which then sifts through all the signals and decides what to do regarding each one.

Some of the clues, or signals, are missing when you use a non-touching glove. No signal is sent to the brain when the moment of touching occurs; therefore, your brain, waiting to make a decision, never receives its clue that a decision is imminent. This lack of sensory information results in our fumbling the attempt to grasp the object, which causes our minds to react with embarrassment, confusion, and frustration. We then conclude that the virtual reality experience is awkward, primitive, and impractical. Such a conclusion is precisely correct, because with a non-touching glove, or a mouse-controlled hand, VR lacks some aspects of effective communication.

The Feedback Loop

Your sensory nerves send messages to your brain, and your brain takes action based upon these messages. This process is referred to as *feedback*. The senses, like the sense of touch, "feed back" to the brain a constant stream of clues about the environment around you.

First you see the kitten in front of you, and your eyes "feed back" to your brain the image of the kitten. Then, if you like kittens, your brain makes a decision to activate your arm muscles to move your hand forward. At the moment of touching, your fingertips "feed back" to your brain the sensation that the fur has been touched. Your brain then orders your arm muscles to stop the forward motion and begin a stroking motion. Therefore, to simulate the sense of touch, VR needs to incorporate feedback mechanisms.

As you can imagine, inventing a feedback system presents quite an engineering problem. The goal is to have the computer "feed back" signals from your gloved hand to your brain, which your brain can interpret as a touching sensation. If you move your gloved hand towards a virtual refrigerator, you want to know when your virtual hand has touched the door or the handle. Ideally, you want to actually feel it just as you do with a real refrigerator. Even better would be a system that lets you feel a different sensation for the

door than the handle. Still better would be to receive a sensation of cold temperature if you open the virtual freezer compartment and put your hand inside. But before any of this can be accomplished, it is necessary to understand how the sensors in our hands and arms work.

Research into the sense of touch has discovered that there are two types of information sources that the brain uses to make judgments about the feedback it receives. This whole framework is called the *haptic system*—and this is only the beginning of your new vocabulary list regarding the sense of touch.

An interesting sidelight about the word "haptic" is that it's the first word I've ever looked up that was not listed in my dictionary—as far as I can remember. Although my loyal and hard-working dictionary is a good one, it is rather aged, so I looked it up in a newer edition, where it is listed.

Apparently it has been added to the English language rather recently—perhaps in the last twenty years or so—by scholars and researchers in the physiological sciences. What's intriguing, once you find it listed, is the original meaning of the Greek root haptein—"to fasten." At first glance, it sounds confusing—is the haptic system, our touch sensors, what we use to "fasten" ourselves to something, like a fastener? When I touch my fork and pick it up, I don't think of myself as being fastened or stuck to it in some way. But if you look a little deeper, you find that the word "fasten" comes to us from the Old English word "faest," which meant "fixed."

Although the word "fixed" has a number of meanings, one antiquated definition is "to get a fix on," or "get your bearings," as a ship in the old days would get a fix on where it was located by checking the locations of the stars. This leads us to the implication that the haptic system includes all the sensory channels that help us get our bearings. We get a fix on the world around us through our haptic system.

But "fix" has a number of other meanings, as well. For instance, "to fix" can mean "to attach" or "to decide," in addition to "to get our bearings." We certainly have evidence that the brain makes decisions based upon our senses, including our sense of touch. And we

are well aware that we build attachments to our surroundings—including our friends, neighbors, and family—with our senses. Look at all the synonyms for "attach": connect, bond, link, relate. Our haptic system is what accomplishes all this. It is the way we get our bearings, connect with the world, decide what to do, and relate with each other. In a way, we are fastened to the world after all.

Whoever chose the word haptic did their homework and found a name rich with meaning. Just think for a moment of the infinitely broad range of connections we use to fasten ourselves to the world and the people around us. If the inventors who are trying to expand the frontiers of virtual reality ever discover or create ways to simulate the haptic system, it will be an achievement second to none in the field of human endeavors.

Interacting with Pressure and Texture

As mentioned above, our haptic system can be divided into two main categories that are so related and intertwined with each other, they are difficult to think of separately. And, this is where we bump into two more new words.

One section of the haptic system is made up of *mechanoreceptors* (think of mechanical receivers). These are layers of cells under the skin that respond to pressure and send signals through the nerves to the brain. We use our mechanoreceptors to feel the texture of objects. There are four kinds of mechanoreceptor cells and each does a specialized job. As their name implies, these cells, in effect, "receive mechanically." An action that is called mechanical is basically an action that involves motion and force, as opposed to other energies, such as electronic, photonic, or acoustic.

A mechanoreceptor cell is not designed to respond to light waves, for example; that's why you don't look at stars with your fingertips. (Of course, theoretically, you could simulate this with a virtual reality system that was designed to turn starlight into pressure on your fingers. Wouldn't that be something to share with your children? "Okay, Son, check out how that star feels." "Wow, Dad, that one's really heavy.")

But when you rub suntan lotion on your arms, catch a high pass in football, or twirl your hair curl next to your cheek, the mechanoreceptor cells are pushed—firmly or lightly—like the power button on your stereo, or the mechanical buttons on your car's dashboard. And, because they are very sensitive, the mechanoreceptor cells "notice" even the slightest touch of a feather. It should now be clear that any attempt to simulate the sense of touch is a significant challenge, especially trying to duplicate the broad range of sensations that we are capable of distinguishing.

There are, however, already some advancements in simulating the sense of touch in virtual reality equipment—by simulating force feedback. One approach has been to modify older technology used in working with virtual atoms and molecules. Fred Brooks' team at the University of North Carolina at Chapel Hill has adapted and computerized a large mechanical arm (developed at the Argonne National Laboratory) that was designed to allow scientists to work with radioactive materials from a safe distance (see Figure 3.4).

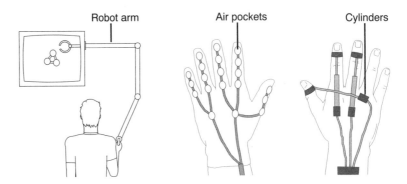

Figure 3.4.

Illustrations of force-feedback methods: robot arm, air-pockets, and cylinders.

This system is used to create computer-generated simulations of chemical molecules. Each atom is displayed in a large size on the screen, and the forces between the atoms are calculated by the computer. Then, when you hold the grip on the metal arm and control an atom, so as to place it in position, the forces between the atoms are fed back to the arm so that you can feel them. This force feedback method allows chemists from pharmaceutical companies to test new combinations of atoms and molecules to see if planned drugs will work as expected. Without force feedback, the process of molecular modeling would be much more difficult.

Other ideas about force feedback and tactile feedback have also been developed. There are systems that use tiny air pockets—like the TeleTact Glove by Airmuscle Ltd.—that inflate and deflate quickly, putting pressure on different parts of the hand. Still other systems use pistons—like the Portable Dextrous Master—that push the fingertips to provide force feedback. (See Figure 3.4.)

But a fascinating technology developed by the TiNi Alloy (pronounced "Tie-Nigh") company uses a special metal called *nitinol* (that's where the "Ni" comes from) that remembers its original shape. By placing an array of wires made of this "shape-memory" metal alloy under the fingers and palm, and electrically heating the wires in certain sequences, feelings of varying textures can be simulated.

There's even a joystick that uses another technique to provide tactile and force feedback. It's called the Sandpaper System, and it was developed by Margaret Minsky and Ming Ouh-young at the MIT Media Lab and the UNC-Chapel Hill. We'll describe it later because it is one of the few devices that begins to include feedback of the type included in the second category of the haptic system.

As much progress as has been made in the realm of mechanoreceptor feedback, however, developers obviously still have a long way to travel before the full range of human touch sensations are duplicated. If you can think of an improved method of simulating the sense of touch, the fledgling tactile feedback industry is waiting to hear from you. The industry is in its infancy, and there is a big open door of opportunity for a creative genius who can invent an advanced interactive haptic device for virtual reality systems.

Interacting with Weight, Shape, and Size

Most of the equipment developed up to now, as we have seen, interacts with the mechanoreceptor half of the haptic system. The other half, which is very closely intertwined with the first half, is called *proprioception*. This fifty-dollar word refers to perception from signals, or stimuli, inside the body.

The first part of the word, "proprio," comes from the same source in Latin ("proprius"—one's own) as "property," something that you

own. So, proprioceptors are receptors, or receivers, that gather information from inside your own body.

It is interesting to study the word "receptor," because it can be broken down to "re" and "ceptor," both of which help explain what it does. The first part, "re," means not only "rebound" but also "again and again." Almost any action that can be described by a single word can be returned to and done again. If you can "insert," you can go back and "reinsert." If you "draw," you can return and "redraw," and so on. In the same way, a cell or a nerve ending can receive information again and again. The second part, "ceptor," derives from the same root as "ceiver" in "receiver." The Latin word "capere" (to take), which is what "capture" and "captor" come from, joined with "re," gave us "receiver" and "receptor." You can see now that a receptor is a mechanism that captures information again and again (the same with a receiver).

What proprioception actually does for us, with our sense of touch, is to provide our bodies with tactile information that is generated inside the body. Unlike a mechanoreceptor, which measures the pressure forces exerted from an object outside the body, a proprioceptor responds to other stimuli that are caused by characteristics such as the weight, shape, and size of the exerting object.

When you pick up a glass of orange juice, your brain receives information about the texture, the smoothness of the glass, and the pressure of the glass against your fingertips. But this kind of information is received by the mechanoreceptors. The muscles in your arm and hand holding the glass are connected to the proprioceptors that signal the information about the weight to the brain.

The mechanoreceptors can't evaluate the weight by themselves because the pressure on the fingertips is mostly from the sides of the glass. Here is where we see how intertwined the two kinds of haptic feedback really are: Even though most of the weight information is picked up by the proprioceptors, it is clear that some information about weight is gained from the increased pressure required by the fingers to keep a larger glass of orange juice from slipping out of your grasp—and therefore is performed by the mechanoreceptors.

The network of proprioceptive muscles and interior sensors, in addition to the clues sent by the mechanoreceptors, help the brain to evaluate how heavy the glass is, what size it is, and shape it is— all while you bring it to your lips for a sip. That's also the reason why you heft an object up and down to gauge its weight. Your brain utilizes the repeated motion to analyze the amount of strain being pulled on the muscles in your arm and hand due to the gravity forces acting on the object. This is proprioception, because it is internal. But at the same time, some of the perception of weight is due to the amount of pressure on the mechanoreceptors.

In many ways, the mechanoreceptors and the proprioceptors work together in a coordinated system to provide the brain with the haptic signals it needs to make decisions. We're back to communication again. The two kinds of receptors communicate with your brain about what your body is touching; the brain then decides what needs to be done and communicates the orders to your muscles. If virtual reality is going to achieve a more complete immersive experience, it must somehow provide feedback to both kinds of haptic perception—the mechanoreceptors and the proprioceptors.

Putting Haptic Clues to Work in Virtual Reality Systems

At the beginning of 1993, the state of virtual reality has not advanced far enough to furnish a great number of proprioceptive clues. Force feedback and tactile feedback devices like the ones discussed earlier focus mainly on the mechanoreceptors, although some proprioception does occur as part of its natural haptic partnership, or symbiosis, with mechanoreception.

But there are a few devices, such as the Sandpaper system alluded to earlier, that are early attempts to provide proprioceptive clues. The Sandpaper system uses a joystick to generate haptic feedback that not only simulates texture, but also mass. By connecting small motors to the lower end of the joystick, varying amounts of force and resistance can be applied to your control of the stick. For instance, by adjusting the motors to a slow, forceful speed, your

hand can get the impression that the stick is stirring a bucketful of syrup or molasses. Another adjustment, where the motors move in a jumpy, jerky manner, makes you feel like you're stirring ice, or even bricks, in the bucket. This is certainly a good way to get your muscles involved!

The Virtual Violin

One of the most fascinating proprioceptive simulators (it's not hard to pick, there are so few proprioceptive devices) is a virtual violin. In Grenoble, France, a team of researchers at the Association for the Creation and Research into Artistic Tools has gradually built a Modular Feedback Keyboard. Jean-Loup Florens, Annie Luciani, and Claude Cadoz have developed a device that allows a musician to simulate playing a violin by placing two fingers into loops attached to a modified computer keyboard. By moving the loops as if moving the bow of a violin, the computer calculates the pressure and motion of the musician's gesture and plays a musical note that sounds just like a violin played in the same way.

Howard Rheingold, in his definitive book *Virtual Reality* (page 328), wrote that, when using this machine, he actually felt as though he were playing a real violin. The experience of feeling a simulation as if it were real requires successfully fooling the proprioceptive sensors in the body—and that is quite a rare achievement in the current state of virtual reality. Cadoz and Florens started their work in 1978, so they have put quite a number of long years of effort into reaching this goal. The keyboard can also be used, when the loops are removed, to simulate a piano; the device is quite versatile.

Do We Need Virtual Instruments?

A common reaction to the notion of expending enormous amounts of time, money, and effort to build a simulation machine that lets you play the piano or a violin is "Why go to all that trouble—why not just play a normal instrument?" This question requires an answer and an explanation.

Certainly, when the motivation is simply to play an instrument, no reason exists to build a synthetic instrument. But researchers have a different paradigm—their motivation is to study and learn regions

of knowledge, such as discovering the secrets of perception and brain function.

A similar question to an automobile manufacturer would be "Why not just study reports of car accidents—why put crash dummies in a car and smash it into a wall?" The answer is, of course, related to control. By crashing test dummies, you can control single factors as desired, rather than being limited to information from random accidents.

In the same way, a computerized synthetic instrument provides control over factors that can then be precisely measured and fully analyzed. The rest of us non-researchers benefit from this drive to create control devices, because the technologies created and invented in the research laboratories are usually improved upon and modified for our enjoyment, comfort, and productivity. Ah, science...what you create sometimes has undesirable consequences we can't foresee, but how different our lives would be without the results of your hard work.

Other Examples of Haptic Interaction

There are several other areas of VR equipment development that are remarkable in their use of proprioception cues and feedback to provide a realistic simulation experience. In addition to the military applications for pilots and soldiers that are built on hydraulic legs that bump, shake, and tilt to provide more proprioceptive realism, there are entertainment simulation cubicles and chairs with similar motions that are in the works for planned VR theaters and arcades. Some are in shopping malls and fairs already.

An earlier application was developed by Autodesk, called High Cycle, in which you climb on a bicycle, like an exercycle, and "ride" through computer-generated landscapes while wearing a head-mounted display. The proprioceptive force feedback capability was added by UNC researchers, who connected a resistance device that made the wheels harder to pedal when you bike uphill and easier when going downhill. This gave the impression that you were really riding up and down hills, when actually you were on a stationary bike bolted to the floor.

Another Autodesk development was the Virtual Racquetball game. A recent announcement by NEC Corporation told of a prototype being created in Japan called Virtual Skiing. Both of these use head-mounted displays with the appropriate equipment—a racquet and skis, respectively.

Virtual Racquetball

The racquetball simulation allows you to swing the racquet at the virtual ball, which bounces off the virtual wall (let's call them v-balls and v-walls) displayed in front of your eyes. The picture of the computer-generated racquet moves in concert with your swing; if it "hits" the v-ball, the computer calculates the v-ball's flight back to the v-wall. It is described as being a lot of fun and fairly realistic, however, the proprioception illusion would be improved if the racquet in your hand responded somehow with a bounce when the v-ball impacts with the v-racquet.

Another racquetball game was developed by *PCVR* magazine using a public domain program called REND386.

Virtual Skiing

The v-skiing prototype has metal plates that you stand on while holding your ski-poles in your hands. The HMD displays the v-hill ahead of you, while your feet move in response to the moguls, bumps, and dips in the slope. As you turn your head, you can see the scene change appropriately; as you lean to the left and right the display shifts and tilts as if you were really on the snowy slopes.

Your proprioceptors can get a good workout on this one. It was pointed out by one of the researchers that the safety of not risking a dangerous fall is a substantial benefit. "Aged people aren't as strong as they used to be, but they want to play the same sports as when they were young. With virtual reality, aged people can ski again," said Asao Kaneko, as reported by David Thurber from the Associated Press.

The NEC Virtual Skiing prototype has one new feature that will be discussed in more detail later when the topic turns to biofeedback. A sensor that measures stress is attached to the user's finger. If the

stress level is low, meaning the skier is calmer and less anxious, the computer automatically adjusts the v-slope to be steeper. When the stress level rises, the computer makes the v-slope more levelled out. These slope changes are coordinated with changes in the incline of the metal plates to increase the realism of the simulation.

The First Commercial VR Venture

One more example needs to be mentioned, but more for its significance than for its contribution to proprioception advancements, although it provides some indirectly induced proprioception cues through an innovative visual association in the program.

A VR system for entertainment arcades, Virtuality, created by an English company called W Industries, was introduced in the United States in January 1992. It marked a solid historical achievement: Virtuality was the first commercial computer-based virtual reality system to appear in the market on a large scale.

This new VR technology was installed in public arcades in eight cities around the country. You could actually stand in line and pay money to try it out, but you couldn't just plunk in a quarter and play for half an hour; a ticket for five minutes cost six dollars.

Virtuality was a sensation. Hundreds of people lined up to find out what the touted VR experience was all about. An important feature of one of the first games (Dactyl Nightmare), which adds a great amount of excitement and makes the adrenaline really start pumping, is that you are in the virtual space with another person. You are each actually standing about twenty feet apart, inside separate padded rings that surround you at waist-level (about three or four feet in diameter). These rings allow you to take a step or two while playing, but protect you from wandering too far—otherwise you might trip and fall over wires or snap the thin cables connecting your head-mounted display to the computer.

The object of the game is for you and your partner to compete in trying to "shoot" each other while hiding behind pillars and other objects on what looks like a giant multi-level chessboard. At the same time, you have to keep an eye out for a large virtual pterodactyl (Dactyl Nightmare, don't forget) that flies around in the v-sky above you. The pterodactyl looks for a chance to swoop down and

grab your v-body or your partner's v-body with its claws. Most people seem to enjoy the game.

The indirect association with proprioception arrives when the pterodactyl carries you up in the sky and suddenly drops you. The illusion of the sense of flying and falling that you experience is prompted by the visual sight of the game board receding quickly from beneath you and then rushing up to meet you again.

Your brain is reduced to delightful confusion because the proprioceptor sensors in your body aren't reporting the confirming signals normally associated with soaring up in the air high above ground. There's no rushing of wind, the soles of your feet are still sensing the pressure of the weight of your body, and there's no jolt felt of being lifted up at the instant of capture.

The Phenomenon of Simulation Sickness

This lack of validation of the visual cues from the proprioceptor senses and the contradictory signals being received by the eyes and the body's sense of its position is exciting to some people, but in others, perhaps ten percent of the population, it causes varying degrees of nauseous feelings in the stomach. This phenomenon has been named *simulation sickness,* or *sim-sickness* for short, and is being studied more frequently in the process of building VR worlds. See the sidebar excerpted from the September 1992 issue of *Andrew's VEE-AR Club Newsletter* for a definition of sim-sickness.

An Excerpt From...

Andrew's VEE-AR Club Newsletter

[Sim-sickness] is induced by the effects of immersion in synthons [synthetic environments, or VR worlds] when [users] are 'flying' or 'whirling,' etc. It's reminiscent of what astronauts report when they enter 'freefall,' or 'sea-sickness' on an ocean liner. It seems to affect some people more than others, and it depends on the activity and the speed of the equipment, but if you are the 'queasy' type when you ride a roller-coaster or a boat, you'll want to prepare yourself for a little sim-sickness when you 'test-drive' a synthon.

It has been observed that some discomfort and even nausea can be noticed during VR experiences if the frame rate is between five and 14 frames-per-second (fps)—especially if the rate is between seven and 10 fps.

It is becoming clear that the effects on the body's sense of its own position—based upon its proprioceptive awareness of what it's doing—during virtual reality experiences can be quite complicated and unpredictable. The sophisticated relationships between the effects of simulations on the body and on brain interpretations are likely to be a rich source of puzzling questions for researchers to focus on as they search for answers in the years to come.

The Potential Power of VR for Training

To conclude this section on the sense of touch, I have an incredible, but true, story that is second to none in terms of the impact it has on a knowledgeable listener—especially on listeners who are pilots.

This story does not directly illustrate the attempts to simulate specific haptic receptors, but it does demonstrate the powerful potential of virtual reality—especially in training applications.

The biggest problem I have with this story is that people who hear it tend to disbelieve it. But, because I have met the man who did it, and because two of his business acquaintances were there to witness it, I can tell this story with complete confidence.

Ronald C. Lindblom, the Director of Business Planning and Automation of a large corporation in Michigan, is a passionate fan of flight simulation software—especially a particularly sophisticated program called Falcon 3.0. Flight simulation programs have been available for several years, but some of the later ones are especially realistic. In some ways, flight simulators were the early commercial forerunners of virtual reality. The early flight simulators provided several of the navigation characteristics and 3-D computer-graphic image capabilities that VR developers later expanded.

Lindblom spent the better part of a year learning the Falcon 3.0 program and becoming quite competent with it on his computer. One day, while flying in his friend's twin-engine plane, Lindblom

asked if he could try out the controls and see what real flying was like. His friend, the pilot, permitted his request and was highly impressed with Lindblom's ability and confident competence.

Later, when Lindblom prepared to hand back the controls to the pilot, his friend asked him if he wanted to try to land the plane. Lindblom reacted with amazement at such a concept, but his friend said not to worry, that he was right there and could take the controls at any time. Due to his time on the flight simulator, Lindblom was able to land the plane correctly on his own, and drove up to the hangar.*

I certainly do not want to be accused of encouraging reckless attempts to duplicate this feat, so let me firmly and clearly state that I do not recommend that anyone try to do what Ron Lindblom was able to do. Perhaps he was lucky. Perhaps he has a great in-born talent to fly. But, in any case, that's not the point.

The message here is that if a person can train himself to such an extent with a flight simulator, which in a sense is a special purpose virtual reality program, then how much more potential exists for a broad range of useful training and development applications with a general purpose VR program? And, further, if a flight simulator—which includes very few haptic clues, since the only device touched is the control stick—is capable of bordering so near to reality, what are the implications for future VR simulations with full-featured haptic systems? Anyone who is young enough to live through the next ten years should be looking forward with great anticipation because this technology is advancing very quickly.

The Other Senses

Out of David Mitchell's list of eight senses, five remain. These are the hardest ones. A few people have had some vague ideas about simulating smell and taste, but the overriding concerns about

---

When speaking to Ron Lindblom about this experience, he mentioned that he previously, in a single engine plane with a flight instructor, had perfectly executed three separate instrument-flying tests with a hood on. The hood prohibits viewing out of the window, but allows instrument viewing, while the instructor puts the plane into an unstable situation. The student then has 30 seconds to stabilize the plane.

sanitation have, up to now, been enough to stifle all apparent attempts. The one exception for the sense of smell was the Sensorama display by Morton Heilig, which generated appropriately timed aromas during the film. But, unless some small VR projects here and there have incorporated feedback to the sense of smell, there are no other known examples that I'm aware of.

These remaining senses—some of which may be argued over by researchers—are simply too much of a problem for virtual reality at this time. How, for example, would a VR system be set up to control your sense of balance? Are there any meaningful feedback clues relating to balance, pheromones (the chemical message system), or the immune system that might improve the illusion of realism? Will future advancements make it possible to define "virtual balance," "virtual pheromones," or "virtual immunity"? These questions have not been analyzed and cannot be answered now. It is difficult enough to attempt to intelligibly frame the questions themselves. Eventual advancements may have to wait for direct brain stimulation methods or some other simulation systems too far in the future for us to think of at this time.

Current VR-Related Software

This writer, in the capacity of introducing computer technology to beginners, is still asked frequently why computer programs are called *software,* so let's start this section by explaining the reason for the word. But first, let me relate a humorous (to me) recent experience that illustrates the potential for confusion in the use of language.

Going into a store to select a gift for my wife, I asked a sales clerk if she would help direct me to the sweaters. She helpfully pointed to another section of the store and said, "Ask Kathy over there to show you the Ladies' Software." I was still tickled by this when I found Kathy, and repeated the directions: "I was told to ask you for the Ladies' Software." Kathy smiled (apparently a computer-literate clerk) and said, "Do you mean Ladies' Soft Lines? They're over here."

Then I realized the obvious—the helpful clerk, trying to remember the department name, "Soft Lines," had thought of "Soft Wear." She may even believe that all software is softwear; after all, computer technology is intimidating to many people, and perhaps she had never the seen the spelling of software. Based on the high percentage of people I deal with who have never learned how software got its name, I think there is a good chance that the charming clerk did not know that software is a computer term. She may have heard the word in passing, and understandably thought the speaker was referring to soft clothing.

So, how did software acquire such a catchy name? It started as a clever play on the word "hardware." If you visit the hardware store in your town, every item you see is something you can touch—it is tangible, concrete. You can put your hands on it, lift it up, and drop it. Hardware is hard. Computer equipment is hardware. The wires, chips, disk drive, monitor, glass, plastic, screws, buttons, keyboard, and cables are all concrete and tangible, also.

But if you remember from Chapter 2, John von Neumann created something new and different from hardware—a set of instructions that is stored in the computer's memory. Those instructions are called a program. There is no way to touch a program, even if you store it on a disk. It is a collection of magnetic blips that only the computer can read. Some of the blips mean "zero" and all the others mean "one." When they are placed in a certain order, the computer can interpret their meaning, but they still do not resemble anything like hardware.

Because of the non-hardware characteristics of magnetic program instructions, someone started calling it software and the name stuck. I don't think anyone expected some of it to be used only for ladies.

Computer programs that use virtual reality principles are called *VR software* and provide varying degrees of realism, navigation, manipulation, three-dimensional graphics, immersion, and haptic feedback. As the equipment (the hardware) becomes more advanced, more powerful, and more capable, there are opportunities for computer programmers to take advantage of the increased sophistication.

For example, IBM-compatible color monitors increasingly displayed more and smaller dots (higher resolution) as they moved from CGA to EGA to VGA, and then towards Super-VGA (SVGA) and beyond. At each step of improved resolution, computer programmers could create new programs that displayed more realistic pictures.

In the same way, as more functions are invented, programmers rush to include the fresh capabilities. As we examine some of the available VR programs, keep two things in mind: All programs require trade-off decisions because of the limitations of existing technologies, and careful consideration of the needs of a program's user is necessary to guide the selection of software.

This overview is intended to illustrate the types of software on the market in relation to specific concepts introduced in this book, and does not attempt in any way to recommend a particular package for a specific set of needs. Readers who plan to purchase commercial software are encouraged to contact either an appropriate consultant for a complete analysis of their needs, or a vendor's representative for precise details on a specific system.

Defining VR-Related Software

There is a good reason why this section is not titled "Defining VR Software"—fundamentally there is no software that can accurately be called "virtual reality software." The fact is no program exists that can support any claim of providing an experience similar to reality. The major significance of the phrase "virtual reality" is due to the power of the concept, and the concept is not fully realized at this time. The imagination can envision the idea, the idea can be described, and programs that integrate portions of the idea may be highlighted, but any attempt to characterize a particular software program as being able to provide "virtual reality" would be foolhardy and arrogant. A clamor of voices protesting "Sure, it's interactive, but it's not realistic," or some other valid objection would also be raised.

The general tendency of the developers and creators in this infant but rapidly growing industry is to avoid implying too much for a product. That is why we refer to a "head-mounted display" rather than a "virtual reality helmet." This second phrase suggests that the

HMD provides an experience similar to reality—and that becomes patently absurd as soon as it surrounds your head.

We must continually clarify that the goal is to reach virtual reality, but the goal has not yet been fully achieved. In fact, if the definition of virtual reality is to include the duplication of all the human senses in a simulation that is imperceptible from reality, then the goal may never be achieved. The implications of establishing universal definitions have been the topic of innumerable conversations for many years, and is likely to be the subject of many more discussions before consensus can be expected.

Looking for Workable Alternatives

The human distaste for confusion, uncertainty, and imprecision has motivated many suggestions for other words and phrases as replacements for the term "virtual reality." Some developers have favored borrowing from the science of cybernetics—the study of control and communication in complex organisms and machines, from the Greek "kybernetes" (steersman)—to suggest *Cyberspace.* Cyberspace refers to a new place, or new space, where innovative control and communication occur—a place in which you can "steer" or "guide" with new tools. (A programmer of Cyberspace environments would become a Cyberspace Engineer, and a participant in Cyberspace would, therefore, be a Cybernaut.)

Other developers, especially Dr. Robert Jacobson with WORLDESIGN, Inc., have recommended *information design,* a down-to-Earth phrase that includes the concept of creating new methods of representing data in three-dimensional space.

The military, in an attempt to avoid some of the confusion and stigma of the VR tag, wants to emphasize the phrase "synthetic environments" as an effective way to combine the manmade aspects and the world-building nature of the technology. Still others, notably Myron Krueger who coined the term in 1970, don't want to change the earlier name "artificial reality" because of its more inclusive boundaries.

The list of phrases that have been put forward is longer than the few mentioned above, but the conclusion is the same—there is a

widespread reaction of uneasiness in response to the phrase "virtual reality." It is cumbersome to explain, somewhat awkward to use, and easy to misunderstand. It can be philosophically provocative and, on occasion, can be perceived as hostile to certain beliefs and doctrines. The phrase gives frequent rise to many-layered puns and forced plays on words, and sometimes even causes tempers to spark and flare.

There are probably a number of solid reasons to stop using the phrase. However, there is one factor that, in its arching simplicity and power, may override all the other forces trying to stop it and change it—the phrase has caught on. Just like the name "American Indians" has been used for several hundred years to describe native Americans because Columbus thought he was landing on the shores of India, the controversial phrase virtual reality might be stuck. When words catch on, rightly or wrongly, sometimes they snag their hooks and barbs too deeply to be easily removed.

Selecting "Domain-Specific" Categories

On balance, the term "virtual reality" seems to have reached "critical mass"—a phrase used to describe the amount of plutonium required to sustain a nuclear explosion. In other words, despite its drawbacks, it has been used frequently enough (several years) and widely enough (all over the world, and throughout all market segments) to achieve stable status. The other phrases—Cyberspace, information design, synthetic environments, and artificial reality— are still available as synonyms, and can be useful to highlight certain aspects, shift perspective, indicate a philosophical orientation, or to distinguish a market focus.

Jacobson, with wisdom derived from experience, recommends an approach that shapes this variety of words into an opportunity to concentrate attention on what a specific application does. He suggests replacing "VR" with descriptions of actual domain-specific systems. For example, "synthetic terrain map" would refer to a program used for urban planning. That's why he doesn't call his company a "virtual reality laboratory," but an "information design studio"—which works well for his purposes because his company designs new ways to present information.

Using Jacobson's suggestion then, the task of identifying VR-related software becomes, first, a process of selecting domain-specific categories. Programs can be classified and grouped by type, and then compared on a more equal footing within the group. All the following categories can be called VR-related because they comprise some aspects of the concept of virtual reality: flight simulator software, 3-D animation software, computer-aided design (CAD) software, rendering software, and other simulation software. The following sections describe these categories in more detail.

Flight Simulator Software

In several ways, the current capabilities of VR are an outgrowth of the early efforts to simulate piloting an airplane. Flight simulators display the inside of a cockpit on the computer screen with your viewpoint facing the controls. A portion of the screen displays a simulated view of what a pilot might see out of the window. Different methods of object manipulation permit you to take actions such as raising the "airplane's" nose by pulling back on a joystick. As the computer calculates the gain in altitude, the simulated altimeter displays appropriate measurements.

You can become quite engrossed in the feeling of how "real" it seems as the computer duplicates the visual characteristics of flying maneuvers. For example, if the program calculates that you have reached a stalling position in flight, you see the warnings and must react just as a pilot would in a real airplane. If you react incorrectly, you risk "crashing" your simulated plane and having to start your flight from takeoff again.

The benefits of flight simulator programs is apparent if you study the records of pilot training schools in the years before flight-simulation software was available. To be a competent pilot, an enormous investment of time and money is required. The long hours of practice in a real airplane to gain the necessary skills and reflexes also carries a constant risk of losing lives and machines. The Air Force quickly saw the advantages of training pilots with simulators, and now has extremely sophisticated and realistic systems. As the story of Ron Lindblom makes clear, the potency of training with

flight simulator programs is remarkable, and affords a glimpse into the successful use of VR for training people for complicated tasks in the future.

Flight simulation software utilizes several components of virtual reality: navigation, allowing flight control of motion in three-dimensions; manipulation of objects, especially of the aircraft fuselage itself; and three-dimensional graphics, which have to be represented on a flat, two-dimensional, screen. The mathematics needed to draw 3-D pictures in a 2-D perspective are quite intricate, and required the labors of brilliant programmers to work out the formulas. This work built the foundation for much of the 3-D graphics structure that was later used to create VR environments.

With so many components, it can be argued that flight simulators are a type of virtual reality—especially if you add immersion with a head-mounted display. But it is clear that flight simulators are special-purpose VR applications. The goal of full-fledged virtual reality enthusiasts is to achieve a general-purpose VR that can be used to create many types of environments.

Shareware

hareware is a category of software that is marketed under an unusual principle in American business—try it before you buy it. The concept operates with a clearly defined agreement that if you don't like the program and you decide not to use it, you are under no obligation to pay any money. However, if you continue to use the software after a temporary period of time, you are expected to send the author a stated amount of money that is usually quite modest, perhaps five to fifty dollars. The term "shareware," of course, is a combined form of the phrase "shared software." This vehicle has been a good channel for small software companies to affordably enter the market—and some of them have experienced resounding success. Most shareware is available through bulletin boards (BBSs). Contact a computer user group in your area to get lists of local BBS phone numbers.

There are dozens of flight simulator programs available, ranging from shareware versions, like "Corncob," all the way up to the most realistic versions, loaded with features, such as the previously mentioned "Falcon 3.0." See the related sidebar on Shareware software.

3-D Animation Software

One of the integral components of VR is the ability to add animation to characters and objects in a created, or synthetic, world. If you enter an environment with a partner, you will want to see your partner's virtual shape walk, point, sit, and move in numerous other ways, otherwise the simulation will be quite unsatisfactory. In addition, cars should roll, balls should bounce, and knobs should turn.

The resource for developing these motions, or animations, is 3-D animation software. These tools have built-in functions that facilitate the creation of moving three-dimensional objects. For example, suppose you want to display a rotating ferris wheel. You would start with a blank screen, or "canvas," and select the functions that let you draw the carnival ride. Once satisfied with the details of the framework, you would choose the "rotate" function and define the axis of rotation and the degrees of rotation; the program takes care of the rest. Your ferris wheel will then rotate around the centerpoint slowly or quickly, depending on your choice of degrees of rotation per frame.

The concept of *frame* is borrowed from the video film concept, because it works quite similar. Close examination of a reel of film reveals thousands of little pictures, or frames, lined up in a row. There is no motion in any of the pictures, and each section of the film has a series of pictures that look exactly the same. If you study two sequential pictures carefully you might notice tiny differences.

When you run the film through a projector, the pictures are shown so swiftly that the tiny differences look like motion. In the same manner, animation software is designed to divide time into tiny slices. During each fraction of a second, an entire picture is drawn on the screen. This picture is called a frame. Then, in the next time slice, the computer calculates the new position—based upon the degrees of rotation you decided—and draws a slightly different picture. This is the next frame. By continuing this process, the ferris wheel looks like it goes all the way around.

Frames per second is the measure of how realistic animation is, or how similar it looks to real motion. The slowest rate that looks like "smooth" motion is about thirty frames per second. That's because

our eyes "hold" an image for about one-thirtieth of a second before it fades from our retina.

Here is an experiment you can try. Look at your hand. Now, without moving your head, close your eyes for a few seconds. Suddenly, just once, blink your eyes open and shut as fast as you can. You'll notice the image of your hand remains for a short period of time—even after your eyelid is shut again. You can "see" your hand after your eyes are closed because your retina is still signaling to your brain its reaction to the light rays bouncing off your hand.

At thirty frames per second, each picture is sent to your eye before the last frame has completely faded. This causes your brain to interpret the sequence as a flowing motion; it doesn't have time to notice that each frame is a still photograph. Professional animators and programmers—and for that matter VR developers—are keenly interested in computer animation packages that run fast enough to reach a minimum of thirty frames per second.

A standard test that measures the frames-per-second capability of a software program is called a *benchmark;* comparisons of software benchmarks is of prime concern in both the animation and the computer industries. Both the program and the computer it is used on affect the benchmark tests. A fast program operated on a slow computer can result in a disappointing benchmark, and vice versa.

If you want to try your hand at creating animations, two of the most affordable packages are "Animator" and "3D Studio." Using one of these programs will give you useful insights into the basic principles involved in three-dimensional animation and a respectful understanding of the issues and skills that must be mastered by not only cartoonists and other animators, but also by the people struggling to create virtual reality. Frames per second is a crucial test of the realism of a synthetic environment.

Computer-Aided Design (CAD) Software

Like the influences of flight simulator and 3-D animation software programs on the development of virtual reality, computer-aided design software assisted the advancement of VR—but in a different way. CAD was the driving force that placed increasingly powerful

computer graphics equipment in thousands of businesses and offices, thereby setting the stage for broader acceptance of the visual medium.

Programs like AutoCAD and PointLine made it possible for designers to create precise drawings of their ideas on the computer and thereby communicate their ideas to clients more easily. With the advent of CAD software, an alternative to drafting blueprints by hand was available. These programs include built-in functions that let you quickly draw lines and shapes. The big T-square is replaced by a grid and cross-hairs displayed on-screen.

When you are finished with your design, if you purchase the 3-D package, you can select the function that shows your concept from a three-dimensional perspective. If you make a mistake, or you decide to move the south wall out four feet, you don't have to reach in the drawer for an eraser; you simply select the "erase" or the "move" function. Once you finalize the drawing, you can print the result on a special printer called a *plotter*. You can even store your work on a disk and transport the disk to your client's office, where your design can be viewed on another computer.

As CAD software became more sophisticated and included more functions, designers of buildings and cars became more familiar with and dependent upon the ability to show precisely what the concept in their minds looked like. Some design firms now will actually refuse to work with you if you don't have the capacity to share CAD files with them, because of the advantages of computer-aided design.

The link between CAD and VR is starting to strengthen. It makes sense, because on the one hand are the thousands of designers who are developing precisely detailed blueprints of cars, offices, hospitals, homes, appliances, and many other products with CAD in two dimensions, and on the other hand is the promise of walking through the designs, testing them, and discovering problems and solutions in them with VR in three dimensions. John Walker, the founder of Autodesk, did much to illustrate this relationship (see the sidebar on John Walker for more information).

Autodesk started a "Cyberia Project," and now there is a program actually called Cyberspace, that allows you to explore your design. It is not too difficult to predict that numerous contributions to virtual reality will probably issue from the CAD industry in the years ahead.

Rendering Software

There is an aspect of displaying pictures that we have not yet discussed in detail. There are several kinds of pictures that the computer can display. Two of them are *polygon pictures* and *photo-realistic pictures*.

The 3-D graphics discussed in the animation section are created by using mathematical formulas that use polygons, or straight-sided shapes, to draw pictures. For example, a square is a polygon; there is a math equation the computer can calculate to draw the sides of the square in a three-dimensional perspective and then color the surface. You can draw a cube by putting six square polygons together—and there is an equation to draw a cube. The result is a computer picture of a cube that looks like it was made from construction paper—all the surfaces have what's called a "flat" color. There is no visual texture and no detail. Some people say it looks like it belongs in a cartoon. (See Figure 3.5.)

John Walker

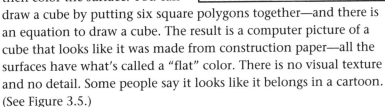

ohn Walker, founder of Autodesk, has directed the company to its current position as the market-leader in producing professional CAD software. Walker envisioned the connection between CAD and VR in detail in 1988. He wrote an inspiring description of it called "Through the Looking Glass: Beyond User Interfaces." This document motivated Howard Rheingold to spend two years traveling around the world trying out VR equipment and writing a definitive book about the history and implications of VR called *Virtual Reality*.

John Walker's paper was a look into the future of computer interaction, in which he explained that in addition to communicating with the computer, people would be exploring other worlds with the computer in Cyberspace. He outlined the ways that Autodesk could build on the foundation of CAD and develop a project to bring a new tool to the design community that would allow this exploration.

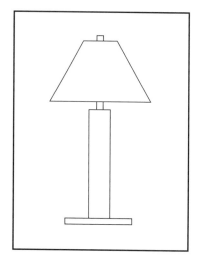 

Figure 3.5.

Comparing a polygon picture and a bit-mapped picture.

Polygon pictures certainly are not reminiscent of what we see in the richly textured world of reality, but they have one advantage—speed. The computer can draw polygons very quickly. If a VR environment is created with thousands of polygons, it is crucial to draw all the polygons swiftly for each frame, because of the need to reach a high frame-per-second benchmark. Virtual reality won't be very convincing if the motion is slow as molasses. Animation software uses mostly polygons for pictures. It's hard to create a recognizable face using only polygons.

In comparison, photographs have a lot of detail and visual texture. You can snap a camera photo of your father's face and recognize him with no trouble. But the computer has difficulty drawing a face quickly because it has to draw the face one dot at a time. If you examine a photograph closely with a microscope, you will see tiny dots—like the dots on a TV screen.

A computer monitor has little dots too, called *pixels* (short for "picture elements"), and the only way to make a computer display a black-and-white photograph is to place each dot from the picture into a pixel. Your computer's memory is made up of little storage places called *bits;* a portion of the memory is assigned to the display on the monitor. So, if you place the information about a dot into a memory bit, it is called *bit-mapping*. One dot per bit. Then the computer places all the bits on-screen, one bit for each pixel or dot.

This takes a lot of processing time. Photo-realistic VR is going to require faster desktop computers than we have now—faster than even large mainframes currently operate. Another problem is that color monitors require an even more complex process than monochrome.

But if you have an application in which speed does not matter as much, then you should consider *rendering software.* To render means to accurately depict a scene. There is a shareware program called Rend386 that lets you do simple rendering, and a commercial rendering program by PIXAR, Inc., called RenderMan.

Photo-VR, a sophisticated photo-realistic program, is available from Straylight Corporation. Not only does Photo-VR allow you to transfer or create high grade (compared to polygons) photo-realistic pictures, it also permits a "walkthrough" function. The ability to walk through a scene is part of the navigation goal of virtual reality, but because of the processing time burden, realtime navigation is not yet achievable with photo-realistic VR. There is a software program for the Macintosh computer actually called "Walk-through," by Virtus, that incorporates a somewhat similar approach.

Lawnmower Man

n appropriate topic for this section is a movie called *Lawnmower Man* that opened in theaters in the spring of 1992. It was written, directed, and co-produced by Brett Leonard, and was the first major motion picture to use the concept of virtual reality as its central plot theme.

Lawnmower Man successfully introduced the idea of virtual reality to the general public, even though some people came away with some confused impressions, such as thinking that so-called "smart drugs" (used as a plot device) were necessary to experience VR. The most incorrect assumption, however, was that the movie showed the current state of the VR art.

The pictures shown in the segments purporting to be the visual views of the protagonists were accepted by most movie-goers as the quality of pictures currently available in a VR system. This is untrue, because those scenes were created by super-computers—taking up to forty minutes for each frame. To put this in perspective, imagine putting an HMD on your head and looking at a scene for forty minutes before seeing the next, slightly different frame.

A movie can show a quicker version of these slow renderings because a movie camera can animate slow pictures by speeding up the film. You can line up the pictures, shoot short sequences of each one, and then run the film. By seeing the film, a movie-goer has no way of knowing that each second of thirty frames required days of patient rendering. Enormous advancements in computer speed and technology are necessary before anyone can experience virtual reality similar to what was shown in *Lawnmower Man*.

Simulation Software

We've already discussed a specialized version of simulation software, the flight simulator. But there are now more generalized simulation software packages, like the manufacturing simulation software by Deneb Robotics, Inc. With a general-purpose simulator program like this, you can control the set-up of an assembly line, for example, starting with a blank screen. You can chose from a selection of pre-created shapes and functions that permit you to simulate automated processes to see how they would work together.

An example would be the "fabrication" of a conveyer belt between work stations. By selecting the frequency of product output from the first machining tool, you can watch the simulated output move down the belt to the next machining location, and analyze the flow requirements for the system. If the output from one station backs up at the next, you can adjust the output frequency until the flow reaches a smooth optimum.

Many kinds of simulators are available now. Some are targeted at specific industries, like manufacturing, while others are more open-ended and flexible. But all simulators provide a method of learning how a myriad of complex factors interrelate and affect one another.

One interesting and affordable simulation program available for desktop computers and Super Nintendo is "Sim-City," one of a series of similar game simulations, like "Sim-Earth" and "Sim-Ant" (aren't all games simulations, though, to one degree or another?).

In Sim-City, you act as mayor of a town that has population growth proportionate to how well you handle issues such as balancing commercial, industrial, and residential sectors, while juggling the effects of such consequences as traffic density, mass-transit needs, and pollution. The levels of taxation and the positioning of police and fire departments affect the rate of growth, the opinion polls of your leadership, and the crime rate.

Although Sim-City is not general-purpose simulation software, it quickly demonstrates the powerful potential of simulation software as a learning tool. While you and your children are having fun, the foundation is being laid for a deeper understanding of the integration of issues, problems, and decisions faced by the real mayor of your real town.

The expectation and hope is that virtual reality, after attaining immersive photo-realism at thirty frames per second with complete freedom of movement and natural manipulation of objects that follows the laws of physics, will provide an unmatched capability of simulation. The question of how society will be changed by such a powerful tool needs thoughtful consideration.

World-Creating Tools Using Virtual Reality Principles

Creating an environment, or a world, on the computer that permits navigation, manipulation, and immersion—including three-dimensional animation and bit-maps—would clearly be an immense job if a programmer was forced to start from scratch. Fortunately, some progressive developers have written world-building tools by combining the basic functions (which can be selected as desired) into authoring programs that save time and effort.

Now you can be a cyberspace engineer—a person who creates virtual reality worlds or environments—without first learning how to be a programmer. There aren't very many world-creating tools to choose from yet, but the existing programs do offer a glimpse of the tools that will be available in the future.

Superscape Development System

In the middle of 1991 a Superscape demonstration program was released that caused great excitement throughout the VR community. It was created by New Dimension International, in England, and showed what was achievable in desktop virtual reality. In the middle of an industrial complex, you can control the actions of a man, two cars, and a helicopter. You can maneuver each object by controlling its speed and movement—even turning it upside down—by pressing keys on the keyboard. You can even "fly" through the air above the rooftops. One of the buildings includes an office, and as the man walks in, the doors open. You can even manipulate a few objects, like the swiveling office chair. Figure 3.6 is a screen from Superscape.

The entire environment with the buildings, the trees, the automobile, the helicopter, the office, the runway, and the man, were created with the Superscape world-building program. You can control the moveable objects via the built-in functions. To create customized functions, a language called "Freescape" is provided to permit script commands, which are a sequence of instructions controlling what happens when objects interact. New Dimension, according to their literature, has sold more of these systems than all other authoring tools combined. Until recently, the system included everything (called a "turn-key" system); the computer and the software together sold for about $15,000, but now the authoring tool can be purchased individually.

NOTE: Images on the cover of this book and the screened pages between the chapters are reproductions of actual images from the Superscape program.

Figure 3.6.

A screen shot from the Superscape program.

Virtual Reality Studio

This authoring tool is an inexpensive spin-off of Superscape, and is correspondingly limited in its abilities. But its one hundred dollar price tag makes VR Studio an affordable way to enter the realm of world-building.

Version 1 was introduced in the United States in October, 1991, and is available for IBM PC-compatible, Amiga, and Radio Shack computers. In England, the name of the program is 3D Toolkit. Version 2 of VR Studio is expected soon, and is understood to have improved features; the first version allows only straight-sided geometric figures, such as the line, triangle, pentagon, hexagon, cube, and pyramid. No curved lines or circles are possible. A complex demonstration game is included that can be examined to learn how certain animations and activations are achieved.

The central screen where worlds are developed includes control buttons that are activated by the mouse to select desired shapes and characteristics such as a color palette. A portion of the screen displays a window where the environment can be viewed.

To create a cube, for example, you click on the Create icon (picture of a button). When you select Cube from the array of shapes, a white cube of predetermined size appears in the window. The next step is to change the cube to a desired size, so you click on the Edit button. This displays another series of choices—such as Shrink, Stretch, and Move—with corresponding arrows. By activating the chosen arrows, the cube adjusts itself under your control. You can then select the colors you want from a palette of 256 colors, and "paint" each surface of the cube. It is all very easy and great entertainment—clicking and creating shapes, forming them, and placing them together to build a world.

Once you have created some shapes and formed them into a room, for example, you may want to add a door that opens when activated, so you select Conditions, and type in the appropriate commands (using the Freescape language) that cause the door to react to activation. This part of world-building becomes increasingly complicated as you add more animation and more conditions. It requires careful persistence and a high tolerance for frustration. A programming background is a great asset if you want to make your world highly interactive.

Two programs on the disk at the end of this book—the Mover program, written by this author, and the Castle program, written by Raymond Holmes in Hawaii—were created with Virtual Reality Studio. As you try them out, notice the lack of curves and arcs. Also, you can see what is meant by the polygon type of graphics using flat colors. Instructions for installing and running these programs can be found in Chapter 7.

Swivel

Unless you work in a research laboratory, you may not have a chance to see worlds created with Swivel, originally programmed by Young Harvill. This is the world-building tool developed by VPL Research, Inc. for use with the systems it created. But Swivel doesn't run alone—it's only one part of a family of programs that must run in combination to control the many different and complex accessories connected to the VPL system.

Another VPL program is Body Electric, which handles the interface with the VPL's VR body suit. Swivel is the world-building tool created by the VPL Research, the premier commercial VR vendor. At this time, due to the uncertainty of the situation since Lanier left, it is not known what the future holds for Swivel.

WorldToolKit

Two of the main developers of Sense8's WorldToolKit, Eric Gullichsen and Patrice Gelband, were programmers at Autodesk when John Walker shaped his vision of Cyberspace. They dreamed of making a less expensive version of virtual reality, and left Autodesk to establish their own company—and see if they could make their vision a reality. Their courage and foresight paid off when they were able to make a working system in 1990. By now Sense8 has established WorldToolKit as a world-building standard in the VR industry. Gullichsen and Gelband have made it possible for many more people to experiment with cyberspace engineering and have pushed VR further down the road to its goal.

WorldToolKit, for about $3500, does not provide an interactive interface such as the interactive screen that comes with VR Studio.

Instead, WorldToolKit uses the C computer language—with a powerful command structure familiar to many programmers. The package includes dozens of pre-written "libraries," in the C language, that provide programming code and algorithms to make world-building easier. But you have to be a C programmer to make it all work.

One of the features in WorldToolKit's repertoire is called *texture-mapping,* a valuable and important capability in a VR environment. The phrase refers to wrapping a texture (that looks like wood-grain or wallpaper) on a polygon shape. After trying out the VR Studio worlds, imagine having realistic-looking textures on those flat surfaces! What a difference texture-mapping makes.

VREAM Virtual Reality Development System

At the time of this writing, VREAM (short for "virtual reality dream"), an elegant and powerful world-building tool by Ed La Hood, is undergoing final testing. It is hoped that it will be on the market by the time this book is published, but software is one human activity that can't be rushed: It's ready when it's ready. La Hood is a prodigy programmer who started hacking code at the age of eleven, and is now on the verge of establishing a new landmark in the history and development of virtual reality.

The VREAM Development System is an interactive world-building tool in which shapes are selected and modified, similar to VR Studio—but the comparison stops there. VREAM is much more sophisticated where VR Studio is primitive. Not only are circles and curves available, but also a sphere and even a torus (doughnut shape).

VREAM uses a far more powerful proprietary language to create customized actions, conditions, and links between objects. It can be connected to many kinds of accessories like HMDs, head-trackers, and gloves—far beyond just the mouse and the joystick. The cornerstone of La Hood's achievement is a computer-generated hand inside the environment, controlled with the mouse or a glove, used to manipulate objects.

Many additional useful features are built-in, but the most exciting development is the recently added ability to attach bit-map graphics to surfaces in the world, adding much realism.

For $1500, VREAM packs a wallop of value. La Hood is likely to make major contributions to the field of virtual reality as the future unfolds.

Where and How Is the Software Used?

This chapter covered a great deal of ground discussing the body's senses and haptic interactions. In addition, we've detailed a wide variety of specific software examples that illustrate some related capabilities available today. Chapter 4 explores a number of practical and useful systems at work in various fields, and the expanding possibilities opening up for VR and 3-D applications.

Chapter 4

3-D
Applications

All life, existence, and events are perceived in three-dimensional space. Even our minds assume that real-life experience happens in three-dimensions. It is taken for granted. Your nightmare would be scary indeed if you dreamed a space warp shrunk the vertical dimension to nothing and squashed you thinner than a piece of paper. Living in three-dimensions, of course, is as important as breathing.

The purpose of this chapter is not to convince you that three dimensions are necessary in real life; we have been convinced of this all of our lives. Instead, this chapter's objective is to establish the importance of three-dimensional perception in computer applications. This chapter presents examples to illustrate the advantage of knowing breadth, width, and height, and the deeper understandings that are possible.

What's Important about 3-D?

First, let's dispose of the objections that may be raised by the first sentence in this chapter. After all, isn't this page a two-dimensional medium? How about a computer screen—don't we talk about the "two-dimensionality of the screen"? Isn't a map an illustration of streets and highways in two-dimensions? If you draw a straight line on a piece of paper, is that not a simple one-dimensional shape? Well, no. The real page has a measurable thickness, regardless of how thin it seems. Otherwise, a one-hundred page book would be thinner than a neutrino.

This is not an attempt to split hairs over technical arguments. The first sentence in this section says "All life, existence, and events are perceived in three-dimensional space." Therefore, a page made of paper—or any other material, for that matter—exists in three-dimensions. Even the ink that forms the readable characters has a measurable thickness. Only in the abstract can the page be called a two-dimensional medium. Our minds can "conceive of" or "imagine" a flat plane with only two-dimensions, but nothing exists in that form—or if it existed we would never see it or know about it. If you doubt this, ask yourself how else you would perceive it.

What we mean when we talk about a medium, screen, or map being in two dimensions is that the information is represented as if it were two-dimensional. The information represented by a map clearly exists in three-dimensions; you can prove this by driving to a landmark positioned on the map and measuring it. Even the street that supports your car exists in three-dimensions—and you see the third dimension when you look at a pothole. But the 3-D streets, buildings, landmarks, and parks are represented on the street map as if they were two-dimensional, as if we were looking straight down on them. There are maps that attempt to show information about the third dimension by using shadows or forty-five degree diagonal lines, but even these are still representing 3-D details as if they were in 2-D.

Our minds have the ability to translate two-dimensional drawings into three-dimensional images, but as powerful as this ability is, it is still no substitute for actually experiencing the real three-dimensional object. Looking at the line between two towns on a

map and imagining the distance in your mind is quite different from actually driving down the highway and discovering how far it really is. This is the gulf that needs to be bridged—and finding ways to span that difference is the goal of the people developing 3-D applications.

This chapter looks at several different disciplines and considers possible software applications that would let you experience the activity rather than just imagining what it would be like. As VR technology advances, these potential 3-D applications for real-world situations are expected to provide deeper levels of understanding for complex processes.

3-D Modeling

The type of modeling covered in this section does not include the kind of modeling done in an artist's studio, unless the artist is a sculptor and builds models for sculptures in wet clay. Three-dimensional modeling, in clay and other materials, has been the responsibility of skilled tradesmen for centuries. When designing a substantial project, like an expensive bronze sculpture or a towering sky-scraper, despite all the work that is expended to draw a detailed blueprint, the architect still needs to find someone who can build a model. A three-dimensional representation of the drawing needs to be seen so that unbalanced portions can be adjusted, or design problems can be worked out.

When the people of France rallied together to fund the Statue of Liberty as a gift to the United States, the sculptor, Frederic Bartholdi, commissioned a series of models, each larger than the last. Each model brought new potential problems to Bartholdi's attention, allowing him to attempt solutions before approaching the next step.

Imagine the immense waste of money and time if Bartholdi had caste the bronze plates for the full-sized statue and then found they didn't fit together? France could not have afforded to continue to make full-size statues until Bartholdi finally got it right. The models themselves were considerably expensive, but far less expensive than making mistakes on the final sculpture.

Building Models

The same procedure is followed in an architect's office. After the plans are drafted, someone is appointed to build a cardboard model—either a junior architect, to gain further experience, or a firm that specializes in such contracting. A base for the model is built, the walls are shaped, the windows are cut out, the roof is placed on, and the grounds are landscaped. It can take weeks of careful effort; at each step the measurements must be double-checked against the blueprints to assure the correct scale is followed.

Architectural models are often built at scales of one-quarter inch to one foot—a ratio of 48 to 1. When the model is finished and carried to the architect's office, the designer walks around it and studies it from different angles to see if the model has the desired design characteristics. If the model builder has made a mistake, the model must go back for corrective repairs and touch-ups. Although it is expensive to build high-quality models, it is much easier and cheaper to correct a mistake on the model than when the contractor's crane is swinging the beams onto the fourth story.

Virtual Models

Applying modeling functions in VR would be useful. The procedure of creating the model would be similar. A cyberspace engineer would use a world-building tool to make the virtual model, carefully following the scale selected. The walls would be shaped, the windows cut out, the roof placed on, and the grounds landscaped.

When finished, the 3-D computer model of the building would be ready for examination. There would be several big advantages over a cardboard model: The VR model would most likely be quicker to build, any changes would be easier to make, and the entire process would save money.

But the most important benefit would be a feature that is impossible with cardboard at a scale of 48 to 1—the designer could "walk-through" the computer model room by room. Evaluating the perspectives of individual rooms and judging the relative sizes of the windows, doors, corridors, and stairways would be an inviting prospect for an architect. Three-dimensional computer modeling

will be an increasingly exciting and useful application for designers of buildings, consumer products, appliances, and many other items.

Models of the Atmosphere

There are other types of 3-D modeling applications, too. For example, you might want a 3-D model of the atmosphere to help you better understand the forces affecting the weather and therefore increase the reliability of your weather forecasting. You can take pictures of the clouds from a satellite in space, but they don't provide an understanding of the inner workings, like the heat reflected from the land and water, the interactions going on at the intersection of cold and warm fronts, or how the inversion layer works.

Imagine inputting the data from atmospheric and weather station readings into a program that creates a three-dimensional simulation of the atmosphere. The model could be adjusted to duplicate the physical forces acting on the air (wind direction, evaporation, cloud reflection, etc.) according to the current readings. You could then have the computer model react to the current conditions.

You could also use the model to see the step-by-step formations of tornadoes and hurricanes. By creating a computer model using the data recorded at the time a tornado or hurricane formed, you can then run the model to show what happens at different points in the cloud structure. You could slow down or speed up the model to gain deeper understandings, or you could start with slightly changed data to check out the variations caused by differing starting points. 3-D atmospheric models are quite effective in their ability to educate weather researchers about complex factors that affect each other in an integrated way.

Object Modeling

Another type of modeling involves much smaller shapes than the Statue of Liberty or the Earth's atmosphere. A toaster, camera, window, or car manufacturer might want to create 3-D computer models of its wares for several purposes: to test planned changes in the design, to animate parts of the product for use in advertising, or to create a visual business presentation.

Creating a 3-D computer model opens up avenues that are not possible with the real object. You can stretch or shrink the shape displayed by the computer. You can change the color with a few keystrokes. You can look at just the outline, distort a doorknob, add luminescence, or make it look reflective or metallic. Once a shape has been modeled on the computer, you can easily perform hundreds or even thousands of graphic actions on it, none of which could be done on the real object—or even a real model—without long, painstaking effort.

The difficult part of making a computer model, however, is figuring out how to tell the computer where many of the points of the three-dimensional object are located. The computer cannot draw a shape that looks like a real object unless many points on the object's surface are translated into the computer's memory storage locations (see the discussion of *shape digitizer* later in this section). To translate a point manually, you must calculate the three-number coordinates of the point—the first number tells the computer how many units to the side the point has to be placed (width), the second number represents how many units back (depth), and the third number locates how many units up (height). (Look back at Figure 1.3 for a detailed example.)

Those three numbers represent the three dimensions. When the computer knows the three numbers, it can display a dot in that location. So, if you wanted to model a pen by hand, you would have to calculate the three numbers, called x, y, and z, for each point on the pen, then type in the three numbers, or coordinates, for each point.

It sounds like a long process, and it certainly is. The time and effort required by this procedure has prompted many attempts to speed up the steps involved (just as the laborious process of typing led people to dream of voice-recognition replacements). But, once the tedious job of creating the computer model is finished, the fun begins. Stretching a segment here, shrinking a component there, scaling the whole model larger and smaller, trying out different effects—it is quite enjoyable to see the visual changes. You can easily test dozens of changes in a short time—and that cannot be done without a computer.

Form Changes

One method of changing a 3-D computer model—a fascinating effect—has been anointed with its own name. It's called *morphing* (from the word *morphology,* which means the study of the forms of organisms, and derives from the Greek word "morphe," meaning "form").

You can create two models with completely different shapes, such as one model with the shape of a rock singer like Michael Jackson, and another model with the shape of a jaguar or leopard. By designing several intermediate 3-D shapes (by locating coordinates, again), you could stretch some of Michael's features into the shape of the first change, then stretch the resulting shape into the next change, and so on until you reach the shape of the jaguar. These gradual steps combine together to produce a morphing change, and the effect of the whole sequence is quite striking. In case you are not aware of it, the producers of the video for Michael Jackson's "Dangerous" album used the exact morphing sequence described here (except it was done in 2-D).

The 3-D tool mentioned previously, the *shape digitizer,* is exciting for programmers who make 3-D models of smaller design shapes because it eliminates much of the work required to make a model of an object. Let's say you want to create a computer-generated model of a flower. You must enter the coordinates of each point on the outline of the flower into the computer. With a three-dimensional shape digitizer, like the digitizing scanner by Cyberware, you would simply place the flower in front of the scanner, instead of calculating and entering each point, as described earlier. Two specialized video cameras record the shape of the object from separate angles. The system then automatically calculates the necessary coordinates for each point and translates the numbers into a format ready for the computer. The result is a professional-looking duplicate of your flower displayed on your computer screen.

Not only is the image impressive, but the time it saves is substantial; the entire scanning procedure is as short as thirteen seconds. Anyone who has created a computer model by hand can hardly avoid an involuntary gasp when confronted with the cutting-edge shape digitizer. As virtual reality and synthetic environments

become capable of transferring digitized shapes into their worlds, the virtual environments will become increasingly realistic and easier to create.

3-D Architecture

What expresses the shaping of three-dimensional space more solidly than architecture? When you walk up the wide concrete steps of a metropolitan courthouse or library with the massive granite columns looming high into the air, doesn't your mind almost feel the sensation of three-dimensional weight? When you think about your home, do you not visualize the size and height of the rooms? If you were an architect, these dimensions and proportions would be your instruments of design—each identified with three measurements.

Suppose you were an architect, with the special gift architects have of visualizing an original design of a building. Let's say you have visualized an appropriate design for a municipal client or a diversified international corporation.

Now you have to communicate your thoughts to the managing committee. You can draw a carefully rendered, colored, three-dimensional perspective to represent the outer shell of your plan. You can draft precise floor-plans of the interior spaces. But you can't afford to spend an unreasonable amount of time preparing costly drawings to convey your concepts, because you have not been awarded the contract yet.

You have a need to communicate a complex plan to several people whose imagination capability is not as well-honed as yours—the architect's—is. But since the committee has not decided which architect to commission for the building yet, you cannot afford the time and money needed to prepare detailed visual representations. You would like them to choose you because you have conceived of solutions for their needs and problems, but you aren't willing to gamble six months of unpaid, expensive preparations to demonstrate the clear advantages of your design without assurance that the committee will give you the contract.

If you could quickly and affordably wire their minds to yours and transfer your ideas for immediate comprehension, the communication puzzle would be solved in an afternoon. But you have not yet

stumbled across the genius who could accomplish such an assignment, so you are stuck with few possible alternatives to achieve success—each of which is only weakly adequate for achieving clear and persuasive understanding.

When the scheduled committee meeting date arrives, you pack your sketches and drawings into your portfolio and head out to rely on your verbal communication skills. Later, while surrounded by a room full of committee members, you discover that several questions based on a misunderstood explanation begin to derail you from your expected track.

3-D Walk-Through

A 3-D application that minimizes misinterpretations as effectively as a direct brain transfer would certainly be a welcome aid for an architect. Imagine a 3-D application in which you arrive at the committee meeting room, exchange pleasantries, and then instruct everyone to utilize a device that places a virtual duplicate of the group inside a three-dimensional computer-generated model of the building that looks like your plan, including the rooms, corridors, and windows of your plan, surrounded by your planned landscaping details. Each participant in the virtual group looks like a corresponding committee member, and each person can control the movements of their virtual representation.

In this imagined scenario, as you describe the justification for the four story atrium in the lobby, everyone sitting in the room can look up and see the artistic statue hanging from the forty-foot-high ceiling, the tiered balconies surrounding the perimeter, and the soft light streaming through the skylights high above. In a slow two-minute scan, the entire committee has realized the effect that you conceived in a flash of inspiration while walking to the coffee machine two weeks earlier. In this short tour, you have achieved better results than you would have in thirty minutes of narration—and avoided another 45 minutes of deflecting side-issues and impractical suggestions.

When a committee member has a question, you point towards the related area and show the answer in three-dimensional detail. Or, if another section of the building is the topic, everyone can move in the appropriate direction to where the new area can be viewed.

In real buildings, after construction, a traditional event takes place called a *walk-through*, in which the client's representatives, the architect, and other principal participants walk in a group together through the building for the first time. The term walk-through can be just as useful in a 3-D application where the group moves together through the virtual building and is introduced to the proposed spaces. And, of course, the significance of a virtual walk-through is the advantage of being able to discover major mistakes before the building is built.

Another feature that architects—and especially clients—might like, would let a participant reach out with a hand device (like a glove) and modify the size of a feature. If you realized a window or a door was too small or too large, you could size it to your liking while you were in the virtual building. Then the others in the group could respond until a consensus was reached about the optimum shape. The next step would be to design another feature that would automatically transfer the size of the changed feature back to the CAD program so the draftsman wouldn't have to duplicate the effort.

No current 3-D tool or application exists that can accomplish all the concepts described above, although some of the capabilities are in the process of development and the remaining features are probably not too far away. A 3-D tool something like the one just described—except that it was limited to one person at a time—was first used to design an auditorium on the campus of the University of North Carolina, Chapel Hill.

The building plans were calculated and programmed into the computer. Students and faculty "walked through" the virtual building and, for example, noticed that one corridor seemed too small. After discussion and examination, the building plans were changed to enlarge the passageway. When the plans were finalized, the ground was broken for construction and the real building was built.

According to people who "walked through" the virtual building and later walked through the real building, the feeling was quite eerie—they felt as though they had seen it all before. And everyone agreed that the small corridor would have been a problem.

3-D Training

As you have seen previously, the power of flight simulation to train pilots in flying maneuvers and the use of controls is well established. But far greater use of 3-D applications for training and development purposes is foreseen. Almost every field you can think of could utilize more efficient and effective training methods. As fields progress, increasingly advanced technology is required to train new recruits and retrain older workers for different jobs.

Several approaches have been envisioned to develop three-dimensional training applications. Naturally, the simulation approach comes immediately to mind. Automobile simulation machines have already been used in high school driver's education classes for several years.

To develop a training simulation application, you first must identify an appropriate skill that people need to learn. Then you analyze the skill to determine the components that can be simulated with hardware and software. For a driving simulator, the steering wheel, accelerator pedal, and brake pedal are necessary pieces of hardware that must be used.

After deciding on the necessary components, you then must think of ways to connect the hardware to software programs that create the simulated scenery of highways, streets, and traffic. For example, when the steering wheel is turned or the pedals are pressed, the scenery must change in a realistic manner. When you're finished, the students can sit in a "driver's seat" and experience driving a real car without the first-time anxieties, and the instructor can grade the students' competence without the worry of potential accidents.

Driver's education cars are still needed, obviously, for later transition to real-life driving, but the driving simulators are useful for the initial training that acclimates the student to driving skills in a safe and secure environment.

Overlays

As practical as simulation programs have proven to be in training, let's imagine the next step in 3-D applications for training. Suppose

it was your responsibility to show ten trainees per week how to place and solder fifty small parts on an electronic circuit board. A traditional training method would involve preparing charts that picture and label each capacitor and connector, and drawing diagrams that indicate the position of each part. You would then spend your week demonstrating the sequence of selecting a component, performing the soldering technique on each small part, and checking each trainee's progress. The cost of wasting incorrectly assembled circuit boards would probably be substantial.

Now, consider creating a 3-D application that combines a simulation with an overlaid image. Software would be developed to duplicate and simulate the circuit board. Each student would wear an HMD designed in such a way that he would see two images: the image of the instructor's real circuit board and the superimposed picture of a virtual circuit board.

As the instructor picks up a piece, the students would watch his hand in their individual visual displays and pick up the identical virtual piece. Then, as the instructor soldered the piece in place while verbally describing the technique and emphasizing the safety precautions, the students would duplicate the hand and finger positions.

Because the students would see instantaneously whether their own virtual hand positions were congruent with the instructor's hand movements, immediate coordination could provide fast learning. It would be similar to a golf instructor standing behind you, reaching around, and placing his hands on yours while you hold a club. With such a training method, you can easily feel the correct position of the hands, the appropriate tension of the muscles, and the relaxed swinging motion of the arms. Verbal descriptions and visual demonstrations in golf training are much less effective.

Three-dimensional applications have yet to reach a point where simulation and overlay technologies can be combined to any large extent, but some initial attempts are being made in some research laboratories and in the military. Broader implementations may not be very far down the road, however, because several promising indicators show that 1993 will likely provide sharp drops in the manufacturing costs of visual displays and other related technologies. At the same time that the cost curve seems ready to head

downward, a great number of companies have announced multi-million dollar development projects for the mid-1990s. The implication of lower costs, combined with more research and development money, historically has resulted in an explosion of new applications.

Converging Forces

There are strong indications that the U.S. government is preparing to encourage the funding of advanced virtual reality and synthetic environment projects. In 1991, Vice President Albert Gore, then a senator from Tennessee, held the first Senate committee hearings on virtual reality (Tom Furness, Director of the HIT Lab at the University of Washington, was one of the speakers).

Gore has vocally supported the belief that the virtual reality industry, which was invented in the United States, should be nurtured and cultivated in this country to avoid losing the resulting benefits, such as job-creation and other major spin-offs. Several indicators seem to hint of a possible surge of VR advancements in 1993. If some of these advancements increase the effectiveness of training and development, perhaps they can help continue to improve the competitiveness of U.S. firms in the global marketplace.

Another vision of future training includes a scenario in which technicians, repair personnel, or mechanics, would carry a small, lightweight visual display, with overlay capabilities, in their toolboxes. When confronted with a broken machine, the technician could then put on the display to begin the repair. While examining the circuits in the machine, the technician could voice requests to see the schematics on the overlay. The supporting equipment back at headquarters would then transmit the requested diagram to the visual display. The technician would have access to all the necessary information without carrying bulky manuals and juggling several items at one time.

The technology from this type of application would be useful in a wide range of industries, such as companies that service furnace and air conditioning units, copy machines, computers, power equipment, and the like. Automobile and aircraft manufacturers might also find cost and performance advantages in such an overlay visual display.

3-D Science

Remarkable progress in the development of advanced 3-D applications has already been achieved in several fields of science. Much of this progress is due to the relatively greater amounts of money available in the sciences and to the great technical expertise and experience of the people involved. Another reason for such fast-paced progress is that science, like architecture, deals with an entire range of physical materials that exist in the world and also with phenomenons that exist in nature—and many of these are three-dimensional. Three-dimensional applications have taken big steps in the realms of chemistry, physics, and medicine.

3-D Chemistry

One of the driving forces behind the rapid advancements in 3-D applications in the chemistry field, and in the related pharmaceutical industries, is the need and desire to use them. When you are in a situation where the materials you work with are so microscopic that you cannot see what's going on, you are likely to search for ways to command a better view. One tool used for magnifying atoms and molecules has been the electron microscope—but even the best images are so blurry and have so little detail they can hardly be called images, unless they are computer enhanced.

Another approach is to create computer-generated displays of atoms and molecules. Although these "pictures" would not show the real atoms, the advantage is that you can make them look very large. Then if you add (through software programming) mathematical reproductions of the atomic and molecular forces interacting between the individual elemental components, you can replicate accurate chemical compounds.

An application that lets you "see" the molecular interactions, however, is only a small part of the many 3-D applications being developed. One of the first force feedback arms, the Argonne ARM, which transferred the "feeling" of the forces in the molecule, was discussed in Chapter 2. The advancements in this technology have led to the development of a controller that is much smaller and more versatile.

NASA's Johnson Space Center (JSC) sponsored an effort at Cybernet Systems in Ann Arbor, Michigan, which introduced the PER-Force handcontroller in the spring of 1992—just one example of the many ways the space program technology benefits us all. This handcontroller reflects, or feeds back, computer-simulated forces to your hand as you manipulate the atoms in the molecule.

For example, if you were a researcher working for a pharmaceutical company, you might want to find a way to improve a proposed prescription drug to minimize side effects discovered through trial experiments. You could duplicate the drug molecule with a 3-D software program—such as HyperChem by Autodesk, or Alchemy III (a Macintosh program) by Tripos Associates—by first building in the accurate chemical structure and the simulated forces between the atoms. Then, by attaching the PER-Force handcontroller to your computer, you can test possible positions for other atoms and see whether they "feel" like the right locations for the desired atomic bonding.

Atoms have complicated bonding forces that are difficult to calculate using only mathematics and two-dimensional representations. Being able to feel the resistance when the atom you're moving gets too close to the boundaries of the electron shells of the atoms, or feeling the "bumpiness" of the atoms reflected in your hand, is very helpful when trying to understand atomic forces. The benefits of three-dimensional chemical applications connected to force-reflection equipment are likely to lead to beneficial discoveries that will result in improved medicines.

3-D Physics

The study of the natural laws of the universe has lead to numerous fields of study because the variations of nature are so vast. From quantum mechanics to the physics of solid matter, the ways of learning about motion, matter, and energy are almost unlimited. And because each of these disciplines, like chemistry and architecture, also deals with the three-dimensionality of natural physical processes, the number of ways to apply 3-D programs is equally broad in scope. And to make matters tougher, each of these fields of physics involves gathering data from natural subjects and then placing the information in a computer in a way that can be easily manipulated and thoroughly analyzed.

Just as the shape digitizer automated the transfer of coordinate data when creating 3-D shape models, the development of equipment to automate the gathering of data from the physical world, *data-acquisition instruments,* has been crucial in the science of physics. These machines acquire data by using sensors located in appropriate locations corresponding to the process being studied. These sensors are attached to wires that transmit the signal readings to an interface, where the information is then converted to a format required by the computer.

To illustrate the usefulness of the data-acquisition function in learning about a physical process, think about how much we've learned from seismographs, the instrument used to measure and record earthquakes. Normally, during the quiet times between earthquakes—called the dormant phase—the pens of a seismograph move gently back and forth, or oscillate, on the paper. But the sudden jolt of the first seismic wave of an earthquake makes the ink pens jump wildly. As the wave subsides, the swaying of the pens tapers until they return to normal levels. When an aftershock hits, the marking pens move in proportion to the forces of the new wave. This collection of tracking marks, known as a seismogram, is used to analyze and compare the geological forces in the Earth— even in layers that are far below ground. Scientists hope that eventually enough information will be accumulated to permit accurate earthquake forecasting.

Analog Instruments

The technology of the seismograph, which was invented a long time ago, uses the technique of measuring known as *analog*—the primary method of scientific measuring available until the digital computer was developed. The analog method is also used in the phonograph record and the tape recorder that supplanted it. The size of the waves mapped by the seismograph's pen is analogous to the forces of the earthquake's seismic waves. The size of the grooves made by the recording needle of the phonograph recorder, and the shape of the magnetic impulses made by the recording heads of the tape recorder, are analogous to the loudness of the sound waves of the artist's voice and instruments. Both words, analog and analogous, derive from the Greek words "ana" meaning "according to,"

and "logus" meaning "proportion." The measuring and recording devices are called analog systems because the quantities they output are analogous, or similar to, the proportions of the input.

What was the other word that meant "similar to," or "almost like"? Virtual. Virtual reality is similar to reality; it is analogous to reality. There are similarities between reality and the goal of virtual reality described throughout this book. We could even call the technology and the concept *Analogous Reality,* or the *Reality Analog Machine,* or even *analog environments.* We could then refer to the main principles as the viewpoint analog, the navigation analog, the manipulation analog, and the immersion analog, because the interactions we're trying to build into the computer are analogous to our built-in human capabilities; the worlds we're trying to build are analogous to the real environment. Although it might be a relief to say "analogous reality" once in a while to avoid overusing the other phrase, it certainly doesn't carry the same zing.

Digital Instruments

An analog data-acquisition instrument processes continuous quantities like the curve of a wave. Because a computer is not based on the analog method, but on the *digital* method, a problem arises when we try to transfer the information to a computer. Just as your fingers are digits, or separate units, a computer stores information in digital units.

If you draw a circle on paper with a pencil, the information about the circle is in analog format. If you form a circle with your fingertips, the information about the circle is in digital format. Figure 4.1 shows the digital and analog circles. Obviously the circle shape formed by your fingertips is not nearly as informative as the drawn circle. If you press your fingertips together in a circular shape, the form is more recognizable, but the circle is much smaller; to accomplish the same semblance of a circle in a larger size you would need more digits.

The pencil-drawn circle is made up of an infinite number of points (the many pieces of lead on the paper), while the finger, or claw-shaped, circle has only five discrete points. To approximate the penciled circle, a digital circle will need thousands of points.

Figure 4.1.

A comparison of a drawn (analog) circle and a fingertip (digital) circle.

A digital data-acquisition instrument developed for the science of physics must translate information recorded by analog sensors into digital format. We've seen the limitations of approximating circular shapes with a few digits. Let's examine ways to overcome those limitations when acquiring physical data on the digital computer.

To utilize the seismic example again, you could produce a simple digital interpretation of the lines on the seismogram by transmitting a signal to the computer for each peak of each wave, and programming the computer to display a corresponding dot for each signal. This would produce a series of dots on the monitor. Like the circle formed by your fingertips, it is not much of a picture yet. But, you could program the computer to draw lines between successive dots. This way you could look at a computer-generated graph depicting the data acquired from the seismograph, like the graph in Figure 4.2.

As you can see from this figure, the computer-generated graph is not a duplicate of the analog signal, but it does show the information researchers would be most interested in—the *amplitude*, or height of the peaks (which reports the force in each wave), and the *frequency*, or distance between the peaks (which communicates time information).

Although seismological physicists could learn from such a graph, as scientists they would not be satisfied with a device that produced such simple graphs. They would call such a piece of digital

equipment a "primitive" data-acquisition instrument. A scientist wants a digital data-acquisition machine to produce a computer-generated graph that duplicates an analog graph and shows all the points along the original line. People always want more, don't they? All right, back to the workbench we go.

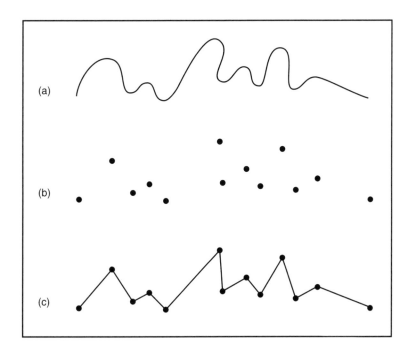

Figure 4.2.

Illustration of (a) a seismo-graph wave, (b) dots that represent the wave peaks, and (c) a computer-generated graph connect-ing the dots.

Because the main limitation of digital equipment is that it is capable of displaying only separate dots, the developers of digital data-acquisition equipment look for ways to transmit more signals more quickly—which the computer then uses to display more dots. Using more dots generates a better reproduction of the original graph. If you could construct a sensor that transmits thousands of signals per second, the computer can display thousands of dots (called *resolution*) on the graph, and the resulting high-resolution digital image would look almost exactly like the analog image source.

It is important for scientists to utilize data-acquisition instruments that generate high-resolution images. Just as the shape-digitizer makes it easier to modify a 3-D computer model, a computer image

of a phenomenon in physics can be manipulated in many ways that are not possible with analog images—including giving data a three-dimensional perspective.

Looking at information about a physical process in a 3-D format leads to a clearer understanding of its interrelated factors. Digital data-acquisition instruments open up avenues of studying physical events and relationships that could otherwise not be examined. And there's another important advantage of a 3-D application beyond merely examining the graph—because the data stored in the computer can be manipulated, physicists can select a set of data points and study the results of a computer simulation of natural forces acting on these points. This simulation capability is also called *modeling*—the same process followed in atmospheric modeling discussed in the section on 3-D modeling.

Controlled modeling in physics research using real-world information obtained through digital data-acquisition equipment has aided in many important scientific discoveries—and as technology advances, controlled modeling will allow further exploration of the mysteries of three-dimensional natural processes.

3-D Medicine

By this point, you have probably concluded that the many different 3-D applications have overlapping boundaries, and it is impossible to define absolutely discrete divisions. Whether the topic is modeling, simulation, improved communication, image manipulation, or computer-generated environments, the definitions and the mental constructs of each topic overlap one another, until the outlines begin to converge.

Of all the fields of science, the medical field may be the most advanced and furthest developed in this convergence or fusion. Besides the greater accessibility of funding than in most other fields, and the bedrock platform of technical expertise built during many decades, the driving force in the medical field for the development of 3-D tools—as in all its research and development—is unique to this field: the demand for effective health-care. The needs are plentiful and tangible—biomedical researchers require better tools to conduct the search for answers, surgeons desire better ways to

repair the human body, and medical schools need practical solutions to the problem of training medical students.

As 3-D technology and equipment improves, so does its utilization in the medical field. From fetal heart monitors to magnetic resonance imaging (MRI), the equipment is developed and implemented to reach important goals—to facilitate improved diagnosis and treatment of the patient's condition. What better place to apply these 3-D tools to improve understanding of three-dimensional processes than in front of the doctor? The patient's organs, nerves, bones, arteries, muscles, injuries, diseases, and tissues are all three-dimensional. Using these 3-D tools is very effective because the surgeon can't see through layers of flesh to perceive the desired object, and the patient is sensitive to any invasion.

Any 3-D imaging capability that facilitates swifter understanding and minimizes recuperation is going to be hastily grabbed and put into service. This use of 3-D applications, unlike many other experimental medical strategies, has the full support of the medical profession, hospital administrations, equipment vendors, the insurance industry, and the patients. After all, everybody wants to be cured as quickly as possible—and with the least conceivable pain and suffering. This section focuses on three key areas of medical 3-D applications: radiation treatment, surgical training, and brain surgery.

3-D Radiation Treatment

The first example was developed by the team under Fred Brooks at UNC Chapel Hill, the premier research laboratory for medical VR applications. The application helps radiologists focus several radioactive beams on a cancerous tumor without affecting the surrounding non-cancerous tissues. Without the 3-D tool to help guide them, the radiologists would have to take many X-ray pictures and calculate the best path for each beam based on their mental reconstruction of the X-ray information.

Without using the 3-D tools, both the patient and the doctor are inconvenienced. To acquire the X-rays, the patient must be strapped down on the table while the X-ray machine rotates around the region taking pictures of the tissues from all directions. This procedure requires the patient to hold still for long periods of time, and is quite burdensome. The patient needs a great deal of patience to remain in this position, especially if the disease has reached a painful state. In addition to the difficulties placed on each patient, the length of time required limits the number of X-rays that can be performed each day.

The UNC approach creates a computer-generated environment combining a virtual (analogous? synthetic? cyber?) image of the patient with a virtual representation of the radiation beams. The computer is connected to the X-ray equipment in such a way that the doctor can see the images of the tissues and the representation of the beams simultaneously. By using a DataGlove, the doctor can reposition a beam by "grabbing" the shaft of the virtual beam and positioning it so that it does not hit any of the nearby organs. The virtual beam shaft is coupled to the real beam generator so that the radiation is directed to the spot the doctor selects. In this manner, the doctor can quickly aim the beams at the target from several directions—the patient does not need to sit still for nearly as long, and many more patients can receive treatment each day. The patients can easily see the benefits of this three-dimensional application.

3-D Surgical Training

There are few stories you'll hear that are as viscerally frightening as those describing a surgical procedure carried out by an inexperienced or insufficiently trained surgeon or doctor. This is a domain that cries out for the development of 3-D training applications. And that is approximately the state of three-dimensional training for beginning surgeons—waiting for development.

Although some initial steps have been taken, the possibilities are mostly conceptual at this point. There is a great deal of development that must be carried out on prototypes and technical procedures before applications in this area will reach maturity. Certainly, the concept of VR surgical applications can be visualized quite easily, and almost all new researchers and developers in the virtual reality field conceive of applying it to the field of surgical training soon after they grasp the principles involved in VR.

The idea of a 3-D system that lets interns practice cutting and slicing on virtual representations of the human body is immediately appealing to all of us. What better way to avoid the tragedy of a real mistake than to equip medical schools with virtual "guinea pig" patients? Let the surgeons-to-be find out which nerves to avoid, the best way to enter the skull, and the most effective angle of the scalpel on a subject who can't feel a thing and won't care what slip-ups result in an incorrectly cut tendon, or worse. Why continue to rely on old training techniques involving cadavers that don't bleed like real people, or other alternatives that don't have the realism necessary for solid experience?

This virtual surgical training application is expected to become a reality, but not for awhile. The technological limitations of current hardware and software are still too restrictive for the full implementation of virtual surgical training, but the pieces are slowly fitting together towards the goal. We've seen how computer graphics capabilities, advancements in processor speeds, force reflection, and realism improvements are converging towards more complex applications. Groups in different areas of the country are even working on separate pieces of the puzzle. Your children may be able to benefit from surgeons getting their first-hand training on virtual reality systems with three-dimensional virtual bodies duplicating the functions of the human.

3-D Brain Surgery

All surgery involves serious decisions, but brain surgery—where the control center of the body is invaded—encompasses some of the most complicated details and procedures, and entails some of the highest risks of surgical errors. The equipment gathered to help the neurosurgeon, therefore, is some of the most complex, advanced, and expensive in the hospital. Sophisticated, digitized, high-resolution, three-dimensional tools can give neurosurgeons the guidance they need to locate positions in the brain more precisely than previous methods.

A recent example at the Cleveland Clinic Foundation—a hospital in Cleveland, Ohio—shows what is possible in 3-D applications for brain surgery. They have developed a system that allows a surgeon to locate a position in the brain within a fraction of an inch.

r. Kormos, Ph.D, and Dr. Barnett, M.D., of the Cleveland Clinic, have created a way to connect a hand-held probe to the computer that uses *ultrasonic* sound waves—sounds so high in pitch that you cannot hear them—to coordinate computer data with the real brain. The doctors must first place a few markers on the patient's head for reference points. The brain is then scanned with an MRI (magnetic resonance imaging) or a CT (computed tomography) system.

The MRI and CT systems are large, expensive machines, each of which is a type of digital data-acquisition instrument combined with shape digitizing capabilities. They collect 3-D information of the human brain from all angles and store the data in fast, advanced computers.

Because the data is referenced to the scalp markers, when the patient enters the operating room the doctor can touch the sonic probe, also called the *magic wand,* to the markers on the patient's head, and the computer will display the stored data superimposed on the images of the real brain. Placing the sonic probe in a part of the brain, the surgeon can look at the computer to see exactly where the position is located in the brain. Remember, we discussed the computer's ability to manipulate images in hundreds of ways. The computer images are designed by the programmer to include reference points that help the doctor determine what section the probe is touching.

Because the brain is a mass of tissue, it is difficult to know exactly what part of it you're looking at. This is a big problem because tiny sections of the brain located next to each other often control different parts of the body. If you think you are operating on section A and your instruments are missing section A by a quarter of an inch, you might be working on section B without knowing it—there are no dividing lines between sections of the brain. The Cleveland Clinic's work in laser surgery has given a great thrust to the computer surgery field. See the related sidebar for details of their work.

To imagine how much this helps the surgeon, let's set up a thought experiment. Visualize yourself as a contestant in an unusual competition. The rules stipulate that you will be carried blindfolded onto an empty football field where the white lines have no numbers. There is a layer of fog so heavy that you can only see your feet when the blindfold is removed. Someone announces over the loudspeaker that a package filled with gold coins has been buried near the center of the fifty-yard line. The coins are yours to keep if you can locate the package.

You can see a white line near you, but you have no way of telling exactly where on the field you are standing. You realize the only way to get your bearings is to start at one end of the field and count

the lines until you reach the fifty-yard line, then estimate the center of the line. Once you reach the goal line, you start walking back towards the fifty-yard line—but you can't see anything except the grass under your feet. Imagine how difficult it would be to find the buried package under these conditions. You could get confused, count wrong, and waste time looking along the wrong line. Even when you count correctly, you still have to find the center of the fifty-yard line. You might have to crawl up and down the fifty-yard line for quite some time looking for the little spot of dirt in the grass where the package was buried.

That's the kind of situation you would face if you were a surgeon operating on the brain without any markings or position indicators. It's like working in the dark or in the fog. You can calculate approximately where you have to go, but when you get there it is difficult to know if you need to move a little to the left or right—especially if you know that a slight miscalculation might mean cutting a portion of the brain that is perfectly healthy.

Now, let's return to the football field. This time, an electrician has hooked up a grid of wires with tiny lights every five feet. Each light is marked with position information, such as "15 feet from goal line, and 30 feet from left edge." The fog is still very heavy, and you can't see more than one light at a time, but this time the announcer tells you that the package is buried next to the light marked "150 feet from goal line, and 45 feet from left edge." Now, you can walk to the nearest light and read the sign, walk to the next light and read its sign, and continue this pattern until you reach the desired location.

A surgeon using a 3-D computer tool can look at the image of the patient's brain and see where the sonic probe is located using the position markers—which are as clear as the tiny lights on the football field. It is almost like being able to see through the brain tissues. It's like turning on the lights in a dark room and suddenly seeing where all the furniture is located. Surgeons can do a better job with the computer helping to "light" the way.

3-D Education

One of the areas where three-dimensional applications are projected to be the most productive is the field of education. In primary, secondary, and university levels, the subjects abound with concepts that could be taught and understood more clearly—and more forcefully—with 3-D representations. The potential implications of learning math fundamentals in geometry (especially solid geometry), algebra, trigonometry, and calculus—as well as in subjects as varied as history, physics, chemistry, computer programming, psychology, foreign languages, and most other areas—are intriguing.

Imagine introducing tools that allow students to see information and objects from different angles and viewpoints, where they can control and manipulate the objects. When you think of this concept after reflecting on our discussions of the powerful impact such applications have in the professional arenas, you begin to realize the educational possibilities. But, as we have also seen, the functions of the computer that permit shaping and massaging of data, like modeling and simulating, open up other avenues of learning such as performing experiments, forming theories and hypotheses, controlling variables, and looking for evidence to support their conclusions.

But there is far more to offer by combining computers and 3-D tools. The ability of a student to explore a virtual environment at his or her own speed and competence level, where the student's own curiosity provides the motivation, becomes an educational force in its own right. Then, by connecting 3-D tools to data-acquisition instruments, and representing the real-world data in three-dimensional images, the students can better learn and understand physical processes.

There is another level of learning that brings a whole new perspective to the use of 3-D tools in education. The fascinating possibilities of this other level outshine even the exploration and experimentation avenues. Imagine letting students build their own worlds and environments with 3-D development systems like VREAM (described later), learning the concepts of "cyberspace engineering," creating geometric shapes, learning the math to

combine these shapes into more sophisticated objects, and learning the logic necessary to create the conditions these objects interact with. There's an aspect of constructing and controlling your own "world" that is so appealing that it can motivate each student to learn while he or she builds.

The advantages of using three-dimensional applications to improve the education process in the schools are both so wide-ranging and persuasive that their eventual implementation is likely—with one main hindrance: a lack of funds. Stuart Vorpagel, Director of Robotics at Gateway Technical College in Kenosha, Wisconsin, along with other educators, has laid out the funding process in terms that relate education to the larger society, in his case represented by the technical industries.

Vorpagel says that because educational funding generally falls short of the needs of education, the schools' choices of which programs to fund are driven by necessity—and the perspective of what constitutes necessity is, in large part, shaped by society. In the case of technical programs like robotics, the college funding programs are influenced by the skills required by the technical industries. If the industry demands a certain skill, then the schools have no choice but to train students for that particular skill—and funding is sought for the equipment and staff needed to teach this skill. This process generates a built-in lag time between a technological advancement and the incorporation of that advancement in the schools; the length of lag time depends on when and whether the technology is implemented in industry.

Understanding the structural cause of this delay in education opens up an opportunity for the developers of technology to coordinate an approach that can decrease the time-lag by short-circuiting the loop. If technology companies purchase subsidized equipment and make it available to qualified school programs, the sequence of technology-industry-school can be modified somewhat. Apple Computer and IBM are well-known examples of companies that have educational purchase programs for this very purpose; their efforts deserve to be applauded and encouraged. As technology companies, the industries, and the schools continue this funding relationship, 3-D tools will continue to appear in schools and provide students with new educational experiences.

An example of a subsidized educational program is a pilot development study sponsored by VRontier worlds of Stoughton, Inc., of which this writer was the facilitator. The objective of the study was to monitor the effects of virtual reality methods when used in a local elementary school. The project was encouraged by the principal, Barbara Wood, who suggested the participation of two teachers, Jan Martin and Judith Reese, in charge of a kindergarten class with 24 children.

The plan was to design an environment with the Virtual Reality Studio development system; the educational objective was to target the concepts of classification and categorization, and to observe the impact of the VR principles on the learning process. A demonstration version of the resulting program, Mover3, is included on the disk in this book.

During several sessions, the students were observed as they explored the environment and discovered different features. Conclusions are preliminary, but it was observed that motivation seemed high as students gained experience in an open-ended learning situation. Because of the primitive nature of the graphics and other limitations of the program, the study was postponed until advancements in hardware and software could be implemented, but several principles were established by the teachers including guidelines for the interaction of students and the modifications necessary for teacher evaluation.

The foundations for educational VR applications and interactive 3-D tools can be built through similar pilot programs sponsored by VR development companies. Important feedback can be provided in return for a modest investment.

3-D Shopping

The versatility of three-dimensional applications becomes more and more evident as we examine the implications of simulating environments on the computer, but selecting kitchen cabinets in cyberspace is usually not one of the first VR possibilities visualized by most people. But it is an existing application right now in Japan.

Matsushita Electric Works (MEW) has a subsidiary in Osaka that provides a system that allows housewives to test their own kitchen design using a virtual reality 3-D tool. The customer enters the virtual kitchen using the head-mounted display and DataGlove, tries out the cabinets desired, and arranges the virtual cabinets in virtual space until a satisfactory design is determined.

Because the customer can try out actions in the virtual kitchen, such as opening the cabinet doors and testing out the sink faucet, she can make sure all the sizes, cabinet placements, and dimensions are correct before placing her order. The VR system then transfers information about the selected pieces to the computer that controls the manufacturing; the cabinets are then built to her specifications.

As Junji Nomura, Ph.D., Senior Staff Researcher at MEW, explains it, most of the present computer-aided manufacturing is geared towards mass production, and the "specifications of products should be more easily changed according to the individual customer's need." The MEW virtual kitchen allows the customer to easily choose custom cabinets, and the manufacturing is able to create the custom design. Designing and building custom cabinets is usually a tiresome process of round-trips between the cabinet store, the contractor's facilities, and the customer's kitchen, plus the error-prone work of making the drawings correctly, and several other steps. Being able to accomplish all of these phases in a single two-hour visit to cyberspace is a remarkable accomplishment; the benefits are clear to anyone who has previously designed and built a kitchen.

3-D Sports

In Chapter 3 we discussed the virtual skiing prototype recently announced by NEC. There are numerous 3-D applications possible, or soon to be possible, that are useful in many sports activities. Simulations of different sports will allow more effective training of beginners and more accessibility to people who are normally denied access to them because of age (like virtual skiing) or disability.

Already there have been simulations made of an Olympic-grade bobsled and a snowboard. David Blackburn, sports aficionado and

founder of the first VR SIG (Special Interest Group) Chapter of the International Interactive Computer Society (IICS) in Los Angeles, is one person who is deeply involved with developing sports-related 3-D tools and virtual reality applications.

He explained to me that the virtual bobsled was built on a motion platform that moves realistically with the virtual motion of the participants in the sled. The description of the motion platform reminded me of the foot plates the virtual skiers stand on in the NEC prototype. The development of realistic motion simulators (for sporting activities) seems to be a recent advancement over the older technology that placed the entire human body in a cubicle or a box. The entire box rolls, tilts, bumps, and shakes while a movie is projected on the front wall. (That reminds me of the little horse ride still sitting in front of many malls where two-year-olds ask their moms for a quarter so they can trot in one place for a minute). As motion simulators are fine-tuned to the point where they provide suitable effects that are in harmony with a particular sport, the coupling of motion simulators to computers in innovative ways may become an industry in itself.

A VR application for baseball was developed in 1992 that analyzed the pitching ability of the five best pitchers in baseball. Their fast pitches were recorded on computer while the paths of the arm and the hand were detailed in fractions of a second. Then, with a DataGlove over their hands, other pitchers were given the opportunity to duplicate the motions with their pitching arm. The aim was to see if their pitches could be improved by imitation. Being able to slow down the pitching motion to visualize each relationship and being able to see the angles of the arm and hand were apparently helpful in improving the speed of the fast pitches—especially since the motion of a pitcher's arm is so fast in real life that it is difficult to follow.

This next story is about an activity that is not typically called a sport, but aside from being a charming story, it may reach the status of a legendary story in the history of virtual reality. It also forcefully demonstrates the dynamic abilities of VR.

When Jaron Lanier, the cofounder of VPL Research, was in the early stages of developing the connections between the DataGlove and the EyePhone, he realized he had a system that might help him

learn something he always had wanted to learn—juggling. So he programmed the computer to display a ball, and he practiced juggling that one virtual ball in the air using the glove. Then he adjusted the program to slow down the motion of the ball and added another ball, then another one. Because the balls were in slow-motion, it was easier to learn the hand and arm motions that are required for juggling.

Once he mastered the juggling motions, he gradually increased the speed until the balls were travelling as fast as they do in the real world. Then, he took off the glove and tested his new skill with three real balls; he found that he had mastered the art of juggling. He had just taught himself juggling—the first person to employ a virtual reality machine to learn how to juggle. It happened approximately in 1986.

3-D Tools for the Physically Challenged

Although most of us find ourselves physically challenged on occasion, the phrase is a recently selected way to refer to people who used to be called disabled or handicapped. Some people with disabilities (and the people who take care of them) put forth a convincing argument that the word "disabled" connotes a meaning they do not like to be associated with (would you?)—a person who is not "able." A disabled automobile is a car that can't do anything. A disabled machine is a piece of equipment that is broken down and cannot perform its job.

A person with a physical problem, the logic continues, is definitely not a "broken-down" human who can't do anything, but a person who is able to work productively at a job and happens to have a physical problem (a challenge). The underlying reason for this effort to modify our use of language is mainly targeted at employers, to underscore the point that people with different kinds of challenges should not be discriminated against by the unintended harm caused by a phrase, or label.

One of the major contributions to this field was first called the Talking Glove, and then refined into the CyberGlove, developed by James Kramer and Larry Leifer at Stanford University. The Talking Glove is connected to a speaker that converts the glove's signals into speech. When a person puts on the glove and spells words using sign language (like that used by the deaf), an electronic circuit interprets the finger positions, selects the word represented by the gesture, and sends the signals to the speaker. The circuit is in a small box attached to a belt around the person's waist; the speaker hangs from a necklace. The glove allows people who cannot talk to communicate with speech through finger and hand motions. The CyberGlove has advancements that are more suited to being interfaced with a virtual environment.

Another leading contribution is Wheelchair VR, which has benefits for a walking person as well as the wheelchair bound. Developed at Hines V.A. Hospital, the wheelchair is really a new input device that provides an alternative to the situation commonly found with the DataGlove. The usual method of signaling the direction you want to move while in a virtual environment wearing the glove is to point your finger in the desired direction. To move forward, you point forward. When you want to stop, you stop pointing. This convention of using pointing gestures to move around is quite workable, but with a few minor drawbacks: You cannot draw someone's attention to an object by pointing at it.

The wheelchair, in contrast, is designed to sit on a pair of parallel rollers, similar to an automobile undergoing a mileage check-up— sitting on a pair of rollers while the mechanic revs the engine. The car doesn't go anywhere, and neither does the wheelchair; the computer is connected to the rollers in a manner that allows it to calculate the distance you want to move in the virtual world while you rotate the chair's wheels (using the same principle, in effect, as the rollers in a mouse pointing device). It is a navigation tool that is operable by persons with lower-body paralysis or other physical limitations.

Building equipment to provide alternatives for people with disabilities is a challenge for research labs and developers of 3-D and VR tools of all kinds, but Gregg Vanderheiden, Ph.D. says there is a larger and more important perspective to consider; this message

should be carefully listened to and its suggestions implemented by all software and hardware VR developers.

Vanderheiden is the Director of the Trace Research and Development Center in the Waisman Center at the University of Wisconsin, Madison. The Trace Center is a research and resource center focused on the issue of guiding the development of technology to benefit human disability. Although the Trace Center does not directly develop VR applications, Vanderheiden and his team—John Mendenhall and Tom Andersen—have used their experience in this field to spotlight some meaningful issues for the future of VR applications; the importance of these issues has generated invitations to speak at disability conferences, such as California State University's annual Technology and Persons with Disabilities Conference.

Vanderheiden's message is simple, but it takes some reflection to sink in. He points to a historical tendency of developers of new technologies to make decisions that unintentionally cause difficulties for people who later try to modify those technologies and make them accessible to people with impairments—the physically challenged.

An example he uses is the graphical user's interface (GUI) that was developed for individuals with full sensory and physical capabilities. He points out that if the GUI had been built in a slightly different way, to allow alternate control or sensory substitution, the interface would have been much easier to modify for impaired individuals.

Depending on the disability, some individuals find it easier to understand the spoken voice, others the written word, and still others the graphic, or visual, icon. If the developers of the GUI had included simple "hooks," or sections of code where these alternate substitutions could have been attached, the GUI could have been more quickly modified for broad access to more people. Vanderheiden pleads the case for future developers to remember to allow easier access to VR environments.

Another instance he describes is, if a phone in a VR world is ringing, a deaf person would not hear it. A simple way to modify this would be to add visual waves emanating from the telephone, providing another layer of information for the deaf. The problem is, if the VR

129

environment is too tightly encoded or encrypted, this type of modification is difficult—perhaps impossible—to achieve, thus leaving the deaf person at a disadvantage in the environment. If the VR developer or world-builder would widen his or her perspective to be aware of the needs of the disabled and leave open some room for appropriate modifications, access to people with visual, hearing, physical, and other impairments could be more equal.

It certainly must be disappointing to users who try to overcome their impairments to discover an obstacle that makes an experience useless to them—especially if the obstacle might have been easily removed with a little forethought. If Vanderheiden and his team's efforts are attended to by the growing VR industry, perhaps virtual reality can be shared by a wider population. The Trace Center is providing a solid service for its patrons in providing an early warning that deserves to be noticed now—not when it is too late.

Putting It All Together

We've now reviewed several three-dimensional applications with great potential for improving the lives and lifestyles of people. The benefits of VR technology are likely to have an increasing impact on millions of people, in areas such as health-care, construction, education, and sports, including special groups of all kinds. But the possibilities don't end there. New opportunities to apply VR are appearing frequently as more people begin to grasp the advantages, and think of ways to apply the capabilities in ever more complex combinations.

A good example of an intriguing new approach is the work being done in the field of data visualization. People who deal with large amounts of numbers are finding more difficulty in knowing the overall picture. Stock market analysts, corporate executives, sales managers, and others in similar positions, are inundated daily with an increasing avalanche of information. An application that might help manage this overload would be a program that converts the raw numbers into 3-D shapes. The objects could easily be color-coded to correspond with the level of action needed (red for "immediate," green for "later," and so forth). Many other combinations can be designed to coordinate information, such as blinking,

rotating, expanding, shrinking, and so on. In fact, data visualization may be one of the "killer apps," as they're called—a business application that is so obviously beneficial and productive everyone feels they have to have it. Spreadsheet and word processing programs were the first "killer apps" that brought millions of desktop computers into business offices.

A data-visualization program now being used to analyze the stock market was highlighted in the June 1992 issue of Forbes magazine. Developed by Paul Marshall of Maxus Systems and programmers at Sense8 Corporation, the program builds a VR world that accepts a stream of numbers from the stock market and creates a 3-D landscape covered with groups of shapes representing stocks. As the prices fluctuate, the shapes automatically reflect changes in color and height as the stocks change value. The analyst using the program can "fly" over this landscape and grasp the meaning of important trends immediately without studying long columns of numbers. Similar approaches could be used to communicate the regional sales performances in a corporation, or the minute-by-minute financial health of a large company.

As more sophisticated uses for VR are imagined, the systems to apply them will have to advance in parallel. We'll look at the capabilities of VR systems as we examine some of the issues involved with them in the next chapter.

Chapter 5

Virtual Reality Systems

This chapter examines issues and problems that an engineer faces when designing components to be integrated into a virtual reality system. We'll look at design problems that have been solved, sometimes in more than one way. We'll detail design questions that are still waiting for answers—or better answers than have been found. We will also turn to open-ended design puzzles to be grappled with in the future.

Exploring Human Factor Issues

The common denominator, the foundation, the framework on which all virtual reality design solutions are built is *human factors* research. The shapes and forms of humans, the sizes of human limbs, the distances from one location on the human body to another, the capabilities and limitations of humans, the position and function of the sense organs, the mechanisms of human muscles and bones, the way humans interpret stimuli, the psychological reactions and compensations of humans—all of these, and many more, are called human factors. Hundreds of organizations—including the automobile companies, the perfume companies, the office seating companies, the washing machine companies, the aircraft and spacecraft manufacturing industries—have spent decades studying human factors to improve the coordination of their products with the human body.

On the other hand, the virtual reality industry is not only quite new, it is also confronted with many unprecedented situations dealing with some of the most intimate associations with the human body. For example, as Bradley Burnett (VP of Research & Development, VRontier worlds of Stoughton, Inc.) says, there is no instruction manual on the topic of building head mounted-displays. An engineer can't just call up an expert and ask "What's the optimum distance a screen should be placed from the eye?"

Standards are not in place for much of VR work. In fact, in some cases, the moment an engineer decides on an innovative solution, that decision becomes the only existing standard. To complicate matters further, as engineers discover every day, turning a concept into an actual piece of VR equipment requires a galaxy of expertise and ability that must be coordinated—and is frequently difficult to find. Most engineers are trained in one or two specialties, while VR solutions need contributions from almost every field; it is hard to find engineers with extensive enough training, who are also creative enough, and who can devote enough time and resources to the challenge. Many engineers refuse to get involved with a project they perceive as inordinately demanding, unless the compensation is equitable.

Up to the present time, virtual reality developers have had to research human factors at the same time they push forward. Doing both presents a situation that is somewhat chaotic, confusing, vague, and frustrating for everyone: people in the field, people who want to contribute to the field (hooray), people who want to understand the field, as well as people who try to explain the field of virtual reality—its achievements and its direction. With this limitation of human factors research in mind, the remainder of this chapter attempts to present the clearest possible description of the

intricate issues and knotty dilemmas involved in one of the most adventuresome projects in human history: the struggle to probe the frontiers of alternate worlds.

Exploring Display Issues

The most essential fact about the human factors involved with the sense of sight is the distance between the pupils of the eyes. The Latin word for "eye" was "oculus," so this measurement is called the *interocular* (between eyes) *distance* (see Figure 5.1). This distance is about 64 millimeters, or about two and a half inches. Some of us have eyes that are a little closer, and some a little wider, but 64 millimeters is a workable average. This distance is so important, it affects all design efforts.

When contemplating a virtual reality display, one of the first concerns is creating a device to hold the screens close to the eyes to provide the illusion of immersion. This immediately leads to questions regarding screen type and screen size.

There are two main types of screens: *cathode ray tubes* (CRT) and *liquid crystal displays* (LCD). A CRT screen is the type used by the big television set in your living room and the monitor used with a desktop computer; an LCD screen is the type used in small portable TVs and portable computers (although some small TVs use tiny CRTs). CRTs are made of glass—even small ones are heavy. LCDs are made of liquid crystal and are lighter in weight. Another crucial difference is that a CRT sprays electrons towards the phosphor coated screen, while an LCD electronically switches cells on and off.

There are two essential reasons you would not want a CRT in front of your eyes: The sheer weight, and the spraying of electrons. The weight is a problem because of the physics of torque (from the Latin word meaning "to twist"). The weight of your arm is the same whether you pick up a fork on the table or reach out to shake an acquaintance's hand, but the torque effect (the amount your shoulder muscles are contracted, or "twisted") increases the farther you extend your reach. In the same way, the heavier the display in front of your head, the more effect on the muscles in your neck. To avoid jamming chiropractor's waiting rooms with patients complaining of neck injuries, VR developers try to minimize the weight of the displays.

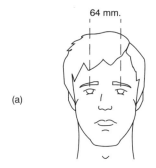

64 mm.

(a)

Interocular distance

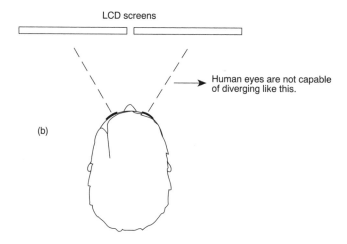

LCD screens

(b)

Human eyes are not capable of diverging like this.

Problem of divergence

Figure 5.1.

Illustration of (a) interocular distance, (b) the problem of divergence, and (c) the wrap-around screen.

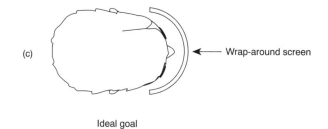

(c)

Wrap-around screen

Ideal goal

When CRTs are used, they are usually placed beside the head facing forward, with lightweight mirrors in front of the eyes reflecting the images into the pupils. This reduces the concern about electrons shooting straight into the eye from the CRT electron gun, also. But, this arrangement has a number of drawbacks—it is expensive to implement, still heavy, difficult to produce an immersion effect with, and awkward to place on and off the head.

The Divergence Problem

The drawbacks of CRTs means that we are left with one choice—LCDs. The weight factor (and therefore, torque) is less, and the electrons are gone. The drawbacks currently include less resolution (which makes the picture less clear than CRTs) and higher cost (because LCDs have been difficult to manufacture). But there is no other real choice, so the decision to use LCDs is easy to make. And that's when the interocular distance hits you right between the eyes. Bad pun. The reason why the interocular distance is important relates to the active centers of the screens—but it requires some explanation.

We need to clarify the design problem by defining it. If nothing else mattered, you would want to have the largest screens possible in front of your eyes, both to achieve the best immersive effect and to increase the resolution. But that doesn't quite state the ideal.

The ideal goal would be to have a screen that wraps completely around your eyes—from left temple to right temple (see Figure 5.1). Well, the truly ideal goal would be to see the virtual environment without screens—but that will probably remain an unfulfilled dream for quite some time. The wraparound screen is not even available yet.

So, to return to the design problem: Right now we're stuck with flat screens. The larger the screen, the better the resolution and immersion, but with the result of increasing *divergence,* where the centers of the screens are further from one another (see Figure 5.1).

Human eyes are coupled together in a fashion that does not allow for divergence past 64 millimeters (see Figure 5.1). You can cross your eyes closer together (called *convergence*), but, with exceptions

so rare they make medical history, your eyes are not capable of diverging any farther than 64 mm from one another.

Without a solution to the divergence problem, the largest screens we can use are ones that, when lined up next to each other, have their active centers no more than 64 millimeters apart. The active center can be different from the center of the actual screen due to screen shifting (see Figure 5.2), a method of moving the image to the left or right, similar to adjusting the horizontal shift on a television set or computer monitor.

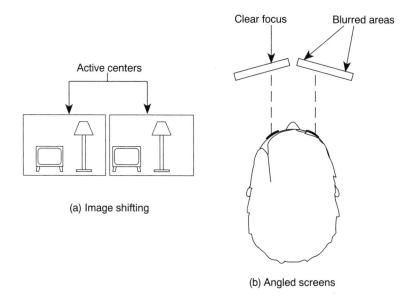

(a) Image shifting

(b) Angled screens

Figure 5.2.

Illustration of (a) image shifting, and (b) angled screens.

The largest LCD screens available that can have their active centers 64 mm apart are about three inches (diagonal measure). The next size available is a four-inch screen, but the active centers are too far apart when placed side by side. Guess what you find when you look inside most HMDs with LCD screens? Yes—three-inch screens, or even 2.7-inch screens (diagonal measure). The breakthrough that led to the use of four-inch screens was related to finding a way to solve the divergence problem. We'll describe the solution when we discuss optics, later in this chapter.

But if you don't shift the active centers, even three-inch screens are slightly too divergent. So one compromise, although unsatisfactory,

that has been implemented when image shifting is not feasible, has been to place the screens at a slight angle to each other (see Figure 5.2). This has the effect of lessening the distance between the centers, but makes some screen positions out of focus, resulting in a partly blurry image. This trade-off is a high price to pay for convergence correction, because a clear image is a high priority.

The Immersion Problem

When you sit and watch TV, or even a movie, you don't feel like you are actually inside the TV. Even when you are caught up in the plot and empathizing with the characters, you are still aware of the real-world environment surrounding the TV screen. Neither can you achieve an immersive feeling by placing your face up against the screen; your left and right eyes will see different parts of the image.

The only way to provide a feeling of being inside the pictures is to display the same image to both eyes. What happens in your brain then is remarkable. Your mind looks at both images and actually interprets them as being just one image. This phenomenon is called *fusing;* if the human brain was not capable of fusing two images together, we would have a much more difficult immersion problem. Fortunately, the brain can fuse images, which provides some additional advantages when we reach the topic of stereoscopic vision. (Using the exact same images is called monoscopic; stereoscopic is a little different.)

If you have looked at a Viewmaster or other stereoscope device, you can recall the way the two images fused in your mind to produce the depth sensation of looking at one scene. Imagine, then, the effect of fusing two moving images in front of your eyes. It is quite an experience. But fusing by itself is not enough to produce a convincing immersive effect. You also must follow some of the rules stated by Eric Howlett, who was mentioned in Chapter 2 as the inventor of VPL Research's EyePhones. We'll hear about him frequently, because of his brilliant contributions to optical advancements.

Howlett identifies a principle of immersion that states that the diameter of the opening, or aperture, your eye looks through to see the screen must be twice the distance between the opening and the

center of the eyeball. So, if the aperture is one inch from the center of your eye, the opening must be twice as much, two inches, in diameter.

This formula results from the way that our eyes see—in a sort of cone shape (see Figure 5.3). Check your eyeglasses—if you wear them. You'll see, if they are the standard shape, that they're probably about one-half inch from your pupil (or about one inch from the center of your eyeball), and they're about two inches in diameter. If you draw an imaginary shape starting at the center of the eyeball and connect it to the perimeter of one of the lenses in your eyeglasses (if you don't wear them, look at a friend's), you'll comprehend the cone shape. When you swivel your eyes as far as possible in each direction (which is your field of view—about 90 degrees total), you find that your line of sight inscribes the outer shape of the cone. (See Figure 5.3.)

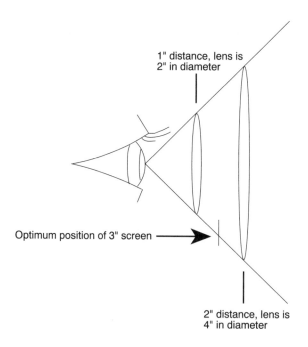

1" distance, lens is 2" in diameter

Optimum position of 3" screen →

2" distance, lens is 4" in diameter

Figure 5.3.

Illustration of how the eye sees in a cone shape. Also, the two sizes of lenses that follow the immersion formula.

If Howlett's rule is not followed, the edges of the scene will be visible—which defeats the immersion principle. The goal is to create a display that provides a feeling of immersion; if you can see the edges of the scene, you might as well go back and watch TV from the couch.

Howlett's Camera

The full effect of Howlett's optical system is beyond words to describe, but it was not designed for a VR system. It was designed in the late 1970s for viewing pictures taken with a very special camera, also designed by Howlett. At this writing, there are only three of Howlett's cameras in existence. As strange as it sounds, a camera that takes pictures so stunningly lifelike and three-dimensional they take your breath away, a camera with an optical system unlike anything ever imagined, a camera with capabilities that may never be achievable again—that camera is not yet available for general use, and is still waiting for funding.

Eric Howlett may be the most inventive person to work on optics since Galileo and Leeuwenhoek, but his greatest achievement has not yet reached the wide market. It can only be called a great tragedy—and an immeasurable loss to science and the world—if the camera doesn't achieve production. Howlett has taken some pictures with it, however, and anyone who has seen at least one of those pictures knows what the world of photography is missing.

The night before I was told the story of the camera, I had been offered a chance to see "something that will change your life." I asked what it was, and I was told that it was indescribable. I made the appointment and lifted up a special viewer to my eyes. There in front of me was a crowd of people, almost breathing, in a park. The view was wide, unlike a regular picture. I could look to the left and see a granite building with doors that looked real enough to walk in, and to the right I could see the green trees and bushes looking as if they were waiting for the breeze to shake their leaves. The depth was outstanding—the people who were farther away seemed as far away as they would be in real life. The little boy with his balloon looked close enough to touch. If I wasn't there with the crowd, sharing their Sunday outing, it was only because no one turned and said "Hi!"

These were slides, but a kind I had never imagined. I was immersed in a picture—an experience I'll never forget. My friend was right, those slides did change my life. They made me want to achieve a new goal—to make virtual reality as realistic as those slides.

Howlett's optics caught the attention of NASA. When the HMD developers saw Howlett's viewer, they must have said, in effect,

143

"We've got to use that system; it's unbelievable. Why use anything else when these are available?" Michael McGreevy and Scott Fisher at NASA had the resources to develop the software that makes Howlett's optical system work.

The effect of Howlett's viewer on people at NASA was so great that no one thought about researching other approaches any further. The result was that one of the most significant issues in building a head-mounted display—solving the divergence problem (more correctly called the *image spacing* problem) in a more affordable way—was going to have to wait a few more years.

LEEP Optics

There were good reasons not to initiate a costly research program in optics in the mid-1980s. Howlett's optical viewer was available. You could buy it and use it right away. It was clearly the best you could hope for. It provided a wide angle picture and an amazing depth of vision. All you had to do was mount two display screens into a plastic shell, place the optical viewer in front of them, and presto, you had an HMD. (Another important reason not to be overlooked is that the largest screens available were 2.7 inches in diagonal measure.)

When Howlett and his wife were discussing the new optical system over cocktails one night in 1979, the phrase "the picture just leaps out at you" was used. Howlett observed that "leap" would be a great name for the system, and then worked out the acronym *LEEP* for *Large Expanse Extra Perspective*.

However, as good as it is, the LEEP optical viewer is only half of the system required to get the kinds of pictures I saw in the slides. The entire LEEP optical system combines both compression and decompression (Howlett calls it "formatting"; he calls the whole system *Wide Angle Orthostereo*). First, a picture is created by lenses that compress (see Figure 5.4), or "push together," all the details from a wide view into a standard size rectangle. Then the LEEP optical viewer is used to decompress, or "spread out," the picture, so it looks wide again (see Figure 5.5).

Figure 5.4.

Illustration of (a) a standard picture and (b) the LEEP compression format of a picture or display.

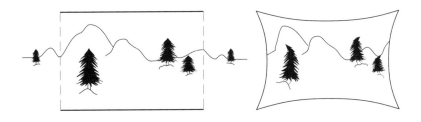

Figure 5.5.

Illustration of (a) a wide-angle Orthostereo view with Howlett's LEEP optical viewer, and (b) a "pin-cushion" effect when looking through the LEEP viewer at a standard picture.

If you look at a standard picture display created with no compression, the LEEP viewer, by no fault of its own, distorts the image; the viewer is designed to "spread out" an image that has previously been "pushed together." Because standard pictures, like the normal ones you see in a magazine, have not been "pushed together," the LEEP viewer "spreads out" a wide view of something that was never meant to be widened. The LEEP optical viewer was never designed to be used in this way. It was meant to be used in conjunction with compressed formatting. Formatting works a little like an alphabet code.

If you ever played spy games when you were young, you know what an alphabet code is like. You set up a code key, such as reversing the alphabet so that "Z" stands for "A," and "Y" stands for "B," and so on. Then you wrote a message to your childhood friend in code, such as "SVOK," and your friend, using the code key, eagerly decoded the word "HELP." This all works fine if both halves of the coding process are present. First, the coding takes place, then the decoding. But if you give your friend the word "HELP," the decoding process results in "SVOK," which doesn't mean anything. In a similar way, the LEEP optical system needs compression, a kind of coding key, to work correctly when it is decoded (viewed).

The main question to ask when you are given the opportunity to look through a LEEP optical viewer is, "Is the image compressed?" If the image is compressed, then you are in for a treat. But if the image is not, be prepared for an image that looks wide and curved outward at the edges. This distortion is called the *pin cushion effect* (see Figure 5.5), because of its similarity with the shape of an old-fashioned pin holder of the same name.

Many people who saw the NASA system didn't realize they were looking at a decompressed image, and thus went away without a full understanding of what the optics required. This led to wide-spread use of the LEEP optics in head-mounted displays—even with screens showing decompressed pictures.

Mark Bolas, with Fake Space Labs, is one person who understood the process. He worked out a way for the computer to compress the image before sending the picture to the screens. The LEEP optics then provide a superior image, resulting in a non-distorted wide view. (The screens also have to receive stereo inputs, as discussed below.) Bolas implemented a math formula, an "algorithm," that functions like the compression optics in Howlett's camera, com-pressing the projection of the virtual scene onto the screens of the display, preparing the picture properly for the LEEP optical viewer.

The drawback of using this algorithm, however, is decreased speed, because of all the extra mathematical computations required. The slowdown in frames-per-second caused by the math algorithm has been countered, up to now, by using faster computers than the PC, such as Silicon Graphics machines, which are also more expensive. Achieving LEEP-like compression on the PC may have to wait until faster PCs are available. But advancements like the Intel 586 chips, the next step after the 486 chip, and *local bus*[*] structural improve-ments could lead to the necessary speed increases.

Everyone interested in VR should realize the implication of achiev-ing fast enough LEEP compression on the PC—the qualities of

---

*Local bus refers to a new kind of connection between the processor chip and a peripheral, like the monitor or the hard drive. This connection passes the signals to the peripheral directly (thus "local") instead of through the standard "bus" connector, which has become a major bottleneck as the number of peripherals has increased. The resulting cost/performance ratio is such that readers need to be warned: If you plan on buying a computer, make certain it has one of the "local bus" architecture.

wide-angle viewing, with stereoscopic depth, will be available on a more affordable platform. Thanks to Eric Howlett, when the PC reaches that level of performance, more realistic virtual reality will be accessible to more people at an affordable price.

Convergence Correction

But wide-angle viewing, with stereoscopic depth, still does not solve the divergence problem (a solution would be called *convergence correction*). Even though a software solution had been implemented for several years, it is a massive effort to achieve convergence correction in software. It is called *software shifting,* and requires two separate computers (one for each eye) and substantial programming time.

The approach is to use one computer to display the image for the left eye, and the other computer to display a shifted view for the right eye. The result is similar to the illustration in Figure 5.2, but the software has much greater shifting abilities than does the screen's control knob. As screens have advanced, they've slowly grown larger. They have more dots, which means higher resolution, which also results in a more detailed picture. But if you want to use four-inch, higher resolution screens, your nose gets pressed right up against the divergence problem. Although an add-on method of applying a special lens (called a *fresnel* lens—because it was invented in France, it has a French pronunciation; the *s* is silent: say "fre-nell") was eventually developed to help correct convergence, fresnel lenses have several drawbacks—including high-maintenance. Lenses with built-in convergence correction for the larger, higher resolution, four-inch (diagonal) screens weren't invented until the end of 1992.

Although advanced screens with higher resolution in small sizes—less than three-inches diagonally—are expected soon (perhaps in 1993), until they are available, the optical method of convergence correction has a far better cost/performance ratio than the software method. When the small, high-resolution screens come on the market, convergence correction won't be necessary; the increased resolution will be able to provide a much more realistic picture. The question of whether they will result in a more satisfactory

immersive experience depends on what methods can be found to preserve Howlett's immersion rule.

VRon Lenses

The story of the VR advancement that led to built-in convergence correction is one I know well, because I work with the man who invented and developed the breakthrough—Bradley Burnett, Vice-President of Research and Development, VRontier worlds of Stoughton, Inc. In addition, I have met and talked to the man who took a chance and helped Burnett in his quest, Bob Davis, Production Manager at an optical company.

The tale of Burnett's quest has never been published. For all who participated, this was a real-world adventure in virtual reality.

Once upon a Time

In some ways, looking back, this almost seems like a fairy tale, but every detail is true and actually happened (see Appendix A). It all began on a night in May, 1992. Burnett was watching TV when he saw a man wearing an interesting head-device. He heard Dr. Henry Fuchs describing how a head-mounted display could be used to provide a virtual reality experience.

This was Burnett's first introduction to the concept of VR—and it intrigued him and inspired him. Lights began to flash as his mind raced ahead with a vision of what might be achieved. Without knowing it, Fuchs had lit a fuse on a firecracker, because Burnett had the training and experience not only to grasp the implications of the concept, but also to combine the technical know-how and the creativity to think in new ways.

Burnett's life changed that day in May, and has never been the same ever since. His burning desire became to first develop a head-mounted display, and then on to the larger challenge of devoting his life to pushing the frontiers of virtual reality forward.

Burnett has been learning about electronics for about seventeen years—and he's only 25. At the age of eight, Burnett was taking apart everything he could find in the house. His parents were

frantic with consternation after coming home one day to discover the radio and TV in pieces. Eventually they found the best way to live in peace was to give their little prodigy old radios, televisions, and appliances.

By the time Burnett was in high school, he was a budding electronics expert, driven by the same force that cast its spell on him eight years earlier: what's in there, and how does it work? A high school teacher, struck by his breadth of knowledge, suggested several times that Burnett should sign up for a test conducted by the neighborhood military recruitment center, but Burnett demurred, responding that he had no interest in military service. Eventually the teacher put a different perspective on the idea, saying that the act of taking the test carried no obligation to join the service, but the results would indicate where Burnett's talents ranked against national scores. This finally convinced him, so he signed up for the examination.

When the recruiters saw Burnett's 100 percent score on the electronics section, they were astounded. The last perfect score had been recorded five years earlier. Their urge to recruit him grew to the point that Burnett was presented with a package that included the best electronics training the military could offer. The benefits were clear, and Burnett signed up.

After his military stint, Burnett found himself in Kenosha, Wisconsin, attending the Gateway Technical Institute. His robotics instructor, Stuart Vorpagel (with a solid reputation of his own—remember our discussion of Vorpagel in Chapter 4), became Burnett's mentor. It was in Kenosha that Burnett was hit by Fuchs' lightning strike, and began a furious scramble to build his first virtual reality equipment.

As Burnett became more impassioned with his goal, the days and nights found him eating little and sleeping less, calling around the country to glean hints and suggestions from people in the VR industry, and hitting roadblocks several times that made him despair of ever finding a way to achieve a finished prototype. Then July 28th came—the beginning of SIGGRAPH '92 in Chicago; Burnett decided to attend and see what he could find out.

Good Timing and Persistence

SIGGRAPH, the *S*pecial *I*nterest *G*roup in *Graph*ics, is the annual conference that showcases the latest advancements in computer graphics and virtual reality technology, where vendors and computer graphics professionals gather from all over the world. SIGGRAPH meets in a different city each year, but by coincidence, it was held in Chicago—only a short drive from Kenosha—just a couple of months after Burnett's ardor began.

At the conference, he was able to try on a working HMD, and talk to key figures in the industry, like Ed La Hood with VREAM, Inc., Bruce Basset with Virtual Research, and Tony Ash with Straylight Corp. He learned of new sources and directions for his helmet work, listened to suggestions for helmet design, and became further infused with a determination to push ahead. La Hood introduced him to the interactivity of VR; Basset suggested using LEEP optics; Ash described desired improvements in the field.

Back in Kenosha, August was a month of starting over several times, ripping out the insides from one plastic shell, and beginning again in another shell. An HMD is unusually challenging because trying to create one requires knowledge from many fields—from plastics design and molding to electronics wiring and circuits to optics to human factors to mechanical construction to the laws of physics. It is a formidable task—one reason why most people who attempt it give up in frustration.

Burnett also found himself embroiled in the white heat of the divergence, immersion, and optical problems, although he hadn't yet discovered Howlett's immersion rule. Being trained in electronics had not prepared him for the myriad of questions that appeared at every turn, but, because of his persistence in cracking the books, teaching himself in the areas of knowledge he lacked, and applying his ingenuity, Burnett was able to finish his first working prototype. Thomas Edison once remarked that invention is one percent inspiration, and 99 percent perspiration. Burnett's hard work— after receiving the spark of Fuch's inspiration—paid off.

The Software Connection

Having a working device, especially an accessory like an HMD, is not sufficient by itself to achieve productive results—it needs to be connected to an application, and in this case, an application means software. Software programs, running on the computer and performing functional tasks, create applications for people to do work.

Burnett knew he needed to forge an alliance with a software developer.

Near the end of August, 1992, his search led him to a bulletin board system (*BBS*) in California, where he noticed a program description that mentioned VR. (See the sidebar on BBSs.) After requesting transfer of the program to his computer, (called *downloading,* which sends the program over the phone line), he discovered that the program had been created by VRontier worlds of Stoughton, a company located in his own state. Eager to find out if a mutual

Bulletin Board Systems

BBS is a computer-controlled message center. There are thousands of computers worldwide that are set up to communicate with other computers by phone line. Using a communications program, you instruct your computer to dial a telephone number that is automatically answered by the BBS program on the computer at the other end of the line. After registering as a user, you can leave messages to other callers, or send and receive other electronic files. The largest commercial BBS is CompuServe, but there are many others, including Prodigy and America On-Line. Many companies have installed a BBS to serve their customers, and many hobbyists and other individuals have installed BBSs in their homes.

interest could be developed, he initiated the first contact; a relationship began that later led to other developments. It was certainly a fortuitous phone call, because unbeknownst to Burnett, VRontier worlds was similarly looking for an association with an appropriate equipment manufacturer.

As a sponsor of Andrew's VEE-AR Club, a family-oriented group of VR enthusiasts, VRontier worlds helped coordinate the first public demonstration of Burnett's HMD prototype—which had never been seen outside his circle of friends and family. On October 10, 1992, at the second annual Virtual Reality Festival in Stoughton, almost one hundred people lined up at the public library to try out the new head-mounted display.

Burnett was encouraged by the great interest, and he began analyzing the observers' responses to get ideas for improvements. The prototype at that time used the LEEP optical viewer, but no corresponding compression was in effect for the displayed image. The resulting distortions began to weigh heavily on Burnett's mind, and he began to focus on some far-reaching ideas.

The Davis Connection

Brad had taught himself enough about optics to realize that he knew very little about an extremely complex subject, so he started looking for some help. For days, every person he contacted in the field of optics refused to get involved with an open-ended project searching for a solution to a problem they barely understood. But finally, Bob Davis—a man who enjoys a challenge—picked up the phone.

As Production Manager of a large lens manufacturing company, Davis had broad experience developing specialty lenses, and he was intrigued by Burnett's description of the problem. He suggested that Burnett bring in the LEEP lenses, and he would see what he could do. They worked together through October and November, trying out different ideas and brainstorming possible approaches. Burnett asked wild questions that normally would have elicited laughter and comments of "No way—that can't be done," but Davis calmly reflected on these new possibilities he had never envisioned, and tried each one out, explaining to Burnett the guiding principles of optometry he had learned over the years.

As the new optical system was taking shape, Davis discovered he was treading in unexplored territory, but he pushed on, trying to make it work, enjoying the process of inquiry and investigation. Davis eventually began taking some of the work home in order to appease his company's management, which was concerned by the amount of time being consumed.

But eventually the package was finished, and the tests showed it was successful. Burnett's creative efforts—and the assistance provided by Davis—had achieved the first optical solution to the problems discovered in the mid-1980s and solved previously only by expensive software shifting—the first optical system to allow

the use of four-inch diagonal screens placed side by side with no software shifting required. They had developed the first light weight, low cost, low maintenance lenses that combined both built-in convergence correction and diffusion—and still preserve Howlett's immersion rule.

It was a remarkable achievement, and deserves acclaim. The invention was soon named *Virtual Reality optical non-distorting* (VRon) lenses, and a patent search—a step towards filing a patent application—was quickly begun. The divergence problem, the immersion problem, and the optical problem were all solved with one stroke.

Stereoscopic Mode

One remaining major topic that involves the HMD has to do with creating a realistic illusion of depth. Simply placing two images in front of each eye does not result in depth perception as realistic as our eyes are normally accustomed to. It is true that our brains can fuse the two images into one, but that's a different capability than perceiving how far away an object is.

There are several different kinds of "cues" used by the brain to calculate distance. One cue, for example, is linear perspective— the way a sidewalk seems to narrow as it recedes in the distance. Drawing pictures in linear perspective to duplicate such diminishing (like a picture of an office building shown from the corner) helps to show depth, but looking at a 3-D linear perspective does not make you "feel" like you are seeing depth—mostly because the picture remains the same, even when you move. Another cue your brain notices when making decisions about distance is that an object that is partly hidden by another object is probably farther from you.

But the most important of these cues is provided by the fact that we have not one, but two eyes. It is the physical distance between our eyes that provides some of the necessary information the brain needs to interpret distance. It is a common childhood discovery that your eyes see different views when you alternate closing left and right eyelids, but it is a rare child who concludes that the brain uses those slightly different views to estimate depth.

It's easy to demonstrate. Just look at two objects in your line of sight. When you focus on the farther object, the nearer one seems to have an outline, and vice versa. In a sense, we always have "double vision," although the brain usually ignores the objects it isn't focused on. When both eyes are focused on the same object, the two views are fused into what the brain thinks is one image.

We can take advantage of how the brain works to create the sense of depth in a two-screen display. The way to do it is to send one image to the left eye, and a slightly different image to the right eye. You only have to follow one rule to make it work. The images have to appropriately duplicate the interocular distance between the eyes.

You can do it with cameras. Set up two cameras side-by-side and make sure the lenses are 64 millimeters apart (about two and half inches). You can even buy cameras aligned in this manner from suppliers like Reel 3-D in California. When you get the two pictures from your camera developed, prop them up in a holder, place your eyes in front, and you can look at your own stereoscopic display.

To do the same thing in an HMD, you attach a separate input (one computer to each input, for now) to each screen, adjust the two images to match the interocular distance using software algorithms, and the result is virtual reality in stereoscopic mode. If the input cables send the same image to each eye, then it's called *monoscopic mode.*

Once you've seen stereoscopic mode, especially in color, you will probably never want to see in mono mode again. But achieving stereo mode technically has been quite difficult and expensive— partly due to the need, until recently, for two computers. Now that it is being accomplished on the PC, the price will go down and the availability will go up. The main stumbling block up to now has been the video card on the PC—it hasn't been possible to split the signal on a standard VGA card—but a few alternative video cards are starting to appear. Stereoscopic mode is one of the key advancements that will make virtual reality much more realistic.

Another, currently more affordable, method of achieving stereoscopic mode is with *shutter glasses,* like Crystal Eyes, from StereoGraphics Corporation, that allow you to use one computer and see in stereo on the monitor. Shutter glasses take advantage of

still another characteristic of the human eyes that we discussed in the section on 3-D Animation Software in Chapter 3—the way the retina "holds" an image for one thirtieth of a second before it fades.

Shutter glasses are designed to work in conjunction with software that "slices" up each second into 60 parts (some systems work with even more slices per second, such as a new system from Stereographics Corp., with 120 f.p.s.). In an alternating fashion, the program sends a left-eye image to the screen for the first slice of time, then a right-eye image for the second slice—a total of 60 images per second. At the same time, the shutter glasses blink off and on, first right, then left, in such a way that each eye only sees the image intended for it, and each eye receives 30 images per second.

The approach works fairly well, and is good value for the money. The main drawback is the perception of flicker, especially if the lights in the room are bright. But if you turn down the lights, you can enjoy stereoscopic vision without buying two computers and an HMD, or a boom display—which we'll discuss next.

Boom Display

A *boom display,* trademarked by Fake Space Labs, is a display attached to a jointed mechanical arm stand similar to those used for boom microphones, but with more joints. There are many applications in which you might not want an HMD sitting on your head. For example, you may want to create a new VR environment, or a 3-D application. With a boom display near you, you could work unencumbered at the keyboard, and then, to check out the appearance of your work, simply reach up, pull the boom display over, and look through the lenses at the display—without having to wrestle with the HMD each time.

One consideration is the tracking advantages of a boom (see the section titled Exploring Tracking Issues later in this chapter). But, another important advantage of a boom display is range of motion. With an HMD on your head, you are required to stay close to the tracking receivers. With a boom display, you can walk around within the maximum reach of the arms, and gain an extra sense of physically being inside the virtual environment.

Retinal Display

The most far-reaching idea in VR display technology has to be the concept of drawing pictures directly on the retina using a laser. This may seem rather shocking at first, but the laser energy would be very low, thus eliminating the chance of damaging the eye. One advantage, in theory, would be extremely high resolution—higher than the eye is capable of seeing (which is about 60 lines per degree)—even higher than retinal rod and cone resolution. Other advantages would be a high frames-per-second rate (lasers are fast) and eye-tracking, or the ability to know exactly what direction your eyes are looking at all times (see the next section, Exploring Tracking Issues).

Until the fall of 1992, most observers of the VR industry would probably have predicted that laser displays on the retina would be several years in the future, but the HIT Lab in Seattle has already demonstrated a "proof-of-concept" machine. The machine sits on a table, so it will be awhile before it is small enough to fit in an HMD (perhaps it will be put on a boom first?), and the picture is in monochrome (red), not full-color, but at least we can say the first laser retinal display has arrived.

Exploring Tracking Issues

The tracking concept is as essential to the goal of immersive VR as the display concepts are. The aim is to send signals to the computer indicating the orientation of your view. The computer must "know" what you're looking at in order to calculate which perspective of the virtual environment to display. If you are wearing an HMD, and you turn your head to the right, you want to see the rightward view. A tracker is designed to communicate to the computer the position and orientation of whatever it tracks. If you put it on your head, it will track your head movements. If you put it on your hand, it will track your hand movements.

There are different types of tracking; three examples are head tracking, boom tracking, and eye tracking. For head tracking, the choices are mainly ultrasonic, such as the Logitech tracking device, or magnetic, like the Polhemus 3SPACE or "The Bird" by Ascension Technology Corp.

Ultrasonic devices use sound waves that are too high for the human ear to hear; these waves are used to communicate with the computer. Different shapes and materials in a room, however, can have strange effects on ultrasonic waves, thus causing anomalies in the functioning of the tracker. The major advantage of the ultrasonic tracker is that it costs substantially less than the magnetic type.

Trackers based on the magnetic approach can be more accurate, but both ultrasonic and magnetic methods share one characteristic: They both have substantial lag time. As you recall from Chapter 4, lag time is the delay between the time you move your head and the time the modified image is displayed. When you move your head to the right, by the time: (1) the tracker computes the new position of your head, (2) the tracker sends the signal, (3) the computer notices the signal, (4) the computer calculates your new viewpoint, and (5) the computer sends the correct image to the display, you might have already moved your head again. Whether or not you moved your head again, you notice the delay—and it is quite disconcerting. Lag time is also called *latency,* and it is the main problem in the field of tracking control.

However, with a boom display, it is possible to minimize this latency. At least step number one in the list above—computing the new position—can be eliminated; the jointed arm of the boom stand can serve as an efficient pointing device to your exact physical location and current viewpoint orientation. Each joint in the movable arm can be fitted with a small potentiometer that accurately measures the tiniest change in position. This method is inexpensive, accurate, and cuts down the latency.

Because of its pinpoint accuracy, eye tracking is the most desired method of determining the user's viewpoint. But current eye-tracking technology is expensive and confined mainly to research labs. If it can eventually be affordably implemented in VR systems, eye tracking would be an advancement over head tracking. Because the head tracker only approximates the location of the viewpoint by measuring the motion of the head, it cannot be as accurate as the eye tracker.

Exploring Manipulation Issues

Because the essence of manipulation is grasping an object with the hand, the item of clothing most closely associated with the hand, a glove, became the likeliest candidate for the development of virtual grasping. The glove permits natural gestures and provides a framework for easily attaching wires and sensors.

But a glove is not the only device that can control the manipulation of virtual objects. A mouse's buttons can be mapped to interface with a virtual hand—thus becoming the least expensive hand controller available. VREAM software, for example, permits the use of a standard three-button mouse to control its virtual hand. Two new devices—the Global Devices 6D Controller and the Polhemus 3BALL, are in the shape of balls. The Polhemus 3BALL actually is a hollow number 3 billiard ball with the sensing device placed inside. You can manipulate objects with an increasing selection of 3-D mice, such as the one being developed by Logitech. There is also a device called a wand, which is a straight stick similar to a magician's wand.

If you had to choose the most natural way to control a virtual hand, you'd have to choose the glove. No matter how you move your fingers while in the glove, the glove moves in exactly the same way. Now all you need is a way to measure the motions of the fingers and relay the results to the computer—then you have the best manipulation device possible. Whether you use fiber optics, strain gauges, cylinders, miniature mechanical arms, or ropes, there's really nothing but the glove shape to achieve the highest level of naturalness possible—until sensors are developed that measure brain-hand nerve signals.

The Patent Issue

At the time of this writing, there is only one issue to be resolved regarding glove manipulation devices—the patenting of future developments in the glove. This question is crucial for several reasons, but first we must backtrack a few steps and look at the invention of the DataGlove.

When Thomas Zimmerman, the inventor of the first glove that connected to a computer (a Commodore 64, by the way), and

Jaron Lanier agreed to cofound VPL Research, Zimmerman assigned his patent to VPL. Then Zimmerman left to pursue other interests. VPL has what is called a *general patent* on the glove, which is different from a *design patent*. A general patent is granted for inventions that are the first of a kind; a design patent is awarded to inventions that modify or change an existing design.

For example, if you were the first person to conceive of a toaster, and no one else had ever thought of an appliance to toast bread, you could be awarded a general patent, because your invention would be the first of its kind. But if you looked at an existing two-slice toaster, and decided to invent a four-slice toaster, you would not be entitled to a general patent. Because you had changed an existing design, you could only receive a design patent. This is a simplified example, but it illustrates the difference.

The patent on VPL's DataGlove was awarded as a general patent, because it was successfully argued that Zimmerman had been the first person to think of connecting a "glove-like device" to a computer. Although it has been pointed out that the DataGlove patent application did not mention some previous fictional concepts that included similar ideas, such as Robert Heinlein's science fiction story *Waldo* from the 1950s, the fact remains that the glove patent was awarded as a general patent.

Whether or not there is a basis for overturning the patent in court, the current situation is that the glove patent is a general patent. A general patent entitles the owner to claim patent infringement against anyone who creates a similar invention. VPL has claimed infringement in the past: VPL sued Jim Kramer over his Talking Glove that helps deaf people turn sign language into speech. The lawsuit was settled out of court, and Kramer agreed not to build additional gloves for one year, but the question of what happens at the end of the year is not decided.

The patent issue became even more clouded: VPL's patents were assumed by a French company, Thompson C.S.F., due to a loan default in which the patents were held as collateral; VPL's employees were let go, including Jaron Lanier, the cofounder; the previous president was reinstalled and efforts were begun to reestablish VPL's position as the leader in the VR research market.

The question of how patent claims will be handled in the future is not clear, but whatever happens, future developments of the glove will be affected one way or another, and all discussions of "glove-like devices" will be overshadowed by a cloud of uncertainty until the situation is clearly resolved.

Exploring Application Issues

With all the discussion about frames-per-second, realistic displays, how to build applications, and trade-offs between different kinds of equipment, there is one point that must always remain firmly at the top of the list. Manipulation is the nitty-gritty of virtual reality. This is where, as Ross Perot so famously said, the rubber hits the road. The concept of manipulation (and interactivity) stands out foremost among the many issues that consume the time and seminars of the developers in the VR industry—including immersion, stereoscopic vision, convergence correction, latency, and all the rest. The user knows the priority and will not be swayed.

In survey after survey, when users of virtual reality systems are asked to rate the importance of different aspects of VR, the overwhelming majority always chooses manipulation and interaction as number one. The average user will wait for the other advancements, but if interaction is not at a high level, the user quickly loses interest.

For business, the priority issue is productivity. If a VR application can save money, pay for itself, facilitate transactions, or provide a better picture of information, then the application will be rated highly. Interactivity is likely to play a key role in a business-oriented application.

Therefore, whatever the application, make it as highly interactive as possible. Build in maximum object manipulation. Make it possible to grab, turn, throw, drop, and otherwise control objects. Set up the maximum amount of object interactions. Make it possible for objects to bump, rebound, respond, and otherwise act on each other. Make it possible for objects to appear, disappear, change color, rotate, respond to gravity, bounce on the floor, and otherwise link with each other. Allow maximum alternative sensory cues, as

recommended by Dr. Vanderheiden, Director of the Trace Center at the University of Wisconsin, in Chapter 4. If VR environment builders focus their efforts on constructing increasing layers of interactivity, their applications will generate the most effective VR experiences.

Objective Rating System

Evaluating the effectiveness of a VR experience is important. In order to foster the maturation of VR into what might be called, more formally, the science of virtual reality, objective evaluation standards will need to be established to provide a structural framework for analysis. Various approaches have been discussed. David Mitchell, the systems operator of the Diaspar VR Network BBS, has contributed a thoughtful suggestion that merits consideration. See the related sidebar for an excerpt from Mitchell's analysis.

An Excerpt From...

Diaspar VR Network

The concept of reality is often thought of as being subjective. The problem becomes worse with a concept of virtual reality. A subjective definition might well be described as "you are there" or participating in a machine-manufactured environment so realistic that you cannot distinguish it from reality. Other possible subjective definitions might describe virtual reality as the ability to interact in an artificially constructed environment or universe, using computer generated artifacts. But, I think there is a better definition that is measurable, and removes the subjective aspect from the definition. My proposed definition of virtual reality is:

Virtual reality is the artificial stimulation of human senses and artificial response to human actions. With this definition, it now becomes possible to say how "VR-like" something is by evaluating how many human sensory systems are interfaced. First, let's look at human senses, not limiting ourselves to the supposed five senses. This is done because, simply, there are more than five senses. Human senses are as follows:

1.   Sight

2.   Sound

3.   Touch

4.   Balance

5.   Smell

6.   Taste

7.   Pheromonal

8.   Immunological

Note that numbers 4, 7, and 8 are not part of the "five senses" we learned in school. Yet, overwhelming scientific evidence supports specific organs and neural nets around these organs. Any real long-term virtual reality endeavors must take into account all human senses. [Mitchell's summary of supporting evidence for these three senses has been excised here—refer back to Chapter 3 for his entire argument.]

From all of this, a simple classification system as to the quality of the virtual reality experienced can be done using a simple scale system with 10 levels. They are:

V0   Reality—what we normally experience.

V1   All eight senses interfaced.

V2   Seven senses interfaced.

V3   Six senses interfaced.

V4   Five senses interfaced.

V5   Four senses interfaced.

V6   Three senses interfaced.

V7   Two senses interfaced.

V8   One senses interfaced.

V9   No senses interfaced.

As an example, a text based system would be V9. While it is true that you might be reading the text using your eyes—the visual system is only a carrier of symbolic information which is converted to mental images by a process we call reading. One is not seeing images directly.

Most things we presently call Virtual Reality, such as sight, sound, and touch (movement being an output function of touch—as touch sensations are generated by movement) are actually only at level V6 (3 senses involved) on the VR scale.

Future treatments and therapies will require V2 or V1 and will probably not be available until well into the 21st century. For EduTainment use, level V3 is the highest needed, since it would

incorporate balance, smell, and taste as well as sight, sound, and touch. And, smell and taste would be needed for EduTainment.

One-hundred percent rating would mean the vision was full-range color binocular with peripheral vision to normal human specifications. If infrared and ultraviolet were folded into human vision range, the rating might be 150% or 200%—based on how much real spectrum is folded into a human perceived spectrum. In emergency aid telepresence, for example, infrared vision for spotting hot spots in a fire might aid fire fighters. So, a VR system for that use might have a sight spectrum in excess of 100%—and might include full 360 degree vision folded onto normal human 190 degree vision fields.

However, with this virtual reality definition system, which does not address content of the virtual reality communication, it is possible to rate systems and determine their applicability for various tasks.

At current rates of progress, we can expect V6 level systems by mid-1994 and V3 systems in the first decade of the 21st century. Level V2 and V1 will come later.[*]

An objective rating system is especially useful when two people attempt to compare VR experiences. Can't you just visualize your descendants talking? "Last night I tried out that new V2 voomie with 120 percent visuals you told me about—wow, you were right. It sure was worth 6K for that experience!"

If an initial recommendation may be offered, it seems slightly confusing trying to remember which scale numbers represent how many senses. V2 is 7 senses. A scale that would coordinate V2 with 2 senses might be more helpful. But the concept is quite a service to the field—it does lay the groundwork for formal studies on virtual reality as a science.

Sidelights on Science

While we're discussing the early shaping of VR as a science in its own right, it is pertinent to mention a notable academic milestone—the first accredited program granting a bachelors degree in virtual reality was established in 1992 at the CAD Institute in

---

[*]*Diaspar VR Network, September 3, 1992.*
Excerpted with permission by David Mitchell.
(See listing of BBS number in Appendix B)

Phoenix, Arizona. John Morrison, the multi-titled director of several disciplines, now has an additional title—Dean of Virtual Reality.

Exploring Navigation Issues

Probably the most important issue in the topic of navigation in a VR environment is whether a consensus can be reached on certain questions. Moving your viewpoint in a virtual world is not as intuitively coupled to an obvious method as manipulating objects was naturally linked to the glove. The navigation method we usually use in the real world, walking with our legs, is not suitable for virtual navigation. You just can't have people walking around, even in a small area, while blinded (to the outside world) by an HMD. A joystick might seem like the most intuitive device, although pointing in the desired direction with your index finger in a glove is equally intuitive. A joystick is limited to two directions, though: forward and backward is one; left and right is the other. It limits the degrees of freedom.

Degrees of freedom? There are six degrees of freedom in navigation. Three are for motion and three are for rotation. Besides the two motion directions listed previously, there is one more: up and down. There is just no intuitive motion on a joystick representing up or down. You can approximate by pushing a button with one finger while pressing on the stick, and although it works, it can be awkward—especially if you are also wearing a glove on your other hand. If you are also wearing an HMD, it becomes almost impossible.

Is this starting to sound awfully complicated? Well, it is. That's why this may be navigation's most significant problem. A great deal of thought has been devoted to this issue, and many devices have been created.

For example, several variations of a ball device have been developed. By pressing your fingers on the ball in different directions, you move around and control your viewpoint. The Spaceball, the 3BALL, and the GLOBAL 3D Controller are three examples. If you think about it, a joystick rotated in space in all directions forms a sphere; therefore, a ball can be viewed as a fancy inflated joystick,

in a sense. Some ball controllers allow you to control your orientation (where you look) as well as other objects, so they are able to reach a high level of versatility. Because a ball can be pushed in any direction, including up and down (as well as rotated), a navigation controller based upon a spherical shape is described as having six degrees of freedom. After a little practice, operating a ball-shaped controller becomes quite intuitive.

Navigating with a glove in a virtual world is also fairly intuitive, because of the almost universal "pointing" convention. To move forward, you simply point forward. To move upwards, you point towards the sky, and so on. But you find a limitation here as well—if you wanted to direct a colleague's attention to a virtual object, you cannot simply point at the object as in the real-world; instead of merely indicating the object, you find yourself moving towards it. Of course, as voice recognition technology becomes more advanced, it will be used as another way to navigate.

Bio-Navigation

Our explorations in this chapter thus far have been limited to contemporary VR technology. We've looked at the cutting-edge developments, but now it is time to look ahead to outlines of future developments. There is at least one concept that carries a rich load of possibilities. It may be closer to reality than it appears; some of us may find this idea unsettling, but to others the concept opens up exciting areas of speculation.

The concept we are talking about is the prediction of harnessing biofeedback processes and direct neural inputs for use in VR. Biofeedback is a method of connecting sensors that measure electrical or other states in the body to a display in such a way that the participant can perceive a visual or auditory representation of the signals.

A simple example would be to strap blood-pressure sensors on your arm and plug wires from them to the computer (another data-acquisition device!). The computer would be programmed to sound varying tones according to the signals received from the sensors, and you would be told to try to lower the tone. The remarkable

result discovered through research is that you can lower your blood-pressure with this approach. The brain and the body use the feedback to learn how to control the blood-pressure. Early experiments were conducted in the 1960s and sophisticated biofeedback machines are now used in therapeutic situations.

The concept of using biofeedback techniques to navigate virtual environments revolves around the possibility that a person could be trained to control a viewpoint by simply thinking. Instead of using a joystick, ball controller, or glove, a person would be wearing a sensor controlled through biofeedback, and the viewpoint would respond and move according to the signals generated by the sensor. Remember the stress level sensor attached to the finger of the skier in NEC's virtual skiing prototype discussed in Chapter 3? Although that sensor is not used for navigation, it is an example of biofeedback being applied right now.

Direct neural inputs are envisioned as the next step after biofeedback. Somehow, though, no one seems to be exactly certain how the brain, or possibly a nerve, can be connected directly to the computer to provide the signals necessary for navigation and interaction—or directly connected to whatever the replacement for the computer may be by that time. The advancements on the horizon for virtual reality are likely to keep the developers busy and the rest of us fascinated for decades. Trying to imagine what will be possible one thousand years from now is beyond prediction.

From Exploring to Discovery

This chapter has shown you the innovations and people behind the current virtual reality applications and worlds. Now it is time to see how the parts are assembled into an operating structure. In the next chapter we will join the engineers and builders of virtual worlds and look at some of the questions that must be asked and contemplated when authoring a virtual reality environment. You can discover for yourself the enjoyment, as well as a few of the complexities, of creating your own worlds.

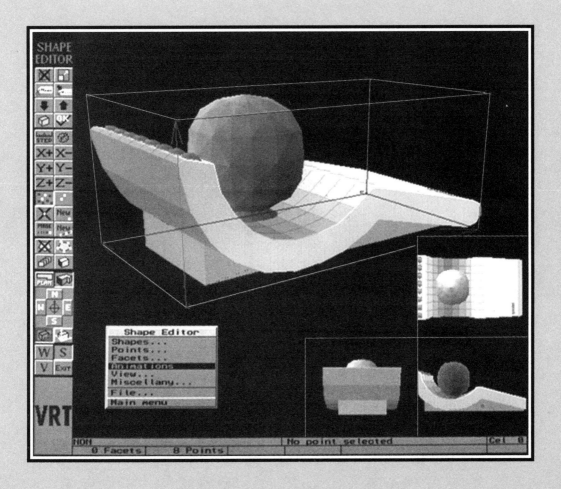

Chapter 6

Authoring a VR Environment

Because the purpose of this book includes the goal of explaining concepts of virtual reality to people who may have little or no experience with computers, the reader with computer expertise might want to skim the following review of programming fundamentals that serves as a framework for subsequent terminology.

Introduction to Building Virtual Worlds

Giving a computer instructions requires a program. Building a virtual world also requires a program. A *program* is a written list of actions that a programmer decides must be carried out. A cook in a kitchen who follows a recipe, which could be called a cooking program, is also carrying out a series of necessary actions.

At first, computer programs had to list the actions in an exact order, called "procedural programming." A program was similar to a recipe for a cake. First do step 1, then do step 2. But a new way of programming was developed that removed the need to follow a predetermined, exact order. It is called *event-driven,* or *event handling,* and it works more like a cooking manual. When you need to know what an angel food cake is, you look up "Cakes" in the table of contents, find the page number, and turn to the correct section. To find the difference between a rump roast and filet mignon, you refer to the section describing cuts of meat.

Event-driven programming is what makes virtual world building possible. It allows the computer to "jump around" and look up appropriate information when necessary. As you might expect, it is far more versatile and adaptable than procedural programming.

Think of how many more choices are available to a concert planner than to a recipe writer. Writing down the steps to follow in a souffle recipe is a more rigid procedure than writing down a list of compositions to be performed in a concert. The concert planner can start with a list of the symphony's repertoire and select whichever arrangement she desires for the opening piece, and then choose succeeding pieces at her discretion. If she wants to add a sonata a week later, she can insert the title wherever she prefers. The souffle planner lacks such freedom of choice.

There is a similar advantage in choosing event-driven programming over procedural programming. A programmer can write separate modules that can be referenced when needed by the computer, just like looking up a topic in a table of contents. Adding another module is as simple as adding another cherry to the middle of a pie. Modifying a procedural program is more like changing a brick in the middle of a stacked wall—you have to either remove the top layers or carefully try to slide the offending brick out without toppling the others. Either way, it involves more time and risk.

Being able to insert objects in a VR program anywhere you desire places much of the decision process in the hands and mind of the virtual world builder—and opens the door of opportunity for people who are not procedural programmers. There are limitations that restrict the world builder, such as the capabilities of the computer selected and the features available in the VR development system utilized.

Before examining the details involved in creating and building virtual spaces, environments, and worlds, let's prepare a larger context by introducing two other viewpoints first.

A Student's Perspective

Sean Lee, Research Director for Andrew's VEE-AR Club, is a student at Madison Area Technical College pursuing a degree in marketing. Lee is an avid collector of articles and information on VR; with a background in robotics, he is but one example of the thousands of new VR devotees preparing for careers related to this widening technology. In late 1992, Lee wrote an essay, "Cyberspace Engineer," on the subject of authoring VR environments. An excerpt from that essay is reprinted here as a sample of the VR research taking place at the college level.

An Excerpt From...

Cyberspace Engineer

... Similar to an empty room that is waiting to be filled and decorated, cyberspace allows engineers to create the virtual worlds where we will work and play.... World building, as it is called by virtual reality enthusiasts, is the creation of artificial environments that one will interact in. The individuals responsible for this synthetic genesis are referred to as cyberspace engineers. These individuals have the task of transforming their ideas and visions to the electronic net of cyberspace and then giving the graphic world substance and life so that the users can interact in it. A cyberspace engineer is like a modern day renaissance man whose knowledge must encompass a broad spectrum, similar to Michelangelo or Leonardo da Vinci. A cyberspace engineer must have a comprehensive understanding of math, physics, spacial relations, art, and psychology.

MATH—A cyberspace engineer...must have an extensive understanding of mathematics.... It is mathematical equations that the computer uses to create and render the virtual reality worlds.... With a solid math background, a cyberspace engineer can create everything from the geometric shape of a box to the sophisticated fractals that make up a mountain range.... The engineer can use math to enhance the reality of the virtual world by duplicating the random effects of nature or by adding specific attributes to objects. Some of the examples of the effects of nature could be wind currents, cloud accumulations, and rain or snow. Some attributes could be gravity,

force feedback, and strength, to name a few. It is these effects of nature and the addition of object attributes that increase the realism and interaction of a virtual world.

PHYSICS— ...In a synthetic environment, the cyberspace engineer must take into account the laws of nature. For example, in the real world when a ball is thrown, one expects the ball to travel in an arc and eventually come down and hit the ground. In a virtual world, if a ball was thrown it would travel in a straight line for infinity without any sense of weight or gravity unless it was programmed otherwise.... Strength, elasticity, malleability, and fragility are also important factors of a virtual reality world. Each object that is created must have innate characteristics.... If one drops a coffee cup it will break because it is fragile. It is the cyberspace engineer's duplication of object characteristics that makes it easy for a novice user of the VR worlds to interact.

SPATIAL RELATIONSHIPS— ...A cyberspace engineer begins his world creation with an empty void. This void has no boundaries or reference points, and travels in all directions to infinity. Essentially, the engineer is floating in empty space until something is created. It is this emptiness that requires the world builder to understand spatial relationships. Most basic is the fact that in a virtual reality world every object, from furniture to a paper clip on a desk, must be three dimensional. The difficulty for the engineer is to create objects in the virtual world and place them so that they become functional in their environment.... Another important aspect of spatial relationships is that of scaling the objects. When programming an object to appear in a virtual world, the cyberspace engineer cannot just simply create an object and place it in the world. As one walks, the size and aspects of any given object are constantly changing. It is the task of the cyberspace engineer to take into account distances and perspectives.

ART— ...How one perceives the different environments in the virtual world is greatly affected by art. If one walks into a room that is primarily made up of colors such as black, brown and gray, it is going to create an effect on the participant of being cold and dark.

PSYCHOLOGY— ...A cyberspace engineer with a competent understanding of psychology can create an environment that is not only functional but also motivational.... The creation of a computer character is very complex. Essentially every facial expression, bodily movement, and verbal response possible would have to be developed.

CONCLUSION— ...More research should be done to find out if any other skills are necessary to create virtual worlds, so that a formal education environment may be created for future cyberspace engineers.[*]

[*]Sean Lee, 1992
Published with permission.

An Ethical Perspective

Nina Adams is a computer consultant with her own firm, Adams Consulting Group. As president of the International Interactive Communications Society (IICS) Chapter in Chicago, founder of the Chicago VR Special Interest Group, and Public Relations Director of the VREAM User's Group, Adams has a special interest in the designing of educational and training systems that use interactive media as well as virtual reality. As you can see in the following excerpt, she brings out an important issue in her essay "Get in Touch with Your Own Design Constraints."

An Excerpt from...

Get in Touch with Your Own Design Constraints

There's an episode from the original TV show "Star Trek" where two cultures are at war. The cultures are very "advanced" and use computers extensively. When a community is "hit," the proper number of people quietly go to some center where they are exterminated. All painless, clean, and neat. They have lost all the gore related to war and have no reason to stop it. Of course, the crew from the Enterprise blows up the computers so the cultures have to relearn "real" war and how devastating it can be.

If you were creating a virtual world simulating this experience, how would it be designed? Would you allow "painless" war to continue? Would the "heroes" be allowed to destroy something that may have been appropriate in that culture? What do you think is right and what is wrong?

I had never really thought about these questions before taking a class on ethics. But now I think about my beliefs and values almost every day. And, I try to make decisions that are congruent with them.

There are so many factors that affect our beliefs and values: culture, economic situation, religion. My beliefs and values may be different from yours and I'm not asking you to change your beliefs. But, if you haven't done so already, I'd like you to figure out what your beliefs and values are. Just spend some time thinking about the following scenarios. What would you do in these situations?

Two game developers create virtual reality war games. One developer shows a person "blowing up" when hit. The second developer never lets anyone get killed. Would you recommend one of these two approaches or something else? Is realism important? Does blood and

guts make the game "better"? What do the game players learn about life and death if no one ever dies?

A friend of yours got a bootlegged copy of a $1,500 program. It's a great program. She couldn't afford to buy the program right now. But, with a copy of the program, she'll be able to make money and plans on buying a legal copy as soon as she is able. Should she have taken the copy of the program? Does planning on buying a copy make it OK?

You were out for drinks with some friends a few weeks ago. During the evening you started brainstorming and came up with some creative ideas on a new VR product. You had a fun evening and never discussed what anyone was going to do with the ideas. You just found out one of your friends took the ideas and sold them to a company. What will you do? Should all of the people who came up with the ideas share in the profits? Should the friend who made the sale give a small portion of the profits to the other friends since they helped develop the ideas? Should the person who made the sale get all the profits since he took the time and effort to develop them further? Since you never discussed what anyone would do, was it OK for your friend to sell the ideas?

You know an avid supporter of pro-Life (or pro-Choice) issues. He's been looking for work for about three months. Out of the clear blue, a pro-Choice (or pro-Life) organization offers him a contract beyond his wildest dreams. Should he take the job? Would being out of work for a year make any difference?

A consultant is hired to develop a virtual world to be used to train employees. In the beginning phases of the project he discovers that training isn't really needed. All that's needed is clarification of job descriptions. What should the consultant do?

A person you know is working on a project. She is having some difficulty with a specific design concept. You attended a meeting of a professional association at which she makes an announcement and asks if anyone knows how to resolve the problem. You've run into the problem and you know how to solve it. It would take you about two hours to help her. Do you offer to help her for no charge? Do you offer to help her and charge her a consulting fee? Do you say nothing?

In all these scenarios you would be making decisions based on your own beliefs and values. If you become more involved in designing virtual worlds, you may be faced with many more decisions.

How would you react if you were asked to develop a virtual world in which:

all objects can be moved through other objects?

there is no gravity?

only black-and-white objects are allowed?

all green people are shorter than blue people?

cigarette smoking is prohibited?

cigarette smoking is exalted?

alien characters are friendly?

alien characters are killers?

a child is killed?

a child is born?

God is depicted?

God is depicted as a woman?

God is depicted as an orange?

The environment is being polluted?

Would you consider working on some of these projects and not working on others? Would that decision change if you were out of work for a month? Would the decision change if you were out of work for a year?

As more virtual worlds are developed, it's going to be more important that they are designed "appropriately" for the audiences. We, as designers and developers, need to be responsible in our efforts. VR has the potential of having more impact on people than any other media since the advent of television. We can shape the future. But shaping the future has pitfalls as well as rewards.

What does "appropriate" mean? I think that's a very personal question. Although I oppose war, for me, it's "appropriate" to have fighter pilots go through extensive battle simulations. I'm not sure about average citizens going through the experience. But I definitely think young children should not be exposed to this type of experience. And, I probably wouldn't be involved in the design of one.

I personally don't think it's ever appropriate for people to shoot at each other. (I don't even like toy guns.) But that's how I feel. I'm not trying to get you to change your values or opinions. I'd just like you to know what your opinions are and design worlds that are consistent with those beliefs.

How do you know if something is "appropriate"? You might ask yourself some questions like:

- Would I want the real world to behave like the virtual world?

- How would I feel if my mother (or the person I respect most) knew I was the key designer of this world?

- Would you like your four-year-old child exploring this world?

Or, develop your own personal ethics statement. You can develop one from scratch or maybe base your statement on sections of those from related professional associations. To develop your own statement, try rereading the questions presented earlier and generalizing what you would do. Add to and modify your ethics statement every time you get a clearer understanding of what's important.

As we develop virtual worlds for others to explore, our design decisions will have an impact on the people who experience our creations. I'm not saying that we all have to make the same decisions. But, we should evaluate how we think our designs will affect others and make decisions that are congruent with our own beliefs.[*]

Talking Terminology

Lee has sketched an outline of the technical proficiencies of the would-be virtual world builder, the cyberspace engineering virtuoso.[**] Adams has colored in the human face, the human heart, the human condition. Both the skill and the wisdom are needed, and both are achieved with difficulty and polished with experience. As we begin authoring each new world, we must remind ourselves to try our best and do it right. We're all on this ride together; let's think of how we might affect each other before we start.

---

[*] *Nina Adams, 1993*
Published with permission.

[**] *An interesting sidelight on the word "virtuoso" (a master of an art) is that it derives from the same Latin word that "virtual" comes from—"virtus" (strength, bravery). "Virtus" came from the earlier Latin word "vir," meaning "man." Virtus, therefore, meant: "manly" or "with strength and bravery like a man." Thus, a nearly unanimous vote has the same strength, or effect, as a unanimous decision, so the vote is "virtually unanimous." A parallel construction with a strongly skilled musician resulted in "virtuoso."*

"In the beginning...." It is not coincidence or blasphemy that causes the echo of biblical phrases to ring in our ears when we consider shaping something out of nothing. We are human. Our words are limited. We search for expressions to convey a meaning when we hardly know what is meant. A world in the computer? Knowing the immensity and variety of the world we inhabit, how do we account for the arrogance implicit in the phrases "virtual world" and "virtual environment"? Virtual room, or virtual building, perhaps, but why "world"? Certainly, "virtual planet" or "virtual universe" is worse, but aren't there any other choices?

There are a few other words we could choose, such as cyberspace, synthetic (man-made) environment, artificial environment, and so on. But the debates could continue regardless of the selection. The more fitting question is, what is the intended meaning of the phrase "virtual world"? And the particular answer depends on what is created and where the boundaries are, because "virtual world" refers to everything created within those boundaries. A four-year-old lives in her own "world" not because she sails the seven seas, but due to the fact that she does not venture beyond definable boundaries. A spaceship is a self-contained world by reason of its enclosed quarters; there is no expectation of finding the continent of Africa in its cargo bay. If you create electronic representations of objects in the memory banks of a computer, you have surely built a virtual world with its own boundaries, properties, laws, and dimensions.

Three-Dimensional Coordinates

And you started with nothing except the limitations of the equipment. If the hardware and the software are more powerful, then you start with nothing except more powerful possibilities. As Lee phrased it in his essay, "A cyberspace engineer begins his world creation with an empty void.... Similar to an empty room that is waiting to be filled and decorated."

If you are moving into a new house and stand in the doorway looking into the bare living room, you have established a viewpoint. This is how you start a virtual world. You pick a viewpoint. But the computer hasn't a clue as to the appearance of a living room, or even the wall of any sort of room. All the computer can start with is a coordinate that is represented by three numbers.

To show how these coordinates work, let's return to where you are, standing at the door frame. You decide that you need some help in planning the placement of the sofa, so you turn to Joe, your contractor, who is standing respectfully at your side (with his own viewpoint), and suggest an unconventional project. Pointing to the far corner of the room, you ask Joe to mark lines on the floor and walls to make visualizing the furniture placement easier. With a sigh, Joe patiently draws black charcoal lines in a grid across the inlaid teak floor and the silk wall fabrics.

Now you can easily tell how far the sofa should stand from the window: two lines over and five lines deep. You can also calculate the location of your viewpoint: 7 lines over, 27 lines deep, and 6 lines up. The computer can handle this kind of information. It may not know what a wall is, but the computer has had some practice with numbers. In a virtual world, you would establish your viewpoint in the same way—7, 27, 6. The numbers are called x, y, and z—x over, y deep, and z up. The same method places the sofa—2 over, 5 deep, 0 up, or 2, 5, 0. Always in the same order—x, y, z.

Creating Objects

Once you have selected a viewpoint in the blank world, you can decide where to place your first object. If your plan is to build a virtual living room, the best approach may be to create the floor and erect the walls before creating the furniture. Each wall is an object in the world, so you will place four wall objects first. In fact, every single item in the world is called an object.

There's a good reason to build the walls before the furniture—because of the question of scale, or relative size. You probably will want all the furniture to look the right size in relation to each other and to the walls. If you created a sofa and then put up the walls, you might end up looking at a giant sofa and a tiny wall, or a miniature sofa and an enormous wall. The scale would be inconsistent and you would have to start all over again.

To build your first wall, you will want to predetermine the size of the room, so you'll need to think about 3-D coordinates again. If you don't plan it out first, the result could be four walls with different shapes, which wouldn't look right. Of course, because this

is a virtual room, you may want to be creative and build an unconventional living room with a radical, avant-garde look. There's no requirement that your virtual world must look just like the real world, unless you decide that is your goal. You are the creator of this room—this world—and you get to decide what you want.

As you prepare to construct the walls of your imagined room, you calculate the expected length, width, and height of each wall. Then you begin the procedure for the first wall. You select an appropriate position in the blank world to place the bottom corner. That position will be a three-dimensional coordinate point that you choose. Continue selecting 3-D coordinate points for each of the other corners.

In effect, you are telling the computer "Start the first line here (the first 3-D point), draw the line over to there (the second 3-D point), next connect the line to the third 3-D point, then over to the fourth point, and finally back down to the first point." The software program uses this information to draw your first object, your first wall, your first polygon shape, from the perspective of your chosen viewpoint. If you selected the 3-D points to form accurate square corners, the object will be a rectangle. Otherwise the object will be some other polygon shape, like a quadrilateral with unequal sides.

Of course, if you have drawn a rectangle or other polygon, then you have created a two-dimensional shape with no width. To indicate how wide you want the wall to be, you must select additional 3-D points slightly shifted from the wall corners, and direct the computer to draw the extra lines as well. This will result in a solid shape, or a solid-looking object, that looks more like a wall than a thin rectangle. You can repeat this process until you have four well-positioned walls for your room.

Grouping Objects

Now you are ready to place your first object inside the four walls. To construct a simple table, for example, you would create five new objects. Four of them would resemble thin pillars, the legs, and the fifth would be the top of the table—a thin, flat shape, similar to a small wall lying on its side. Each object would be created with the

same procedure used to create the four walls; you select the 3-D points that are used to draw the sides connecting from point-to-point. If you have ever drawn dot-to-dot pictures in a coloring book (you're not too old to remember that, are you?), you know exactly what the computer is doing—it draws lines by following the dots you have selected. The difference, naturally, is in the speed. If you—like the computer—could connect thousands or millions of dots every second, you would be more famous than Houdini.

But, to return to our table.... After the pillars and the tabletop are constructed, you'll probably want to place the tabletop horizontally across the vertical pillars or legs. By carefully selecting the correct coordinates, you can line up the legs under the corners of the tabletop. Now you have created your first table—actually, you have lined up five shapes to look like a table.

A problem could arise later if a person who is exploring your world tries to lift the table using a virtual hand. If they grab a leg, the pillar will move by itself. Unless you want them to think the table is broken, you may not be satisfied with this arrangement. You may want the table to move as a unit when lifted. To "unify" the five shapes into an object that moves as if it were a single shape, you need to "group" the objects that make up the table shape. By defining the legs and tabletop as a "table group," all five shapes will act as if they were one single object. In fact, the computer will define the new grouped shape as a single new entity in the world, constructed from the five component objects.

Attributes

Either before or after grouping your objects, you can assign attributes to each component shape. If you color the table brown, the color brown is referred to as an attribute of the table. While you are "operating," or exploring, your virtual world, the computer calculates which objects should be drawn based upon your viewpoint. Objects that are located behind your viewpoint (as if they were behind your head) don't need to be drawn—in fact, can't be drawn—because the defined viewpoint can't "see" those objects. For each object determined to be visible from your viewpoint, the computer looks up the object in the listing (like the table of

contents), checks the coordinates and the attributes, and then draws the object. If the color attribute for the table object is "set" to brown, the table will be colored brown while being drawn.

In addition to color, there can be several other attributes attached to each object. For example, objects can be defined as having attributes such as whether they are movable, and whether they can be thrown. Each attribute can then be set on or off. By setting the table's "moveable" attribute off, no amount of lifting or shoving will budge that table. It has been defined as unmovable, and the computer ignores any attempt to push the table in any direction. Usually an attribute is established with the use of parameters, or numbers, that control the attribute. A zero parameter usually means that the attribute is set to "off," and the number one means it is set to "on." So, to change the moveability attribute from off to on, you would simply change the value from 1 to 0.

Many different kinds of attributes can be defined, and each at-tribute can be set to "on" or "off." For example, objects can be rotatable or penetrable. They can respond to gravity and fall to the floor when dropped, or they can be elastic and bounce up and down when they hit the ground. To design each object, you would set the attached attributes off or on according to the desired interac-tions. As you add objects, the world becomes more populated with increasingly complex shapes and interactions. At some appropriate point, when you feel satisfied with the results (virtual worlds, like programs, never seem to be finished), you can call yourself a cyberspace engineer.

Types of World-Building Tools

Establishing viewpoints, using 3-D coordinates, grouping objects, and setting attributes are all common elements of building virtual worlds, but there are three main methods used to develop virtual worlds. One way is to use a programming language to create your own routines from scratch. This is the most difficult avenue, requiring virtuoso programming skills, constant patience, and years of painstaking work. Another approach is to purchase a world-building tool that includes pre-developed routines, created with a programming language, that you can combine, modify, and

connect in varying integrations. These commonly used routines are called "libraries," and eliminate a great deal of work. A popular world-building tool called WorldToolKit, by Sense8 Corporation, is based on this method of integrated libraries of code.

As computer and VR capabilities have progressed, some far-sighted programmers have realized that a third approach, development tool, or world editor program, if properly arranged, would be able to provide effective results for would-be world builders. Like a word processing program that includes selectable text functions to easily carry out tasks normally requiring a great deal of effort, a virtual reality development tool places an array of three-dimensional graphical tools at a world builder's fingertips. VR Studio is an example of an affordable development tool, but is quite restricted in its ability to connect with peripherals. Freescape, developed by the English corporation New Dimension International Limited, is an example of a quite powerful and versatile development tool for desktop VR, but costs several thousand dollars. VREAM is the name of another development tool that might be on the market by the time this book is published. A sample of the VREAM tool is on the disk enclosed with this book. One demonstration program created with VREAM is also included on the disk.

Building Worlds with a World-Editing System

VR development systems at this time incorporate the use of a GUI Interface to facilitate the creation and animation of objects, as well as interacting with these objects using selected peripherals and accessories. A world typically starts with a screen containing a viewport, or window, of the virtual world, surrounded by an array of icons representing choices. By clicking the icons with a mouse cursor or arrow, you can select appropriate choices to accomplish varied tasks. For example, to create an object, you select a shape, and that shape appears in the window. Readers who have experience with painting and drawing programs, such as PaintBrush, can visualize a similar screen with a "window," or "canvas," where you draw and doodle, surrounded by an assortment of drawing tool icons. A world-editing system has a comparable GUI interface.

A system like this that allows you to easily edit, or change, your world with functions designed to save time and effort is more accessible and more interactive. For example, if you are unsatisfied with the position of an object after you have placed it, you merely click on the icon that represents the "Move" command, and select the new position. The editing system moves the object to your chosen spot. You do not have to keep track of each of the coordinates of the object's starting position. You do not have to calculate the x, y, z numbers of the new coordinates. You simply indicate the new position with the mouse. The editing system keeps track of all the numbers needed to move the object from there to here. After all, the computer is a commutation machine—why not let it do its job?

In essence, the world-building system is like the leather straps and harness on a horse: It controls the power of the beast and directs it to produce work. Planning, creating, and building the program that controls the editing process are time-consuming and frustrating processes for a programmer. The complexity of all the functions and tools—which harness the ability of the computer to keep track of numbers in such a way that the world-builder can be freed from some of the drudgery—is a difficult challenge for the system developer.

But after one person does all the hard work making the editing system, the world-builders who use the system benefit greatly. It's very much like enjoying the benefits of power steering on the car. The inventor who conceived the idea must have spent a great deal of time and effort making it possible, but the result helps millions of people every day.

Putting the computer to work assisting itself in its job is an accomplishment and a service. The investment in time and energy saves the rest of us time and energy, and makes easily possible what is otherwise difficult. The developers of virtual reality world-editing systems deserve a big round of applause and appreciation for their struggles and their creative foresight.

Script Commands

A cyberspace engineer using an editing system, however, is not able to wave a hand, or click a mouse button, and accomplish everything imaginable in the world. There will be frequent occasions when a desired function or capability is not included in the tools provided. At the times when an idea is not achievable within the constraints of the editing system, the world-builder is forced to look for alternate methods. This is when you have to delve into the mysteries of *script commands*.

The developers of editing systems realize that they cannot include every function or capability that might possibly be needed, so they typically provide a way for world-builders to type in manual instructions. These lists of typed commands are generally called scripts. If you want a phone to ring at a certain time, for example, that is called a *condition*. Conditions are usually similar to "If this happens, then make that happen," which is called an IF-THEN statement. "IF the time becomes 2:30 p.m., THEN start the phone ringing."

A condition is well suited for inclusion in a script. You can type a script command for many types of conditions—and the more commands available for a script, the more flexibility is available for the world builder. But here's where things get complicated. You can't just type "IF the time becomes 2:30 p.m., THEN start the phone ringing." You have to follow the rules. The rules might not allow the word "the" or the word "start." The rules for the commands are set up in advance by the developer of the editing system. All the rules and all the commands, taken together, are called a language—a computer language. Here's a short example of a condition written in computer language that might follow the rules for a script command:

```
IF a = 1
THEN b = b + 2
```

If this script command looks like programming, that's because it is like programming. Using a script is a way of instructing, or programming, the computer to do things in the virtual world that are not already defined in the editing system. This makes it possible to customize a particular world or environment to achieve complex actions.

After typing the script commands (using the language provided and the format required), you will want to save your work in a stored reproduction called a script file. Then, when you test the condition in the virtual world and find that it is not working just the way you envisioned, you can call up the script file again and make changes to it without retyping all the commands. Or, if you think of a new action, you can add more commands to your script file.

In a typical virtual world system, the script files are performed between each frame. In other words, after the computer has displayed the objects on the screen (which is one frame), it then runs through all the script files before displaying the objects again (the next frame). That way, if a condition is met—such as the time becoming 2:30 p.m.—the response will be implemented during the next frame—the phone will be activated.

Script files expand the power of world-editing to include more features and more flexibility, but they also require more study and persistence from the cyberspace engineer than built-in functions require. Learning the script command language is the first step— learning how to use the commands is the second step. It's a big help if you have already learned programming before trying to learn a script language, because many of the principles are similar.

Several programs on the disk at the end of the book—such as Mover and Castle—contain scripts. Also, the "Adventure in VREAM" demonstration program is generated with one large script file. You won't be able to read it, however, because it has been compiled into a machine-readable—binary—format to make it operate more quickly. An example of a script file that is used in Mover is a list of commands that check to see whether you have activated the pink moving cart with the mouse cursor (using the right button). If the cart is moving when you activate it, it stops moving; it starts moving again if it is stopped at the time you activate it.

The user of a world, sometimes called a "cybernaut" (a traveler in cyberspace, analogous to "astronaut"—a traveler in star space), never sees a script file—only the computer sees the script files. The computer uses the script files to determine whether conditions are True or False, and to induce the instructed response to the conditions when they're found to be True. The world-builder also sees—

185

in fact, plans—the script commands that instruct the computer during the time when the world is being constructed—called the *edit* or *development mode*. When editing is finished, and the world or environment is ready, then all the instructions are compiled into a form that is suitable for the computer to operate. When the computer is actually executing, or "running," the instructions, it is called *run-time mode*.

Creating Advanced Worlds

Returning to the concept of designing a living room in a virtual world—let's expand the idea to include the entire house.

Suppose your house has ten rooms. This would be considered an advanced world. There are two ways to approach the construction of ten rooms—you can choose to put all ten rooms in one complete world, or you can establish several worlds. You could build one world for each room, resulting in ten separate environments. Both approaches will allow you to walk through all the rooms in run-time mode, but in different ways.

With the first method—ten rooms in one world—you would construct the entire house the same way it is done in real life: put up all the walls, connect them to each other, install the doors and windows, and then fill the rooms with furniture. Walking from room to room, then, would be accomplished just like in a real house. You could even look through an open doorway and see into the next room, or look out of the window onto the yard. But you would pay a price for such realism. You would have to pay for a substantial amount of memory. The instructions for virtual worlds fill up considerable amounts of computer memory.

The second method, with isolated environments—one or more rooms to each—is less demanding of computer memory. You can bring one environment at a time into the memory area. Then how do you walk from one room to another? You simply set up more conditions. A sample condition would be, in effect, "If the viewpoint crosses through a doorway, replace current room in memory with next room"—this is called an entrance condition. Each room, or group of rooms, is a separate segment in the complete world, and each segment is called an *environment*.

The advantage of linking entrances to and from environments is the substantial savings in the amount of computer memory needed. If you need only enough memory capacity for the space required for one room, then making separate environments connected by entrances will save you money. But, to be clear, entrances in virtual worlds are not obliged to be limited to doorways between rooms. You can set up an entrance condition for any object or portion of an object—even for an event or an action. If the instructions specify an entrance condition when a cybernaut bumps into the lamp, then the room could be replaced with an environment representing the inside of the lamp's light bulb. This is a virtual world. There's no reason why you have to limit yourself to real world restrictions. Creating advanced worlds opens up many opportunities to use your imagination freely.

Large-Scale Advanced Worlds

Nina Adams, who contributed the ethical perspective near the beginning of this chapter, has generously offered to share an outline of her knowledge about issues involved in managing a development project when teams of people participate towards one goal. This expertise is based on her vast experience in managing educational and software system design projects over the last 25 years. Some readers might find this section more useful than others, depending on their level of group involvement. With the numerous layers of complexities and skills to be managed and coordinated in a larger project, such as a commercial virtual reality application, these pointers may be helpful to readers responsible for organizing a team effort. I have condensed Nina's suggestions into a list of project phases.

First, consider what you want to accomplish with your world:

- Are you creating it for fun, for research, for training?
- Do you have some overall perspective of the world?
- Will it follow the rules of the real world, or will it be something totally different?

You will probably find it easier to design something if you have a goal in mind before you start.

Virtual World Development Project Phases

Feasibility

Define: Project scope and objectives
Project requirements
Staffing needs
Cost projections
Benefit projections

Project Planning

Set up: Tasks and deadlines
User interfaces
Subcontractor interfaces
Status and budget monitoring and reporting guidelines
Contingency plans
Standards

If a large virtual world is developed, it may have to be segmented—requiring more than one developer. However, all segments must look as if they were built by one person. Therefore, standards are necessary before the project starts. Company-wide standards and application-specific standards may be implemented.

Select: Hardware
Software
Staff

Project Management

Follow-up and report on project development and implement contingency plans, if needed.

Frequent progress reviews with the client. Ensure that the client is aware, and approves, of each step to avoid costly redo work.

Design

Develop detailed specifications and evaluation criteria.

World Development

Develop world to meet specifications.

Testing and Quality Control

Make sure the world being developed conforms to standards and meets all the specifications.

Pilot

Test the world with a small number of actual end-users to make sure it does what it is supposed to do.

Implement

Distribute the world to everyone who is supposed to have it.

Evaluate

After the world has been in use for a while, find out if it actually met the goals established at the beginning of the project. Decide how the world-building process could have been done more effectively. Learn from the mistakes made.

Regardless of the number of suggestions, large-scale virtual world building is quite a challenge. If you join such a project, you will find yourself learning new skills and discovering a deeper under-standing of the integration of hardware and software required for advanced world-building. The cybernauts who will explore your worlds hope you will find ways to create abundant interactivity, interesting places to visit, and high levels of immersion—using as many of the senses as possible. Best wishes in your cybernautic efforts!

Time for the Fun!

Now that you have learned the fundamentals of building your own
virtual world, it is time for some virtual reality fun and entertainment. In the next chapter, you'll find instructions and tips on
installing and operating the 3-D and VR programs on the disk with
this book. You can see and experience the adventures for yourself.
Jump right in—the perceptions are fine!

Chapter 7

Virtual Reality Arcade

Here's where you can put into practice everything you've learned about VR concepts and experiences in the first six chapters. The programs included with this book represent some of the latest and best PC-based developments in 3-D graphic programs.

Installing and Operating the Software on the Enclosed Disk

The programs have been carefully selected to include examples of different features and capabilities, all designed to be instructive as well as entertaining. By wearing the enclosed red and blue 3-D glasses, you will be able to see two

impressive demonstrations of the depth effect—the Anaglyph and the FLY the Grand Canyon programs. You can explore several worlds (Castle, Mover, and MinoDino) created with VR Studio—a remarkably affordable program. And, to top it all off—if you have access
to a computer with enough power—you can also enjoy the first book-based demonstration of the most interactive, feature-packed, flexible, and affordable virtual reality program for the IBM-compatible PC yet devised: a virtual world called Adventure in VREAM.

Each program is comprised of several files that are all combined into one compressed file. Compression squeezes more information into a smaller space—so all the programs can fit onto one disk. Without compression, the programs would have required the space of several disks, which would have forced a higher price for the book; there's always a trade-off. The price you pay for compression, though, is the little extra time it will take to expand the files. The programs will automatically decompress themselves, however, so there's nothing complicated about the procedure—and you only have to do it once. Just follow the steps one at a time, and in a few minutes you'll be able to enjoy the programs.

Understanding More about Installing the Program Files

On the last page of this book there are step-by-step directions for installing the program files. The instructions assume that you know a little about DOS commands. If you don't know what DOS means, then you won't know what the instructions mean either, so you'll need to get someone to help you follow the directions. The following pointers explain helpful hints for each step, but the installation instructions on the last page list the steps for the exact procedure you should follow.

1. First, turn to the detailed description of each program in this chapter and make sure that you have the kind of computer equipment required for the program. The most powerful computer required is for the VREAM program—a 486. If you do not have the necessary computer for a program, try to

think of a friend, neighbor, or associate who might let you see the program on their computer in return for letting them try out the programs.

2. If your computer is appropriate for the program, then select or create a directory where you want to store a copy of the program (the instructions on the last page suggest a directory name).

3. Place the floppy disk included with this book into your 3 ½ inch drive. If you have only a 5 ¼ inch floppy drive, you probably can find someone who will be willing to transfer the programs onto another disk. Or, your nearby computer store should have personnel with enough foresight to take a moment to help you—especially if you buy a disk or a box of disks from them.

4. Copy the desired program from the floppy drive to the selected directory on the hard drive. The filename extension should be .EXE.

5. Change your default directory to the selected directory—if you haven't already done so.

6. Type the name listed as the compressed filename of the program. This will start the automatic process of decompressing the program's files. You will see the name of each file listed on-screen as the file is being decompressed.

7. When the decompressing procedure is finished, you will see the DOS command prompt again. At this time, type the name of the executable program (listed in the detailed description for that program in this chapter). Press the Enter key. The computer will start the program, and you will begin your virtual odyssey.

NOTE: The ANAGLYPH program requires a shape name in addition to the program name.

Instructions for the Programs Requiring 3-D Glasses

Although these programs that demonstrate the method of achieving a 3-D effect with shifted images are not examples of the kinds of virtual worlds represented by the other programs, they do show what is possible when you shift images and present alternate displays to each eye. Compared to expensive stereoscopic systems, red and blue 3-D glasses generate a three-dimensional depth illusion that can be slightly disorienting or disconcerting. But, when you consider the remarkable effect provided by two simple pieces of translucent colored plastic, it is clear that the value of the 3-D viewer lies in permitting us to discover another talent of the human brain and trying to make sense of whatever signals it receives.

The 3-D viewing glasses enclosed with this book are not magic lenses. You will want to have some realistic expectations of the effect you can expect. It takes a little while for your brain to become acclimated to the depth cues it receives from the left and right images. First, you will want to hold the glasses correctly in front of your eyes. The red lens is meant for your left eye and blue lens for your right eye. Reversing them will provide the wrong image for each eye; your brain will try to interpret the shifted images in the wrong direction. It will be as confusing as putting your arms into your jacket sleeves backwards.

Readers who wear glasses can place the 3-D viewer inside the frames for hands-free viewing. You won't have to hold on to the 3-D viewer with one hand while simultaneously pressing keys on the keyboard. If you are without the advantage of a built-in holder, you can choose between remaining temporarily one-handed, or finding a way to affix the 3-D viewer to your face. Placing a small piece of tape at the top center of the 3-D glasses and the bridge over the nose has been found to be quite effective.

You will probably find it more efficient at first to launch the program before positioning the 3-D viewing glasses. Later, when you are more familiar with the disorienting effect, you should find it somewhat easier to adjust to looking at the keyboard while wearing them. Once the program is launched and you have

positioned the viewer, you may wonder at first what all the fuss has been about. Ignore such rebellious thoughts. Wait for a minute or two while looking at the images. Give your brain a chance to adjust. You'll probably discover a sensation of gradually gaining an increasing perspective of depth. Try to identify the lines that look furthest away and compare them with lines that look closer. Then you might want to estimate the perceived distance between them. While you're trying to analyze what you are seeing, you should notice your brain slowly interpreting more and more depth in the scene. Get ready to say "Wow!"

Description and Instructions for FLY the Grand Canyon Demo

Equipment needed:

> IBM-compatible computer.
> VGA graphics capability.
> 3-D viewing glasses.

Compressed file name:

> FLY_DEMO.EXE

Execution file name:

> FLYDEMO

Source:

> Hyacinth (address in Appendix B).
> Written by Fred Tuck.

Related programs:

> FLY the Grand Canyon $ 69.00 (Commercial version).

One of the world's greatest natural wonders is the Grand Canyon. This Grand Canyon simulation program has to be one of the best 3-D stereoscopic programs available for use with red and blue glasses. It is advertised as the first stereo 3-D flying simulation for the personal computer, and as far as is known, is the only one of its kind. This is a demonstration version that enables you to fly across

a 100-square-mile area of the Grand Canyon. A fascinating aspect of this program is that the information for the contours came from aerial photographs from a U.S. Geological Survey. This is the real shape of the canyon you're going to fly, not a programmer's concept of what it should look like.

To start the FLY the Grand Canyon program, type FLYDEMO. Because this a demo, the section of the canyon you can explore is limited to 100 square miles. The full version is 1800 square miles, comprised of over three million data points, which represents the contours of the entire canyon. If you like the effect of the demo, you'll really like the full version because it will let you fly over a much larger area—plus it includes several other features not available in the demo. The full commercial version permits you to look at 3-D topological maps of any section, with three different magnification levels. In addition, you can select any time of day and see a shadow map, where the shadows of the contours are displayed according to where the sun is located.

The first screen of the FLYDEMO version has a 3-D map of the complete canyon topology shown as if you were in an airplane looking down. If you wear the glasses while looking at the canyon map, you will gradually sense more and more depth, and the bottom level of the canyon will seem farther and farther away. The text boxes will seem as though they are the closest to you.

When you want to continue, press any key and the screen will display a series of instructions. At the end of the instructions you will be given the choice of a pre-determined, or canned, tour where you can just sit back and enjoy the flight without worrying about the controls, or the "fly-it-yourself" mode, which allows you to fly wherever you want. You might want to take the tour first to see what the flight is like.

On the bottom of the screen (see Figure 7.1) is a display of the "instrument" panel that shows information such as the altitude of the plane. During the flight, the contours of the cliffs and outcroppings are rendered in low detail wire-frame mode. As you watch with the 3-D viewer, your brain will increasingly converge the shifted blue and red images into an illusion of depth. You might want to try different distances from the monitor to find the best position for convergence.

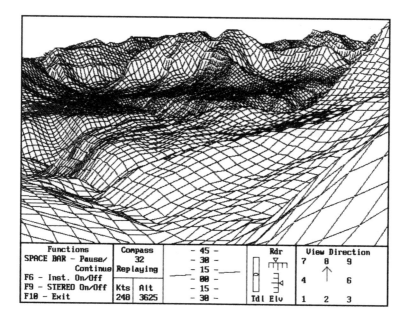

Functions	Compass		– 45 –	Rdr	View Direction
SPACE BAR – Pause/	32		– 30 –		7 8 9
Continue	Replaying		– 15 –		
F6 – Inst. On/Off			– 00 –		4 ↑ 6
F9 – STEREO On/Off	Kts	Alt	– 15 –		
F10 – Exit	248	3625	– 30 –	Idl Elv	1 2 3

Figure 7.1.

A sample screen from FLY the Grand Canyon.

Because the computer needs to calculate, or "crunch," the large amount of mathematics necessary to draw all the lines between the data points while you are flying, the low level of detail is represented by large polygons. If you want to see a higher level of detail at any time, however, just press the space bar. The motion of the flight will stop, and your viewpoint will pause, but you will see much more detail. Because you have stopped moving, the computer has time to fill in all the missing lines. This is where you get a much more accurate picture of the shapes in the contours.

This is a good illustration of the limitations caused by the speed of the personal computer—the PC can't keep up with all the math of the high detail and still continue flying. As desktop computers advance in speed (one measure of their power), increasing amounts of detail will be possible even while flying. Imagine what it might be like someday flying with the high detail displayed!

After watching the demonstration tour, try flying yourself. Start the program again. This time select number 2 after the instructions end. Use the number pad to select the view you want. Number 8 shows you what it looks like straight ahead, as if you were the pilot. Number 2 shows you what you would see behind you. The other numbers show the view from the side, as if you were looking out

the window like a passenger. To bank the plane left and right, use the left and right arrow keys. To lift the nose of the aircraft, or gain altitude, press the down arrow. To lower the nose and head towards the ground, press the up arrow. At any time, you can press the End key and return all controls to the center position.

Several of the function keys cause special actions. To end the flying session and exit the program, press F10. If you want to fly without having the stereoscopic 3-D effect (if you would like to try it without the 3-D glasses), press F9. To increase the size of the window by removing the instrument panel, press F6—of course, then you're flying without instruments; you'd better get familiar with the controls first. If you crash, the screen will be surrounded with what looks like shards of glass, but after a couple of seconds you are given another chance to try your flying skills. FLY the Grand Canyon provides a truly enjoyable 3-D experience using the red and blue anaglyph method.

Description and Instructions for ANAGLYPH

Equipment needed:

IBM-compatible computer.
EGA graphics capability.
3-D viewing glasses.

Compressed file name:

ANAGLYPH.EXE

Execution file name:

STEREO plus parameters (see instructions).

Source:

Schreiber Instruments (address in Appendix B).
Written by Ed Schreiber.

If you have ever run your fingers over a cameo figure on a brooch, or examined the stamped design on the base of a lamp or on the handle of a fork, then you have been introduced to an anaglyph.

From two Greek words meaning to "carve up" ("ana" is "up," and "glyphein" is "to carve"), anaglyph has come to mean a shape, or ornament, in low relief. In architecture, a "glyph" can be a groove or channel; more generally, a glyph is any incised or raised figure. The Egyptian hieroglyphs were so named because of the early "sacred carvings" found on the walls of the monuments and on discovered tablets. The concept of relief, high or low, derives from a Latin word "relevare," meaning to "lift or raise up" (related to "levee," "lever," and "levitation"—a raised embankment, a tool to raise things, and raising into the air, respectively).

So, an anaglyph is a figure in relief, or raised above the surface. It is a subtle way of indicating the third dimension, the depth. If a surface represents the first two dimensions, (x and y), then anything raised above the surface is projected into the third spatial dimension (z). A surface can be a floor, a smooth brooch, riverside land, or a computer monitor screen. With the ingenious 3-D program ANAGLYPH, you explore figures that look like they have depth; figures that are raised, or projected, beyond the surface.

To start the ANAGLYPH program, type STEREO CUBE and press Enter. (From now on, these directions will omit instructing you to press Enter—all statements that require typing a command also require pressing Enter. It's the method used to indicate to the computer that you are finished typing your command.) Typing STEREO CUBE will display a rotating cube on the screen. Wearing the 3-D glasses, watch the motion and become adjusted to the image. Soon you should see a three-dimensional cube. The color of the lines should be a light bluish-white. You can move closer and farther from the screen to see the effect distance has on the image, but the normal span between the monitor and your chair is usually fine. If you notice some reddish and bluish double lines now and then, it's because your brain isn't converging your eyes exactly right at that moment. You can move the shape using the keys listed below.

When you start STEREO with a shape name, a help menu first appears on the screen. The following list summarizes the keys to use:

Arrow keys, Ins, Del to rotate

Shift-(arrow keys) to pan out

PgUp, PgDn to zoom

Shift-PgUp, Shift-PgDn to move in, out

+ (plus) to speed up, - (minus) to slow down

Home to restore initial view

Shift-Home to reset speed

End to toggle autorotation

Esc to exit

? for help

NOTE: Only the arrow keys on the numeric pad can be used to pan in and out.

There are several shapes you can try out with the STEREO program. Each shape has a corresponding file with a .3D extension.

When you try a different shape, type STEREO and one of the shape names, like you did with STEREO CUBE. There's no need to type the .3D extension, but it's fine if you do. The more complex shapes, such as ROBOT, take longer to execute. To exit from any shape, press the ESC key.

You can even make your own shapes, because STEREO can handle any text file that meets some simple requirements. The file should contain lines with x, y, z points separated by spaces or tabs. Look at one of the ANAGLYPH files in an editor to see how it is done. A blank line indicates a start of a new "polyline," and consecutive non-blank lines contain the vertices. The file should have the extension .3D. It might help to try the smaller files first to get practice in the interactive operation of STEREO.

One last note on STEREO. Ed Schreiber wrote this program several years ago, and is now involved with other software for engineers, so the company is not planning to continue supporting STEREO. You shouldn't have any problems with the program, but if you do, try to have a friend help you instead of contacting the source company. They have begun to focus their efforts on their current work. The

program is included with this book because of the interactive nature of its 3-D effect. Read the included STEREO.DOC file for documentation.

Description and Instructions for MOVER

Equipment needed:

> IBM-compatible computer.
> VGA graphics capability.
> Mouse or joystick.

Compressed file name:

> MOVR7.EXE

To execute the file, enter the desired number, one through eight, to install the corresponding actions.

Source:

> VRontier worlds of Stoughton (address in Appendix B).
> Created with Virtual Reality Studio.

This program was developed for a pilot study at an elementary school. The participating teachers were Jan Martin and Judith Reese, and the targeted objective was to create a computer environment using some of the VR principles, such as navigation and interaction, that could be incorporated into a curriculum involving the concepts of classification and categorization.

VR Studio was chosen as the authoring tool primarily because of its affordable cost, to learn what methods and techniques were successful, and to analyze the potential impact of open-ended exploration on the students' learning experience. The purpose of including it here is to show what is achievable without spending thousands of dollars—and to demonstrate some of the basic fundamentals of creating a world.

You begin with your viewpoint located a few inches above the surface of a road, and a pink flatbed cart is racing towards you. If you don't get out of the way, you will be placed on top of the cart. For a few seconds, all operator navigation is temporarily suspended

while you are automatically transported high in the sky for a panoramic view of the world below. Then you are allowed to fall towards the cart at high speed, but are stopped just in time to be placed gently on the surface again. At this time the cart moves off down the road, with you taking a ride.

If no action is taken, you may ride around the world indefinitely and "sightsee." But you are not restricted to sitting on the surface of the cart while riding. By positioning the arrow cursor, controlled by the mouse, on the pink triangle icon, you may rise into the air while still moving with the cart. While in the air, you may look around with the LOOK DOWN and LOOK UP icons, or look left and right with the TURN LEFT and TURN RIGHT icons, or tilt the view with the TILT LEFT and TILT RIGHT icons.

As long as actions are limited to the orientation of the viewpoint, the ride will continue. But, as soon as you use the motion icons like FORWARD, BACKWARD, LEFT, or RIGHT, you risk falling off the cart, because if you cross over the edge of the cart in any direction, you will fall off and land on the ground. But you won't get hurt, and you land in such a way that your viewpoint is facing horizontally.

There are two ways to climb back on top of the cart. You can either stop the cart and get on, or you can collide with it while it is moving. Stopping the cart requires being near enough to it—by either maneuvering your position or waiting until it returns back around again. If you're close enough, and you want to stop the cart, you move the mouse cursor into the window of the world (where the cursor becomes a "cross-hair"), place the cross-hairs on the cart, and press the right button on the mouse. This is called "activating the object;" the cart should stop immediately. Activating the cart again will make it start moving once again—but you might want to climb on first. To do that, simply use the FORWARD icon to collide with the cart. This will place you on top of the cart again. Then you can activate the cart and off you go. The other way to return to the top of the cart is to maneuver your viewer position to a point on the road where the cart is expected to travel. This makes the cart collide with you and off you go.

Try activating other objects in the environment, such as the orange pyramids and the blue boxes. You must stop the cart in front of these objects first, or nothing will happen, because the cart will be too far away. Activate the tall, upside-down pyramid and ride with

it. There is a difference in riding with the tall pyramid, because you can maneuver, or navigate, anywhere you wish, and still travel with it. There is only one way to get off the tall pyramid. You must return to the top and activate the blue surface. Try activating the brown sign and see what appears.

This is a full-featured, animated, rich environment using VR principles developed for an elementary school, but VR is intriguing for adults too. (Some features are sophisticated but do not impede young children.) Use a mouse to move freely in all directions—even "fly." Learn spatial relationships, control of a computer, categorizing, and classification (group blue or orange objects on a moving pink flatbed cart). Stop, start, and ride on the moving cart. Activate objects, make objects appear and disappear, explore behind the walls, and find secret entrances to hidden areas. (Can you find the helicopter?) The program has seven levels: Starting with "forward" and "back" motions, each level adds another dimension of movement.

Instructions:

The way to get started:

1. Select the version, or level, you wish to enter (1 through 7). The numbers (commands) have the following actions:

Number	Action
1	'Forward' and 'back' motion controls.
2	Add 'left' and 'right' motion controls.
3	Add 'turn left' and 'turn right' motion controls.
4	Add 'look up' and 'look down' motion controls.
5	Add 'move up' and 'move down' motion controls.
6	Add 'tilt left' and 'tilt right' motion controls.
7	Add 'reset view' control — Full featured MOVER program.
8	Read instructions on screen.
9	Exit to DOS.

2. Select Keyboard, Joystick, or Mouse.

3. MOVER was developed to allow simplified access for elementary school children and has 7 steps or versions (numbered from 1 to 7). Each version is completely separate from the others and can be entered at any time. The first version allows only forward and backward motion. This was designed to minimize confusion for young children as they begin to learn how to use the mouse buttons. Each subsequent version adds an additional pair of motion controls: for instance, version two adds the ability to move left and right. Users can enter any version they feel comfortable with.

4. You change your viewpoint by placing the cursor on an icon at the right side of the screen and pressing a mouse button.

5. On the motion controls, the right button lets you move quickly, the left button lets you move slowly.

6. If you get disoriented, click the left mouse button on the box marked RESET VIEW.

7. Sometimes colliding with an object can make something happen (such as getting a ride on the moving cart).

8. Sometimes activating an object can cause action (such as stopping and starting the moving cart). *Activating* is achieved by moving the cursor to an object in the picture and clicking the right mouse button. Activation is only effective if you are close enough to the object.

Controls:

Large red arrow—Move forward.

Large blue arrow—Move backward.

Yellow triangle—Move left.

Green triangle—Move right.

Yellow arrow—Turn left.

Green arrow—Turn right.

Pink eye box—Look up.

Blue eye box—Look down.

Pink triangle—Move up.

Blue triangle—Move down.

Left tilted head—Tilt left.

Right tilted head—Tilt right.

Horizon box—Reset view.

Esc—Start again.

Shift-Esc—Exit MOVER.

Sounds:

A scraping sound means you are colliding with an object.

Other sounds are related to certain actions.

Hints:

Whether you are walking or flying, you are restricted to the green area bounded by blue ocean.

The centerpoint of the picture is marked with a + (plus) sign. To walk straight down a path, turn in such a way that the path points directly at the centerpoint.

To toggle the + (plus) sign on and off, press *C*.

The large *N* means North. (Ask the student to point to East, West, and South.)

Read the included MOVER.DOC file for documentation.

You can activate:

- the green direction arrow on the road

- the brown sign (makes art gallery visible)

- the pink moving flatbed

- the blue boxes and the orange pyramids (if the moving cart is parked next to them)

- the oscillating art in the gallery

- the tall pillar pyramid (puts you on top—the only way to get off is to activate the blue top of the pyramid)

- any white cube

NOTE: Suggestion for teachers:

Evaluating a student's readiness to continue on to a subsequent version can be accomplished by asking the student if he or she can describe how the controls work, and which motions are caused by which icons.

If you stop the flatbed next to the group of blue boxes or the group of orange pyramids and activate each box or pyramid, the objects will move and position themselves on the top of the flatbed. If you have three of the same objects on top of the flatbed when you go through the tunnel, you time-warp to another area. The objects move off the flatbed and it disappears. To return to the first area, move close to the white cube and activate it. After returning to the first area, you can pick up another load.

NOTE: You might find it more rewarding in the long run to let the children discover for themselves how they want to explore and what portion of the world they want to explore—and teach each other what they have found out. Within a short time, what seemed a little complicated will become familiar.

If the mouse is a little awkward for the hand of a kindergarten student, there are smaller mice available on the market. Also, you may find that the students can manipulate a joystick a little easier than a mouse. You could also show the student how to hold the mouse steady with one hand, and press the buttons with the other.

Description and Instructions for MINO-DINO Demo

Equipment needed:

IBM-compatible computer.
VGA graphics capability.
Mouse or joystick.

Compressed file name:

MINODINO.EXE

Execution file name:

1.BAT

Source:

VRontier worlds of Stoughton (address in Appendix B).
Created with Virtual Reality Studio.

Because VR Studio is restricted to shapes that have no curves, MINO-DINO was created to discover how much could be achieved towards the goal of combining straight sided shapes to approximate a rounded animal shape. The Tyrannosaurus Rex was chosen both for its popularity and for the challenge it presented. The attempt was partially successful in that the result is a recognizable shape, but the inability to use curves is such a severe limitation that the shape still remains somewhat "blocky." A seemingly obvious solution would be to utilize many more small shapes to accomplish the task, but another fundamental restriction in VR Studio makes this impossible.

When creating worlds with VR Studio, only about sixty objects are allowed in one environment. Each tooth in the Rex's mouth is an object—so the teeth alone represent about ten objects, leaving a balance of fifty objects with which to build the rest of the body and the mountains. Even the cave doors are separate objects, so this environment pushes the limit of what's possible in VR Studio.

However, VR Studio does permit 254 different environments, or areas, in one world, so when you go down the dinosaur's throat or enter one of the cave entrances, you are transferred into another environment, and then another 60 objects are available in the new area. Although 254 areas provide sufficient room for most applications, the problem is that no area can be viewed from another. It would be much better if less areas were available and more than sixty objects could be constructed in each area. Typically, there is a far greater need for large numbers of objects in a single area than for many areas containing few objects.

To start the MINO-DINO program, type DINO. The graphical interface for MINO-DINO is similar to the MOVER program. Your first

position in the world faces the feet of the dinosaur. If you press the left button of the mouse while the cursor is on the BACK icon, you will back up and see more of the body.

There are two cave entrances in the hills, one on either side of the dinosaur. Travelling down the steps and turning the corner, you will see a gold door ahead of you. After walking close to it, you can activate the door by placing the mouse cursor on the door (the cursor will change to cross-hairs). Press the right button and the door will slide upward. You can now enter the bright, multi-colored room. As you pass the purple pedestal, the door will close automatically behind you. To exit, you can reopen the first door by reactivating it or activating the other door. If you mistakenly find yourself outside the tunnel walls, you will have to maneuver through a chink in the wall to return to the tunnels.

Instructions:

Look a dinosaur in the eye. Go in its mouth. Walk up its back. Watch out when it jumps. Explore the caves. Use a mouse or joystick to move freely in all directions, even "fly."

Virtual reality attempts to let you do things you couldn't do in real life. While children are exploring the dinosaurs, they are also learning about spatial relationships and computers—all at their own pace and at their own independent level.

1. To begin the exploration, type 1.BAT.

2. Select Keyboard, Joystick, or Mouse.

3. You change your viewpoint by placing the cursor on an icon at the right side of the screen, and pressing a mouse button.

4. On the motion controls, the right button lets you move quickly, the left button lets you move slowly.

5. If you get disoriented, click the left mouse button on the box marked RESET VIEW.

6. Sometimes, colliding with an object can make something happen (such as going into the cave).

7. Sometimes activating an object can cause action (such as opening a door).

"Activating" is achieved by clicking the right mouse button on an object. Activation is only effective if you are close enough to the object.

Controls:

Large red arrow—Move forward.

Large blue arrow—Move backward.

Yellow triangle—Move left.

Green triangle—Move right.

Yellow arrow—Turn left.

Green arrow—Turn right.

Pink eye box—Look up.

Blue eye box—Look down.

Pink triangle—Move up.

Blue triangle—Move down.

Left tilted head—Tilt left.

Right tilted head—Tilt right.

Horizon box—Reset view.

Esc—Start again.

Shift-Esc—Exit MINO-DINO.

Sounds:

A scraping sound means you are colliding with an object.

Other sounds are related to certain actions.

Hints:

Whether you are walking or flying, you are restricted to the area bounded by mountains.

The centerpoint of the picture is marked with a + (plus) sign. To walk straight down a path, turn in such a way that the path points directly at the centerpoint. To toggle the + (plus) sign on and off, press C.

You can activate:

> The two gold doors, the gold bar in the large room in the cave, and the white cube in another area (activating, or colliding with, the white cube returns you to the dinosaur). Activating (or colliding with) the cave entrances moves you inside the caves.

Description and Instructions for CASTLE

Equipment needed:

> IBM-compatible computer.
> VGA graphics capability.
> Mouse or joystick.

Compressed file name:

> CASTLE.EXE

Execution file name:

> CSTL

Source:

> Raymond Holmes (address in Appendix B).
> Created with Virtual Reality Studio.

Some interesting techniques and animations are showcased in this program, which demonstrates a different scale with massive castle walls and doors. You start in front of an inviting castle drawbridge lowered over a moat. If you don't walk carefully over the bridge, you'll fall into the moat and find yourself standing far from the bridge. Once you successfully cross the bridge into the castle entrance, you find yourself facing a massive wooden gate. But, a lever is on the wall that you can activate (by placing the mouse cursor on it and pressing the right button). It's fascinating to watch the lever raise the gate.

Continue on straight ahead or turn into one of the doors on either side. As you explore the corridors in the castle walls, you will see

torches and more doors. In the corner dungeons are ladders that can be activated also—you will be transported up or down. Once you are up on the ramparts, it is not obvious how to get back down, so here's how: look down at the black opening and activate it.

Raymond has plans to extend the features of this program, but at the present time, although it is called the Castle of Doom, it has no monsters or ghosts.

Instructions:

The meaning of the arrow icons is self-evident. Navigation is similar to MOVER and MINO-DINO. Place the mouse cursor on the icon and hold down the left or right mouse button until you want to stop. Use the left button for slow speed, and the right button for fast speed. "Walking" is the only navigation mode supported.

The two triangles provide LOOK UP and LOOK DOWN modes; the circle between the triangles will RESET your view if you become disoriented.

Activation is accomplished by positioning the mouse cursor on an object and pressing the right button once. Attack objects with left mouse button.

Press *C* to remove the center crosshairs. Press Esc to restart. Press Shift-Esc to quit, or exit.

Description and Instructions for Adventure in VREAM

Equipment needed:

IBM-compatible computer, with a 386 and math coprocessor or better (such as 386 25MHz with math coprocessor, 486DX, or better).

At least 4 megabytes of extended memory, with no Upper Memory Blocks (UMBs).

A hard (or fixed) drive with at least 3MB of free space.

VGA graphics capability.

2- or 3-button mouse, (a 3-button mouse is recommended) and keyboard.

Memory setup:

Use HIMEM.SYS (but not EMM386).

Compressed file name:

SEEVREAM.EXE

Execution file name:

VREAMADV

Source:

VREAM, Inc. (address in Appendix B).

Related programs:

VREAM Runtime System	$ 89.00
VREAM Advanced Runtime System	$ 395.00
VREAM Virtual Reality Development System	$1495.00

Readers who do not yet have a 486 computer, a 386 computer with a co-processor chip, or a 3-button mouse may want to consider making an arrangement with a friend or associate with access to this type of system. With the increasing availability of faster computers, and the advent of the Intel 586, this should be less and less difficult. The fact of the relatively limited market penetration of higher-end machines was considered before selecting "Adventure in VREAM" for this book. The possibility of disappointing some readers was a concern that was carefully weighed. But the benefits of making it possible to view one of the most ingenious and interactive virtual reality capabilities now available were finally too persuasive to think of leaving it out.

The VREAM virtual reality development system, with all of its accessibility and intriguing features, was accomplished by just one man—Ed La Hood, who started programming at the age of fourteen. The scope of his achievement, we think you'll agree, is deserving of the highest acclaim and the widest possible distribution. For readers who have the necessary system, this may be your first opportunity to check out this latest and most exciting contribution to the field of VR. After all, VREAM stands for "virtual reality dream."

To start the program, type VREAMADV. This will launch "Adventure in VREAM," which is a run-time demonstration of a few basic

features of this innovative system. After a few seconds, you will find yourself in a main room with three blocks on one end, a fan in the middle, and a TV in the other end. There are other objects in the room, such as pictures on the wall, and a door in the wall. In the attic, you'll find two beach balls and a jukebox. But the description of the objects is only the beginning. There are many interactions you can enjoy with this adventure.

Before describing all the details of the features and interactions, there is an important issue to discuss and clarify. Any developer of a program has to select what is included in a demonstration program. Clearly, this is a difficult and frustrating process. If you were a developer, you would be faced with the following dilemma: on the one hand, you would want to include every ingenious feature you have struggled to devise. You would think of all the late nights, tired muscles, and sore eyes you endured. You would think, "How can I leave out that feature or this function?"

But, you simply can't include everything in a demo. It would be too large, take too long, or require too much explanation and documentation. A demo must remain a demo. To make a demonstration program, you will be forced to cut, slash, and maim—until you are looking at a weak shadow of the powerful performance you wish you could demonstrate. It's like cutting off your arm. If that seems melodramatic, just ask a programmer who has had to clip his pet software.

Being aware of this problem is especially important when you look at "Adventure in VREAM." Let's take one simple example—the lack of sound. In a fully functional VREAM world, the dimension of sound adds another layer of immersion for your ears. When you turn on the TV or press a button on the jukebox, the strains of music or other samples of sound pour from the speakers, providing extra enjoyment for the virtual world experience. But the programmer was forced by circumstances beyond his control to remove the sound capability from the demonstration world—because of the large size of the sound files. They simply wouldn't fit on the disk, even when compressed.

The result of this sacrifice may annoy you. It is natural for you to want to try out the sound capabilities, but it's perplexingly frustrating for the programmer who invested the time to crowbar the sound function in, and now has to take it out.

But the only other choice was even worse: not making the VREAM demo available to you. So, although you won't be able to experience all of the enthralling features of VREAM, at least you can try out quite a large number of them. A summary of some of the additional features available in the full version of VREAM can be found at the end of this section.

Actions and Interactions

Here's a quick review of the actions you can check out in your VREAM adventure. You can:

- Move your viewpoint (also called "the viewer") to any position within the virtual world, including going inside objects.

- Control both the viewer and the 3-D hand at the same time.

- Interact fully with objects by controlling the 3-D hand.

- Grab objects, pick them up, and manipulate them in 3-D space.

- Activate objects by "grabbing" them (such as the ceiling fan).

- Activate objects by "pushing" them (such as the TV or the juke box).

- Throw objects in 3-D space and watch them drop due to gravity (such as the beach balls).

- See photorealistic textures (such as the pictures on the wall and the images on the TV).

- See text (such as the blocks, the juke box, and the front of the building).

- See real-time shading of objects based on light source position (the surface colors change when moved).

- Move between multiple environments within a virtual world.

- "Walk" through walls and doors, and "fly" through the air and up in the sky.

- Place blocks in the air, stack them on top of each other, and place them on the table.

VREAM Runtime System Instructions

The following are some general hints for the demo:

- The viewer can be controlled by the keys on the keyboard; the 3-D hand can be controlled by the mouse.

- The viewer movement keys always move the viewer relative to its current orientation in space. The orientation of the viewer in space is determined by the viewer rotation keys on the keyboard (see the following section for a full list of commands).

- The viewer moves faster if the Shift key is pushed in combination with any of the viewer movement or rotation keys.

- The F5 key turns the hand on and off within each environment.

- The mouse can be used to move the 3-D hand forward and backward by holding down the right mouse button and moving the mouse forward and backward.

- You can generally tell when you are close enough to an object to grab it by moving towards it until the hand disappears behind the object. At this point, you can pull the hand back from behind the object and be in position to grab the object with the hand.

- Press F10 to quit.

Adventure in VREAM Instructions

This virtual world is a simple demonstration world that illustrates some of the basic capabilities of virtual worlds developed with the VREAM system.

Start-Up

The world begins with the viewer in the main room of a house. There are two rooms in the house: the main room and the attic. The viewer can move to the outside environment to gain an external view of the house.

Main Room

When the virtual adventure begins, the viewer is in the main room of a house looking at three blocks and a picture on the wall. Behind the viewer is a ceiling fan, a TV, and another picture.

The viewer can move towards the blocks, or pick up and move any of the blocks by "grabbing" them with the 3-D hand. Once grabbed, a block can be moved or rotated with the 3-D hand, or carried along with the viewer. This illustrates the ability to grab and fully manipulate objects in 3-D space.

The picture on the wall illustrates the ability to incorporate photo-realistic textures into virtual worlds. This picture can also be grabbed and fully manipulated with the 3-D hand.

The ceiling fan in the middle of the room can be turned on and off by "grabbing" the cord that hangs down from the fan. In order to get close enough to the cord to grab it, the user should move towards the ceiling fan cord until the hand is displayed behind the cord. At this point the user can back up until the hand is once again in front of the cord and grab the cord with the hand.

The user can also view images on the TV by "pushing" the top or bottom button on the TV with the index finger of the hand. The buttons on the TV will turn from white to yellow when the hand is close enough to push them. Each of the two buttons on the TV will display a different image when pushed. The TV can also be grabbed and manipulated by the 3-D hand. Grabbing the TV and moving it after an image has been displayed provides a good interactive visual effect.

The user can go inside all of the objects in the main room.

The user can pass through any of the walls of the main room. By passing through the ceiling of the main room, the viewer will enter the attic. By passing through any of the other walls of the main room, the viewer will enter the outside environment.

Attic

All the objects in the attic can be grabbed and moved with the hand. Within the attic, there is a juke box and two beach balls.

Both of the beach balls adhere to gravity. If they are grabbed by the hand, lifted above the floor, and released, they will drop back to the floor. Both beach balls can also be thrown by the user. This is accomplished by grabbing a beach ball, moving it with the hand, and releasing the ball while the hand is still in motion. The blue and green beach ball is elastic and will bounce. The red and white beach ball is not elastic and will not bounce.

The user can push any of the four juke box buttons. The buttons on the juke box will turn from white to yellow when the hand is close enough to push them. If the sound files were present, each button would select a song that would play.

The user can go inside of all of the objects in the attic. The user can pass through any of the walls of the attic. By passing through the floor, the viewer will enter the main room. By passing through the ceiling or any of the walls of the attic, the viewer will enter the outside environment.

Outside Environment

While outside of the house, the viewer will be in an outside environment and will have an external view of the house. The front of the house has text that reads "VREAM."

The user can move anywhere in the outside environment without limitation.

If the user goes below the ground level, the grass will disappear, allowing the user to look up and view all of the objects from a below ground perspective.

The user may reenter the house by passing through any of the walls of the house. The room entered will depend on where the user enters the house.

Interface Guide

To move the viewpoint with the keyboard, press the appropriate keys listed below. Hold the key down until you reach the viewpoint position you desire. (Pressing any key while the Shift key is depressed will cause the motion to increase in speed.)

Keyboard Controls:

	Viewer Movement:		
Key	**Action**	**Key**	**Action**
Q	viewer move left	W	viewer move right
A	viewer move backward	S	viewer move forward
Z	viewer move down	X	viewer move up

	Viewer Rotation:		
Key	**Action**	**Key**	**Action**
E	viewer yaw left	R	viewer yaw right
D	viewer pitch down	F	viewer pitch up
C	viewer roll left	V	viewer roll right

	System Control:
Key	**Action**
F5	hand on/off
F6	wireframe on/off
F7	solid on/off
F8	hidden wireframe on/off
F10	quit and exit
Shift	viewer move and rotate faster

NOTE: Be careful to turn wireframe on if you turn solid off.

To control the 3-D hand with the mouse, press the appropriate button(s) listed below. Hold the button(s) down until you are finished with the desired action. (If you have a 2-button mouse, ignore the actions requiring the middle button):

Mouse Controls:

Hand Movement:	
Mouse	**Action**
mouse left	hand move left
mouse right	hand move right
mouse up	hand move up
mouse down	hand move down
right button + mouse up	hand move forward
right button + mouse down	hand move backward

Hand Rotation:	
Mouse	**Action**
middle button + mouse right	hand yaw left (3-button mouse required)
middle button + mouse left	hand yaw right (3-button mouse required)
middle button + mouse down	hand pitch down (3-button mouse required)
middle button + mouse up	hand pitch up (3-button mouse required)
right button + mouse left	hand roll left
right button + mouse right	hand roll right

Hand Finger Movement:	
Mouse	**Action**
left button	make fist (hand grab)
right button + left button	index finger in (hand push)
right button + middle button	thumb in (hand point) (3-button mouse required)

After practicing these keys and mouse combinations for a short time, you'll begin to feel more comfortable with the relationships between the actions you take and the movements on-screen. It will help to keep in mind one pointer: Pushing an object is done with the index finger; grabbing an object is achieved by making a fist.

Summary of VREAM Virtual Reality Development System Features

In addition to the basic interactivity demonstrated with "Adventure in VREAM" as reviewed in the last section, the full-featured version of the VREAM Development System includes a 3-D World Editor in which a person can create unlimited types of worlds, and a separate Runtime System that allows users to explore and interact with the worlds created with the World Editor. Taken together, the VREAM 3-D World Editor and the VREAM Runtime System make up the complete VREAM Development System, which includes the following features:

- Stereo sound.
- Compatibility with a variety of interface devices (joystick, gloves, HMDs, trackers, and so forth).
- Ability to launch external programs from within the virtual reality environment.
- Ability to generate on-screen text for counters, timers, help screens, and so forth.
- Ability to incorporate full hierarchical rotations and translations.
- A full set of 3-D drawing tools within the 3-D World Editor.
- Ability to import 3-D objects defined within .DXF files.
- Utilization of the full amount of extended memory available, allowing for extremely large virtual worlds.

Have Fun!

In many ways, we are all on an adventure together, through life, through space, through time. The curious, the talented, and the indifferent will shape the face of the future. The glowing embers of creativity and innovation will kindle the passion to push against the constraints of "what is known" and reach out for "what can be discovered" and "what can be built." In the real universe, the music of the spheres is played by physics, and engineers of real equipment have to dance to the music. But, in the virtual universe, the cyberspace engineer can compose a new kind of music, coloring it with imaginative chords, following the melody wherever it leads, savoring the notes of freedom.

One hundred years from now, a book like this might not be a book like this. Paper, ink, pictures, and digital magnetic pulses—those are the vehicles that now bring you information, thought, and experience—constitute today's book. If you feel more informed, if you feel challenged and stimulated by new thoughts, if you feel exhilarated by the novel 3-D experiences on the disk, then the goal of this book has been achieved. Welcome to the entertaining and fascinating world of virtual reality.

Appendixes

Virtual Reality and Technology

Beep...bop...beep...bop. This is the sound of the little square ball bouncing off my rectangular paddle and bouncing off the sides of the screen. A higher pitch beep sounds as the square goes past my father's paddle and into the goal. We're on the edge of our seats because we have never experienced so much high speed excitement. In 1975, it was hard for my eight-year-old mind to comprehend this cutting edge technology in my very own living room. My father, who had never seen a TV until he was ten, was also overwhelmed. An interactive game that is actually played on the television was enough to make him tell all his friends of his experiences with it.

Because virtual reality is so new, much of the discussion about it is still in the philosophical stage. It is these philosophical arguments that will impel its continuing development. This essay will reflect current facts about VR technology, and, perhaps more importantly, will present my personal philosophy based on my experiences developing an HMD. Because I view philosophy as simply well thought out opinions, I feel it necessary to tell you a little about myself so you can better understand my perspective.

Opinions, in my opinion, are another form of expressing feelings on an issue, therefore I don't debate them. Only facts can be debated. Someone said that genius is the ability to sort facts. Unfortunately, I am not a genius. However, I have spent a great deal of effort learning how to sort out facts. I say this so everyone understands that some of this discussion is based solely on my outlook of it. My opinions are no more right than yours and I would encourage you to form your own.

Tom Hayward, the author of this book, has given me many wonderful opportunities, one of which is to write this very appendix.

I can think of nothing I'd enjoy more than writing a book not just on the philosophies of VR, but taking you step by step through the designing of a head-mounted display and the writing of a 3-D software application. If you would like to know more about how it all works, how you can build it and put it on your home computer, as well as ideas on how you can have a career in VR, please write me at the address in Appendix B.

The Quest for Knowledge

I was obsessed with technology as a child. I took apart every toy—and nearly everything else in the house—just to look inside and see all the little colored parts. I would have done anything to understand even how just one of them worked. Unfortunately, no one I knew understood what was behind all of this magic. In fact, they thought it a little strange that it was so important to me.

My grandmother had a drawer in the kitchen with some old tools in it that had belonged to my late grandfather. Now armed with these mechanical opportunities to open things, nothing in the house was safe. It seemed every time I got an electronic toy, the first thing my grandmother would say is "Now, don't go taking it apart."

As time went on, I dreamed of making a robot. I remember going to the hardware store when I was ten and telling the guy what I

wanted to do, and how he laughed at me. Later that year I made a four-foot robot with an arm made from an erector set and motors ripped out of toys.

Today I hold my degree in electromechanical technology (slang termed—robotics). Sometimes I would like to go into that hardware store again and thank the old man for making me so angry. Finally, when I was twelve years old and my favorite thing to do was build electronic kits alone, I began to think that maybe I was a little nuts. Then, all of a sudden, my life all came together that same year.

For Halloween in 1979, my neighbor, Joseph Marchese of Norristown, Pennsylvania, designed the most advanced electronic costume I had ever seen. It was based on a character from the famous *Star Wars* movie. I latched onto him that very night, and to this day, a part of me has never let go. He told me things about a whole worldwide industry called electronics. He told me of his hero Thomas Edison. In the weeks to come he took me into his basement and showed me his own little shop. He told me that it is all right to wonder about life in space—in fact, it would be ignorant not to. He harnessed my creative thoughts, convinced me that anything is possible, and taught me that I could do anything I wanted. And yes, it's even OK to be a little nuts. Any innovations of mine are dedicated to him.

Springtime was much welcomed in Kenosha, Wisconsin, in May of 1992. It was hard to believe I actually could not wait for a Monday to come. Our public broadcasting station, of all channels, was running a miniseries on the history of computers. It started out with developments in the 1800s, and for five weeks on Monday night, would show the progress of evolution of the computers in 20-year increments. The show was so good I couldn't wait for Monday night to roll around. Little did I know that this Monday night would change the course of the rest of my life.

Henry Fuchs walked on a treadmill wearing a large helmet. Down in the corner of the screen was a picture of what he was seeing. He was walking through a house that had not even been built yet. The view he saw in the helmet corresponded to the direction he looked. Moments later, Fuchs described what that helmet was and how it could change the world. After that, more developers from the University of North Carolina showed a different helmet. This time

they were walking through giant molecules. I sat speechless...then suddenly the show ended. Good thing I taped it so I could make my wife watch it 22 more times that night.

Needless to say my destiny unfolded before me. I had to have a helmet—and for me, to buy one would be a failure. I tried to call Fuchs, but I could never get through. They did, however, send me a lot of papers. One of my dreams to this day is to meet Dr. Henry Fuchs.

Since that day, my life has never been the same. I worked night and day to build my first helmet. I took this prototype to several trade shows, and it went over incredibly well. Today, I am proud to be the Vice President of Research and Development at VRontier worlds of Stoughton. VRontier is becoming pretty well known thanks to the unbelievable efforts and talents of its founder, Tom Hayward.

The product I have developed, *Tier1,* is a stereo input head mount. It has a lot of new features, but I am most proud of the VRon (*V*irtual *R*eality *O*ptical *N*on-Distorting) optical system. We are a month away from shipping to our customers, and we are all very anxious.

Virtual Reality and Technology— The Big Fact

From his earliest cave days, man has always daydreamed about doing something other than what he was doing, or being somewhere else. Later, as man became more socialized, people would gather to watch actors pretend that they were in fact other people, in other places. When people go to plays, they sometimes become so involved in the scene that they feel as if they really are the characters. They no longer feel like they are merely sitting in a theater, nor are they necessarily aware of the curtain that frames the stage.

Let's take this another step. Literature is one of the most powerful things we have in our society. It allows people to take the perspectives of different characters and walk in their shoes—in any place, at any time. Literature is limited only by the author's ability

to create and effectively communicate an idea. An author has the power to so interest a reader in the story that the reader projects himself into the imagination of the author—in much the same way the viewer of the play does.

In the early part of the 1900s, the radio came about. People would gather around to hear the stories that stimulated their minds into believing that for a moment they were the people being described. In the mid-1900s, television came into the picture. Now a family can sit in front of a box intensively projecting themselves into the story. Again, during this time, they have a lower awareness for the real environment around them.

So, is virtual reality a relatively new concept? Is there no other way to convince people that they are in an alternative reality than through a total-immersion head mount with 180-degree viewing? Before we can form an opinion about virtual environments, we must first define virtual reality and identify its goal. If you look at most definitions, you will see that they mention wearing a bunch of hardware that fools the mind into perceiving a reality that is not present. But current technology cannot accomplish this at 100% effectiveness. This type of definition is based solely on the current technological state we are in—and this forsakes the whole idea of what virtual reality is all about.

The fact is—you cannot, and should not, include technology in the basic definition of VR. Technology is just the current state of the vehicle that most people relate to when describing virtual reality. My definition of virtual reality is:

A perception-generating device that entails human interaction.

The benefit of this definition is that it does not include an implied assumption of the vehicle used to accomplish the goal. The goal is to achieve a simulation that is indistinguishable from a real life event, but is not limited to real life experiences.

Somehow, people are reading into it that computers and head mounts are the only way to go. They think that these current head mounts are the first attempts, and that we ultimately need to develop the best head mount possible. Again this is a reflection of our times. I think that somewhere in this definition lies the purpose for plays, books, radio stories, and movies. If, before head mounts

and computers were commonplace, you told the average person my definition of virtual reality and asked him to tell you how this goal could be accomplished, he probably would have said through plays, books, radio stories, or movies. He would never have said "What about a head mount or a computer?"—he probably could not even have dreamed of it. Now let's take this a step further.

What is the closest thing we have today that matches the definition? You say VR. Let me rephrase the question. I am asking you what VR is. I guarantee the tendency is to define VR by the current state of technology. But this state is merely an aspect of VR. Modern technology is merely one vehicle of achieving it. You may argue that a book cannot be considered a VR attempt because there is no interaction from the user. The fact that a reader projects himself into the story and adds details the author left out proves that there is interaction!

The ultimate VR will never be achieved with a head mount. It will be done through direct neural input. In other words, you close your eyes, put a pair of probes on your head, and you're there. For this reason, we must have a definition for VR forsaking technology. Otherwise, we would have to redefine it every time we make an advancement and create a new vehicle to achieve it.

It is said that a new vehicle such as neural implanting will be a long time coming. I say that this does not have to be the case. True, it does seem infinitely complicated to control billions of neurons. Thinking about billions of neurons, all existing without any apparent order, is almost as overwhelming as going back to the 1600s and asking a machinist and a mathematician to build a device controlling billions of electrons to do what the average pocket calculator does today.

New Ways of Thought

So how did we do more in the 100 years following the industrial revolution than we had ever done before? It was a new outlook, a way of thinking that did it. Once new ways to approach problems were achieved, more and more approaches unfolded themselves. Finally, with the advent of computers, we can quickly perform

complex calculations, and keep track of and sort facts in ways never before possible.

Today we have the hot new concept of virtual reality. So how do we push ahead and jump farther with it under the current conditions? The driving force behind the industrial revolution was finding new ways to approach problems. We have to examine our limitations of artificial intelligence in order to simulate a realistic reality. We have to think above our conventional restrictions and stop them from limiting our new ways of thinking and the approaches we allow ourselves to take. We have to bravely turn our backs on the normal, and view it merely as a foundation, and not all that they can be.

There are only two restrictions for scientific possibility:

1. Physics and chemistry are at the core of reality. Though the reality is potentially limitless, we must always work within physics and chemistry.

2. The person's abilities to understand what they have to work with, as well as their creativity to harness it.

The former is a given. We cannot change the basic laws of nature. We can, however, focus our efforts on the latter. It seems that creative people are born that way. An uneducated person can be taught, but seldom can a noncreative person be taught to be creative if he or she truly is not. One of the biggest crimes in technology is not recognizing the importance of creativity. An even bigger crime is when a creative person snuffs out a great opportunity because his or her education says that it is not the correct thing to do.

Deducing the Unknown Order

Science comes from a Latin word "scientia," which means "to know." The goal of science is to examine the unknown, establish as many knowns as possible, and then derive the answer to the unknown. The only difference between what we understand and what we do not understand is order.

If you look at the Sunday comics under a magnifying lens, you see a bunch of random dots. You do not make out a tangible image from

it because your brain cannot find the order to the image from that narrow perspective. If all you ever saw were the dots, you might think that they were all separate entities of random colors in random order; you would never really define their purpose.

The ideology in real science is to use validity and logic to form a known. It is then handed along through education so that we all can share these knowns. We then must use that education, along with more logic and validity, to find more knowns in the unknown. The problem is that validity is not always credible in every circumstance, and the fine line between validity and logic breaks down. Here is an example of validity:

Bill only likes girls.   condition 1
Bill likes Sarah.   condition 2
Therefore, Sarah must be a girl.   solution

Validity worked well here. Now consider this:

Bill likes girls.   condition 1
Girls like girls.   condition 2
Therefore, Bill must be a girl.   solution

The latter is valid, but not logical. To a computer, which lacks common sense, it would have been easy to make this mistake. When people are dealing with unknown factors, these mistakes happen all the time. A new way of thinking will have to involve minimizing these mistakes.

The failures in artificial intelligence seem to frustrate scientists. They cannot figure out how to make a computer simulate common sense. To date, computers cannot be programmed to have common sense. You cannot give it some fundamentals and have it continue to learn from its environment. It can only do just what it is told and nothing else. It does not think for itself. Why is this? Does it need more memory or speed? How about a new hard drive? Nope! It is because of math. The whole computer is based entirely on math. The problem is not the computer—it does what it is designed to do. Several artificial intelligence (AI) professors have admitted that while AI programs are more functional than ever before, they still work within the confines of an "IF-THEN-ELSE" structured architecture.

The problem is in thinking that one could use math to represent complex thinking. Human common sense and reasoning is the higher order. Math, a lower order, is derived from human common sense and reasoning. You cannot take a narrow derivative from a high order, give the lower order to someone else and expect him or her to figure out the higher. You cannot define all of reality and intelligence using math as a means. If I tell you to think of a cube, which has a side of three inches, you can picture it in your head. You used math to gauge the size, but the other attributes of the cube—like color and texture—came from other things in your head.

Burnett's Formula for Innovation

One new thought I have in trying to get people to harness their creativity is a formula for innovation: Innovations equals Radical Desires divided by (Obstacles minus Individual Solutions), or:

$$\text{Innovations} = \frac{\text{Radical Desires}}{(\text{Obstacles} - \text{Individual Solutions})}$$

The terms in the formula have the following definitions:

Radical Desires—Allow yourself to brainstorm. Do not limit the focus of what you want to end up with by your current understanding of how you think you will get there. First and foremost, lay out exactly what you want.

Obstacles—Every attempt you make to do something in an innovative way, you will find multiple obstacles. You should view each one of these as an opportunity to learn. As each obstacle disappears, your innovation will become more of a reality. These obstacles can only disappear through individual solutions.

Individual Solutions—Great solutions are often a result of indirect approaches. An example of an indirect approach is to find the force with which a ball was thrown by measuring the speed it traveled and the distance it went. Great solutions also require determination, creativity, and new approaches.

Education is only the foundation of building with our creativity. In much the same way that a lot is the foundation for a building and does not determine how high that building can go, you should

never let education limit your creativity. A broad educational background is needed to make VR evolve. I look to the past—even as recent as the 1800s—to see that all the Earth's elements employed in today's technology have always been with us.

The growth was not realized until man decided to do more than dream—he had to face the fear of change, and even endure ridicule from his colleagues. He had to embark on a new road, with only his dreams to guide him.

VR—Real Life Adventures

The hallway is long and narrow. I can see the steel door up ahead; I'm certain it leads to another hallway that looks just like this one. The question is who will be on the other side of it? My heart is beating strongly as I get closer. My machine gun is aiming straight ahead; I have 44 bullets left. Clang! The door opens. Whew! No one here.

Suddenly I hear the horror of the door opening behind me. As I turn to fire, I hear an enemy guard shouting at me. I hear the shot, and everything flashes red. I have been hit once. Now I'm mad. I turn to see three uniformed adversaries. They are about my size, and they are way down the hall. "Bring it on," I yell as I gun them all down and see blood flying everywhere. I spin back around a little more calm now.

I open the next door. Wow! I'm face to face with this guy. I have forgotten the fact that this world is made up of dots. I am responding to this guy as though I have opened a door and was surprised to see another person. Enemy guards in VR have no fear, nor do they ever feel surprised. They are the perfect specimen of what the government tries to make its military become. I once strived to be this good myself. Alas, VR warriors are absolute; they fear no death; they are silent; they are very deadly.

One of my father's friends, Jim Croce, once wrote a line in a song that says what we do makes us what we are. I am not a killer. I felt no shame being put down by the best of the best. I am only glad it is a simulation. I popped the helmet off and decided to go for a snack. When I get to the kitchen, almost out of some primitive reflex, I quickly check behind the door.

The Youngest Warrior

"Me see, me see!" No, this is not another language. This is how Amanda Burnett instructs her father to allow her to see something. You see, Amanda is only 2 years old.

Carefully I hold the helmet over my daughter's head and hit "play" on the remote of the VCR. On the TV, I see everything that Amanda sees. A horse runs across the screen. The horse jumps a fence, and Amanda is laughing so hard it is difficult to keep the helmet hovered over her head. She reaches her hands out and stomps her feet as though she is trying to chase the horse.

I stop and think about this for a moment. I think about how lucky I am to work in this field, and how wonderful it was to share it with this beautiful little girl. What sorts of new things will her children have to try out someday? I can only hope that they will have a souvenir from the past that was once mine. Something that will show them my foot prints in the sand and inspire them as they wonder and play in the new vrontier.

Bradley Burnett
Vice President of Research & Development,
VRontier worlds of Stoughton, Inc.

Virtual Reality Resource Information

This appendix lists a number of resources that may be useful to readers who desire to expand their knowledge of virtual reality.

Disk Software Sources

"Adventure in VREAM"

VREAM, Inc.,
2568 N. Clark St., #250
Chicago, IL 60614
(312) 477-0425

VRontier worlds of Stoughton,
809 E. South St.
Stoughton, WI 53589
(608) 873-8523

ANAGLYPH

(*Note:* This program has been discontinued and is no longer supported.)

Schreiber Instruments,
4800 Happy Canyon Road, Suite 250
Denver, CO 80237
(303) 759-1024

CASTLE

Raymond Holmes,
673 Ululani Street
Kailua, HI 96734
(CompuServe 73737,2704)

FLY the Grand Canyon

Hyacinth,
Dept. Q,
5508 Chimney Hollow
Norcross, GA 30093
(404) 925-4333

MOVER, MINO-DINO

VRontier worlds of Stoughton,
809 E. South St.
Stoughton, WI 53589
(608) 873-8523

VR Newsletters, Associations, Organizations, and Groups

The listings in this section with *(BBS)* following the name are called *Bulletin Board Systems,* and are on computers. There are thousands of BBSs all over the world, therefore this listing only includes some

of the major ones. To join a BBS, contact the voice phone line of the BBS and follow the sign-up procedure. When your account is activated, you will be able to connect your computer with the BBS and send messages to and transfer files with other members.

Adams Consulting Group
3952 Western Ave.
Western Springs, IL 60558
(708) 246-0766
(CompuServe 71052,1373)
Contact: Nina Adams, President

Andrew's VEE-AR Club (and Newsletter)
624 Jackson Street
Stoughton, WI 53589
Contact: Andrew or Tom Hayward

Boston Computer Society, Virtual Reality Group
BCS VR Group, Building 1400
One Kendall Square
Cambridge, MA 02139
(508) 921-6846
Contact: Paul Matthews

CompuServe VR Forum (BBS)
CompuServe Information Service
P.O. Box 20212
Columbus, OH 43220-0212
Customer Service: (800) 848-8990
Outside US: (614) 457-8650
GO GRAPHDEV (on-line)
   (Use this last line to reach the VR Forum after connecting to
   CompuServe.)

Cyber Edge Journal
#1 Gate Six Road, Suite G
Sausalito, CA 94965
(415) 331-EDGE (3343)
Editors: Ben Delaney
          Sherry Epley

Cyber Society
2016 Main Street, Suite 1207
Houston, TX 77002-8843
(713) 752-0761
Contact: Greg Klein

Diaspar VR Network (BBS)
424 Glenneyre
Laguna Beach, CA 92651
System Operator: David Mitchell
(714) 831-1776 (Voice)
9600 Baud: (714) 376-1234
2400 Baud: (714) 376-1200
    Connects to Internet

Electronic Frontiers Foundation
155 Second Street
Cambridge, MA 02140
(617) 864-0665
Fax: (617) 864-0866
Contact: John Perry Barlow

Les Virtualistes
90 avenue de Paris
92320 Chatillon
France

Long Beach Virtual Reality Group
2041 San Anseline, Apt. 4
Long Beach, CA 90815
(310) 594-9394
Contact: Mike Heim

Networked Virtual Art Museum
Studio for Creative Inquiry
Carnegie Mellon University
Pittsburgh, PA 15213
(412) 268-3452
Contact: Carl E. Loeffler

PCVR Magazine (Homebrew VR for PC)
1706 Sherman Hill Road, Unit #A
Laramie, WY 82060
(307) 742-7675 (Voice and Fax)
Editor: Joseph Gradecki

PRESENCE: Teleoperators & Virtual Environments
MIT Press Journals
55 Hayward Street
Cambridge, MA 02142-1399
(800) 356-0343 or (617) 628-8569
Editors: Thomas Sheridan,
          Nathaniel Durlach,
          Thomas Furness, III

Sci.virtual-worlds (BBS)
A Usenet Newsgroup on Internet.
Internet is a global BBS available through universities and increas-
ingly available through commercial BBSs like CompuServe, the
WELL, and Diaspar. Sci.virtual-worlds is a forum on virtual reality.

Society for Virtual Reality (Virtuele Realiteit)
Lichtaartsesteenweg 55
B-2275 Poederlee
Lille, Belgium
Contact: Philippe Van Nedervelde, President ad interim

University of Waterloo Virtual Reality Group
Univ. of Waterloo
Dept. of Computer Science
Waterloo, Ontario N2L 3G1
(519) 888-4870

Virtual Reality Information Line—24 hours
Up-to-date news, events, job-line. $1.25 per minute.
1 (900) VIRTUAL (847-8825)

Virtual Reality News
32969 Hamilton Court, Suite 215
Farmington Hills, MI 48334
Editor: Brian Lareau

Virtual Reality Report (Newsletter)
Meckler Corporation
11 Ferry Lane West
Westport, CT 06880
(203) 226-6967
Editor-in-Chief: Sandra K. Heisel

Virtual Reality Special Interest Group (VR SIG),
Los Angeles Chapter
Virtual Ventures
1300 The Strand, Suite A
Manhattan Beach, CA 90266
(310) 545-0369

Virtual Reality Special Interest Group (VR SIG),
Louisville Chapter
P.O. Box 43003
Louisville, KY 40253
Contact: Andrew Prell
(502) 495-7186

Virtual Reality Special Interest Group (VR SIG),
Chicago Chapter
3952 Western Ave.
Western Springs, IL 60558
(708) 246-0766
(CompuServe 71052,1373)
Contact: Nina Adams

Virtuality Entertainment Games
(Try out VR for yourself—Locations across the USA)
Horizon Entertainment
P.O. Box 14020
St. Louis, MO 63178-4020
(800) ILLUSION (455-8746)
Contact: Bill Freund
(314) 331-6000

VRASP (VR Alliance for Students & Professionals)
Newsletter: *PIX-Elation*
P.O. Box 4139
Highland Park, NJ 08904-4139
Contact: Karin August
(CompuServe: 71033,702)

VR News—Virtual Reality Newsletter
P.O. Box 2515
London, N4 4JW
England
Editor: Mike Bevan

VR Monitor—The Journal of Virtual Reality
Matrix Information Services
18560 Bungalow Drive
Lathrup Village, MI 48076
(313) 559-1526
Sr. Editor: Frank Dunn
Tech. Editor: Steve Aukstakalnis

VR User Group
2 Beacon Road
London, SE13 6EH
England
Contact: Kim Baukham

VREAM User's Group (*Z Axis* Newsletter)
        Memberships and Subscriptions:
        Tom Hayward
        624 Jackson Street
        Stoughton, WI 53589
        (CompuServe 70550,2702)

        Newsletter Editor:
        Tim Gifford
        Argus Productions
        25 Torwood Street
        Hartford, CT 06114
        (CompuServe 71223,7933)

        Public Relations:
        Nina Adams
        3952 Western Ave.
        Western Springs, IL 60558
        (CompuServe 71052,1373)

The WELL VR Forum (BBS)
Whole Earth 'Lectronic Link
27 Gate 5 Road
Sausalito, CA 94965-9976
(415) 332-4335 (To sign up)
(415) 332-6106 (Modem phone number)
GO VR (on-line)

VR and 3-D Events

Because of the increasing interest in virtual reality and the decreasing costs of VR equipment, hundreds of conferences and conventions have sprung up around the world dealing with VR and related topics. Because of the vast number of conferences and the fact that their conventions are often held annually at differing locations, it is not feasible to include an exhaustive list of conferences. You should consult a VR newsletter for information regarding the dozens of conferences and conventions.

VR Articles, Books, Periodicals, and References

You can locate hundreds of magazine articles on the subject of VR in your local library. Most of the titles listed here are larger works.

3-D TV Products
(Catalog)
3-D TV Corporation
P.O. Box Q
San Rafael, CA 94913-4316
(415) 479-3516

Artificial Reality II
(Book)
Author: Myron W. Krueger
Addison-Wesley, 1991

"Birth of an Industry: Virtual Reality Today"
(Research Reference)
CyberEdge Journal
#1 Gate Six Road, Suite G
Sausalito, CA 94965
(415) 331-EDGE (3343)
Editors: Ben Delaney
         Sherry Epley

Computers as Theatre
(Book)
Author: Brenda Laurel
Addison-Wesley, 1991

Cyberspace—First Steps
(Book)
Collection of Essays on VR
The MIT Press, 1992
(800) 356-0343 or (617) 628-8569

"Marvels of Virtual Reality"
(Article)
Fortune Magazine,
June 3, 1991
Author: Gene Bylinsky

Media Magic
(Free Catalog of books, videotapes, and software)
P.O. Box 507
Nicasio, CA 94946

Multi-Index to Cyberspace, Virtual and Artificial Reality
(Periodical)
Carande Press
P.O. Box 453
Pine Valley, CA 91962-0453
(619) 473-0164

Reel 3-D Enterprises, Inc.
(3-D equipment)
P.O. Box 2368
Culver City, CA 90231
(310) 837-2368
Contacts: Susan Pinsky
          David Starkman

247

Senate Subcommittee on Science and Technology Hearing on VR.
(Videotape)
The Virtual Reality Film Documentary
2330 Williams Street
Palo Alto, CA. 94306
(415) 723-6632
Contact: Robert Miller

Silicon Mirage: The Art and Science of Virtual Reality
(Book)
Authors: Steve Aukstakalnis
           David Blatner
Peachpit Press, 1992

Virtual Reality: Adventures in Cyberspace
(Book)
Author: Francis Hamit
Miller, Freeman, 1991

"Virtual Reality:
How a Computer Generated World Could Change the Real World"
(Magazine Article)
Business Week Magazine, October 5, 1992

Virtual Reality Playhouse
(Book and disk)
Author: Nicholas Lavroff
Waite Group Press, 1992

Virtual Reality Sourcebook
(Directory)
SophisTech Research
6936 Seaborn Street
Lakewood, CA 90713-2832
(800) 4VR SOURCE (Orders)
(310) 421-7295
Contact: Gregory Panos

Virtual Reality: Theory, Practice, and Promise
(Book)
Authors: Sandra Heisel
           Judith Roth
Meckler Corp., 1990

Virtual Reality: Through the new looking glass
(Book)
Authors: Ken Pimentel
          Kevin Teixeira
Intel/Windcrest/McGraw-Hill, Inc., 1993

Virtual Reality:
The Revolutionary Technology of Computer-Generated Artificial
Worlds—and How It Promises and Threatens to Transform Business and
Society
(Book)
Author: Howard Rheingold
Summit Books, 1991

Virtual Worlds: A Journey into Hype and Hyperreality
(Book)
Author: Benjamin Woolley
Blackwell Publications, 1992

VR Equipment Distribution
(Catalog)
Spectrum Dynamics
2016 Main Street, Suite 1207
Houston, TX 77002-8843
(713) 752-0761 or (713) 658-3881
Contact: Gregory Klein

VR Patent Collection
(Patent Service)
Matrix Information Services
Circulation Department
18560 Bungalow Drive
Lathrup Village, MI 48076
(313) 559-1526

WAX or the Discovery of Television Among the Bees
(Film)
P.O. Box 174
Cooper Station
New York, NY 10276
Director: David Blair

249

VR Research Laboratories and Academic Centers

CAD Institute
(First accredited undergraduate course in VR)
4100 E. Broadway, Suite 180
Phoenix, AZ 85040
(800) 658-5744
Dean: John Morrison

HIT (Human Interface Technology Laboratory)
University of Washington, FJ-15
Seattle, WA 98195
(206) 543-5075
Director: Dr. Thomas A. Furness III

Institute for Simulation and Training Laboratory
University of Central Florida
12424 Research Parkway, Suite 300
Orlando, FL 32826
Director: Dr. Michael Moshell

UNC Laboratory
University of North Carolina, Chapel Hill
Computer Science Department
Chapel Hill, NC 27599-3175
Director: Dr. Frederick Brooks

US Navy—Cyberview
David Sarnoff Research Center
Mark Long, CN5300
Princeton, NJ 08543-5300

Wheelchair VR
Hines Rehabilitation and R&D Center
P.O. Box 20
Hines, IL 60141
Contact: Dr. John Trimble

Index

Symbols

3-D animation software, 82-83
3-D architecture, 104-106
3-D education, 122-124
3-D glasses, 193, 196-197
3-D medicine, 116-121
  brain surgery, 119-121
  radiation treatment, 117-118
  surgical training, 118-119
3-D modeling, 99-104
3-D science, 110-121
  chemistry, 110-111
  physics, 111-116
3-D shopping, 124-125
3-D sports, 125-127
3-D training, 107-109, 118-121
3-D walk-throughs, 105-106
3BALL, 164
3D Studio, 83
3D Toolkit (VR Studio), 91-92

A

Advanced Research Projects
  Agency (ARPA), 41
Adventure in VREAM, *see*
  VREAM
Alchemy III, 111
ANAGLYPH program, 195,
  200-203
Animator, 83
architecture, 3-D, 104-106
Argonne ARM, 110
Atari (Warren Robinett), 40
atoms, 40
AutoCAD, 84
Autodesk
  Cyberia
  Project, 85

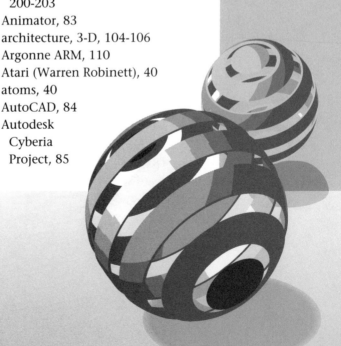

B

Babbage, Charles, 35
balance, 54
BBSs (bulletin board systems), 151
    Diaspar VR Network, 161
benchmarks, frames per second, 83
bicycle simulation, 69
bio-navigation, 165-166
biofeedback, 165
bit-mapping, 86
blood-pressure sensors, 165
Body Electric, 92
boom display, 155-157
booting, 31
brain surgery, 119-121
Brooks, Frederick, 39
building worlds, 169-176
    3-D coordinates, 177-178
    advanced, 186-189
    cyberspace, 171
    development phases, 188-189
    editing system, 182-187
    ethics, 173-177
    mathematics, 171
    MOVER program, 203
    objects, 178-181
    physics, 172
    psychology, 172
    script commands, 184-186
    spatial relationships, 172
    tools, 181-186
bulletin board systems, *see* BBSs
Burnett, Bradley, 148-149
Bush, Vannevar, 36

C

C computer language, 93
CAD (Computer Aided Design)
    software, 38, 84
        AutoCAD, 84
        PointLine software, 84
        see also Sutherland, Ivan
CASTLE program, 92, 212-213
cathode ray tube (CRT), 137
chemistry (3-D)
    atom displays, 110
    molecular interactions, 110
    software
        Alchemy III, 111
        HyperChem, 111
compression (files), 194-195
Computer Aided Design, *see* CAD
computers
    communication, 31-34
    history, 27-34
    monitors, 33, 36
    punch cards, 32
conditions (script commands), 184
convergence correction, 147-148
Convolvotron, 57-58
coordinates
    object modeling, 102
    world building, 177-179
CRT (cathode ray tube), 137
CyberGlove, 59
    sign language, 128
Cyberia Project, 85
Cybernet Systems, 111
    PER-Force handcontroller, 111
Cyberspace, 11, 78, 85
    world building, 171-172

D

Dactyl Nightmare, 71
data-acquisition instruments, 112
DataGlove, 47, 52
  kitchen simulation, 125
  radiation treatment, 118
Davis, Bob, 152-153
depth
  HMDs, 153-155
  monoscopic mode, 154
  shutter glasses, 154
desktop VR, 21, 89
development phases, world-
  building, 188-189
Diaspar VR Network
  BBSs, 161
  Mitchell, David, 53
digital instruments, 113-116
dimensions, 98-99
  see also 3-D
displays, 137-156
  boom display, 155, 157
  convergence, 147-148
  divergence, 139-141
  fresnel lenses, 147
  HMDs, stereoscopic mode,
    153-155
  Howlett's camera, 143-144
  immersion, 141-148
  LCDs (liquid crystal displays),
    137
  LEEP optics, 144
  shutter glasses, 154
  software, 151-152
  VRon lenses, 148-153
  Wide Angle Orthostereo, 144
distortion, 145-146
divergence, 139-141

drawing
  CAD software, 83-85
  PointLine software, 84
  VR Studio, 91-92

E

editing worlds, 182-187
Englebart, Douglas, 36, 38
ethics in world building, 173-177
exo-skeleton glove, 59
EXOS Dextrous Hand Master, 59
Experience Theater, 38
eye tracking, 156, 157
EyePhones HMD, 47
  Howlett, Eric, 141
  see also LEEP system

F

Falcon 3.0 flight simulator, 73
feedback, 30, 61-63
  force, 41, 64
    Argonne ARM, 110
  Sandpaper System, 65
  tactile, 65
  see also biofeedback
Fisher, Scott, 46
flight simulation, 42, 73-74, 80-81
FLY the Grand Canyon, 197-200
Focal Point 3-D Audio, 58
force feedback, 41, 64, 110
Foster, Scott, 57
frames, 73, 82
Freescape (Superscape), 90
fresnel lenses, 147
Fuchs, Henry, 39-40
Furness, Thomas, 43

G

GLOBAL 3D Controller, 164
gloves, 52, 165
    CyberGlove, 59, 128
    DataGlove, 52
    exo-skeleton, 59
    EXOS Dextrous Hand Master, 59
    Portable Dextrous Master, 65
    PowerGlove, 52
    Talking Glove, 128
    TeleTact, 65
GLOWFLOW, 39
Gore, Albert, Jr., 109
Gravis 3-D sound card, 58
grouping objects in world building, 179-181
GUI (graphical user interface), 33-34, 129, 209

H

handicapped users, 127
haptic system, 62-63, 69-74
    mechanoreceptors, 63
    Sandpaper system, 67
head tracking, 20, 156
head-mounted display, *see* HMD
Heilig, Morton
    head-mounted display, 38
    Sensorama, 38, 75
High Cycle, 69
HIT Lab (Human Interface Technology Laboratory), 43
HMDs (head-mounted display), 20
    depth, 153-155
    EyePhones (NASA), 47
    Heilig, Morton, 38
    Howlett's camera, 143
    Howlett's optical viewer, 144
    monoscopic mode, 154

    skiing, 70
    software, 151-152
Howlett, Eric, 47, 143-144
    EyePhones, 141
    Howlett's camera, 143-144
    Howlett's optical viewer, 144
human factors, 135-137
Human Interface Technology Laboratory (HIT Lab), 43
HyperChem, 111

I

immersion, 12, 18-21, 141-148
    head-trackers, 20
    HMD (head-mounted display), 20
    WOW (window-on-world), 21
immune sensors, 54
information design, 11, 78
Information Processing Techniques Office (IPTO), 37
    see also Licklider, J. C. R.
installing included software, 193-195
International Interactive Computer Society (IICS), 126
interocular distance, 137

J–K

Johnson Space Center (JSC), 111

Krueger, Myron, 39
    Artificial Reality, 38
    GLOWFLOW, 39
    video equipment, 39

L

lag-time, 157
Lanier, Jaron, 46
large-scale advanced worlds, 187
LCDs (liquid crystal displays), 137

LEEP system, 47, 144
lenses
    fresnel, 147
    VRon, 148-153
Licklider, J. C. R., 36-38
liquid crystal displays (LCDs), 137
Logitech tracking devices, 156

M

manipulation, 12, 17-18, 158-160
    gloves, 158
    GUIs, 34
    mouse, 158
mathematics in world building, 171
Matsushita Electric Works (MEW),
    125
McGreevy, Walter, 46
mechanoreceptors, 63
medicine
    3-D, 116-121
    brain sugery, 119-121
    radiation treatment, 117-118
    surgical training, 118-119
MEW (Matsushita Electric Works),
    125
military, 41-48
MINO-DINO program, 208-212
Mitchell, David, 53
modeling, 37, 116
    3-D, 99-104
    objects, 101-103
    world-building tools, 100
    see also Licklider, J. C. R.
monitors, 36
    history, 33
    pixels, 86
    resolution, 77
monoscopic mode, 154
morphing, 103-104
MOVER program, 92, 203-208

N

NASA, 41-48
    DataGlove, 47
    EyePhones HMD, 47
navigation, 12, 15-16, 164-166
    3BALL, 164
    bio-navigation, 165-166
    GLOBAL 3D Controller, 164
    gloves, 165
    GUIs, 34
    neural inputs, 166
    Spaceball, 164
    walk-through, 16
    worlds, 16
NEC Virtual Skiing, 70
neural inputs, 166
New Dimension International, Inc.
    Freescape, 90
    Superscape, 89-91
Nintendo
    PowerGlove, 52
    Sim-City, 88
nitinol metal, 65
non-touching gloves, 59-60

O

objects
    groups, attributes, 180-181
    modeling, 101-103
    world building, 178-180
optical lenses, LEEP system, 47
overlays, 40
    3-D training, 107-109

P

patents, gloves, 158
PER-Force handcontroller, 111
perspective, see viewpoint
pheromones, 54

photo-realistic pictures, 85-87
Photo-VR rendering software, 87
physics
    3-D, 111-116
    analog instruments, 112-113
    digital instruments, 113-116
    in world building, 172
pixels, 86
plotters, 84
PointLine software, 84
points, object modeling, 102
polygon pictures, 85-87
Port of Seattle, 43
Portable Dextrous Master, 65
PowerGlove (Mattel), 52
programming, 170
    see also script commands
programs, 169
    3-D glasses, 196-197
    ANAGLYPH, 200-203
    CASTLE, 212-213
    FLY the Grand Canyon, 197-200
    MINO-DINO, 208-212
    MOVER, 203-208
    VREAM, 59-60, 213-222
    see also software
proprioception, 65-68
prototypes, design, 17
psychology in world building, 172

R

radiation treatment, 117-118
racquetball, 70
read-only memory, *see* ROM
rendering software, 85-87
    Photo-VR, 87
    RenderMan, 87
    Rend386 shareware, 87
resolution, 77, 86, 115
retinal display, 156

Rheingold, Howard, 85
Robinett, Warren, 40
ROM (read-only memory), 32

S

Sandpaper system, 65-67
science (3-D), 110-121
    see also medicine
screens
    CRTs (cathode ray tubes), 137
    LCDs (liquid crystal displays),
     137
    see also displays
script commands, 184-186
Sense8 WorldToolKit, 92-93
senses, 53-55, 74-75, 161-163
    balance, 54
    immune sensors, 54
    pheromones, 54
    simulation, 54
    sound, 55-58
    touch, 58-74
Sensorama, 38, 75
sensors, motion detection, 45
shapes
    ANAGLYPH, 195, 202
    MINO-DINO program, 209
    shape digitizer, 103
    textures, 93
shareware, 87
SIGGRAPH (Special Interest Group
  in Graphics), 150
sign language (CyberGlove), 128
SIGs (Special Interest Group), 126
Sim-City, 88
sim-sickness, 72-73
simulation
    bicycle, 69
    flight, 73-74, 80-81, 197-200
    sense, 54

software, 88-89
sound, 3-D, 56, 58
touch, 59, 64-65, 68
training (3-D), 107
skiing, 70-71
smell, 75
software, 75-89
   3-D animation, 82-83
      3D Studio, 83
      Animator, 83
   3-D glasses, 193, 196-197
   ANAGLYPH, 200-203
   Body Electric, 92
   CAD (computer-aided design), 83-85
      AutoCAD, 84
      PointLine software, 84
   CASTLE, 92, 212-213
   chemistry
      Alchemy III, 111
      HyperChem, 111
   flight simulation, 73, 80-81
   FLY the Grand Canyon, 197-200
   HMDs, 151-152
   installation, 193-195
   MINO-DINO, 208-212
   MOVER, 203-208
   rendering software, 85-87
   simulation, 88-89
   Swivel, 92
   VR Studio, 91
   VREAM, 93-94, 213-222
   see also programs
sound, 55-58
sound waves, 157
Spaceball, 164
Special Interest Groups (SIGS), 126
sports
   3-D, 125-127
   baseball, 126

bobsled, 126
racquetball, 70
skiing, 70-71
stereoscopic mode, 153-155
Super Nintendo, Sim-City, 88
Superscape, 89-90
surgical training, 118-121
Sutherland, Ivan, 37
   see also CAD
Swivel, 92
synthetic environments, 11, 78

T

tactile feedback, 65
Talking Glove, 128
tank (military) simulators, 42
telepresence, 44-46
TeleTact glove, 65
text files, ANAGLYPH program, 202
textures, 66
   ANAGLYPH program, 201
   mechanoreceptors, 63
   shapes, 93
   simulation, 65
TiNi Alloy company, 65
tools, world-building, 181-186
torque, displays, 137
touch, 58-74
   feedback
      force, 64, 110
      Sandpaper System, 65
      tactile, 65
   gloves
      EXOS Dextrous Hand Master, 59
      Portable Dextrous Master, 65
      TeleTact, 65
   haptic system, 62-63
   nitinol metal, 65
   PER-Force handcontroller, 111

pressure, 66
proprioception, 65-68
texture, 65-66
tracking, 156-157
 boom tracking, 156
 eye tracking, 156
 head position, 156-157
 Logitech devices, 156
training, 73-74
 3-D, 107-109
 surgical training, 118-119

U–V

viewpoint, 12-15
 GUIs, 34
 world building, 177-178
 see also perspective
violin simulation, 68
Virtual Audio Systems, 3-D sound, 58
virtual prototype design, 17
Virtual Raquetball, 70
virtual reality goals, 11-21
Virtual Reality, 68
Virtuality (W Industries), 71-72
von Neumann, John, 29, 31-33
VPL Research, Inc., 46
 Body Electric, 92
 DataGlove, 47
 Swivel, 92
VR Studio, 52, 91-92
VREAM, 60, 93-94, 213-222
VRon lenses, 148-153

W

W Industries, 71-72
walk-throughs, 16
 3-D, 105-106
Walker, John, 85
Wenzel, Elizabeth, 57
Wide Angle Orthostereo, 144
Wightman, Dr. Frederick, 57
 Convolvotron, 57
 sound perception, 58
window-on-world VR (WOW), 21
worlds, 16, 89-94
 building, 169-176
 3-D coordinates, 177-178
 development phases, 188-189
 editing system, 182-187
 ethics, 173-177
 objects, 178-181
 physics, 172
 psychology, 172
 script commands, 184-186
 spatial relationships, 172
 tools, 181-186
 environments, 209
 modeling, 100
 Sense8 WorldToolKit, 92-93
 Swivel, 92
 VR Studio, 91-92
 VREAM, 93-94, 217-222
 see also environments

X–Y–Z

x-rays, *see* radiation treatment

Zimmerman, Thomas, 47
 DataGlove, 52

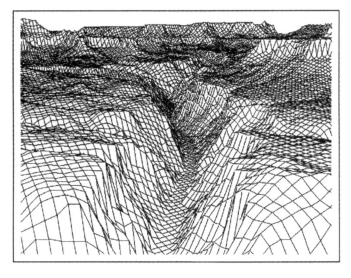

Disk Installation

Each file on the disk included with this book is a compressed collection of files. Do *not* try to decompress them before transferring them to a hard disk with a sufficient amount of free space. The space required is listed with each program. There is no space available on the 3 ½-inch floppy disk for decompression. Make sure you copy the files to the hard disk as instructed before typing their names, or the process will fail.

The disk contains the following six subdirectories:

Subdirectory name	Space required on hard drive for decompression	Name of compressed file
\A-VREAM	2.2M	SEEVREAM.EXE.
\ANAGLYPH	200K	ANAGLYPH.EXE.
\CASTLE	150K	CASTLE.EXE.
\FLYGC	1.3M	FLY_DEMO.EXE.
\MINODINO	160K	MINODINO.EXE.
\MOVER	700K	MOVR7.EXE.

To access these files, copy the desired file to your hard disk by following the procedure outlined below:

1. Make a subdirectory on your hard disk. The names listed above are suggested, but not mandatory.

2. Copy the desired file from the floppy to the newly created subdirectory on the hard disk (for example, type COPY B:\A-VREAM*.* C:\A-VREAM*.*).

3. Move to the new hard disk subdirectory (in this case, type CD C:\A-VREAM).

4. Extract the contents of the .EXE file by typing its name and pressing Enter (in this case, type SEEVREAM.EXE).

5. You will see the names of the compressed programs listed on the screen as they are automatically extracted.

6. If you wish, you can delete the compressed file from the hard disk (in this case, type DEL SEEVREAM.EXE).

7. Refer to each program's start-up instructions in Chapter 7.

Visual C++ Programming

Visual C++
Programming

Steven Holzner

||||Brady

New York   London   Toronto   Sydney   Tokyo   Singapore

Brady Publishing
A Division of Prentice Hall Computer Publishing
15 Columbus Circle
New York, NY 10023

ISBN: 1-56686-048-2

Library of Congress Catalog No.: 93-1204

96 95 94 93   4 3 2

Printing Code: The rightmost double-digit number is the year of the book's printing; the rightmost single-digit number is the number of the book's printing. For example, 93-1 shows that the first printing of the book occurred in 1993.

Manufactured in the United States of America

Limits of Liability and Disclaimer of Warranty

Trademarks

Credits

Publisher
Michael Violano

Managing Editor
Kelly D. Dobbs

Acquisitions Director
Jono Hardjowirigo

Editor
Susan Hunt

Production Editor
Bettina Versaci

Developmental Editor
Michael Sprague

Copy Editors
Gail S. Burlakoff
Kathy Murray Sabotin

Editorial Assistant
Lisa Rose

Book Designers
Michele Laseau
Kevin Spear

Cover Designer
HUB Graphics

Production Team
Diana Bigham, Katy Bodenmiller, Tim Cox, Mark Enochs,
Linda Koopman, Tom Loveman, Sean Medlock, Roger Morgan,
Joe Ramon, Carrie Roth, Greg Simsic

Contents

INTRODUCTION ....**XI**

CHAPTER 1. C++ PRIMER 1

All About Windows..2
   A Brief History of Windows..2
   Dissecting a Window 3
   Preserving the Feel of Windows 5
Our First Program 6
Entering the C++ World 9
   The C++ Predefined I/O Streams 11
Just What Is an Object? 13
   C with Classes..14
The Stack Object Example 18
Initializing Objects 29
Class Inheritance 34
Customizing Classes: Function Overriding 38
Function Overloading..41
Overloaded Functions with Different Parameter Numbers 46
Wrapping Up the C++ Primer...47

CHAPTER 2. ANATOMY OF A C++ WINDOWS PROGRAM 49

All About Windows Programming 50
   Hungarian Notation 51
Your First True Windows Program 53
Dissecting a C++ Windows Program 61
   Visual C++ Views and Documents 66
The CFirstApp Object 69
The CMainFrame Object 78
The FirstDoc Object 84
The FirstView Object 90

CHAPTER 3. KEYBOARD AND MOUSE INPUT 99

Using the Keyboard in Windows...100
   Windows Keyboard Input Conventions 100

Designing the First Document...101
Designing Your First View 103
    Storing the New Character 111
    The this Keyword..112
Adding a Caret to the Window 122
The Mouse and Mouse Events 134
    Using the Mouse in Code 136

CHAPTER 4. MENUS 149

Menu Conventions 149
Adding Menus to Your Programs 150
    Creating the Menu 151
    Connecting Menu Items to Code...................................157
Adding Shortcut Keys in Windows 160
Adding Accelerator Keys in Windows 162
Checking Menu Items 171
Graying Menu Items 174
Handling User-Interface Update Messages 176
Adding Menu Items in Code 177

CHAPTER 5. DIALOG BOXES: BUTTONS AND TEXT BOXES 203

Message Boxes..204
Designing Dialog Boxes 208
    Using CDialog Member Functions to Update Data 213
    Using Visual C++ Member Variables to Update Data 216
A Calculator Example 229
A Notepad Example 243

CHAPTER 6. DIALOG BOXES:
LISTBOXES, GRIDS—AND A SPREADSHEET..................................261

A Database Example 262
List Boxes 263
Combo Boxes 283
A Spreadsheet Example 284
Using VBX Controls in Code..288
Using a Dialog Box as the Main Window 298

CHAPTER 7. GRAPHICS AND A MOUSE-DRIVEN PAINT PROGRAM 305

Creating the Paint Program's Menus 306
Writing the Paint Program 308
Setting Individual Pixels in Windows 314
Freehand Drawing in the Paint Program 316
    Drawing Lines 320
    Selecting Colors and Pens 322
    Drawing Rectangles 325
    Drawing Ellipses 329
Filling Figures with Color 331
"Stretching" Graphics Figures 333

CHAPTER 8. FILES 355

MFC File Handling 356
A CFile Class Example 357
    Writing a File 358
    Reading a File 361
Sequential and Random Access Files 363
Updating the Notepad to Handle Files 370
    The Document's Modified Flag 373
Updating the Database to Handle Files 376
How to Customize Serialization 381

CHAPTER 9. MULTIPLE DOCUMENTS AND MULTIPLE VIEWS 399

Multiple Document Interface (MDI) Programs 400
Adding Scroll Bars 407
Multiple Views 415
Splitter Windows 420

CHAPTER 10. EXCEPTION HANDLING AND DEBUGGING 437

Exception Handling 438
    The Debug Window 444
    Catching Multiple Exceptions 448
Debugging 455
    Testing Programs 456
    Debugging at Work 457

    Breakpoints 459

    Single Stepping 463

That Is It 470

APPENDIX A. WINDOWS PROGRAM DESIGN 471

Windows Programming Philosophy 471

Mouse Actions 473

Keyboard Actions 473

The Edit Menu 477

The File Menu 477

The Help Menu 478

APPENDIX B. ABOUT THE DISKETTE 479

INDEX 483

Introduction

Programming on a small scale is usually an enjoyable experience. Small, bite-sized programs are usually quick to compile and run—it's a rare programmer who hasn't had some fun with small-scale programming and gotten the satisfaction of seeing things work the first time. In fact, as originally created, computers—and especially microcomputers—were designed to work only with small-scale programs. The few hobbyists that had their own computers were lucky if they had more than a few kilobytes of RAM.

But times change, and they change nowhere faster than in the computer field. As technology developed, the cost of equipment started to fall. Disks became larger, more and more RAM became available, and CPUs kept getting faster. In microcomputing, what had been a hobby became an industry—an industry in which customers today demand more functionality from their hardware and software. Following the hardware, the size of programs has grown tremendously over the last decade. It rapidly became apparent that creating a program ten times larger than what you had was not going to be ten times easier.

With the standard programming languages, there almost seems to be an inverted economy of scale—the faster a program increases in size, the faster it becomes unwieldy and unmanageable. Errors can proliferate and penetrate all parts of the program. One section of code conflicts with another. Debugging a large program becomes less of an exercise, more of a career.

This is because the standard programming languages were designed for small-scale projects (by today's standards). The parts of a program often have access to all the other parts of the program, especially if many of its variables are global. The way you store and use data in the whole program has to be kept in mind as you work on any part of the code. When you start to debug, you find yourself debugging 10,000 lines of interdependent code and data—the whole program at once—instead of manageable pieces.

In fact, as programs grew, the solution to their unwieldiness was to cut them up into manageable pieces. In assembly language, for example, everything in a file is *global* (accessible by other parts of the program)—but you don't often write large programs in assembly language. In the early BASIC, you could use GOSUB subroutines to cut up your code—but all of the data was still global between the subroutine and the main body of the program. Languages like FORTRAN started sup-porting functions and subroutines with purely local data; you could transfer data between them by passing it explicitly or with COMMON statements. Then the C language appeared. Its strong emphasis on typing (and, for that matter, data structures), helps to ensure that what you send to and receive from other parts of the program is just what you wanted. As programs grew larger, the programmer's strategy became to divide and conquer, a process now referred to as *encapsulation*.

Even the idea of data local to a specific function wasn't enough; as programs became more complex, programmers often found that other functions also needed access to that data. They wanted to wrap together whole sections of the program—data and code—into something beyond a simple function: something now called an *object*.

If you think of a large program as, say, a workshop, then programmers want to be able to stock it with self-contained tools. That is, they don't want to be concerned with the internal data and functions necessary in an oscilloscope—they simply want to be able to have an oscilloscope ready for use. In a real oscilloscope, the internal data and functions are purely *private*—we don't see what is going on inside. All we see is that we have an oscilloscope, ready for use. Programming is at exactly that stage—we want to be able to package data and functions together so that the internal details of complex parts of a program simply slip out of sight. The idea, quite literally, is "out of sight, out of mind." That can be done only when data and the functions that maintain and work with that data are packaged together. In this way, you are able to break a large unwieldy program into a collection of easily thought-of tools and resources.Because of this capability, C++ is the language we are looking for as our programs grow.

Nowhere is this more true today for the PC programmer than in Windows programming. If you have done any Windows programming, you know how difficult it can be—just getting a simple window on the screen can take dozens of lines of complex code, five or so files, and a steep learning curve.

Now that has changed. C++ not only enables us to wrap our program's sections into easily conceptualized objects, but also makes possible *class libraries*—whole libraries that can generate many different types of objects. Microsoft created the Microsoft Foundation Class (MFC) library for use with Windows. That library is also the foundation of this book. If we want to create a window in our code, we will be able to derive it as a self-contained object from the Microsoft class library. If we want a dialog box, same thing. Based on readily creatable objects, Windows programs in C++ are *dramatically* shorter than their C cousins. Visual C++ makes the whole thing even easier by giving us software design tools that will actually write the code for us. Writing Windows programs has become even easier for the C programmer who moves up to C++.

Our Approach

This book is designed expressly for you if you have had some Microsoft C or C++ programming experience and want to move on to Visual C++. The book assumes that you already know C; most programmers turn to C++ only after they have some C experience under their belts. The first chapter brings you up to speed in C++ and you will learn more about it as you need to. If you already know C++, you may be able to skip Chapter 1 and dig right into Windows.

Because Visual C++ is a language for programmers, and because this is a book for would-be programmers, it is oriented toward seeing programs work. In other words, we will see what the language can do for us—not the other way around. We are not going to work through long, academic arguments about abstractions—those kinds of discussions would be out of place. This is a book for programmers, one that intends to help you unleash the full power of Visual C++ in its own environment, Windows.

You should know from the beginning, however, that there is a good deal to learn before you can really use Visual C++—or even C++ itself. There is no way around learning the difference between a class and an object, between overloading functions and overriding them, between using Windows programs and writing them. All in all, you have to learn about many things: virtual functions, built-in I/O classes, nested classes, constructors, destructors, and inheritance, to name a few. In other words, we are going to get serious about learning Visual C++— and there is a lot to learn.

This book is filled with plenty of examples, ready to run. There is no better way to learn than by example, and you will see some good ones here. And we will develop the longer examples line by line, using boldface type in a gray shaded box to indicate where we are as we work through a program. There are lots of figures, notes, and—an added bonus—tips. A tip might be a way to make a program run twice as fast, it might be about some other part of Visual C++ that is unexpectedly handy for the current situation, and it might even give you some insights about what is going on behind the scenes in Visual C++. Whatever the tip, it will show you some aspects of Visual C++ from the professional programmer's point of view—giving you a little extra power, a little extra control.

That is the approach—learning Visual C++ by seeing it work, by starting near the beginning and carefully building expertise. We will go from the most basic—the very foundations of Windows object-oriented programming—to the most powerful in Visual C++, from the most simple to the most advanced. Take a moment now to look over what the book covers.

What Is in This Book

The C++ language is capable of wonderful speed and precision—and we are going to put it to work. To start, you will spend some time learning C++ itself (as the need arises, you will learn more). The following list is an overview of some of the C++ subjects you will learn to master.

▼ Classes

▼ Objects

▼ Function overloading

▼ Using memory in C++

▼ Inheritance

▼ Default parameters

▼ The I/O class libraries

▼ Virtual functions

After you get some C++ expertise, you will see why the combination of C++ and Windows is such a natural. You will master the following Windows topics and more as you make full use of Visual C++.

▼ Creating windows

▼ Menus

▼ File-handling in Windows

▼ Dialog boxes

▼ Scroll bars

▼ List boxes

▼ The mouse

▼ Windows graphics

▼ Reading keystrokes in Windows

▼ Windows messages

▼ Debugging in Visual C++

▼ The MultiDocument Interface (MDI)

These and other topics are waiting for you in Visual C++ to show you how simple C-derived Windows programming can be. We will create many useful examples, including a pop-up notepad, a paint program, a spreadsheet program, a database program, a complete file editor, and others.

To use this book, you will need some knowledge of C. Visual C++ builds on Microsoft C, and you need a good foundation in C before you can tackle C++. The software we will be using is Visual C++ version 1.0 and Windows 3+. If you want to use the Visual Basic custom controls discussed in Appendix A, you will need a copy of those controls—it comes in the Professional Edition of Visual Basic.

That's it; you are ready to begin—to unleash the full power of Visual C++. You are going to see it at work almost immediately because, in programming, there is no substitute for the real thing—seeing it in action. If you want to master Visual C++ and become a power programmer, let's start at once with Chapter 1 so that you can come up to speed in C++. Then, when you are ready, you will begin your guided tour of Windows programming.

C++ Primer

Welcome to Visual C++, one of the most exciting programming packages now available for Windows, and one of the components of a revolution in Windows programming. This powerful package is one of the new generations of programming tools that are beginning to open up Windows programming as never before. No longer does it take a great deal of patience, experience, and expensive software to produce valuable Windows applications—under Visual C++ (and programs like it), developing Windows programs is easier than ever. In this chapter, we will put together our first Visual C++ programs. Although they are not true Windows programs, Visual C++ will run them for us under Windows 3+. You will see that doing this is easier than you might expect, because Visual C++ handles most of the details.

If you have done any programming for Windows, you will find that this is where C++ really shines. The Windows programming interface is extensive; much of it has to do with the enormous number of options we programmers have for window styles, ways of running the program, window dimensions, memory allocation, and so on.

The great majority of Windows programs do not need such great ranges of choices, however—which is why C++ is perfect here. All of the option selections can be wrapped up into standard *classes*, and we can derive our own *objects* from them. In this way, the details become hidden from view and the *surface area* of the Windows programming interface shrinks rapidly back to a manageable size. This is just what C++ is for: dividing potentially large programs into manageable—and *self-contained*—objects. These objects themselves can take care of all the operations they need—such as writing themselves to a disk file. You will see how this modularity helps, again and again throughout the book.

To handle such objects, you must be familiar with C++ and such C++ terms as classes, objects, and function overriding. You will get that familiarity in this chapter. In the next chapter, you will put what you have learned to work in Windows. That doesn't mean you have to wait to see our programs run under Visual C++, as you will soon find out. Before doing anything, however, you should make sure that you are familiar with the host environment—Windows.

All About Windows

Many people believe—and they could be right—that Graphical User Interfaces (GUIs) are the wave of the future in microcomputing. Certainly, Windows 3.0 was the fastest-selling software package in history (500,000 copies in its first six weeks; 3,000,000 in its first nine months). In most significant ways, Windows is a full operating environment by itself.

Windows is very different from DOS. One of the most fundamental differences—that Windows is a Graphical User Interface (GUI)—introduces many new concepts. One of the primary ideas here is that most of the available options are presented to the user at once, in the form of objects on the screen, much like tools ready to be used. The utility of this simple approach is surprising—instead of remembering complex techniques and keywords, a user can simply select the correct tool for the task at hand and begin work. In this way, graphical interfaces fulfill much of the promise of computers as endlessly adaptable tools. Let's take a look at some of the background of this operating environment.

A Brief History of Windows

Microsoft started working on Windows in 1983, only two years after the PC appeared. But the original version, Windows 1.01, didn't actually ship until 1985. This version was supposed to run on the standard machine of that time: An IBM PC with two 360K disk drives, 256K, and an 8088. The display was automatically tiled; that is, the windows were arranged to cover the whole screen. It looked very two dimensional—and far from impressive.

The next major version, Windows 2, came out two years later. For the first time, windows could overlap on the screen. Windows 2 could run only in 80x86 real mode, however, which meant that it was limited to a total of one megabyte of memory. For a while, Windows even split into Windows 286 and Windows 386 to take advantage of the capabilities of the (then new) 80386 chip. Although progress had been made, much more was needed.

In May of 1990, Microsoft introduced Windows 3.0. The look and feel of Windows 3.0 was a great improvement over its ancestors. Version 3.0 featured proportional fonts, which made displays look more refined and also had better support for DOS programs. Version 3.1, introduced in April of 1992, improved on version 3.0, especially in the way files are managed. Many people now use Windows as their primary operating environment for the PC.

The MS-DOS Executive of earlier versions was replaced by a trinity of windows that manage Windows: the *Program Manager*, the *Task List*, and the *File Manager*. From a programming point of view, one of the most important features of Windows 3+ is that it can support extended memory: up to 16 megabytes of RAM. In its 386-enhanced mode, Windows uses the built-in virtual memory capabilities of the 80/3/4/586—that is, it can store sections of memory temporarily on disk—to give programmers access to up to four times the amount of installed memory. In a machine that has 16 megabytes, Windows can provide 64 megabytes. One of the advantages of OS/2 has always been its removal of memory restrictions, but now, more and more programmers are coming back to Windows. With Windows 3+, Windows has at last arrived.

Dissecting a Window

Before we go on, you should be familiar with a typical Windows 3+ window, its parts, and their names (see figure 1.1). You are probably aware that it is important for us to know what a user expects from a Windows application before we write one. Let's spend a little time reviewing

Windows terminology; this review will help us later in the book. At the upper left corner of the window is a system menu box, that, when selected, displays a menu that typically enables the user to move the window, close it, or minimize it. At the top center is the title or caption bar, which provides an easy way to label an application.

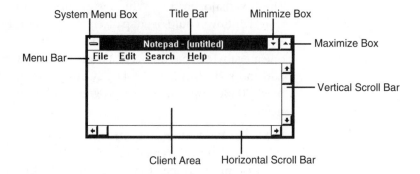

Figure 1.1. A Windows 3+ window.

To the right of to the title bar are the Minimize and Maximize boxes, which enable the user to reduce the window to an icon (called an application's *iconic* state), or expand it fully, usually to the whole screen. Under the title bar, a menu bar usually offers the menu options currently available for the application. Almost every stand-alone application has a menu bar with at least one menu item in it: the File menu. The Exit item usually is at the bottom of this menu (see figure 1.2).

Always Have an Exit Item.
Because the Exit item is the usual way for users to leave an application, when your application supports file handling, you should include the Exit item at the bottom of the File menu. (In fact, Windows applications that don't even use files often have a File menu to provide an Exit item.)

Under the menu bar, the *client area*—the area the window is designed to display—is the whole window except for the borders and scroll bars. This is the drawing area, the area you will work with directly in Visual C++. On this part of the window you will place buttons, list boxes, text boxes, and the other parts of your programs. In Windows, these visual objects are called *controls*.

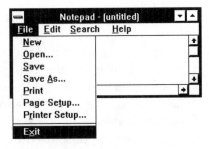

Figure 1.2. A Windows 3+ window with a file menu.

To the right of the client area is a vertical scroll bar, a common part of windows that displays text. When there is too much text to fit in the window at one time, scroll bars let you move through the document to look at some subsection of the whole. (The small square that moves up and down, and which you use to manipulate your position in the scroll bar is called a *thumb*.) Across the bottom of the window is the horizontal scroll bar, that scrolls the text in the client area horizontally.

Everything in the window *except* the client area is called the *nonclient* area—even the border is part of the nonclient area. Windows is responsible for maintaining the nonclient area of the window; we will be responsible for the client area.

Preserving the Feel of Windows

As I have already mentioned, when you program in Visual C++ you should be familiar with the way the user expects Windows programs to work and feel. In particular, you should be at home with the language of mouse clicks and double clicks, and anticipating what the user might expect from your application.

Part of the Windows interface you will be programming in, for example, is the fact that the File menu usually has an Exit item and that item—if present—is always last. Before you produce applications yourself, you should be familiar with the many other aspects of the way users expect Windows applications to work; in other words, there are many Windows conventions you should adhere to. Although these conventions are described in this book's discussion of the appropriate topics, there is no substitute for working with existing Windows applications to get the feel of the Windows interface.

After some time, these conventions become automatic. For example, in file list boxes, where the program is showing you which files are available to be opened, one click of the mouse should highlight a file name—the process is called *selecting* Two clicks should open the file—this is called *choosing*. On the other hand, because using Windows without a mouse—just with the keyboard—is also supposed to be possible, you should provide keyboard support also. (In this case, the user would use the Tab key to move the cursor to the correct box, the arrow keys to highlight a file name, and the Enter key to choose it.)

NOTE

For the purposes of program design, this book assumes that you have a mouse as well as C++. Although it is possible to use Windows *applications* without a mouse, not having one hampers Windows *programmers* (or even experienced Windows users), seriously crippling their productivity.

Windows users expect other conventions. They expect to be able to move an object around the screen by dragging it with the mouse. They expect accelerator keys in menus, system menus that let them close a window, and windows that can be moved, resized, or minimized. The best way to know what will be expected of your program is to work with existing Windows applications.

Our First Program

Start Visual C++ now. You will see the Visual C++ Workbench, shown in figure 1.3. You will become familiar with all of its parts in this book.

To get us started, we can run a DOS-style C program in Visual C++. We can use the traditional first program of C books, for example, which appears as follows:

```c
#include <stdio.h>
void main()
{
    printf("Hello world.");
}
```

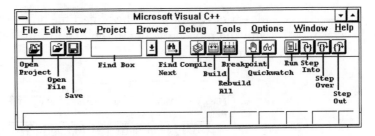

Figure 1.3. The Visual C++ Workbench.

Although Visual C++ can handle this program, you will see in the next chapter that programming in Windows is very different from programming in DOS. To create this hello.c program, select the New item in Visual C++'s File menu. A new window appears in Visual C++ (see figure 1.4).

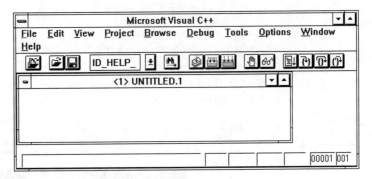

Figure 1.4. A new file window.

Now type the preceding program. Figure 1.5 shows what your screen should look like.

Save this file as hello.c by using Visual C++'s Save As... menu item in the File menu. In other words, click on Save As... in the File menu, type **hello.c** as the file name, and then click on OK. This creates hello.c on disk.

At this point, we are ready to run. Visual C++ handles the programs you develop as *projects*, in much the same way other Microsoft programming environments do. Many different files can be associated with a project, but we will work with only two as we develop this program: hello.c and hello.mak—the project file itself. Visual C++ keeps a project file—a .mak file—for every project. The project file holds a list of the files associated with the project. Before we build and run hello.exe, then, we have to create hello.mak.

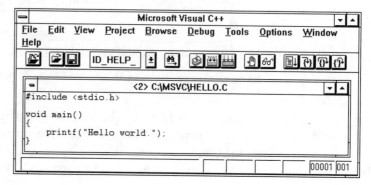

Figure 1.5. Our first C program.

To create hello.mak, select the New... item in Visual C++'s Project menu. The New Project window opens (see figure 1.6). Click the down-arrow next to the Project Type box. A drop-down list box, also shown in figure 1.6, opens.

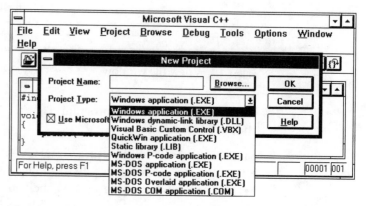

Figure 1.6. Creating a new project.

Remember—we are not creating a true Windows program here. (We are learning about C++, and hello.c is a DOS-style program to get us started.) To inform Visual C++ of that fact, select the QuickWin Application (.EXE) item in the drop-down list box and then click on OK in the New project dialog box.

At this point, an Edit dialog box opens (see figure 1.7). This box enables you to associate the files you want with the project hello.mak. Select hello.c and click the OK button. Visual C++ creates hello.mak.

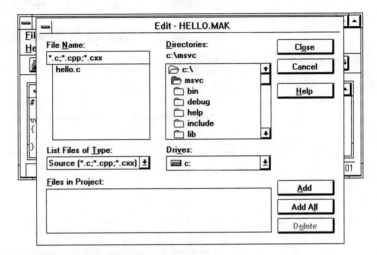

Figure 1.7. Creating hello.mak.

Finally, to create and run hello.exe, select the Build HELLO.EXE menu item in the Project menu. Visual C++ creates hello.exe and places an Output window on the screen (see figure 1.8). The results of compiling hello.c and building hello.exe appear in this window. Because there are no errors, select the Close item in the Output window's system menu. (In other words, click on the button in the window's upper left corner.)

To run hello.exe, select the Execute HELLO.EXE line in the Project menu. When you do, the program runs and we see `Hello world.` (see figure 1.9). That's it; our first program was a success. To end it, select the Close menu item in the Hello window's File menu.

Entering the C++ World

Now you will start seeing exactly why C++ is an improvement over C. First you will see some unique—and very popular—features of C++. Then we will turn to what has made it famous: the capability to work with objects.

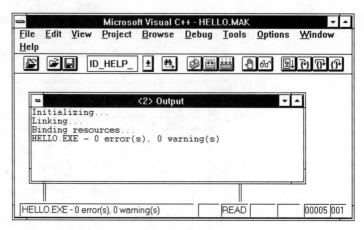

Figure 1.8. Building hello.exe.

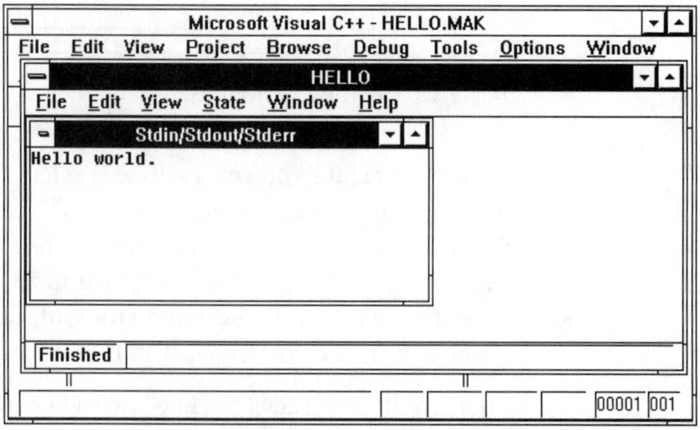

Figure 1.9. Running hello.exe.

The driving force behind objects is *modularity*, a concept that has already been stressed. Originally, as was mentioned earlier, C++ was written to be used when C programs got very long (although C++ has so many flexible features that thousands of programmers prefer it to C for all uses).

In long programs, it is often hard to remember all of the details about all of the parts. Remembering is much easier when we can combine associated functions and the data they need into a conceptual object, which we can then think of as a single entity. We will be able to think of the whole object in terms of its overall use, without having to remember all of the details of its internal data handling. In fact, an object is very much like a new kind of structure—except that it can hold data and functions.

One common example of an object is a *stack*—a specially dedicated area of memory used for storing data in a particular way. You push values on the stack, and later pop them to retrieve them. When you pop them, they come off in reverse order—if you pushed the values 1, 2, 3, 4, and 5 onto the stack, then popping values off the stack successively would yield 5, 4, 3, 2, and 1.

To make your own stack, you need the memory space used for storage as well as the functions that do the pushing and the popping. The stack may even have internal functions that monitor the stack. All of these details can be distracting when you have lots of other things on your mind. It's easier if you can wrap them all (the C++ term is *encapsulate*) into one logical idea—a stack. With this example in mind, let's begin working with C++.

The C++ Predefined I/O Streams

You already know the standard C streams: stdin, stdout, stderr, and stdlog. In C++, there are some additional predefined streams named cin, cout, cerr, and clog. They are tied to the same devices, but we use them in a different way. Let's look at an example, which shows how to use *cout* to print to the screen. The following shows how to use C++ to print Hello, world. on the screen.

```
#include <iostream.h>

void main()
{
    cout << "Hello world.";       // Print "Hello, world."
}
```

To use the predefined C++ streams, we had to include the header file iostream.h. Next, print the string by using the << operator, as follows:

```
#include <iostream.h>

void main()
{
    cout << "Hello world.";       // Print "Hello, world."
}
```

In normal C, << is a left-shift operator; it works on integer values by shifting their bits left by a specified number of places. In C++, the << and >> operators still function as left- and right-shift operators—but operators can have more than one meaning. In this case, << might be used to also send output to cout (it is called the *insertor operator* because it inserts data into the cout stream); because >> might be used to also read input from cin, it is called the *extractor*. Giving an operator multiple uses, depending on the types of data you are using it with, is called *operator overloading*—it's an important part of C++.

Say, for example, that you define some complex data structure and you want to be able to define the operation of addition on such structures. In C++, you can overload the + operator to handle it without problems. In fact, almost any of the usual C operators—except for some special ones like ?: or the dot operator (.)—can be overloaded in C++.

Why << is Better Than printf( ).
One reason << is a better choice than printf( ) is that printf( ) does not perform reliable type-checking on the data being sent to the screen.

The corresponding keyboard input stream is called *cin*, and when you want to read a value, you can do it the following way:

```
void main()
{
    int our_int;

    cout << "Please type an integer: ";
    cin >> our_int;
}
```

But because Windows has its own way of printing to the screen and passing keystrokes to our programs, we won't use cin here. Streams like these become very important in Chapter 7, when we deal with files.

You might also notice a new method of using comments in programs. We put a one-line comment in the program by prefacing it with the // symbol.

```
"// Print Hello, world."
```

This is a new addition to C++. It works for one-line comments only; that is, C++ ignores the rest of the line following the // symbol. (The older /* */ method is still available, of course, but C++ programmers often use the // one-line comments, reserving the /* */ method for multiline ones.)

The next step is to type this program into a file and get it to run. (Because C++ uses the .cpp extension, the file is named hello.cpp.) Close the project hello.mak by using the Close item in the Project menu. Select the New... item in the File menu. Type in the following new C++ program:

```cpp
#include <iostream.h>

void main()
{
    cout << "Hello world.";        // Print "Hello, world."
}
```

Now save it as hello2.cpp and create a new project called, say, hello2.mak. Associate hello2.cpp with hello2.mak when the Edit Hello2.Mak dialog box opens. Finally, build and run hello2.exe. You can see the results in figure 1.10.

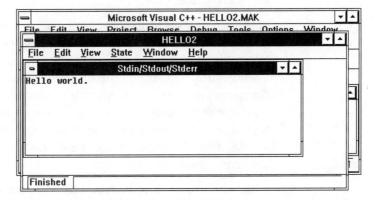

Figure 1.10. Running the first C++ program.

That's it; we have gotten our first C++ program to run. It was that simple. Now let's take the next step in C++ and learn about objects themselves.

Just What Is an Object?

In C++, a long program is less a mass of uncoordinated functions and interconnecting data structures than a collection of easily-managed tools and resources, ready to be put to use.

That is the way we usually think of our programs—as self-contained sections neatly wrapped up into concepts. You might stock your kitchen, for example, with a refrigerator, an oven, and a dishwasher—each thought of as a discrete unit. When you put food in the refrigerator, you don't want to be concerned with the internal operation of the refrigerator—you simply want your food kept cold.

Imagine what your kitchen would be like if you had to deal simultaneously with every detail of the timers and thermostats and pumps inside all of your appliances by setting, adjusting, and coordinating them all at once. That's much the way a large-scale, purely function-oriented program works today—you can't wrap into easily managed tools the data and the internal functions needed to work on and maintain that data. The function is the standard unit of program design. In the real world, however, people don't think of functions—they think in terms of objects and their various uses.

That is what C++ is all about—creating objects that are easy to think about and manage—conceptually much like the operation of refrigerators and ovens. Many internal functions may be needed to maintain an object like a refrigerator. Setting the thermostat of your refrigerator causes many things to occur inside the refrigerator. You don't need to concern yourself with any of these internal functions. They—and the way they interact with each other—are set into motion when you change the thermostat setting. You don't need to see the details, and that is what makes the appliance worth owning.

In the same way, a programming object provides a carefully designed and intentionally limited interface to the rest of the program. Until now, there was no way to wrap up the functions with data they use and need to form anything bigger than another function. Now, however, programmers can work with objects, which can have data and functions that are private to the object (internal data and functions), or available to anyone (public data and functions). Let's see how objects work.

C with Classes

The most significant programming improvement of C++ over C is that it can use *classes*. In fact, C++ was originally called C with Classes. Briefly, a class is something like a data structure in C, except that a class can be defined to hold functions as well as data. A class makes up a formal type, just as when you declare the fields of a structure. When you declare variables of that type, the variables themselves are the objects.

Remember, in C++, classes are the formal types and objects are the specific variables of that type. (Understanding this point is important. Forgetting it can cause confusion.)

You set up a class just as you might a structure with struct, except that a class definition can also hold function prototypes as follows:

```
class the_class {
    int private_data;
public:
    int public_data;
    int public_function(int t);
};
```

NOTE

All functions in C++ need prototypes.

When you declare variables of this type, those variables will be objects, which is how classes are related to objects. In the preceding example, we're setting up a class named the_class. This class includes some data: public_data and private_data. It also includes a function, named public_function(). If this had been a structure, we could only have included data, as follows:

```
struct some_struct {
    int public_data;
    int private_data;
};
```

Then we could have declared variables of this structure type, as follows:

```
void main()
{
    some_struct the_struct
        :
```

Next, we could have reached the members of the_struct with the dot operator, as follows:

```
struct some_struct {
    int public_data;
    int private_data;
};

void main()
{
    some_struct the_struct
    the_struct.public_data = 5;
        :
```

It works the same way with classes. When we declare a variable of class the_class, it is an object like the_object, as follows:

```
class the_class {
    int private_data;
public:
    int public_data;
    int public_function(int t);
};

void main()
{
    the_class the_object;
        :
```

Now we can reach the member data of the_object as follows, just as we could with the_struct.

```
class the_class {
    int private_data;
public:
    int public_data;
    int public_function(int t);
};

void main()
{
    the_class the_object;
    the_object.public_data = 5;
        :
```

Now, however, we can also refer to its functions—called *member functions*—the same way.

```
class the_class {
    int private_data;
public:
    int public_data;
    int public_function(int t);
};

void main()
{
    the_class the_object;
    the_object.public_data = 5;
    the_object.public_function(5);
        :
```

This is something new. We have associated not only data but also a function with the_object. And we did that simply by including its prototypes in the declaration of the_class, as follows:

```
class the_class {
    int private_data;
public:
    int public_data;
    int public_function(int t);
};
```

Did you notice the keyword *public* in the class declaration? There are three ways to include member data and functions in a class—as *private*, *public*, or *protected*. By default, all members of a class are private, which is why we don't include that keyword.

If something is private, no part of the program can refer to it outside its object. In the_class, private_data is private; the *only* parts of the program that can reach it are the functions associated with the objects of that class (in other words, the member functions). Functions (as well as data) can be private.

It is good to remember the spirit of C++ here—to increase the modularity of programs, as much of the object should be made as private as possible in most cases. This is an important part of the C++ style, and it is the reason that all of the member data and functions are private by default (that's the whole idea behind encapsulation). The *protected* keyword is used when you derive one class from another—a process called *inheritance*—and want to give only the derived classes access to specific members. You will learn more about this throughout the book.

Note that if everything in an object were private, no part of it could be reached—it would be useless. Here, however, because both the variable public_data and the function public_function( ) are declared as public, we can reach them from other places in the program, as follows:

```
    the_object.public_data = 5;          // Set public_data
    the_object.public_function(3);       // Use
public_function()
```

The functions that should be left private are those that are purely internal to the object; they are usually used only by other member functions.

Now that you have an overall idea of what objects are about, let's take the time to work through a specific example and get all of the details down pat. One of the simplest examples of an object is a numerical stack, which is not only of real use to programmers, but is also easy to implement. Let's examine the process of building a stack object.

The Stack Object Example

First, let's review the way a stack works. A stack is made up of a section of memory in which we store data in a special way. Say, for example,the following is part of the stack in memory:

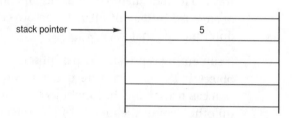

Notice the stack pointer, which points at a particular location called the top of the stack. When you put a value, such as 7, onto the stack, the stack pointer is incremented by one place to point to the next location, and the 7 is placed at that location as follows:

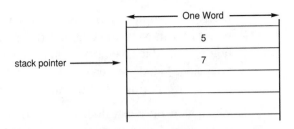

In this way, you *push* a value onto the stack. You can retrieve these values by popping them off the stack. When you pop one value from the stack, it is the last value pushed (7), and the stack pointer moves back, as follows:

Popping the stack again yields a value of 5. Note that the order in which values come off is the reverse of that in which they were put on. That's the way the stack works. If you push the values 1, 2, and 3, then popping values off the stack yields 3, 2, and 1. Stacks like this are popular programming constructions, but there is no direct support for them in C++. We can add that ourselves, however, with a stack class.

Designing the stack class is easy. First, you need some space for the stack itself. You can set that aside as data internal to the stack object in an array called stack_data[], as follows:

```
class stack_class {
    int stack_data[100];
        :
};
```

Note that because we have left it private, only member functions will have access to the stack. The rest of the program doesn't have to bother with it, and it won't clutter up the global data space. In addition, we have to store the stack pointer—our index in the array stack_data[]—which points at the element that will be popped next, as follows:

```
class stack_class {
    int stack_data[100];
    int stack_ptr;      // stack_ptr = -1      stack is empty
};
```

This stack pointer is private, because only member functions are concerned about the value of the stack pointer. The rest of the program only needs to push and pop values; it does not need to examine the stack pointer itself. Note the comment, which indicates that when stack_ptr holds -1, the stack is empty. That is, -1 is an impossible index value for the array stack_data[]. When you decrement stack_ptr to that value, you have popped everything off of the stack.

When you push a value, it goes into the first element of the array, stack_data[0], and stack_ptr becomes 0. The next time you push a value, it goes into stack_data[1], and stack_ptr becomes 1 also. When you pop a value, stack_ptr goes back to 0. After you pop that value too, stack_ptr becomes -1 and nothing is left on the stack—you can't pop off any more values.

Let's set up the prototypes for the two functions that will actually do the pushing and popping. They should be public so that the rest of the program can use them. Also, some stack operations—such as popping an empty stack or attempting to push data onto a full stack— ought to generate an error. For that reason, let's have push() and pop() return integer values—0 for failure and 1 for success, as follows:

```
class stack_class {
    int stack_data[100];
    int stack_ptr;       // stack_ptr = -1 stack is empty
public:
    int pop(int *pop_to);
    int push(int push_this);
};
```

Note that because pop() has to change the value of the argument passed to it, you have to pass a pointer to it—exactly as you do with scanf(). You should also include an initialization function to set the stack pointer to -1 (an empty stack) at the beginning of the program, as follows:

```
class stack_class {
    int stack_data[100];
    int stack_ptr;                  // stack_ptr = -1   stack is empty
public:
    void init(void);
    int pop(int *pop_to);
    int push(int push_this);
};
```

```
void CFirstView::OnDraw(CDC* pDC)
{
  CString hello_string = "Hello, world.";
  CFirstDoc* pDoc = GetDocument();

  pDC->TextOut(0, 0, hello_string, hello_string.GetLength() );
}
```

This code is designed specifically to handle one type of event: when a window is *redrawn* (or *refreshed*)—that is, when the window is first drawn or uncovered when another window moves. Typically, your Windows C++ programs will be collections of code sections like this, including other *On* events like OnMouseMove, OnButtonPress, and so on. That is how event-driven programming works: you design code primarily around the I/O interface. These programs do not have *modes* (unlike an editor, which can have insert mode, marking mode, and so on). Rather, all the options available at one time are represented on-screen, ready to be used. You will see how this works soon.

In addition to being event-driven, Windows programming is also naturally object-oriented. That is easy enough to see on the screen: just pick up an *object*—an icon or paintbrush—and move it around. This corresponds closely to *object*-oriented programming, as you will see. In Windows programming, in a natural way, you can break a program into discrete objects, each with its own code and data. Each object can be independent of the others.

Object-oriented programming is perfect for event-driven software because it breaks the program into discrete, modular objects. This is the way you will treat windows and all the buttons, text boxes, and such that you put in them—as objects.

Hungarian Notation

Before you begin, you should be familiar also with the naming convention for Windows variables. Because Windows programs can be so long, losing track of what all the variables mean is easy. *Hungarian notation* (a Windows convention named for the nationality of its inventor, Charles Simonyi, a Microsoft programmer) can help. Hungarian notation provides letters that can be used as prefixes (see table 2.1). (You might want to refer to this table often as you read this book.) The letters can also be combined; lpszMyString, for example, means *a long pointer to a zero-terminated string named MyString*. If lpszMyString were a member of some class, its name would be m_lpszMyString in the Microsoft Foundation Class libraries. (This book is largely an exploration of those libraries.)

Table 2.1. Hungarian Notation

Prefix	Meaning
a	Array
b	Bool (int)
by	Unsigned char (byte)
c	Char
cb	Count of bytes
cr	Color reference value
cx, cy	Short (count of x, y length)
dw	Unsigned long (dword)
fn	Function
h	Handle
i	Integer
m	Data member of a class
n	Short or int
np	Near pointer
p	Pointer
l	Long
lp	Long pointer
s	String
sz	String terminated with a zero
tm	Text metric
w	Unsigned int (word)
x, y	Short (x or y coordinate)

Now that you have the background, let's take a look at a C++ program for Windows.

Your First True Windows Program

You are going to create your first true Windows program—one that prints `Hello, World.` in a window. Start Visual C++ now. Visual C++ includes several *wizards* that help you with the programming process, as follows:

▼ App Wizard writes C++ programs.

▼ Class Wizard writes classes and connects menu items and buttons to code.

▼ App Studio designs Windows resources like dialog boxes and menus.

You will use the first of these wizards, AppWizard, to create your new project and write the skeleton code. Then you will customize the code yourself. Having a wizard write the code for you is a big help (the process is referred to as *CASE*—computer-aided software design).

Start AppWizard by selecting the AppWizard... item in the Project menu. AppWizard opens, with a screen that looks like figure 2.1.

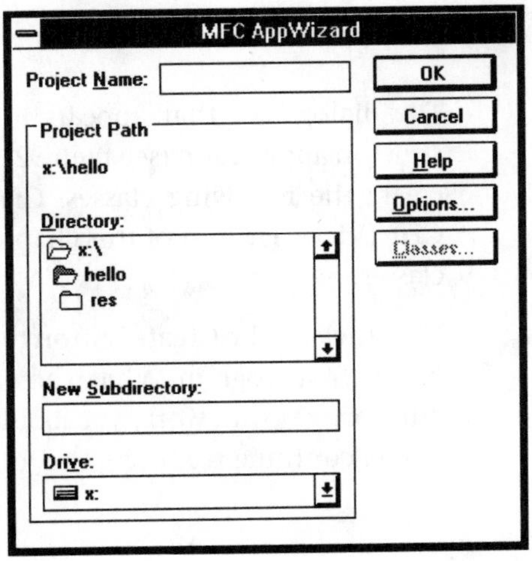

Figure 2.1. AppWizard.

Give this new project the name first.mak (type `first` in the Project Name box). Now click on the Options button, opening the Options dialog box shown in figure 2.2. Click on the top check box, which currently reads `Multiple Document Interface`, to remove the X from the box. (You do not need multiple windows in your first program.) Note the options—a toolbar and printing support—that AppWizard will put in the program. Click on OK to close the Options dialog box, and click on OK in AppWizard itself.

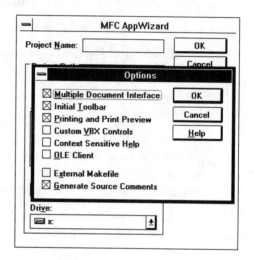

Figure 2.2. AppWizard's options.

The dialog box that appears indicates that AppWizard will create a skeleton application (see figure 2.3). It also indicates that AppWizard will create the following classes: CFirstApp, CMainFrame, CFirstDoc, and CFirstView. The rest of this chapter is about an exploration of these new classes.

Now click on the Create button to have AppWizard create the framework of your first program. What it actually creates is a set of 19 files in the \first directory. (Do not worry yet about what is in these files—you will find out as you continue reading.) The following is a list of the files:

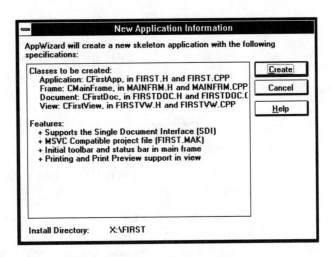

Figure 2.3. AppWizard's info box.

File Name	Description
FIRST.CLW	Class Wizard data
README.TXT	General information
FIRST.H	Header file
FIRST.CPP	Program C++ file
FIRST.DEF	Definition of project's Windows modules
MAINFRM.H	Main frame window header file
MAINFRM.CPP	Main frame window C++ code
STDAFX.H	Standard application frameworks header
STDAFX.CPP	Standard application frameworks C++ code
FIRSTDOC.H	Document class header
FIRSTDOC.CPP	Document class C++ code
FIRSTVW.H	View class header
FIRSTVW.CPP	View class C++ code
RES	Subdirectory (includes FIRST.RC2, FIRST.ICO,TOOLBAR.BMP)

continues

File name	Description
RESOURCE.H	Resource file header
FIRST.RC	General resource file (menu, and so on)
FIRST.MAK	Project file

As you can imagine, creating all these files yourself and integrating them into the project first.mak would take some time; here, AppWizard has done it all for you.

Now add the few lines you need to place Hello, World. in the window, so that you can run first.exe. To add lines, select the Open... menu item in the File menu and open the file \first\firstvw.cpp. This code supports the program's *view class*, which AppWizard has called CFirstView, and which controls the way data appears in the window. Now find the member function CFirstView::OnDraw(), that currently appears as follows:

```
void CFirstView::OnDraw(CDC* pDC)
{
CFirstDoc* pDoc = GetDocument();

//TODO: add draw code here
}
```

You can see the comment AppWizard has left for you: add draw code here. For now, just add the following code lines (then you will examine what they mean and what they do), as follows:

```
void CFirstView::OnDraw(CDC* pDC)
{
CString hello_string = "Hello, world.";
CFirstDoc* pDoc = GetDocument();

pDC->TextOut(0, 0, hello_string, hello_string.GetLength() );
}
```

You are creating a string object, hello_string, which holds the string Hello, world..

CString is one of the many predefined classes Visual C++ has in the Microsoft Foundation Class (MFC) library. You will see more about CString as you go on, but it is worth noting that the CString class is a near-perfect example of all that makes object-oriented programming worth-while.

The data in a CString object is held internally. You can reach it by assigning strings to it, as follows:

```
CString hello_string = "Hello, world.";
```

This self-contained object also has functions you can use—that is, functions you do not have to write yourself. These functions, which are logically part of the CString programming object, let you handle the whole idea of a string as an easy conceptual object. CString objects include such member functions as the following:

Function	Description
Find( )	Find a character or substring in the string
GetLength( )	Gets the string's length in characters
Left( )	Return n leftmost characters
Mid( )	Return substring from middle
Right( )	Return n rightmost characters

In C++, as in C, you can use the index operator [] with a CString object, like this: hello_string[4]. C++ has other operations also, such as concatenating two strings together, which works in the following way:

```
final_string = hello_string + second_string;
```

Everything about this object is self-contained, wrapping the string up in a neat package.

To print such string objects in a window, you use a function named TextOut( ). TextOut( ) is a member function of the *device context* class. All drawing or graphics manipulation in Windows is done in device contexts. These device contexts can correspond to various things: A window (or part of one), the whole screen, a printer, and so on. By unifying the varying environments into a device context (in which Windows-defined standard tools and functions are available), Windows lets you operate in a device-independent way.

In C++, you get a device context *object* of class CDC (Class Device Context). All of the functions that one can perform with a device context are member functions of device context objects. Table 2.2 lists the member functions of the CDC class.

Table 2.2. Member Functions of the CDC Class

AbortDoc	ExcludeClipRect	GetMapMode
Arc	ExcludeUpdateRgn	GetNearestColor
Attach	ExtFloodFill	GetOutlineTextMetrics
BitBlt	ExtTextOut	GetOutputCharWidth
CDC	FillRect	GetOutputTabbedTextExtent
Chord	FillRgn	GetOutputTextExtent
CreateCompatibleDC	FloodFill	GetOutputTextMetrics
CreateDC	FrameRect	GetPixel
CreateIC	FrameRgn	GetPolyFillMode
DeleteDC	GetAspectRatioFilter	GetROP2
DeleteTempMap	GetBkColor	GetSafeHdc
Detach	GetBkMode	GetStretchBltMode
DPtoLP	GetBoundsRect	GetTabbedTextExtent
DrawFocusRect	GetBrushOrg	GetTextAlign
DrawIcon	GetCharABCWidths	GetTextCharacterExtra
DrawText	GetCharWidth	GetTextColor
Ellipse	GetClipBox	GetTextExtent
EndDoc	GetCurrentPosition	GetTextFace
EndPage	GetDeviceCaps	GetTextMetrics
EnumObjects	GetFontData	GetViewportExt
Escape	GetGlyphOutline	GetViewportOrg
	GetKerningPairs	

GetWindowExt	RealizePalette	SetBrushOrg
GetWindowOrg	Rectangle	SetMapMode
GrayString	RectVisible	SetMapperFlags
IntersectClipRect	ReleaseAttribDC	SetOutputDC
InvertRect	ReleaseOutputDC	SetPixel
InvertRgn	ResetDC	SetPolyFillMode
IsPrinting	RestoreDC	SetROP2
LineTo	RoundRect	SetStretchBltMode
LPtoDP	SaveDC	SetTextAlign
MoveTo	ScaleViewportExt	SetTextCharacterExtra
OffsetClipRgn	ScaleWindowExt	SetTextColor
OffsetViewportOrg	ScrollDC	SetTextJustification
OffsetWindowOrg	SelectClipRgn	SetViewportExt
PaintRgn	SelectObject	SetViewportOrg
PatBlt	SelectPalette	SetWindowExt
Pie	SelectStockObject	SetWindowOrg
PlayMetaFile	SetAbortProc	StartDoc
Polygon	SetAttribDC	StartPage
Polyline	SetBkColor	StretchBlt
PolyPolygon	SetBkMode	TabbedTextOut
PtVisible	SetBoundsRect	TextOut
QueryAbort		UpdateColors

Now, to get back to the program you have written. In OnDraw( ), you get a pointer to a device context passed directly to you; your job is to draw with it (the results could appear on screen or printer). That pointer is called pDC. In C++, you can use the arrow operator (->) to reach member functions from an object pointer (just as you can reach data members of a structure in C with the -> operator used on a pointer to that structure).

TextOut() takes four parameters: the x and y position at which text is displayed in the window (you will use (0, 0), the upper left corner of the window); the string `Hello, world.` itself (in a CString object); and the length of the string (which you can find with the CString member function CString::GetLength()). Using TextOut(), the code appears as follows:

```
void CFirstView::OnDraw(CDC* pDC)
{
CString hello_string = "Hello, world.";
CFirstDoc* pDoc = GetDocument();
```

```
pDC->TextOut(0, 0, hello_string, hello_string.GetLength() );
}
```

That's it for the code. You are printing `Hello, world.` at location (0,0) in the client area, as follows:

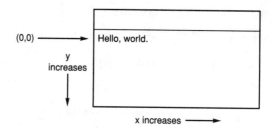

Now you can create first.exe and run it. Notice that with the help of AppWizard, you did not have to write many more lines than are in the DOS version of this program, as follows:

```
#include <iostream.h>

void main()
{
cout << "Hello ";
cout << "World.\n";
}
```

Now, to create first.exe, select the Build FIRST.EXE line in Visual C++'s Project menu. After Visual C++ creates this file, run it by selecting the Execute FIRST.EXE line (also in the Project menu). When you do, you see the `Hello, World.` message in a window (see figure 2.4).

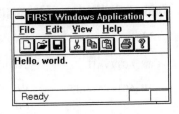

Figure 2.4. Your first program at work.

That's it; you have created and run your first true Windows program. Your project is a success. Now you can take it apart and see what is going on inside it.

Dissecting a C++ Windows Program

The first.exe program has two main objects. One, named CFirstApp, is derived from the Microsoft Foundation Class CWinApp; the other, named CMainFrame, is derived from the MFC class CFrameWnd, as follows:

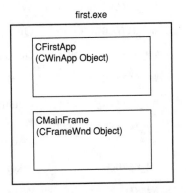

CFirstApp represents the program and CMainFrame represents the window. CFirstApp is your interface to Windows. When an event occurs in Windows, a message is sent to the program—CFirstApp—to let it know what is happening. When a key is pressed, for example, the special message WM_KEYDOWN is sent to CFirstApp. The program interfaces to Windows through messages. Table 2.3 lists some of the 150 messages Windows might pass to you in the following way:

Table 2.3. Windows Messages

Message	Explanation
WM_ACTIVATE	Windows becoming active or inactive
WM_ACTIVATEAPP	Window being activated belongs to a different application
WM_CANCELMODE	Cancels system mode
WM_CHILDACTIVATE	Child window moved
WM_CLOSE	Window was closed
WM_CREATE	Window is being created; CreateWindow function was called
WM_CTLCOLOR	Control or message box about to be drawn
WM_DESTROY	DestroyWindow function was called
WM_ENABLE	Window was enabled or disabled
WM_ENDSESSION	Session is ending
WM_ENTERIDLE	Waiting for user action
WM_ERASEBKGND	Window background needs to be erased
WM_GETDLGCODE	Query to control's input procedure
WM_GETMINMAXINFO	Get size information about the window
WM_GETTEXT	Copies text corresponding to window
WM_GETTEXTLENGTH	Gets length of text associated with window
WM_ICONERASEBKGND	Iconic window background needs to be erased
WM_KEYDOWN	A key was pressed
WM_KILLFOCUS	Window losing the input focus
WM_MENUSELECT	User has selected a menu item
WM_MOVE	Window was moved
WM_PAINT	Request to repaint a portion of window
WM_PAINTICON	Request to repaint a portion of icon
WM_PARENTNOTIFY	Child window is created or destroyed
WM_QUERYDRAGICON	User about to drag an iconic window
WM_QUERYENDSESSION	User chose End Session command

Message	Explanation
WM_QUERYNEWPALETTE	Window about to realize its color palette
WM_QUERYOPEN	User requests icon be opened
WM_QUIT	Terminate application; program should quit and exit
WM_SETFOCUS	Window received input focus
WM_SETFONT	Font changed
WM_SETREDRAW	Sets or clears redraw flag
WM_SETTEXT	Sets title text of window
WM_SHOWWINDOW	Window is to be hidden or shown
WM_SIZE	Size of window changed; window was sized or resized

The prefix WM stands for *window message*. These messages are sent to a function in CFirstApp. The function, named WinMain(), handles them in a messsage loop; after some preliminary processing, the messages are sent on to your window object, as follows:

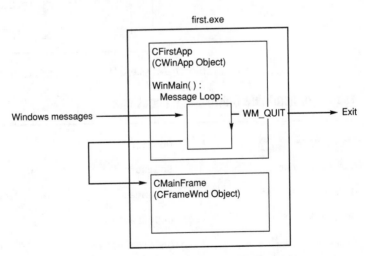

The CMainFrame object is derived from CFrameWnd, which is derived from the CWnd class. When a window gets a message which indicates that you should redraw its contents, OnPaint(), a CMainFrame function that comes from base class CWnd is called. Similarly, other functions are called for other Windows messages. To customize a program, you just have to override those functions and add code to them yourself.

Say, for example, that you want to handle the WM_PAINT message (your window needs to be redrawn), the WM_SIZE message (the window's size was changed), and the WM_CLOSE message (your window was closed). All you need to do is set up three functions: OnPaint(), OnSize(), and OnClose(). They will be member functions of the CMainFrame object, and will be called when your window receives the corresponding message as follows:

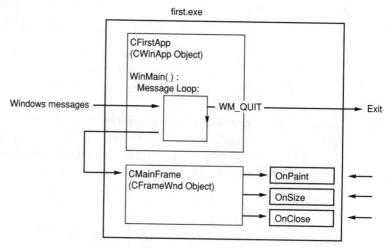

The available OnMessage functions appear in table 2.4.

Table 2.4. Available OnMessage Functions

OnActivate	OnChildActivate	OnDeleteItem
OnActivateApp	OnClose	OnDestroy
OnAskCbFormatName	OnCommand	OnDestroyClipboard
OnCancel	OnCompacting	OnDevModeChange
OnCancelMode	OnCompareItem	OnDrawClipboard
OnChangeCbChain	OnCreate	OnDrawItem
OnChar	OnCtlColor	OnEnable
OnCharToItem	OnDeadChar	OnEndSession

OnEnterIdle	OnMouseMove	OnQueryNewPalette
OnEraseBkgnd	OnMove	OnQueryOpen
OnFontChange	OnNcActivate	OnRButtonDblClk
OnGetDlgCode	OnNcCalcSize	OnRButtonDown
OnGetMinMaxInfo	OnNcCreate	OnRButtonUp
OnHScroll	OnNcDestroy	OnRenderAllFormat
OnHScrollClipboard	OnNcHitTest	OnRenderFormat
OnIconEraseBkgnd	OnNcLButtonDblClk	OnSetCursor
OnIdle	OnNcLButtonDown	OnSetFocus
OnInitDialog	OnNcLButtonUp	OnSetFont
OnInitMenu	OnNcMButtonDblClk	OnShowWindow
OnInitMenuPopup	OnNcMButtonDown	OnSize
OnKeyDown	OnNcMButtonUp	OnSizeClipboard
OnKeyUp	OnNcMouseMove	OnSpoolerStatus
OnKillFocus	OnNcPaint	OnSysChar
OnLButtonDblClk	OnNcRButtonDblClk	OnSysColorChange
OnLButtonDown	OnNcRButtonDown	OnSysCommand
OnLButtonUp	OnNcRButtonUp	OnSysDeadChar
OnMButtonDblClk	OnOK	OnSysKeyDown
OnMButtonDown	OnPaint	OnSysKeyUp
OnMButtonUp	OnPaintClipboard	OnTimeChange
OnMDIActivate	OnPaintIcon	OnTimer
OnMeasureItem	OnPaletteChanged	OnVKeyToItem
OnMenuChar	OnParentNotify	OnVScroll
OnMenuSelect	OnQueryDragIcon	OnVScrollClipboard
OnMouseActivate	OnQueryEndSession	OnWinIniChange

Dividing code in this way makes it much easier to write—one function to handle one Windows message (that is, one type of Windows event).

The default Visual C++ program (built by AppWizard) offers more functionality at the cost of a little more complexity, however. The next section examines that program.

Visual C++ Views and Documents

Currently, your window might appear as follows:

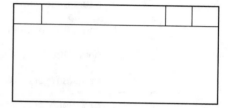

If you want some text in it, you can simply place it there by using TextOut( ), as follows:

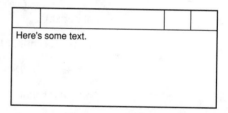

In Windows, however, a program can handle multiple documents (have multiple files open), each of which might contain different text. You might want to work with only one of them at a time, as follows:

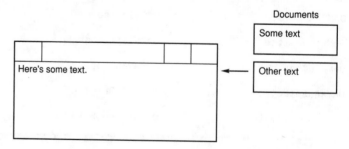

In this case, you have to handle the process of displaying the data from the correct document and swapping between the documents yourself.

Alternatively, you might have a really long document and want to display only part of it at a time, as follows:

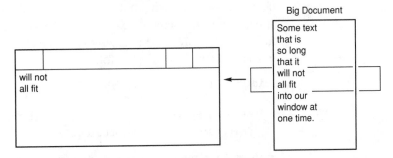

In other words, you only want to *view* a section of the long document. In fact, you might have several long documents and want to view only a section of each one, switching between them as the user directs.

For that reason, Visual C++ expects you to store data in a class it created (named CFirstDoc, for document). You can create multiple documents (when the user clicks on the File menu's New or Open items) just by creating new objects of this class. When the user opens, saves, or closes a document, member functions of that document's object will be called, letting you know what is going on.

Additionally, at least one *view* into every Visual C++ document exists. The document stores the data; the view indicates how that data is to be displayed. Member functions of CFirstView (a class created by Visual C++) will handle such Windows events as keystrokes, mouse movements, and so on. When a view has to draw, it gets the data from the document object and then displays it, using functions like TextOut( ), as follows:

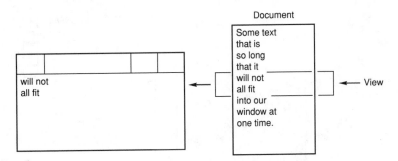

The reason views are separate from documents is to enable you to have multiple views into the same document. A view is actually a *child window* of the main window in your program. This means that the view is a window that appears wholly in the client area of the main window (usually covering the whole client area). When the data you are displaying needs to be (re)drawn (that is, when your window is uncovered or first appears on the screen), the main window calls the view's member function OnDraw(). That is why you placed your TextOut() instruction in CFirstView::OnDraw() as follows:

```
void CFirstView::OnDraw(CDC* pDC)
{
    CString hello_string = "Hello, world.";
    CFirstDoc* pDoc = GetDocument();

    pDC->TextOut(0, 0, hello_string, hello_string.GetLength() );
}
```

Other calls are made between these four fundamental parts of a Visual C++ program. Schematically, it appears as follows (not all possible calls are shown):

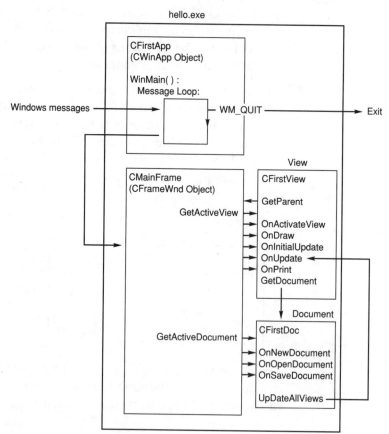

Visual C++ maintains these four parts of the program in the following files, class by class.

Class	Files	Code listing
CFirstApp	first.cpp, first.h	Listing 2.1
CMainFrame	mainfrm.cpp, mainfrm.h	Listing 2.2
CFirstDoc	firstdoc.cpp, firstdoc.h	Listing 2.3
CFirstView	firstvw.cpp, firstvw.h	Listing 2.4

The class declarations themselves appear in the header files; the member function definitions appear in the .cpp files. You will be examining programs like this throughout the book. (For reference, these files appear in listings 2.1, 2.2, 2.3, and 2.4.) Now you will take them apart and examine exactly how your first program put Hello, world. on the screen. Because the real work in Visual C++ goes on in the view and document classes, the CFirstApp and CMainFrame objects are covered only briefly.

The CFirstApp Object

A general understanding of the way the parts of your first program work is important because, in later chapters, you will be making modifications to the code AppWizard writes for you.

The CFirstApp class is the foundation of the program—note that the foundation is not the window itself. (A Windows program actually does not need to have any windows at all.) That class is derived from CWinApp in first.h, as follows:

```
class CFirstApp : public CWinApp
{
public:
    CFirstApp();
    virtual BOOL InitInstance();
    //{{AFX_MSG(CFirstApp)
    afx_msg void OnAppAbout();
```

```
        // NOTE - the ClassWizard will add and remove member functions here.
        //     DO NOT EDIT what you see in these blocks of generated code !
    //}}AFX_MSG
    DECLARE_MESSAGE_MAP()
};
```

Visual C++—in particular, Class Wizard, the second wizard you have at your disposal—will handle a large section at the end of this file for you. This wizard makes the process of adding members to the program's classes easier by automatically propagating the changes you make throughout the program. Do not worry about that now—you will see more about Class Wizard later. AppWizard adds a declaration like this to all the classes it writes; you should not edit this section because it will be handled for you, as you will see.

Note also the virtual declaration of the function InitInstance(), as follows:

```
class CFirstApp : public CWinApp
{
public:
    CFirstApp();
    virtual BOOL InitInstance();
    :
```

Functions are declared *virtual* when you expect to override them; in this case, AppWizard is indicating that InitInstance() can be overridden. Windows can run multiple copies of a program simultaneously. Each copy is called an *instance*. When you start a new instance of the program, you can execute initialization code by placing it in the InitInstance() function. Even though you can have multiple instances of first.exe running, only *one* object of type CFirstApp exists. If you want to execute initialization code when the program is first run (and before any other instances start), you place it in CFirstApp's constructor. The next block of code from first.cpp shows you CFirstApp's constructor as well as the skeleton version of the InitInstance() override that AppWizard has prepared. (For the complete listing of first.cpp, see listing 2.1.) Note the declaration of theApp, the one and only object of class CFirstApp that your program uses, is as follows:

```
#include "first.h"
CFirstApp::CFirstApp()
```

```
{
    // TODO: add construction code here,
    // Place all significant initialization in InitInstance
}
CFirstApp NEAR theApp;          // The one and only declaration of theApp
BOOL CFirstApp::InitInstance()
{
    SetDialogBkColor();         // set dialog background color to gray
    LoadStdProfileSettings();   // Load standard INI file options
    AddDocTemplate(new CSingleDocTemplate(IDR_MAINFRAME,
            RUNTIME_CLASS(CFirstDoc),
            RUNTIME_CLASS(CMainFrame),          // main SDI frame window
            RUNTIME_CLASS(CFirstView)));


    // create a new (empty) document
    OnFileNew();

    if (m_lpCmdLine[0] != '\0')
    {
        // TODO: add command line processing here
    }

    return TRUE;
}
```

You may have wondered how all the main classes—CFirstApp, CMainFrame, CFirstDoc, and CFirstView—are connected. As you will see in the coming chapters, that is done with a *document template*; in code, it looks as follows:

```
BOOL CFirstApp::InitInstance()
{
    SetDialogBkColor();         // set dialog background color to gray
    LoadStdProfileSettings();   // Load standard INI file options
```

```
AddDocTemplate(new CSingleDocTemplate(IDR_MAINFRAME,
        RUNTIME_CLASS(CFirstDoc),
        RUNTIME_CLASS(CMainFrame),        // main SDI frame window
        RUNTIME_CLASS(CFirstView)));
                :
```

Now every time a new instance of the program is started, a frame window, a document, and a view will be associated with the object of class CFirstApp. Note that RUNTIME_CLASS( ) is written in uppercase letters, which indicates that it is a macro supplied by the MFC class library.

In addition, InitInstance( ) creates a new and empty document by calling the function OnFileNew( ), a member function of CFirstDoc. AppWizard also sets up a skeleton application if conditional that enables you to handle any command-line input. A long pointer to the command-line text is stored in the CFirstApp pointer array m_lpCmdLine[] (m_ = member, lp = long pointer). You can reach it as follows:

```
BOOL CFirstApp::InitInstance( )
{
    SetDialogBkColor();           // set dialog background color to gray
    LoadStdProfileSettings();     // Load standard INI file options

    AddDocTemplate(new CSingleDocTemplate(IDR_MAINFRAME,
            RUNTIME_CLASS(CFirstDoc),
            RUNTIME_CLASS(CMainFrame),        // main SDI frame window
            RUNTIME_CLASS(CFirstView)));


    // create a new (empty) document
    OnFileNew();

    if (m_lpCmdLine[0] != '\0')
    {
```

```
    // TODO: add command line processing here
    }

    return TRUE;
}
```

That is it for CFirstApp, which launches your program. Although CFirstApp is the actual interface between you and Windows, you will see it only rarely in this book because you will be more concerned with views and documents. You just need to understand how it works in a general way: the details are handled fully when an object of class theApp is created. That is how easily you can create a Windows program in C++—all you really need is an object of the CWinApp class, which connects itself automatically to Windows. That object handles Windows messages and sends them on to your window. The next section examines the window object—the main window itself, derived from the CMainFrame class. (You will see this object occasionally in this book, but certainly not as often as views and documents.) But first, here is listing 2.1, the complete listing for the first.cpp and first.h files.

 Listing 2.1. First.Cpp and First.H

```
******************** first.h
```

```
// first.h : main header file for the FIRST application
//

#ifndef __AFXWIN_H__
    #error include 'stdafx.h' before including this file for PCH
#endif

#include "resource.h"        // main symbols


/////////////////////////////////////////////////////////////
///////////////////////////
// CFirstApp:
// See first.cpp for the implementation of this class
```

continues

Listing 2.1. continued

```
//

class CFirstApp : public CWinApp
{
public:
    CFirstApp();

// Overrides
    virtual BOOL InitInstance();

// Implementation

    //{{AFX_MSG(CFirstApp)
    afx_msg void OnAppAbout();
        // NOTE - the ClassWizard will add and remove member functions here.
        //    DO NOT EDIT what you see in these blocks of generated code !
    //}}AFX_MSG
    DECLARE_MESSAGE_MAP()
};


******************** first.cpp


////////////////////////////////////////////////////////////
/////////////////////
// CMainFrame message handlers
// first.cpp : Defines the class behaviors for the application.
//

#include "stdafx.h"
#include "first.h"

#include "mainfrm.h"
#include "firstdoc.h"
#include "firstvw.h"

#ifdef _DEBUG
#undef THIS_FILE
```

```
static char BASED_CODE THIS_FILE[] = __FILE__;
#endif


/////////////////////////////////////////////////////////
/////////////////////////
// CFirstApp


BEGIN_MESSAGE_MAP(CFirstApp, CWinApp)
        //{{AFX_MSG_MAP(CFirstApp)
    ON_COMMAND(ID_APP_ABOUT, OnAppAbout)
        // NOTE - the ClassWizard will add and remove mapping macros here.
        //    DO NOT EDIT what you see in these blocks of generated code !
    //}}AFX_MSG_MAP
    // Standard file based document commands
    ON_COMMAND(ID_FILE_NEW, CWinApp::OnFileNew)
    ON_COMMAND(ID_FILE_OPEN, CWinApp::OnFileOpen)
    // Standard print setup command
    ON_COMMAND(ID_FILE_PRINT_SETUP, CWinApp::OnFilePrintSetup)
END_MESSAGE_MAP()


/////////////////////////////////////////////////////////
/////////////////////////
// CFirstApp construction


CFirstApp::CFirstApp()
{
    // TODO: add construction code here,
    // Place all significant initialization in InitInstance
}


/////////////////////////////////////////////////////////
/////////////////////////
// The one and only CFirstApp object


CFirstApp NEAR theApp;


/////////////////////////////////////////////////////////
/////////////////////////
```

continues

Listing 2.1. continued

```
// CFirstApp initialization

BOOL CFirstApp::InitInstance()
{
    // Standard initialization
    // If you are not using these features and wish to reduce the size
    //  of your final executable, you should remove from the following
    //  the specific initialization routines you do not need.

    SetDialogBkColor();           // set dialog background color to gray
    LoadStdProfileSettings();  // Load standard INI file options

    // Register the application's document templates. Document templates
    //  serve as the connection between documents, frame windows and views.

    AddDocTemplate(new CSingleDocTemplate(IDR_MAINFRAME,
            RUNTIME_CLASS(CFirstDoc),
            RUNTIME_CLASS(CMainFrame),      // main SDI frame window
            RUNTIME_CLASS(CFirstView)));


    // create a new (empty) document
    OnFileNew();

    if (m_lpCmdLine[0] != '\0')
    {
        // TODO: add command line processing here
    }

    return TRUE;
}
```

```
/////////////////////////////////////////////////////////
////////////////////////
// CAboutDlg dialog used for App About

class CAboutDlg : public CDialog
{
public:
    CAboutDlg();

// Dialog Data
    //{{AFX_DATA(CAboutDlg)
    enum { IDD = IDD_ABOUTBOX };
    //}}AFX_DATA


// Implementation
protected:
    virtual void DoDataExchange(CDataExchange* pDX);
// DDX/DDV support
    //{{AFX_MSG(CAboutDlg)
        // No message handlers
    //}}AFX_MSG
    DECLARE_MESSAGE_MAP()
};

CAboutDlg::CAboutDlg() : CDialog(CAboutDlg::IDD)
{
    //{{AFX_DATA_INIT(CAboutDlg)
    //}}AFX_DATA_INIT
}

void CAboutDlg::DoDataExchange(CDataExchange* pDX)
{
    CDialog::DoDataExchange(pDX);
    //{{AFX_DATA_MAP(CAboutDlg)
    //}}AFX_DATA_MAP
}

BEGIN_MESSAGE_MAP(CAboutDlg, CDialog)
    //{{AFX_MSG_MAP(CAboutDlg)
    // No message handlers
    //}}AFX_MSG_MAP
```

continues

Listing 2.1. continued

```
END_MESSAGE_MAP()

// App command to run the dialog
void CFirstApp::OnAppAbout()
{
    CAboutDlg aboutDlg;
    aboutDlg.DoModal();
}
```

The CMainFrame Object

When a new instance of your program runs, new objects are created according to the document template. Those objects include a new CMainFrame object, a new CFirstDoc object, and a CFirstView object. Because CMainFrame is derived from the CFrameWnd (*frame window,* that is a standard window) class, a standard window appears on-screen. The document is created next, followed by the view. When the view is created, it is attached to the frame window as a child window, covering the frame window's client area. That is the reason views are more important to you than the main window (because you will be working almost exclusively with the client area). A general overview of the CMainFrame object is important also.

When the program starts, then, the object theApp makes sure that an object is created dynamically from the CMainFrame class (because that class is specified in the document template) and that the corresponding window is placed on the screen. CMainFrame is derived from the MFC class CFrameWnd, a standard frame window in the MFC class library. CMainFrame already has member functions to handle the Windows messages such a window usually has to handle (including resizing the window, collapsing it to the iconic state, and so on). Because these functions are already there, you do not have to write them—the MFC library has saved you a great deal of effort. (If you customize such a window, however, you have to override those functions.)

The derivation of CMainFrame from the CFrameWnd class as it appears in mainframe.h (see listing 2.2 for the complete listing of mainframe.h) is as follows:

```
class CMainFrame : public CFrameWnd
{
protected: // create from serialization only
    CMainFrame();
    DECLARE_DYNCREATE(CMainFrame)
        :
```

First, note the *protected* keyword. As you saw in the last chapter, you can use three keywords—public, private, and protected—to give a program access to members of a class. If members are public, the rest of the program has access to them; if they are private, it does not. And if some members of a base class are *protected*, access is the same as private for all parts of the program *except* derived classes.

That is, if you declare a member of a base class protected, as follows:

```
class animal {
protected:
    void eat(void);
    void sleep(void);
    void breathe(void);
};
```

Those members are private to the rest of the program, except classes derived from this one, as follows:

```
class animal {
protected:
    void eat(void);
    void sleep(void);
    void breathe(void);
};

class elephant : public animal {
public:
    void trumpet(void);
    void stampede(void);
};
```

Here, the protected members of animal become protected members of elephant. They are inaccessible to all parts of the program except member functions of elephant and classes derived from it. In other words, you use the keyword protected when you want to keep members of a class private in a base class and in all classes derived from it; protected enables certain members to stay hidden from the rest of the program, even in derived classes. In this case, CMainFrame's constructor is declared as a protected function.

```
class CMainFrame : public CFrameWnd
{
protected: // create from serialization only
    CMainFrame();
    DECLARE_DYNCREATE(CMainFrame)
        :
```

Next, notice the DECLARE_DYNCREATE( ) line. This macro, which is part of the MFC class library, appears in all classes that can be created dynamically from a document template by an object of class CWinApp. App Wizard and Class Wizard handle this automatically.

In mainframe.cpp, the window's constructor and destructor are ready for you to add code if you want to do so when the main window is created or destroyed.

```
CMainFrame::CMainFrame()
{
    // TODO: add member initialization code here
}

CMainFrame::~CMainFrame()
{
}
```

That is it for mainframe.h and mainframe.cpp. Together, they define the CMainFrame class, which has all the member functions needed to handle the routine Windows messages a normal window gets—you do not have to write them all yourself. Listing 2.2 is the complete listing for these two files.

 Listing 2.2. Mainfrm.Cpp and Mainfrm.h

```
******************** mainfrm.h

// mainfrm.h : interface of the CMainFrame class
//
```

```
/////////////////////////////////////////////////////////////
/////////////////////

class CMainFrame : public CFrameWnd
{
protected: // create from serialization only
    CMainFrame();
    DECLARE_DYNCREATE(CMainFrame)

// Attributes
public:

// Operations
public:

// Implementation
public:
    virtual ~CMainFrame();
#ifdef _DEBUG
    virtual     void AssertValid() const;
    virtual     void Dump(CDumpContext& dc) const;
#endif

protected:     // control bar embedded members
    CStatusBar      m_wndStatusBar;
    CToolBar       m_wndToolBar;

// Generated message map functions
protected:
    //{{AFX_MSG(CMainFrame)
    afx_msg int OnCreate(LPCREATESTRUCT lpCreateStruct);
        // NOTE - the ClassWizard will add and remove member functions here.
        //      DO NOT EDIT what you see in these blocks of generated code !
    //}}AFX_MSG
    DECLARE_MESSAGE_MAP()
};


******************** mainfrm.cpp
```

continues

Listing 2.2. continued

```cpp
// mainfrm.cpp : implementation of the CMainFrame class
//

#include "stdafx.h"
#include "first.h"

#include "mainfrm.h"

#ifdef _DEBUG
#undef THIS_FILE
static char BASED_CODE THIS_FILE[] = __FILE__;
#endif


/////////////////////////////////////////////////////////////////
/////////////////////////
// CMainFrame

IMPLEMENT_DYNCREATE(CMainFrame, CFrameWnd)

BEGIN_MESSAGE_MAP(CMainFrame, CFrameWnd)
    //{{AFX_MSG_MAP(CMainFrame)
        // NOTE - the ClassWizard will add and remove mapping macros here.
        //     DO NOT EDIT what you see in these blocks of generated code !
    ON_WM_CREATE()
    //}}AFX_MSG_MAP
END_MESSAGE_MAP()


/////////////////////////////////////////////////////////////////
/////////////////////////
// arrays of IDs used to initialize control bars

// toolbar buttons - IDs are command buttons
static UINT BASED_CODE buttons[] =
{
    // same order as in the bitmap 'toolbar.bmp'
    ID_FILE_NEW,
    ID_FILE_OPEN,
```

```
        ID_FILE_SAVE,
        ID_SEPARATOR,
        ID_EDIT_CUT,
        ID_EDIT_COPY,
        ID_EDIT_PASTE,
        ID_SEPARATOR,
        ID_FILE_PRINT,
        ID_APP_ABOUT,
};

static UINT BASED_CODE indicators[] =
{
    ID_SEPARATOR,                   // status line indicator
    ID_INDICATOR_CAPS,
    ID_INDICATOR_NUM,
    ID_INDICATOR_SCRL,
};

/////////////////////////////////////////////////////////////
////////////////////////
// CMainFrame construction/destruction

CMainFrame::CMainFrame()
{
    // TODO: add member initialization code here
}

CMainFrame::~CMainFrame()
{
}

int CMainFrame::OnCreate(LPCREATESTRUCT lpCreateStruct)
{
    if (CFrameWnd::OnCreate(lpCreateStruct) == -1)
        return -1;

    if (!m_wndToolBar.Create(this) ¦¦
        !m_wndToolBar.LoadBitmap(IDR_MAINFRAME) ¦¦
        !m_wndToolBar.SetButtons(buttons,
          sizeof(buttons)/sizeof(UINT)))
```

continues

Listing 2.2. continued

```
    {
        TRACE("Failed to create toolbar\n");
        return -1;         // fail to create
    }

    if (!m_wndStatusBar.Create(this) ||
        !m_wndStatusBar.SetIndicators(indicators,
          sizeof(indicators)/sizeof(UINT)))
    {
        TRACE("Failed to create status bar\n");
        return -1;         // fail to create
    }

    return 0;
}


/////////////////////////////////////////////////////////////////////
////////////////////////////
// CMainFrame diagnostics

#ifdef _DEBUG
void CMainFrame::AssertValid() const
{
    CFrameWnd::AssertValid();
}

void CMainFrame::Dump(CDumpContext& dc) const
{
    CFrameWnd::Dump(dc);
}

#endif //_DEBUG
```

The next section looks at the document class, CFirstDoc.

The FirstDoc Object

As I have mentioned, the document and view objects are the most important to you; the rest of the program—called the *framework* in Visual C++—is mostly handled automatically.

Understanding what the document and view objects are doing in a program is important because they form the basis of data storage and display in Visual C++ programs. As mentioned earlier, the document object stores data and the view object (a child window of the main window, which usually takes up the whole client area) is responsible for displaying it the way you want it. The main objects in a program communicate through function calls. The document object fits in, as follows:

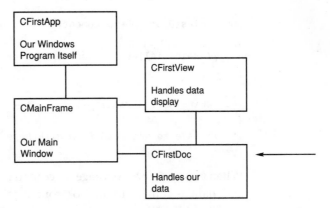

The CFirstDoc class is declared in firstdoc.h and is derived from the MFC class CDocument class like this in the following way:

```
class CFirstDoc : public CDocument
{
protected: // create from serialization only
    CFirstDoc();
    DECLARE_DYNCREATE(CFirstDoc)

// Attributes
public:

// Operations
public:
    :

        :
```

Note also the declaration of the class's constructor and the inclusion of the DECLARE_DYNCREATE() macro, which enables this class to be created on the fly (that is, when a new document is created). The firstdoc.cpp file simply contains skeleton code for functions that are discussed later.

```
CFirstDoc::CFirstDoc()
{
    // Constructor
}

CFirstDoc::~CFirstDoc()
{
    // Destructor
}

BOOL CFirstDoc::OnNewDocument()
{
    // Reinitialize new documents here
}

void CFirstDoc::Serialize()
{
    // Save to and load from disk here
}
```

When you want to add storage space for data to the document, you simply add data members to it. To store data in a CString object named m_data_string (the m_ is for member), for example, you add its declaration to the declaration of CFirstDoc, as follows:

```
class CFirstDoc : public CDocument
{
protected: // create from serialization only
    CFirstDoc();
    DECLARE_DYNCREATE(CFirstDoc)

// Attributes
public:
    CString m_data_string;

// Operations
public:
    :
```

Now you can reach that data member from the view (which is where all the action is) with GetDocument(), which returns a pointer to your document, pDoc. That pointer is used as follows:

```
pDoc->m_data_string
```

We will see a great deal more about using pointers and pointers to objects. For reference, the complete listing of firstdoc.cpp and firstdoc.h is in listing 2.3.

 Listing 2.3. Firstdoc.cpp and Firstdoc.h

```
******************** firstdoc.h
```

//
////////////////////////
```
// firstdoc.h : interface of the CFirstDoc class
//
```
//
////////////////////////

```
class CFirstDoc : public CDocument
{
protected: // create from serialization only
    CFirstDoc();
    DECLARE_DYNCREATE(CFirstDoc)

// Attributes
public:

// Operations
public:

// Implementation
public:
    virtual ~CFirstDoc();
    virtual void Serialize(CArchive& ar);      // overridden for document i/o
#ifdef _DEBUG
    virtual    void AssertValid() const;
    virtual    void Dump(CDumpContext& dc) const;
#endif
protected:
```

continues

Listing 2.3. continued

```
     virtual    BOOL    OnNewDocument();

// Generated message map functions
protected:
    //{{AFX_MSG(CFirstDoc)
        // NOTE - the ClassWizard will add and remove member functions here.
        //      DO NOT EDIT what you see in these blocks of generated code !
    //}}AFX_MSG
    DECLARE_MESSAGE_MAP()
};


********************* firstdoc.cpp

/////////////////////////////////////////////////////////////
/////////////////////////
// CFirstApp commands
// firstdoc.cpp : implementation of the CFirstDoc class
//

#include "stdafx.h"
#include "first.h"

#include "firstdoc.h"

#ifdef _DEBUG
#undef THIS_FILE
static char BASED_CODE THIS_FILE[] = __FILE__;
#endif


/////////////////////////////////////////////////////////////
/////////////////////////
// CFirstDoc

IMPLEMENT_DYNCREATE(CFirstDoc, CDocument)

BEGIN_MESSAGE_MAP(CFirstDoc, CDocument)
    //{{AFX_MSG_MAP(CFirstDoc)
        // NOTE - the ClassWizard will add and remove mapping macros here.
        //      DO NOT EDIT what you see in these blocks of generated code !
```

```
        //}}AFX_MSG_MAP
END_MESSAGE_MAP()


/////////////////////////////////////////////////////////
/////////////////////
// CFirstDoc construction/destruction

CFirstDoc::CFirstDoc()
{
    // TODO: add one-time construction code here
}


CFirstDoc::~CFirstDoc()
{
}


BOOL CFirstDoc::OnNewDocument()
{
    if (!CDocument::OnNewDocument())
        return FALSE;
    // TODO: add reinitialization code here
    // (SDI documents will reuse this document)
    return TRUE;
}


/////////////////////////////////////////////////////////
/////////////////////
// CFirstDoc serialization

void CFirstDoc::Serialize(CArchive& ar)
{
    if (ar.IsStoring())
    {
        // TODO: add storing code here
    }
    else
    {
        // TODO: add loading code here
    }
}
```

continues

Listing 2.3. continued

```
/////////////////////////////////////////////////////////////////
/////////////////////////
// CFirstDoc diagnostics

#ifdef _DEBUG
void CFirstDoc::AssertValid() const
{
    CDocument::AssertValid();
}

void CFirstDoc::Dump(CDumpContext& dc) const
{
    CDocument::Dump(dc);
}

#endif //_DEBUG
```

The FirstView Object

Finally, the view object is responsible for displaying data the way you want it. This object, which is of the CFirstView class, fits into the whole program as follows:

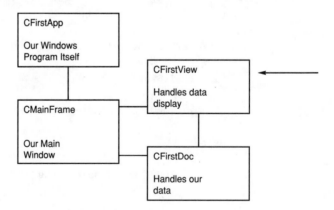

CFirstView is derived from the MFC class CView in firstvw.h, as follows:

```
class CFirstView : public CView
{
protected: // create from serialization only
    CFirstView();
    DECLARE_DYNCREATE(CFirstView)

// Attributes
public:
    CFirstDoc* GetDocument();
        :
```

When a Windows event (a mouse movement, for example) occurs, a function in the view object is called—here, that function would be OnMouseMove(). (You start adding these functions in the next chapter.) Inside such functions, you need to update the data in the document; to do that, you use the built-in function GetDocument(), which returns a pointer to the document object. This is how you connect view and document objects.

The view object is made up of a collection of OnXXX() functions that handle Windows events. You have already seen OnDraw(), for example, the function called by the CMainFrame object when the view needs to be (re)drawn (as when the client area is uncovered). To handle such redrawing, you placed the string printing code in CFirstView::OnDraw().

```
void CFirstView::OnDraw(CDC* pDC)
{
    CString hello_string = "Hello, world.";
    CFirstDoc* pDoc = GetDocument();

    pDC->TextOut(0, 0, hello_string, hello_string.GetLength());
}
```

Note that your program stores no data in the document; you do that in the next chapter.

Here you have created a CString object, hello_string, with the string Hello, world. in it. Note the call to GetDocument() that AppWizard has put in for you.

```
void  CFirstView::OnDraw(CDC*  pDC)
{
    CString hello_string = "Hello, world.";
    CFirstDoc* pDoc = GetDocument();

    pDC->TextOut(0, 0, hello_string, hello_string.GetLength());
}
```

If you wanted to, you could get data for display from the document object by using the pointer pDoc. In this program, however, you just want to display the string named hello_string; to do so, you use the device context member function TextOut(). A pointer to a device context object is passed to you in OnDraw(), and you use it to display hello_string, as follows:

```
void CFirstView::OnDraw(CDC* pDC)
{
    CString hello_string = "Hello, world.";
    CFirstDoc* pDoc = GetDocument();

    pDC->TextOut(0, 0, hello_string, hello_string.GetLength());
}
```

Finding the Member Functions of an MFC Class.
You might wonder which MFC classes have which member functions. To find out, look up the particular class in the *Class Library Reference* that comes with Visual C++. It lists each MFC class, along with all its members and what they do.

You will see more about views soon.

Listing 2.4 is the complete listing of firstvw.cpp and firstvw.h.

Listing 2.4. Firstvw.cpp and Firstvw.h

```
********************* firstvw.h
```

```
//////////////////////////////////////////////////////////////////
///////////////////////////
// firstvw.h : interface of the CFirstView class
```

```
//
////////////////////////////////////////////////////////
/////////////////////////

class CFirstView : public CView
{
protected: // create from serialization only
    CFirstView();
    DECLARE_DYNCREATE(CFirstView)

// Attributes
public:
    CFirstDoc* GetDocument();

// Operations
public:

// Implementation
public:
    virtual ~CFirstView();
    virtual void OnDraw(CDC* pDC);  // overridden to draw this view
#ifdef _DEBUG
    virtual void AssertValid() const;
    virtual void Dump(CDumpContext& dc) const;
#endif

    // Printing support
protected:
    virtual BOOL OnPreparePrinting(CPrintInfo* pInfo);
    virtual void OnBeginPrinting(CDC* pDC, CPrintInfo* pInfo);
    virtual void OnEndPrinting(CDC* pDC, CPrintInfo* pInfo);

// Generated message map functions
protected:
    //{{AFX_MSG(CFirstView)
        // NOTE - the ClassWizard will add and remove member functions here.
        //     DO NOT EDIT what you see in these blocks of generated code !
```

continues

Listing 2.4. continued

```
    //}}AFX_MSG
    DECLARE_MESSAGE_MAP()
};


#ifndef _DEBUG      // debug version in firstvw.cpp
inline CFirstDoc* CFirstView::GetDocument()
    { return (CFirstDoc*) m_pDocument; }
#endif



******************** firstvw.cpp


////////////////////////////////////////////////////////////
////////////////////////
// CFirstDoc commands
// firstvw.cpp : implementation of the CFirstView class
//

#include "stdafx.h"
#include "first.h"

#include "firstdoc.h"
#include "firstvw.h"

#ifdef _DEBUG
#undef THIS_FILE
static char BASED_CODE THIS_FILE[] = __FILE__;
#endif


////////////////////////////////////////////////////////////
////////////////////////
// CFirstView

IMPLEMENT_DYNCREATE(CFirstView, CView)


BEGIN_MESSAGE_MAP(CFirstView, CView)
    //{{AFX_MSG_MAP(CFirstView)
        // NOTE - the ClassWizard will add and remove mapping macros here.
```

```
        //    DO NOT EDIT what you see in these blocks of generated code !
    //}}AFX_MSG_MAP
    // Standard printing commands
    ON_COMMAND(ID_FILE_PRINT, CView::OnFilePrint)
    ON_COMMAND(ID_FILE_PRINT_PREVIEW, CView::OnFilePrintPreview)
END_MESSAGE_MAP()


/////////////////////////////////////////////////////////////
////////////////////////
// CFirstView construction/destruction

CFirstView::CFirstView()
{
    // TODO: add construction code here
}


CFirstView::~CFirstView()
{
}


/////////////////////////////////////////////////////////////
////////////////////////
// CFirstView drawing

void CFirstView::OnDraw(CDC* pDC)
{
    CString hello_string = "Hello, world.";
    CFirstDoc* pDoc = GetDocument();

    pDC->TextOut(0, 0, hello_string, hello_string.GetLength());
    // TODO: add draw code here
}


/////////////////////////////////////////////////////////////
////////////////////////
// CFirstView printing

BOOL CFirstView::OnPreparePrinting(CPrintInfo* pInfo)
```

continues

95

Listing 2.4. continued

```
{
    // default preparation
    return DoPreparePrinting(pInfo);
}


void CFirstView::OnBeginPrinting(CDC* /*pDC*/, CPrintInfo* /*pInfo*/)
{
    // TODO: add extra initialization before printing
}


void CFirstView::OnEndPrinting(CDC* /*pDC*/, CPrintInfo* /*pInfo*/)
{
    // TODO: add cleanup after printing
}


/////////////////////////////////////////////////////////////
////////////////////////
// CFirstView diagnostics

#ifdef _DEBUG
void CFirstView::AssertValid() const
{
    CView::AssertValid();
}

void CFirstView::Dump(CDumpContext& dc) const
{
    CView::Dump(dc);
}


CFirstDoc* CFirstView::GetDocument() // non-debug version is inline
{
    ASSERT(m_pDocument->IsKindOf(RUNTIME_CLASS(CFirstDoc)));
    return (CFirstDoc*) m_pDocument;
}
```

```
#endif //_DEBUG
```

///
/////////////////////////////
// CFirstView message handlers

That is it for the parts of your first program. You have seen a general overview of a Visual C++ program, but are short on specifics. All you have done so far is display a string in a window—you have not read any input or stored any data in the document. (All in all, your first program is not that useful.)

In the next chapter, you have a chance to put Visual C++ to work. You will start reading mouse and keyboard data, and storing it in the document.

Keyboard and Mouse Input

I

n this chapter, you are going to put Visual C++ to work in Windows by enabling your programmers to accept input, which in Windows, means accepting keyboard and mouse input.

First you will learn the different ways to read keyboard input (because this is Windows, that input comes to you through Windows messages). The two types of keyboard messages are those generated by the action of a key (like WM_KEYDOWN and WM_KEYUP) and those generated after Windows translates such messages into ASCII (WM_CHAR messages). This chapter shows you how to use them, and then shows you a sample program that reads input from the keyboard and displays it in a window.

Next, you work with the mouse, examining the variety of mouse-specific Windows messages you might receive (such as WM_MOUSEMOVE and WM_LBUTTONDOWN). You put the messages to work in a sample program of their own. Note that because you not only are accepting input, but also displaying the results of the programs, this chapter shows you a little more about text output as well. In particular, you learn that using a variable-width font (the Windows default) can create some interesting problems when you want to display and change strings in a window.

Using the Keyboard in Windows

Even in a multitasking windowing environment, you have only one keyboard. This means that even though a dozen windows might be displayed simultaneously, only *one* can actively accept keyboard input. In Windows terminology, that window has the current *focus*; the window that has the focus is the *currently active* window. You can tell which window is currently active in a Windows session: Windows highlights the caption bar at the top of the window or, if the window does not have a caption bar, Windows highlights the window's frame. Even an icon can be the active window; if it is, Windows highlights the caption text under the icon. When you use the keyboard, a stream of keyboard messages is sent to the window with the focus.

Windows Keyboard Input Conventions

In Windows, a flashing cursor (often either a vertical bar or an I-beam shape) usually indicates where text that you type will go. Note that the mouse cursor is usually referred to as the *cursor* in Windows, and what you call the cursor in DOS is called the *insertion point* or *caret* in Windows. That is, when you type text, it appears at the insertion point or caret; when you move the mouse, you are moving the cursor (not the insertion point or caret).

Also, when several buttons, listboxes, or text boxes—what Windows calls *controls*—are in a window, the user ordinarily can select which control has the focus by clicking it with the mouse. If a button has the current focus, the highlighted border indicates that the user can choose the button by pressing Enter. If the user clicks a text box instead of the highlighted button, a flashing insertion point appears in the box (and as the button loses the focus, its border returns to normal).

Furthermore, under Windows, the user expects to be able to press the Tab key to move the focus between controls in a window. That is, if the text box just mentioned follows the button in the window's *tab order*, then the user can move from the button to the text box by pressing the Tab key.

In general, the user is supposed to be able to circulate around a window's controls simply by pressing the Tab key. Note also that frequently, when a dialog box first appears, one of the buttons is already highlighted (often the button marked OK); in that case, that button is said to have the *default focus*.

In addition, certain keys do certain things. The F1 key, for example, usually is reserved for Help. F2 is supposed to correspond to the New item in menus—as in New Game, New File..., or New Spreadsheet.... If the File menu is open, Alt-X is supposed to mean the same as Exit—and so on. (To see which key conventions are standard, just use Windows applications.)

One final point about the keyboard—from the user's point of view—is that, under Windows, the user is supposed to be able to use the keyboard instead of the mouse for input operations. In some cases, this is more theoretically true than actually true—as in a graphics paint program—but in most applications, the keyboard should be able to duplicate the mouse's actions. You need to keep that in mind when you design Windows applications.

Designing the First Document

Start Visual C++ and use AppWizard to create a new project named key.mak. Select the Options... button in AppWizard and deselect the Multiple Document Interface check box as before, then create the key.mak project.

The plan of action here is to read keyboard input and store it in the document object in a string you might call data_string, as follows:

Document

data_string

Although the document stores the data, the view is responsible for reading keystrokes and updating the screen. You will arrange it so that when the user presses a key and a WM_CHAR message is generated, a member function in the view named OnChar( ) is called. The view adds the character to data_string by calling GetDocument( ) to get a pointer to the document object named pDoc, and reaching the data string like this: pDoc->data_string. After adding the new character to the data_string, the view also draws the string (now a longer one) in the window. Schematically, drawing the string in the window appears as follows:

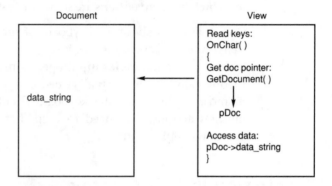

Begin by opening keydoc.h, the header file for the document class (use the Open... item in Visual C++'s File menu). Here you find the declaration of CKeyDoc, the document class, as follows:

```
class CKeyDoc : public CDocument
{
protected: // create from serialization only
    CKeyDoc();
    DECLARE_DYNCREATE(CKeyDoc)

// Attributes
public:

// Operations
public:
     :
};
```

Your only job here is to customize the document so that it holds the data, data_string. You can make this string an MFC CString object, which enables you to use predefined member functions such as GetLength( ) (which you have already seen). Because the MFC classes are built to handle strings stored in CString objects (as well as normal C strings), using a CString object is convenient. You can add the data_string object by making it an *embedded object* in the CKeyDoc class, as follows:

```
class CKeyDoc : public CDocument
{
protected: // create from serialization only
    CKeyDoc();
    DECLARE_DYNCREATE(CKeyDoc)

// Attributes
public:
    CString data_string;

// Operations
public:
    :
};
```

Now the CString object data_string will be a public member of any CKeyDoc object. That is it for the document. Now that you have added space for the data, the next step is to customize the view class, CKeyView.

Designing Your First View

The first step in designing the view class is to add key-handling capability. You have to customize CKeyView to handle keystrokes. There are only five keystroke messages (sent to the window with the current focus), as follows:

Message	Meaning
WM_KEYDOWN	Key was pressed
WM_SYSKEYDOWN	System key was pressed
WM_KEYUP	Key was released
WM_SYSKEYUP	System key was released
WM_CHAR	Translated key

As you might expect, WM_KEYDOWN is generated when a key is pressed; WM_KEYUP, when the key is released.

NOTE

In addition, Windows makes a distinction for system keystrokes (keystrokes that are commands to Windows, usually in combination with the Alt key), including Alt-Esc, which switches the active window. The messages are WM_SYSKEYDOWN and WM_SYSKEYUP—but you will not work with the system keyboard messages here.

In Visual C++, the functions OnKeyDown( ) and OnKeyUp( ) handle the WM_KEYDOWN and WM_KEYUP messages, as follows:

```
void OnKeyDown(UINT nChar, UINT nRepCnt, UINT nFlags);
void OnKeyUp(UINT nChar, UINT nRepCnt, UINT nFlags);
```

These functions are generated for you when you indicate that you want to handle the WM_KEYDOWN and WM_KEYUP messages. The parameter nFlags, which is passed to you, is coded bit by bit as follows:

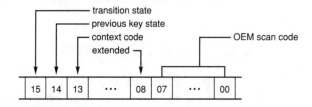

The transition state is 0 if the key was just pressed (for WM_KEYDOWN messages) and 1 if just released (WM_KEYUP messages). The previous key state is 0 if the key was previously up; 1, if previously down. The context code is 1 if the Alt key is pressed; usually it is 0 for WM_KEYDOWN and WM_KEYUP, and 1 for system messages. Also, the extended flag is 1 if the keystroke is the result of pressing or releasing one of the additional keys on the IBM enhanced keyboard (the one used with the PS/2)—note that programs usually do not use this flag.

For each keystroke or valid combination of keystrokes (such as Shift-a), the keyboard generates a unique *scan code*. This is the raw, untranslated information from the keyboard port (port 60h) on the I/O bus. You will not use this information until it has been translated (into ASCII) by Windows. The *OEM* (original equipment manufacturer) scan field holds the key's scan code as generated by the keyboard itself.

The repeat count is an indication of typematic action. If you hold down a key and generate automatic repetitions of that key, this field holds the number of repetitions. Usually, Windows does not produce a separate WM_KEYDOWN or WM_SYSKEYDOWN message for typematic action (which would flood the message queue); rather, it bunches them together and places a nonzero value in the repeat count parameter, nRepCnt.

You might notice that you still do not really know which key was pressed. The nChar parameter contains a *virtual key code*, which *does* tell you which key was pressed. A constant is defined for each keystroke (see table 3.1).

Table 3.1. Virtual Key Codes

VK_LBUTTON	VK_NEXT	VK_NUMPAD2	VK_F3
VK_RBUTTON	VK_END	VK_NUMPAD3	VK_F4
VK_CANCEL	VK_HOME	VK_NUMPAD4	VK_F5
VK_MBUTTON	VK_LEFT	VK_NUMPAD5	VK_F6
VK_BACK	VK_UP	VK_NUMPAD6	VK_F7
VK_TAB	VK_RIGHT	VK_NUMPAD7	VK_F8
VK_CLEAR	VK_DOWN	VK_NUMPAD8	VK_F9
VK_RETURN	VK_SELECT	VK_NUMPAD9	VK_F10
VK_SHIFT	VK_PRINT	VK_MULTIPLY	VK_F11
VK_CONTROL	VK_EXECUTE	VK_ADD	VK_F12
VK_MENU	VK_SNAPSHOT	VK_SEPARATOR	VK_F13
VK_PAUSE	VK_INSERT	VK_SUBTRACT	VK_F14
VK_CAPITAL	VK_DELETE	VK_DECIMAL	VK_F15
VK_ESCAPE	VK_HELP	VK_DIVIDE	VK_F16
VK_SPACE	VK_NUMPAD0	VK_F1	VK_NUMLOCK
VK_PRIOR	VK_NUMPAD1	VK_F2	VK_A-VK_Z, VK_0-VK_9

Note that table 3.1 contains codes for keys that do not normally generate a printable character, such as the function keys (VK_F1 to VK_F16) and the keyboard arrow keys (VK_UP and VK_LEFT). In fact, this is the usual way for Windows programs to read such keys. You might think that you can read all of the keys this way, because even the letters (VK_A to VK_Z) are defined—but there is a problem. Although you can figure out which key was pressed (including the keys from VK_A to VK_Z), you cannot tell the difference between upper- and lowercase letters like *A* and *a*. That is, whether you press *A* or *a*, wParam holds the value VK_A.

One way to resolve this difficulty is to use the Windows function GetKeyState( ), which can indicate the state of the Shift key (or any other key, including the mouse buttons). You use it in the following way:

```
GetKeyState(VK_SHIFT)
```

If this value is negative, the Shift key was down when the keystroke you are currently processing was generated.

NOTE

It is important to realize that GetKeyState( ) returns not the real-time state of a key, but rather the state of the key at the time the keyboard message you currently are analyzing was generated.

Reading Nonprinting Characters.
Keep in mind that WM_KEYDOWN and WM_KEYUP messages enable you to process nonprinting keys like function keys and the right- and left-arrow keys.

This is a very clumsy way to read keyboard input, however, if you are looking for characters like those in the string "Hello World." A better way is to use the WM_CHAR message, whose message-handling function is OnChar( ), is as follows:

```
void OnChar(UINT nChar, UINT nRepCnt, UINT wFlags);
```

Here the first parameter, nChar, is the ASCII code of the key that was pressed, which is what you want. You set up OnChar( ) in the View class as outlined previously, as follows:

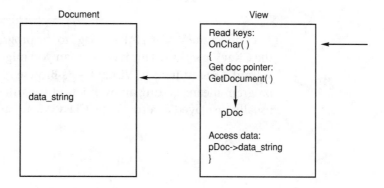

Here, your goal is to read the keys the user types. As keys are pressed, you can echo them in the window, starting at the upper left location—coordinates (0, 0). That is, when you type the letter **T**, the following appears:

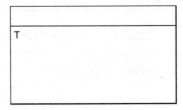

The location (0, 0) is the upper left corner of the client area; y increases going down and x increases to the right, as follows:

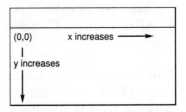

Now you can keep going, typing other characters as follows:

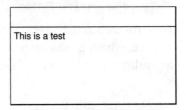

To connect the WM_CHAR message to the program, you have to work on the CKeyView class. This is easier than you might think. Select the Class Wizard... menu item in Visual C++'s Browse menu. (*Browsing* in a C++ program means getting an overview of the inherited class connections, usually displayed as a tree.) The Class Wizard appears (see figure 3.1).

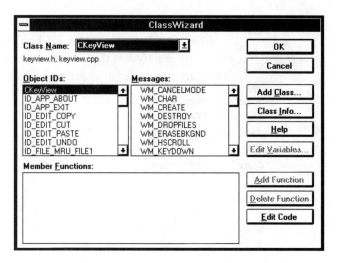

Figure 3.1. Using Class Wizard.

You can see a list of all the classes in the Object IDs box. A list of the messages those classes can intercept is in the Messages box. CKeyView is already selected at the top of the Object IDs box. Now double click the WM_CHAR line in the Messages box. The function OnChar( ) appears in the Member functions box (see figure 3.2).

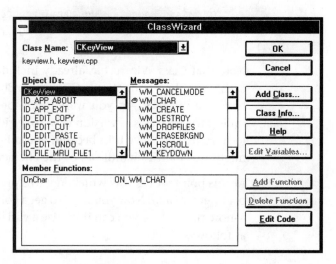

Figure 3.2. Creating a member function.

That is all it takes; now click OK to create a skeletal OnChar( ) function in CKeyView. After the Class Wizard box has disappeared, open the file keyview.cpp and look at the definition of the member functions. You can see OnChar( ) at the end, as follows:

```cpp
#include "key.h"
#include "keydoc.h"
#include "keyview.h"

CKeyView::CKeyView()
{
}

CKeyView::~CKeyView()
{
}

void CKeyView::OnDraw(CDC* pDC)
{
    CKeyDoc* pDoc = GetDocument();
}

void CKeyView::OnChar(UINT nChar, UINT nRepCnt, UINT nFlags)
{
    // TODO: Add your message handler code here and/or call default
    CView::OnChar(nChar, nRepCnt, nFlags);
}
```

Note that Class Wizard has already included code here to call the base class's OnChar( ) function—CView::OnChar( ). If you do not plan to handle a message—or you want some preliminary processing done—calling the base class's version of an overridden function is often a good idea. Here, you leave it in because you might adapt OnChar( ) later and might not want to handle all of the character messages.

At this point, you know which key was pressed—its ASCII code is in the parameter nChar. Now you need to get a pointer to the document like this —note that in C++ you can initialize a variable with a call to a function— as follows:

```
void CKeyView::OnChar(UINT nChar, UINT nRepCnt, UINT nFlags)
{
    CKeyDoc* pDoc = GetDocument();
        :
    CView::OnChar(nChar, nRepCnt, nFlags);
}
```

Now the pointer pDoc points to the document, which means that the data string in which you want to place nChar can be reached as follows:

```
pDoc->data_string
```

Storing the New Character

You already know that you can overload functions in C++. You can overload *operators*, as well. To overload the + operator, for example, all you have to do is write a function overloading the + operator as follows:

```
Cstring Cstring::operator+(Cstring second_string)
{
    //New function here.
}
```

Doing this overloads the + operator with respect to the CString class, which means that you can add two CString objects together, like this:

```
string1 = string2 + string3;
```

Visual C++ has already done this for you. You can add individual characters as well as strings to strings. To add the character in nChar to pDoc->data_string, all you have to do is to execute the following line:

```
void CKeyView::OnChar(UINT nChar, UINT nRepCnt, UINT nFlags)
{
    CKeyDoc* pDoc = GetDocument();
    pDoc->data_string += nChar;
    CView::OnChar(nChar, nRepCnt, nFlags);
     :
}
```

That is it. You have stored the new data in the document, as you planned.

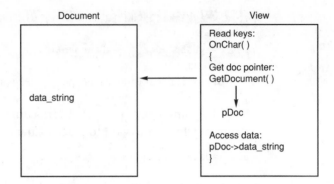

The next step is to display this data on the screen (that is the view's job). You do that by getting a device context in which to work. (Earlier, in OnDraw( ), a pointer to a device context was passed to you—here you have to get one yourself.) The simplest way to create a device context is to use the CClientDC class to create a new device context object that corresponds to the client area of the view (which is also the client area of the window). To attach a client-area device context to the view object, you need to pass a pointer to that object to CClientDC's constructor. You use the this keyword to pass the pointer.

The this Keyword

The this keyword is implicit in all objects in C++; in fact, it is a built-in pointer to the current object. The stack class's push( ) function, for example, was written as follows:

```
int stack_class::push(int push_this)
{
    if(stack_ptr >= 99)
        return 0;
    else
        stack_data[++stack_ptr] = push_this;
            return 1;
}
```

But you *could* have written the code by prefacing each variable with the this keyword, used as a pointer (note that stack_ptr becomes this->stack_ptr, and so on), as follows:

```
int stack_class::push(int push_this)
{
```

```
        if(this->stack_ptr >= 99)
                return 0;
        else
                this->stack_data[++this->stack_ptr] = push_this;
        return 1;
    }
```

Sometimes the this keyword is used just as it is here—to pass a function a pointer to the current object. In OnChar( ), it works as follows:

```
void CKeyView::OnChar(UINT nChar, UINT nRepCnt, UINT nFlags)
{
    CKeyDoc* pDoc = GetDocument();
    pDoc->data_string += nChar;
    CView::OnChar(nChar, nRepCnt, nFlags);

    CClientDC dc(this);
        :
}
```

Note that you can declare variables and objects in the middle of C++ programs this way.

Now you have a device context attached to the view. You can print in it, using TextOut( ), as you have seen before. The process of printing looks like the following code, which prints the pDoc->data_string.

```
void CKeyView::OnChar(UINT nChar, UINT nRepCnt, UINT nFlags)
{
    CKeyDoc* pDoc = GetDocument();
    pDoc->data_string += nChar;
    CView::OnChar(nChar, nRepCnt, nFlags);

    CClientDC dc(this);
    dc.TextOut(0, 0, pDoc->data_string, pDoc->data_string.GetLength());
        :
}
```

And that is really all there is to OnChar( ). At this point, the string appears on-screen as you type it, as shown in figure 3.3. You have completed your first true Windows program.

Figure 3.3. Using your first true Windows program.

You can do one or two other things here. If there were multiple views into this same document (if you split the window to show two sections of the same document, for example), you would somehow have to inform the other views that this view, the current view, had updated the document with data. That is done with the CDocument class function UpdateAllViews( ). When you call it, the document calls the OnUpDate( ) function in all currently active views, enabling them to update their displays as well.

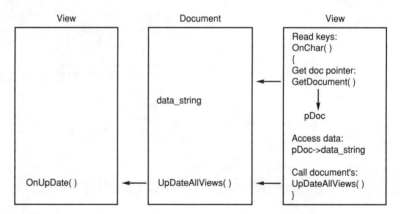

You will see more about this later. Adding it to the program is easy; just add the following line to OnChar( ):

```
void CKeyView::OnChar(UINT nChar, UINT nRepCnt, UINT nFlags)
{
    CKeyDoc* pDoc = GetDocument();
    pDoc->data_string += nChar;
    CView::OnChar(nChar, nRepCnt, nFlags);
```

```
        CClientDC dc(this);
        dc.TextOut(0, 0, pDoc->data_string, pDoc->data_string.GetLength());
        pDoc->UpdateAllViews(this, 0L, 0);
}
```

This is a typical last line in message-handling functions of view classes.

One last improvement to the program might be to add drawing code in the OnDraw( ) function so that the data is displayed correctly if the window needs to be redrawn (if the window is uncovered when another window is moved). You can do that as follows:

```
void CKeyView::OnDraw(CDC* pDC)
{
    CKeyDoc* pDoc = GetDocument();
    pDC->TextOut(0, 0, pDoc->data_string, pDoc->data_string.GetLength());
}
```

That is it. The code for this program (keyview.cpp) is in listing 3.1.

 Listing 3.1. A Key-reading Program (Key.Mak, on the disk)

```
// keyview.h : interface of the CKeyView class
//
////////////////////////////////////////////////////////////////////////
////

class CKeyView : public CView
{
protected: // create from serialization only
    CKeyView();
    DECLARE_DYNCREATE(CKeyView)

// Attributes
public:
    CKeyDoc* GetDocument();

// Operations
public:

// Implementation
```

continues

Listing 3.1. continued

```
public:
    virtual ~CKeyView();
    virtual void OnDraw(CDC* pDC);   // overridden to draw this view
#ifdef _DEBUG
    virtual void AssertValid() const;
    virtual void Dump(CDumpContext& dc) const;
#endif

    // Printing support
protected:
    virtual BOOL OnPreparePrinting(CPrintInfo* pInfo);
    virtual void OnBeginPrinting(CDC* pDC, CPrintInfo* pInfo);
    virtual void OnEndPrinting(CDC* pDC, CPrintInfo* pInfo);

// Generated message map functions
protected:
    //{{AFX_MSG(CKeyView)
    afx_msg void OnChar(UINT nChar, UINT nRepCnt, UINT nFlags);
    //}}AFX_MSG
    DECLARE_MESSAGE_MAP()
};

#ifndef _DEBUG  // debug version in keyview.cpp
inline CKeyDoc* CKeyView::GetDocument()
    { return (CKeyDoc*) m_pDocument; }
#endif

/////////////////////////////////////////////////////////////////
//////////
// keyview.cpp : implementation of the CKeyView class
//

#include "stdafx.h"
#include "key.h"

#include "keydoc.h"
#include "keyview.h"

#ifdef _DEBUG
#undef THIS_FILE
static char BASED_CODE THIS_FILE[] = __FILE__;
```

```
#endif

//////////////////////////////////////////////////////////////////////
// CKeyView

IMPLEMENT_DYNCREATE(CKeyView, CView)

BEGIN_MESSAGE_MAP(CKeyView, CView)
    //{{AFX_MSG_MAP(CKeyView)
    ON_WM_CHAR()
    //}}AFX_MSG_MAP
    // Standard printing commands
    ON_COMMAND(ID_FILE_PRINT, CView::OnFilePrint)
    ON_COMMAND(ID_FILE_PRINT_PREVIEW, CView::OnFilePrintPreview)
END_MESSAGE_MAP()

//////////////////////////////////////////////////////////////////////
// CKeyView construction/destruction

CKeyView::CKeyView()
{
    // TODO: add construction code here
}


CKeyView::~CKeyView()
{
}


//////////////////////////////////////////////////////////////////////
// CKeyView drawing

void CKeyView::OnDraw(CDC* pDC)
{
    CKeyDoc* pDoc = GetDocument();
    pDC->TextOut(0, 0, pDoc->data_string, pDoc >data_string.GetLength());
}
```

continues

Listing 3.1. continued

```
//////////////////////////////////////////////////////////////
////////////
// CKeyView printing

BOOL CKeyView::OnPreparePrinting(CPrintInfo* pInfo)
{
    // default preparation
    return DoPreparePrinting(pInfo);
}

void CKeyView::OnBeginPrinting(CDC* /*pDC*/, CPrintInfo* /
*pInfo*/)
{
    // TODO: add extra initialization before printing
}

void CKeyView::OnEndPrinting(CDC* /*pDC*/, CPrintInfo* /*pInfo*/)
{
    // TODO: add cleanup after printing
}


//////////////////////////////////////////////////////////////
////////////
// CKeyView diagnostics

#ifdef _DEBUG
void CKeyView::AssertValid() const
{
    CView::AssertValid();
}

void CKeyView::Dump(CDumpContext& dc) const
{
    CView::Dump(dc);
}

CKeyDoc* CKeyView::GetDocument() // non-debug version is inline
{
    ASSERT(m_pDocument->IsKindOf(RUNTIME_CLASS(CKeyDoc)));
    return (CKeyDoc*) m_pDocument;
}
```

```
#endif //_DEBUG

/////////////////////////////////////////////////////////////////////
//////
// CKeyView message handlers

void CKeyView::OnChar(UINT nChar, UINT nRepCnt, UINT nFlags)
{
    // TODO: Add your message handler code here and/or call default

    CKeyDoc* pDoc = GetDocument();

    pDoc->data_string += nChar;

    CView::OnChar(nChar, nRepCnt, nFlags);

    CClientDC dc(this);

    dc.TextOut(0, 0, pDoc->data_string, pDoc->data_string.GetLength());

    pDoc->UpdateAllViews(this, 0L, 0);
}


// keydoc.h : interface of the CKeyDoc class
//
/////////////////////////////////////////////////////////////////////
//////

class CKeyDoc : public CDocument
{
protected: // create from serialization only
    CKeyDoc();
    DECLARE_DYNCREATE(CKeyDoc)

// Attributes
public:

// Operations
public:
    CString data_string;
```

continues

Listing 3.1. continued

```
// Implementation
public:
    virtual ~CKeyDoc();
    virtual void Serialize(CArchive& ar);     // overridden for document i/o
#ifdef _DEBUG
    virtual void AssertValid() const;
    virtual void Dump(CDumpContext& dc) const;
#endif
protected:
    virtual BOOL    OnNewDocument();

// Generated message map functions
protected:
    //{{AFX_MSG(CKeyDoc)
        // NOTE - the Class Wizard will add and remove member functions here.
        //     DO NOT EDIT what you see in these blocks of generated code !
    //}}AFX_MSG
    DECLARE_MESSAGE_MAP()
};


//////////////////////////////////////////////////////////////////////////
// keydoc.cpp : implementation of the CKeyDoc class
//

#include "stdafx.h"
#include "key.h"

#include "keydoc.h"

#ifdef _DEBUG
#undef THIS_FILE
static char BASED_CODE THIS_FILE[] = __FILE__;
#endif


//////////////////////////////////////////////////////////////////////////
// CKeyDoc

IMPLEMENT_DYNCREATE(CKeyDoc, CDocument)

BEGIN_MESSAGE_MAP(CKeyDoc, CDocument)
    //{{AFX_MSG_MAP(CKeyDoc)
```

```
        // NOTE - the Class Wizard will add and remove mapping macros here.
        //     DO NOT EDIT what you see in these blocks of generated code !
    //}}AFX_MSG_MAP
END_MESSAGE_MAP()


/////////////////////////////////////////////////////////////////////////////
// CKeyDoc construction/destruction

CKeyDoc::CKeyDoc()
{
    // TODO: add one-time construction code here
}


CKeyDoc::~CKeyDoc()
{
}


BOOL CKeyDoc::OnNewDocument()
{
    if (!CDocument::OnNewDocument())
        return FALSE;
    // TODO: add reinitialization code here
    // (SDI documents will reuse this document)
    return TRUE;
}


/////////////////////////////////////////////////////////////////////////////
// CKeyDoc serialization

void CKeyDoc::Serialize(CArchive& ar)
{
    if (ar.IsStoring())
    {
        // TODO: add storing code here
    }
    else
    {
        // TODO: add loading code here
    }
}
```

continues

Listing 3.1. continued

```
///////////////////////////////////////////////////////////////////
////////////
// CKeyDoc diagnostics

#ifdef _DEBUG
void CKeyDoc::AssertValid() const
{
    CDocument::AssertValid();
}

void CKeyDoc::Dump(CDumpContext& dc) const
{
    CDocument::Dump(dc);
}

#endif //_DEBUG


///////////////////////////////////////////////////////////////////
////////////
// CKeyDoc commands
```

Adding a Caret to the Window

You have been able to read characters and type them in the window as follows:

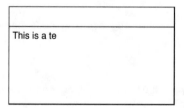

But normal Windows programs use a *caret* (the short blinking line called a cursor in DOS) to indicate where the next key you press will appear on-screen as follows:

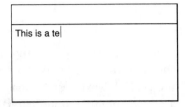

Next, you are going to add a caret to the program. Because carets are associated with objects of the CWnd class, and the view class is derived from CView (which in turn comes from CWnd), you can associate a caret with the view.

The six main caret functions are as follows:

```
CreateCaret()
CreateSolidCaret()
SetCaretPos()
ShowCaret()
HideCaret()
DestroyCaret()
```

To add a caret, you must first create it by using CreateSolidCaret( ) when the view is created. Next, you use ShowCaret( ) to start it at position (0, 0), as follows:

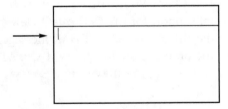

Then you use SetCaretPos( ) to advance the caret as you type, showing where the next character goes, as follows:

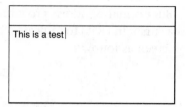

This is a test|

You might begin by starting a project named caret.mak and adding to it the code from key.mak. So far, this program does everything the key project did. Next, reserve space for the caret's location in the window in a CPoint object named caret_location. This object has two members: caret_location.x and caret_location.y. Because the caret is associated with the view, you add this object to the view class in caretvw.h, as follows:

```
class CCaretView : public CView
{
protected: // create from serialization only
    CCaretView();
    DECLARE_DYNCREATE(CCaretView)

// Attributes
public:
    CCaretDoc* GetDocument();
    CPoint caret_location;

// Operations
public:
```

Next, you have to design and display the caret when the view is created. Use Class Wizard (the last item in the Browse menu) to add skeletal support for the *OnCreate( )* view class member function. When you did this for the WM_CHAR message, the result was OnChar( ); repeat the process now for the WM_CREATE message (see figure 3.4), to add OnCreate( ) to caretvw.cpp.

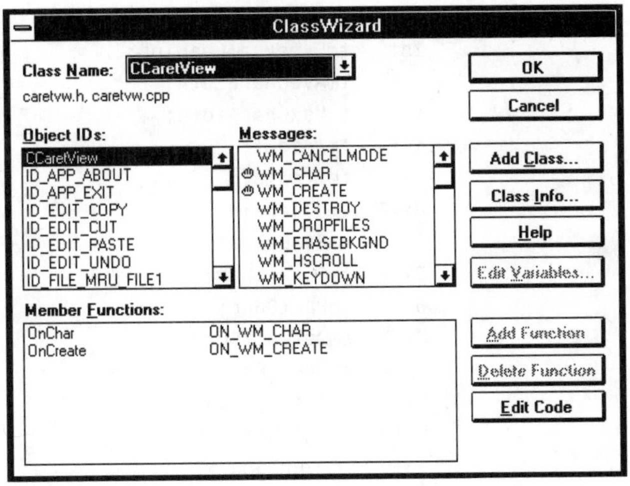

Figure 3.4. Creating a function to intercept the WM_CREATE message.

This produces the following outline for OnCreate( ), as follows:

```
int CCaretView::OnCreate(LPCREATESTRUCT lpCreateStruct)
{
    if (CView::OnCreate(lpCreateStruct) == -1)
        return -1;


    return 0;
}
```

This is the appropriate place to create the caret (not in the constructor, because the view window has not yet been created there). You can do that with the function CreateSolidCaret( ). You have to indicate the size and shape of the caret you want; to do *that* you need to determine some characteristics of the view—in particular, the average width and height of characters. That is done by creating a device context object and using its member function GetTextMetrics( ). The following code shows how the GetTextMetrics( ) function takes a pointer to a structure of type TEXTMETRIC, which holds characteristics of the font you are using.

```
typedef struct tagTEXTMETRIC
    {
    int    tmHeight;
    int    tmAscent;
    int    tmDescent;
```

```
int    tmInternalLeading;
int    tmExternalLeading;
int    tmAveCharWidth;
int    tmMaxCharWidth;
int    tmWeight;
BYTE   tmItalic;
BYTE   tmUnderlined;
BYTE   tmStruckOut;
BYTE   tmFirstChar;
BYTE   tmLastChar;
BYTE   tmDefaultChar;
BYTE   tmBreakChar;
BYTE   tmPitchAndFamily;
BYTE   tmCharSet;
int    tmOverhang;
int    tmDigitizedAspectX;
int    tmDigitizedAspectY;
} TEXTMETRIC;
```

You create a caret one-eighth the width of the average character (tmAveCharWidth/8) and the same height as the characters themselves (tmHeight). The process of creating a caret appears as follows in OnCreate( ):

```
int CCaretView::OnCreate(LPCREATESTRUCT lpCreateStruct)
{
    TEXTMETRIC tm;

    if (CView::OnCreate(lpCreateStruct) == -1)
        return -1;

    CClientDC dc(this);
    dc.GetTextMetrics(&tm);

    CreateSolidCaret(tm.tmAveCharWidth/8, tm.tmHeight);
        :
}
```

Now all you have to do is initialize the caret_location object to (0, 0) with SetCaretPos( ) and display the caret with ShowCaret( ), as follows:

```
int CCaretView::OnCreate(LPCREATESTRUCT lpCreateStruct)
{
    TEXTMETRIC tm;
```

```
    if (CView::OnCreate(lpCreateStruct) == -1)
        return -1;

    CClientDC dc(this);
    dc.GetTextMetrics(&tm);

    CreateSolidCaret(tm.tmAveCharWidth/8, tm.tmHeight);

    caret_location.x = caret_location.y = 0;
    SetCaretPos(caret_location);
    ShowCaret();

    return 0;
}
```

That is it. At this point, you can barely see the blinking caret in the upper left corner of the window's client area (see figure 3.5).

Figure 3.5. The window's caret.

The next step, of course, is to move the caret to the end of the text as you read and type. So far, OnChar( ) appears as follows:

```
void CCaretView::OnChar(UINT nChar, UINT nRepCnt, UINT nFlags)
{
    CView::OnChar(nChar, nRepCnt, nFlags);
    CCaretDoc* pDoc = GetDocument();
    pDoc->data_string += nChar;

    CClientDC dc(this);
    dc.TextOut(0, 0, pDoc->data_string, pDoc->data_string.GetLength());
}
```

Each time through, you print the full string; your job is to add the caret following the text displayed on-screen. To do so, you need to use the device context member function GetTextExtent( ), which gives you an easy way to determine how long a string will be when it is displayed. The characters in most Windows fonts vary in width. The GetTextExtent( ) function returns an object of type CSize; the length of the string you pass is stored in that object's cx member, which means that you can set the caret's x location, as follows:

```
void CCaretView::OnChar(UINT nChar, UINT nRepCnt, UINT nFlags)
{
    CView::OnChar(nChar, nRepCnt, nFlags);
    CCaretDoc* pDoc = GetDocument();
    pDoc->data_string += nChar;

    CClientDC dc(this);
    dc.TextOut(0, 0, pDoc->data_string, pDoc->data_string.GetLength());

    CSize string_size = dc.GetTextExtent(pDoc->data_string, \
        pDoc->data_string.GetLength());
    caret_location.x = string_size.cx;
        :
}
```

Now all you have to do is set the caret location on the screen to match this new location and make sure that it is displayed with ShowCaret( ). In fact, the best thing to do is hide the caret before printing and then show it again after you finish. The code appears as follows, in OnChar( ):

```
void CCaretView::OnChar(UINT nChar, UINT nRepCnt, UINT nFlags)
{
    CView::OnChar(nChar, nRepCnt, nFlags);
    CCaretDoc* pDoc = GetDocument();
    pDoc->data_string += nChar;

    CClientDC dc(this);
    HideCaret();
    dc.TextOut(0, 0, pDoc->data_string, pDoc->data_string.GetLength());

    CSize string_size = dc.GetTextExtent(pDoc->data_string, \
        pDoc->data_string.GetLength());
```

```
    caret_location.x = string_size.cx;
    SetCaretPos(caret_location);
    ShowCaret();
}
```

That is it for displaying the caret. The results of the new program appear in figure 3.6, and the new versions of caretvw.h and caretvw.cpp appear in listing 3.2. Now that you can handle text, you are ready to move on to handling the mouse.

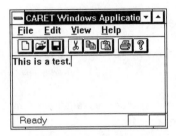

Figure 3.6. The program with working Windows caret.

Listing 3.2. Key-reading Program With Caret

```
// caretvw.h : interface of the CCaretView class
//
/////////////////////////////////////////////////////////////////
////////////

class CCaretView : public CView
{
protected: // create from serialization only
    CCaretView();
    DECLARE_DYNCREATE(CCaretView)

// Attributes
public:
    CCaretDoc* GetDocument();
    CPoint caret_location;
// Operations
public:

// Implementation
```

continues

Listing 3.2. continued

```
public:
    virtual ~CCaretView();
    virtual void OnDraw(CDC* pDC);   // overridden to draw this view
#ifdef _DEBUG
    virtual void AssertValid() const;
    virtual void Dump(CDumpContext& dc) const;
#endif

    // Printing support
protected:
    virtual BOOL OnPreparePrinting(CPrintInfo* pInfo);
    virtual void OnBeginPrinting(CDC* pDC, CPrintInfo* pInfo);
    virtual void OnEndPrinting(CDC* pDC, CPrintInfo* pInfo);

// Generated message map functions
protected:
    //{{AFX_MSG(CCaretView)
    afx_msg void OnChar(UINT nChar, UINT nRepCnt, UINT nFlags);
    afx_msg int OnCreate(LPCREATESTRUCT lpCreateStruct);
    //}}AFX_MSG
    DECLARE_MESSAGE_MAP()
};

#ifndef _DEBUG   // debug version in caretvw.cpp
inline CCaretDoc* CCaretView::GetDocument()
    { return (CCaretDoc*) m_pDocument; }
#endif

/////////////////////////////////////////////////////////////////////
/////////
// caretvw.cpp : implementation of the CCaretView class
//

#include "stdafx.h"
#include "caret.h"

#include "caretdoc.h"
#include "caretvw.h"

#ifdef _DEBUG
#undef THIS_FILE
```

```
static char BASED_CODE THIS_FILE[] = __FILE__;
#endif

//////////////////////////////////////////////////////////////////
////////////
// CCaretView

IMPLEMENT_DYNCREATE(CCaretView, CView)

BEGIN_MESSAGE_MAP(CCaretView, CView)
    //{{AFX_MSG_MAP(CCaretView)
    ON_WM_CHAR()
    ON_WM_CREATE()
    //}}AFX_MSG_MAP
    // Standard printing commands
    ON_COMMAND(ID_FILE_PRINT, CView::OnFilePrint)
    ON_COMMAND(ID_FILE_PRINT_PREVIEW, CView::OnFilePrintPreview)
END_MESSAGE_MAP()

//////////////////////////////////////////////////////////////////
////////////
// CCaretView construction/destruction

CCaretView::CCaretView()
{
    // TODO: add construction code here
}

CCaretView::~CCaretView()
{
}

//////////////////////////////////////////////////////////////////
////////////
// CCaretView drawing

void CCaretView::OnDraw(CDC* pDC)
{
    CCaretDoc* pDoc = GetDocument();

    // TODO: add draw code here
}
```

continues

Listing 3.2. continued

```
/////////////////////////////////////////////////////////////////////
/////////
// CCaretView printing

BOOL CCaretView::OnPreparePrinting(CPrintInfo* pInfo)
{
    // default preparation
    return DoPreparePrinting(pInfo);
}

void CCaretView::OnBeginPrinting(CDC* /*pDC*/, CPrintInfo* /*pInfo*/)
{
    // TODO: add extra initialization before printing
}

void CCaretView::OnEndPrinting(CDC* /*pDC*/, CPrintInfo* /*pInfo*/)
{
    // TODO: add cleanup after printing
}


/////////////////////////////////////////////////////////////////////
/////////
// CCaretView diagnostics

#ifdef _DEBUG
void CCaretView::AssertValid() const
{
    CView::AssertValid();
}

void CCaretView::Dump(CDumpContext& dc) const
{
    CView::Dump(dc);
}

CCaretDoc* CCaretView::GetDocument() // non-debug version is inline
```

```
    {
        ASSERT(m_pDocument->IsKindOf(RUNTIME_CLASS(CCaretDoc)));
        return (CCaretDoc*) m_pDocument;
    }


    #endif //_DEBUG


    /////////////////////////////////////////////////////////////////////
    //////
    // CCaretView message handlers

    void CCaretView::OnChar(UINT nChar, UINT nRepCnt, UINT nFlags)
    {
        CView::OnChar(nChar, nRepCnt, nFlags);
        CCaretDoc* pDoc = GetDocument();
        pDoc->data_string += nChar;

        CClientDC dc(this);
        HideCaret();
        dc.TextOut(0, 0, pDoc->data_string, pDoc >data_string.GetLength());

        CSize string_size = dc.GetTextExtent(pDoc->data_string, \
            pDoc->data_string.GetLength());
        caret_location.x = string_size.cx;
        SetCaretPos(caret_location);
        ShowCaret();


    }


    int CCaretView::OnCreate(LPCREATESTRUCT lpCreateStruct)
    {
        TEXTMETRIC tm;

        if (CView::OnCreate(lpCreateStruct) == -1)
            return -1;


        CClientDC dc(this);
        dc.GetTextMetrics(&tm);


        CreateSolidCaret(tm.tmAveCharWidth/8, tm.tmHeight);
```

continues

Listing 3.2. continued

```
caret_location.x = caret_location.y = 0;
SetCaretPos(caret_location);
ShowCaret();

return 0;
}
```

The Mouse and Mouse Events

As you might expect, mouse events such as clicking, double-clicking, and moving are communicated to you through Windows messages as follows:

Message	Meaning
WM_MOUSEMOVE	Mouse was moved
WM_LBUTTONUP	Left button up
WM_LBUTTONDBLCLK	Left button double-click
WM_LBUTTONDOWN	Left button down
WM_RBUTTONUP	Right button up
WM_RBUTTONDBLCLK	Right button double-click
WM_RBUTTONDOWN	Right button down
WM_MBUTTONUP	Middle button up
WM_MBUTTONDBLCLK	Middle button double-click
WM_MBUTTONDOWN	Middle button down

Note also that Windows does not generate a WM_MOUSEMOVE message for every pixel location over which the mouse cursor travels. Instead, as the mouse moves, Windows sends only so many messages a second, as you will see when you construct the paint application.

> **Controlling the Mouse.**
> Another important bit of information is that if the user moves the mouse out of the window—in Windows, moving the mouse and the mouse cursor are treated as semantically equal—you may get a WM_LBUTTONDOWN message without ever getting a WM_LBUTTONUP message (or the reverse). Beware of programming these messages in pairs.

The preceding mouse messages all refer to the client area of the window—the area under your control. But the program also sees messages that refer to other areas (such as the menu bar; the system menu, if one exists; and so on). Using these messages, Windows knows when to move, resize, or close the window. Although Windows applications rarely use such messages, here they are for reference (note that *NC* stands for *nonclient area*).

Message	Meaning
WM_NCMOUSEMOVE	Nonclient mouse move
WM_NCLBUTTONDOWN	Nonclient left button down
WM_NCLBUTTONUP	Nonclient left button up
WM_NCLBUTTONDBLCLK	Nonclient left button double-click
WM_NCRBUTTONDOWN	Nonclient right button down
WM_NCRBUTTONUP	Nonclient right button up
WM_NCRBUTTONDBLCLK	Nonclient right button double-click
WM_NCMBUTTONDOWN	Nonclient middle button down
WM_NCMBUTTONUP	Nonclient middle button up
WM_NCMBUTTONDBLCLK	Nonclient middle button double-click

Note that because these messages refer to nonclient areas, they cannot use client-area coordinates (unless they use negative values). Rather, they use *screen-area coordinates* like this (starting in the screen's upper left corner), as follows:

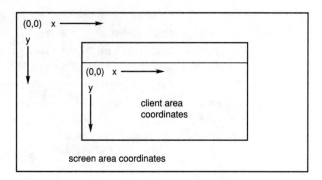

For you, the most important messages involve the right and left buttons—WM_LBUTTONDOWN, WM_LBUTTONUP, WM_RBUTTONDOWN, and WM_RBUTTONUP. By using these messages and decoding the data sent to you in the associated OnXXX() functions, you can determine the location of the mouse cursor some action was taken with the buttons.

Using the Mouse in Code

Mouse messages make using information from the direct mouse easy. To move the text insertion point to a new location on the screen, you start at (0,0), as follows:

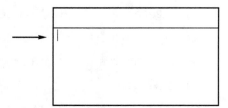

With the caret at that location, you can type the following message:

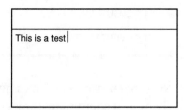

Next, you might move the mouse cursor somewhere else and click the mouse. The caret should then move to that location, as follows:

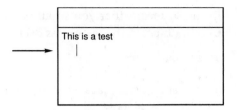

You should be able to type again, as follows:

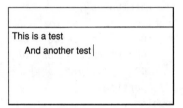

You do this by keeping track not only of the caret location (in caret_location), but also the location at the beginning of the string, in a new origin on the screen called origin_location.

You always print the string starting at the position origin_location in the window. When you start the program, origin_location is set to the point (0, 0) in the client area, as follows:

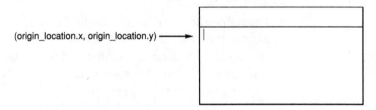

If the mouse moves the caret to some other location, you reset the origin_location there so that you can print text starting at that point, as follows:

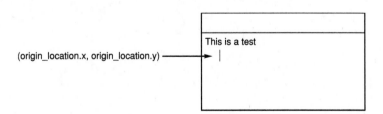

Doing so means that you should add origin_location as an embedded CPoint object in the view class declaration in caretvw.h.

```
class CCaretView  :  public CView
{
protected:  //  create from serialization only
    CCaterView () ;
    DECLARE_DYNCREATE(CCaretView)

// Attributes
public:
    CCaretDoc* GetDocument();
    CPoint caret_location;
    CPoint origin_location;
// Operations
public:
        :
```

(Note that because setting a new origin affects only the way data is displayed, not the way it is stored, you do not make this change to the document class.)

Now you have to enable the program to handle button clicks—specifically, you want to move the origin location when the user clicks the mouse somewhere in the window's client area.

To enable the program to handle button clicks, because you need to handle the WM_LBUTTONDOWN message, you use Class Wizard to create a skeletal function named OnLButtonDown( ). Start Class Wizard (the last item in the Browse menu) and add the WM_LBUTTONDOWN message to CCaretView (see figure 3.7).

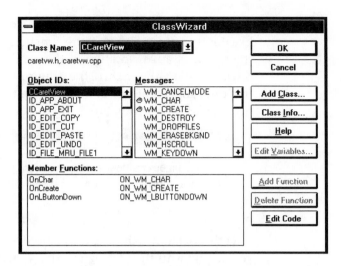

Figure 3.7. Intercepting a mouse message.

Click on the OK button now to add OnLButtonDown( ) to the class CCaretView. In caretvw.cpp, that function appears as follows:

```
void CCaretView::OnLButtonDown(UINT nFlags, CPoint point)
{
    CView::OnLButtonDown(nFlags, point);

}
```

The nFlags parameter is an unsigned integer that can take the following values, which indicate the state of the mouse buttons (and associated keyboard keys).

Value	Explanation
MK_CONTROL	Control key was down
MK_LBUTTON	Left mouse button down
MK_MBUTTON	Middle mouse button down
MK_RBUTTON	Right mouse button down
MK_SHIFT	Shift key was down

The point parameter, an object of class CPoint, holds the screen location like this: (point.x, point.y). If this function is called, the user has clicked the mouse at a new location in the window; you should set both the origin_location (the origin of the string on-screen) and the caret_location (the caret goes at the end of the string, but you set the string length to 0 here to start a new string) to the new mouse location, as follows:

```
void CCaretView::OnLButtonDown(UINT nFlags, CPoint point)
{
    CView::OnLButtonDown(nFlags, point);
    origin_location = caret_location = point;
        :
}
```

After the user moves the origin, you need to clear the string's data, which you can do with the CString member function Empty( ). First, you use GetDocument( ) to reach the document. Then you clear the string, as follows:

```
void CCaretView::OnLButtonDown(UINT nFlags, CPoint point)
{
    CView::OnLButtonDown(nFlags, point);
    origin_location = caret_location = point;

    CCaretDoc* pDoc = GetDocument();

    pDoc->data_string.Empty();
        :
}
```

Finally, you hide the caret, move it to its new position, and display it again as follows:

```
void CCaretView::OnLButtonDown(UINT nFlags, CPoint point)
{
    CView::OnLButtonDown(nFlags, point);
    origin_location = caret_location = point;

    CCaretDoc* pDoc = GetDocument();

    pDoc->data_string.Empty();

    HideCaret();
    SetCaretPos(caret_location);
```

```
    ShowCaret();
}
```

Note that hiding the caret before moving it is a good idea—otherwise, you might leave its image in the old location (if it was blinking on when you moved it).

Now, of course, you have to update OnChar( ). When the user presses keys, you want the text displayed to start at the new location, origin_location. You do that like this in the TextOut( ) call, as follows:

```
void CCaretView::OnChar(UINT nChar, UINT nRepCnt, UINT nFlags)
{
    CView::OnChar(nChar, nRepCnt, nFlags);

    CCaretDoc* pDoc = GetDocument();

    pDoc->data_string += nChar;

    CClientDC dc(this);
    HideCaret();
    dc.TextOut(origin_location.x, origin_location.y, \
        pDoc->data_string, pDoc->data_string.GetLength());
        :
}
```

The string is displayed starting at the new origin, as it should be. Now that you have printed the string, you want to set the new caret position to the end of the string, which starts at origin_location, not (0, 0). (Caret_location.y was already set when the user moved the mouse and clicked.) You update caret_location.x as follows:

```
void CCaretView::OnChar(UINT nChar, UINT nRepCnt, UINT nFlags)
{
    CView::OnChar(nChar, nRepCnt, nFlags);

    CCaretDoc* pDoc = GetDocument();

    pDoc->data_string += nChar;

    CClientDC dc(this);
    HideCaret();
    dc.TextOut(origin_location.x, origin_location.y, \
        pDoc->data_string, pDoc->data_string.GetLength());
```

```
CSize string_size = dc.GetTextExtent(pDoc->data_string, \
    pDoc->data_string.GetLength());
caret_location.x = origin_location.x + string_size.cx;
SetCaretPos(caret_location);
ShowCaret();


}
```

That is all there is to it. Now you can type in the window, click the mouse in a new location, and type there, as shown in figure 3.8. The new caretvw.h, and caretvw.cpp files are in listing 3.3. You should add code to OnDraw( ) if you want the window redrawn properly after it is uncovered.

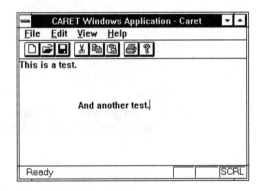

Figure 3.8. Moving the insertion caret.

 Listing 3.3. Mouse-enabled CCaretView Class

```
// caretvw.h : interface of the CCaretView class
//
/////////////////////////////////////////////////////////////////////
////////////

class CCaretView : public CView
{
protected: // create from serialization only
    CCaretView();
    DECLARE_DYNCREATE(CCaretView)
```

```
// Attributes
public:
    CCaretDoc* GetDocument();
    CPoint caret_location;
    CPoint origin_location;
// Operations
public:

// Implementation
public:
    virtual ~CCaretView();
    virtual void OnDraw(CDC* pDC);   // overridden to draw this view
#ifdef _DEBUG
    virtual void AssertValid() const;
    virtual void Dump(CDumpContext& dc) const;
#endif

    // Printing support
protected:
    virtual BOOL OnPreparePrinting(CPrintInfo* pInfo);
    virtual void OnBeginPrinting(CDC* pDC, CPrintInfo* pInfo);
    virtual void OnEndPrinting(CDC* pDC, CPrintInfo* pInfo);

// Generated message map functions
protected:
    //{{AFX_MSG(CCaretView)
    afx_msg void OnChar(UINT nChar, UINT nRepCnt, UINT nFlags);
    afx_msg int OnCreate(LPCREATESTRUCT lpCreateStruct);
    afx_msg void OnLButtonDown(UINT nFlags, CPoint point);
    //}}AFX_MSG
    DECLARE_MESSAGE_MAP()
};

#ifndef _DEBUG  // debug version in caretvw.cpp
inline CCaretDoc* CCaretView::GetDocument()
    { return (CCaretDoc*) m_pDocument; }
#endif

/////////////////////////////////////////////////////////////////
//////////
// caretvw.cpp : implementation of the CCaretView class
//
```

continues

Listing 3.3. continued

```
#include "stdafx.h"
#include "caret.h"

#include "caretdoc.h"
#include "caretvw.h"

#ifdef _DEBUG
#undef THIS_FILE
static char BASED_CODE THIS_FILE[] = __FILE__;
#endif


/////////////////////////////////////////////////////////////////
////////////
// CCaretView

IMPLEMENT_DYNCREATE(CCaretView, CView)

BEGIN_MESSAGE_MAP(CCaretView, CView)
    //{{AFX_MSG_MAP(CCaretView)
    ON_WM_CHAR()
    ON_WM_CREATE()
    ON_WM_LBUTTONDOWN()
    //}}AFX_MSG_MAP
    // Standard printing commands
    ON_COMMAND(ID_FILE_PRINT, CView::OnFilePrint)
    ON_COMMAND(ID_FILE_PRINT_PREVIEW, CView::OnFilePrintPreview)
END_MESSAGE_MAP()


/////////////////////////////////////////////////////////////////
////////////
// CCaretView construction/destruction

CCaretView::CCaretView()
{
    // TODO: add construction code here
}

CCaretView::~CCaretView()
{
}
```

```
///////////////////////////////////////////////////////////////////
//////////
// CCaretView drawing

void CCaretView::OnDraw(CDC* pDC)
{
    CCaretDoc* pDoc = GetDocument();

    // TODO: add draw code here
}


///////////////////////////////////////////////////////////////////
//////////
// CCaretView printing

BOOL CCaretView::OnPreparePrinting(CPrintInfo* pInfo)
{
    // default preparation
    return DoPreparePrinting(pInfo);
}

void CCaretView::OnBeginPrinting(CDC* /*pDC*/, CPrintInfo* /*pInfo*/
)
{
    // TODO: add extra initialization before printing
}

void CCaretView::OnEndPrinting(CDC* /*pDC*/, CPrintInfo* /*pInfo*/)
{
    // TODO: add cleanup after printing
}




///////////////////////////////////////////////////////////////////
//////////
// CCaretView diagnostics

#ifdef _DEBUG
```

continues

Listing 3.3. continued

```
void CCaretView::AssertValid() const
{
    CView::AssertValid();
}

void CCaretView::Dump(CDumpContext& dc) const
{
    CView::Dump(dc);
}

CCaretDoc* CCaretView::GetDocument() // non-debug version is inline
{
    ASSERT(m_pDocument->IsKindOf(RUNTIME_CLASS(CCaretDoc)));
    return (CCaretDoc*) m_pDocument;
}

#endif //_DEBUG


/////////////////////////////////////////////////////////////////////
//////////
// CCaretView message handlers

void CCaretView::OnChar(UINT nChar, UINT nRepCnt, UINT nFlags)
{
    // TODO: Add your message handler code here and/or call default

    CView::OnChar(nChar, nRepCnt, nFlags);

    CCaretDoc* pDoc = GetDocument();

    pDoc->data_string += nChar;

    CClientDC dc(this);
    HideCaret();
    dc.TextOut(origin_location.x, origin_location.y, \
        pDoc->data_string, pDoc->data_string.GetLength());

    CSize string_size = dc.GetTextExtent(pDoc->data_string, \
        pDoc->data_string.GetLength());
    caret_location.x = origin_location.x + string_size.cx;
```

```
        SetCaretPos(caret_location);
        ShowCaret();


}


int CCaretView::OnCreate(LPCREATESTRUCT lpCreateStruct)
{
    TEXTMETRIC tm;

    if (CView::OnCreate(lpCreateStruct) == -1)
        return -1;

    CClientDC dc(this);
    dc.GetTextMetrics(&tm);

    CreateSolidCaret(tm.tmAveCharWidth/8, tm.tmHeight);

    caret_location.x = caret_location.y = 0;
    origin_location.x = origin_location.y = 0;
    SetCaretPos(caret_location);
    ShowCaret();


    // TODO: Add your specialized creation code here

    return 0;
}


void CCaretView::OnLButtonDown(UINT nFlags, CPoint point)
{
    CView::OnLButtonDown(nFlags, point);
    origin_location = caret_location = point;

    CCaretDoc* pDoc = GetDocument();

    pDoc->data_string.Empty();

    HideCaret();
    SetCaretPos(caret_location);
    ShowCaret();
}
```

That is how to put the mouse to work—by using the mouse messages. You learn more about using the mouse later, when you put together the paint program. Meanwhile, you are going to learn about another popular Windows topic—how to create and use menus.

Menus

We are all familiar with menus, an extraordinarily popular feature of Windows. Through menus, users can select from among a variety of program options. In this chapter, which shows you all of the techniques you need to handle menus, you learn how to do the following:

▼ Interface a menu to your program

▼ Add accelerator keys

▼ Gray (disable) menu items

▼ Add check marks to menu items

You even see how to add menu items at run time (when you write a telephone book program that enables you to add people's names to a menu at run time).

Menu Conventions

You will be adding *pop-up menus*—also called *drop-down menus* or *submenus*—to your programs; this type of menu appears on command. At the top of the window, directly below the title bar, is the program's *menu bar*—also called the *main menu* or *top-level menu,* as follows:

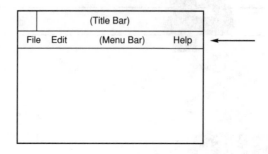

This example includes three of the most common menus: File, Edit, and Help. When the user selects one of these names, using either the mouse or keyboard, the corresponding pop-up menu appears. Suppose, for example, that the user selects the File menu, as follows:

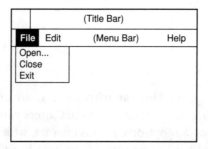

It is standard for Windows applications to have a File menu (even if they do not handle files), because users expect it. The final menu item in the File menu is almost always the Exit item, which enables the user to quit the program. Note the *ellipsis*—three dots—that follow the Open... item; an ellipsis indicates to the user that selecting this item opens a dialog box. Other standard ways of working with menu items include graying inappropriate menu items and adding check marks in front of items to indicate that a certain option is (and will remain) selected. Your programs should adhere to these user expectations.

Adding Menus to Your Programs

You can create a menu example yourself. Note that Visual C++ gives your window a File, Edit, View, and Help menu by default. You can add a Hello menu with one item (call it the Hello item), as follows:

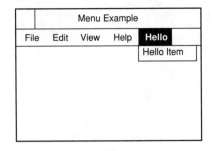

When the user selects that item, you can print `Hello, world.` in the window's client area, as follows:

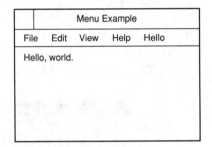

In Windows, you (usually) design *resources*—menus, icons, and dialog boxes—before adding them to a program. Before you write any C++ code, for example, you can design the shape, location, type, and size of dialog boxes (using the App Studio) and place that specification into a *resource file* (with the extension .rc). You can also design menus by using the App Studio. After you design the menu, we will examine the lines App Studio added to the .rc file.

Creating the Menu

Now, by using App Wizard, you can create the menu project (menu.mak). Make it a single window—make sure that the Multiple Document Interface check box is not checked. After you create this new project, Visual C++ automatically opens it. If you create and run menu.exe at this point, you will see the window shown in figure 4.1, which already includes the basic Visual C++ menus.

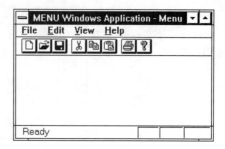

Figure 4.1. Beginning the menu project.

Now, to add your own Hello menu, start App Studio from the Tools menu. In App Studio's Type box, click on the menu icon; a menu icon called IDR_MAINFRAME appears in the Resources box (see fig. 4.2). The *IDR* prefix stands for *resource ID*; when you create menu items, they have the prefix *IDM* (for *menu ID*), following the standard Windows procedure.

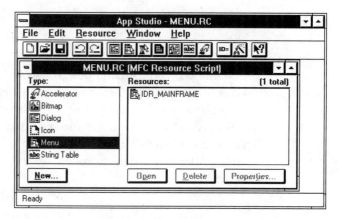

Figure 4.2. Visual C++'s App Studio.

The reason you see IDR_MAINFRAME here is that the menus are connected to the main (frame) window, not to your view. Note that this makes matters a little trickier when you need to alter that menu from inside the view. Double click IDR_MAINFRAME now to open your program's menu system (see figure 4.3).

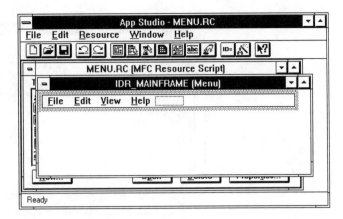

Figure 4.3. The Menu Editor.

The small dotted box in the menu bar indicates that App Studio is ready to add a new menu to the menu bar; here, you will be adding the Hello menu. Double click the dotted box in the menu bar now, to open the Menu Item Properties box shown in figure 4.4. Type Hello as the new menu's Caption (see figure 4.4). Now close the dialog box by clicking the small system box in its upper left corner.

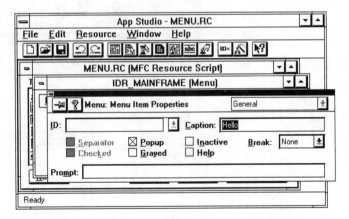

Figure 4.4. Creating a new menu.

Figure 4.5 shows the new menu in your program's menu bar. As you can see, the dotted-line box has moved one space to the right, ready for you to add another menu.

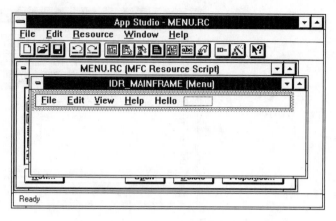

Figure 4.5. The new menu.

Instead of adding a new menu, open the new Hello menu by clicking it. A new dotted box appears in it, as shown in figure 4.6. Double-click that box now; the Menu Item Properties box opens again.

Figure 4.6. Creating a new menu item.

Give this new menu item the ID IDM_HELLO and the caption Hello Item, as shown in figure 4.7. App Studio gives this constant, IDM_HELLO, a value by itself—what is important for you is the name IDM_HELLO, which you can use now in Class Wizard. Now save the new menu system with App Studio's Save menu item and then exit App Studio.

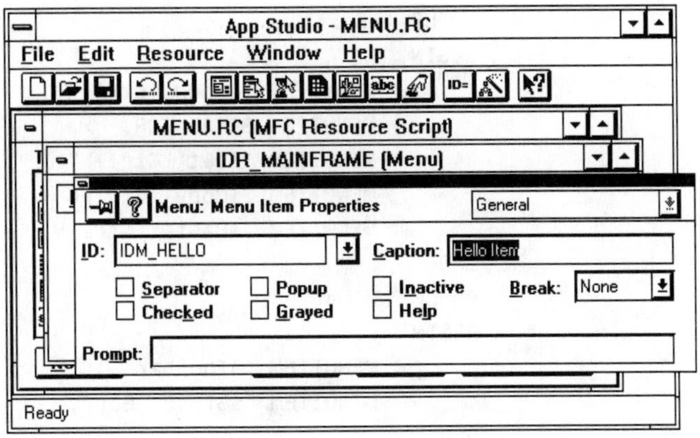

Figure 4.7. Editing the new menu item.

Now take a look at what App Studio has actually done. Look inside your project's resource file (menu.rc) at the section that sets up the menu system, which appears as follows:

```
IDR_MAINFRAME MENU PRELOAD DISCARDABLE
BEGIN
    POPUP "&File"
    BEGIN
        MENUITEM "&New\tCtrl+N",        ID_FILE_NEW
        MENUITEM "&Open...\tCtrl+O",     ID_FILE_OPEN
        MENUITEM "&Save\tCtrl+S",        ID_FILE_SAVE
        MENUITEM "Save &As...",          ID_FILE_SAVE_AS
        MENUITEM SEPARATOR
        MENUITEM "&Print...\tCtrl+P",    ID_FILE_PRINT
        MENUITEM "Print Pre&view",       ID_FILE_PRINT_PREVIEW
        MENUITEM "P&rint Setup...",      ID_FILE_PRINT_SETUP
        MENUITEM SEPARATOR
        MENUITEM "Recent File",          ID_FILE_MRU_FILE1, GRAYED
        MENUITEM SEPARATOR
        MENUITEM "E&xit",                ID_APP_EXIT
    END
```

```
        POPUP "&Edit"
        BEGIN
                MENUITEM "&Undo\tCtrl+Z",        ID_EDIT_UNDO
                MENUITEM SEPARATOR
                MENUITEM "Cu&t\tCtrl+X",          ID_EDIT_CUT
                MENUITEM "&Copy\tCtrl+C",         ID_EDIT_COPY
                MENUITEM "&Paste\tCtrl+V",        ID_EDIT_PASTE
        END
        POPUP "&View"
        BEGIN
                MENUITEM "&Toolbar",             ID_VIEW_TOOLBAR
                MENUITEM "&Status Bar",          ID_VIEW_STATUS_BAR
        END
        POPUP "&Help"
        BEGIN
                MENUITEM "&About MENU...",        ID_APP_ABOUT
        END
        POPUP "Hello"
        BEGIN
                MENUITEM "Hello Item",            IDM_HELLO
        END
END
```

Almost all of this file has to do with the default menus Visual C++ places in your program. Soon you will more thoroughly examine the options used there. For now, however, take a look at the last four lines, which specify the menu and menu item you have just created. These lines appear as follows:

```
    POPUP "Hello"
    BEGIN
            MENUITEM "Hello Item",            IDM_HELLO
    END
```

As you can see, the Hello menu is a pop-up menu that contains one item—"Hello Item"—to which the constant value IDM_HELLO is connected.

The value App Studio has given to IDM_HELLO is at the top of the file resource.h, as follows:

```
// App Studio generated include file.
// Used by MENU.RC
//
    #define IDR_MAINFRAME                      2
    #define IDD_ABOUTBOX                     100
    #define IDM_HELLO                      32768
        .
        .
        .
```

You do not have to worry about providing values for IDM constants or editing the resource file menu.rc. Windows programmers used to have to work directly with the lines of a resource file, but App Studio handles that for you here.

Now that you have added the Hello menu with its Hello Item menu item to your program, the next step is to connect it to your code so that you can print your message when that item is selected, as follows:

```
┌──┬───────────────────────────────────┐
│  │           Menu Example            │
├──┴────┬──────┬──────┬──────┬─────────┤
│ File  │ Edit │ View │ Help │ Hello   │
├───────┴──────┴──────┴──────┴─────────┤
│ Hello, world.                        │
│                                      │
│                                      │
│                                      │
│                                      │
│                                      │
└──────────────────────────────────────┘
```

The next section shows you how to do that with Class Wizard.

Connecting Menu Items to Code

You might recall that you were able to use Class Wizard to connect Windows messages like WM_CREATE to your program. As you might expect, a Windows message lets you know when the user selects a menu item. Start Class Wizard from the Browse menu and make sure that the view class CMenuView is selected in the Class Name box (see figure 4.8). You will add the code that handles the Hello item to your view class (because you will not store any data here).

Now you will connect a function to the Object ID IDM_HELLO. After you connect it, that function will be called when the Hello Item menu item is selected. Find IDM_HELLO in the Object IDs box and click on it, as shown in figure 4.8.

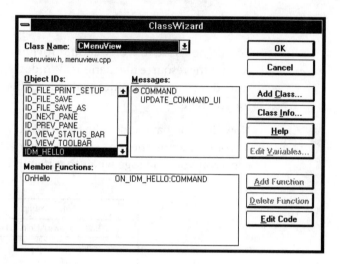

Figure 4.8. Connecting a menu item to code.

Two types of Windows messages—COMMAND and UPDATE_ COMMAND_UI—will appear in the Messages box. Click on COMMAND here. (A WM_COMMAND message is actually what is generated when a menu item is selected.) You will see more about the other type of message, UPDATE_COMMAND_UI, later.

In a dialog box, Class Wizard suggests the name OnHello() for this new function. Accept that name and close Class Wizard. Now, open menuview.cpp so that you can see OnHello(), the new member function in your view class, CMenuView, as follows:

```
void CMenuView::OnHello( )
{
    // TODO: Add your command handler code here

}
```

All you want to do here is print your message in the window. First, set up the text in a CString object, as follows:

```
void CMenuView::OnHello()
{
 CString hello_string = "Hello, world.";
    :

}
```

Next, you create a device context object and use its member function, TextOut(), to print the following message:

```
void CMenuView::OnHello()
{
    CString hello_string = "Hello, world.";
    CClientDC dc(this);


    dc.TextOut(0, 0, hello_string, hello_string.GetLength());

}
```

And that is it. The new menu looks like the one in figure 4.9; selecting it causes your message to appear (see figure 4.10). Your first menu program is a success. You have seen how to create entirely new menus as well as menu items. Although the menu you created here is an entirely new one, note that you can use this process to add menu items to the default menus.

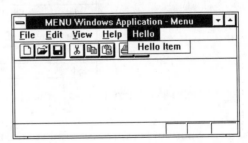

Figure 4.9. The menu at work.

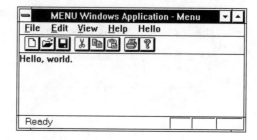

Figure 4.10. Your menu program's message.

Adding Shortcut Keys in Windows

In some Windows menus and menu items, underlined letters indicate *shortcut* keys (see figure 4.11). When a menu with shortcut keys is open, the user can select a particular menu or menu item by simply pressing Alt and the shortcut key. The user can press Alt-F, for example, to open the File menu when the user is running your program (see figure 4.11).

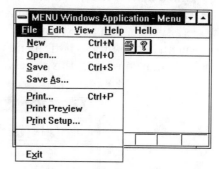

Figure 4.11. Shortcut keys in the File menu.

Shortcut keys are easy to add to the menu. To add them, open App Studio again and select the menu IDR_MAINFRAME, which corresponds to your main frame window's menu system. Now double-click on the Hello menu; the Menu Item Properties dialog box opens.

NOTE

One important rule about shortcut keys is that, to avoid confusion, they must be unique at their own level. In other words, no two menu names should have the same shortcut key in the same menu bar.

To choose the shortcut key for the Hello menu, you need to see which letters are used for other menus. Because *H* is already used by the Help menu and *E* is used by the Edit menu, you can use the first *L* in Hello as this menu's shortcut key. To design a shortcut key, you type an ampersand (&) in front of the appropriate letter in the name of the menu (or menu item). Here, you will change Hello to He&llo. Then close the Menu Item Properties box by clicking its system box. Next, open the Hello menu by clicking it and double-click on the Hello Item. You can make the *I* in Item the shortcut key here; change the name of this item to Hello &Item, as shown in figure 4.12. Finally, save the changes with App Studio's Save by selecting that menu item.

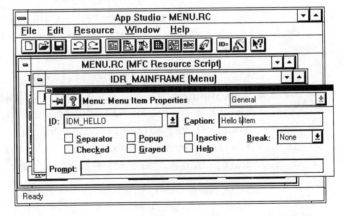

Figure 4.12. Designing shortcut keys.

Now when you rebuild and run the program, you can see that shortcut keys have been added to the menu and menu item (see figure 4.13).

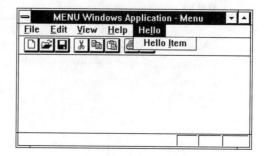

Figure 4.13. Your new shortcut keys.

Adding Accelerator Keys in Windows

Accelerator keys are another Windows feature. You might have noticed them in figure 4.11. They are the key combinations to the right of several menu items—the accelerator key corresponding to the New... item is Ctrl+N and the accelerator key for Open... is Ctrl+O, for example. You can use accelerator keys (unlike shortcut keys) even though a menu is not open. Because accelerator keys are always valid, you should choose key combinations that will not interfere with the keystrokes the user normally uses while running your program.

You can add accelerator keys to your program by using App Studio. Open App Studio again and open IDR_MAINFRAME. Next, double-click on Hello Item in the Hello menu, opening the Menu Item Properties box. Your job here is to change the menu item's caption so that the accelerator key is displayed. To make the accelerator key Ctrl+H, change the text in the Caption box to read `Hello &Item\tCtrl+H`, as shown in figure 4.14.

Here, the \t works just like the normal C printf() code for a tab; its job is to move the accelerator key to the right of the menu. Then you type the name of the key, which is Ctrl+H here. Other valid options include Alt+, Shift+, and the function keys, F1–F12. App Studio simply places this new text in the menu (see figure 4.15). You have not made it active yet.

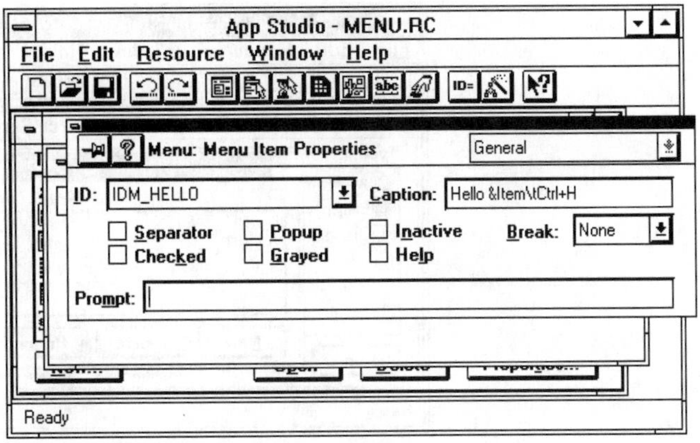

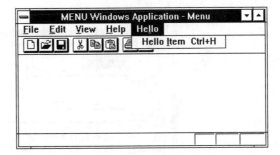

Figure 4.14. Designing an accelerator key.

Figure 4.15. The new accelerator key.

Connecting an accelerator key to a menu item is easy; you use the Accelerator Table Editor. Open App Studio again and click on the accelerator resource icon—the top icon in the Type list box—rather than on the menu resource icon. This indicates that you want to work on the *accelerator table* instead of on menu items. Accelerators are treated as separate resources in Windows, as you will see.

When you select the accelerator icon, a dialog box showing the current accelerator keys for your program appears (see figure 4.16). Note that because your accelerator key does not exist yet, the box does not contain an entry for it. Click on the New button at the bottom of the dialog box to open the Accelerator Table Editor, shown in figure 4.17.

Figure 4.16. Accelerator key dialog box.

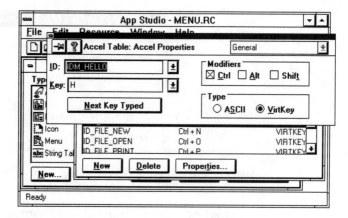

Figure 4.17. The Accelerator Table Editor.

To associate the accelerator key Ctrl+H with the IDM_HELLO message (so that an IDM_HELLO message will be sent to your program when the user presses Ctrl+H), type **IDM_HELLO** in the ID box.

Next, to set up the accelerator key itself, type **H** in the Key box and click on the Ctrl check box in the Modifiers box (refer to figure 4.17). That is all there is to it. Now, when the user presses Ctrl+H, you get an IDM_HELLO message whether a menu is open or not. (Now you can understand why accelerators are treated as a separate resource: because they are not dependent on menus, you can use them anytime.)

Close the Accelerator Table Editor now and save the changes, using App Studio's Save menu item. When you run the new program, you will be able to use the new Ctrl+H accelerator key.

Note the declaration connected to Ctrl+H in the accelerator table, which is stored in the file menu.rc and appears as follows:

```
IDR_MAINFRAME ACCELERATORS PRELOAD MOVEABLE PURE
BEGIN
    "C",    ID_EDIT_COPY,  VIRTKEY,CONTROL, NOINVERT
    "H",    IDM_HELLO,     VIRTKEY,CONTROL, NOINVERT
    "N",    ID_FILE_NEW,   VIRTKEY,CONTROL, NOINVERT
    "O",    ID_FILE_OPEN,  VIRTKEY,CONTROL, NOINVERT
    "P",    ID_FILE_PRINT, VIRTKEY,CONTROL, NOINVERT
    "S",    ID_FILE_SAVE,  VIRTKEY,CONTROL, NOINVERT
    "V",    ID_EDIT_PASTE, VIRTKEY,CONTROL, NOINVERT
    VK_BACK,        ID_EDIT_UNDO,  VIRTKEY,ALT, NOINVERT
    VK_DELETE,      ID_EDIT_CUT,   VIRTKEY,SHIFT, NOINVERT
    VK_F6, ID_NEXT_PANE, VIRTKEY,NOINVERT
    VK_F6, ID_PREV_PANE, VIRTKEY,SHIFT, NOINVERT
    VK_INSERT,      ID_EDIT_COPY,  VIRTKEY,CONTROL, NOINVERT
    VK_INSERT,      ID_EDIT_PASTE, VIRTKEY,SHIFT, NOINVERT
    "X",    ID_EDIT_CUT,   VIRTKEY,CONTROL, NOINVERT
    "Z",    ID_EDIT_UNDO,  VIRTKEY,CONTROL, NOINVERT
END
```

You have come pretty far, creating a menu with a menu item, complete with shortcut key and accelerator. The code for menuview.cpp is in listing 4.1; listing 4.2 holds the menu section of menu.rc.

Listing 4.1. Menuview.cpp

```
// menuview.cpp : implementation of the CMenuView class
//

#include "stdafx.h"
```

continues

Listing 4.1. continued

```
#include "menu.h"

#include "menudoc.h"
#include "menuview.h"

#ifdef _DEBUG
#undef THIS_FILE
static char BASED_CODE THIS_FILE[] = __FILE__;
#endif


//////////////////////////////////////////////////////////////////
////////////
// CMenuView

IMPLEMENT_DYNCREATE(CMenuView, CView)

BEGIN_MESSAGE_MAP(CMenuView, CView)
   //{{AFX_MSG_MAP(CMenuView)
   ON_COMMAND(IDM_HELLO, OnHello)
   //}}AFX_MSG_MAP
   // Standard printing commands
   ON_COMMAND(ID_FILE_PRINT, CView::OnFilePrint)
   ON_COMMAND(ID_FILE_PRINT_PREVIEW, CView::OnFilePrintPreview)
END_MESSAGE_MAP()

//////////////////////////////////////////////////////////////////
////////////
// CMenuView construction/destruction

CMenuView::CMenuView()
{
   // TODO: add construction code here
}

CMenuView::~CMenuView()
{
}
```

```
///////////////////////////////////////////////////////////////////
///////
// CMenuView drawing

void CMenuView::OnDraw(CDC* pDC)
{
   CMenuDoc* pDoc = GetDocument();

   // TODO: add draw code here
}


///////////////////////////////////////////////////////////////////
///////
// CMenuView printing

BOOL CMenuView::OnPreparePrinting(CPrintInfo* pInfo)
{
   // default preparation
   return DoPreparePrinting(pInfo);
}

void CMenuView::OnBeginPrinting(CDC* /*pDC*/, CPrintInfo* /*pInfo*/)
{
   // TODO: add extra initialization before printing
}

void CMenuView::OnEndPrinting(CDC* /*pDC*/, CPrintInfo* /*pInfo*/)
{
   // TODO: add cleanup after printing
}


///////////////////////////////////////////////////////////////////
///////
// CMenuView diagnostics

#ifdef _DEBUG
void CMenuView::AssertValid() const
{
   CView::AssertValid();
}
```

continues

Listing 4.1. continued

```
void CMenuView::Dump(CDumpContext& dc) const
{
   CView::Dump(dc);
}

CMenuDoc* CMenuView::GetDocument() // non-debug version is inline
{
   ASSERT(m_pDocument->IsKindOf(RUNTIME_CLASS(CMenuDoc)));
   return (CMenuDoc*) m_pDocument;
}

#endif //_DEBUG

/////////////////////////////////////////////////////////////////////
////////////
// CMenuView message handlers

void CMenuView::OnHello()
{
   // TODO: Add your command handler code here
   CString hello_string = "Hello, world.";
   CClientDC dc(this);

   dc.TextOut(0, 0, hello_string, hello_string.GetLength());

}
```

Listing 4.2. Menu Section of Menu.rc

```
//Microsoft App Studio generated resource script.
//
#include "resource.h"

IDR_MAINFRAME ICON        DISCARDABLE          "RES\\MENU.ICO"

/////////////////////////////////////////////////////////////////////
////////////
```

```
//
// Bitmap
//

IDR_MAINFRAME BITMAP          MOVEABLE PURE
"RES\\TOOLBAR.BMP"


/////////////////////////////////////////////////////////////////
/////////////
//
// Menu
//

IDR_MAINFRAME MENU PRELOAD DISCARDABLE
BEGIN
    POPUP "&File"
    BEGIN
            MENUITEM "&New\tCtrl+N",     ID_FILE_NEW
            MENUITEM "&Open...\tCtrl+O",  ID_FILE_OPEN
            MENUITEM "&Save\tCtrl+S",     ID_FILE_SAVE
            MENUITEM "Save &As...",       ID_FILE_SAVE_AS
            MENUITEM SEPARATOR
            MENUITEM "&Print...\tCtrl+P", ID_FILE_PRINT
            MENUITEM "Print Pre&view",    ID_FILE_PRINT_PREVIEW
            MENUITEM "P&rint Setup...",   ID_FILE_PRINT_SETUP
            MENUITEM SEPARATOR
            MENUITEM "Recent File",       ID_FILE_MRU_FILE1, GRAYED
            MENUITEM SEPARATOR
            MENUITEM "E&xit",             ID_APP_EXIT
    END
    POPUP "&Edit"
    BEGIN
            MENUITEM "&Undo\tCtrl+Z",     ID_EDIT_UNDO
            MENUITEM SEPARATOR
            MENUITEM "Cu&t\tCtrl+X",      ID_EDIT_CUT
            MENUITEM "&Copy\tCtrl+C",     ID_EDIT_COPY
```

continues

Listing 4.2. continued

```
            MENUITEM "&Paste\tCtrl+V",      ID_EDIT_PASTE
    END
    POPUP "&View"
    BEGIN
            MENUITEM "&Toolbar",            ID_VIEW_TOOLBAR
            MENUITEM "&Status Bar",         ID_VIEW_STATUS_BAR
    END
    POPUP "&Help"
    BEGIN
            MENUITEM "&About MENU...",      ID_APP_ABOUT
    END
    POPUP "He&llo"
    BEGIN
            MENUITEM "Hello &Item\tCtrl+H",       IDM_HELLO
    END
END


/////////////////////////////////////////////////////////////
/////////////
//
// Accelerator
//

IDR_MAINFRAME ACCELERATORS PRELOAD MOVEABLE PURE
BEGIN
    "C",    ID_EDIT_COPY,   VIRTKEY,CONTROL, NOINVERT
    "H",    IDM_HELLO,      VIRTKEY,CONTROL, NOINVERT
    "N",    ID_FILE_NEW,    VIRTKEY,CONTROL, NOINVERT
    "O",    ID_FILE_OPEN,   VIRTKEY,CONTROL, NOINVERT
    "P",    ID_FILE_PRINT,  VIRTKEY,CONTROL, NOINVERT
    "S",    ID_FILE_SAVE,   VIRTKEY,CONTROL, NOINVERT
    "V",    ID_EDIT_PASTE,  VIRTKEY,CONTROL, NOINVERT
    VK_BACK,        ID_EDIT_UNDO,  VIRTKEY,ALT, NOINVERT
    VK_DELETE,      ID_EDIT_CUT,   VIRTKEY,SHIFT, NOINVERT
    VK_F6, ID_NEXT_PANE, VIRTKEY,NOINVERT
```

```
VK_F6,    ID_PREV_PANE,   VIRTKEY,SHIFT, NOINVERT
VK_INSERT,    ID_EDIT_COPY,   VIRTKEY,CONTROL, NOINVERT
VK_INSERT,    ID_EDIT_PASTE, VIRTKEY,SHIFT, NOINVERT
"X",    ID_EDIT_CUT,    VIRTKEY,CONTROL, NOINVERT
"Z",    ID_EDIT_UNDO,   VIRTKEY,CONTROL, NOINVERT
END
```

The next step in menu handling—changing the appearance of menu items as the program runs—moves you up to the next level of control. In the following section, you learn how to mark a menu item with a check mark (to indicate that the item represents a selected option). Then you will find out how to gray menu items (to indicate that they are disabled).

Checking Menu Items

In the Menu Item Properties box shown in figure 4.4, you might have noticed the check boxes marked Checked, Grayed, Inactive, and so on. These boxes indicate the *initial condition* of a menu item. By using these check boxes, you can select the appearance of a menu (or menu item) when the program first runs. To select one of these initial conditions, simply check the appropriate box when you design your menu.

Placing Separator Lines in Menus.
The Separator check box in the Menu Item Properties box enables you to place separators in a menu. Separator lines are horizontal lines that let you separate menu items into logical groups in a menu. (You might set File Open... and File Save... apart from Exit this way, for example.)

You can perform these actions—setting menu item conditions—when your program is running, also. You will add a check mark to the Hello item after it has been selected, for example, to indicate that the "Hello, world." string is already printed. Figure 4.18 shows the checked menu item.

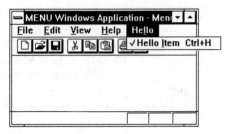

Figure 4.18. Adding check marks to menus.

To add the check mark, you add code to the OnHello() member function, which currently appears as follows:

```
void CMenuView::OnHello()
{
    CString hello_string = "Hello, world.";
    CClientDC dc(this);

    dc.TextOut(0, 0, hello_string, hello_string.GetLength());
}
```

The CheckMenuItem() function is the one you want. That function works as follows:

```
CheckMenuItem(nItem, nFlags)
```

Here, nItem indicates—either by ID number (IDM_HELLO, for example) or by position (0 corresponds to the first menu or menu item)—the menu item you want checked. The nFlags parameter indicates which of these addressing schemes you want and what action to take (these values can be ORed together), as follows:

nFlags	Meaning
MF_BYCOMMAND	Indicates, by menu ID value, what menu item to work on (the default)
MF_BYPOSITION	Indicates, by passing the 0-based position ofmenu item, what menu item to work on

nFlags	Meaning
MF_CHECKED	Check the menu item
MF_UNCHECKED	Remove check mark

That means that you can check the Hello item, as follows:

```
CheckMenuItem(IDM_HELLO, MF_CHECKED)
```

But the menu system is attached to the main frame window, not to the view. How can you reach it?

As you may recall, the view is a child window of the main window. You can get a pointer to the main window by using a function called GetParent(), as follows:

```
void CMenuView::OnHello()
{
    CString hello_string = "Hello, world.";
    CClientDC dc(this);

    dc.TextOut(0, 0, hello_string, hello_string.GetLength());

    CWnd* pParent = GetParent();
        :


}
```

Next, you get a pointer to the main window's menu object, which is an object of class CMenu, as follows:

```
void CMenuView::OnHello()
{
    CString hello_string = "Hello, world.";
    CClientDC dc(this);

    dc.TextOut(0, 0, hello_string, hello_string.GetLength());
```

```
   CWnd* pParent = GetParent( );
   CMenu* pMenu = pParent->GetMenu( );
       :
}
```

At this point, you have a pointer to your program's menu system. To execute CheckMenuItem(IDM_HELLO, MF_CHECKED), you just do the following:

```
void CMenuView::OnHello( )
{
   CString hello_string = "Hello, world.";
   CClientDC dc(this);

   dc.TextOut(0, 0, hello_string, hello_string.GetLength( ));

   CWnd* pParent = GetParent( );
   CMenu* pMenu = pParent->GetMenu( );
   pMenu->CheckMenuItem(IDM_HELLO, MF_CHECKED);

}
```

And that is it; now the menu item appears with a check mark.

Graying Menu Items

To gray menu items, you use EnableMenuItem( ), a function that works in the following way:

```
EnableMenuItem(nItem, nFlags)
```

Again, nItem indicates, either by ID number (IDM_HELLO, for example) or by position (0 corresponds to the first menu or menu item), the menu item you want checked. And again, the nFlags parameter indicates which of the two addressing schemes you want and what action to take (the values can be ORed together), as follows:

nFlags	Meaning
MF_BYCOMMAND	Indicates, by menu ID value, which menu item to work on (the default)
MF_BYPOSITION	Indicates which menu item to work on by passing that menu item's 0-based position
MF_DISABLED	Disables menu item so that it cannot be selected, but does not gray it
MF_ENABLED	Enables menu item
MF_GRAYED	Dims and disables menu item

You can indicate the menu item you want to change either by menu ID value (the default—MF_BYCOMMAND) or by position (MF_BYPOSITION). If you select a menu item by position, the first item in a menu is item 0, the next is item 1, and so on. You might be surprised to learn, however, that the following code (in which you use MF_BYPOSITION) grays the *File* item in the menu bar, not Hello, the first item in that menu:

```
CMenu* pMenu = GetMenu();
pMenu->EnableMenuItem(0, MF_BYPOSITION | MF_GRAYED);
```

The reason this happens is that pMenu is a pointer to the menu object for the whole menu system (that is, for all menus that appear in the menu bar). When you refer to the first item in the menu system, that item is the first *menu*, *not* not the first menu item, as follows:

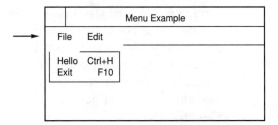

The next menu in this example (Edit) is item 1, and so on. You did not have to worry about this when you selected menu items with MF_BYCOMMAND (the default), because only one menu item in the entire menu system has the ID IDM_HELLO. Here, however, to indicate the menu item's correct position, you have to make the File pop-up menu an object before you can use the following:

```
pMenu->EnableMenuItem(0, MF_BYPOSITION | MF_GRAYED)
```

You can create that object with GetSubMenu( ). In the preceding example, GetSubMenu(0) returns a pointer to the menu object that holds the first submenu, File, as follows:

```
CMenu* pMenuBar = GetMenu( );
CMenu* pMenu = pMenuBar->GetSubMenu(0);
pMenu->EnableMenuItem(0, MF_BYPOSITION | MF_GRAYED);
```

Now pMenu *is* a pointer to the File menu; the preceding lines will gray the first item in that menu. Note that to gray this item, you had to get two pointers to menu objects, as follows:

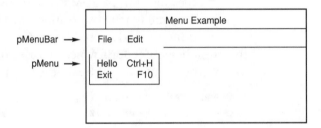

Handling User-Interface Update Messages

We have called many menu functions (like EnableMenuItem( )). Visual C++ provides another mechanism here. You can set a menu item's state another way; Visual C++'s philosophy is that the best object to handle that task is the object that handles the menu item itself. In other words, because the CMenuView object handles the Hello Message menu item, Visual C++ will send a message asking your view object whether the status should be enabled or disabled before displaying that menu item. In this way, the view object does not have to interact with the insides of the CMenu object.

This kind of message—sent just before a menu item or button is displayed—is called an UPDATE_COMMAND_UI message (*UI* stands for *user interface*). You can use Class Wizard to intercept those messages as well. In Class Wizard, notice that the menu item IDM_HELLO (refer to figure

4.8) is connected to two types of messages for which you can write handlers: COMMAND messages (the menu item was selected by the user), and UPDATE_COMMAND_UI messages (the menu item is about to be displayed and you are being asked about its state). Associate a function with IDM_HELLO's UPDATE_COMMAND_UI message now; accept the name that Class Wizard gives it: OnUpdateHello( ), as follows:

```
void CMenuView::OnUpdateHello(CCmdUI* pCmdUI)
{
    pCmdUI->Enable(FALSE);
}
```

The pCmdUI parameter is a pointer to the object about which you are being queried—in this case, the Hello menu item. To gray it so that it is displayed as disabled, you can use the Enable( ) member function as follows:

```
void CMenuView::OnUpdateHello(CCmdUI* pCmdUI)
{
    pCmdUI->Enable(FALSE);
}
```

In this way, Visual C++ enables you to handle the state of menu items without worrying about the parent window's menu system. Your code becomes more modular. Instead of having to use GetParent( ) and GetMenu( ) to modify a menu item's state, you just handle UPDATE_COMMAND_UI messages.

Adding Menu Items in Code

Another exiting thing about using menus is the possibility of adding menu items at run time. To see how this works, you can design a phonebook. Say, for example, that you type the name Albert, and a telephone number, as follows:

File	Edit	View	Help	Phonebook	Help
Albert	(314)	159-2653			

Then you select the Add Name menu item in the Phonebook menu, as follows:

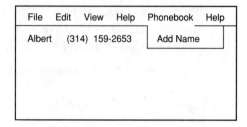

To erase the string you typed and add the name Albert to your Phonebook menu, as follows:

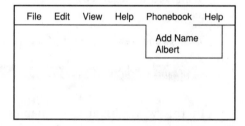

You can add other names the same way, as follows:

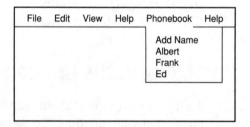

Then, when you select a name (Albert, for example) from the Phonebook, the original string (including the telephone number) is displayed, as follows:

```
File   Edit   View   Help   Phonebook   Help

Albert    (314)  159-2653
```

To begin the Phonebook, start App Wizard and create an SDI (Single Document Interface) project named phone.mak. Open the menu system, add a menu named &Phonebook to the menu bar (to the left of the Help menu), and give that menu one item—Add Name, with the ID IDM_ADDNAME. Figure 4.19 shows the results of the program—so far.

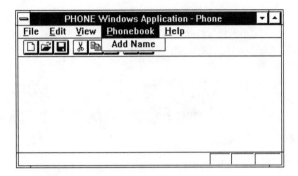

Figure 4.19. Beginning the Phonebook application.

Next, connect the IDM_ADDNAME ID to a new function in CPhoneView you can create with Class Wizard—a function named OnAddname(). Selecting the Add name item causes the code in this function to execute, as follows:

```
void CPhoneView::OnAddname()
{

}
```

This is where you add the code that appends items to the Phonebook menu. First, however, because you must have a typed-in string to append, you need to add a function named OnChar() to CPhoneView. (Use Class Wizard to connect it to WM_CHAR.) Next, add the following character-reading code, which is exactly like the code you have seen before for this purpose, to OnChar().

```
void CPhoneView::OnChar(UINT nChar, UINT nRepCnt, UINT nFlags)
{
    out_string += nChar;
    CClientDC dc(this);
    dc.TextOut(0, 0, out_string, out_string.GetLength());

    CView::OnChar(nChar, nRepCnt, nFlags);
}
```

Here you use a CString object named out_string to hold the characters as they are typed (you do not want to store them in the document until the user selects the Add Name menu item). Add that object to phonevw.h, as follows:

```
class CPhoneView : public CView
{
protected: // create from serialization only
   CPhoneView( );
   DECLARE_DYNCREATE(CPhoneView)

// Attributes
public:
   CString out_string;

// Operations
public:
       :
```

Now the characters you type are stored in out_string, as follows:

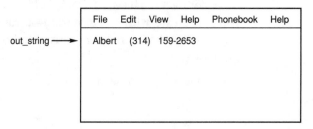

After typing the string, the user can select the Add Name menu item, calling the function OnAddName(). At this point, you are supposed to add this name to the Phonebook menu. You can get a pointer to the parent window and then to the menu bar, as follows:

```
void CPhoneView::OnAddname( )
{
   CWnd* pParent = GetParent( );
   CMenu* pMenuBar = pParent->GetMenu( );
          :
}
```

Here you have to use pointers to the parent window's menu system because soon you will have to use the CMenu member function, AppendMenu( ).

Next, you need to get a pointer to the menu to which you want to append items. (Use GetSubMenu( ), as before.) The Phonebook menu you have designed is menu number 3 (File = 0) in the menu bar, as follows:

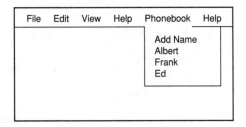

That means you can get the pointer you need, as follows:

```
void   CPhoneView::OnAddname( )
{
    CWnd* pParent = GetParent( );
    CMenu* pMenuBar = pParent->GetMenu( );
    CMenu* pMenu = pMenuBar->GetSubMenu(3);
        :
}
```

In the next step, you simply append to the menu the name the user has typed. To do that, use the CMenu member function AppendMenu( ) to append out_string to the Phonebook menu. This CMenu member function takes three parameters. The first is a constant indicating what kind of menu item you are adding (see table 4.1). (You will use MF_STRING, which indicates that the item you are adding is a string.) The second parameter is the menu ID value. The third item is a pointer to the new menu item's text.

Table 4.1. AppendMenu( ) Values

MF Value	Meaning
MF_CHECKED	Place check mark next to item
MF_DISABLED	Disables menu item
MF_ENABLED	Enables menu item
MF_GRAYED	Disables menu item and dims it
MF_MENUBARBREAK	Places menu on new column in menu bar

continues

Table 4.1. continued

MF Value	Meaning
MF_MENUBREAK	Places item on new column in pop-up menus
MF_OWNERDRAW	An owner-draw item like a bitmap
MF_POPUP	New menu item has pop-up menu associated with it
MF_SEPARATOR	Draws separator bar
MF_STRING	Menu item is a string
MF_UNCHECKED	Remove check next to item

To append only the name, not the typed telephone number to the menu, you append all text up to the first space in your out_strings, which now looks like this: "Albert (314) 159-2653". To find the first space, use the CString function Find( ); to use only the text up to that location (so that you can add it to the menu), use the CString function Left(*n*)—which returns the leftmost n characters of a string—as follows:

```
void CPhoneView::OnAddname( )
{
  CWnd* pParent = GetParent( );
  CMenu* pMenuBar = pParent->GetMenu( );
  CMenu* pMenu = pMenuBar->GetSubMenu(3);
  pMenu->AppendMenu(MF_STRING | MF_ENABLED, new_menu_ID++, \
          out_string.Left(out_string.Find(" ")));
      :
}
```

Now, provided that you can find a good value for new_menu_ID, the person's name will be added to the Phonebook menu, as follows:

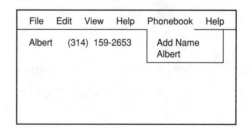

(You have not yet erased out_string in the window.)

The problem is finding a good value for the new menu item's ID, new_menu_ID. Visual C++ gets in the way here by insisting that new menu items be associated with an ID number which is already connected to an Onxxx() function. (IDM_ADDNAME is already connected to OnAddname(), for example.) If you use an ID that is not already connected to a function (you simply make up an ID number), Visual C++ displays the new menu item as grayed (disabled) and does not let you enable it. That is a problem, because none of the new menu items (like Albert) is connected to Onxxx() functions. In other words, Visual C++ will not let you enable a menu item unless that item is already connected to a function.

A typical solution here is to create a number of dummy menu IDs connected to dummy functions and then to use those ID values. To do that, use App Studio to add a new (dummy) menu after the Help menu. Because you do not want this new menu displayed, give it the caption " " and mark it as Inactive (see figure 4.20). The user will not be able to select it (and it will be invisible).

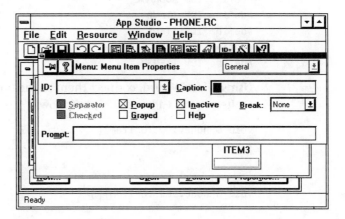

Figure 4.20. Designing a dummy menu.

Next, add the menu items ITEM0 through ITEM3, as shown in figure 4.21, and give them the IDs IDM_ITEM0 through IDM_ITEM3.

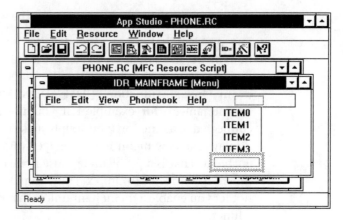

Figure 4.21. Designing dummy menu items.

New values are created for your dummy menu items in resource.h, as follows:

```
#define IDR_MAINFRAME               2
#define IDD_ABOUTBOX                100
#define IDM_ADDNAME                 32768
#define IDM_ITEM0                   32772
#define IDM_ITEM1                   32773
#define IDM_ITEM2                   32774
#define IDM_ITEM3                   32775
```

Using Class Wizard, connect them to the functions OnItem0() through OnItem3() in CPhoneView, as follows:

```
void CPhoneView::OnItem0()
{
}

void CPhoneView::OnItem1()
{
}

void CPhoneView::OnItem2()
{
}

void CPhoneView::OnItem3()
{
}
```

Now you can use the legal ID numbers IDM_ITEM0 to IDM_ITEM3 in AppendMenu( ). To keep track of the values you are using, you add an unsigned integer—new_menu_ID—to phonevw.h, right after out_string, as follows:

```
class CPhoneView : public CView
{
protected: // create from serialization only
  CPhoneView( );
  DECLARE_DYNCREATE(CPhoneView)

// Attributes
public:
  CString out_string;
  UINT new_menu_ID;

// Operations
public:
```

Next, you initialize it with IDM_ITEM0, the first of your legal menu IDs, in CPhoneView's constructor (phonevw.cpp), as follows:

```
CPhoneView::CPhoneView( )
{
                                        new_menu_ID = IDM_ITEM0;
// TODO: add construction code here
}
```

That is it; now you are free to add the person's name from out_string to your Phonebook menu, as follows:

```
void CPhoneView::OnAddname( )
{
  CWnd* pParent = GetParent( );
  CMenu* pMenuBar = pParent->GetMenu( );
  CMenu* pMenu = pMenuBar->GetSubMenu(3);
  CPhoneDoc* pDoc = GetDocument( );
  pMenu->AppendMenu(MF_STRING | MF_ENABLED, new_menu_ID++, \
          out_string.Left(out_string.Find(" ")));
          :
}
```

(Note that you increment new_menu_ID. In a real application, make sure that it does not go past IDM_ITEM3.)

The remaining steps here are to store the data (the complete string typed by the user—now in out_string) in the document and to erase it from the screen so that the user can enter another name and number. To store the data, you set up an array of four CStrings named data_string[] in phonedoc.h, as follows:

```
class CPhoneDoc : public CDocument
{
protected: // create from serialization only
   CPhoneDoc( );
   DECLARE_DYNCREATE(CPhoneDoc)

// Attributes
public:
   CString data_string[4];

// Operations
public:
   :
```

That is where the data—now in out_string—will be stored. Because you also have to keep track of your location in the data_string[] array, add an index to that array (named data_index), as follows:

```
class CPhoneDoc : public CDocument
{
protected: // create from serialization only
   CPhoneDoc( );
   DECLARE_DYNCREATE(CPhoneDoc)

// Attributes
public:
   CString data_string[4];
   int data_index;

// Operations
public:
   :
```

Now add out_string to data_string[] in the document, as follows:

```
void  CPhoneView::OnAddname( )
{
  CWnd* pParent = GetParent( );
  CMenu* pMenuBar = pParent->GetMenu( );
  CMenu* pMenu = pMenuBar->GetSubMenu(3);
  CPhoneDoc* pDoc = GetDocument( );
  pMenu->AppendMenu(MF_STRING | MF_ENABLED, new_menu_ID++, \
          out_string.Left(out_string.Find(" ")));

  pDoc->data_string[pDoc->data_index++] = out_string;
          :
}
```

(Note that you also increment data_index.)

The final step is to erase out_string from the screen, which you can do by typing over it, using text that has been set to the window's background color (a typical method of erasing text in Windows). You do so by getting a device context object and setting the Text color in it to the background color, using SetTextColor() and GetBkColor(), as follows:

```
void  CPhoneView::OnAddname( )
{
  CWnd* pParent = GetParent( );
  CMenu* pMenuBar = pParent->GetMenu( );
  CMenu* pMenu = pMenuBar->GetSubMenu(3);
  CPhoneDoc* pDoc = GetDocument( );
  pMenu->AppendMenu(MF_STRING | MF_ENABLED, new_menu_ID++, \
          out_string.Left(out_string.Find(" ")));

  pDoc->data_string[pDoc->data_index++] = out_string;
  CClientDC dc(this);
  DWORD OldTextColor = dc.SetTextColor(dc.GetBkColor( ));
          :
}
```

Note that SetTextColor() returns the current text color, a DWORD (doubleword) value, which you store in OldTextColor so that you can restore it later. In fact, all you have to do is type out_string again to erase it, restore the text color, and clear out_string in preparation for a new name and number, as follows:

```
void   CPhoneView::OnAddname( )
{
    CWnd* pParent = GetParent( );
    CMenu* pMenuBar = pParent->GetMenu( );
    CMenu* pMenu = pMenuBar->GetSubMenu(3);
    CPhoneDoc* pDoc = GetDocument( );
    pMenu->AppendMenu(MF_STRING ¦ MF_ENABLED, new_menu_ID++, \
             out_string.Left(out_string.Find(" ")));

    pDoc->data_string[pDoc->data_index++] = out_string;
    CClientDC dc(this);
    DWORD OldTextColor = dc.SetTextColor(dc.GetBkColor( ));
    dc.TextOut(0, 0, out_string, out_string.GetLength( ));
    dc.SetTextColor(OldTextColor);
    out_string.Empty( );
}
```

That is it for OnAddname( ). Now the user can type a name and number,
select Add Name, and see the name added to the Phonebook menu (and
the window is cleared to prepare it for the next name and number), as
follows:

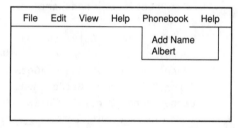

The question now is: how do you connect the new menu items to your
program? When the first item is selected, OnItem0() is called, when the
second item is selected, OnItem1() is called, and so on, as follows:

```
void CPhoneView::OnItem0( )
{
}

void CPhoneView::OnItem1( )
{
}
```

```
void  CPhoneView::OnItem2()
{
}

void CPhoneView::OnItem3()
{
}
```

You could place code in each of these dummy functions, responding when each one is called. But this gets awkward—what if you have ten or more dummy functions? A better option is to go behind the scenes in Visual C++ and intercept the calls to OnItem0() through OnItem3() before they are made. (This gives you considerably more Visual C++ expertise.)

When a menu item is selected, the main window gets a WM_COMMAND Windows message, which is handled in the OnCommand() function in CMainFrame. That function comes from the base class CFrameWnd (CMainFrame is derived from CFrameWnd). But you can override it in CMainFrame by designing your own OnCommand() function in mainfrm.cpp, as follows:

```
BOOL CMainFrame::OnCommand(WPARAM wParam, LPARAM lParam)
{
}
```

The menu item's ID is in the wParam parameter. You can intercept those messages as follows:

```
BOOL CMainFrame::OnCommand(WPARAM wParam, LPARAM lParam)
{
    if(wParam >= IDM_ITEM0 && wParam <= IDM_ITEM3){
            ... Handle our menu items ...
    }
    else

    CFrameWnd::OnCommand(wParam, lParam);
}
```

Note that because you passed all messages—except the ones you plan to handle—to the base class's version of OnCommand(), your dummy functions will no longer be called; instead, you can handle the menu items yourself.

All you have to do here is print the string in data_string[] that matches the menu item selected. Because that item is number wParam - IDM_ITEM0, you have to print the following in your view's window:

```
data_string[wParam - IDM_ITEM0]
```

To do that, you have to reach both the view and the document from the CMainFrame object.

This is something you have never done before, but it is not difficult. The CMainFrame class has two member functions, GetActiveView() and GetActiveDocument(), which return pointers to the currently active CView and CDocument objects. That is almost what you want—you need pointers to the derived CPhoneView and CPhoneDoc objects (derived from CView and CDocument). Only pointers to your derived objects will be able to reach members you have added in those objects, like data_string[] (which is not part of the CDoc class).

You can use a cast to get the pointers you want. First you inform Visual C++ of the structure of CPhoneView and CPhoneDoc by including their header files in mainframe.cpp, as follows:

```
// mainfrm.cpp : implementation of the CMainFrame class
//

    #include "stdafx.h"
    #include "phone.h"
    #include "phonedoc.h"
    #include "phonevw.h"

    #include "mainfrm.h"
```

Next you cast the pointers you get from GetActiveView() and GetActiveDocument() correctly in OnCommand(), as follows:

```
BOOL CMainFrame::OnCommand(WPARAM wParam, LPARAM lParam)
{
    if(wParam >= IDM_ITEM0 && wParam <= IDM_ITEM3){
        CPhoneView* pView = (CPhoneView*) GetActiveView();
        CPhoneDoc* pDoc = (CPhoneDoc*) GetActiveDocument();
        :
    }
    else
    CFrameWnd::OnCommand(wParam, lParam);
```

```
        return  TRUE;
    }
```

You are almost done. All that remains is to get a device context for your view and display the correct string from the document in it, as follows:

```
BOOL  CMainFrame::OnCommand(WPARAM  wParam,  LPARAM  lParam)
{
  if(wParam >= IDM_ITEM0 && wParam <= IDM_ITEM3){
        CPhoneView* pView = (CPhoneView*) GetActiveView();
        CPhoneDoc* pDoc = (CPhoneDoc*) GetActiveDocument();
        CClientDC dc(pView);
        dc.TextOut(0, 0, pDoc->data_string[wParam - IDM_ITEM0],\
               pDoc>data_string[wParam - IDM_ITEM0].GetLength());
    }
    else
    CFrameWnd::OnCommand(wParam, lParam);

    return TRUE;
}
```

And that is it—the phonebook application is complete. The user can place names in the Phonebook menu, as follows:

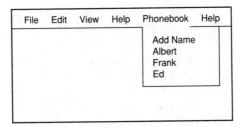

To retrieve the names, the user selects them in that menu, causing the full text to reappear, as follows:

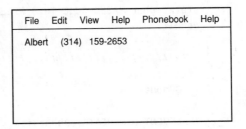

That completes the program. Figure 4.22 shows the working Phonebook—a success.

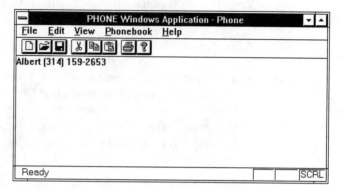

Figure 4.22. The functioning Phonebook application.

The file phonevw.cpp appears in listing 4.3; mainfrm.cpp is in listing 4.4; phonedoc.cpp, in listing 4.5.

 Listing 4.3. Phonevw.pp

```
// phonevw.cpp : implementation of the CPhoneView class
//

#include "stdafx.h"
#include "phone.h"

#include "phonedoc.h"
#include "phonevw.h"

#ifdef _DEBUG
#undef THIS_FILE
static char BASED_CODE THIS_FILE[] = __FILE__;
#endif


/////////////////////////////////////////////////////////////////////
////////////
// CPhoneView

IMPLEMENT_DYNCREATE(CPhoneView, CView)
```

```
BEGIN_MESSAGE_MAP(CPhoneView,  CView)
    //{{AFX_MSG_MAP(CPhoneView)
         ON_WM_CHAR( )
         ON_COMMAND(IDM_ADDNAME, OnAddname)
         ON_COMMAND(IDM_ITEM1, OnItem1)
         ON_COMMAND(IDM_ITEM2, OnItem2)
         ON_COMMAND(IDM_ITEM3, OnItem3)
         ON_COMMAND(IDM_ITEM0, OnItem0)
         //}}AFX_MSG_MAP
    // Standard printing commands
    ON_COMMAND(ID_FILE_PRINT, CView::OnFilePrint)
    ON_COMMAND(ID_FILE_PRINT_PREVIEW, CView::OnFilePrintPreview)
END_MESSAGE_MAP( )

/////////////////////////////////////////////////////////////////////
/////////
// CPhoneView construction/destruction

CPhoneView::CPhoneView( )
{
    new_menu_ID = IDM_ITEM0;        // TODO: add construction code here
}


CPhoneView::~CPhoneView( )
{
}


/////////////////////////////////////////////////////////////////////
/////////
// CPhoneView drawing

void CPhoneView::OnDraw(CDC* pDC)
{
    CPhoneDoc* pDoc = GetDocument( );

    //CString hello_string = "Hello!";
    CClientDC dc(this);

    dc.TextOut(0, 0, out_string, out_string.GetLength( ));
}
```

continues

Listing 4.3. continued

```
///////////////////////////////////////////////////////////////////
//////////
// CPhoneView printing

BOOL CPhoneView::OnPreparePrinting(CPrintInfo* pInfo)
{
      // default preparation
      return DoPreparePrinting(pInfo);
}


void CPhoneView::OnBeginPrinting(CDC* /*pDC*/, CPrintInfo* /*pInfo*/)
{
      // TODO: add extra initialization before printing
}


void CPhoneView::OnEndPrinting(CDC* /*pDC*/, CPrintInfo* /*pInfo*/)
{
      // TODO: add cleanup after printing
}


///////////////////////////////////////////////////////////////////
/////
// CPhoneView diagnostics

#ifdef _DEBUG
void CPhoneView::AssertValid() const
{
      CView::AssertValid();
}


void CPhoneView::Dump(CDumpContext& dc) const
{
      CView::Dump(dc);
}


CPhoneDoc* CPhoneView::GetDocument() // non-debug version is inline
{
      ASSERT(m_pDocument->IsKindOf(RUNTIME_CLASS(CPhoneDoc)));
```

```
        return  (CPhoneDoc*)  m_pDocument;
}


#endif //_DEBUG


/////////////////////////////////////////////////////////////////////////////
// CPhoneView message handlers

void CPhoneView::OnChar(UINT nChar, UINT nRepCnt, UINT nFlags)
{
        // TODO: Add your message handler code here and/or call default

   out_string += nChar;
   CClientDC dc(this);
        dc.TextOut(0, 0, out_string, out_string.GetLength());

        CView::OnChar(nChar, nRepCnt, nFlags);
}

void CPhoneView::OnAddname()
{
   CWnd* pParent = GetParent();
   CMenu* pMenuBar = pParent->GetMenu();
   CMenu* pMenu = pMenuBar->GetSubMenu(3);
   CPhoneDoc* pDoc = GetDocument();
   pMenu->AppendMenu(MF_STRING ¦ MF_ENABLED, new_menu_ID++, \
        out_string.Left(out_string.Find(" ")));

   pDoc->data_string[pDoc->data_index++] = out_string;
   CClientDC dc(this);
   DWORD OldTextColor = dc.SetTextColor(dc.GetBkColor());
   dc.TextOut(0, 0, out_string, out_string.GetLength());
   dc.SetTextColor(OldTextColor);
   out_string.Empty();
}


void CPhoneView::OnItem0()
{
   // TODO: Add your command handler code here
}
```

continues

Listing 4.3. continued

```cpp
void CPhoneView::OnItem1()
{
   // TODO: Add your command handler code here
}


void CPhoneView::OnItem2()
{
   // TODO: Add your command handler code here
}


void CPhoneView::OnItem3()
{
   // TODO: Add your command handler code here
}
```

Listing 4.4. Mainframe.cpp

```cpp
// mainfrm.cpp : implementation of the CMainFrame class
//

#include "stdafx.h"
#include "phone.h"
#include "phonedoc.h"
#include "phonevw.h"

#include "mainfrm.h"

#ifdef _DEBUG
#undef THIS_FILE
static char BASED_CODE THIS_FILE[] = __FILE__;
#endif


/////////////////////////////////////////////////////////////////
////////////////
// CMainFrame

IMPLEMENT_DYNCREATE(CMainFrame, CFrameWnd)
```

```
BEGIN_MESSAGE_MAP(CMainFrame, CFrameWnd)
    //{{AFX_MSG_MAP(CMainFrame)
            // NOTE - the Class Wizard will add and remove mapping macros here.
            //    DO NOT EDIT what you see in these blocks of generated code !
    ON_WM_CREATE()
    //}}AFX_MSG_MAP
END_MESSAGE_MAP()

/////////////////////////////////////////////////////////////////////////////
// arrays of IDs used to initialize control bars

// toolbar buttons - IDs are command buttons
static UINT BASED_CODE buttons[] =
{
    // same order as in the bitmap 'toolbar.bmp'
    ID_FILE_NEW,
    ID_FILE_OPEN,
    ID_FILE_SAVE,
            ID_SEPARATOR,
    ID_EDIT_CUT,
    ID_EDIT_COPY,
    ID_EDIT_PASTE,
            ID_SEPARATOR,
    ID_FILE_PRINT,
    ID_APP_ABOUT,
};

static UINT BASED_CODE indicators[] =
{
    ID_SEPARATOR,   // status line indicator
    ID_INDICATOR_CAPS,
    ID_INDICATOR_NUM,
    ID_INDICATOR_SCRL,
};

/////////////////////////////////////////////////////////////////////////////
// CMainFrame construction/destruction

CMainFrame::CMainFrame()
```

continues

Listing 4.4. continued

```
{
    // TODO: add member initialization code here
}

CMainFrame::~CMainFrame()
{
}

int CMainFrame::OnCreate(LPCREATESTRUCT lpCreateStruct)
{
    if (CFrameWnd::OnCreate(lpCreateStruct) == -1)
            return -1;

    if (!m_wndToolBar.Create(this) ||
            !m_wndToolBar.LoadBitmap(IDR_MAINFRAME) ||
            !m_wndToolBar.SetButtons(buttons,
            sizeof(buttons)/sizeof(UINT)))
    {
            TRACE("Failed to create toolbar\n");
                            return -1;      // fail to create
    }

    if (!m_wndStatusBar.Create(this) ||

!m_wndStatusBar.SetIndicators(indicators,
                            sizeof(indicators)/sizeof(UINT)))
    {
                            TRACE("Failed to create status bar\n");
                            return -1;      // fail to create
    }

    return 0;
}


/////////////////////////////////////////////////////////////////
////////////
// CMainFrame diagnostics

#ifdef _DEBUG
void CMainFrame::AssertValid() const
```

```
{
    CFrameWnd::AssertValid();
}

void CMainFrame::Dump(CDumpContext& dc) const
{
    CFrameWnd::Dump(dc);
}


#endif //_DEBUG


/////////////////////////////////////////////////////////////////////////
/////
// CMainFrame message handlers

BOOL CMainFrame::OnCommand(WPARAM wParam, LPARAM lParam)
{
    if(wParam >= IDM_ITEM0 && wParam <= IDM_ITEM3){
            CPhoneView* pView = (CPhoneView*) GetActiveView();
            CPhoneDoc* pDoc = (CPhoneDoc*) GetActiveDocument();
            CClientDC dc(pView);
            dc.TextOut(0, 0, pDoc->data_string[wParam - IDM_ITEM0], \
                    pDoc->data_string[wParam - IDM_ITEM0].GetLength());
    }
    else
            CFrameWnd::OnCommand(wParam, lParam);

    return TRUE;
        }
```

 Listing 4.5. Phonedoc.cpp

```
// phonedoc.cpp : implementation of the CPhoneDoc class
//

#include "stdafx.h"
#include "phone.h"
```

continues

Listing 4.5. continued

```
#include "phonedoc.h"

#ifdef _DEBUG
#undef THIS_FILE
static char BASED_CODE THIS_FILE[] = __FILE__;
#endif

/////////////////////////////////////////////////////////////////////////
// CPhoneDoc

IMPLEMENT_DYNCREATE(CPhoneDoc, CDocument)

BEGIN_MESSAGE_MAP(CPhoneDoc, CDocument)
    //{{AFX_MSG_MAP(CPhoneDoc)
            // NOTE - the Class Wizard will add and remove mapping macros here.
            //      DO NOT EDIT what you see in these blocks of generated code !
      //}}AFX_MSG_MAP
END_MESSAGE_MAP()

/////////////////////////////////////////////////////////////////////////
// CPhoneDoc construction/destruction

CPhoneDoc::CPhoneDoc()
{
   data_index = 0;
   // TODO: add one-time construction code here
}

CPhoneDoc::~CPhoneDoc()
{
}

BOOL CPhoneDoc::OnNewDocument()
{
   if (!CDocument::OnNewDocument())
         return FALSE;
   // TODO: add reinitialization code here
```

```
   // (SDI documents will reuse this document)
   return TRUE;
}


//////////////////////////////////////////////////////////////
////////////
// CPhoneDoc serialization

void CPhoneDoc::Serialize(CArchive& ar)
{
   if (ar.IsStoring())
   {
         // TODO: add storing code here
   }
   else
   {
         // TODO: add loading code here
   }
}


//////////////////////////////////////////////////////////////
////////////
// CPhoneDoc diagnostics

#ifdef _DEBUG
void CPhoneDoc::AssertValid() const
{
   CDocument::AssertValid();
}

void CPhoneDoc::Dump(CDumpContext& dc) const
{
   CDocument::Dump(dc);
}

#endif //_DEBUG


//////////////////////////////////////////////////////////////
////////////
// CPhoneDoc commands
```

That completes the survey of menus, for now. As you can see, there is a great deal of power in Visual C++'s menu-handling functions. You have created menus, grayed and disabled menu items, and added check marks, accelerator keys, and shortcut keys to menus. You also tailored your menus directly at run time. This all adds up to a powerful package. Clearly, you still have a great deal more to learn about Windows. Now that you understand menus, you can move on to the next chapter where you learn about dialog boxes.

Dialog Boxes: Buttons and Text Boxes

In Windows, dialog boxes represent the standard way of receiving control input from the user beyond the menu level. Through dialog boxes, the Windows user opens files, renames files, customizes windows and application parameters, selects colors—almost anything a simple menu selection cannot specify. Because dialog boxes are so common, the user already knows that menu items followed by an ellipsis, such as Save As..., open dialog boxes.

In this chapter, you will start putting together dialog boxes of your own. And you will get an idea of the kinds of objects the user can manipulate in dialog boxes—specifically, buttons and text boxes. In Windows, these types of objects are called *controls*. (Controls include buttons, text boxes—which are also called *edit controls*—scroll bars, list boxes, and so on.) With Visual C++, the once difficult task of designing dialog boxes is much easier. You will start by learning a quick way to place dialog boxes on the screen.

Message Boxes

The quickest way to put a simple dialog box on the screen is with the Windows MessageBox( ) function, as follows:

```
int MessageBox(lpText, lpCaption = NULL, wType = MB_OK);
```

Here, lpText is a far pointer to the text you want in the message box (you can use a CString object); lpCaption is a far pointer to the caption text you want to appear in the message box's title bar (you can use a CString object here, as well); and wType specifies the controls you can have in the message box, as you will see.

NOTE

The term controls include buttons, text boxes, scroll bars, list boxes, and so on (in other words, just about every active element in a Windows program that is not itself a window).

Note also the "= NULL" and "= MB_OK" string in the following MessageBox's declaration:

```
int MessageBox(lpText, lpCaption = NULL, wType = MB_OK);
```

These are C++ *default* values. In C++, you can declare default values in a function's declaration, like this. If you then omit values for these parameters when you call that function, the default values are used. You could simply use MessageBox( ) in the following way:

```
CString hello_string = "Hello, world."
MessageBox(hello_string);
```

This passes NULL for the long pointer to the message box caption (so that the caption will give the name of the project) and the value MB_OK for wType (a single button, marked OK, will appear in the message box).

MessageBox( ) lets you design a dialog box to a certain extent, and enables the user to communicate to the program through buttons: OK, Cancel, Abort, Retry, Ignore, Yes, or No. To see how MessageBox( ) works, you might create a small program that places on screen a window in which a menu named Message has a menu item named Message Box....

Using App Wizard, create a new project named msg.mak. Add a Message menu with App Studio, and give that menu one item with the caption Message... and the ID value IDM_MESSAGE. Next, use Class Wizard to connect IDM_MESSAGE to a new view class function named OnMessage(). Double-click OnMessage() in Class Wizard, opening OnMessage() in msgview.cpp, as follows:

```
void CMsgView::OnMessage()
{

}
```

Now just place the code there, like this:

```
void CMsgView::OnMessage()
{
    CString hello_string = "Hello, world."
    MessageBox(hello_string);
}
```

The resulting menu is shown in figure 5.1. (Note that you include three dots after the name Message Box in the corresponding Menu item, to indicate that a dialog box will appear.)

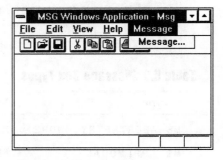

Figure 5.1. Message Box menu.

When the user selects the Message Box... item, the program calls the OnMessage() member function and the message box appears (see fig. 5.2).

You can pass certain specific values—the ones shown in table 5.1—in the wType parameter. (If you want to use more than one, OR them together.) Two of the more important MB types are MB_APPLMODAL and MB_SYSTEMMODAL. A dialog box is said to be *modal* when the user has to deal with it before continuing with the rest of the program (as opposed to *nonmodal* dialog boxes, which can appear and operate side by side with other windows). An MB_APPLMODAL message box is modal on the application level; that is, before the user can continue using the application, he or she has to finish with dialog box. Clicking any other windows belonging to the application causes a beep. With an MB_SYSTEMMODAL message box, the user must close the message box before he tries to switch to another application.

Figure 5.2. Message box example.

About Cancel Buttons.
Almost every dialog box that has buttons should have a Cancel button—Windows users expect them. Cancel buttons enable users to close the dialog box without changing the operations of the rest of the program.

Table 5.1. Message Box Types

wType	Meaning
MB_ABORTRETRYIGNORE	Abort, Retry, Ignore buttons
MB_APPLMODAL	Modal on application level
MB_DEFBUTTON1	First button is default
MB_DEFBUTTON2	Second button is default
MB_DEFBUTTON3	Third button is default
MB_ICONASTERISK	Same as MB_ICONINFORMATION
MB_ICONEXCLAMATION	Include exclamation point icon
MB_ICONHAND	Same as MB_ICONSTOP

MB_ICONINFORMATION	Include circle icon
MB_ICONQUESTION	Include question mark icon
MB_ICONSTOP	Include stop sign icon
MB_OK	OK button
MB_OKCANCEL	OK and Cancel buttons
MB_RETRYCANCEL	Retry and Cancel buttons
MB_SYSTEMMODAL	Modal on system level
MB_YESNO	Yes and No buttons
MB_YESNOCANCEL	Yes, No, Cancel buttons

When the user clicks a button in a message box, or closes the box, the Message Box() returns an integer value corresponding to one of the following constants:

wType	Meaning
IDABORT	User clicked Abort Button
IDCANCEL	User clicked Cancel Button
IDIGNORE	User clicked Ignore Button
IDNO	User clicked No Button
IDOK	User clicked OK Button
IDRETRY	User clicked Retry Button
IDYES	User clicked Yes Button

By checking the return value of MessageBox() against this list, you can determine what action the user took.

As helpful as MessageBox() is, you can go much farther when you design your own dialog boxes, as you will see. If you wanted to add a text box to the message box shown in figure 5.2, for example, you would have to design your own dialog box. Fortunately, the Dialog Editor makes that an easy job, as you are about to discover.

Designing Dialog Boxes

Say that your goal is simply to set up a dialog box similar to the one in figure 5.2, except that you want to add a text box and a button marked Click Me. When the user clicks on this button, the phrase "Hello, world." appears in the text box. The dialog box appears as follows:

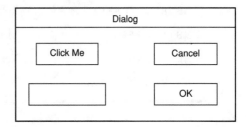

After the user clicks on the Click Me button the dialog box appears as follows:

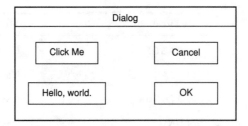

To set up this box, use App Wizard to create a new project named dlg.mak. Make it an SDI (single document interface) application. Now, to design the dialog box, open App Studio and click on the dialog resource type (the third icon down in the Type box on the left). The built-in dialog box you already have, an About box, appears in the Resources box as resource IDD_ABOUTBOX. Because you want to create your own dialog box, click on App Studio's New... button. A box opens, asking what new type of resource you want; select Dialog to create a new dialog resource named IDD_DIALOG1 and open the dialog editor (see fig. 5.3).

The vertical button bar you see in figure 5.3 is called the *toolbar*; it is filled with the types of controls that you can add to the dialog box. Two buttons (OK and Cancel) are already in this dialog box and, as you will see, functioning code is connected to them.

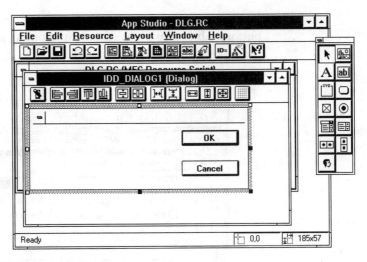

Figure 5.3. App Studio's dialog editor.

To add a button with the caption Click Me, position the mouse cursor over the button tool in the toolbar (the third tool down on the right). Next, *drag* the button (press and hold down the left mouse button while you move the mouse) over to the dialog box you are designing (see fig. 5.4).

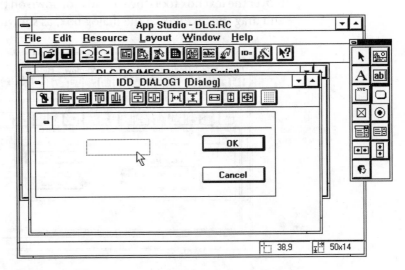

Figure 5.4. Placing a button in the dialog box.

Now release the mouse button to create the new button. Click on the new button to bring up the Push Button Properties box, and give this button the caption Click Me (see fig. 5.5).

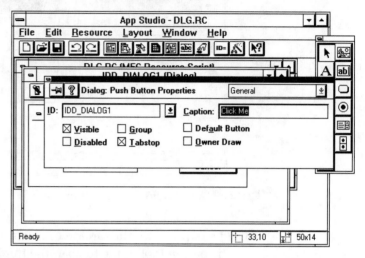

Figure 5.5. The Push Button Properties box.

Next, you can create the text box. Press the mouse button while the cursor is over the text box tool (the second tool down on the right in the toolbar) and drag the text box to the dialog box, as shown in figure 5.6.

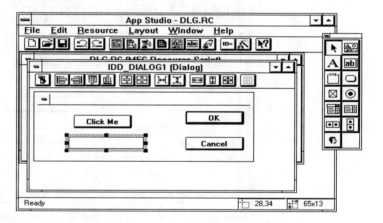

Figure 5.6. A new text box.

The eight small squares around the periphery of the new text box are called *sizing handles*. You can use them with the mouse to reshape controls the way you want them. When you double-click on this text box, the dialog editor gives it the ID IDC_EDIT1 (*IDC* stands for *control ID*). That completes the dialog box design.

At this point, then, you have completed the dialog box (resource number IDD_DIALOG1). Save it now, using App Studio's Save menu item. This dialog box specification is added to dlg.rc, as follows:

```
IDD_DIALOG1 DIALOG DISCARDABLE  0, 0, 185, 57
STYLE DS_MODALFRAME ¦ WS_POPUP ¦ WS_VISIBLE ¦ WS_CAPTION ¦WS_SYSMENU
FONT 8, "MS Sans Serif"
BEGIN
    DEFPUSHBUTTON       "OK",IDOK,129,6,50,14
    PUSHBUTTON          "Cancel",IDCANCEL,129,34,50,14
    PUSHBUTTON          "Click Me",IDC_BUTTON1,33,10,50,14
    EDITTEXT IDC_EDIT1,28,34,65,13,ES_AUTOHSCROLL
END
```

The complete dialog box—from the font used, to the location of the controls—is specified. Your next step is to associate variables with the new controls you have created. To do that, you first have to create a new class for the dialog box. This class is derived from the CDialog MFC class. Open Class Wizard (one of the items in AppStudio's Resource menu) now to create the new dialog class, which you might call CHelloDlg.

Realizing that this is a new class, the first thing Class Wizard does is to open a dialog box that asks for a name for the new class. (Note that class type CDialog is already selected.) Give the name CHelloDlg and click on the Create Class button. Now Class Wizard itself opens, displaying the class and its object IDs (see fig. 5.7).

Because you want to handle button pushes, add a member function named OnClickMeButton() now. Select the name given to the push button (IDC_BUTTON1) now in Class Wizard. The Messages box displays the messages connected with this button: BN_CLICKED and BN_DOUBLECLICKED. Select BN_CLICKED, the button message you want to handle, and click Class Wizard's Add Function button, as shown in figure 5.8.

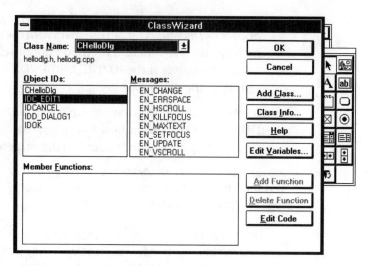

Figure 5.7. Designing the Dialog class.

Figure 5.8. Creating Dialog member functions.

When Class Wizard asks for the name of the new function in the Add Member Function dialog box, give it the name OnClickMeButton(). This creates a new member function of the CHelloDlg class (see fig. 5.8). The code for this function in class CHelloDlg appears as follows:

```
void CHelloDlg::OnClickMeButton()
{

}
```

When the user clicks the button, the code you place here is executed—and what you want to do is to place the text Hello, world. in the text box (its ID is IDC_EDIT1). You can do this in either of two ways—by using the CDialog member function SetDlgItemText() or by using the new Visual C++ member variable methods. Both ways are examined here.

Using CDialog Member Functions to Update Data

To use the CDialog member function SetDlgItemText(), you first set up a string named hello_string, as follows:

```
void CHelloDlg::OnClickMeButton()
{
    CString hello_string;

}
```

Now you use SetDlgItemText(). Because the text box has the ID value IDC_EDIT1, all you have to do is the following:

```
void CHelloDlg::OnClickMeButton()
{
    CString hello_string;

    SetDlgItemText(IDC_EDIT1, hello_string);
}
```

Now the CHelloDlg class is complete. To make the dialog box pop up on-screen, however, you have to tie it to a menu item. Use App Studio to add a Hello... item (ID value IDM_HELLO) to the program's File menu, as shown in figure 5.9.

Now use Class Wizard to connect a function named OnHello() to IDM_HELLO. Then open OnHello() by double-clicking on OnHello() in Class Wizard, as follows:

```
void CMainFrame::OnHello()
{

}
```

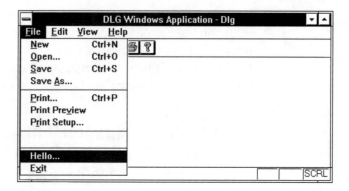

Figure 5.9. The program's Hello . . . Menu item.

This is the function that is executed when the user selects the Hello... menu item. To display the dialog box, you just have to create an object of class CHelloDlg, as follows:

```
void CMainFrame::OnHello()
{
    CHelloDlg dlg;
        :
}
```

Then you display it with the CDialog function DoModal(), which pops up the dialog box on the screen as a modal dialog box, as follows:

```
void CMainFrame::OnHello()
{
  CHelloDlg dlg;
  dlg.DoModal();
}
```

Note also that you have to include hellodlg.h at the top of the same file, mainfrm.cpp, so that the compiler knows about the CHelloDlg class, as follows:

```
// mainfrm.cpp : implementation of the CMainFrame class
//

#include "stdafx.h"
#include "dlg.h"

#include "mainfrm.h"
```

```
#include "hellodlg.h"
    :
```

That is it—now the dialog box program is ready to use. When the user selects the Hello... item, your program creates a dialog box of class CHelloDlg and then displays it, using the member function DoModal(). DoModal() returns values like IDOK or IDCancel. From the drop-down list box in the Push Button Properties box, you can select any of the following for the buttons:

DoModal( ) Return Values	Meaning
IDABORT	User clicked Abort Button
IDCANCEL	User clicked Cancel Button
IDIGNORE	User clicked Ignore Button
IDNO	User clicked No Button
IDOK	User clicked Ok Button
IDRETRY	User clicked Retry Button
IDYES	User clicked Yes Button

(Be sure to make each button's caption match its intended function.)

When the dialog box is open, the user can click on the button marked Click Me to execute this function, as follows:

```
void CHelloDlg::OnClickMeButton()
{
  CString hello_string;
  SetDlgItemText(IDC_EDIT1, hello_string);
}
```

At that point, the message appears in the following text box:

215

Figure 5.10 shows the completed dialog box.

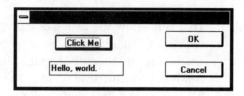

Figure 5.10. Your first custom dialog box.

Using SetDlgItemText( ) is one way to fill the text box with text. Another way is to use Visual C++ to connect data members to the controls. You do that next.

Using Visual C++ Member Variables to Update Data

So far, you have connected the function OnClickMeButton( ) to the Click Me button with Class Wizard, as follows:

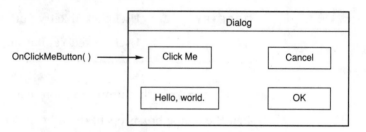

As you know, object-oriented programming enables you to connect member data as well as member functions to objects. You can use Class Wizard to create a member function m_EditBoxText, for example, that holds the string in the following text box:

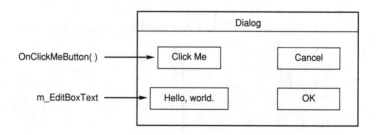

Then, in OnClickMeButton( ), you can update the data in the text box, like this:

```
void CHelloDlg::OnClickMeButton()
{
  m_EditBoxText = "Hello, world.";
          :
}
```

To do this, start Class Wizard now and select the class CHelloDlg (see fig. 5.11).

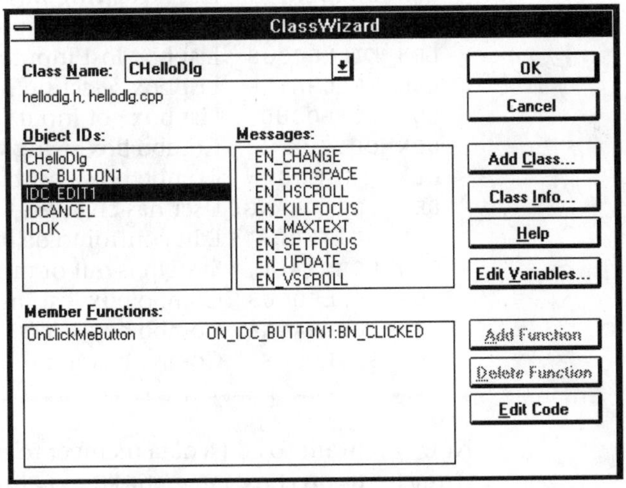

Figure 5.11. Class CHelloDlg open in Class Wizard.

The Messages box displays the messages a text box can send. The EN_CHANGE message (*EN_CHANGE* stands for *edit notification change*) is issued when the text in the box is changed, for example. You can connect member functions to messages that are called when the corresponding event occurs. Table 5.2 lists some of the more common notification messages from Windows controls.

Table 5.2. Windows Controls Notification Codes

Message	Meaning
BN_CLICKED	Button has been clicked
BN_DOUBLECLICKED	Button has been double-clicked

continues

Table 5.2. continued

Message	Meaning
EN_CHANGE	Edit control (text box) contents changed
EN_ERRSPACE	Edit control is out of space
EN_HSCROLL	Edit control's horizontal scroll clicked
EN_KILLFOCUS	Edit control lost input focus
EN_MAXTEXT	Insertion exceeded specified number of characters
EN_SETFOCUS	Edit control got input focus
EN_UPDATE	Edit control to display altered text
EN_VSCROLL	Edit control's vertical scroll clicked
LBN_DBLCLK	List box string was double-clicked
LBN_ERRSPACE	System is out of memory
LBN_KILLFOCUS	List box lost input focus
LBN_SELCHANGE	List box selection has changed
LBN_SETFOCUS	List box got input focus
CBN_DBLCLK	Combo box string was double-clicked
CBN_DROPDOWN	Combo box's list box to be dropped down
CBN_EDITCHANGE	User has changed text in the edit control
CBN_EDITUPDATE	Edit control to display altered text
CBN_ERRSPACE	System is out of memory
CBN_KILLFOCUS	Combo box lost input focus
CBN_SELCHANGE	Combo box selection was changed
CBN_SETFOCUS	Combo box got input focus

Now, you want to add a data member to the CHelloDlg class to hold the string in the text box. Open the Edit Member Variables dialog box, shown in figure 5.12, by selecting the Edit Variables... button.

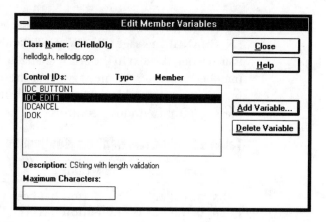

Figure 5.12. The Edit Member variables box.

Select the Add Variable... button to open the Add Member Variable box (see fig. 5.13).

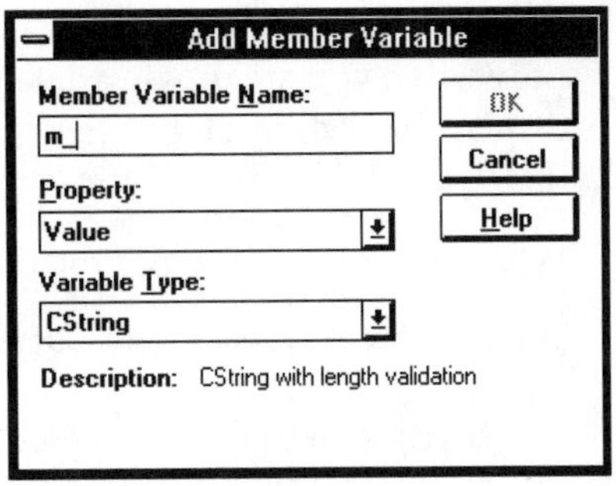

Add Member Variable

Member Variable **N**ame:

m_|

OK

Cancel

Property:

Value

Help

Variable **T**ype:

CString

Description: CString with length validation

Figure 5.13. The Add Member Variable box.

You can see that the type CString is already selected. Just type **m_EditBoxText** (the name of this new variable), click on OK, and close Class Wizard. Now you have a member variable named m_EditBoxText in the CHelloDlg class. To reach it, simply add this code in CHelloDlg::OnClickMeButton( ), as follows:

```
void CHelloDlg::OnClickMeButton()
{
  m_EditBoxText = "Hello, world.";
        :
}
```

By itself, this does not update the text in the text box. You have to call a function named UpdateData( ), in the following way:

```
void CHelloDlg::OnClickMeButton()
{
  m_EditBoxText = "Hello, world.";
  UpdateData(FALSE);      //FALSE write to screen
}
```

Calling UpdateData( ) with an argument of FALSE makes the program update the text in the text box (that is, FALSE causes UpdateData( ) to update the data member). An argument of TRUE causes the member variable to be updated from the text box. In Visual C++, using UpdateData( ) is called *DDX* (for *dialog data exchange*).

Note that when a dialog box is displayed or hidden, the appropriate version of UpdateData() is called automatically, transferring data, if the user clicked the OK button. If the user clicked the Cancel button, UpdateData() is not called. This means that you have to use UpdateData() only when you are moving data between controls while the dialog box is displayed or while it is hidden—but not just before you display or hide the dialog box.

With the new version of OnClickMeButton(), as follows:

```
void CHelloDlg::OnClickMeButton()
{
  m_EditBoxText = "Hello, world.";
  UpdateData(FALSE);      //FALSE write to screen
}
```

the data member m_EditBoxText is updated and the string Hello, world. is displayed in the following way:

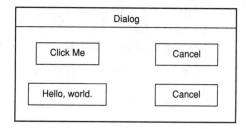

This version of the code is ready; the program works as before (refer to fig. 5.10). The listing of mainfrm.cpp is in listing 5.1; dlg.rc is in listing 5.2; hellodlg.h, in listing 5.3; and hellodlg.cpp, in listing 5.4.

Listing 5.1. Mainfrm.cpp

```
// mainfrm.cpp : implementation of the CMainFrame class
//

#include "stdafx.h"
#include "dlg.h"

#include "mainfrm.h"
#include "hellodlg.h"
#ifdef _DEBUG
#undef THIS_FILE
static char BASED_CODE THIS_FILE[] = __FILE__;
```

```
#endif

////////////////////////////////////////////////////////////////
///////////
// CMainFrame

IMPLEMENT_DYNCREATE(CMainFrame, CFrameWnd)

BEGIN_MESSAGE_MAP(CMainFrame, CFrameWnd)
  //{{AFX_MSG_MAP(CMainFrame)
  ON_WM_CREATE()
  ON_COMMAND(IDM_Hello, OnHello)
  //}}AFX_MSG_MAP
END_MESSAGE_MAP()

////////////////////////////////////////////////////////////////
///////////
// arrays of IDs used to initialize control bars

// toolbar buttons - IDs are command buttons
static UINT BASED_CODE buttons[] =
{
  // same order as in the bitmap 'toolbar.bmp'
  ID_FILE_NEW,
  ID_FILE_OPEN,
  ID_FILE_SAVE,
  ID_SEPARATOR,
  ID_EDIT_CUT,
  ID_EDIT_COPY,
  ID_EDIT_PASTE,
  ID_SEPARATOR,
  ID_FILE_PRINT,
  ID_APP_ABOUT,
};

static UINT BASED_CODE indicators[] =
{
    ID_SEPARATOR,                    // status line indicator
    ID_INDICATOR_CAPS,
    ID_INDICATOR_NUM,
    ID_INDICATOR_SCRL,
};
```

```
//////////////////////////////////////////////////////////////
////////////
// CMainFrame construction/destruction

CMainFrame::CMainFrame()
{
  // TODO: add member initialization code here
}

CMainFrame::~CMainFrame()
{
}

int CMainFrame::OnCreate(LPCREATESTRUCT lpCreateStruct)
{
  if (CFrameWnd::OnCreate(lpCreateStruct) == -1)
      return -1;

  if (!m_wndToolBar.Create(this) ||
      !m_wndToolBar.LoadBitmap(IDR_MAINFRAME) ||
      !m_wndToolBar.SetButtons(buttons,
        sizeof(buttons)/sizeof(UINT)))
  {
      TRACE("Failed to create toolbar\n");
      return -1;              // fail to create
  }

  if (!m_wndStatusBar.Create(this) ||
      !m_wndStatusBar.SetIndicators(indicators,
        sizeof(indicators)/sizeof(UINT)))
  {
      TRACE("Failed to create status bar\n");
      return -1;              // fail to create
  }

  return 0;
}
```

```
///////////////////////////////////////////////////////////////
///////////////
// CMainFrame diagnostics

#ifdef _DEBUG
void CMainFrame::AssertValid() const
{
  CFrameWnd::AssertValid();
}

void CMainFrame::Dump(CDumpContext& dc) const
{
  CFrameWnd::Dump(dc);
}


#endif //_DEBUG

///////////////////////////////////////////////////////////////
///////////////
// CMainFrame message handlers

void CMainFrame::OnHello()
{
  CHelloDlg dlg;

  dlg.DoModal();
}
```

Listing 5.2. Pertinent Sections of Dlg.rc

```
//Microsoft App Studio generated resource script.
//
#include "resource.h"

///////////////////////////////////////////////////////////////
/////////////
//
// Icon
//
```

```
IDR_MAINFRAME              ICON        DISCARDABLE
"RES\\DLG.ICO"


/////////////////////////////////////////////////////////////////
/////////////
//
// Bitmap
//

IDR_MAINFRAME              BITMAP        MOVEABLE PURE
"RES\\TOOLBAR.BMP"


/////////////////////////////////////////////////////////////////
/////////////
//
// Menu
//

IDR_MAINFRAME MENU PRELOAD DISCARDABLE
BEGIN
  POPUP "&File"
  BEGIN
    MENUITEM "&New\tCtrl+N",
  ID_FILE_NEW
    MENUITEM "&Open...\tCtrl+O",
  ID_FILE_OPEN
    MENUITEM "&Save\tCtrl+S",
  ID_FILE_SAVE
    MENUITEM "Save &As...",
  ID_FILE_SAVE_AS
    MENUITEM SEPARATOR
    MENUITEM "&Print...\tCtrl+P",
  ID_FILE_PRINT
    MENUITEM "Print Pre&view",
  ID_FILE_PRINT_PREVIEW
    MENUITEM "P&rint Setup...",
  ID_FILE_PRINT_SETUP
    MENUITEM SEPARATOR
    MENUITEM "Recent File",
```

```
        ID_FILE_MRU_FILE1, GRAYED
          MENUITEM SEPARATOR
          MENUITEM "Hello...",
    IDM_Hello
          MENUITEM "E&xit",
    ID_APP_EXIT
    END
    POPUP "&Edit"
    BEGIN

          MENUITEM "&Undo\tCtrl+Z",
    ID_EDIT_UNDO
          MENUITEM SEPARATOR
          MENUITEM "Cu&t\tCtrl+X",
    ID_EDIT_CUT
          MENUITEM "&Copy\tCtrl+C",
    ID_EDIT_COPY
          MENUITEM "&Paste\tCtrl+V",
    ID_EDIT_PASTE
    END
    POPUP "&View"
    BEGIN
          MENUITEM "&Toolbar",
    ID_VIEW_TOOLBAR
          MENUITEM "&Status Bar",
    ID_VIEW_STATUS_BAR
    END
    POPUP "&Help"
    BEGIN
          MENUITEM "&About DLG...",
    ID_APP_ABOUT
    END
END


/////////////////////////////////////////////////////////////////////
/////////////
//
// Accelerator
//
```

```
IDR_MAINFRAME ACCELERATORS PRELOAD MOVEABLE PURE
BEGIN
    "N",            ID_FILE_NEW, VIRTKEY,CONTROL
    "O",            ID_FILE_OPEN, VIRTKEY,CONTROL
    "S",            ID_FILE_SAVE, VIRTKEY,CONTROL
    "P",            ID_FILE_PRINT, VIRTKEY,CONTROL
    "Z",            ID_EDIT_UNDO, VIRTKEY,CONTROL
    "X",            ID_EDIT_CUT, VIRTKEY,CONTROL
    "C",            ID_EDIT_COPY, VIRTKEY,CONTROL
    "V",            ID_EDIT_PASTE, VIRTKEY,CONTROL
    VK_BACK,        ID_EDIT_UNDO, VIRTKEY,ALT
    VK_DELETE,      ID_EDIT_CUT, VIRTKEY,SHIFT
    VK_INSERT,      ID_EDIT_COPY, VIRTKEY,CONTROL
    VK_INSERT,      ID_EDIT_PASTE, VIRTKEY,SHIFT
    VK_F6,          ID_NEXT_PANE,   VIRTKEY
    VK_F6,          ID_PREV_PANE, VIRTKEY,SHIFT
END


/////////////////////////////////////////////////////////////
/////////////
//
// Dialog
//

IDD_ABOUTBOX DIALOG DISCARDABLE  34, 22, 217, 55
STYLE DS_MODALFRAME ¦ WS_POPUP ¦ WS_CAPTION ¦ WS_SYSMENU CAPTION"About DLG"
FONT 8, "MS Sans Serif"
BEGIN
    ICON
    IDR_MAINFRAME,IDC_STATIC,11,17,20,20
    LTEXT           "DLG Application Version 1.0",IDC_STATIC,40,10,119,8
    LTEXT           "Copyright \251 1993",IDC_STATIC,40,25,119,8
    DEFPUSHBUTTON           "OK",IDOK,176,6,32,14,WS_GROUP
END

IDD_DIALOG1 DIALOG DISCARDABLE  0, 0, 185, 57
STYLE DS_MODALFRAME ¦ WS_POPUP ¦ WS_VISIBLE ¦ WS_CAPTION ¦ WS_SYSMENU
```

```
FONT 8, "MS Sans Serif"
BEGIN
    DEFPUSHBUTTON  "OK",IDOK,129,6,50,14
    PUSHBUTTON     "Cancel",IDCANCEL,129,34,50,14
    PUSHBUTTON     "Click Me",IDC_BUTTON1,33,10,50,14
    EDITTEXT       IDC_EDIT1,28,34,65,13,ES_AUTOHSCROLL
END
```

Listing 5.3. Hellodlg.h

```
// hellodlg.h : header file
//

/////////////////////////////////////////////////////////////////////
/////////////
// CHelloDlg dialog

class CHelloDlg : public CDialog
{
// Construction
public:
    CHelloDlg(CWnd* pParent = NULL);     // standard
constructor

// Dialog Data
    //{{AFX_DATA(CHelloDlg)
    enum { IDD = IDD_DIALOG1 };
    CString     m_EditBoxText;
    //}}AFX_DATA

// Implementation
protected:

    virtual void DoDataExchange(CDataExchange* pDX);
    // DDX/DDV support

    // Generated message map functions
    //{{AFX_MSG(CHelloDlg)
    afx_msg void OnClickMeButton();
    //}}AFX_MSG
    DECLARE_MESSAGE_MAP()
};
```

Listing 5.4. Hellodlg.cpp

```cpp
// hellodlg.cpp : implementation file
//

#include "stdafx.h"
#include "dlg.h"
#include "hellodlg.h"

#ifdef _DEBUG
#undef THIS_FILE
static char BASED_CODE THIS_FILE[] = __FILE__;
#endif


/////////////////////////////////////////////////////////////////
////////////
// CHelloDlg dialog

CHelloDlg::CHelloDlg(CWnd* pParent /*=NULL*/)
  : CDialog(CHelloDlg::IDD, pParent)
{
  //{{AFX_DATA_INIT(CHelloDlg)
  m_EditBoxText = "";
  //}}AFX_DATA_INIT
}


void CHelloDlg::DoDataExchange(CDataExchange* pDX)
{
  CDialog::DoDataExchange(pDX);
  //{{AFX_DATA_MAP(CHelloDlg)
  DDX_Text(pDX, IDC_EDIT1, m_EditBoxText);
  //}}AFX_DATA_MAP
}

BEGIN_MESSAGE_MAP(CHelloDlg, CDialog)
  //{{AFX_MSG_MAP(CHelloDlg)
  ON_BN_CLICKED(IDC_BUTTON1, OnClickMeButton)
  //}}AFX_MSG_MAP
END_MESSAGE_MAP()


/////////////////////////////////////////////////////////////////
////////////
```

```
// CHelloDlg message handlers

void CHelloDlg::OnClickMeButton()
{
  m_EditBoxText = "Hello, world.";
  UpdateData(FALSE);  //FALSE write to screen


}
```

A Calculator Example

Now that you know the details, you can work faster. Now, working with the controls you are familiar with so far (buttons and text boxes), you are going to create a simple pop-up calculator that enables you add numbers. With App Studio, create a new (SDI) project named calc.mak. Start the App Studio once again and give a new dialog box the caption Calculator. Next, add two text boxes (see fig. 5.14).

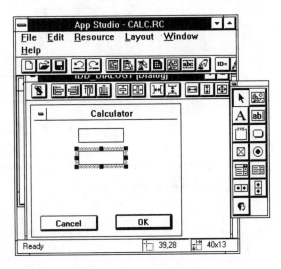

Figure 5.14. Calculator template with two text boxes.

Now, to make the dialog box look like the one in figure 5.15, add a push button under the text boxes (make its caption an equal sign (=), and use the Text tool (the first tool down on the toolbar's left) to place a plus sign (+) next to the second text box.

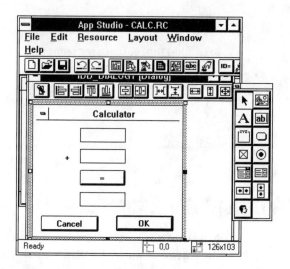

Figure 5.15. Completed Calculator template.

At this point, you have arranged the controls, as follows:

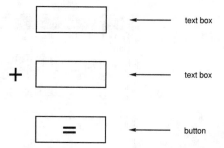

The user can place numbers in the two text boxes when the dialog box is active, as follows:

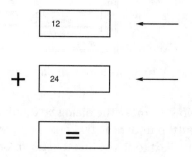

The next step is to display the answer when the user clicks on the = button, as follows:

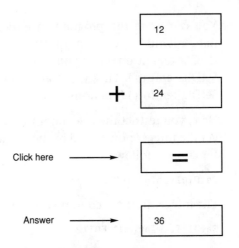

Place a text box below the = button (refer to fig. 5.15).

Now save your work and select the Class Wizard menu item. Give the new dialog class the name CCalcDlg and click on the Create Class button. The IDs of the controls are as follows:

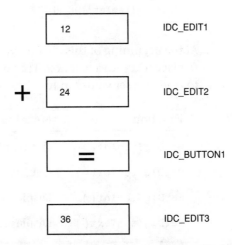

Using Class Wizard, connect a function to IDC_BUTTON1 and name it OnClickedButton1() in the dialog box class, CCalcDlg, as follows:

```
void CCalcDlg::OnClickedButton1()
```

```
{

}
```

You can write the program in either of two ways: you can connect data members to each of the controls and work with them in OnClickedButton1(), or you can use the functions GetDlgItemInt() and SetDlgItemInt(). First you learn how to use the GetDlgItemInt() and SetDlgItemInt() functions.

Here, you restrict the calculator to using only integer values, so you can get the integer now stored in the top text box with the GetDlgItemInt() function as follows:

```
GetDlgItemInt(IDC_EDIT1)
```

The integer in the second text box appears as follows:

```
GetDlgItemInt(IDC_EDIT2)
```

You can add those two values and place them in the result box with SetDlgItemInt(), as follows:

```
void CCalcDlg::OnClickedButton1()
{
  SetDlgItemInt(IDC_EDIT3, GetDlgItemInt(IDC_EDIT1) + \
    GetDlgItemInt(IDC_EDIT2);
}
```

At the beginning of this chapter you used the SetDlgItemText() function to place text into a text box. That function is one of four that you can use to read and set values in text boxes and labels.

Function	Meaning
GetDlgItemInt()	Get text from dialog control
GetDlgItemText()	Get int value as displayed in control
SetDlgItemInt()	Display text in dialog control
SetDlgItemText()	Displayed int value in control

Now connect the calculator dialog box to a menu item in the File menu
named Calculator... in the view class, CCalcView, and add the following
code to OnCalculator( ):

```
void CCalcView::OnCalc()
{
  CCalcDlg dlg;
  dlg.DoModal();
}
```

Finally, include the file calcdlg.h in the beginning of calcview.cpp with
#include, so that the compiler knows about CCalcDlg; compile and link
the program and give it a try. When you bring up the calculator, you can
plug integer values into the two text boxes, click the = button, and see the
answer (see fig. 5.16). Your calculator is a success.

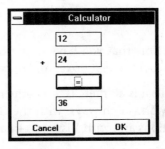

Figure 5.16. Your new Calculator.

The other way to write this program is to use Class Wizard to connect
member variables to the text boxes. In addition to Cstrings, you can
connect other types of variables to text boxes—in particular, you can

233

connect integer variables to them by selecting the int type in the Add Member Variable box's Variable Type box. Do that now to add three member int variables to the CCalcDlg class, in the following way:

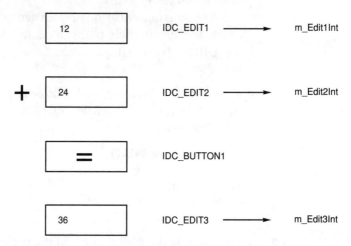

Now the function CCalcDlg::OnClickedButton1() appears as follows:

```
void  CCalcDlg::OnClickedButton1()
{
  UpdateData(TRUE);
  m_Edit3Int = m_Edit1Int + m_Edit2Int;
  UpdateData(FALSE);
}
```

(Note that you have to use UpdateData() twice—once to read the data from the text boxes and once to write it.)

That is all there is to it—the result is the same as before. Your calculator works both ways: with the GetDlgItemInt() and SetDlgItemInt() functions and with Visual C++ data members.

So much for the calculator (calcview.cpp is in listing 5.5; calcdlg.cpp, in listing 5.6; and calc.rc, in listing 5.7).

Listing 5.5. Calcview.cpp

```
// calcview.cpp : implementation of the CCalcView class
//

#include "stdafx.h"
```

```
#include "calc.h"
#include "calcdlg.h"
#include "calcdoc.h"
#include "calcview.h"

#ifdef _DEBUG
#undef THIS_FILE
static char BASED_CODE THIS_FILE[] = __FILE__;
#endif

/////////////////////////////////////////////////////////////////
/////////////
// CCalcView

IMPLEMENT_DYNCREATE(CCalcView, CView)

BEGIN_MESSAGE_MAP(CCalcView, CView)
  //{{AFX_MSG_MAP(CCalcView)
  ON_COMMAND(IDM_CALC, OnCalc)
  //}}AFX_MSG_MAP
  // Standard printing commands
  ON_COMMAND(ID_FILE_PRINT, CView::OnFilePrint)
  ON_COMMAND(ID_FILE_PRINT_PREVIEW, CView::OnFilePrintPreview)
END_MESSAGE_MAP()

/////////////////////////////////////////////////////////////////
/////////////
// CCalcView construction/destruction

CCalcView::CCalcView()
{
  // TODO: add construction code here
}

CCalcView::~CCalcView()
{
}

/////////////////////////////////////////////////////////////////
/////////////
// CCalcView drawing

void CCalcView::OnDraw(CDC* pDC)
```

```
{
  CCalcDoc* pDoc = GetDocument();

  // TODO: add draw code here
}


///////////////////////////////////////////////////////////////////
////////
// CCalcView printing

BOOL CCalcView::OnPreparePrinting(CPrintInfo* pInfo)
{
  // default preparation
  return DoPreparePrinting(pInfo);
}

void CCalcView::OnBeginPrinting(CDC* /*pDC*/, CPrintInfo* /*pInfo*/)
{
  // TODO: add extra initialization before printing
}

void CCalcView::OnEndPrinting(CDC* /*pDC*/, CPrintInfo* /*pInfo*/)
{
  // TODO: add cleanup after printing
}


///////////////////////////////////////////////////////////////////
////////
// CCalcView diagnostics

#ifdef _DEBUG
void CCalcView::AssertValid() const
{
  CView::AssertValid();
}

void CCalcView::Dump(CDumpContext& dc) const
{
  CView::Dump(dc);
}
```

```
CCalcDoc* CCalcView::GetDocument() // non-debug version is
inline
{
  ASSERT(m_pDocument->IsKindOf(RUNTIME_CLASS(CCalcDoc)));
  return (CCalcDoc*) m_pDocument;
}

#endif //_DEBUG

/////////////////////////////////////////////////////////////////////
////////////
// CCalcView message handlers


void CCalcView::OnCalc()
{
  CCalcDlg dlg;
  dlg.DoModal();

}
```

Listing 5.6. Calcdlg.cpp

```
// calcdlg.cpp : implementation file
//

#include "stdafx.h"
#include "calc.h"
#include "calcdlg.h"

#ifdef _DEBUG
#undef THIS_FILE
static char BASED_CODE THIS_FILE[] = __FILE__;
#endif

/////////////////////////////////////////////////////////////////////
////////////
// CCalcDlg dialog

CCalcDlg::CCalcDlg(CWnd* pParent /*=NULL*/)
```

```
                : CDialog(CCalcDlg::IDD, pParent)
    {
        //{{AFX_DATA_INIT(CCalcDlg)
      m_Edit1Int = 0;
      m_Edit2Int = 0;
      m_Edit3Int = 0;
      //}}AFX_DATA_INIT
    }

    void CCalcDlg::DoDataExchange(CDataExchange* pDX)
    {
      CDialog::DoDataExchange(pDX);
      //{{AFX_DATA_MAP(CCalcDlg)
      DDX_Text(pDX, IDC_EDIT1, m_Edit1Int);
      DDX_Text(pDX, IDC_EDIT2, m_Edit2Int);
      DDX_Text(pDX, IDC_EDIT3, m_Edit3Int);
      //}}AFX_DATA_MAP
    }

    BEGIN_MESSAGE_MAP(CCalcDlg, CDialog)
      //{{AFX_MSG_MAP(CCalcDlg)
      ON_BN_CLICKED(IDC_BUTTON1, OnClickedButton1)
      //}}AFX_MSG_MAP
    END_MESSAGE_MAP()

    /////////////////////////////////////////////////////////////////
    ////////////
    // CCalcDlg message handlers

    void CCalcDlg::OnClickedButton1()
    {
      UpdateData(TRUE);
      m_Edit3Int = m_Edit1Int + m_Edit2Int;
      UpdateData(FALSE);
    }
```

Listing 5.7. Calc.rc

```
//Microsoft App Studio generated resource script.
//
#include "resource.h"
```

```
#define  APSTUDIO_READONLY_SYMBOLS
/////////////////////////////////////////////////////////////////////
///////
//
// Generated from the TEXTINCLUDE 2 resource.
//
#include "afxres.h"


/////////////////////////////////////////////////////////////////////
///////
#undef APSTUDIO_READONLY_SYMBOLS

#ifdef APSTUDIO_INVOKED
/////////////////////////////////////////////////////////////////////
//////
//
// TEXTINCLUDE
//

1 TEXTINCLUDE DISCARDABLE
BEGIN
  "resource.h\0"
END

2 TEXTINCLUDE DISCARDABLE
BEGIN
  "#include ""afxres.h""\r\n"
  "\0"
END

3 TEXTINCLUDE DISCARDABLE
BEGIN
  "#include ""res\\calc.rc2""  // non-App Studio edited resources\r\n"
  "\r\n"
  "#include ""afxres.rc""  // Standard components\r\n"
  "#include ""afxprint.rc""  // printing/print preview resources\r\n"
  "\0"
END
```

```
/////////////////////////////////////////////////////////////////
/////////////////
#endif
//   APSTUDIO_INVOKED


/////////////////////////////////////////////////////////////////
////////////
//
// Icon
//

IDR_MAINFRAME ICON DISCARDABLE "RES\\CALC.ICO"

/////////////////////////////////////////////////////////////////
////////////
//
// Bitmap
//

IDR_MAINFRAME BITMAP MOVEABLE PURE    "RES\\TOOLBAR.BMP"

/////////////////////////////////////////////////////////////////
////////////
//
// Menu
//

IDR_MAINFRAME MENU PRELOAD DISCARDABLE
BEGIN
 POPUP "&File"
 BEGIN
   MENUITEM "&New\tCtrl+N",
ID_FILE_NEW
   MENUITEM "&Open...\tCtrl+O",
ID_FILE_OPEN
   MENUITEM "&Save\tCtrl+S",
ID_FILE_SAVE
```

```
                MENUITEM "Save &As...",
ID_FILE_SAVE_AS
                  MENUITEM SEPARATOR
                  MENUITEM "&Print...\tCtrl+P",
ID_FILE_PRINT
                  MENUITEM "Print Pre&view",
ID_FILE_PRINT_PREVIEW
                  MENUITEM "P&rint Setup...",
ID_FILE_PRINT_SETUP
                  MENUITEM SEPARATOR
                  MENUITEM "Recent File",
ID_FILE_MRU_FILE1, GRAYED
                  MENUITEM SEPARATOR
                  MENUITEM "Calculator...",          IDM_CALC
                  MENUITEM "E&xit",
ID_APP_EXIT
                END
                POPUP "&Edit"
                BEGIN
                  MENUITEM "&Undo\tCtrl+Z",
ID_EDIT_UNDO
                  MENUITEM SEPARATOR
                  MENUITEM "Cu&t\tCtrl+X",
ID_EDIT_CUT
                  MENUITEM "&Copy\tCtrl+C",
ID_EDIT_COPY
                  MENUITEM "&Paste\tCtrl+V",
ID_EDIT_PASTE
                END
                POPUP "&View"
                BEGIN
                  MENUITEM "&Toolbar",
ID_VIEW_TOOLBAR
                  MENUITEM "&Status Bar",
ID_VIEW_STATUS_BAR
                END
                POPUP "&Help"


       BEGIN
```

```
                    MENUITEM "&About CALC...",        ID_APP_ABOUT
          END
    END


///////////////////////////////////////////////////////////////////////
/
//
// Accelerator
//

IDR_MAINFRAME ACCELERATORS PRELOAD MOVEABLE PURE
BEGIN
  "N",            ID_FILE_NEW, VIRTKEY,CONTROL
  "O",            ID_FILE_OPEN, VIRTKEY,CONTROL
  "S",            ID_FILE_SAVE, VIRTKEY,CONTROL
  "P",            ID_FILE_PRINT, VIRTKEY,CONTROL
  "Z",            ID_EDIT_UNDO, VIRTKEY,CONTROL
  "X",            ID_EDIT_CUT, VIRTKEY,CONTROL
  "C",            ID_EDIT_COPY, VIRTKEY,CONTROL
  "V",            ID_EDIT_PASTE, VIRTKEY,CONTROL
  VK_BACK,        ID_EDIT_UNDO, VIRTKEY,ALT
  VK_DELETE,      ID_EDIT_CUT, VIRTKEY,SHIFT
  VK_INSERT,      ID_EDIT_COPY, VIRTKEY,CONTROL
  VK_INSERT,      ID_EDIT_PASTE, VIRTKEY,SHIFT
  VK_F6,          ID_NEXT_PANE, VIRTKEY
  VK_F6,          ID_PREV_PANE, VIRTKEY,SHIFT
END


///////////////////////////////////////////////////////////////////////
/
//
// Dialog
//

IDD_ABOUTBOX DIALOG DISCARDABLE  34, 22, 217, 55
STYLE DS_MODALFRAME ¦ WS_POPUP ¦ WS_CAPTION ¦ WS_SYSMENU CAPTION "About CALC"
            FONT 8, "MS Sans Serif"
```

```
BEGIN
    ICON
    IDR_MAINFRAME,IDC_STATIC,11,17,20,20
    LTEXT        "CALC Application Version 1.0",IDC_STATIC,40,10,119,8
    LTEXT        "Copyright \251 1993",IDC_STATIC,40,25,119,8
    DEFPUSHBUTTON  "OK",IDOK,176,6,32,14,WS_GROUP
END

IDD_DIALOG1 DIALOG DISCARDABLE  0, 0, 135, 116
STYLE DS_MODALFRAME ¦ WS_POPUP ¦ WS_VISIBLE ¦ WS_CAPTION ¦ WS_SYSMENU
CAPTION "Calculator"
FONT 8, "MS Sans Serif"
BEGIN
  DEFPUSHBUTTON  "OK",IDOK,78,102,50,14
  PUSHBUTTON     "Cancel",IDCANCEL,10,102,50,14
  EDITTEXT       IDC_EDIT1,45,15,40,13,ES_AUTOHSCROLL
  EDITTEXT       IDC_EDIT2,45,36,40,13,ES_AUTOHSCROLL
  PUSHBUTTON     "=",IDC_BUTTON1,46,57,39,14
  EDITTEXT       IDC_EDIT3,45,79,40,13,ES_AUTOHSCROLL
  LTEXT          "+",IDC_STATIC,29,39,9,8
END
```

The next example gives you more experience with dialog boxes and shows you how to communicate with the controls. Because you can rely on Window's text boxes to handle most of the details of text-handling, putting together a notepad—complete with word wrap and Cut and Paste capabilities—is very easy. That is what you are going to do now.

A Notepad Example

Using App Wizard, create a new application named pad.mak; then start App Studio, creating a new dialog box. Using the text box tool, add a large text box like the one shown in figure 5.17.

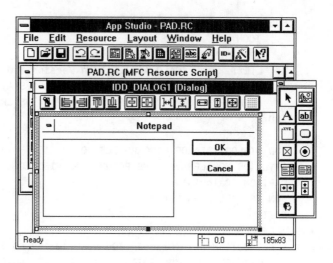

Figure 5.17. Starting the Notepad template.

Next, give this dialog box the name Notepad in the Caption box and click twice on the text box to open the Edit Properties dialog box. In the upper right corner of this box, select Styles in the drop-down list box so that you can specify the style for the text box (see fig. 5.18).

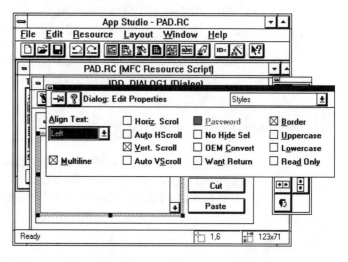

Figure 5.18. The Edit Field Styles dialog box.

Visual C++ Programming

To create the notepad, click on the Multiline and Vert. Scroll boxes. Then make sure that Auto HScroll is *not* clicked. Now click on the OK button, making this a multiline notepad with a vertical scroll bar. Finally, add two buttons labelled Cut (ID = IDC_CUT) and Paste (ID = IDC_PASTE), as shown in figure 5.19.

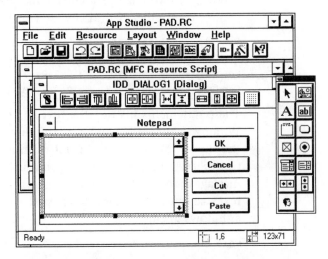

Figure 5.19. The Completed Notepad template.

About Horizontal Scrolling.
By making sure that automatic horizontal scroll is off in a text box, you ensure that automatic word wrap is turned on.

At this point, you are ready to integrate the new notepad into the program. Open Class Wizard (from App Studio's Resources menu) and associate a class named CPadDlg with the new dialog box. Next, use Class Wizard to connect two functions, OnCut() and OnPaste(), with IDC_CUT and IDC_PASTE to CPadDlg. Open OnCut(), as follows:

```
void CPadDlg::OnCut()
{

}
```

The text box itself (IDC_EDIT1) handles most of the details of text entry, and even lets the user select text. (The user can highlight text, for example, by pressing the left mouse button at one location and moving the cursor to another location; when he or she releases the button, the text in between is highlighted.) You can operate on any selected text with SendDlgItemMessage( ) statements like these, in which the text box has control ID number 101, in OnCut( ) and OnPaste( ), as follows:

```
SendDlgItemMessage(101, WM_CUT, 0, 0L);        //Cut text
SendDlgItemMessage(101, WM_COPY, 0, 0L);       //Copy text
SendDlgItemMessage(101, WM_CLEAR, 0, 0L);      //Clear text
SendDlgItemMessage(101, WM_PASTE, 0, 0L);      //Paste text
```

These statements instruct the text box to cut the selected text (to the Windows clipboard), copy it (to the clipboard), clear it, or paste it (from the clipboard). Thus, cutting and pasting is very simple. Whenever the Cut or Paste button is clicked, you just have to send the appropriate message to the text box—it handles all the details for you. (Note that if no text is selected, no text is cut or pasted over.) Cutting and pasting appears as follows in OnCut():

```
void CPadDlg::OnCut()
{
   SendDlgItemMessage(IDC_EDIT1, WM_CUT);
}
```

In OnPaste( ), it appears as follows:

```
void CPadDlg::OnPaste()
{
   SendDlgItemMessage(IDC_EDIT1, WM_Paste);
}
```

That is all you need to make the Cut and Paste buttons active. In fact, that is all you need to make the notepad dialog box work.

To make sure that the notepad is displayed, use Class Wizard to add a Notepad... menu item to the program's File menu, giving it the ID IDC_NOTEPAD. Now add a function named OnNotepad( ) to the view class (CPadView) that handles this menu item in the following way:

```
void CPadView::OnNotepad()
{

}
```

All you have to do is place the following lines here:

```
void CPadView::OnNotepad()
{
  CPadDlg dlg;
  dlg.DoModal();
}
```

You store the pad's data in the document as well, so that you can restore it to the pad if the pad is put back on-screen. (When the pad is removed from the screen, its destructor is called and the data is erased.) To provide space for that data, add a CString object named m_PadText to the document in paddoc.h.

```
// paddoc.h : interface of the CPadDoc class
//
/////////////////////////////////////////////////////////////////////
///////////////

class CPadDoc : public CDocument
{
protected: // create from serialization only
  CPadDoc();
  DECLARE_DYNCREATE(CPadDoc)

// Attributes
public:
  CString m_PadText;

// Operations
```

This is where you store the data. Now you get a pointer to the document in OnNotepad() in the view, in the following way:

```
void CPadView::OnNotepad()
{
  CPadDoc* pDoc = GetDocument( );
  CPadDlg dlg;
  dlg.DoModal();
        :
}
```

Use Class Wizard to connect a CString member variable named m_PadText to the text box (that is, use the Edit Variables... button, followed by the

Add Variable button). In this way, before showing the pad on the screen, you can restore CPadDlg::m_PadText from the document's copy of this string (pDoc->m_PadText), as follows:

```
void CPadView::OnNotepad()
{
  CPadDoc* pDoc = GetDocument();
  CPadDlg dlg;
  dlg.m_PadText = pDoc->m_PadText;
  dlg.DoModal( );
            :
}
```

Because UpdateData() is called automatically when a dialog box is displayed or hidden, you can omit the function here. After the pad is closed, you can retrieve its data (before the dlg object goes out of scope and its destructor is called) as follows:

```
void CPadView::OnNotepad()
{
  CPadDoc* pDoc = GetDocument();
  CPadDlg dlg;
  dlg.m_PadText = pDoc->m_PadText;
  dlg.DoModal();
  pDoc->m_PadText = dlg.m_PadText;
}
```

Now you can use a pop-up notepad that preserves its contents every time you pop it up. The notepad program is a success.

Figure 5.20 shows the final notepad. If you want to, you can mark text for cutting and pasting (see fig. 5.21). It is that simple to make and use.

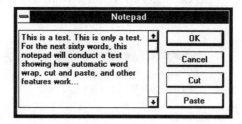

Figure 5.20. The Notepad at work.

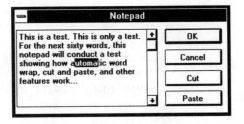

Figure 5.21. The Cut and Paste options.

The file padview.cpp is in listing 5.8; pad.rc, in listing 5.9; paddlg.cpp, in listing 5.10; and paddoc.h, in listing 5.11.

Listing 5.8. Padview.cpp

```
// padview.cpp : implementation of the CPadView class
//

#include "stdafx.h"
#include "pad.h"
#include "paddlg.h"

#include "paddoc.h"
#include "padview.h"

#ifdef _DEBUG
#undef THIS_FILE
static char BASED_CODE THIS_FILE[] = __FILE__;
#endif


/////////////////////////////////////////////////////////////////
////////////
// CPadView

IMPLEMENT_DYNCREATE(CPadView, CView)

BEGIN_MESSAGE_MAP(CPadView, CView)
    //{{AFX_MSG_MAP(CPadView)
    ON_COMMAND(IDM_NOTEPAD, OnNotepad)
```

continues

Listing 5.8. continued

```
    //}}AFX_MSG_MAP
    // Standard printing commands
    ON_COMMAND(ID_FILE_PRINT, CView::OnFilePrint)
    ON_COMMAND(ID_FILE_PRINT_PREVIEW,
CView::OnFilePrintPreview)
END_MESSAGE_MAP()


/////////////////////////////////////////////////////////
////////////////////////
// CPadView construction/destruction

CPadView::CPadView()
{
    // TODO: add construction code here
}


CPadView::~CPadView()
{
}


/////////////////////////////////////////////////////////
////////////////////////
// CPadView drawing

void CPadView::OnDraw(CDC* pDC)
{
    CPadDoc* pDoc = GetDocument();

    // TODO: add draw code here
}


/////////////////////////////////////////////////////////
////////////////////////
// CPadView printing

BOOL CPadView::OnPreparePrinting(CPrintInfo* pInfo)
{
    // default preparation
    return DoPreparePrinting(pInfo);
}
```

```
void  CPadView::OnBeginPrinting(CDC*  /*pDC*/,  CPrintInfo*  /
*pInfo*/)
{
    // TODO: add extra initialization before printing
}

void CPadView::OnEndPrinting(CDC* /*pDC*/, CPrintInfo* /*pInfo*/)
{
    // TODO: add cleanup after printing
}




/////////////////////////////////////////////////////////////
////////////////////////
// CPadView diagnostics

#ifdef _DEBUG
void CPadView::AssertValid() const
{
    CView::AssertValid();
}

void CPadView::Dump(CDumpContext& dc) const
{
    CView::Dump(dc);
}

CPadDoc* CPadView::GetDocument() // non-debug version is inline
{
    ASSERT(m_pDocument->IsKindOf(RUNTIME_CLASS(CPadDoc)));
    return (CPadDoc*) m_pDocument;
}

#endif //_DEBUG

/////////////////////////////////////////////////////////////
////////////////////////
    // CPadView message handlers
```

continues

Listing 5.8. continued

```
void  CPadView::OnNotepad()
{
    CPadDoc* pDoc = GetDocument();
    CPadDlg dlg;
    dlg.m_PadText = pDoc->m_PadText;
    dlg.DoModal();
    pDoc->m_PadText = dlg.m_PadText;

}
```

Listing 5.9. Pertinent Sections of Pad.rc

```
//Microsoft App Studio generated resource script.
//
#include "resource.h"

#define APSTUDIO_READONLY_SYMBOLS
/////////////////////////////////////////////////////////////
///////////////////
//
// Generated from the TEXTINCLUDE 2 resource.
//
#include "afxres.h"


/////////////////////////////////////////////////////////////
/////////////////////////
#undef APSTUDIO_READONLY_SYMBOLS

#ifdef APSTUDIO_INVOKED
/////////////////////////////////////////////////////////////
/////////////////////////
//
// TEXTINCLUDE
//

1 TEXTINCLUDE DISCARDABLE
BEGIN
    "resource.h\0"
```

```
          END

2  TEXTINCLUDE  DISCARDABLE
BEGIN
    "#include ""afxres.h""\r\n"
    "\0"
END

3 TEXTINCLUDE DISCARDABLE
BEGIN
    "#include ""res\\pad.rc2""  // non-App Studio edited resources\r\n"
    "\r\n"
    "#include ""afxres.rc""  // Standard components\r\n"
    "#include ""afxprint.rc""  // printing/print preview resources\r\n"
    "\0"
END


/////////////////////////////////////////////////////////
/////////////////////////
#endif
// APSTUDIO_INVOKED


/////////////////////////////////////////////////////////
/////////////////////////
//
// Icon
//

IDR_MAINFRAME          ICON   DISCARDABLE
                       "RES\\PAD.ICO"


/////////////////////////////////////////////////////////
/////////////////////////
//
// Bitmap
//

IDR_MAINFRAME          BITMAP      MOVEABLE PURE
                       "RES\\TOOLBAR.BMP"
```

continues

Listing 5.9. continued

```
///////////////////////////////////////////////////////////
///////////////////////
//
// Menu
//

IDR_MAINFRAME MENU PRELOAD DISCARDABLE
BEGIN
    POPUP "&File"
    BEGIN

        MENUITEM "&New\tCtrl+N", ID_FILE_NEW

        MENUITEM "&Open...\tCtrl+O", ID_FILE_OPEN

        MENUITEM "&Save\tCtrl+S", ID_FILE_SAVE

        MENUITEM "Save &As...", ID_FILE_SAVE_AS

        MENUITEM SEPARATOR

        MENUITEM "&Print...\tCtrl+P", ID_FILE_PRINT

        MENUITEM "Print Pre&view", ID_FILE_PRINT_PREVIEW

        MENUITEM "P&rint Setup...", ID_FILE_PRINT_SETUP

        MENUITEM SEPARATOR

        MENUITEM "Recent File", ID_FILE_MRU_FILE1, GRAYED

        MENUITEM SEPARATOR

        MENUITEM "E&xit", ID_APP_EXIT
    END
    POPUP "&Edit"
    BEGIN
        MENUITEM "&Undo\tCtrl+Z", ID_EDIT_UNDO
        MENUITEM SEPARATOR
```

```
                MENUITEM "Cu&t\tCtrl+X", ID_EDIT_CUT
                  MENUITEM "&Copy\tCtrl+C", ID_EDIT_COPY
                  MENUITEM "&Paste\tCtrl+V", ID_EDIT_PASTE
        END
        POPUP "&View"
        BEGIN
            MENUITEM "&Toolbar", ID_VIEW_TOOLBAR
            MENUITEM "&Status Bar", ID_VIEW_STATUS_BAR
        END
        POPUP "&Help"
        BEGIN
            MENUITEM "&About PAD...", ID_APP_ABOUT
        END
        POPUP "&Notepad"
        BEGIN
            MENUITEM "Notepad...", IDM_NOTEPAD
        END
END


/////////////////////////////////////////////////////
/////////////////////
//
// Accelerator
//

IDR_MAINFRAME ACCELERATORS PRELOAD MOVEABLE PURE
BEGIN
        "N",            ID_FILE_NEW, VIRTKEY,CONTROL
        "O",            ID_FILE_OPEN, VIRTKEY,CONTROL
        "S",            ID_FILE_SAVE, VIRTKEY,CONTROL
        "P",            ID_FILE_PRINT, VIRTKEY,CONTROL
        "Z",            ID_EDIT_UNDO, VIRTKEY,CONTROL
        "X",            ID_EDIT_CUT, VIRTKEY,CONTROL
        "C",            ID_EDIT_COPY, VIRTKEY,CONTROL
        "V",            ID_EDIT_PASTE, VIRTKEY,CONTROL
        VK_BACK,        ID_EDIT_UNDO, VIRTKEY,ALT
        VK_DELETE,      ID_EDIT_CUT, VIRTKEY,SHIFT
        VK_INSERT,      ID_EDIT_COPY, VIRTKEY,CONTROL
        VK_INSERT,      ID_EDIT_PASTE, VIRTKEY,SHIFT
        VK_F6,          ID_NEXT_PANE, VIRTKEY
        VK_F6,          ID_PREV_PANE, VIRTKEY,SHIFT
```

continues

Listing 5.9. E N D continued

```
////////////////////////////////////////////////////////////////
//////////////
//
// Dialog
//


IDD_ABOUTBOX DIALOG DISCARDABLE  34, 22, 217, 55
STYLE DS_MODALFRAME ¦ WS_POPUP ¦ WS_CAPTION ¦ WS_SYSMENU
CAPTION "About PAD"
FONT 8, "MS Sans Serif"
BEGIN
    ICON
    IDR_MAINFRAME,IDC_STATIC,11,17,20,20
    LTEXT           "PAD Application Version1.0",IDC_STATIC,40,10,119,8
    LTEXT           "Copyright \251 1993",IDC_STATIC,40,25,119,8
    DEFPUSHBUTTON   "OK",IDOK,176,6,32,14,WS_GROUP
END


IDD_DIALOG1 DIALOG DISCARDABLE  0, 0, 185, 83
STYLE DS_MODALFRAME ¦ WS_POPUP ¦ WS_VISIBLE ¦ WS_CAPTION ¦ WS_SYSMENU
CAPTION "Notepad"
FONT 8, "MS Sans Serif"
BEGIN
    DEFPUSHBUTTON   "OK",IDOK,130,6,50,14
    PUSHBUTTON      "Cancel",IDCANCEL,130,25,50,14
    EDITTEXT        IDD_DIALOG1,1,6,123,71,ES_MULTILINE ¦ WS_VSCROLL
    PUSHBUTTON      "Cut",IDC_CUT,130,44,50,14
    PUSHBUTTON      "Paste",IDC_PASTE,130,63,50,14
END


////////////////////////////////////////////////////////////
//////////////////////
//
// String Table
//
```

Listing 5.10. Paddlg.cpp

```cpp
    // paddlg.cpp : implementation file
//

#include "stdafx.h"
#include "pad.h"
#include "paddlg.h"
#include "paddoc.h"
#include "padview.h"

#ifdef _DEBUG
#undef THIS_FILE
static char BASED_CODE THIS_FILE[] = __FILE__;
#endif

/////////////////////////////////////////////////////////
/////////////////////////
// CPadDlg dialog

CPadDlg::CPadDlg(CWnd* pParent /*=NULL*/)
    : CDialog(CPadDlg::IDD, pParent)
{
    //{{AFX_DATA_INIT(CPadDlg)
    m_PadText = "";
    //}}AFX_DATA_INIT
}

void CPadDlg::DoDataExchange(CDataExchange* pDX)
{
    CDialog::DoDataExchange(pDX);
    //{{AFX_DATA_MAP(CPadDlg)
    DDX_Text(pDX, IDC_EDIT1, m_PadText);
    //}}AFX_DATA_MAP
}

BEGIN_MESSAGE_MAP(CPadDlg, CDialog)
    //{{AFX_MSG_MAP(CPadDlg)
    ON_BN_CLICKED(IDC_CUT, OnCut)
    ON_BN_CLICKED(IDC_PASTE, OnPaste)
    //}}AFX_MSG_MAP
END_MESSAGE_MAP()
```

continues

257

Listing 5.10. continued

```
/////////////////////////////////////////////////////
/////////////////////////
// CPadDlg message handlers

void CPadDlg::OnCut()
{
    SendDlgItemMessage(IDC_EDIT1, WM_CUT);

}

void CPadDlg::OnPaste()
{

    SendDlgItemMessage(IDC_EDIT1, WM_PASTE);
}
```

Listing 5.11. Paddoc.h

```
// paddoc.h : interface of the CPadDoc class
//
/////////////////////////////////////////////////////
/////////////////////////

class CPadDoc : public CDocument
{
protected: // create from serialization only
    CPadDoc();
    DECLARE_DYNCREATE(CPadDoc)

// Attributes
public:
    CString m_PadText;

// Operations
public:

// Implementation
public:
```

Listing 5.11. continued

```
    virtual ~CPadDoc();
    virtual void Serialize(CArchive& ar);     // overridden for document i/o
#ifdef _DEBUG
    virtual          void AssertValid() const;
    virtual          void Dump(CDumpContext& dc) const;
#endif
protected:
    virtual  BOOL        OnNewDocument();

// Generated message map functions
protected:
    //{{AFX_MSG(CPadDoc)
    // NOTE - the Class Wizard will add and remove member functions here.
    //    DO NOT EDIT what you see in these blocks of generated code !
    //}}AFX_MSG
    DECLARE_MESSAGE_MAP()
};
```

That ends the discussion of the notepad as well as the coverage of buttons and text boxes in dialog boxes. In the next chapter, you continue exploring dialog boxes and learn about some new controls—grid controls and list boxes.

Dialog Boxes: Listboxes, Grids— and a Spreadsheet

Windows users are very familiar with listboxes. A listbox presents you with a number of text string choices to select from; clicking one of the listed choices highlights and selects that choice. Listboxes are used when you have a number of pre-determined options that you want to present to the user. In this chapter, you will put together a small database example, showing you how to add items to a listbox, and retrieve them on command.

In addition, there is a popular dialog-box control that comes with Visual C++—*grids*. A *grid* is one of a special class of controls that originally comes to Visual C++ from Visual Basic, and it is supported in a .vbx file that you will install in Visual C++. Other such controls are available separately—controls that support modems, graph data, display Windows gauges, and so on—and we will see how to handle these kinds of popular controls by using the Visual C++ CVBControl class. In particular, you will write a spreadsheet example by using the Grid control.

You may have noticed how easy it is to add controls to dialog boxes—all you have to do is to draw what you want by using tools from the toolbar. You probably want to do the same thing with the main window—draw controls where you want them. There is a way of doing that in Visual C++, where you derive your view class from the dialog box, enabling you to use dialog-box controls in the main window. You will see how that works at the end of this chapter.

First, however, let's see how listboxes work by putting together a short database example.

A Database Example

The example will be to put together a small database program by using a list box to display your data. For example, say that you had loaned money to a number of people and wanted to keep track of those loans as follows:

> Frank owes $36 due on 12/19
>
> Charles owes $400 due on 2/21
>
> Jeff owes $45 due on 3/2

As in the phone book program, you type a name followed by the data you need to store in the main window, as follows:

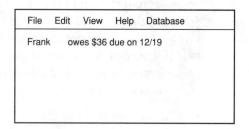

You could have an Add Item selection in a Database menu that would add *Frank* to a list box. After you enter all of the data, bring up the list box by clicking another File menu item—for example, Find Item...—and the following dialog box would come up:

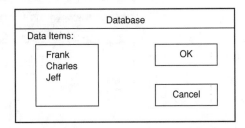

You need to let the user choose a database item with the mouse—for example, Frank—from the list box. When they do, you can close the dialog box and display that item's data in the main window, as follows:

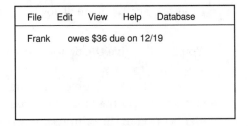

In other words, this process is like the phone book application, except that you present the list of data items in a list box, not in a menu. To adapt this program into a real database program, you need to tailor each entry into a complete record with an entire collection of CString objects that can be stored and retrieved by selecting the appropriate keyword in the list box.

There are two ways of selecting items from a list box like this: by selecting—highlighting—an item and clicking an OK button; or by double-clicking that item in the list box, and you should allow for both methods in our program. To start, you need to learn about list boxes.

List Boxes

Create a new SDI application called db.mak, by using App Wizard. Next, bring up App Studio, and create a new dialog box (IDD_DIALOG1). You need to use the list box tool to draw a list box, by stretching it as shown in figure 6.1.

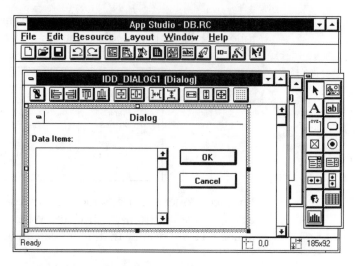

Figure 6.1. The Database dialog box template.

You need to give the dialog box the caption Database, and label the list box *Data Items:*, with the text tool—first down on the left—as shown in figure 6.1. Now double-click the new list box itself, bringing up its options. Select the Styles option in the drop-down list box in the upper right corner in the options box, displaying the list box options as shown in figure 6.2.

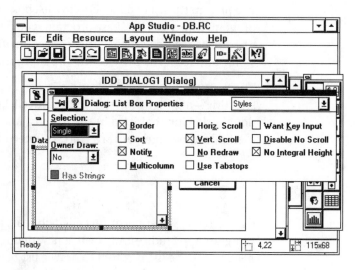

Figure 6.2. List box options.

Note in particular the Sort, Notify, and Vert. Scroll Bar options. Deselect Sort; when you click it, all of the entries in the list box are sorted in alphabetical order. It will simplify things in your example program if you leave the entries in the order in which they are inserted, because their location in the list box corresponds to their location in the arrays of strings. The Notify option, that is already set, ensures that you are notified when all of the changes are made in the list box. That is exactly what you want: to get messages from the list box when changes are made to it. These are the list box notification (prefix: LBN) codes that we can get from a list box as follows:

LBN_ERRSPACE	List box cannot get enough memory space
LBN_SELCHANGE	Selection was changed
LBN_DBLCLK	List box selection was double-clicked
LBN_SELCANCEL	Selection was canceled
LBN_SETFOCUS	List box got the focus
LBN_KILLFOCUS	List box lost the focus

The list box notification you are interested in is LBN_DBLCLK, that you will see when a selection is clicked twice. Another way to make a selection in your example is by clicking the OK button, to get a message from the OK button, not the list box). Let's put this process to work.

Save the new dialog box in a file with App Studio's Save item, adding these lines to db.rc—note the declaration of the list box, as follows:

```
IDD_DIALOG1 DIALOG DISCARDABLE  0, 0, 185, 92
STYLE DS_MODALFRAME ¦ WS_POPUP ¦ WS_VISIBLE ¦ WS_CAPTION ¦
WS_SYSMENU CAPTION "Database"
FONT 8, "MS Sans Serif"
BEGIN
    DEFPUSHBUTTON   "OK",IDOK,129,23,50,14
    PUSHBUTTON          "Cancel",IDCANCEL,129,44,50,14
    LTEXT           "Data Items:",IDC_STATIC,0,9,49,7
    LISTBOX
IDC LIST1,4,22,115,68,LBS_NOINTEGRALHEIGHT ¦ WS_VSCROLL ¦ WS_TABSTOP
END
```

Select the Class Wizard item in App Studio's Resource menu, by giving the new dialog class a name—for example, CDataDlg. Create this class by opening Class Wizard. The first thing to do in Class Wizard is to add code to the view class to handle keyboard input. We do that as before, by adding code to handle the WM_CHAR message named OnChar(), as follows:

```
void CDbView::OnChar(UINT nChar, UINT nRepCnt, UINT nFlags)
{
        out_string += nChar;
        CClientDC dc(this);
        dc.TextOut(0, 0, out_string, out_string.GetLength());
        CView::OnChar(nChar, nRepCnt, nFlags);
}
```

Also, add out_string to dbview.h as a CString object like this:

```
// dbview.h : interface of the CDbView class
//
/////////////////////////////////////////////////////////////////////
// class CDbView : public CView
{
protected: // create from serialization only
    CDbView();
    DECLARE_DYNCREATE(CDbView)
// Attributes
public:
    CDbDoc* GetDocument();
    CString out_string;
// Operations
public:
    :
```

Now your program is ready to accept keystrokes as follows:

File	Edit	View	Help	Database
Frank	owes $36 due on 12/19			

The next step is to handle that data with the Add Item menu item, that will store the data in your document—and erase out_string from the window, as follows:

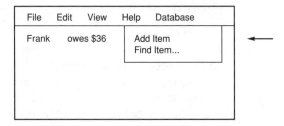

You need to add two menu items to the IDR_MAINFRAME menu by using App Studio: Add Item—give it the ID IDM_ADDITEM—and Find Item... (ID IDM_FINDITEM), and connect them to the functions OnAdditem() and OnFinditem() respectively. Currently, OnAdditem() appears as follows:

```
void CDbView::OnAdditem()
{
}
```

Your primary goal is to store what has been typed in the document. You need to add a CString array called data_string[], and an index in that array called data_index to your document (dbdoc.h) as follows:

```
class CDbDoc : public CDocument
{
protected: // create from serialization only
        CDbDoc();
        DECLARE_DYNCREATE(CDbDoc)
// Attributes
public:
    CString data_string[10];
    int data_index;
            :
```

In addition, you need to set the data_index to 0 in CDbDoc's constructor (in dbdoc.cpp), as follows:

```
CDbDoc::CDbDoc()
{
```

```
        data_index = 0;
}
```

Now, in OnAdditem(), you store out_string in pDoc->data_string[pDoc->data_index], and erase it from the screen in preparation for accepting more data, as follows:

```
void CDbView::OnAdditem()
{
CDbDoc* pDoc = GetDocument();
pDoc->data_string[pDoc->data_index++] = out_string;
CClientDC dc(this);
DWORD OldTextColor = dc.SetTextColor(dc.GetBkColor());
dc.TextOut(0, 0, out_string, out_string.GetLength());
dc.SetTextColor(OldTextColor);
    out_string.Empty();
}
```

That is all for OnAdditem(). After the data has been stored, you add it to the dialog box's list box. You can do that in the OnFinditem(), that is called when you click on Find Item... in the Database menu.

Until now, you have declared the dialog box objects in the function that used them in the following way:

```
void CDbView::OnFinditem()
{
    CDataDlg dlg;
    dlg.DoModal;
}
```

However, this means that the dialog box object goes out of scope when you leave the function, making it inaccessible to the rest of the program. If you want other functions to have access to data in the dlg object, you can declare it as an embedded object, by using it in dbview.h—notice that you also include datadlg.h to tell the compiler about the CDataDlg class, as follows:

```
// dbview.h : interface of the CDbView class
//
/////////////////////////////////////////////////////
///////////////////////// #include "datadlg.h"
class CDbView : public CView
{
```

```
protected: // create from serialization only
                CDbView();
                DECLARE_DYNCREATE(CDbView)
// Attributes
public:
                CDbDoc* GetDocument();
                CString out_string;
        CDataDlg dlg;
// Operations
public:
        :
```

How do you transfer data from the document's data_string[] array, and data_index variable to the dlg object? You can add a similar array and data item to the CDataDlg class, as follows in datadlg.h.

```
// datadlg.h : header file
//
///////////////////////////////////////////////////////////////////////////
// CDataDlg dialog
class CDataDlg : public CDialog
{
// Construction
public:
    CString data_string[10];
    int data_index;
                    :
```

figure 6.

Now you can transfer data to your dlg object in OnFinditem(),as follows:

```
void CDbView::OnFinditem()
{
        CDbDoc* pDoc = GetDocument();
for (int loop_index = 0;
loop_index < pDoc->data_index;
loop_index++){
dlg.data_string[loop_index] = pDoc->data_string[loop_index];
        }
        dlg.data_index = pDoc->data_index;
                :
}
```

That is it; the data has been transferred. The next step is to show the following dialog box:

```
void CDbView::OnFinditem()
{
CDbDoc* pDoc = GetDocument();
for (int loop_index = 0;
loop_index < pDoc->data_index;
loop_index++){
dlg.data_string[loop_index] = pDoc->data_string[loop_index];
        }
        dlg.data_index = pDoc->data_index;
    dlg.DoModal();
                                    :

}
```

When the dialog box is being prepared for display, you can add the data strings in data_string[] to the list box. You can do that by sending an LB_INSERTSTRING message to the list box (ID number IDC_LIST1). The messages you can send to list boxes appear in table 6.1.

Table 6.1. List Box Control Messages

List Box Message	Means
LB_ADDSTRING	Add a string
LB_INSERTSTRING	Insert a string
LB_DELETESTRING	Delete a string
LB_RESETCONTENT	Clear box
LB_SETSEL	Set selection state
LB_SETCURSEL	Set currently selected item
LB_GETSEL	Get selection state
LB_GETCURSEL	Get currently selected item
LB_GETTEXT	Get item at some index
LB_GETTEXTLEN	Get item's text length
LB_GETCOUNT	Get number of items in list box
LB_SELECTSTRING	Select a string
LB_DIR	Display directory files

List Box Message	Means
LB_GETTOPINDEX	Get item at top (not 0 if box is scrolled)
LB_FINDSTRING	Locate a string
LB_GETSELCOUNT	Get selection count
LB_GETSELITEMS	Get indices of selected items
LB_SETTABSTOPS	Set tabs
LB_GETHORIZONTALEXTENT	Width in pixels box can be scrolled horizontally
LB_SETHORIZONTALEXTENT	Width in pixels box can be scrolled vertically
LB_SETCOLUMNWIDTH	Set col. width in multi-column boxes
LB_SETTOPINDEX	Set top item's index
LB_GETITEMRECT	Get bounding rectangle for item
LB_GETITEMDATA	Get user supplied data associated with item
LB_SETITEMDATA	Set user supplied data associated with item
LB_SELITEMRANGE	Set a range of items

To add the data strings to the list box, use Class Wizard to connect a function named OnInitDialog() to the WM_INITDIALOG message in the CDataDlg class. That is the correct place to add items to a list box, not the dialog box's constructor, because the actual list box does not exist at that point. You only need the first word of the data strings—for example, up to the first space—added to the list box, so you cycle through the data_string[] array like the following CDataDlg::OnInitDialog().

```
BOOL CDataDlg::OnInitDialog()
{
    CDialog::OnInitDialog();
for (int loop_index = 0;
loop_index < data_index;
loop_index++){
```

```
SendDlgItemMessage(IDC_LIST1, LB_INSERTSTRING, loop_index, \
(LONG) (LPSTR) (const char*) \
data_string[loop_index].Left(data_string[loop_index].Find(" ")));
    }
return TRUE;   // return TRUE  unless you set the focus to a control
}
```

Note the parameters you used in SendDlgItemMessage(), as follows:

```
    SendDlgItemMessage(IDC_LIST1, LB_INSERTSTRING, loop_index, \
(LONG) (LPSTR) (const char*) \
data_string[loop_index].Left(data_string[loop_index].Find(" ")));
```

The first item is the list box's ID number, the next is the message you want to send. This is followed by the new item's location in the list box—0-based—and a long value that holds a pointer to the string you want to add. This long value is a little tricky because your data is stored in a CString object. You need to cast the CString object to a char string first. You do that with (const char*)—the "const" is important because we are pointing to private CString data that we are not allowed to change—for example, you cannot cast a CString object to a simple char*. Next, we cast the last char* string to another type: a Windows long pointer to a string, using the (LPSTR) cast (defined in windows.h). Finally, we cast that long pointer into a long value with (LONG) and we are set, without any loss of data.

There are other operations you could perform with SendDlgItemMessage() on list boxes. For example, the length of the current selection in that list box, appears as follows:

```
nLen = (int) SendDlgItemMessage(IDC_LIST1, LB_GETTEXT, nIndex, \
(LONG) (LPSTR) szString);
```

Or, you could have highlighted an item—for example, selected it—with index nIndex, as follows:

```
SendDlgItemMessage(IDC_LIST1, LB_SETCURSEL, nIndex, 0L);
```

You can even get the length of the current selection, as follows:

```
nLen = SendDlgItemMessage(IDC_LIST1, LB_GETTEXTLEN, nIndex, 0L);
```

That is it; now your list box is filled with key words and the dialog box appears as follows:

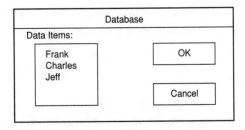

When you double-click one of the items, or select one and click OK, you want to display the matching data string as follows:

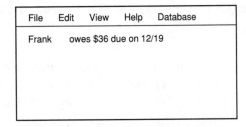

You do that by connecting a function to the list box's `LBN_DBLCLK` notification message in Class Wizard, as shown in figure 6.3.

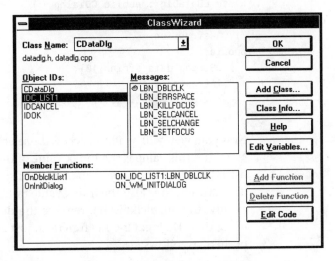

Figure 6.3. Connecting to the LBN_DBLCLK notification.

The name Class Wizard gives this function is CDataDlg::OnDblclkList1(). You can open it by double-clicking it in Class Wizard, as follows:

```
void CDataDlg::OnDblclkList1()
{
}
```

You need to communicate to the rest of the program what item was selected. You do that by sending a LB_GETCURSEL message to IDC_LIST1, as follows:

```
void CDataDlg::OnDblclkList1()
{
selected_item = (int) SendDlgItemMessage(IDC_LIST1, LB_GETCURSEL, 0, 0L);
    :
}
```

The usual return value for SendDlgItemMessage() is a long procedure, but you cast it into an integer value named selected_item that you can add to CDataDlg in datadlg.h, as follows:

```
// datadlg.h : header file
// ////////////////////////////////////////////////////////
/////////////////////// // CDataDlg dialog
class CDataDlg : public CDialog
{
// Construction
public:
    CString data_string[10];
    int data_index;
    int selected_item;
        :
```

Now your view will be able to access the selected item as dlg.selected_item. Note that this value is the index value of the item selected by you in the list box—and because you loaded the list box directly from the array data_string[], it is also the index value in that array of the selected item. Finally, in OnDblclkList1(), remove the dialog box from the screen by using the CDialog::OnOK() function, just as if the OK button had been pushed, as follows:

```
void CDataDlg::OnDblclkList1()
{
    selected_item = (int) SendDlgItemMessage(IDC_LIST1, LB_GETCURSEL, 0, 0L);
    CDialog::OnOK();
}
```

That is your other option—pushing the OK button after making a selection—so you need to intercept the OK button's code here as well. To do that, use the Class Wizard to connect a function to the BN_CLICKED notification message of the OK button (ID = IDOK). You will find that the function, appears as follows:

```
void CDataDlg::OnOK()
{
    CDialog::OnOK();
}
```

Add the code here to make sure that selected_item is set correctly, as follows:

```
void CDataDlg::OnOK()
{
selected_item = (int) SendDlgItemMessage(IDC_LIST1, LB_GETCURSEL, 0, 0L);
CDialog::OnOK();
}
```

That is it; now the item you want to display on the screen is pDoc->data_string[dlg.selected_item] from the view's perspective, therefore you put that full string on the screen, as follows:

```
void CDbView::OnFinditem()
{
        CDbDoc* pDoc = GetDocument();
    for (int loop_index = 0; loop_index < pDoc->data_index; loop_index++){
        dlg.data_string[loop_index] = pDoc->data string[loop index];
        }
        dlg.data_index = pDoc->data_index;
        dlg.DoModal();
    CClientDC dc(this);
    dc.TextOut(0, 0, pDoc->data_string[dlg.selected_item], \
pDoc->data_string[dlg.selected_item].GetLength());
}
```

That's all there is to it; your database is a success. You can fill it with values as shown in figure 6.4, and retrieve them as shown in figure 6.5.

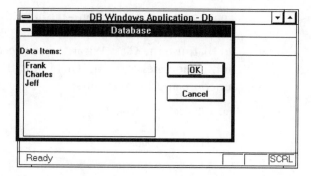

Figure 6.4. The List Box with items in it.

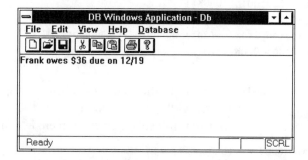

Figure 6.5. Retrieving database items.

The file datadlg.cpp appears in listing 6.1; dbview.h in appears in listing 6.2; and dbdoc.h appears in listing 6.3.

Clicking a Button From Code.
You make the OK button appear to click itself when you double-click the list box selection by using the following code:

```
SendDlgItemMessage(IDOK, BM_SETSTATE, 1, 0L);
SendDlgItemMessage(IDOK, BM_SETSTATE, 0, 0L);.]
```

Listing 6.1. Datadlg.Cpp

```cpp
// datadlg.cpp : implementation file
//
#include "stdafx.h"
#include "db.h"
#include "dbdoc.h"
#include "dbview.h"
#ifdef _DEBUG
#undef THIS_FILE
static char BASED_CODE THIS_FILE[] = __FILE__;
#endif
/////////////////////////////////////////////////////////////////////////////
// CDataDlg dialog
CDataDlg::CDataDlg(CWnd* pParent /*=NULL*/)
        : CDialog(CDataDlg::IDD, pParent)
{
        //{{AFX_DATA_INIT(CDataDlg)
    m_ListText = "";
    //}}AFX_DATA_INIT
}
void CDataDlg::DoDataExchange(CDataExchange* pDX)
{
    CDialog::DoDataExchange(pDX);
    //{{AFX_DATA_MAP(CDataDlg)
    DDX_LBString(pDX, IDC_LIST1, m_ListText);
    //}}AFX_DATA_MAP
}
BEGIN_MESSAGE_MAP(CDataDlg, CDialog)
    //{{AFX_MSG_MAP(CDataDlg)
    ON_LBN_DBLCLK(IDC_LIST1, OnDblclkList1)
    //}}AFX_MSG_MAP
END_MESSAGE_MAP()
/////////////////////////////////////////////////////////////////////////////
// CDataDlg message handlers
BOOL CDataDlg::OnInitDialog()
{
    CDialog::OnInitDialog();
for (int loop_index = 0; loop_index < data_index;
loop_index++){
```

continues

```
    SendDlgItemMessage(IDC_LIST1, LB_INSERTSTRING, loop_index, \
(LONG) (LPSTR) (const char*) \
data_string[loop_index].Left(data_string[loop_index].Find(" ")));
    }
return TRUE;   // return TRUE  unless you set the focus to a control
}
void CDataDlg::OnDblclkList1()
{
selected_item = (int) SendDlgItemMessage(IDC_LIST1, LB_GETCURSEL, 0, 0L);
CDialog::OnOK();
}
void CDataDlg::OnOK()
{
selected_item = (int) SendDlgItemMessage(IDC_LIST1, LB_GETCURSEL, 0, 0L);
CDialog::OnOK();
}
```

Listing 6.2. Dbview.H

```
// dbview.h : interface of the CDbView class
// /////////////////////////////////////////////////////
//////////////////////// #include "dbdlg.h"
#include "datadlg.h"
class CDbView : public CView
{
protected: // create from serialization only CDbView();
DECLARE_DYNCREATE(CDbView)
// Attributes
public:
    CDbDoc* GetDocument();
    CString out_string;
    CDataDlg dlg;
// Operations
public:
// Implementation
public:
        virtual ~CDbView();
        virtual void OnDraw(CDC* pDC);  // overridden to draw this view
#ifdef _DEBUG
```

```
        virtual void AssertValid() const;
        virtual void Dump(CDumpContext& dc) const;
#endif
        // Printing support
protected:
virtual BOOL OnPreparePrinting(CPrintInfo* pInfo);
virtual void OnBeginPrinting(CDC* pDC, CPrintInfo* pInfo);
virtual void OnEndPrinting(CDC* pDC, CPrintInfo* pInfo);
// Generated message map functions
protected:
        //{{AFX_MSG(CDbView)
afx_msg void OnChar(UINT nChar, UINT nRepCnt, UINT nFlags);
afx_msg void OnAdditem();
        afx_msg void OnFinditem();
        //}}AFX_MSG
        DECLARE_MESSAGE_MAP()
};
#ifndef _DEBUG        // debug version in dbview.cpp inline CDbDoc*
CDbView::GetDocument()
   { return (CDbDoc*) m_pDocument; }
#endif
//////////////////////////////////////////////////////////////////////
figure 6.

// dbview.cpp : implementation of the CDbView class
//
#include "stdafx.h"
#include "db.h"
#include "dbdoc.h"
#include "dbview.h"
#ifdef _DEBUG
#undef THIS_FILE
static char BASED_CODE THIS_FILE[] = __FILE__;
#endif
////////////////////////////////////////////////////////////////////// //
CDbView
IMPLEMENT_DYNCREATE(CDbView, CView)
BEGIN_MESSAGE_MAP(CDbView, CView)
        //{{AFX_MSG_MAP(CDbView)
        ON_WM_CHAR()
        ON_COMMAND(IDM_ADDITEM, OnAdditem)
```

continues

Listing 6.2. continued

```
                ON_COMMAND(IDM_FINDITEM, OnFinditem)
            //}}AFX_MSG_MAP
            // Standard printing commands
ON_COMMAND(ID_FILE_PRINT, CView::OnFilePrint)
ON_COMMAND(ID_FILE_PRINT_PREVIEW, CView::OnFilePrintPreview)
END_MESSAGE_MAP()
///////////////////////////////////////////////////////////
/////////////////////
// CDbView construction/destruction
CDbView::CDbView()
{
    // TODO: add construction code here
}
CDbView::~CDbView()
{
}
///////////////////////////////////////////////////////////
/////////////////////
// CDbView drawing
void CDbView::OnDraw(CDC* pDC)
{
    CDbDoc* pDoc = GetDocument();
    // TODO: add draw code here
}
///////////////////////////////////////////////////////////
/////////////////////
// CDbView printing
BOOL CDbView::OnPreparePrinting(CPrintInfo* pInfo)
{
    // default preparation
    return DoPreparePrinting(pInfo);
}
void CDbView::OnBeginPrinting(CDC* /*pDC*/, CPrintInfo* /*pInfo*/)
{
    // TODO: add extra initialization before printing
}
void CDbView::OnEndPrinting(CDC* /*pDC*/, CPrintInfo* /*pInfo*/)
{
    // TODO: add cleanup after printing
}
```

```
/////////////////////////////////////////////////////////
/////////////////////
// CDbView diagnostics
#ifdef _DEBUG
void CDbView::AssertValid() const
{
    CView::AssertValid();
}
void CDbView::Dump(CDumpContext& dc) const
{
    CView::Dump(dc);
}
CDbDoc* CDbView::GetDocument() // non-debug version is inline
{
    ASSERT(m_pDocument->IsKindOf(RUNTIME_CLASS(CDbDoc)));
    return (CDbDoc*) m_pDocument;
}
#endif //_DEBUG
/////////////////////////////////////////////////////////
/////////////////////
// CDbView message handlers
void CDbView::OnChar(UINT nChar, UINT nRepCnt, UINT nFlags) {
                out_string += nChar;
                CClientDC dc(this);
                dc.TextOut(0, 0, out_string, out_string.GetLength());
                CView::OnChar(nChar, nRepCnt, nFlags);
}
void CDbView::OnAdditem()
{
CDbDoc* pDoc = GetDocument();
pDoc->data_string[pDoc->data_index++] = out_string;
CClientDC dc(this);
DWORD OldTextColor = dc.SetTextColor(dc.GetBkColor());
dc.TextOut(0, 0, out_string, out_string.GetLength());
dc.SetTextColor(OldTextColor);
        out_string.Empty();
}
void CDbView::OnFinditem()
{
                CDbDoc* pDoc = GetDocument();
for (int loop_index = 0;
loop_index < pDoc->data_index;
```

continues

Listing 6.2. continued

```
loop_index++){
dlg.data_string[loop_index] = pDoc->data_string[loop_index];
            }
            dlg.data_index = pDoc->data_index;
            dlg.DoModal();
            CClientDC dc(this);
dc.TextOut(0, 0, pDoc->data_string[dlg.selected_item], \
pDoc->data_string[dlg.selected_item].GetLength());
}
```

Listing 6.3. Applicable Section of Dbdoc.H

```
// dbdoc.h : interface of the CDbDoc class
// /////////////////////////////////////////////////////
/////////////////////
class CDbDoc : public CDocument
{
protected: // create from serialization only
            CDbDoc();
            DECLARE_DYNCREATE(CDbDoc)
// Attributes
public:
    CString data_string[10];
    int data_index;
// Operations
public:
// Implementation
public:
            virtual ~CDbDoc();
            virtual void Serialize(CArchive& ar);
#ifdef _DEBUG
            virtual        void AssertValid() const;
            virtual        void Dump(CDumpContext& dc) const;
#endif
protected:
            virtual        BOOL        OnNewDocument();
// Generated message map functions
protected:
        //{{AFX_MSG(CDbDoc)
// NOTE - the ClassWizard will add and remove member functions.
```

```
// DO NOT EDIT what you see in these blocks of generated code !
    //}}AFX_MSG
    DECLARE_MESSAGE_MAP()
};
///////////////////////////////////////////////////////
/////////////////////////
```

Combo Boxes

In addition to using list boxes, you can also use combo boxes—list boxes with an added text box. This way, the user is not restricted to selecting items as presented in a list, but can enter his own text in the text box.

We can draw combo boxes with the combo box tool in the App Studio's toolbox—fourth tool down on the right. By using combo boxes, you get many of the same types of messages as you have already seen in list boxes as follows—CBN stands for combo box notification, as follows:

CBN_ERRSPACE	Combo box cannot get enough memory space
CBN_SELCHANGE	Selection was changed
CBN_DBLCLK	Combo box selection was double-clicked
CBN_SETFOCUS	Combo box got the focus
CBN_KILLFOCUS	List box lost the focus

In addition, however, you can also get these notification codes in wParam when the text in the text box is changed, as follows:

CBN_EDITCHANGE	Text in text box edited
CBN_EDITUPDATE	Text in text box updated from list
CBN_DROPDOWN	Drop-down combo box was opened

You handle combo boxes in the same way as you have handled list boxes—with the SendDlgItemMessage(). The combo box control messages available, as shown in table 6.2, are much like the ones you saw for the list boxes.

Table 6.2. Combo Box Control Messages

Combo Box Message	Means
CB_GETEDITSEL	Get text box selection
CB_LIMITTEXT	Limit text length in text box
CB_SETEDITSEL	Selects characters in the text box
CB_ADDSTRING	Add a string to the list box
CB_DELETESTRING	Delete a string from the list box
CB_DIR	Display directory data
CB_GETCOUNT	Get count of items in list box
CB_GETCURSEL	Get index of selected item if any
CB_GETLBTEXT	Get string from list box
CB_GETLBTEXTLEN	Get length of string in list box
CB_INSERTSTRING	Insert a string
CB_RESETCONTENT	Clear list and text boxes
CB_FINDSTRING	Find a string
CB_SELECTSTRING	Select string matching a prefix
CB_SETCURSEL	Select a string
CB_SHOWDROPDOWN	Shows or hides drop–down list box
CB_GETITEMDATA	Get user supplied data for this item
CB_SETITEMDATA	Set user supplied data for this item

A Spreadsheet Example

Another popular dialog box control is the Grid control, that looks like a spreadsheet. It is not exactly a spreadsheet, because you cannot edit the individual cells to place text in them—although some programs move a text box over the active cell by using the MoveWindow() function so that it looks like you can move them.

In Visual C++ we can create a spreadsheet that looks something like this, where we will enter the numerical data in the data text box, as follows:

Spreadsheet						
	A	B	C	D		Ok
1						
2						Cancel
3						Data:
4						
5						

After you type a number in the data text box and click a cell, that value will appear in the cell. For this example, you might also program it to add the values in column A and display the resultant sum at the bottom—cell A5, as follows:

Spreadsheet						
	A	B	C	D		Ok
1	12					
2	24					Cancel
3						Data:
4						
Sum → 5	36					

In order to do this, you need to install the Grid control in App Studio with its Install Controls... menu item. When you select that item, the Install Controls dialog box opens, as shown in figure 6.6.

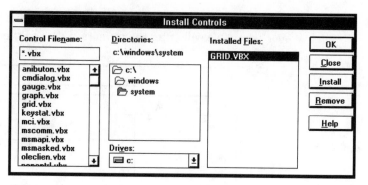

Figure 6.6. App Studios' Install controls box.

The file grid.vbx—the.vbx extension originally stood for a Visual Basic control—comes with Visual C++, and it is installed in the windows\system subdirectory. Select it to add it to App Studio. The Grid control appears in the toolbar as shown in figure 6.7.

Figure 6.7. The Grid control tool.

Create a new project with App Wizard, and make it an SDI application by deselecting the Multiple Document Interface check box in the Options dialog box. Click the Custom VBX Controls box in that same Options box and your program will support the use of the Grid control. Give this new project a name—for example, spread.mak.

Add a dialog box to the project—IDD_DIALOG1—with App Studio and draw a grid in it. Double–click the grid, bringing up the Grid Properties box, and select the Styles item in the drop-down list box in the upper right corner. The properties of the grid are displayed, as shown in figure 6.8. Click the Cols item and give it a value of 5 to give your spreadsheet five columns, as also shown in figure 6.8. In addition, give it six rows by setting the Rows property. Close the Grid Properties box. Add a text box to the dialog box you are designing and label it *Data:* as shown in figure 6.9. Your dialog box template is complete.

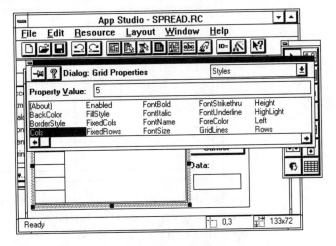

Figure 6.8. Setting a VBX control's properties.

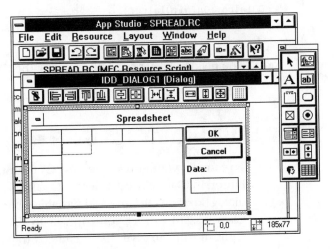

Figure 6.9. The Spreadsheet template.

You need to select the Class Wizard item in App Studio's Resource menu to open Class Wizard and create a class for this dialog box; call it

CSpreadDlg. You need to label your spreadsheet's cells with letters and numbers, as follows:

Spreadsheet					
	A	B	C	D	Ok
1					
2					Cancel
3					Data:
4					
5					

You can do that in CSpreadDlg::OnInitDialog(). Connect that function to CSpreadDlg's WM_INITDIALOG message by using Class Wizard. You can open that function, as follows:

```
BOOL CSpreadDlg::OnInitDialog()
{
    CDialog::OnInitDialog();
    return TRUE;  // return TRUE  unless you set the focus to a control
}
```

You need to label your cells by using the CVBControl class. This process is discussed in the next section.

Using VBX Controls in Code

To connect your grid to the class CVBControl, click the Edit Variables... button in Class Wizard. Select IDC_GRID1 in the Edit Member Variables dialog box, and click the Add Variable... button. The only type of variable Class Wizard will let you connect to IDC_GRID1 is a variable of type CVBControl*, so give that member variable the name m_GridControl. This CVBControl object, that you can point to with m_GridControl, will be your interface to the grid.

The new object m_GridControl includes these member functions, that you will use to set and retrieve the grid's property values, as follows:

SetNumProperty()	Set numerical property
SetStrProperty()	Set string property
GetNumProperty()	Get numerical property's value
GetStrProperty()	Get string property's string

The grid properties that you will be interested in are the Row, Col, and Text properties. Only one cell is active at a time in a grid, and its location is given by (Row, Col). The text in that grid is held in the Text property. That means you can set the Row property of your grid to 0 in OnInitDialog(), as follows (note that SetNumProperty takes a long integer value).

```
BOOL CSpreadDlg::OnInitDialog()
{
    CDialog::OnInitDialog();
    m_GridControl->SetNumProperty("Row", 0L);
        :
    return TRUE;  // return TRUE  unless you set the focus to a control
}
```

Next, we can load the letters 'A' to 'D' in the spreadsheet's columns. For this simple character operation, we will not use CString objects, but rather a character array holding one character, because we can increment that character easily. That is, we label the columns in the following way:

```
BOOL CSpreadDlg::OnInitDialog()
{
    CDialog::OnInitDialog();
    char out_char[] = "A";
    m_GridControl->SetNumProperty("Row", 0L);
for(long loop_index = 1;
loop_index < 5;
loop_index++){
m_GridControl->SetNumProperty("Col", loop_index);
m_GridControl->SetStrProperty("Text", (LPSTR) out_char);
out_char[0]++;
    }
    :
    return TRUE;  // return TRUE  unless you set the focus to a control
}
```

Next, you can label the rows as follows:

```
BOOL CSpreadDlg::OnInitDialog()
{
    CDialog::OnInitDialog();
    char out_char[] = "A";
    m_GridControl->SetNumProperty("Row", 0L);
for(long loop_index = 1;
loop_index < 5;
loop_index++){
m_GridControl->SetNumProperty("Col", loop_index);
m_GridControl->SetStrProperty("Text", (LPSTR)
out_char);
out_char[0]++;
    }
    out_char[0] = '1';
    m_GridControl->SetNumProperty("Col", 0L);
    for(loop_index = 1; loop_index < 6; loop_index++){
        m_GridControl->SetNumProperty("Row", loop_index);
        m_GridControl->SetStrProperty("Text", (LPSTR)out_char);
        out_char[0]++;
    }
    return TRUE;  // return TRUE  unless you set the focus to a control }
```

Your rows and columns are labeled just the way you want them, shown as follows:

Spreadsheet					
	A	B	C	D	Ok
1					
2					Cancel
3					Data:
4					
5					

You can place the values in the data text box. When you click on the spreadsheet, the active cell will be set to that location, and a VBN_CLICK

(Visual basic control Click notification) message will be generated. You can intercept that message in Class Wizard, and connect the function CSpreadDlg::OnClickGrid1() to that message now and open it, as follows:

```
void CSpreadDlg::OnClickGrid1(UINT, int, CWnd*, LPVOID)
{
}
```

When you click on the grid, the active cell is set to that (Row, Col), and you need to place the text from the Data: text box in the cell also. You can get that text with the GetDlgItemText() function and place it in the currently active cell's Text property, as follows:

```
void CSpreadDlg::OnClickGrid1(UINT, int, CWnd*, LPVOID)
{
    const CHARS = 20;
    char data_string[CHARS];
    GetDlgItemText(IDC_DATAENTRY, (LPSTR) data_string, CHARS);
    m_GridControl->SetStrProperty("Text", (LPSTR) data_string);
        :
```

Note that you used the GetDlgItemText() function to retrieve the text from the text box IDC_DATAENTRY—the last parameter it needs holds the number of characters to retrieve. Now you have the text from the Data: text box in data_string[], and have placed it into the currently active cell. The next step is to add all of the cells' values in column 1, and display the sum at the bottom. You can find the sum where you will use atol() to read the values from the cells, as follows:

```
void CSpreadDlg::OnClickGrid1(UINT, int, CWnd*, LPVOID)
{
    const CHARS = 20;
    char data_string[CHARS];
    GetDlgItemText(IDC_DATAENTRY, (LPSTR) data_string, CHARS);
    m_GridControl->SetStrProperty("Text", (LPSTR) data_string);
    long sum = 0;
    CString temp;
    long oldrow = m_GridControl->GetNumProperty("Row");
    long oldcol = m_GridControl->GetNumProperty("Col");
    m_GridControl->SetNumProperty("Col", 1L);
    for(long loop_index = 1;
    loop_index < 5;
    loop_index++){
```

```
m_GridControl->SetNumProperty("Row", loop_index);
temp = m_GridControl->GetStrProperty("Text");
        sum += atol(temp);
    }
```

Note that you saved the old Row and Col values to replace them later. Now the sum of the values in column 1 is held in the variable sum. You can place that value as text in the string data_string[] with the function wsprintf(), that prints numerical data to strings, as follows:

```
void CSpreadDlg::OnClickGrid1(UINT, int, CWnd*, LPVOID)
{
    const CHARS = 20;
    char data_string[CHARS];
    GetDlgItemText(IDC_DATAENTRY, (LPSTR) data_string, CHARS);
    m_GridControl->SetStrProperty("Text", (LPSTR) data_string);
    long sum = 0;
    CString temp;
    long oldrow = m_GridControl->GetNumProperty("Row");
    long oldcol = m_GridControl->GetNumProperty("Col");
    m_GridControl->SetNumProperty("Col", 1L);
    for(long loop_index = 1;
    loop_index < 5;
    loop_index++){
    m_GridControl->SetNumProperty("Row", loop_index);
    temp = m_GridControl->GetStrProperty("Text");
        sum += atol(temp);
    }
    wsprintf(data_string, "%ld", sum);
        :
```

All you have to do is display the result and restore the grid's Col and Row properties, that you can do as follows:

```
void CSpreadDlg::OnClickGrid1(UINT, int, CWnd*, LPVOID)
{
    const CHARS = 20;
    char data_string[CHARS];
    GetDlgItemText(IDC_DATAENTRY, (LPSTR) data_string, CHARS);
    m_GridControl->SetStrProperty("Text", (LPSTR) data_string);
    long sum = 0;
    CString temp;
    long oldrow = m_GridControl->GetNumProperty("Row");
```

```
long oldcol = m_GridControl->GetNumProperty("Col");
m_GridControl->SetNumProperty("Col", 1L);
for(long loop_index = 1;
loop_index < 5;
loop_index++){
m_GridControl->SetNumProperty("Row", loop_index);
temp
= m_GridControl->GetStrProperty("Text");
    sum += atol(temp);
}
wsprintf(data_string, "%ld", sum);
m_GridControl->SetNumProperty("Row", loop_index++);
m_GridControl->SetStrProperty("Text", (LPSTR) data_string);
m_GridControl->SetNumProperty("Row", oldrow);
m_GridControl->SetNumProperty("Col", oldcol);
}
```

That is it; add a menu named Spreadsheet to your main window and an item in it named Spreadsheet.... Next, connect the function OnSpreadsheet() to that item in the CSpreadView class. Finally, place the usual code there to display our dialog box, as follows:

```
void CSpreadView::OnSpreadsheet()
{
    CSpreadDlg dlg;
    dlg.DoModal();
}
```

The spreadsheet works as shown in figure 6.10. The program is a success, and you can adapt it into a functioning spreadsheet with some additional programming. The listing of your spreadsheet dialog box's header is in listing 6.4; the code is in listing 6.5; and the view class' code is in listing 6.6, spreavw.cpp.

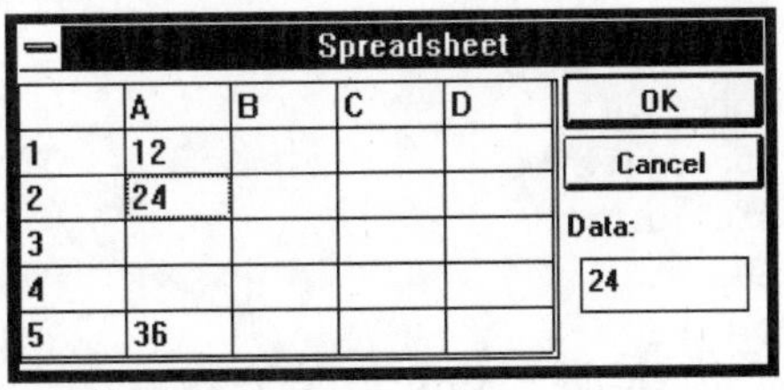

Figure 6.10. The functioning spreadsheet.

Listing 6.4. Spreaddl.H

```
// spreaddl.h : header file
//
//////////////////////////////////////////////////////////
////////////////////////
// CSpreadDlg dialog
class CSpreadDlg : public CDialog
{
// Construction
public:
    CSpreadDlg(CWnd* pParent = NULL);      // standard constructor
// Dialog Data
    //{{AFX_DATA(CSpreadDlg)
    enum { IDD = IDD_DIALOG1 };
    CVBControl*    m_GridControl;
    //}}AFX_DATA
// Implementation
protected:
    virtual void DoDataExchange(CDataExchange* pDX);
// DDX/DDV support
    // Generated message map functions
    //{{AFX_MSG(CSpreadDlg)
    virtual BOOL OnInitDialog();
    afx_msg void OnClickGrid1(UINT, int, CWnd*, LPVOID);
    //}}AFX_MSG
    DECLARE_MESSAGE_MAP()
};
```

Listing 6.5. Spreaddl.Cpp

```
// spreaddl.cpp : implementation file
//
#include "stdafx.h"
#include "spread.h"
#include "spreaddl.h"
#include <stdlib.h>
#ifdef _DEBUG
#undef THIS_FILE
static char BASED_CODE THIS_FILE[] = __FILE__;
#endif
//////////////////////////////////////////////////////////
////////////////////////
```

```
// CSpreadDlg dialog
CSpreadDlg::CSpreadDlg(CWnd* pParent /*=NULL*/)
    : CDialog(CSpreadDlg::IDD, pParent)
{
    //{{AFX_DATA_INIT(CSpreadDlg)
    m_GridControl = NULL;
    //}}AFX_DATA_INIT
}
void CSpreadDlg::DoDataExchange(CDataExchange* pDX)
{
    CDialog::DoDataExchange(pDX);
    //{{AFX_DATA_MAP(CSpreadDlg)
    DDX_VBControl(pDX, IDC_GRID1, m_GridControl);
    //}}AFX_DATA_MAP
}
BEGIN_MESSAGE_MAP(CSpreadDlg, CDialog)
    //{{AFX_MSG_MAP(CSpreadDlg)
    ON_VBXEVENT(VBN_CLICK, IDC_GRID1, OnClickGrid1)
    //}}AFX_MSG_MAP
END_MESSAGE_MAP()
/////////////////////////////////////////////////////////
/////////////////////
// CSpreadDlg message handlers
BOOL CSpreadDlg::OnInitDialog()
{
    CDialog::OnInitDialog();
    char out_char[] = "A";
    m_GridControl->SetNumProperty("Row", 0L);
    for(long loop_index = 1;
    loop_index < 5;
    loop_index++){
    m_GridControl->SetNumProperty("Col", loop_index);
    m_GridControl->SetStrProperty("Text", (LPSTR) out_char);
    out_char[0]++;
    }
    out_char[0] = '1';
                m_GridControl->SetNumProperty("Col", 0L);
    for(loop_index = 1;
    loop_index < 6;
    loop_index++){
    m_GridControl->SetNumProperty("Row", loop_index);
    m_GridControl->SetStrProperty("Text", (LPSTR) out_char);
```

continues

Listing 6.5. continued

```
    out_char[0]++;
    }
    return TRUE;  // return TRUE   unless you set the focus to a control }
    void CSpreadDlg::OnClickGrid1(UINT, int, CWnd*, LPVOID)
{

    const CHARS = 20;
    char data_string[CHARS];
    GetDlgItemText(IDC_DATAENTRY, (LPSTR) data_string, CHARS);
    m_GridControl->SetStrProperty("Text", (LPSTR) data_string);
    long sum = 0;
    CString temp;
    long oldrow = m_GridControl->GetNumProperty("Row");
    long oldcol = m_GridControl->GetNumProperty("Col");
    m_GridControl->SetNumProperty("Col", 1L);
    for(long loop_index = 1;
    loop_index < 5;
    loop_index++){
    m_GridControl->SetNumProperty("Row", loop_index);
    temp = m_GridControl->GetStrProperty("Text");
    sum += atol(temp);
    }
wsprintf(data_string, "%ld", sum);
m_GridControl->SetNumProperty("Row", loop_index++);
m_GridControl->SetStrProperty("Text", (LPSTR) data_string);
m_GridControl->SetNumProperty("Row", oldrow);
m_GridControl->SetNumProperty("Col", oldcol);
}
```

Listing 6.6. Spreavw.Cpp

```cpp
// spreavw.cpp : implementation of the CSpreadView class
//
#include "stdafx.h"
#include "spread.h"
#include "spreaddl.h"
#include "spreadoc.h"
#include "spreavw.h"
#ifdef _DEBUG
#undef THIS_FILE
static char BASED_CODE THIS_FILE[] = __FILE__;
#endif
```

```
/////////////////////////////////////////////////////////
////////////////////
// CSpreadView
IMPLEMENT_DYNCREATE(CSpreadView, CView)
BEGIN_MESSAGE_MAP(CSpreadView, CView)
    //{{AFX_MSG_MAP(CSpreadView)
    ON_COMMAND(IDM_SPREADSHEET, OnSpreadsheet)
    //}}AFX_MSG_MAP
    // Standard printing commands
ON_COMMAND(ID_FILE_PRINT, CView::OnFilePrint) ON_COMMAND(ID_FILE_PRINT_PREVIEW,
CView::OnFilePrintPreview)
END_MESSAGE_MAP()
/////////////////////////////////////////////////////////
/////////////////////
// CSpreadView construction/destruction
CSpreadView::CSpreadView()
{
    // TODO: add construction code here
}


CSpreadView::~CSpreadView()
{
}
/////////////////////////////////////////////////////////
/////////////////////
// CSpreadView drawing
void CSpreadView::OnDraw(CDC* pDC)
{
    CSpreadDoc* pDoc = GetDocument();
    // TODO: add draw code here
}
/////////////////////////////////////////////////////////
/////////////////////
// CSpreadView printing
BOOL CSpreadView::OnPreparePrinting(CPrintInfo* pInfo)
{
    // default preparation
    return DoPreparePrinting(pInfo);
}
void CSpreadView::OnBeginPrinting(CDC* /*pDC*/, CPrintInfo* /*pInfo*/)
{
    // TODO: add extra initialization before printing
```

continues

Listing 6.6. continued

```
}
void CSpreadView::OnEndPrinting(CDC* /*pDC*/, CPrintInfo* /*pInfo*/)
{
    // TODO: add cleanup after printing
}
/////////////////////////////////////////////////////////
//////////////////////////
// CSpreadView diagnostics
#ifdef _DEBUG
void CSpreadView::AssertValid() const
{
    CView::AssertValid();
}
void CSpreadView::Dump(CDumpContext& dc) const
{
    CView::Dump(dc);
}
CSpreadDoc* CSpreadView::GetDocument() // non-debug version is inline
{
    ASSERT(m_pDocument->
IsKindOf(RUNTIME_CLASS(CSpreadDoc)));
    return (CSpreadDoc*) m_pDocument;
}
#endif //_DEBUG
/////////////////////////////////////////////////////////
//////////////////////////
// CSpreadView message handlers
void CSpreadView::OnSpreadsheet()
{
    CSpreadDlg dlg;
    dlg.DoModal();
}
```

Using a Dialog Box as the Main Window

You have seen the most common controls in dialog boxes already—and you have seen how easy it is to put them there. You can design your view the same way so that you can use controls in your main window just as you can in a dialog box. It is called creating a *Form View*.

Form views are just like normal views, except that they can be designed with App Studio. You can put the controls you want right in, and connect Onxxx() functions to those controls just as you would for any Visual C++ project.

To get started, just design the form view as a dialog box, by putting all the controls you want in it—in this case, just use a large text box. Next, double-click the dialog box, opening the Dialog Properties box. Select Styles from the drop–down list box at upper right and do the following: select Child in the Style box, select None in the Border box, and deselect the Visible property, as shown in figure 6.11.

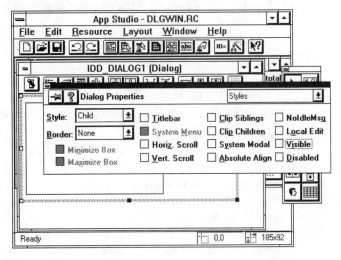

Figure 6.11. Designing a Form View.

The next step is to select General from the drop–down list box at upper right, and erase the dialog box's caption so that nothing appears in the Caption box. Finally, close the Dialog Properties box. Your form view has been designed.

Now you need to connect it to a class derived from CFormView. To do that, open Class Wizard from App Studio and select CFormView as the base class in the Class Type box. Give this class a name of, say, CDlgView and click OK. This creates the class we need, CDlgView.

The final step is to replace the current view class—the default class CDlgwinView—with your newly-designed class, CDlgView. To do that, you need to alter the program's document template. The document template is in the main application file, dlgwin.cpp. Check the InitInstance() function, and you will find the following code:

```
BOOL CDlgwinApp::InitInstance()
{
SetDialogBkColor();          // set dialog background
color to gray LoadStdProfileSettings();
// Load standard INI file options EnableVBX();
// Initialize VBX support
// Register the application's document templates.  Document templates
//   serve as the connection between documents, frame windows and views.
        AddDocTemplate(new CSingleDocTemplate(IDR_MAINFRAME,
        RUNTIME_CLASS(CDlgwinDoc),
        RUNTIME_CLASS(CMainFrame),       // main SDI frame window
        RUNTIME_CLASS(CDlgwinView)));
:
```

Change CDlgwinView in the last line to CDlgView, by using the Form View class you have created for the dialog box, as follows:

```
BOOL CDlgwinApp::InitInstance()
{
SetDialogBkColor();          // set dialog background
color to gray LoadStdProfileSettings();
// Load standard INI file options EnableVBX();
// Initialize VBX support
// Register the application's document templates.  Document templates
//   serve as the connection between documents, frame windows and views.
AddDocTemplate(new CSingleDocTemplate(IDR_MAINFRAME,
        RUNTIME_CLASS(CDlgwinDoc),
        RUNTIME_CLASS(CMainFrame),       // main SDI frame window
        RUNTIME_CLASS(CDlgView)));
```

That is it; the Form View program—in which you have only placed a text box—appears in figure 6.12. The listing of dlgwin.cpp appears in listing 6.7.

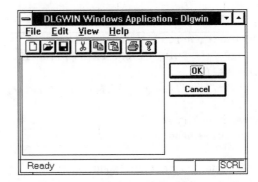

Figure 6.12. The Form View at work.

Listing 6.7. Dlgwin.Cpp

```
// dlgwin.cpp : Defines the class behaviors for the application.
//
#include "stdafx.h"
#include "dlgwin.h"
#include "mainfrm.h"
#include "dlgwidoc.h"
#include "dlgwivw.h"
#include "dlg2view.h"
#ifdef _DEBUG
#undef THIS_FILE
static char BASED_CODE THIS_FILE[] = __FILE__;
#endif
/////////////////////////////////////////////////////////////
///////////////////////
// CDlgwinApp
BEGIN_MESSAGE_MAP(CDlgwinApp, CWinApp)
    //{{AFX_MSG_MAP(CDlgwinApp)
    ON_COMMAND(ID_APP_ABOUT, OnAppAbout)
// NOTE - the ClassWizard will add and remove mapping macros here.
//    DO NOT EDIT what you see in these blocks of generated code !
    //}}AFX_MSG_MAP
    // Standard file based document commands
ON_COMMAND(ID_FILE_NEW, CWinApp::OnFileNew)
ON_COMMAND(ID_FILE_OPEN, CWinApp::OnFileOpen)
```

continues

301

Listing 6.7. continued

```
// Standard print setup command
ON_COMMAND(ID_FILE_PRINT_SETUP, CWinApp::OnFilePrintSetup)
END_MESSAGE_MAP()
////////////////////////////////////////////////////////////////
/////////////////////
// CDlgwinApp construction
CDlgwinApp::CDlgwinApp()
{
    // TODO: add construction code here,
    // Place all significant initialization in InitInstance
}
///////////////////////////////////////////////////////////////
/////////////////////////
// The one and only CDlgwinApp object
CDlgwinApp NEAR theApp;
///////////////////////////////////////////////////////////////
/////////////////////////
// CDlgwinApp initialization
BOOL CDlgwinApp::InitInstance()
{
    // Standard initialization
// If you are not using these features and wish to reduce the size
//  of your final executable, you should remove from the following
//   the specific initialization routines you do not need.
SetDialogBkColor();
// set dialog background
color to gray LoadStdProfileSettings();
// Load standard INI file options EnableVBX();
// Initialize VBX support
// Register the application's document templates.  Document templates
//   serve as the connection between documents, frame windows and views.
AddDocTemplate(new CSingleDocTemplate(IDR_MAINFRAME, RUNTIME_CLASS(CDlgwinDoc),
RUNTIME_CLASS(CMainFrame),    // main SDI frame window
RUNTIME_CLASS(CDlgView)));
    // create a new (empty) document
    OnFileNew();
    if (m_lpCmdLine[0] != '\0')
    {
        // TODO: add command line processing here
```

```
    }
    return TRUE;
}
/////////////////////////////////////////////////////
/////////////////////
// CAboutDlg dialog used for App
About
class CAboutDlg : public CDialog
{
public:
    CAboutDlg();
// Dialog Data
    //{{AFX_DATA(CAboutDlg)
    enum { IDD = IDD_ABOUTBOX };
    //}}AFX_DATA
// Implementation
protected:
virtual void DoDataExchange(CDataExchange* pDX);
// DDX/DDV support
//{{AFX_MSG(CAboutDlg)
        // No message handlers
    //}}AFX_MSG
    DECLARE_MESSAGE_MAP()
};
CAboutDlg::CAboutDlg() : CDialog(CAboutDlg::IDD)
{
    //{{AFX_DATA_INIT(CAboutDlg)
    //}}AFX_DATA_INIT
}
void CAboutDlg::DoDataExchange(CDataExchange* pDX)
{
    CDialog::DoDataExchange(pDX);
    //{{AFX_DATA_MAP(CAboutDlg)
    //}}AFX_DATA_MAP
}
BEGIN_MESSAGE_MAP(CAboutDlg, CDialog)
    //{{AFX_MSG_MAP(CAboutDlg)
        // No message handlers
    //}}AFX_MSG_MAP
END_MESSAGE_MAP()
// App command to run the dialog
```

continues

Listing 6.7. continued

```
void CDlgwinApp::OnAppAbout()
{
    CAboutDlg aboutDlg;
    aboutDlg.DoModal();
}
/////////////////////////////////////////////////////////
///////////////////////////////
// VB-Event registration
// (calls to AfxRegisterVBEvent will be placed here by ClassWizard)
//{{AFX_VBX_REGISTER_MAP()
//}}AFX_VBX_REGISTER_MAP
/////////////////////////////////////////////////////////
////////////////////////////
// CDlgwinApp commands
```

That is it for the Form View program, and for the coverage of dialog boxes. You have come far, learning how to design dialog boxes, and how to use the most popular controls in them. In the next chapter, you will continue your exploration of Visual C++ as you learn how to create graphics, and display them in a mouse-driven paint program.

Graphics and a Mouse-driven Paint Program

any of you are familiar with paint programs. By using a Paint Program, you can draw graphics images by selecting and using graphics tools. For example, you can select a line drawing tool, press the left mouse button at the location where you want to anchor one end of the line, move to the other end of the line you want to draw, and release the mouse button. When you do that, the program draws the line for you. This is the kind of program you are going to develop in this chapter. With this program, you will be able to create graphics images just like any Paint Program, and, more importantly, you will get an idea of how to work with graphics in Windows.

Creating the Paint Program's Menus

You can design the paint program's menus first by setting up the file paint.rc. Create an SDI application named paint.mak with App Wizard and open the IDR_MAINFRAME menu system with App Wizard. You will see the traditional menus already there—File, Edit, View, and Help. Add a menu named Tools as shown in figure 7.1.

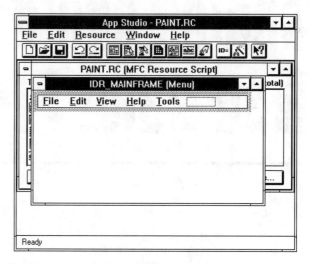

Figure 7.1. The paint program's tool menu.

The Tools menu will hold the painting tools for the program. Add the following items to that menu: Point, IDM_POINT—draw a single point; Draw, IDM_DRAW—freehand drawing; Line, IDM_LINE; Rectangle, IDM_RECTANGLE; Ellipse, IDM_ELLIPSE; and Fill, IDM_FILL—fill a figure with solid color. These menu items appear in figure 7.2.

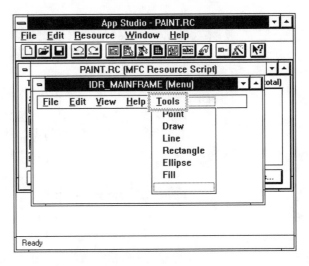

Figure 7.2. Paint program's tool menu items.

Save this and App Studio adds the menu to paint.rc. The menu section of that file now appears as follows:

```
IDR_MAINFRAME MENU PRELOAD DISCARDABLE
BEGIN
    POPUP "&File"
    BEGIN
        MENUITEM "&New\tCtrl+N",        ID_FILE_NEW
        MENUITEM "&Open...\tCtrl+O",     ID_FILE_OPEN
        MENUITEM "&Save\tCtrl+S",        ID_FILE_SAVE
        MENUITEM "Save &As...", ID_FILE_SAVE_AS
        MENUITEM SEPARATOR
        MENUITEM "&Print...\tCtrl+P",    ID_FILE_PRINT
        MENUITEM "Print Pre&view",       ID_FILE_PRINT_PREVIEW
        MENUITEM "P&rint Setup...",      ID_FILE_PRINT_SETUP
        MENUITEM SEPARATOR
        MENUITEM "Recent File", ID_FILE_MRU_FILE1, GRAYED
        MENUITEM SEPARATOR
        MENUITEM "E&xit",               ID_APP_EXIT
    END
    POPUP "&Edit"
    BEGIN
        MENUITEM "&Undo\tCtrl+Z",        ID_EDIT_UNDO
        MENUITEM SEPARATOR
```

```
                MENUITEM "Cu&t\tCtrl+X",        ID_EDIT_CUT
                MENUITEM "&Copy\tCtrl+C",       ID_EDIT_COPY
                MENUITEM "&Paste\tCtrl+V",      ID_EDIT_PASTE
        END
        POPUP "&View"
        BEGIN
                MENUITEM "&Toolbar",    ID_VIEW_TOOLBAR
                MENUITEM "&Status Bar", ID_VIEW_STATUS_BAR
        END
        POPUP "&Help"
        BEGIN
                MENUITEM "&About PAINT...",     ID_APP_ABOUT
        END
        POPUP "&Tools"
        BEGIN
                MENUITEM "Point",       IDM_POINT
                MENUITEM "Draw",        IDM_DRAW
                MENUITEM "Line",        IDM_LINE
                MENUITEM "Rectangle",   IDM_RECTANGLE
                MENUITEM "Ellipse",     IDM_ELLIPSE
                MENUITEM "Fill",        IDM_FILL
        END
END
```

Similarly, the new constants, IDM_POINT to IDM_FILL, are defined in resource.h, as follows:

```
#define IDM_POINT                   32768
#define IDM_DRAW                    32769
#define IDM_LINE                    32770
#define IDM_RECTANGLE               32771
#define IDM_ELLIPSE                 32772
#define IDM_FILL                    32773
```

Now the menu system is ready to go and you can put together the program's code.

Writing the Paint Program

When you select a drawing tool from the menu you have just designed, it should remain active until another tool is chosen. You can do that by setting a Boolean flag. For example, if you select the Line option, you can set a Boolean flag named bLine inside of the window object and leave it set until you choose another drawing tool. When any part of the object needs to know what drawing tool is currently active, it can check these flags. You can define them as BOOL in the view object's header, paintvw.h, as follows:

```
// paintvw.h : interface of the CPaintView class
//
///////////////////////////////////////////////////////////////////
////////////
class CPaintView : public CView
{
protected: // create from serialization only
    CPaintView();
    DECLARE_DYNCREATE(CPaintView)
    BOOL bPoint;
    :   BOOL bDraw;
    :   BOOL bLine;
    :   BOOL bRectangle;
    :   BOOL bEllipse;
    BOOL bFill;


// Attributes
public:
        CPaintDoc* GetDocument();
// Operations
public:
    :
```

These flags will be set when the user selects one of the drawing options—Line, Point, Ellipse, and so on. Only one flag—bLine—will be TRUE at any time. Therefore, every part of the program—that will be divided into mouse move events and so on—will know what you are supposed to be drawing. You will need Onxxx( ) functions to respond to menu selections and to set these flags appropriately, so add them now. You can do that in Class Wizard. Connect OnLine( ) to IDM_LINE, OnRectangle( ) to IDM_RECTANGLE, and so on. Note that you need to use a name like OnDrawItem( ) for IDM_DRAW because, you already have a function named OnDraw( ). In addition, connect functions to the UPDATE_COMMAND_UI too—such as OnUpdatePoint( ), OnUpdateDraw( ) and so on—enabling you to set the check marks in the Tools menu correctly—for example, that is what the UPDATE_COMMAND_UI is for. The functions produced are as follows:

```
void CPaintView::OnPoint()
{
}
void CPaintView::OnDrawItem()
{
}
void CPaintView::OnLine()
{
}
void CPaintView::OnRectangle()
{
}
void CPaintView::OnEllipse()
{
}
void CPaintView::OnFill()
{
}
void CPaintView::OnUpdatePoint(CCmdUI* pCmdUI)
{
}
void CPaintView::OnUpdateDraw(CCmdUI* pCmdUI)
{
}
void CPaintView::OnUpdateLine(CCmdUI* pCmdUI)
{
}
void CPaintView::OnUpdateRectangle(CCmdUI* pCmdUI)
{
}
void CPaintView::OnUpdateEllipse(CCmdUI* pCmdUI)
{
}
void CPaintView::OnUpdateFill(CCmdUI* pCmdUI)
{
}
```

Let's write some code. The beginning point is the constructor, that sets things up the way you want them. In this case, all you have to do is to set bPoint to TRUE, because the Point drawing tool is your default drawing tool—it is the first one in the Tools menu—and set the other ones FALSE, as follows:

```
CPaintView::CPaintView()
{
    bPoint = TRUE;
    bDraw = FALSE;
    bLine = FALSE;
    bRectangle = FALSE;
    bEllipse = FALSE;
    bFill = FALSE;
}
```

Now you can start working on the functions that respond to the Tools menu items—OnPoint( ), OnDrawItem( ), OnLine( ), OnRectangle( ), OnEllipse( ), and OnFill( ). The only job of those functions will be to set the Boolean flags bPoint, bDraw, bLine, bRectangle, bEllipse, and bFill. Then, when the real action takes place with the mouse, you can check what type of figure you are supposed to be drawing—for example, when the mouse button goes up, you are supposed to draw the correct graphics figure on the screen. In addition, you need to set all of the other flags to FALSE. To save some code, you can define a function named SetFlagsFalse( ) as follows:

```
void CPaintView::SetFlagsFalse()
{
    bPoint = FALSE;
    bDraw = FALSE;
    bLine = FALSE;
    bRectangle = FALSE;
    bEllipse = FALSE;
    bFill = FALSE;
}
```

You can add it manually to your view's header, paintvw.h, as follows:

```
// paintvw.h : interface of the CPaintView class
/////////////////////////////////////////////////////////////////
////////////////
class CPaintView : public CView
{
protected: // create from serialization only
    CPaintView();
    DECLARE_DYNCREATE(CPaintView)
    BOOL bPoint;
    BOOL bDraw;
    BOOL bLine;
```

```
    BOOL bRectangle;
    BOOL bEllipse;
    BOOL bFill;
    void SetFlagsFalse();
// Attributes
public:
    :
```

Now you can respond to menu items as follows:

```
void CPaintView::OnPoint()
{
        SetFlagsFalse();
        bPoint = TRUE;
}
void CPaintView::OnDrawItem()
{
        SetFlagsFalse();
        bDraw = TRUE;
}
void CPaintView::OnLine()
{
        SetFlagsFalse();
        bLine = TRUE;
}
void CPaintView::OnRectangle()
{
        SetFlagsFalse();
        bRectangle = TRUE;
}
void CPaintView::OnEllipse()
{
        SetFlagsFalse();
        bEllipse = TRUE;
}
void CPaintView::OnFill()
{
        SetFlagsFalse();
        bFill = TRUE;
}
```

In addition, you need to ensure that the check marks are set correctly when the Tools menu appears, and that is what the OnUpdatexxx() functions are for. You may recall that Update() functions get a pointer to the user interface object in OnUpdatePoint(), as follows:

```
void CPaintView::OnUpdatePoint(CCmdUI* pCmdUI)
{
}
```

If the corresponding tool's Boolean flag is set, you need to make sure that menu item is marked with a check mark, as follows:

```
void CPaintView::OnUpdatePoint(CCmdUI* pCmdUI)
{
        if (bPoint)
            pCmdUI->SetCheck(1);
                    :
}
```

Here you give the SetCheck( ) function a value of 1, that places a check mark in from of the matching user interface object. However, when the flag is not set, you need to remove the check mark from the matching user interface if there is one.

```
void CPaintView::OnUpdatePoint(CCmdUI* pCmdUI)
{
    if (bPoint)
        pCmdUI->SetCheck(1);
    else
            pCmdUI->SetCheck(0);
}
_H
```

That is it; the following user-interface functions ensure that the check marks are set correctly.

```
_G
void CPaintView::OnUpdatePoint(CCmdUI* pCmdUI)
{
    if (bPoint)
        pCmdUI->SetCheck(1);
    else
        pCmdUI->SetCheck(0);
}
void CPaintView::OnUpdateDraw(CCmdUI* pCmdUI)
{
    if (bDraw)
        pCmdUI->SetCheck(1);
    else
        pCmdUI->SetCheck(0);
```

```
    }
    void CPaintView::OnUpdateLine(CCmdUI* pCmdUI)
    {
        if (bLine)
            pCmdUI->SetCheck(1);
        else
            pCmdUI->SetCheck(0);
    }
    void CPaintView::OnUpdateRectangle(CCmdUI* pCmdUI)
    {
        if (bRectangle)
            pCmdUI->SetCheck(1);
        else
            pCmdUI->SetCheck(0);
    }
    void CPaintView::OnUpdateEllipse(CCmdUI* pCmdUI)
    {
        if (bEllipse)
            pCmdUI->SetCheck(1);
        else
            pCmdUI->SetCheck(0);
    }
    void CPaintView::OnUpdateFill(CCmdUI* pCmdUI)
    {
        if (bFill)
            pCmdUI->SetCheck(1);
        else
            pCmdUI->SetCheck(0);
    }
```

When you make a menu selection, the check mark appears in front of that menu item to indicate that that tool is the current drawing tool, and the correct Boolean flag will be set. Now let's see what we can do about drawing in our window.

Setting Individual Pixels in Windows

The drawing action will take place when you use the mouse. For example, say that you have selected the first drawing tool, Point, that sets individual points. To use it, you need to move the mouse cursor to a certain location and click the (left) mouse button. When the mouse button goes up, you can draw the point at that location. To do that, you will need to ensure that you are supposed to be drawing points—for example, bPoint is TRUE—and then you can use the device context function SetPixel( ) in the function that you need to connect to the WM_LBUTTONUP( ) message. Connect a function to that message now named OnLButtonUp( ) with Class Wizard, that creates the following prototype:

```
void CPaintView::OnLButtonUp(UINT nFlags, CPoint point)
{
}
```

You can get the location of the mouse cursor at the time that the button went up from the CPoint object point like this: (point.x, point.y). Next, pass those coordinates to SetPixel( ) as well as the color you want the pixel to be.

You can set the color of the pixel to black with the RGB( ) macro. This macro returns a value of type COLORDEF, that is how Windows declares colors. RGB( ) takes three parameters that range from 0 to 255, and that represent one of the primary color values—in order, red, green, and blue. This is the way to design colors in Windows, with separate values for the red, green, and blue components. Here, you are setting the pixel to black—for example, all of the color components are 0: RGB(0, 0, 0).

```
void CPaintView::OnLButtonUp(UINT nFlags, CPoint point)
{
    if(bPoint){
        CClientDC dc(this);
        dc.SetPixel(point.x, point.y, RGB(0, 0, 0));
    }
    :
}
```

Note that the three values RGB( ) takes can range from 0 to 255. For example, if you want a red dot, you specify it like this: RGB(255, 0, 0). That's it for drawing points; now when you want to set individual pixels, you only have to select Point from the tools menu as shown in figure 7.3— setting bPoint TRUE. Click the mouse button when the cursor is at the desired location—generating WM_LBUTTONDOWN and WM_LBUTTONUP events—drawing points as shown in figure 7.4.

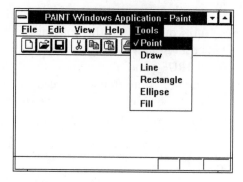

Figure 7.3. The paint program's point item.

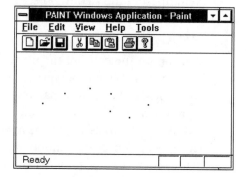

Figure 7.4. Points in the paint program.

That's it—you are drawing already, and all you needed was the OnLButtonUp( ) function. The next tool in the Tools menu, and the next graphics operation to cover is freehand drawing.

Freehand Drawing in the Paint Program

To draw freehand, you need to use the WM_MOUSEMOVE event. This event is generated as the mouse moves across the screen. Connect a function now in Class Wizard to WM_MOUSEMOVE named OnMouseMove( ). Class Wizard creates the function as follows:

```
void CPaintView::OnMouseMove(UINT nFlags, CPoint point)
    {
    }
```

Here, point holds the current mouse cursor position—x = point.x, y = point.y—and nFlags is encoded bit by bit to indicate what mouse buttons are down as follows (MK stands for mouse key):

MK_LBUTTON   Left button is down

MK_MBUTTON   Middle button is down

MK_RBUTTON   Right button is down

That is it, nFlags is made up of the appropriate combination of these constants, ORed together. When you need to draw, hold the left mouse button and move the mouse. You can check the left button and also determine whether or not the Draw tool is active by checking bDraw as follows:

```
void CPaintView::OnMouseMove(UINT nFlags, CPoint point)
{
    if((nFlags && MK_LBUTTON) && bDraw){
            :
    }
}
```

To get a device context object, you need to do the following:

```
void CPaintView::OnMouseMove(UINT nFlags, CPoint point)
{
    if((nFlags && MK_LBUTTON) && bDraw){
    CClientDC dc(this);
            :
    }
}
```

The next step is to draw on the screen. Although you might want to use the SetPixel( ) here, mouse move events are not generated for every pixel you pass over. However, a limited number of these events are generated per second; if you simply drew a dot on the screen, you would end up with an unconnected trail of pixels. Instead, you need to store the previous mouse location and draw a line from that location to your current position. The effect on the screen will be of a continuous path of set pixels, following the mouse cursor in the window.

Unlike setting individual pixels, you need two points for a line. When you press the left mouse button to start drawing, set one end of the line, that you can call the anchor point. Next, you need to move the cursor, and draw a line. In code, that means that you should set the anchor point, that you can store as (xAnchor, yAnchor) in paintvw.h, as follows:

```
// paintvw.h : interface of the CPaintView class
////////////////////////////////////////////////////////////////////
////////////////
class CPaintView : public CView
{
protected: // create from serialization only
        CPaintView();
        DECLARE_DYNCREATE(CPaintView)
        int xAnchor;
        int yAnchor;
        BOOL bPoint;
        BOOL bDraw;
        BOOL bLine;
        BOOL bRectangle;
        BOOL bEllipse;
        BOOL bFill;
        void SetFlagsFalse();
// Attributes
public:
        CPaintDoc* GetDocument();
                        :
```

In CPaintView::OnLButtonDown( )—for example, the function called when the mouse button goes down—you can set the anchor point as follows, so you can use it in CPaintView::OnMouseMove( ) later.

```
void CPaintView::OnLButtonDown(UINT nFlags, CPoint point)
{
        xAnchor = point.x;
        yAnchor = point.y;
}
```

In the WM_MOUSEMOVE event, you need to draw a line from (xAnchor, yAnchor) to (point.x, point.y). To draw lines, you use the MoveTo( ) and LineTo( ) functions. You can only pass the location of one point to LineTo( ), and it draws a line from the current position to that point. To set the current position to the anchor point, use MoveTo( ), as follows:

```
void CPaintView::OnMouseMove(UINT nFlags, CPoint point)
{
    if((nFlags && MK_LBUTTON) && bDraw){
        CClientDC dc(this);
        dc.MoveTo(xAnchor, yAnchor);
                    :
        }
}
```

And then we can draw the line connecting the dots with LineTo( ), as follows:

```
void CPaintView::OnMouseMove(UINT nFlags, CPoint point)
{
    if((nFlags && MK_LBUTTON) && bDraw){
        CClientDC dc(this);
        dc.MoveTo(xAnchor, yAnchor);
        dc.LineTo(point.x, point.y);
                    :
        }
}
```

Finally, you need to update the anchor point so the next time a mouse move event is generated, you will connect to the end of the line you just drew (note that the anchor point is only updated if bDraw is TRUE—that is, if you are drawing freehand).

```
void CPaintView::OnMouseMove(UINT nFlags, CPoint point)
{
    if((nFlags && MK_LBUTTON) && bDraw){
        CClientDC dc(this);
        dc.MoveTo(xAnchor, yAnchor);
        dc.LineTo(point.x, point.y);
        xAnchor = point.x;
        yAnchor = point.y;
    }
}
```

That is it; when you select the Draw tool, you can hold the left mouse button down and move the mouse cursor around, drawing as shown in figure 7.5.

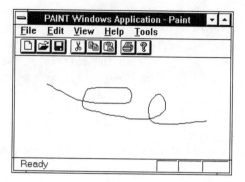

Figure 7.5. Freehand drawing with the Paint Program.

The next step, and the next drawing tool, is Line. This tool will enable you to draw lines on the screen.

Drawing Lines

The usual way for the user to draw lines in a Paint Program is to select the Line tool, press the left button at one point on the screen.

a

Move the cursor to the other end of the line, as follows:

a   b

Release the left button. At that time, the program connects the two points—for example, the location where the left button went down and the location where it went up, as follows:

a ————————————— b

We already set the anchor point, which you will use as the first end of the line, in the WM_LBUTTONDOWN event, as follows:

```
void CPaintView::OnLButtonDown(UINT nFlags, CPoint point)
{
    xAnchor = point.x;
    yAnchor = point.y;
}
```

When the button goes back up in OnLButtonUp( ), you can complete the line. Since we want to draw a line from (xAnchor, yAnchor) to the new location, that is encoded in point as (point.x, point.y), you can draw the line as follows:

```
void CPaintView::OnLButtonUp(UINT nFlags, CPoint point)
{
    if(bPoint){
        CClientDC dc(this);
        dc.SetPixel(point.x, point.y, RGB(0, 0, 0));
    }
    if(bLine){
        CClientDC dc(this);
        dc.MoveTo(xAnchor, yAnchor);
        dc.LineTo(point.x, point.y);
    }
}
```

That's it. Now you can draw lines, as shown in figure 7.6. Just select the Line tool—setting bLine TRUE; press the left mouse button at some location—setting the anchor point in the OnLButtonDown( ) function—; move to the final location and release the mouse button—drawing the line with MoveTo( ) and LineTo( ) in OnLButtonUp( ).

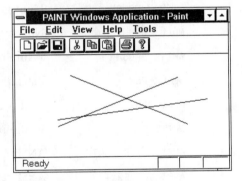

Figure 7.6. Drawing lines in the Paint Program.

There are more options, however, that can draw in different colors as well.

Selecting Colors and Pens

You do not specify the drawing colors for lines in the same way that you do for points—where you included a color value in the SetPixel( ) call. However, you have to design a new *pen*. You can draw figures in Windows with pens, and fill the figures in with *brushes*. After you place a pen into a device context object, it stays there until changed. To change the pen in a device context object, you can use SelectStockObject( ) as follows:

```
dc.SelectStockObject(STOCK_OBJECT);
```

The available stock objects are shown in table 7.1; you can select from these three options: NULL_PEN, BLACK_PEN, and WHITE_PEN. Another option is to design your own pen.

Table 7.1. Device Context Stock Objects

Stock Object	Means
BLACK_BRUSH	Black brush.
DKGRAY_BRUSH	Dark gray brush.
GRAY_BRUSH	Gray brush.
HOLLOW_BRUSH	Hollow brush.
LTGRAY_BRUSH	Light gray brush.
NULL_BRUSH	Null brush.
WHITE_BRUSH	White brush.
BLACK_PEN	Black pen.
NULL_PEN	Null pen.
WHITE_PEN	White pen.
ANSI_FIXED_FONT	ANSI fixed system font.
ANSI_VAR_FONT	ANSI variable system font.
DEVICE_DEFAULT_FONT	Device-dependent font.
OEM_FIXED_FONT	OEM-dependent fixed font.
SYSTEM_FONT	The system font.
SYSTEM_FIXED_FONT	The fixed-width system font.
DEFAULT_PALETTE	Default color palette.

Let's say that you wanted to draw blue lines. You could create a solid blue pen, one pixel wide with the CPen member function CreatePen(). CreatePen() takes three parameters—a pen style, a pixel width for the pen, and a color. The different pen styles, from solid to dotted, are shown in figure 7.7. These pen styles are as follows (PS stands for pen style—use these constants in CreatePen()):

Pen Styles	Meaning
PS_SOLID	Solid line
PS_DASH	Dashed line
PS_DOT	Dotted line
PS_DASHDOT	Dash-dot line
PS_DASHDOTDOT	Dash-dot-dot line
PS_NULL	Null line (does not draw)
PS_INSIDEFRAME	Draw inside boundaries

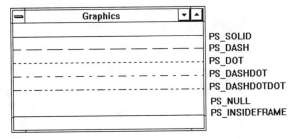

Figure 7.7. Windows pen styles.

Drawing Closed Figures.
The last pen type above, PS_INSIDEFRAME, is used when you are drawing closed figures with a border width greater than one pixel, but don't want to draw outside the figure. For example, if you set the pen style to PS_INSIDEFRAME and then draw a rectangle with the Rectangle() function (that is coming up), the border line, no matter how thick, will stay inside the rectangle's boundary. The other pen styles will overlap outside the rectangle.

323

To draw a solid blue line, you need to choose PS_SOLID. In addition, you want a pen width of one pixel, therefore the first two parameters for CreatePen( ), are as follows:

```
CPen* pPen = new CPen;
 pPen->CreatePen(PS_SOLID, 1...);
```

Finally, you need to specify the color of the pen. To create a solid blue pen, you can do the following:

```
CPen* pPen = new CPen;
pPen->CreatePen(PS_SOLID, 1, RGB(0, 0, 255));
```

RGB(255, 0, 0) would have been all red, RGB(0, 255, 0) would have been green.

Drawing in White.
You can specify white with RGB( ) like this: RGB(255, 255, 255).
In addition, the standard gray in Windows is RGB(128, 128, 128).

Now you can use SelectObject( ) to install this pen. In general, you use SelectObject( ) as follows:

```
SelectObject(pGdi)
```

Here, pGdi is a pointer to an object of class CGdiObject (a graphics device interface object), which can point to any of these classes, as follows:

CPen	Pen object
CBrush	Brush Object
CFont	Font Object
CBitmap	Bitmap Object

SelectObject( ) returns a pointer to the object it is replacing, and it is usually a good idea to store that handle and reinstall it when you are finished. You can do that by declaring a variable of type CGdiObject* that you can call pPenOld, as follows:

```
void CPaintView::OnLButtonUp(UINT nFlags, CPoint point)
{
    CGdiObject* pPenOld;
    if(bPoint){
```

```
                    CClientDC dc(this);
                    dc.SetPixel(point.x, point.y, RGB(0, 0, 0));
        }
        if(bLine){
                CClientDC dc(this);
                CPen* pPen = new CPen;
                pPen->CreatePen(PS_SOLID, 1, RGB(0, 0, 255));
                pPenOld = dc.SelectObject(pPen);
dc.MoveTo(xAnchor, yAnchor);
dc.LineTo(point.x, point.y);
:
        }
}
```

When you are done drawing, replace the original pen as follows:

```
void CPaintView::OnLButtonUp(UINT nFlags, CPoint point)
{
    CGdiObject* pPenOld;
    if(bPoint){
                CClientDC dc(this);
                dc.SetPixel(point.x, point.y, RGB(0, 0, 0));
        }
        if(bLine){
                CClientDC dc(this);
CPen* pPen = new CPen;
pPen->CreatePen(PS_SOLID, 1, RGB(0, 0, 255));
pPenOld = dc.SelectObject(pPen);
dc.MoveTo(xAnchor, yAnchor);
dc.LineTo(point.x, point.y);
                dc.SelectObject(pPenOld);
                delete pPen;
        }
}
```

This code enables you to draw blue lines—now you are drawing in color. The next tool in your Paint Program is Rectangle. That will enable you to draw rectangles, a process that works like drawing lines.

Drawing Rectangles

After you select the Rectangle tool, press the mouse button at the location of one corner, move the cursor to the other corner, and release it. At that point, the program draws the rectangle. When drawing a line, you had to use two points as follows:

a ———————————————————— b

When drawing a rectangle, you also need to specify two points, as follows:

a

b

However, you don't have to use MoveTo( ) to set the current position; instead, the device context Rectangle( ) member function can take the coordinates of both points at once, as follows:

```
dc.Rectangle(ax, ay, bx, by);
```

This call draws a rectangle with the current pen from (ax, ay) to (bx, by). In your case, the anchor point is set when you press the left mouse button and place the rectangle-drawing code in the WM_LBUTTONUP case. In particular, the rectangle you want to draw goes from (xAnchor, yAnchor) to (point.x, point.y). That means that you can draw rectangles as follows:

```
void CPaintView::OnLButtonUp(UINT nFlags, CPoint point)
{
    CGdiObject* pBackup;
    if(bPoint){
        CClientDC dc(this);
        dc.SetPixel(point.x, point.y, RGB(0, 0, 0));
    }
    if(bLine){
        CClientDC dc(this);
        dc.MoveTo(xAnchor, yAnchor);
        dc.LineTo(point.x, point.y);
    }
    if(bRectangle){
        CClientDC dc(this);
        dc.Rectangle(xAnchor, yAnchor, point.x, point.y);
    }
}
```

It looks as though this should work. You are passing the anchor point and the point at which the left button went up to Rectangle( ). However, there is a problem. When Windows draws rectangles or other closed figures, it fills them in with the background color by default, covering over what was there before. That means that when you draw a rectangle, anything behind it will be obliterated; that is not the standard for paint programs.

Instead, you should draw the figures and fill them transparently, so whatever is behind them is preserved. To do that, you need to select a new *brush*. Just as pens are used for drawing, so brushes are used for filling. And, just as there are some stock pens you can use with SelectStockObject( ), so there are stock brushes—BLACK_BRUSH, DKGRAY_BRUSH, GRAY_BRUSH, HOLLOW_BRUSH, LT_GRAY_BRUSH, NULL_BRUSH, and WHITE_BRUSH. To load, say BLACK_BRUSH into the device context, and to fill it with black, use the following call:

```
pBackup = dc.SelectStockObject(BLACK_BRUSH);
```

Deleting Text in Windows.
You can delete text by covering it with a filled rectangle. You can use GetBkColor( ) to get the background color and create both a pen and solid brush of that color. Then, using GetTextMetrics( ), you can determine how high the current font is, and using GetTextExtent( ), you can determine how long the string is you want to delete. Finally, you can delete the text with Rectangle( ).

In this case, you need to use NULL_BRUSH, that ensures that your figures will not be filled. Save the old brush object that you are replacing—for example, you get a pointer to the old brush from SelectStockObject( )), and restore it when you are finished, as follows:

```
void CPaintView::OnLButtonUp(UINT nFlags, CPoint point)
{
    CGdiObject* pBackup;
    if(bPoint){
        CClientDC dc(this);
        dc.SetPixel(point.x, point.y, RGB(0, 0, 0));
    }
    if(bLine){
        CClientDC dc(this);
        dc.MoveTo(xAnchor, yAnchor);
        dc.LineTo(point.x, point.y);
    }
    if(bRectangle){
        CClientDC dc(this);
        pBackup = dc.SelectStockObject(NULL_BRUSH);
```

```
        dc.Rectangle(xAnchor, yAnchor, point.x, point.y);
—>              dc.SelectObject(pBackup);
    }
}
```

Now you are able to draw objects in the application without disturbing what was underneath. However, there are one or two more points about brushes that should still be covered. You can create pens in the same way that you created brushes. In fact, there are two standard ways of creating brushes in Windows—with the CBrush member functions CreateSolidBrush( ) and CreateHatchBrush( ).

To create a solid brush—a solid brush will paint regions with a solid color—you can use CreateSolidBrush( ). You can pass the color you want the pen to be in the following way to create a green brush:

```
CBrush* pBrush = new CBrush;
pBrush->CreateSolidBrush(RGB(0, 255, 0));
pBackup = SelectObject(pBrush);
```

You can also create a hatch brush that has a predefined pattern in it with CreateHatchBrush( ). Here, you pass two parameters: the hatch style we want and the color we want. The allowed hatch styles are (HS stands for hatch style): HS_HORIZONTAL, HS_VERTICAL, HS_FDIAGONAL, HS_BDIAGONAL, HS_CROSS, and HS_DIAGCROSS, as shown in figure 7.8. For example, if we wanted to create a gray hatch brush of style HS_DIAGCROSS, we could do that as follows:

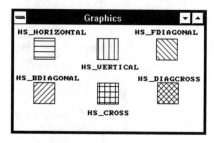

Figure 7.8. Windows hatch styles.

```
CBrush* pBrush = new CBrush;
pBrush->CreateHatchBrush(HS_DIAGCROSS, RGB(128, 128, 128);
pBackup = SelectObject(pBrush);
```

In this way, we can fill our figures with colored patterns.

> **Creating Your Own Brush Patterns.**
> You can even create your own brush patterns with the Windows functions CreatePatternBrush( ) or CreateBrushIndirect( ).

At this point, you can draw rectangles, as shown in figure 7.9. The next drawing tool in the Paint Program is Ellipse. Drawing ellipses is very similar to drawing rectangles.

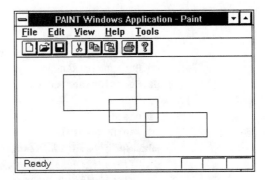

Figure 7.9. Drawing rectangles with the Paint Program.

Drawing Ellipses

When you select the Ellipse tool, press the left mouse button, setting an anchor point, move the cursor to a new location, and release the mouse button. When you release the button, draw an ellipse framed by those points.

You can do that with the Ellipse( ) function, whose arguments are identical to the Rectangle( ) function. In this case, however, an ellipse is inscribed inside the rectangle whose coordinates you pass. One corner of the rectangle will be (xAnchor, yAnchor) and the other will be (point.x, point.y). To do this, check if the bEllipse flag is set in OnLButtonUp( ), and, when it is, you proceed as if you were drawing a rectangle — but use Ellipse( ) instead, as follows:

```
void CPaintView::OnLButtonUp(UINT nFlags, CPoint point)
{
    CGdiObject* pBackup;
    if(bPoint){
        CClientDC dc(this);
        dc.SetPixel(point.x, point.y, RGB(0, 0, 0));
    }
    if(bLine){
        CClientDC dc(this);
        dc.MoveTo(xAnchor, yAnchor);
        dc.LineTo(point.x, point.y);
    }
    if(bRectangle){
        CClientDC dc(this);
        pBackup = dc.SelectStockObject(NULL_BRUSH);
        dc.Rectangle(xAnchor, yAnchor, point.x, point.y);
        dc.SelectObject(pBackup);
    }
    if(bEllipse){
        CClientDC dc(this);
        pBackup = dc.SelectStockObject(NULL_BRUSH);
        dc.Ellipse(xAnchor, yAnchor, point.x, point.y);
        dc.SelectObject(pBackup);
    }
}
```

You install a NULL_BRUSH before drawing the ellipse so that the background graphics is not covered. Your new operation is a success. Now you are able to add ellipses to the Paint Program, as shown in figure 7.10.

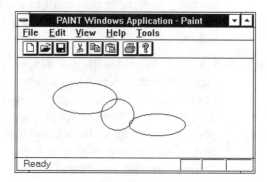

Figure 7.10. Drawing ellipses in the paint program.

There is one last painting tool that you placed in the Tools menu, and that is Fill. The Fill tool enables you to fill figures in.

Filling Figures with Color

To fill figures in in Windows, all you need to do is use the device context FloodFill( ) member function. You position the mouse cursor inside a figure on the screen, click it, and the figure fills with color. What's happening here is that you get the location of the mouse cursor from point in the OnLButtonUp( ) function, and then you pass that set of coordinates on to FloodFill( ), along with a handle to your device context and a *bounding color.*

The *bounding color* is the color of the border of the figure that you are filling in. You pass that color so that FloodFill( ) knows when to stop filling. For example, all of the figures you have drawn so far have been black, so the bounding color of your figures is black. To fill the figures in with black, you will use the function SetROP2(R2_BLACK). This function specifies the way you draw in your device context. The following indicates that all pixels you draw should be black.

```
void CPaintView::OnLButtonUp(UINT nFlags, CPoint point)
{
    CGdiObject* pBackup;
    if(bPoint){
        CClientDC dc(this);
        dc.SetPixel(point.x, point.y, RGB(0, 0, 0));
    }
    if(bLine){
        CClientDC dc(this);
        dc.MoveTo(xAnchor, yAnchor);
        dc.LineTo(point.x, point.y);
    }
    if(bRectangle){
        CClientDC dc(this);
        pBackup = dc.SelectStockObject(NULL_BRUSH);
        dc.Rectangle(xAnchor, yAnchor, point.x, point.y);
        dc.SelectObject(pBackup);
    }
    if(bEllipse){
            CClientDC dc(this);
```

```
pBackup = dc.SelectStockObject(NULL_BRUSH);
dc.Ellipse(xAnchor, yAnchor, point.x, point.y);
dc.SelectObject(pBackup);
    }
    if(bFill){
            CClientDC dc(this);
            dc.SetROP2(R2_BLACK);
                :
    }
}
```

Next, you just fill the figure with FloodFill( )—note that we're indicating that the bounding color is black, RGB(0, 0, 0).

```
void CPaintView::OnLButtonUp(UINT nFlags, CPoint point)
{
    CGdiObject* pBackup;
    if(bPoint){
        CClientDC dc(this);
        dc.SetPixel(point.x, point.y, RGB(0, 0, 0));
    }
    if(bLine){
        CClientDC dc(this);
        dc.MoveTo(xAnchor, yAnchor);
        dc.LineTo(point.x, point.y);
    }
    if(bRectangle){
        CClientDC dc(this);
        pBackup = dc.SelectStockObject(NULL_BRUSH);
        dc.Rectangle(xAnchor, yAnchor, point.x, point.y);
        dc.SelectObject(pBackup);
    }
    if(bEllipse){
        CClientDC dc(this);
        pBackup = dc.SelectStockObject(NULL_BRUSH);
        dc.Ellipse(xAnchor, yAnchor, point.x, point.y);
        dc.SelectObject(pBackup);
    }
    if(bFill){
        CClientDC dc(this);
        dc.SetROP2(R2_BLACK);
        dc.FloodFill(point.x, point.y, RGB(0, 0, 0));
    }
}
```

That's it; now you can fill in your figures, as shown in figure 7.11.

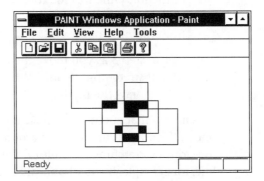

Figure 7.11. Filling with color in the Paint Program.

The Paint Program is done and you were able to draw all kinds of graphics figures—lines, rectangles, and ellipses. In fact, there are a few embellishments that you might want to add. For example, it is customary for paint programs to show lines, rectangles, or ellipses as they are being sized, giving you the illusion of *stretching* the figure into shape.

"Stretching" Graphics Figures

When you move the mouse, you get WM_MOUSEMOVE messages. You can give the appearance of stretching lines, rectangles, or ellipses as you do. Let's begin with lines. You will start off at the anchor point; when you move the cursor, draw a line from the anchor point to the new mouse position. When the cursor is moved again, you need to erase the old line and draw a new one from the anchor point to the new cursor location. This will give the impression that you are stretching a line from the anchor point to the mouse cursor's position.

To do this, you will have to store the end point of the previous line so that you can erase it before drawing new ones. In other words, the process will go as follows:

1. Set the anchor point in OnLButtonDown( ).

2. In OnMouseMove( ), draw a line from (xAnchor, yAnchor) to (point.x, point.y), and save (point.x, point.y) as (xold, yold).

3. The next time OnMouseMove( ) is called, erase the line from (xAnchor, yAnchor) to (xold, yold), and draw a new line to the new coordinates, (point.x, point.y). Then update (xold, yold) from (point.x, point.y).

4. Repeat step 3 as you move the mouse around, giving the impression of stretching the line. When OnLButtonUp( ) is called, you should draw the final line.

This means that you need to erase the old line before you draw the new one as the mouse cursor moves around. In addition, make sure that the line you are stretching is visible on the screen—if you just stretch a black line, for example, it will disappear as you move over a black filled figure. One way to do this is to specify the current pen's *drawing mode*. This indicates the way that the current pen will interact with what is on the screen in a bit-by-bit fashion. The options range from ignoring what is already on the screen entirely and drawing with the pen, to ignoring the pen entirely and leaving the screen alone. There are 16 different options, and they are listed in table 7.2 (the R2 prefix stands for binary raster operation).

Table 7.2. Windows Drawing Modes

Operation	Windows Drawing Mode
BLACK	R2_BLACK
~(PEN ¦ SCREEN)	R2_NOTMERGEPEN
~PEN & SCREEN	R2_MASKNOTPEN
~PEN	R2_NOTCOPYPEN
PEN & ~SCREEN	R2_MASKPENNOT
~SCREEN	R2_NOT
PEN ^ SCREEN	R2_XORPEN
~(PEN & SCREEN)	R2_NOTMASKPEN
PEN & SCREEN	R2_MASKPEN
~(PEN ^ SCREEN)	R2_NOTXORPEN
SCREEN	R2_NOP
~PEN ¦ SCREEN	R2_MERGENOTPEN

Operation	Windows Drawing Mode
PEN	R2_COPYPEN [the default]
PEN ¦ ~SCREEN	R2_MERGEPENNOT
PEN ¦ SCREEN	R2_MERGEPEN
WHITE	R2_WHITE

Use the R2_NOT drawing mode, that simply inverts what is on the screen in a bit-by-bit fashion. That is, when you draw with a R2_NOT pen, white (RGB(255, 255, 255)) will become black (RGB(0, 0, 0)), and black will become white. In addition, when you draw the same line over again with an R2_NOT pen, overwriting the first time, the original screen pixels will be restored, and that is what you want. In other words, you can rewrite the four steps above to use the R2_NOT pen as follows:

1. Set the anchor point in OnLButtonDown( ).

2. In OnMouseMove( ), draw a line with a R2_NOT pen, inverting screen pixels to make sure the line is visible, from (xAnchor, yAnchor) to (point.x, point.y), and save (point.x, point.y) as (xold, yold).

3. The next time OnMouseMove( ) is called, erase the line from (xAnchor, yAnchor) to (xold, yold), simply by drawing it again with a R2_NOT pen, and draw a new R2_NOT line, inverting screen pixels, to the new coordinates, (point.x, point.y). Then update (xold, yold) from (point.x, point.y).

4. Repeat step 3 as you move the mouse around, giving the impression of stretching the line. When OnLButtonUp( ) is called, you should draw the final line with R2_COPYPEN.

To stretch the line, you can add code to OnMouseMove( ). You can do that first by checking if the left mouse button is down—for example, if (nFlags && MK_LBUTTON) is TRUE—and if you are actually drawing lines—for example, if bLine is TRUE. If these conditions are true, we create a device context object, as follows:

```
void CPaintView::OnMouseMove(UINT nFlags, CPoint point)
{
    if((nFlags && MK_LBUTTON) && bLine){
        CClientDC dc(this);
        :
    }
}
```

Now you get the old drawing mode with the Windows function GetROP2( ) (i.e., Get binary raster operation mode) and save it in an integer variable called nDrawMode, then set the drawing mode to R2_NOT with SetROP2( ), as follows:

```
void CPaintView::OnMouseMove(UINT nFlags, CPoint point)
{
    int nDrawMode;

        if((nFlags && MK_LBUTTON) && bLine){
        CClientDC dc(this);
        nDrawMode = dc.GetROP2();
        dc.SetROP2(R2_NOT);
                :
        }
}
```

Next, you need to erase the old line from the previous WM_MOUSEMOVE event before drawing the new one. The old line runs from (xAnchor, yAnchor) to (xold, yold). To set aside space for xold and yold, place them in paintvw.h, as follows:

```
// paintvw.h : interface of the CPaintView class
//
/////////////////////////////////////////////////////////////////////
////////////
class CPaintView : public CView
{
protected: // create from serialization only
    CPaintView();
    DECLARE_DYNCREATE(CPaintView)
    int xAnchor;
    int yAnchor;
    int xold;
    int yold;
```

```
        BOOL bPoint;
        BOOL bDraw;
        BOOL bLine;
        BOOL bRectangle;
        BOOL bEllipse;
        BOOL bFill;
        void SetFlagsFalse();
// Attributes
public:
        CPaintDoc* GetDocument();
// Operations
public:
    :
```

Note that (xold, yold) must hold a valid point from the very beginning of the drawing operation, so we set it to (xAnchor, yAnchor) when the left button originally goes down in OnLButtonDown( ), as follows:

```
void CPaintView::OnLButtonDown(UINT nFlags, CPoint point)
{
    xAnchor = point.x;
    yAnchor = point.y;
    xold = xAnchor;
    yold = yAnchor;
}
```

Just erase the old line by drawing it again with the drawing mode set to R2_NOT, and draw the new line from the anchor point to your current position as follows:

```
void CPaintView::OnMouseMove(UINT nFlags, CPoint point)
{
                int nDrawMode;
                if((nFlags && MK_LBUTTON) && bLine){
                    CClientDC dc(this);
                    nDrawMode = dc.GetROP2();
                    dc.SetROP2(R2_NOT);
                    dc.MoveTo(xAnchor, yAnchor);
                    dc.LineTo(xold, yold);
                    dc.MoveTo(xAnchor, yAnchor);
                    dc.LineTo(point.x, point.y);
                        :
    }
}
```

All that remains now is to update (xold, yold) for the next time, and to reset the drawing mode as follows:

```
void CPaintView::OnMouseMove(UINT nFlags, CPoint point)
{
    int nDrawMode;
    if((nFlags && MK_LBUTTON) && bLine){
            CClientDC dc(this);
            nDrawMode = dc.GetROP2();
            dc.SetROP2(R2_NOT);
            dc.MoveTo(xAnchor, yAnchor);
            dc.LineTo(xold, yold);
            dc.MoveTo(xAnchor, yAnchor);
            dc.LineTo(point.x, point.y);
            xold = point.x;
            yold = point.y;
            dc.SetROP2(nDrawMode);
    }
}
```

That's all there is to it. Now when you set the anchor point and move around the screen when drawing lines, you stretch a line from the anchor point to the current cursor position, as in figure 7.12.

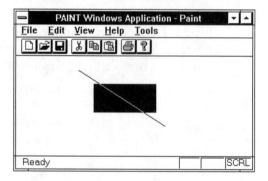

Figure 7.12. Stretching lines in the Paint Program.

You can do the same thing for ellipses and rectangles easily. All you have to do is to set the drawing mode to R2_NOT, draw over old rectangles as the cursor moves around the screen and draw new ones, just as you did for lines. That appears as follows in OnMouseMove( ):

```
void CPaintView::OnMouseMove(UINT nFlags, CPoint point)
{
    CGdiObject* pBackup;
    int nDrawMode;
    if((nFlags && MK_LBUTTON) && bDraw){
            CClientDC dc(this);
            dc.MoveTo(xAnchor, yAnchor);
            dc.LineTo(point.x, point.y);
            xAnchor = point.x;
            yAnchor = point.y;
    }
    if((nFlags && MK_LBUTTON) && bLine){ CClientDC dc(this);
            nDrawMode = dc.GetROP2();
            dc.SetROP2(R2_NOT);
            dc.MoveTo(xAnchor, yAnchor);
            dc.LineTo(xold, yold);
            dc.MoveTo(xAnchor, yAnchor);
            dc.LineTo(point.x, point.y);
            xold = point.x; yold = point.y;
            dc.SetROP2(nDrawMode);
    }
    if((nFlags && MK_LBUTTON) && bRectangle){
            CClientDC dc(this);
            nDrawMode = dc.GetROP2();
            dc.SetROP2(R2_NOT);
            pBackup = dc.SelectStockObject(NULL_BRUSH);
            dc.Rectangle(xold, yold, xAnchor, yAnchor);
            dc.Rectangle(xAnchor, yAnchor, point.x, point.y);
            dc.SelectObject(pBackup);
            xold = point.x;
            yold = point.y;
            dc.SetROP2(nDrawMode);
    }
    if((nFlags && MK_LBUTTON) && bEllipse){
            CClientDC dc(this);
            nDrawMode = dc.GetROP2();
            dc.SetROP2(R2_NOT);
            pBackup = dc.SelectStockObject(NULL_BRUSH);
            dc.Ellipse(xold, yold, xAnchor, yAnchor);
            dc.Ellipse(xAnchor, yAnchor, point.x, point.y);
            dc.SelectObject(pBackup);
            xold = point.x;
            yold = point.y;
            dc.SetROP2(nDrawMode);
        }
}
```

339

Now all of your functions are complete. That's it. The rest of the code simply defines your main window, and creates it as you have done many times before. The entire listing of paintvw.cpp appears in listing 7.1, paintvw.h in listing 7.2, and paint.rc in listing 7.3.

Listing 7.1. Paintvw.Cpp

```
_G
// paintvw.cpp : implementation of the CPaintView class
//
#include "stdafx.h"
#include "paint.h"
#include "paintdoc.h"
#include "paintvw.h"
#ifdef _DEBUG
#undef THIS_FILE
static char BASED_CODE THIS_FILE[] = __FILE__;
#endif
/////////////////////////////////////////////////////////////////////////
//
// CPaintView
IMPLEMENT_DYNCREATE(CPaintView, CView)
BEGIN_MESSAGE_MAP(CPaintView, CView)
    //{{AFX_MSG_MAP(CPaintView)
    ON_COMMAND(IDM_POINT, OnPoint)
    ON_UPDATE_COMMAND_UI(IDM_POINT, OnUpdatePoint)
    ON_UPDATE_COMMAND_UI(IDM_DRAW, OnUpdateDraw)
    ON_COMMAND(IDM_DRAW, OnDrawItem)
    ON_COMMAND(IDM_LINE, OnLine)
    ON_UPDATE_COMMAND_UI(IDM_LINE, OnUpdateLine)
    ON_COMMAND(IDM_RECTANGLE, OnRectangle)
    ON_UPDATE_COMMAND_UI(IDM_RECTANGLE, OnUpdateRectangle)
    ON_COMMAND(IDM_ELLIPSE, OnEllipse)
    ON_UPDATE_COMMAND_UI(IDM_ELLIPSE, OnUpdateEllipse)
    ON_COMMAND(IDM_FILL, OnFill)
    ON_UPDATE_COMMAND_UI(IDM_FILL, OnUpdateFill)
    ON_WM_LBUTTONDOWN()
    ON_WM_LBUTTONUP()
    ON_WM_MOUSEMOVE()
    //}}AFX_MSG_MAP
// Standard printing commands ON_COMMAND(ID_FILE_PRINT, CView::OnFilePrint)
ON_COMMAND(ID_FILE_PRINT_PREVIEW, CView::OnFilePrintPreview)
        END_MESSAGE_MAP()
```

```
///////////////////////////////////////////////////////////////////
///////
// CPaintView
construction/destruction
CPaintView::CPaintView()
{
    bPoint = TRUE;
    bDraw = FALSE;
    bLine = FALSE;
    bRectangle = FALSE;
    bEllipse = FALSE;
    bFill = FALSE;
}
CPaintView::~CPaintView()
{
}
///////////////////////////////////////////////////////////////////
///////
// CPaintView drawing
void CPaintView::OnDraw(CDC* pDC)
{
    CPaintDoc* pDoc = GetDocument();
    // TODO: add draw code here
}
///////////////////////////////////////////////////////////////////
///////
// CPaintView printing
BOOL CPaintView::OnPreparePrinting(CPrintInfo* pInfo)
{
    // default preparation
    return DoPreparePrinting(pInfo);
}
void CPaintView::OnBeginPrinting(CDC* /*pDC*/, CPrintInfo* *pInfo*/)
{
    // TODO: add extra initialization before printing
}
void CPaintView::OnEndPrinting(CDC* /*pDC*/, CPrintInfo* *pInfo*/)
{
    // TODO: add cleanup after printing
}
    ///////////////////////////////////////////////////////////
    ////////////
    // CPaintView diagnostics
    #ifdef _DEBUG
```

continues

341

Listing 7.1. continued

```
void CPaintView::AssertValid() const
{
    CView::AssertValid();
}
void CPaintView::Dump(CDumpContext& dc) const
{
    CView::Dump(dc);
}
CPaintDoc* CPaintView::GetDocument() // non-debug version is inline
{
    ASSERT(m_pDocument->IsKindOf(RUNTIME_CLASS(CPaintDoc)));
    return (CPaintDoc*) m_pDocument;
}
#endif //_DEBUG
///////////////////////////////////////////////////////////////////
//////////
// CPaintView message handlers
void CPaintView::SetFlagsFalse()
{
    bPoint = FALSE;
    bDraw = FALSE;
    bLine = FALSE;
    bRectangle = FALSE;
    bEllipse = FALSE;
    bFill = FALSE;
}
void CPaintView::OnPoint()
{
    SetFlagsFalse();
    bPoint = TRUE;
}
void CPaintView::OnUpdatePoint(CCmdUI* pCmdUI) {
    if (bPoint)
        pCmdUI->SetCheck(1);
    else
        pCmdUI->SetCheck(0);
}
void CPaintView::OnUpdateDraw(CCmdUI* pCmdUI) {
    if (bDraw)
        pCmdUI->SetCheck(1);
```

```cpp
    else
            pCmdUI->SetCheck(0);
}
void CPaintView::OnDrawItem()
{
    SetFlagsFalse();
    bDraw = TRUE;
}
void CPaintView::OnLine()
{
    SetFlagsFalse();
    bLine = TRUE;
}
void CPaintView::OnUpdateLine(CCmdUI* pCmdUI) {
    if (bLine)
                pCmdUI->SetCheck(1);
    else
                pCmdUI->SetCheck(0);
}
void CPaintView::OnRectangle()
{
    SetFlagsFalse();
    bRectangle = TRUE;
}
void CPaintView::OnUpdateRectangle(CCmdUI* pCmdUI)
{
    if (bRectangle)
                pCmdUI->SetCheck(1);
    else
                pCmdUI->SetCheck(0);
}
void CPaintView::OnEllipse()
{
    SetFlagsFalse();
    bEllipse = TRUE;
}
void CPaintView::OnUpdateEllipse(CCmdUI* pCmdUI)
{
    if (bEllipse)
                pCmdUI->SetCheck(1);
    else
                pCmdUI->SetCheck(0);
```

continues

Listing 7.1. continued

```
}
void CPaintView::OnFill()
{
    SetFlagsFalse();
    bFill = TRUE;
}
void CPaintView::OnUpdateFill(CCmdUI* pCmdUI)
{
    if (bFill)
                pCmdUI->SetCheck(1);
    else
                pCmdUI->SetCheck(0);
}
void CPaintView::OnLButtonDown(UINT nFlags, CPoint point) {
    xAnchor = point.x;
    yAnchor = point.y;
    xold = xAnchor;
    yold = yAnchor;
    CView::OnLButtonDown(nFlags, point);
}
void CPaintView::OnLButtonUp(UINT nFlags, CPoint point)
{
    CGdiObject* pBackup;
    if(bPoint){
        CClientDC dc(this);
        dc.SetPixel(point.x, point.y, RGB(0, 0, 0));
    }
    if(bLine){
        CClientDC dc(this);
        dc.MoveTo(xAnchor, yAnchor);
        dc.LineTo(point.x, point.y);
    }
    if(bRectangle){
        CClientDC dc(this);
        pBackup = dc.SelectStockObject(NULL_BRUSH);
        dc.Rectangle(xAnchor, yAnchor, point.x, point.y);
        dc.SelectObject(pBackup);
    }
    if(bEllipse){
        CClientDC dc(this);
        pBackup = dc.SelectStockObject(NULL_BRUSH);
        dc.Ellipse(xAnchor, yAnchor, point.x, point.y);
        dc.SelectObject(pBackup);
```

```
        }
    if(bFill){
        CClientDC dc(this);
        dc.SetROP2(R2_BLACK);
        dc.FloodFill(point.x, point.y, RGB(0, 0, 0));
    }
    CView::OnLButtonUp(nFlags, point);
}
void CPaintView::OnMouseMove(UINT nFlags, CPoint point) {
    CGdiObject* pBackup;
    int nDrawMode;
    if((nFlags && MK_LBUTTON) && bDraw){
        CClientDC dc(this);
        dc.MoveTo(xAnchor, yAnchor);
        dc.LineTo(point.x, point.y);
        xAnchor = point.x;
        yAnchor = point.y;
    }
    if((nFlags && MK_LBUTTON) && bLine){ CClientDC dc(this);
        nDrawMode = dc.GetROP2();
        dc.SetROP2(R2_NOT);
        dc.MoveTo(xAnchor, yAnchor);
        dc.LineTo(xold, yold);
        dc.MoveTo(xAnchor, yAnchor);
        dc.LineTo(point.x, point.y);
        xold = point.x;
        yold = point.y;
        dc.SetROP2(nDrawMode);
    }
    if((nFlags && MK_LBUTTON) && bRectangle){
        CClientDC dc(this);
        nDrawMode = dc.GetROP2();
        dc.SetROP2(R2_NOT);
        pBackup = dc.SelectStockObject(NULL_BRUSH);
        dc.Rectangle(xold, yold, xAnchor, yAnchor);
        dc.Rectangle(xAnchor, yAnchor, point.x, point.y);
        dc.SelectObject(pBackup);
        xold = point.x;
        yold = point.y;
        dc.SetROP2(nDrawMode);
    }
```

continues

345

Listing 7.1. continued

```
if((nFlags && MK_LBUTTON) && bEllipse){
        CClientDC dc(this);
        nDrawMode = dc.GetROP2();
        dc.SetROP2(R2_NOT);
        pBackup = dc.SelectStockObject(NULL_BRUSH);
        dc.Ellipse(xold, yold, xAnchor, yAnchor);
        dc.Ellipse(xAnchor, yAnchor, point.x, point.y);
        dc.SelectObject(pBackup);
        xold = point.x;
        yold = point.y;
        dc.SetROP2(nDrawMode);
    }
    CView::OnMouseMove(nFlags, point);
}
```

Listing 7.2. Paintvw.H

```
// paintvw.h : interface of the CPaintView class
//
/////////////////////////////////////////////////////////////////////
////////////
class CPaintView : public CView
{
protected: // create from serialization only
    CPaintView();
    DECLARE_DYNCREATE(CPaintView)
    int xAnchor;
    int yAnchor;
    int xold;
    int yold;
    BOOL bPoint;
    BOOL bDraw;
    BOOL bLine;
    BOOL bRectangle;
    BOOL bEllipse;
    BOOL bFill;
    void SetFlagsFalse();
// Attributes
```

```
public:
    CPaintDoc* GetDocument();
// Operations
public:
// Implementation
public:
    virtual ~CPaintView();
    virtual void OnDraw(CDC* pDC);  // overridden to draw this
view
#ifdef _DEBUG
    virtual void AssertValid() const;
    virtual void Dump(CDumpContext& dc) const;
#endif
    // Printing support
protected:
    virtual BOOL OnPreparePrinting(CPrintInfo* pInfo);
    virtual void OnBeginPrinting(CDC* pDC, CPrintInfo* pInfo);
    virtual void OnEndPrinting(CDC* pDC, CPrintInfo* pInfo);
// Generated message map functions
protected:
    //{{AFX_MSG(CPaintView)
    afx_msg void OnPoint();
    afx_msg void OnUpdatePoint(CCmdUI* pCmdUI);
    afx_msg void OnUpdateDraw(CCmdUI* pCmdUI);
    afx_msg void OnDrawItem();
    afx_msg void OnLine();
    afx_msg void OnUpdateLine(CCmdUI* pCmdUI);
    afx_msg void OnRectangle();
    afx_msg void OnUpdateRectangle(CCmdUI* pCmdUI);
    afx_msg void OnEllipse();
    afx_msg void OnUpdateEllipse(CCmdUI* pCmdUI);
    afx_msg void OnFill();
    afx_msg void OnUpdateFill(CCmdUI* pCmdUI);
    afx_msg void OnLButtonDown(UINT nFlags, CPoint point);
    afx_msg void OnLButtonUp(UINT nFlags, CPoint point);
    afx_msg void OnMouseMove(UINT nFlags, CPoint point);
    //}}AFX_MSG DECLARE_MESSAGE_MAP()
};
#ifndef _DEBUG    // debug version in paintvw.cpp
inline CPaintDoc* CPaintView::GetDocument()
{ return (CPaintDoc*) m_pDocument; }
#endif
/////////////////////////////////////////////////////////////////
////////////
```

Listing 7.3. Paint.Rc

```
//Microsoft App Studio generated resource script.
//
#include "resource.h"
#define APSTUDIO_READONLY_SYMBOLS /////////////////////////////////
/////////////////////////////////////////
//
// Generated from the TEXTINCLUDE 2 resource.
//
#include "afxres.h"
//////////////////////////////////////////////////////////////////
/////////////// #undef APSTUDIO_READONLY_SYMBOLS
#ifdef APSTUDIO_INVOKED /////////////////////////////////////////////
//////////////////////////////////// //
// TEXTINCLUDE
//
1 TEXTINCLUDE DISCARDABLE
BEGIN
        "resource.h\0"
END
2 TEXTINCLUDE DISCARDABLE
BEGIN
        "#include ""afxres.h""\r\n"
        "\0"
END
3 TEXTINCLUDE DISCARDABLE
BEGIN
"#include ""res\\paint.rc2""  // non-App Studio edited
resources\r\n"
        "\r\n"
        "#include ""afxres.rc""  // Standard components\r\n"
"#include ""afxprint.rc""  // printing/print preview
resources\r\n"
        "\0"
END
//////////////////////////////////////////////////////////////////
/////////////// #endif    // APSTUDIO_INVOKED
//////////////////////////////////////////////////////////////////
/////////////
//
// Icon
//
IDR_MAINFRAME              ICON    DISCARDABLE     "RES\\PAINT.ICO"
```

```
///////////////////////////////////////////////////////////
/////////////////  //
// Bitmap
//
IDR_MAINFRAME              BITMAP    MOVEABLE PURE
"RES\\TOOLBAR.BMP"
///////////////////////////////////////////////////////////
/////////////// //
// Menu
//
IDR_MAINFRAME MENU PRELOAD DISCARDABLE
BEGIN
    POPUP "&File"
    BEGIN
        MENUITEM "&New\tCtrl+N",        ID_FILE_NEW
        MENUITEM "&Open...\tCtrl+O",    ID_FILE_OPEN
        MENUITEM "&Save\tCtrl+S",       ID_FILE_SAVE
        MENUITEM "Save &As...", ID_FILE_SAVE_AS
        MENUITEM SEPARATOR
        MENUITEM "&Print...\tCtrl+P",   ID_FILE_PRINT
        MENUITEM "Print Pre&view",      ID_FILE_PRINT_PREVIEW
        MENUITEM "P&rint Setup...",     ID_FILE_PRINT_SETUP
        MENUITEM SEPARATOR
        MENUITEM "Recent File", ID_FILE_MRU_FILE1, GRAYED
        MENUITEM SEPARATOR
        MENUITEM "E&xit",        ID_APP_EXIT
    END
    POPUP "&Edit"
    BEGIN
        MENUITEM "&Undo\tCtrl+Z",       ID_EDIT_UNDO
        MENUITEM SEPARATOR
        MENUITEM "Cu&t\tCtrl+X",        ID_EDIT_CUT
        MENUITEM "&Copy\tCtrl+C",       D_EDIT_COPY
        MENUITEM "&Paste\tCtrl+V",      ID_EDIT_PASTE
    END
    POPUP "&View"
    BEGIN
        MENUITEM "&Toolbar",    ID_VIEW_TOOLBAR
        MENUITEM "&Status Bar", ID_VIEW_STATUS_BAR
    END
    POPUP "&Help"
    BEGIN
```

continues

Listing 7.3. continued

```
            MENUITEM "&About PAINT...",     ID_APP_ABOUT
        END
        POPUP "&Tools"
        BEGIN
            MENUITEM "Point",       IDM_POINT
            MENUITEM "Draw",        IDM_DRAW
            MENUITEM "Line",        IDM_LINE
            MENUITEM "Rectangle",   IDM_RECTANGLE
            MENUITEM "Ellipse",     IDM_ELLIPSE
            MENUITEM "Fill",        IDM_FILL
        END
END
/////////////////////////////////////////////////////////////////
///////////// //
// Accelerator
//
IDR_MAINFRAME ACCELERATORS PRELOAD MOVEABLE PURE
BEGIN
    "N",  ID_FILE_NEW,    VIRTKEY,CONTROL
    "O",  ID_FILE_OPEN,   VIRTKEY,CONTROL
    "S",  ID_FILE_SAVE,   VIRTKEY,CONTROL
    "P",  ID_FILE_PRINT,  VIRTKEY,CONTROL
    "Z",  ID_EDIT_UNDO,   VIRTKEY,CONTROL
    "X",  ID_EDIT_CUT,    VIRTKEY,CONTROL
    "C",  ID_EDIT_COPY,   VIRTKEY,CONTROL
    "V",  ID_EDIT_PASTE,  VIRTKEY,CONTROL
    VK_BACK,        ID_EDIT_UNDO,   VIRTKEY,ALT
    VK_DELETE,      ID_EDIT_CUT,    VIRTKEY,SHIFT
    VK_INSERT,      ID_EDIT_COPY,   VIRTKEY,CONTROL
    VK_INSERT,      ID_EDIT_PASTE,  VIRTKEY,SHIFT
    VK_F6,          ID_NEXT_PANE,   VIRTKEY
    VK_F6,          ID_PREV_PANE,   VIRTKEY,SHIFT
END
/////////////////////////////////////////////////////////////////
///////////// //
// Dialog
//
IDD_ABOUTBOX DIALOG DISCARDABLE  34, 22, 217, 55
STYLE DS_MODALFRAME | WS_POPUP | WS_CAPTION | WS_SYSMENU
CAPTION "About PAINT"
FONT 8, "MS Sans Serif"
```

```
BEGIN
    ICON  IDR_MAINFRAME,IDC_STATIC,11,17,20,20
    LTEXT "PAINT Application Version 1.0",IDC_STATIC,40,10,119,8
    LTEXT "Copyright \251 1993",IDC_STATIC,40,25,119,8
    DEFPUSHBUTTON "OK",IDOK,176,6,32,14,WS_GROUP
END
/////////////////////////////////////////////////////////////////////////////
//
// String Table
//
STRINGTABLE PRELOAD DISCARDABLE
BEGIN
    IDR_MAINFRAME           "PAINT Windows Application\nPaint\nPAINT Document"
END
STRINGTABLE PRELOAD DISCARDABLE
BEGIN
    AFX_IDS_APP_TITLE       "PAINT Windows Application"
    AFX_IDS_IDLEMESSAGE     "Ready"
END
STRINGTABLE DISCARDABLE
BEGIN
    ID_INDICATOR_EXT        "EXT"
    ID_INDICATOR_CAPS       "CAP"
    ID_INDICATOR_NUM        "NUM"
    ID_INDICATOR_SCRL       "SCRL"
    ID_INDICATOR_OVR        "OVR"
    ID_INDICATOR_REC        "REC"
END
STRINGTABLE DISCARDABLE
BEGIN
    ID_FILE_NEW   "Create a new document"
    ID_FILE_OPEN  "Open an existing document"
    ID_FILE_CLOSE "Close the active document"
    ID_FILE_SAVE  "Save the active document"
    ID_FILE_SAVE_AS         "Save the active document with a new name"
    ID_FILE_PAGE_SETUP      "Change the printing options"
    ID_FILE_PRINT_SETUP     "Change the printer and printing options"
```

continues

Listing 7.3. continued

```
        ID_FILE_PRINT "Print the active document"
        ID_FILE_PRINT_PREVIEW         "Display full pages"
END
STRINGTABLE DISCARDABLE
BEGIN
        ID_APP_ABOUT  "Display program information
        ID_APP_EXIT   "Quit the application; prompts to save documents"
END
STRINGTABLE DISCARDABLE
BEGIN
        ID_FILE_MRU_FILE1    "Open this document"
        ID_FILE_MRU_FILE2    "Open this document"
        ID_FILE_MRU_FILE3    "Open this document"
        ID_FILE_MRU_FILE4    "Open this document"
END
STRINGTABLE DISCARDABLE
BEGIN
        ID_NEXT_PANE "Switch to the next window pane"
        ID_PREV_PANE "Switch back to the previous window pane"
END
STRINGTABLE DISCARDABLE
BEGIN
        ID_EDIT_CLEAR "Erase the selection"
        ID_EDIT_CLEAR_ALL     "Erase everything"
        ID_EDIT_COPY  "Copy the selection and put it on the Clipboard"
        ID_EDIT_CUT   "Cut the selection and put it on the Clipboard"
        ID_EDIT_FIND  "Find the specified text"
        ID_EDIT_PASTE "Insert Clipboard contents"
        ID_EDIT_REPEAT        "Repeat the last action"
        ID_EDIT_REPLACE       "Replace specific text with different text"
        ID_EDIT_SELECT_ALL    "Select the entire document"
        ID_EDIT_UNDO  "Undo the last action"
        ID_EDIT_REDO  "Redo the previously undone action"
END
STRINGTABLE DISCARDABLE
BEGIN
        ID_VIEW_TOOLBAR       "Show or hide the toolbar"
        ID_VIEW_STATUS_BAR    "Show or hide the status bar"
END
```

```
STRINGTABLE  DISCARDABLE
BEGIN
    AFX_IDS_SCSIZE        "Change the window size"
    AFX_IDS_SCMOVE        "Change the window position"
    AFX_IDS_SCMINIMIZE    "Reduce the window to an icon"
    AFX_IDS_SCMAXIMIZE    "Enlarge the window to full size"
    AFX_IDS_SCNEXTWINDOW "Switch to the next document window"
    AFX_IDS_SCPREVWINDOW "Switch to the previous document window"
    AFX_IDS_SCCLOSE       "Close the active window
END
STRINGTABLE DISCARDABLE
BEGIN
AFX_IDS_SCRESTORE         "Restore the window to normal size"
AFX_IDS_SCTASKLIST        "Activate Task List"
END
#ifndef APSTUDIO_INVOKED ///////////////////////////////////////
/////////////////////////////////////// //
// Generated from the TEXTINCLUDE 3 resource.
//
#include "res\paint.rc2"  // non-App Studio edited resources
#include "afxres.rc"  // Standard components
#include "afxprint.rc"  // printing/print preview resources
///////////////////////////////////////////////////////////////
////////// #endif     // not APSTUDIO_INVOKED
```

Saving and Restoring the Paint Image.
You can add code to the OnDraw( ) function to restore the paint
program's client area when it is uncovered, if you want. To do
that, you should create a new (memory-only) device context that
matches the view's device context with the member function
CreateCompatibleDC( ). Store the resulting pointer in the document; when you draw in the view, also draw in that new compatible device context. When it is time to update the view from that
device context in OnDraw( ), use the member function BitBlt( )
to copy the graphical data back to the view.

That's it for my coverage of graphics and for the development of your
Paint Program. You have come far in this chapter—now you are able to
draw lines, points, ellipses, and so on. In the next chapter, I will start with
the process of saving all of your work on disk and in files.

353

Files

U p to this point, you have written many powerful programs, but you have yet to produce anything permanent—something that will last after you turn the computer off. You can store data on computer disks in the form of files, and that's what this chapter is about. If computers did not allow you to store data in some permanent fashion, working with computers—and learning programming techniques—would be pointless.

Working with files is integral to programming, and the file-handling capabilities in Visual C++ are good ones. In this chapter, you will see how to interface file-handling capabilities with your programs. The first program simply saves a string to disk. After that, you will learn to work with records and random access files. Next, you will update the notepad and db programs to handle files through the process of *serialization* (the MFC method of automatic file processing). Finally, you will discover how to handle serialization yourself—from the ground up. The next section gets you started with file handling in Visual C++.

MFC File Handling

Some aspects of programming are not spelled out in the C++ standard because they vary from computer to computer. File handling in Visual C++ under Windows is one of these areas, because here you can't use the standard file stream functions fopen( ), fread( ), fwrite( ), and fclose( ) functions you have seen in C. The reason for this is that Windows is a multitasking environment that does not support streams in the standard way; Windows has its own (non-stream) method of handling file functions. Instead, the usual way of working with files in Visual C++ is based on the CFile class already defined in the MFC libraries, and this chapter is largely an exploration of that class.

Actually, declaring and using an object of class CFile is much like working with an I/O stream in C. In C, you might print the text "Hello, world." to the file hello.txt as the following example shows. Notice that you open the file with fopen( ), write to it with fwrite( ), and close it with fclose( ).

```
#include <stdio.h>
void main( )
{
    FILE *file_pointer;
    if((file_pointer = fopen("hello.txt", "w")) != NULL) {
        fwrite("Hello, world.", strlen("Hello, world."),    0, \
file_pointer);
    fclose(file_pointer);
    }
    else printf("Error writing hello.txt\n");
}
```

In Visual C++, you use the CFile member functions Open( ), Write( ), and Close( ), so the process is parallel. In fact, Visual C++ makes it even easier because you use the CFile constructor to open a file, and the CFile destructor automatically closes a file when the object goes out of scope. The CFile member functions appear in table 8.1.

Table 8.1. CFile's Member Functions

Member	Means
CFile	Constructor
Close	Closes file, deletes object
Duplicate	Duplicates object

Member	Means
Flush	Flushes data
GetLength	Gets length of the file
GetPosition	Gets file pointer
GetStatus	Gets status of the specified file
LockRange	Locks range of file bytes
Open	Opens a file (with error-testing option)
Read	Reads data from file
Remove	Deletes specified file
Rename	Renames specified file
Seek	Moves file pointer
SeekToBegin	Moves file pointer to beginning of file
SeekToEnd	Moves file pointer to end of file
SetLength	Changes length of file
SetStatus	Sets status of specified file
UnlockRange	Unlocks range of file bytes
Write	Writes to current file position
~CFile	Destructor

The following section uses an example to show how all this works.

A CFile Class Example

First, create a new application with App Wizard named, for example, file.mak, and add two file handling items to the File menu. You can name the items File Write (ID = IDM_FILEWRITE) and File Read (ID = IDM_FILEREAD), as shown in figure 8.1.

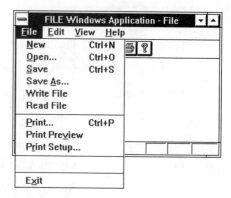

Figure 8.1. The file example's File menu.

Next, connect two view class functions to those menu items named OnFileWrite( ) and OnFileRead( ) by using ClassWizard, as follows:

```
void CFileView::OnFilewrite( )
{
}
void CFileView::OnFileread( )
{
}
```

Now you are ready to write some data.

Writing a File

In OnFileWrite( ), you can write the text "Hello, world." to the file hello.txt; and in OnFileRead( ), you can read it back in again. These actions are triggered by selecting the appropriate menu item. Start by declaring the CFile object in OnFileWrite( ), which you might call simply *file*, and by opening it, as follows:

```
void CFileView::OnFilewrite( )
{
    CFile file;
    file.Open("hello.txt", CFile::modeCreate ¦ CFile::modeWrite);
        :
}
```

Notice that two CFile members, CFile::modeCreate and CFile::modeWrite, are Or'ed together, specifying that you want to create this file if it doesn't already exist and that you intend to write to it. Other Open() options of CFile appear in table 8.2. Notice that you do not check for errors here—because if there is an error, Visual C++ generates an exception. (You learn how to handle exceptions in Chapter 10.)

Table 8.2. CFile Open( ) Options

CFile Member	Meaning
CFile::modeCreate	Creates a new file or truncates to 0 length
CFile::modeNoInherit	File cannot be inherited by child processes
CFile::modeRead	Opens the file for reading only
CFile::modeReadWrite	Opens the file for reading and writing
CFile::modeWrite	Opens the file for writing only
CFile::shareCompat	Opens the file in compatibility mode
CFile::shareDenyNone	Opens the file without denying any access
CFile::shareDenyRead	Opens the file and denies others read access
CFile::shareDenyWrite	Opens the file and denies others write access
CFile::shareExclusive	Opens the file and denies others all access
CFile::typeBinary	Sets binary mode
CFile::typeText	Special processing for <cr><lf> pairs

In fact, you can choose an easier way to create the file hello.txt and open it. Just use the CFile constructor (when you create a CFile object, a logical assumption is that you want to open it, so Visual C++ adds that capability to the constructor). That appears as follows:

```
void CFileView::OnFilewrite()
{
    CFile file("hello.txt", CFile::modeCreate | CFile::modeWrite);
        :
}
```

That's it. Now the file is open for use, ready to be written to (although it has zero length), as follows:

Hello.txt

Next, you can add a CString object named hello_string to hold your text and write it to disk with CFile::Write( ), as the following example shows. You need only to pass the character string and its length to Write( ), as follows:

```
void CFileView::OnFilewrite()
{
    CString hello_string = "Hello, world.";
    CFile file("hello.txt", CFile::modeCreate | CFile::modeWrite);
    file.Write(hello_string, hello_string.GetLength());
        :
}
```

In general, when using CFile::Write( ), you simply pass a pointer to a data buffer (which can hold any type of data—numerical, text, etc.) as the first parameter and the number of bytes to write as the second. Note that if you don't know how big a certain object is, you can always use sizeof( ). Note also that you do not have to use file handles here (as you do in standard C), because you are using member functions of the file object, so the file you are working with is obvious. At this point, then, the text has been written to disk, as follows:

Hello.txt

CString "Hello, world."

The final step is to close the file now that the text has been written. You can do that with the CFile function Close( ). In fact, you don't need to use Close( ) because it is automatically invoked by the CFile destructor when the corresponding object goes out of scope. Often, however, you may find it useful to close a file in order to save memory and to indicate that you are done with it in the folowing way:

```
void CFileView::OnFilewrite()
{
    CString hello_string = "Hello, world.";
CFile file("hello.txt", CFile::modeCreate | CFile::modeWrite);
    file.Write(hello_string, hello_string.GetLength());
    file.Close();
}
```

Reading a File

That's all there is to writing the text file. Next, you need to read it back in OnFileRead( ). That works much as it did in OnFileWrite( )—you start by opening the file. This time, however, open it by using CFile::modeRead, as follows:

```
void CFileView::OnFileread()
{
    CFile file("hello.txt", CFile::modeRead);
        :
}
```

After that, set aside space for the data you want to read in with a constant length character string named data_string, as follows:

```
void CFileView::OnFileread()
{
    const MAX_LEN = 20;
    char data_string[MAX_LEN];
    CFile file("hello.txt", CFile::modeRead);
        :
}
```

Now you read the file hello.txt with the CFile member function Read( ). You pass a data buffer pointer to Read( ), along with the number of bytes you want to read. This function returns the number of bytes actually read as an unsigned integer, and you store that value in a variable named number_read, as follows:

```
void CFileView::OnFileread()
{
    const MAX_LEN = 20;
    char data_string[MAX_LEN];
    CFile file("hello.txt", CFile::modeRead);
    UINT number_read = file.Read(data_string, MAX_LEN);
        :
}
```

The final step is to print out the result of reading in the file. Do that with TextOut(), as follows:

```
void CFileView::OnFileread()
{
    const MAX_LEN = 20;
    char data_string[MAX_LEN];
    CFile file("hello.txt", CFile::modeRead);
    UINT number_read = file.Read(data_string, MAX_LEN);
    CClientDC dc(this);
    dc.TextOut(0, 0, data_string, number_read);
        :
}
```

Now you have written your file and read it back in, as shown in figure 8.2. The program is a success.

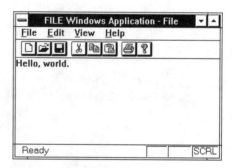

Figure 8.2. Reading the file back in.

Sequential and Random Access Files

So far, you have treated your file as a *sequential* file. Sequential files are ordinarily used for text files, where you write the file from beginning to end and read it the same way; that is, you don't jump around inside the file. Working with sequential files is like using cassette tapes; if you want to hear something at the end of the tape, you have to pass by everything in front of it first.

If sequential files are like cassette tapes, then *random* files—the next type—are like compact discs. Although you must fast-forward to the parts you want in a cassette tape, you can simply move around at will on a CD, without going through all the intervening tracks. The price you pay is that the data in a random access file has to be carefully sectioned into records so that you know exactly where the data you want is located. For example, if the records developed for the database application were all the same size, they would work perfectly in a random access file; when you want the twentieth record, you can simply skip over the first 19 records and then start reading.

CFile objects support this kind of file access with the Seek() member function. For example, you might write four constant-length character arrays (the "records") to a file named data.dat in the following way:

data.dat

"This"
"is"
"a"
"test."

The CFile class maintains a file pointer for use with the Seek() function. Using it is easy; for example, if you want to read the second record in the file data.dat, you simply position the file pointer there by using Seek(), as follows:

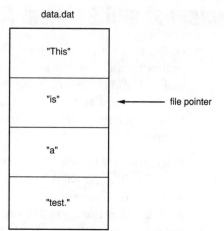

data.dat

"This"

"is" ← file pointer

"a"

"test."

When you next read a record from the file, that'll be the record you read. Let's see this in action. First, you can write the file in OnFileWrite(). Next, open it in OnFileRead() and read in only the second record, using Seek().

Writing the file is easy with CFile::Write(). First, set the constant-length character array records (the records could be anything, including structures and objects). Notice that CString objects are not used here because they expand or contract to fit the size of their internal strings, and records must be a constant length.

```
void CFileView::OnFilewrite( )
{
    const MAX_LEN = 20;
    const MAX_ITEMS = 4;
    char output_string[MAX_ITEMS][MAX_LEN];
    strcpy(output_string[0], "This");
    strcpy(output_string[1], "is");
    strcpy(output_string[2], "a");
    strcpy(output_string[3], "test.");
         :

}
```

Now your data is ready to be written. Open a file called, for example, random_file, and write the data out in the following way:

```
void CFileView::OnFilewrite( )
{
    const MAX_LEN = 20;
    const MAX_ITEMS = 4;
    CString hello_string = "Hello, world.";
```

```
        CFile file("hello.txt", CFile::modeCreate | CFile::modeWrite);
        file.Write(hello_string, hello_string.GetLength( ));
        file.Close( );
        char output_string[MAX_ITEMS][MAX_LEN];
        strcpy(output_string[0], "This");
        strcpy(output_string[1], "is");
        strcpy(output_string[2], "a");
        strcpy(output_string[3], "test.");
        CFile random_file("data.dat", CFile::modeCreate | CFile::modeWrite);
        for (int loop_index = 0; loop_index < MAX_ITEMS; loop_index++)
{random_file.Write(output_string [loop_index], MAX_LEN);
        }
        random_file.Close( );
}
```

Now you have created data.dat on disk, as follows:

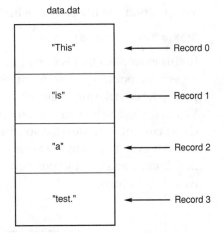

data.dat

The next step reads in only the second record; here, that is record 1 (in the 0-based system). You do that in OnFileRead(). First, create a character array large enough to hold a single record and open the file for reading, as follows:

```
void CFileView::OnFileread( )
{
        const MAX_LEN = 20;
        char input_string[MAX_LEN];
        CFile random_file("data.dat", CFile::modeRead);
            :
}
```

Now position the file pointer at record 1, as follows:

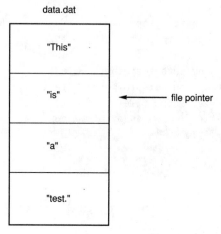

You position the file pointer with Seek( ), in the following format:

```
Seek(offset, method),
```

In this example, *offset* is the offset in bytes you want to move. How you move the pointer depends on the second parameter, method. This parameter can take three values: CFile::begin, CFile::current, and CFile::end. You use these values to indicate the origin of the offset. For example, CFile::current indicates that you want to move the file pointer offset bytes (the value can be positive or negative) with respect to the current position. In this case, you want to position the pointer immediately after the first record, as follows:

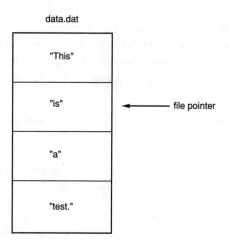

In code, that works in the following way:

```
void CFileView::OnFileread()
{
    const MAX_LEN = 20;
    char input_string[MAX_LEN];
    CFile random_file("data.dat", CFile::modeRead);
    random_file.Seek(MAX_LEN, CFile::begin);
        :
}
```

Now that the file pointer is positioned, you can read in the data. Here, you can cheat a little because you know that the second record contains only two bytes of data—so you ask for two bytes to be read. Finally, print out the result and close the file, as follows:

```
void CFileView::OnFileread()
{
    const MAX_LEN = 20;
    char input_string[MAX_LEN];
    CFile random_file("data.dat", CFile::modeRead);
    random_file.Seek(MAX_LEN, CFile::begin);
    number_read = random_file.Read(input_string, 2);
    dc.TextOut(0, 0, input_string, number_read);
    random_file.Close();
}
```

The program is a success. That's it for your first file example. The code for fileview.cpp appears in listing 8.1.

Listing 8.1. Fileview.Cpp

```
// fileview.cpp : implementation of the CFileView class
//
#include "stdafx.h"
#include "file.h"
#include <string.h>
#include "filedoc.h"
#include "fileview.h"
#ifdef _DEBUG
#undef THIS_FILE
static char BASED_CODE THIS_FILE[] = __FILE__;
#endif
```

continues

Listing 8.1. continued

```
//////////////////////////////////////////////////////////////////////////
// CFileView
IMPLEMENT_DYNCREATE(CFileView, CView)
BEGIN_MESSAGE_MAP(CFileView, CView)
    //{{AFX_MSG_MAP(CFileView)
    ON_COMMAND(IDM_FILEWRITE, OnFilewrite)
    ON_COMMAND(IDM_FILEREAD, OnFileread)
    //}}AFX_MSG_MAP
    // Standard printing commands
    ON_COMMAND(ID_FILE_PRINT, CView::OnFilePrint)
    ON_COMMAND(ID_FILE_PRINT_PREVIEW, CView::OnFilePrintPreview)
END_MESSAGE_MAP()
//////////////////////////////////////////////////////////////////////////
// CFileView construction/destruction
CFileView::CFileView()
{
    // TODO: add construction code here
}
CFileView::~CFileView()
{
}
//////////////////////////////////////////////////////////////////////////
// CFileView drawing
void CFileView::OnDraw(CDC* pDC)
{
    CFileDoc* pDoc = GetDocument();
    // TODO: add draw code here
}
//////////////////////////////////////////////////////////////////////////
// CFileView printing
BOOL CFileView::OnPreparePrinting(CPrintInfo* pInfo)
{
    // default preparation
    return DoPreparePrinting(pInfo);
}
void CFileView::OnBeginPrinting(CDC* /*pDC*/, CPrintInfo* /*pInfo*/)
{
    // TODO: add extra initialization before printing
}
```

```
void CFileView::OnEndPrinting(CDC* /*pDC*/, CPrintInfo* /*pInfo*/)
{
    // TODO: add cleanup after printing
}
/////////////////////////////////////////////////////////////////////////////
// CFileView diagnostics
#ifdef _DEBUG
void CFileView::AssertValid() const
{
    CView::AssertValid();
}
void CFileView::Dump(CDumpContext& dc) const
{
    CView::Dump(dc);
}
CFileDoc* CFileView::GetDocument() // non-debug version is inline
{
    ASSERT(m_pDocument->IsKindOf(RUNTIME_CLASS(CFileDoc)));
    return (CFileDoc*) m_pDocument;
}
#endif //_DEBUG
/////////////////////////////////////////////////////////////////////////////
// CFileView message handlers
void CFileView::OnFilewrite()
{
    const MAX_LEN = 20;
    const MAX_ITEMS = 4;
    CString hello_string = "Hello, world.";
    CFile file("hello.txt", CFile::modeCreate |
    CFile::modeWrite);
    file.Write(hello_string, hello_string.GetLength());
    file.Close();
    char output_string[MAX_ITEMS][MAX_LEN];
    strcpy(output_string[0], "This");
    strcpy(output_string[1], "is");
    strcpy(output_string[2], "a");
    strcpy(output_string[3], "test.");
    CFile random_file("data.dat", CFile::modeCreate | CFile::modeWrite);
    for (int loop_index = 0; loop_index < MAX_ITEMS; loop_index++){
```

continues

Listing 8.1. continued

```
        random_file.Write(output_string[loop_index], MAX_LEN);
    }
    random_file.Close();
}
void CFileView::OnFileread()
{
    const MAX_LEN = 20;
    char data_string[MAX_LEN];
    CFile file("hello.txt", CFile::modeRead);
    UINT number_read = file.Read(data_string, MAX_LEN);
    CClientDC dc(this);
    dc.TextOut(0, 0, data_string, number_read);
    char input_string[MAX_LEN];
    CFile random_file("data.dat", CFile::modeRead);
    random_file.Seek(MAX_LEN, CFile::begin);
    number_read = random_file.Read(input_string, 2);
    dc.TextOut(0, 0, input_string, number_read);
    random_file.Close();
}
```

Updating the Notepad to Handle Files

With all this preparation for file handling, you may be surprised at the ease with which you can add file handling to two of your major programs: the notepad and database programs. Visual C++ has already built into the applications most of the file handling capability you need. And you can customize the rest easily because MFC objects support a process called *serialization*. This means, as you see in detail later in this chapter, that MFC objects can write themselves automatically to a CFile object.

In particular, when any of the built-in File menu items are used, the program serializes the document by itself. To customize data storage (and retrieval), you need only to add code to the Serialize() function in your document class, which currently looks like the following. (Visual C++ has already written this code in your program.)

```
void CPadDoc::Serialize(CArchive& ar)
{
    if (ar.IsStoring())
    {
    }
    else
    {
    }
}
```

The data you want to store is the text from the notepad, which is stored in a CString object named m_PadText (from paddoc.h), as follows:

```
class CPadDoc : public CDocument
{
protected: // create from serialization only
    CPadDoc();
    DECLARE_DYNCREATE(CPadDoc)
// Attributes
public:
```
CString m_PadText;
```
                :
```

The Serialize( ) function passes a reference to an archive object. (A *reference* in C++ is another name for an object or variable.) Normally, when you pass an object to a function, a copy of the object is passed so that the function can't change the contents of the original object. Using the ampersand (&) as shown in the following code, however, indicates that you want to pass parameters by reference (as many languages do) instead of by value (the C++ default):

void CPadDoc::Serialize(CArchive& ar)
```
{
    if (ar.IsStoring())
    {
    }
    else
    {
    }
}
```

Here you are placing data in the archive object, so you need some way to reach it. Because the reference you get to the archive object can be thought of as another name for that object itself, you can send data to it much as you did in Chapter 1 with cout, as follows:

```
#include <iostream.h>
void main( )
{
    cout << "Hello world.";        // Print "Hello, world."
}
```

In Serialize(), check the archive member function IsStoring() to determine whether the data is being written to disk, and then simply serialize
m_PadText in the following way:

```
void CPadDoc::Serialize(CArchive& ar)
{
    if (ar.IsStoring( ))
    {
        ar << m_PadText;
    }
    else
    {
        ar >> m_PadText;
    }
}
```

That's all that is necessary to add file handling to your document. Now the
notepad program can save files with the Save As... menu item, which
opens the dialog box shown in figure 8.3. Additionally, the program can
open files with the Open... menu item, which opens the dialog box
shown in figure 8.4. The process is that easy; when the Serialize() function
is called, the data is stored or loaded as needed. All the details have been
handled for you. The listing for paddoc.cpp appears in listing 8.2.

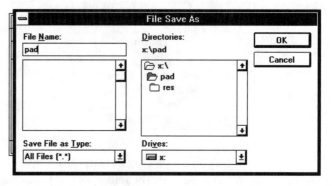

Figure 8.3. The notepad's File Save As... box.

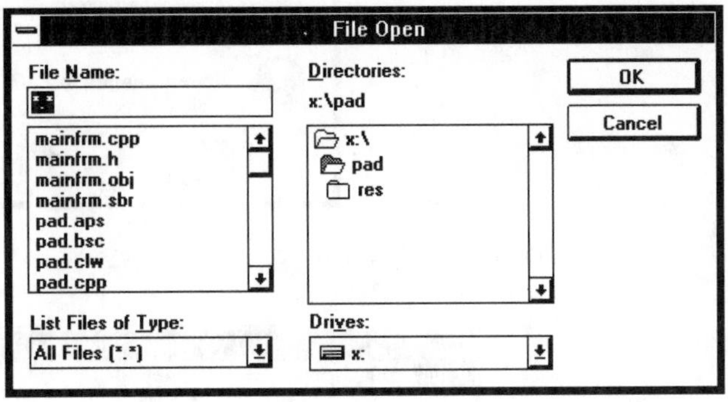

Figure 8.4. The notepad's File Open box.

The Document's Modified Flag

You can make one more change to the notepad program. When you modify the data in the document's m_PadText data member, you can set the document's modified flag with the member function SetModifiedFlag( ) as shown in the following example (you are storing the data after closing the notepad).

```
void CPadView::OnNotepad( )
{
    CString display_string;
    CPadDoc* pDoc = GetDocument( );
    CPadDlg dlg;
    dlg.m_PadText = pDoc->m_PadText;
    dlg.DoModal( );
    pDoc->m_PadText = dlg.m_PadText;
    pDoc->SetModifiedFlag( );
}
```

Now if the user quits without saving the notepad's data, a message box appears on the screen asking whether the user wants to save the data, as shown in figure 8.5. In addition, the program now automatically maintains a Most Recently Used (MRU) list of files ready to be opened in the File menu, as shown in figure 8.6. All this functionality is built into Visual C++ applications.

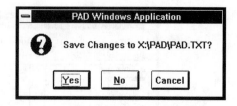

Figure 8.5. File warning.

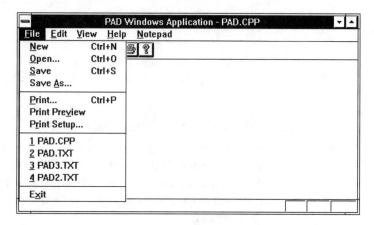

Figure 8.6. The pad's most recently used list.

Listing 8.2. Paddoc.Cpp

```
// paddoc.cpp : implementation of the CPadDoc class
//
#include "stdafx.h"
#include "pad.h"
#include "paddoc.h"
#ifdef _DEBUG
#undef THIS_FILE
static char BASED_CODE THIS_FILE[ ] = __FILE__;
#endif
/////////////////////////////////////////////////////////////////////////////
CPadDoc
IMPLEMENT_DYNCREATE(CPadDoc, CDocument)
BEGIN_MESSAGE_MAP(CPadDoc, CDocument)
    //{{AFX_MSG_MAP(CPadDoc)
    // NOTE - the ClassWizard will add and remove mapping macros here.
    // DO NOT EDIT what you see in these blocks of generated code !
    //}}AFX_MSG_MAP
END_MESSAGE_MAP( )
```

```
//////////////////////////////////////////////////////////////////////
///////////
// CPadDoc construction/destruction
CPadDoc::CPadDoc( )
{
    // TODO: add one-time construction code here
}
CPadDoc::~CPadDoc( )
{
}
BOOL CPadDoc::OnNewDocument( )
{
    if (!CDocument::OnNewDocument( ))
        return FALSE;
    // TODO: add reinitialization code here
    // (SDI documents will reuse this document)
    return TRUE;
}
//////////////////////////////////////////////////////////////////////
///////////
// CPadDoc serialization
void CPadDoc::Serialize(CArchive& ar)
{
    if (ar.IsStoring( ))
    {
        ar << m_PadText;
    }
    else
    {
        ar >> m_PadText;
    }
}
//////////////////////////////////////////////////////////////////////
///////////
// CPadDoc diagnostics
#ifdef _DEBUG
void CPadDoc::AssertValid( ) const
{
    CDocument::AssertValid( );
}
void CPadDoc::Dump(CDumpContext& dc) const
{
    CDocument::Dump(dc);
}
```

continues

Listing 8.2. continued

```
#endif //_DEBUG
////////////////////////////////////////////////////////////////////
////////////
// CPadDoc commands
```

Updating the Database to Handle Files

You can add file handling to the database program as well. In the database program, you stored data in an array named data_string[] and stored the number of items in the integer data_index, as follows:

```
class CDbDoc : public CDocument
{
protected: // create from serialization only
     CDbDoc();
     DECLARE_DYNCREATE(CDbDoc)
// Attributes
public:
     CString data_string[10];
     int data_index;
              :
```

You can serialize that data by using the document's Serialize() function, as follows:

```
void CDbDoc::Serialize(CArchive& ar)
{
     if (ar.IsStoring())
     {
          ar << data_index;
          for (int loop_index = 0; loop_index < data_index; loop_index++)
          { ar << data_string[loop_index];
          }
     }
     else
     {
          ar >> data_index;
          for (int loop_index = 0; loop_index < data_index; loop_index++)
          { ar >> data_string[loop_index];
          }
     }
}
```

Because of multiple overloading in Visual C++, however, sending integers to an archive object is an ambiguous operation. You can solve that ambiguity by changing the integer data_index to a long instead:

```
class CDbDoc : public CDocument
{
protected: // create from serialization only
    CDbDoc( );
    DECLARE_DYNCREATE(CDbDoc)
    // Attributes
    public:
    CString data_string[10];
    long data_index;
            :
```

You also can set the document's modified flag when the user adds an item to the database, in the following way:

```
void CDbView::OnAdditem( )
{
    CDbDoc* pDoc = GetDocument( );
    pDoc->data_string[pDoc->data_index++] = out_string;
    pDoc->SetModifiedFlag(TRUE);
    CClientDC dc(this);
    DWORD OldTextColor = dc.SetTextColor(dc.GetBkColor( ));
    dc.TextOut(0, 0, out_string, out_string.GetLength( ));
    dc.SetTextColor(OldTextColor);
    out_string.Empty( );
}
```

The final version of dbdoc.cpp appears in listing 8.3. You can add one more customization here, and that has to do with the default file types used by the file system. As the program stands, it suggests a file named *db* when you want to save a file, as shown in figure 8.7.

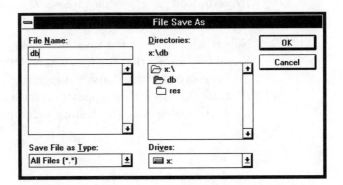

Figure 8.7. Default file types in the database program.

You can customize that with the Visual C++ String Table Editor in App Studio. Open App Studio now and select the String Table resource, as shown in figure 8.8.

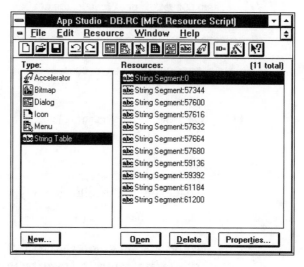

Figure 8.8. The Visual C++ String Table Editor.

Next, double-click String Segment 0, which opens the String Table Editor and displays the current string in the following way:

```
IDR_MAINFRAME          "DB Windows Application\nDb\nDB Document"
```

This is the default identification string for the main frame window. You can add the text "\nDB Files(*.dat)\n.dat" to the string; this indicates that the files you want to use have the extension .dat and allow the user to choose them easily. Add that string now in the String Table Editor and save the complete string, as follows:

```
IDR_MAINFRAME          "DB Windows Application\nDb\nDB
    Document\nDB Files (*.dat)\n.dat"
```

Now when you open the Save As... dialog box, as shown in figure 8.9, Visual C++ knows that the files you are interested in end with .dat and display files with that extension, suggesting a name of db.dat. In addition, the text "DB Files (*.dat)" appears in the drop-down list box in the lower left of the dialog box. This feature adds a little utility to the program.

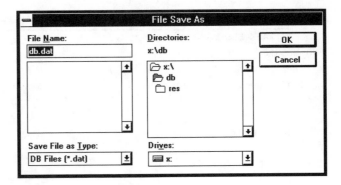

Figure 8.9. Improved default file types.

TIP

You easily can set your program's window title. Use the String Table Editor to change the string called AFX_IDS_APP_TITLE, which is the name of your program that will appear in your window's title.

Listing 8.3. Dbdoc.Cpp

```
// dbdoc.cpp : implementation of the CDbDoc class
//
#include "stdafx.h"
#include "db.h"
#include "dbdoc.h"
#ifdef _DEBUG
#undef THIS_FILE
static char BASED_CODE THIS_FILE[ ] = __FILE__;
#endif
////////////////////////////////////////////////////////////////////////
// CDbDoc
IMPLEMENT_DYNCREATE(CDbDoc, CDocument)
BEGIN_MESSAGE_MAP(CDbDoc, CDocument)
     //{{AFX_MSG_MAP(CDbDoc)
     // NOTE - the ClassWizard will add and remove mapping macros here.
     // DO NOT EDIT what you see in these blocks of generated code !
```

continues

Listing 8.3. continued

```
     //}}AFX_MSG_MAP
END_MESSAGE_MAP()
/////////////////////////////////////////////////////////////////////////////
// CDbDoc construction/destruction
CDbDoc::CDbDoc()
{
    data_index = 0;
}
CDbDoc::~CDbDoc()
{
}
BOOL CDbDoc::OnNewDocument()
{
    if (!CDocument::OnNewDocument())
        return FALSE;
    // TODO: add reinitialization code here
    // (SDI documents will reuse this document)
    return TRUE;
}
/////////////////////////////////////////////////////////////////////////////
// CDbDoc serialization
void CDbDoc::Serialize(CArchive& ar)
{
    if (ar.IsStoring())
    {
        ar << data_index;
        for (int loop_index = 0;
        loop_index < data_index; loop_index++){
            ar << data_string[loop_index];
        }
    }
    else
    {
        ar >> data_index;
        for (int loop_index = 0;
        loop_index < data_index; loop_index++){
            ar >> data_string[loop_index];
        }
```

```
        }
}
///////////////////////////////////////////////////////////////////////
////////////
// CDbDoc diagnostics
#ifdef _DEBUG
void CDbDoc::AssertValid( ) const
{
    CDocument::AssertValid( );
}
void CDbDoc::Dump(CDumpContext& dc) const
{
    CDocument::Dump(dc);
}
#endif //_DEBUG
///////////////////////////////////////////////////////////////////////
////////////
// CDbDoc commands
```

Now that you have seen serialization at work, you need to probe that process for yourself. In particular, serialization only works on MFC objects—what if you want to create your own objects and save them? What if you want to save data outside the document? You learn how to solve these problems next.

How to Customize Serialization

One big advantage of using MFC objects is that they can serialize themselves, which means—as you have seen—that they can write themselves out to disk. You might want to create your own classes and serialize them yourself, however. The next sample program shows you how to do this—independent of a document—to illustrate how the serialization process works.

You might use this program to keep track of some friends. Suppose that you have a class named Friend_Class and that the objects of that class keep track of the CStrings FirstName and LastName. Also assume that you have two objects as follows:

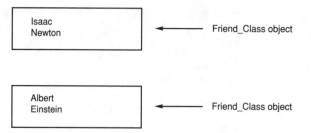

You could place the objects in an object list to keep track of them; support already exists in the MFC libraries with the CObList Class. Lists are used, as you might expect, to maintain lists of objects. In particular, the plan is to place the objects in a CObList-based class called, for example, Friend_ClassList. Such a list is really a collection of pointers, as follows:

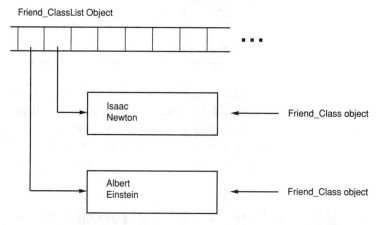

After you set up the list, you automatically can send it out to disk and read it back in later. Objects you can serialize in this fashion must be derived from the base class CObject, so you can set up the class that holds the friends' names (Friend_Class), in the header file as follows:

```
class Friend_Class : public CObject
{
};
```

Here you derive Friend_Class (the class that will hold the names "Isaac Newton" and "Albert Einstein" in two of its objects) from the MFC class CObject so that you will be able to serialize the list. CObject's member functions and data appear in table 8.3.

Table 8.3. CObject's Member Functions and Data

Member	Means
AssertValid	Is object valid?
CObject	Copies constructor
CObject	Default constructor
Dump	Creates diagnostic dump
GetRuntimeClass	Gets CRuntimeClass structure
IsKindOf	Tests relationship to given class
IsSerializable	Tests if can be serialized
operator =	Assignment
operator delete	Deletes operator
operator new	New operator
Serialize	Loads or stores to or from archive
~CObject	Destructor
DECLARE_DYNAMIC	Macro Gives access to run-time class information
DECLARE_SERIAL	Macro Allows serialization
IMPLEMENT_DYNAMIC	Macro Implements access to run-time class information
IMPLEMENT_SERIAL	Macro Implements serialization
RUNTIME_CLASS	Macro Gets CRuntimeClass structure

TIP

Another reason to use CObject-based objects is that they allow you to determine which class you're dealing with at run-time and to allocate new ones as well. This information usually doesn't exist in .exe files but can be implemented in CObject-based objects with the DECLARE_DYNAMIC and IMPLEMENT_DYNAMIC macros.

Next, you declare two constructors for Friend_Class: Friend_Class() and Friend_Class(CString First, CString Last). The first one, without arguments, is necessary for classes that you want to serialize, simply so that CObject's constructor will be called. You use the other one, which takes two CString arguments, to initialize the FirstName and LastName member strings. For example, the declaration Friend_Class Friend1("Isaac," "Newton") gives you an object in the following way:

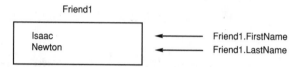

Here's how those prototypes appear in the class definition (also in the header file):

```
class Friend_Class : public CObject
{
    Friend_Class(){};
        :
public:
    Friend_Class(CString First, CString Last);
    CString         FirstName;
    CString         LastName;
        :
};
```

In addition, you do two more things to support initialization: include the macro DECLARE_SERIAL in the class definition and indicate that you will override the function Serialize(), as follows:

```
class Friend_Class : public CObject
{
    Friend_Class(){};
    DECLARE_SERIAL(Friend_Class);
public:
    Friend_Class(CString First, CString Last);
    CString         FirstName;
    CString         LastName;
    void Serialize(CArchive& archive);
};
```

Visual C++ expands the DECLARE_SERIAL macro into the prototypes it needs for serialization. In the function Serialize(), you indicate which class data you want to send out to disk and in what order.

Next comes the list class Friend_ClassList, which makes up the list of your objects of class Friend_Class, as follows:

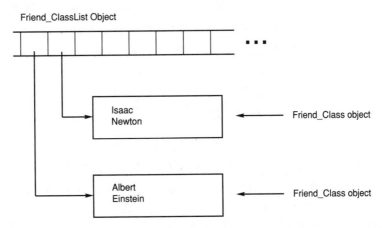

You declare the list class FriendClassList in a similar fashion, with a constructor that takes no arguments (necessary for all classes that can be serialized) and with the DECLARE_SERIAL macro. This class is a list, so instead of deriving it from CObject, you derive it from COblist, a class whose member functions and data appear in table 8.4.

```
class Friend_Class : public CObject
{
Friend_Class( ){}; DECLARE_SERIAL(Friend_Class);
public:
Friend_Class(CString First, CString Last); CString
FirstName;
     CString        LastName;
void Serialize(CArchive& archive);
};
class Friend_ClassList : public CObList
{
public:
     Friend_ClassList( ){};
     DECLARE_SERIAL(Friend_ClassList)
};
```

Table 8.4. CObList's Member Functions and Data

Member	Means
AddHead	Adds element to head of the list
AddTail	Adds element to the tail of the list
CObList	Constructor (makes an empty list)
Find	Gets position of an element
FindIndex	Gets position of an element specified by index
GetAt	Gets element at specified position
GetCount	Gets number of elements in list
GetHead	Gets the head element of the list
GetHeadPosition	Gets the position of the head element
GetNext	Gets the next element
GetPrev	Gets the previous element
GetTail	Gets the tail element
GetTailPosition	Gets the position of the tail
InsertAfter	Inserts new element after specified position
InsertBefore	Inserts new element before specified position
IsEmpty	Tests for the empty list
RemoveAll	Removes all the elements from the list
RemoveAt	Removes an element at specified position
RemoveHead	Removes element from the head of list
RemoveTail	Removes element from the tail of list
SetAt	Sets the element at specified position
~CObList	Destructor

Now that your class declarations are complete, you can write the code for the Friend_Class constructor, which will load two CString objects into the Friend_Class::FirstName and Friend_Class::LastName CStrings, as follows:

```
Friend_Class::Friend_Class(CString First, CString Last)
{
    FirstName = First;
    LastName = Last;
}
```

You can also define the Friend_Class::Serialize() function, which handles the process of sending your data out to disk. This function is defined for the individual objects in the list, not for the list as a whole. That's the way it works in general: If you want to serialize a collection of objects, you define the function Serialize() for those objects. Here, you are using the CArchive class, which handles serialization of data in a binary fashion, as follows:

```
Archive <— data <— Serialize()
```

As you have seen, archive streams are specially created to handle this serialization process, and you send data to them (which in turn sends data to the disk) as follows:

```
Archive << Friend1.FirstName << Friend1.Lastname
```

The CArchive member functions and data appear in table 8.5. As before, you check the IsStoring() member function to see whether you are writing data out to the disk or reading it back in. In addition, you must first serialize the base class CObject, and you do that by calling the base class' Serialize() function. The whole thing appears as follows:

```
Friend_Class::Friend_Class(CString First, CString Last)
{
    FirstName = First;
    LastName = Last;
}
void Friend_Class::Serialize(CArchive& archive)
{
    CObject::Serialize(archive);
    if (archive.IsStoring()) archive << FirstName << LastName;
    else archive >> FirstName >> LastName;
}
IMPLEMENT_SERIAL(Friend_Class, CObject, 0)
IMPLEMENT_SERIAL(Friend_ClassList, CObList, 0)
```

Table 8.5. CArchive's Member Functions and Data

Member	*Means*
CArchive	Constructor
Close	Flushes data and disconnects from CFile
Flush	Flushes data
GetFile	Gets the CFile pointer
IsLoading	Is the archive loading?
IsStoring	Is the archive storing?
operator <<	Loads objects
operator >>	Stores objects
Read	Reads bytes
ReadObject	Calls Serialize function for loading
Write	Writes bytes
WriteObject	Calls Serialize function for storing
~CArchive	Destructor

Notice that the macro IMPLEMENT_SERIAL is used at the end, which is where C++ adds the functions actually needed for serialization. You use IMPLEMENT_SERIAL for both the list Friend_ClassList and the elements of that list, which are of type Friend_Class. Notice also that you indicate the base classes from which each of them are derived. (The last parameter in the macro, 0, is intended to hold the version number of your software, and it is there for your convenience, so you can use any value you want.)

Now you are ready to write the code that puts this all to work. You need to create two objects and put them in a list, as follows:

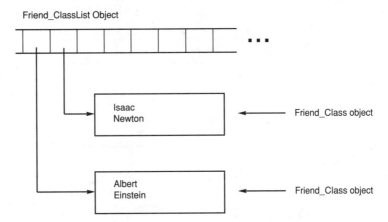

Friend_ClassList Object

Isaac
Newton

Friend_Class object

Albert
Einstein

Friend_Class object

To do that, you need only to use new to allocate two objects of class Friend_Class and one list of class Friend_ClassList. You get pointers to the two objects, which you can call friend_ptr_1 and friend_ptr_2, and a pointer to the list, which you can call data_list_ptr. You fill the friend objects with data when you construct them, and you can add them to the list with the AddHead( ) function (a member function of CObList). If you wrote an application with a menu item called Testing... to test the serialization process, it might appear as follows in OnTesting( ):

```
void CTestView::OnTesting( )
{
    Friend_Class* friend_ptr_1 = new Friend_Class("Isaac",  "Newton");
    Friend_Class* friend_ptr_2 = new Friend_Class("Albert", "Einstein");
    Friend_ClassList* data_list_ptr = new Friend_ClassList;
    data_list_ptr->AddHead(friend_ptr_1);
    data_list_ptr->AddHead(friend_ptr_2);
        :
```

AddHead( ) simply adds an element to the list at the position called the head. In general, the head of a list is the position at which new items are added. After adding two items, the head of the list is in the third position appears as follows:

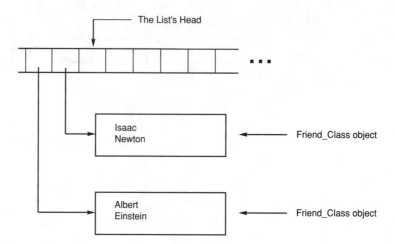

At this point, the list is complete and you are ready to send it out to disk. You can call the disk file friends.dat, and you can open that file as a CFile object. Next, you associate an archive object with this file by passing a pointer to the file object to CArchive's constructor and indicating that this archive is used for storing data, as follows:

```
void CTestView::OnTesting()
{
    CFile the_file;
    CFileException exc;
    char* pfilename = "friends.dat";
    Friend_ClassList* data_list_ptr = new Friend_ClassList;
    Friend_Class* friend_ptr_1 = new Friend_Class("Isaac", "Newton");
    Friend_Class* friend_ptr_2 = new
    Friend_Class("Albert", "Einstein");
    data_list_ptr->AddHead(friend_ptr_1); data_list_ptr->AddHead(friend_ptr_2);
    the_file.Open(pfilename, CFile::modeCreate | CFile::modeWrite, &exc);
    CArchive the_out_Archive(&the_file, CArchive::store);
        :
```

You might notice that when you open the_file, you include a pointer to a CFileException object named exc. This is where you find information if there is a problem opening the file. (More about exceptions is explained in Chapter 10.)

An archive object can be associated with either storing or loading data—but not both (that is, you must create a new archive object to read back in the data). Now you are ready to send your list to the archive stream, which sends it to the disk file friends.dat, as follows:

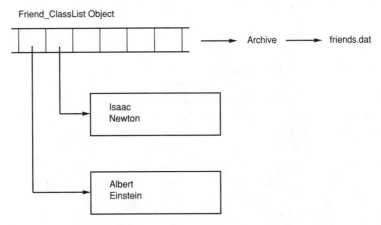

Friend_ClassList Object

To serialize the list of objects (that is, to write it out to disk), you send it to the output archive simply by passing that archive the pointer to the list as follows:

```
the_out_Archive << data_list_ptr;
```

Then, close both the archive and the file:

```
void CTestView::OnTesting()
{
    CFile the_file;
    CFileException exc;
    char* pfilename = "friends.dat";
    Friend_ClassList* data_list_ptr = new Friend_ClassList;
    Friend_Class* friend_ptr_1 = new Friend_Class("Isaac",  "Newton");
    Friend_Class* friend_ptr_2 = new Friend_Class("Albert", "Einstein");
    data_list_ptr->AddHead(friend_ptr_1);
    data_list_ptr->AddHead(friend_ptr_2);
    the_file.Open(pfilename, CFile::modeCreate | CFile ::modeWrite, &exc);
    CArchive the_out_Archive(&the_file, CArchive::store);
    the_out_Archive << data_list_ptr;
    the_out_Archive.Close();
    the_file.Close();
        :
```

At this point, the list of objects is stored in the file friends.dat. You have successfully stored it on disk. To read it back in, reverse the process, creating a new input archive called the_in_archive and reading the list back in the following way:

```
void CTestView::OnTesting( )
{
    CFile the_file;
    CFileException exc;
    char* pfilename = "friends.dat";
    Friend_ClassList* data_list_ptr = new Friend_ClassList;
    Friend_Class* friend_ptr_1 = new Friend_Class("Isaac", "Newton");
    Friend_Class* friend_ptr_2 = new Friend_Class("Albert", "Einstein");
    data_list_ptr->AddHead(friend_ptr_1);
    data_list_ptr->AddHead(friend_ptr_2);
    the_file.Open(pfilename, CFile::modeCreate | CFile::modeWrite, &exc);
    CArchive the_out_Archive(&the_file, CArchive::store);
    the_out_Archive << data_list_ptr;
    the_out_Archive.Close( );
    the_file.Close( );
    the_file.Open(pfilename, CFile::modeRead, &exc);
    CArchive the_in_Archive(&the_file, CArchive::load);
    the_in_Archive >> data_list_ptr;
    the_in_Archive.Close( );
    the_file.Close( );
       :
```

Now that the list is read back in, the head position is set back to the first element. You can get pointers to the objects in the list with GetHeadPosition( )—which returns a value of type POSITION as defined in Visual C++—and GetNext( )—which takes a value of type POSITION and allows you to increment through the list. Finally, you can even print data from the objects retrieved in the window.

```
void CTestView::OnTesting( )
{
    CFile the_file;
    CFileException exc;
    char* pfilename = "friends.dat";
    Friend_ClassList* data_list_ptr = new Friend_ClassList;
    Friend_Class* friend_ptr_1 = new Friend_Class("Isaac", "Newton");
```

```
    Friend_Class* friend_ptr_2 = new Friend_Class("Albert", "Einstein");
    data_list_ptr->AddHead(friend_ptr_1);
    data_list_ptr->AddHead(friend_ptr_2);
    the_file.Open(pfilename, CFile::modeCreate | CFile::modeWrite, &exc);
    CArchive the_out_Archive(&the_file, CArchive::store);
    the_out_Archive << data_list_ptr;
    the_out_Archive.Close();
    the_file.Close();
    the_file.Open(pfilename, CFile::modeRead, &exc);
    CArchive the_in_Archive(&the_file, CArchive::load);
    the_in_Archive >> data_list_ptr;
    the_in_Archive.Close();
    the_file.Close();
    POSITION pos = data_list_ptr->GetHeadPosition();
    friend_ptr_1 = (Friend_Class*)data_list_ptr->GetNext(pos);
    friend_ptr_2 = (Friend_Class*)data_list_ptr->GetNext(pos);
    ClientDC dc(this);
    dc.TextOut(0, 0, friend_ptr_2->FirstName, \
    friend_ptr_2->FirstName.Getlength());
}
```

And that's it. You have created a list of MFC objects, serialized the list, and examined the objects. The program is a success, and the result appears in figure 8.10. The header file, testview.h, appears in listing 8.4, and testview.cpp appears in listing 8.5.

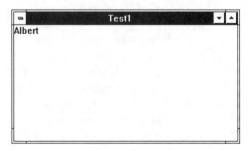

Figure 8.10. The customized serialization example.

Listing 8.4. Testview.H

```
// testview.h : interface of the CTestView class
//
//////////////////////////////////////////////////////////////////
////////////
class CTestView : public CView
{
protected: // create from serialization only
   CTestView( );
   DECLARE_DYNCREATE(CTestView)
// Attributes
public:
   CTestDoc* GetDocument( );
// Operations
public:
// Implementation
public:
   virtual ~CTestView( );
   virtual void OnDraw(CDC* pDC);  // overridden to
draw this view
#ifdef _DEBUG
   virtual void AssertValid( ) const;
   virtual void Dump(CDumpContext& dc) const;
#endif
         // Printing support
protected:
   virtual BOOL OnPreparePrinting(CPrintInfo* pInfo);
   virtual void OnBeginPrinting(CDC* pDC, CPrintInfo* pInfo);
   virtual void OnEndPrinting(CDC* pDC, CPrintInfo* pInfo);
// Generated message map functions
protected:
   //{{AFX_MSG(CTestView)
   afx_msg void OnTesting( );
   //}}AFX_MSG
   DECLARE_MESSAGE_MAP( )
};
#ifndef _DEBUG    // debug version in testview.cpp
inline CTestDoc* CTestView::GetDocument( )
    { return (CTestDoc*) m_pDocument; }
```

```
#endif
////////////////////////////////////////////////////////////////
////////////
class Friend_Class : public CObject
{
    Friend_Class( ){};
    DECLARE_SERIAL(Friend_Class);
public:
Friend_Class(CString First, CString Last);
    CString    FirstName;
    CString    LastName;
    void Serialize(CArchive& archive);
};
class Friend_ClassList : public CObList
{
public:
    Friend_ClassList( ){};
    DECLARE_SERIAL(Friend_ClassList)
};
```

Listing 8.5. Testview.Cpp

```
// testview.cpp : implementation of the CTestView class
//
#include "stdafx.h"
#include "test.h"
#include "testdoc.h"
#include "testview.h"
#ifdef _DEBUG
#undef THIS_FILE
static char BASED_CODE THIS_FILE[ ] = __FILE__;
#endif
////////////////////////////////////////////////////////////////
////////////// CTestView
IMPLEMENT_DYNCREATE(CTestView, CView)
IMPLEMENT_SERIAL(Friend_Class, CObject, 0)
IMPLEMENT_SERIAL(Friend_ClassList, CObList, 0)
BEGIN_MESSAGE_MAP(CTestView, CView)
    //{{AFX_MSG_MAP(CTestView)
    ON_COMMAND(IDM_TESTING, OnTesting)
    //}}AFX_MSG_MAP
```

continues

Listing 8.5. continued

```
      // Standard printing commands
      ON_COMMAND(ID_FILE_PRINT, CView::OnFilePrint)
      ON_COMMAND(ID_FILE_PRINT_PREVIEW, CView::OnFilePrintPreview)
END_MESSAGE_MAP( )
///////////////////////////////////////////////////////////////////////////
//
// CTestView construction/destruction
CTestView::CTestView( )
{
      // TODO: add construction code here
}
CTestView::~CTestView( )
{
}
///////////////////////////////////////////////////////////////////////////
//
// CTestView drawing
void CTestView::OnDraw(CDC* pDC)
{
      CTestDoc* pDoc = GetDocument( );
      // TODO: add draw code here
}
///////////////////////////////////////////////////////////////////////////
//
// CTestView printing
BOOL CTestView::OnPreparePrinting(CPrintInfo* pInfo)
{
      // default preparation
      return DoPreparePrinting(pInfo);
}
void CTestView::OnBeginPrinting(CDC* /*pDC*/, CPrintInfo* /*pInfo*/)
{
      // TODO: add extra initialization before printing
}
void CTestView::OnEndPrinting(CDC* /*pDC*/, CPrintInfo* /*pInfo*/)
{
      // TODO: add cleanup after printing
}
```

```
/////////////////////////////////////////////////////////////////////////
// CTestView diagnostics
#ifdef _DEBUG
void CTestView::AssertValid() const
{
    CView::AssertValid();
}
void CTestView::Dump(CDumpContext& dc) const
{
    CView::Dump(dc);
}
CTestDoc* CTestView::GetDocument() // non-debug version is inline
{
    ASSERT(m_pDocument->IsKindOf(RUNTIME_CLASS(CTestDoc)));
    return (CTestDoc*) m_pDocument;
}
#endif //_DEBUG
/////////////////////////////////////////////////////////////////////////
// CTestView message handlers
void CTestView::OnTesting()
{
    CFile the_file;
    CFileException exc;
    char* pfilename = "friends.dat";
    Friend_ClassList* data_list_ptr = new Friend_ClassList;
    Friend_Class* friend_ptr_1 = new Friend_Class("Issac", "Newton");
    Friend_Class* friend_ptr_2 = new Friend_Class("Albert", "Einstein");
    data_list_ptr->AddHead(friend_ptr_1); data_list_ptr- >AddHead(friend_ptr_2);
    the_file.Open(pfilename, CFile::modeCreate | CFile::modeWrite, &exc);
    CArchive the_out_Archive(&the_file, CArchive::store);
    the_out_Archive << data_list_ptr;
    the_out_Archive.Close();
    the_file.Close();
    the_file.Open(pfilename, CFile::modeRead, &exc);
    CArchive the_in_Archive(&the_file, CArchive::load);
    the_in_Archive >> data_list_ptr;
    the_in_Archive.Close();
    the_file.Close();
    POSITION pos = data_list_ptr->GetHeadPosition();
    friend_ptr_1 = (Friend_Class*)data_list_ptr->GetNext(pos);
```

continues

397

Listing 8.5. continued

```
    friend_ptr_2 = (Friend_Class*)data_list_ptr->GetNext(pos);
    CClientDC dc(this);
    dc.TextOut(0, 0, friend_ptr_2->FirstName, \
    friend_ptr_2->FirstName.GetLength( ));
}
Friend_Class::Friend_Class(CString First, CString Last)
{
    FirstName = First;
    LastName = Last;
}
void Friend_Class::Serialize(CArchive& archive)
{
    CObject::Serialize(archive);
    if (archive.IsStoring( )) archive << FirstName << LastName;
    else archive >> FirstName >> LastName;
}
```

That ends the discussion of Visual C++ file handling. Next, however, you can go wild in Chapter 9, exploring alternate views and MDI programs.

Multiple Documents and Multiple Views

I n the examples up to this point in the book, you have worked with applications that use only a single document and a single view. This chapter, however, shows you how to use multiple documents and multiple views in Visual C++ applications. The example in this chapter constructs a multi-window editor in which you can handle multiple documents at once. Each document will have its own window inside of the single main window, and the user will be able to open as many documents as needed with the New or Open… menu items.

After you learn to support multiple documents, the next step is to enable the user to open multiple views in a single document. This feature is controlled by the New Window menu item in the program's Window menu. When the user selects this item, a new window will open, showing a new view into the current document. Additionally, this chapter helps you learn to enable independent scrolling in the two views.

399

Finally, this chapter shows you how to support splitter windows in Visual C++. A *splitter window* allows you two or more views into the same document, but handles them all in the same window. The next section begins by explaining how you can design the multi-window editor and enable the user to edit multiple documents.

Multiple Document Interface (MDI) Programs

Start App Wizard now to create the project editor.mak. This time, you are creating an MDI application, so do not deselect the MDI option. Create editor.mak simply by giving the project that name and by clicking first the OK button and then the Create button.

In the SDI programs, the main window was derived from the base class CFrameWnd, as follows:

```
class CMainFrame : public CFrameWnd
{
protected: // create from serialization only
    CMainFrame();
    DECLARE_DYNCREATE(CMainFrame)
        :
```

Now, in the new MDI application, the main window is derived from the CMDIFrameWnd class (in mainfrm.h), as follows:

```
class CMainFrame : public CMDIFrameWnd
{
    DECLARE_DYNAMIC(CMainFrame)
public:
    CMainFrame();
        :
```

This means that the main window will now support MDI children, and at this stage, one such child window per document is used, as follows:

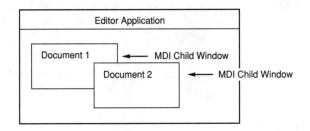

Originally, the document template (invoked when a document is opened) supported only the main window itself, as follows:

```
BOOL CPadApp::InitInstance()
{
    // Standard initialization
    // If you are not using these features and wish to reduce the size
    //  of your final executable, you should remove from the following
    //  the specific initialization routines you do not need.
    SetDialogBkColor();          // set dialog background color to gray
    LoadStdProfileSettings(); // Load INI file options (including MRU)
    // Register the application's document templates. Document templates
    //  serve as the connection between documents, frame  windows and views.
    AddDocTemplate(new CSingleDocTemplate(IDR_MAINFRAME,
        RUNTIME_CLASS(CPadDoc),
        RUNTIME_CLASS(CMainFrame),   // main SDI frame window
        RUNTIME_CLASS(CPadView)));
            :
```

Now, however, each time a new document is opened, you get a new MDI child window, as derived from the CMDIChildWnd (from editor.cpp), as follows:

```
BOOL CEditorApp::InitInstance()
{
    // Standard initialization
    // If you are not using these features and wish to reduce the size
    //  of your final executable, you should remove from the following
    //  the specific  initialization routines you do not need.
    SetDialogBkColor();  // set dialog background color to gray
    LoadStdProfileSettings(); // Load INI options (including MRU)
    // Register the application's document templates. Document templates
    //  serve as the connection between documents, frame windows and views.
    AddDocTemplate(new CMultiDocTemplate(IDR_EDITORTYPE,
        RUNTIME_CLASS(CEditorDoc),
        RUNTIME_CLASS(CMDIChildWnd), //standard MDI child frame
        RUNTIME_CLASS(CEditorView)));
            :
```

These child windows will hold the various open documents, and all of the details will be handled for you by Visual C++. For example, when the user clicks the New item in the File menu, another document is created and its window opens, as shown in figure 9.1. Nothing is going on in each document yet—you still must add the code that will respond to the various windows events.

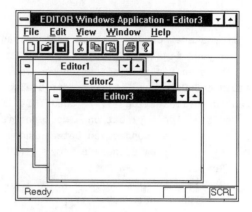

Figure 9.1. The MDI Editor application.

Each of the MDI child windows supports the normal type of view, derived from the CView class, as follows:

```
class CEditorView : public CView
{
protected: // create from serialization only
    CEditorView();
    DECLARE_DYNCREATE(CEditorView)
// Attributes
public:
    CEditorDoc* GetDocument();
        :
```

This means that you are free to work with messages like WM_CHAR and WM_MOUSEMOVE as before. Because you want to design a multi-window editor, use Class Wizard now to connect a function, OnChar(), to the view class, intercepting the WM_CHAR message. Next, open that function in the following way:

```
void CEditorView::OnChar(UINT nChar, UINT nRepCnt, UINT nFlags)
{
}
```

The editor will not have exceptional word-processing capabilities (this is a chapter about multiple documents and views, not about word processing). This example enables users to type what they want in the window, press Enter, and save or retrieve the file to or from disk. When the user presses Enter, the code is supposed to skip to the next line, so you handle that case separately, as follows:

```
void CEditorView::OnChar(UINT nChar, UINT nRepCnt, UINT nFlags)
{
    if(nChar == '\r'){
        [*** Skip to next line ***]
    }
    else{
        [*** Store the character ***]
    }
}
```

You can keep track of the text in a CString array named data_string[ ] and the line number in a long variable named line_number (note that Visual C++ places the document name in the MDI child window's title), as follows:

MDI Child Window

Editor1		
This	◄─── data_string[0]	line_number = 0
is	◄─── data_string[1]	line_number = 1
a	◄─── data_string[2]	line_number = 2
test.	◄─── data_string[3]	line_number = 3

The top line in the window corresponds to line_number 0, the text is in data_string[0], the next line is line_number 1, the text is in data_string[1], and so on. Storing the data like this makes it easier to display because you won't have to search each CString object to find carriage returns.

You can add those two data members, line_number and data_string[ ], to the document header in editodoc.h, where you can set aside space for, say, 100 lines, as follows:

```
const MAX_LINES = 100;
class CEditorDoc : public CDocument
{
```

```
protected: // create from serialization only
    CEditorDoc();
    DECLARE_DYNCREATE(CEditorDoc)
    CSize m_sizeDoc;
// Attributes
public:
    CSize GetDocSize() {return m_sizeDoc;}
    // Operations
public:
    CString data_string[MAX_LINES];
    long line_number;
        :
```

Next, you can set line_number to 0 when you start in CEditorDoc's constructor (in editodoc.cpp), as follows:

```
//////////////////////////////////////////////////////////////////////
//////////////// CEditorDoc construction/destruction
CEditorDoc::CEditorDoc()
{
line_number = 0;
}
```

As far as reading characters in CEditorView::OnChar(), then, you have only to increment pDoc->line_number if Enter was pressed, moving processing to the next line, as follows:

```
void CEditorView::OnChar(UINT nChar, UINT nRepCnt, UINT nFlags) {
    CEditorDoc* pDoc = GetDocument();
    if(nChar == '\r'){
        pDoc->line_number++;
    }
    else{
    }
}
```

If, on the other hand, the key you pressed (now in nChar) was not Enter, you need to display it. You do that in CEditorView::OnChar() first by storing it in pDoc->data_string[pDoc->line_number], the document's string array, as follows:

```
void CEditorView::OnChar(UINT nChar, UINT nRepCnt, UINT nFlags)
{
    CEditorDoc* pDoc = GetDocument();
    if(nChar == '\r'){
        pDoc->line_number++;
```

```
        }
    else{
            pDoc->data_string[pDoc->line_number] +=nChar;
                :
    }
}
```

Now you can display it. To make sure that you display the current line of text in the correct line in the view, use line_number. You also use dc.GetTextMetrics() to fill a TEXTMETRIC structure and determine the height of one line (that is, the tmHeight member). That means that the current string (stored in pDoc->data_string[pDoc->line_number]) should be displayed at (0, pDoc->line_number * tm.tmHeight), as follows:

```
void CEditorView::OnChar(UINT nChar, UINT nRepCnt, UINT nFlags)
{
    CEditorDoc* pDoc = GetDocument();
    CClientDC dc(this);
    if(nChar == '\r'){
        pDoc->line_number++;
    }
    else{
        pDoc->data_string[pDoc->line_number] +=nChar;
        TEXTMETRIC tm;
        dc.GetTextMetrics(&tm);
        dc.TextOut(0, (int) pDoc->line_number *
        tm.tmHeight,
                pDoc->data_string[pDoc->line_number],
                pDoc->data_string[pDoc->line_number].GetLength());
    }
}
```

Finally, you set the document's modified flag to make sure the user doesn't quit without first saving the current data, and you also call the base class function CView::OnChar(), as follows:

```
void CEditorView::OnChar(UINT nChar, UINT nRepCnt, UINT nFlags)
{
    CEditorDoc* pDoc = GetDocument();
    CClientDC dc(this);
    if(nChar == '\r'){
        pDoc->line_number++;
    }
```

```
        else{
            pDoc->data_string[pDoc->line_number] +=nChar;
            TEXTMETRIC tm;
            dc.GetTextMetrics(&tm);
            dc.TextOut(0, (int) pDoc->line_number * tm.tmHeight,
                pDoc->data_string[pDoc->line_number],
                pDoc->data_string[pDoc >line_number].GetLength());
        }
        pDoc->SetModifiedFlag();
        CView::OnChar(nChar, nRepCnt, nFlags);
}
```

That's it for OnChar(); the next step is to add similar code to OnDraw() so that the text is displayed when the window is uncovered or resized. Having this code in OnDraw() will be useful when you add scrolling because the window must be redrawn after it is scrolled. This code simply displays the data from the document, as follows:

```
void CEditorView::OnDraw(CDC* pDC)
{
    CEditorDoc* pDoc = GetDocument();
    TEXTMETRIC tm;
    pDC->GetTextMetrics(&tm);
    int yval = 0;
    for(int loop_index = 0; loop_index <= pDoc->line_number; loop_index++){
            pDC->TextOut(0,yval, pDoc-> data_string[loop_index],
            pDoc->data_string [loop_index].GetLength());
            yval += tm.tmHeight;
    }
}
```

Finally, you can add code to the Serialize() function to store the current number of lines in the document (that is, line_number), followed by the CString objects themselves.

```
void CEditorDoc::Serialize(CArchive& ar)
{
    if (ar.IsStoring())
    {
        ar << line_number;
        for (int loop_index = 0; loop_index < line_number; loop_index++){
        ar << data_string[loop_index];
        }
    }
```

```
    else
    {
        ar >> line_number;
        for (int loop_index = 0; loop_index < line_number; loop_index++){
        ar >> data_string[loop_index];
        }
    }
}
```

This means that you will be able to store and retrieve files to and from disk (but note that you are using your own format—a long int followed by CString objects—so you should not use the editor on general text files).

Now the editor is active, and you can type text as well as store it, as shown in figure 9.2. In addition, you can open a new document using the New item in the File menu and start working on that as well, as shown in figure 9.3. When a new document is opened, the program creates and keeps track of the new document automatically—which allows you to handle multiple documents. The program is a success so far.

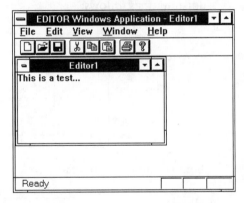

Figure 9.2. The editor at work.

Adding Scroll Bars

A user easily can type more lines than the space in the MDI child window allows. For a limited time, you can increase the size of the window, up to a maximum of the screen size. After that, there's no option for resizing the window—as the program is currently written. You can fix matters by adding scroll bars to your MDI child windows.

407

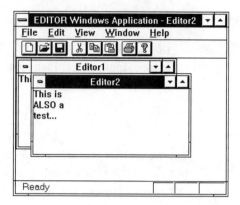

Figure 9.3. Multiple documents in the editor.

Adding scroll bars takes a little work because now you have to keep track of two coordinate systems—the document's coordinate system and your view's coordinate system (so that the view can be scrolled independent of the document). In other words, now the view can be at any location in the document, as follows:

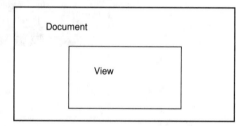

Both of these systems can have different origins, as follows:

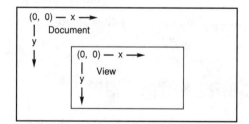

In the language of Windows, the document's coordinates are called *logical coordinates*, and the view's coordinates are called *device coordinates*, as follows:

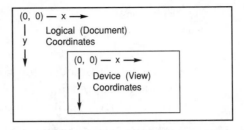

If the user clicks the mouse in the view after it has been scrolled, the mouse click location is returned in terms of device (view) coordinates. The code must translate the coordinates into logical (document) coordinates before working with that data.

Ready to try this out? Much of the work is handled automatically by Visual C++'s CScrollView class. As the program stands, the view is derived from the CView class, as usual (from editovw.h), as follows:

```
class CEditorView : public CView
{
protected: // create from serialization only
    CEditorView(); DECLARE_DYNCREATE(CEditorView)
// Attributes
public:
    CEditorDoc* GetDocument();
    void OnInitialUpdate();
    virtual void OnUpdate(CView* pSender, LPARAM lHint = 0L,
        CObject* pHint = NULL);
// Operations
public:
    :
```

Change that now to CScrollView as shown in the next code example. (CScrollView itself is derived from CView, but it also supports scroll bars.)

```
class CEditorView : public CScrollView
{
protected: // create from serialization only
    CEditorView(); DECLARE_DYNCREATE(CEditorView)
// Attributes
public:
    CEditorDoc* GetDocument();
    void OnInitialUpdate();
    virtual void OnUpdate(CView* pSender, LPARAM lHint = 0L,
        CObject* pHint = NULL);
```

```
// Operations
public:
    :
```

Next, you need to modify the code in editovw.cpp to indicate that
CEditorView is derived from CScrollView. As it is, two Visual C++ macros
still refer to CView in editovw.cpp, as follows:

```
IMPLEMENT_DYNCREATE(CEditorView, CView)
BEGIN_MESSAGE_MAP(CEditorView, CView)
    //{{AFX_MSG_MAP(CEditorView)
    ON_WM_CHAR()
    //}}AFX_MSG_MAP
    // Standard printing commands
    ON_COMMAND(ID_FILE_PRINT, CView::OnFilePrint)
    ON_COMMAND(ID_FILE_PRINT_PREVIEW, CView::OnFilePrintPreview)
END_MESSAGE_MAP()
    :
```

Change the macros to indicate that CEditorView is actually derived from
CScrollView like this, as follows:

```
IMPLEMENT_DYNCREATE(CEditorView, CScrollView)
BEGIN_MESSAGE_MAP(CEditorView, CScrollView)
    //{{AFX_MSG_MAP(CEditorView)
    ON_WM_CHAR()
    //}}AFX_MSG_MAP
    // Standard printing commands
    ON_COMMAND(ID_FILE_PRINT, CView::OnFilePrint)
    ON_COMMAND(ID_FILE_PRINT_PREVIEW,
    CView::OnFilePrintPreview)
END_MESSAGE_MAP()
    :
```

That's all there is to it; now the view class is derived from CScrollView, not
CView.

More remains to be done here, however. At this point, you have to set a
size for the document so CScrollView will know how to handle it (that is,
the view has to know the scrolling boundaries of the document). Do that
with the CScrollView member function SetScrollSizes(). First, you store
the size of the document in the document header, editodoc.h, by using
a CSize object named m_sizeDoc. (A CSize object has two members, cx
and cy, which hold coordinates.)

```
// editodoc.h : interface of the CEditorDoc class
//
/////////////////////////////////////////////////////////////////
/////////////// const MAX_LINES = 100;
class CEditorDoc : public CDocument
{
protected: // create from serialization only
    CEditorDoc();
    DECLARE_DYNCREATE(CEditorDoc)
    CSize m_sizeDoc;
        :
```

In addition, you can define a function that returns the document size to the rest of the program in the following way:

```
// editodoc.h : interface of the CEditorDoc class
//
/////////////////////////////////////////////////////////////////
//////////
// const MAX_LINES = 100;
class CEditorDoc : public CDocument
{
protected: // create from serialization only
    CEditorDoc();
    DECLARE_DYNCREATE(CEditorDoc)
    CSize m_sizeDoc;

// Attributes
public:
CSize GetDocSize() {return m_sizeDoc;}
        :
```

Now if you want to get the document's (protected) size, you are able to use the (public) function GetDocSize(). All that remains here is to set m_sizeDoc to an actual value when you start (that is, in CEditorDoc's constructor). For this example, you might choose a size of 800 by 1000 pixels in the following way:

```
/////////////////////////////////////////////////////////////////
////////////
// CEditorDoc construction/destruction
CEditorDoc::CEditorDoc()
{
    line_number = 0;
    m_sizeDoc = CSize(800, 1000);
}
```

You now have a size connected to the document, a size you can retrieve with GetDocSize(). You need that size to initialize the scrolling functions of CScrollView when the view is first created. Such initialization is done in the function CEditorView::OnInitialUpdate() with the function SetScrollSizes().

A view receives updates from the rest of the program when the document has been changed by another view. You handle such updates in a function named OnUpdate(). In addition, the function OnInitialUpdate() is called when the view is first created, which means that you can set CScrollView's scrolling parameters in that function. The next example shows this in CEditorView::OnInitialUpdate(). (Visual C++ already has created a skeleton version of this function.)

```
void CEditorView::OnInitialUpdate()
{
    SetScrollSizes(MM_TEXT, GetDocument()-
    >GetDocSize());
}
```

Here you are informing CScrollView of the size of the document. The first parameter, MM_TEXT, indicates that the document is a text document. Other options are shown in table 9.1. The second parameter is the CSize object holding the document's size.

Table 9.1. Mapping Mode Options

Mapping Mode	Scroll Unit
MM_HIENGLISH	0.001 inch
MM_HIMETRIC	0.01mm
MM_LOENGLISH	0.01 inch
MM_LOMETRIC	0.1 mm
MM_TEXT	1 pixel
MM_TWIPS	1/1440 inch

Now the scrolling view is set up. You should examine a few more items before running the program, however. One of the following items is OnDraw().

```
void CEditorView::OnDraw(CDC* pDC)
{
    CEditorDoc* pDoc = GetDocument();
    TEXTMETRIC tm;
    pDC->GetTextMetrics(&tm);
    int yval = 0;
    for(int loop_index = 0; loop_index <= pDoc->line_number; loop_index++){
        pDC->TextOut(0, yval,
        pDoc->data_string[loop_index],
        pDoc->data_string[loop_index].GetLength());
        yval += tm.tmHeight;
    }
}
```

Notice that the end of this function prints the string using what appears to be document coordinates, as follows:

```
int yval = 0;
for(int loop_index = 0; loop_index <= pDoc->line_number; loop_index++){
    pDC->TextOut(0, yval, pDoc->data_string [loop_index],
        pDoc->data_string[loop_index].GetLength());
        yval += tm.tmHeight;
}
```

In fact, Visual C++ has already called a function named OnPrepareDC() to prepare the device context passed in OnDraw(), as follows:

```
void CEditorView::OnDraw(CDC* pDC)
{
```

This function sets the device context's origin to the document's origin. Originally, the view's origin is wherever it has been scrolled to, as follows:

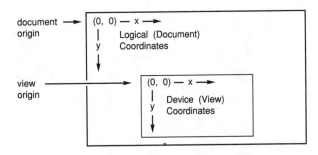

After OnPrepareDC() is called, the origin of the device context is moved to correspond to the document's origin, as follows:

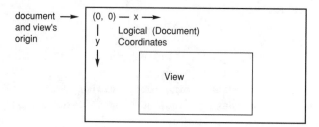

Now when you draw the document, the part that appears in the view will also be drawn automatically, and you can draw the whole thing with document (logical) coordinates. That means you don't have to change OnDraw() because the origin of the device context was moved automatically to match the document's origin.

OnChar() is a different story, however. With this function, you create your own device context, in the following way:

```
void CEditorView::OnChar(UINT nChar, UINT nRepCnt, UINT nFlags)
{
    CEditorDoc* pDoc = GetDocument();
    CClientDC dc(this);
    if(nChar == '\r'){
        pDoc->line_number++;
            :
    }
    else{
        pDoc->data_string[pDoc->line_number] +=nChar;
            :
    }
}
```

That means you have to re-orient this device context yourself by using OnPrepareDC(), and you do that in the following way:

```
void CEditorView::OnChar(UINT nChar, UINT nRepCnt, UINT nFlags)
{
    CEditorDoc* pDoc = GetDocument();
    CClientDC dc(this);
    OnPrepareDC(&dc);
    if(nChar == '\r'){
        pDoc->line_number++;
            :
```

```
      }
    else{
         pDoc->data_string[pDoc->line_number] +=nChar;
              :
    }
}
```

If you want explicitly to convert points (for example, mouse click locations) between device and logical coordinates, you could use the device context functions DPtoLP() and LPtoDP().

Now you are ready to run, and your program supports scrolling, as shown in figure 9.4. The editor is a success so far; now you can even scroll documents as necessary.

Let's move on to the process of supporting multiple views in the same document.

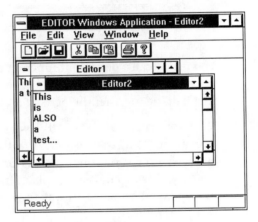

Figure 9.4. The scrolling multi-window editor.

Multiple Views

If the user selects the new Window item in the program's Window menu, a new (and scrollable) view into the document is opened. That is fine—but what if the user types in one of the views, but not the other? The result is something like what you see in figure 9.5; one view displays the new character(s), but the other one does not. (Notice that the views display

415

view numbers, such as Editor1:2, which means document Editor1, view 2.) Now you need to find some way to coordinate the views.

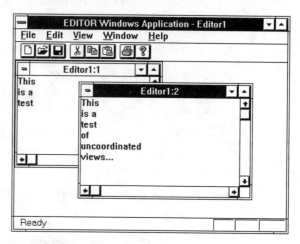

Figure 9.5. Uncoordinated multiple views.

You may recall a document function named UpdateAllViews() that you saw briefly in Chapter 2. That function is part of a group of such functions that help tie together the parts of a Visual C++ program, as follows:

Here you can use UpdateAllViews() after any view has changed the document. Doing so makes sure that the function OnUpdate() is called in all views except the one that performed the modification and called UpdateAllViews() in the first place. In CEditorView::OnChar(), you can call UpdateAllViews() this way (now that you have modified the document), as follows:

```
void CEditorView::OnChar(UINT nChar, UINT nRepCnt, UINT nFlags)
{
    CEditorDoc* pDoc = GetDocument();
    CClientDC dc(this);
    OnPrepareDC(&dc);
    if(nChar == '\r'){
        pDoc->line_number++;
    }
    else{
        pDoc->data_string[pDoc->line_number] +=nChar;
        TEXTMETRIC tm;
        dc.GetTextMetrics(&tm);
```

```
            dc.TextOut(0, (int) pDoc->line_number * tm.tmHeight,
            pDoc->data_string[pDoc->line_number],
            pDoc->data_string[pDoc->line_number].GetLength());

    }
    pDoc->UpdateAllViews(this, 0L, NULL);
    pDoc->SetModifiedFlag();
    CView::OnChar(nChar, nRepCnt, nFlags);

}
```

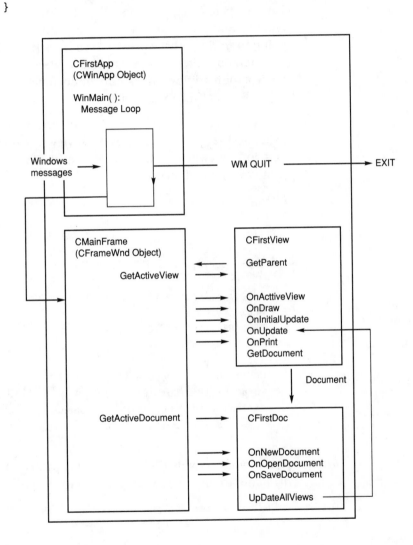

Notice that you pass three parameters to UpdateAllViews()—a this pointer, indicating which view is making the modification, a long parameter, and a value of NULL. This last value is actually a pointer to an object of type CObject; in general, UpdateAllView()'s prototype appears as follows:

```
void UpdateAllViews(CView* pSender, LPARAM lHint = 0,
    CObject* pHint = NULL);
```

The long parameter, lHint, usually contains information concerning the type of modification the view made to the document; pHint usually points to an object that will help you process the update. For example, one common object to use as the hint is a CRect object holding the coordinates of the modification made to the document. Here, simply leave these values 0 and NULL for simplicity.

Now you need to add the OnUpdate() function to the view class in order to handle the updates caused by other views. To do that, you override the function CView::OnUpdate(), so you must add it to the view's header file (editovw.h), as follows:

```
// editovw.h : interface of the CEditorView class
//
/////////////////////////////////////////////////////////////////////
/////////////
class CEditorView : public CScrollView
{
protected: // create from serialization only
    CEditorView();
    DECLARE_DYNCREATE(CEditorView)
// Attributes
public:
    CEditorDoc* GetDocument();
    void OnInitialUpdate();
    virtual void OnUpdate(CView* pSender, LPARAM lHint = 0L,
        CObject* pHint = NULL);
            :
```

Finally, you can write CEditorView::OnUpdate(). Add this function now (by hand) to the view's source file, editovw.cpp, as follows:

```
void CEditorView::OnUpdate(CView*, LPARAM, CObject*)
{
}
```

If this function gets called, another view has changed the document's contents, and you should redisplay it. To do that, simply mark the view as invalid. Marking any section of a window invalid causes a WM_PAINT message to be sent; that message causes the function CWnd::OnPaint() to be called, which in turn calls the function OnDraw(). If the modified section of the document is in the view's current display, the document is redrawn. To invalidate the entire view, simply call Invalidate() in the following way:

```
void CEditorView::OnUpdate(CView*, LPARAM, CObject*)
{
    Invalidate();
}
```

Now, whenever any view modifies the document, it also calls pDoc->UpdateAllViews(), which in turn calls OnUpdate() in all the other views attached to this document, updating all displays. That results in the coordinated system you see in figure 9.6, in which all views work together. When you type anything in one view, you can see it echoed in the other view(s).

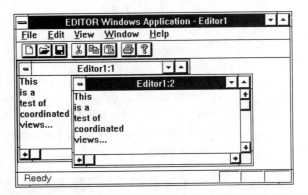

Figure 9.6. Coordinated views in the editor.

You have come far in working with the multiple-window editor. You can handle multiple documents, scrollable views, and now multiple views. But that's not all that's possible here—you can also add splitter windows to the editor application.

Splitter Windows

You have already worked with multiple views, but they have been in multiple windows, as follows:

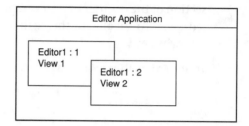

Sometimes you will find it more convenient to work with multiple, scrollable views in the same MDI Child window, as follows:

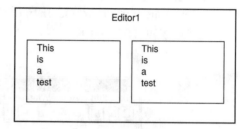

This type of window is called a *splitter window*, and it is something you can add to editor.mak. To do that, start Class Wizard now and use it to create a new class by pressing the Add Class button. Call this new class CEdSplitFrame, for example, and choose splitter for the class type, as shown in figure 9.7.

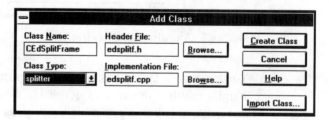

Figure 9.7. Creating a new class with Class Wizard.

Next, click the Create Class button to create the class and then close Class Wizard. Class Wizard creates the CEdSplitFrame class like this in the file edsplitf.h, as follows:

```
// edsplitf.h : header file
//
/////////////////////////////////////////////////////////////////////////////
// CEdSplitFrame frame with splitter
#ifndef __AFXEXT_H__
#include <afxext.h>
#endif
class CEdSplitFrame : public CMDIChildWnd
{
    DECLARE_DYNCREATE(CEdSplitFrame)
protected:
    CEdSplitFrame();    // protected constructor used by dynamic creation
// Attributes
protected:
    CSplitterWnd    m_wndSplitter;
public:
        :
};
```

CEdSplitFrame is derived from CMDIChildWnd because it is part of an MDI application. The member object m_wndSplitter is the actual window that will cover your splitter window's client area and support the splitter functions. To install this class as the new view class, you need to change editor.cpp. The following example shows how to include edsplitf.h and then install CEdSplitFrame in the document template.

```
/////////////////////////////////////////////////////////////////////////////
// editor.cpp : Defines the class
behaviors for the application.
//
#include "stdafx.h"
#include "editor.h"
#include "edsplitf.h"
#include "mainfrm.h"
#include "editodoc.h"
#include "editovw.h"
        :
        :
```

```
BOOL CEditorApp::InitInstance()
{
    // Standard initialization
    // If you are not using these features and wish to reduce the size
    //  of your final executable, you should remove from the following
    //  the specific initialization routines you do not need.
    SetDialogBkColor();         // set dialog background color to gray
    LoadStdProfileSettings();   // Load standard INI options (including MRU)
    // Register the application's document templates. Document templates
    //  serve as the connection between documents, frame windows and views.
    AddDocTemplate(new CMultiDocTemplate(IDR_EDITORTY PE,
        RUNTIME_CLASS(CEditorDoc),
        RUNTIME_CLASS(CEdSplitFrame),          //
        standard MDI child frame
        RUNTIME_CLASS(CEditorView)));
            :
```

That's all there is to creating splitter windows. Now you can use splitter windows in the editor. To do so, run the program and drag one of the small split boxes (next to the arrows in the scroll bars). A dividing line appears; drag it to where you want it in the window. This adds a new view to the window, as shown in figure 9.8.

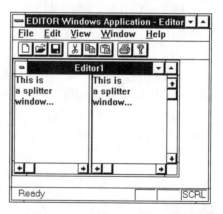

Figure 9.8. The editor with splitter windows.

The editor is a complete success—you have even been able to add splitter windows. The listings (all of which you've modified) appear in listings 9.1 to 9.8, as follows:

Listing #	Listing Name	Description
Listing 9.1	editodoc.h	Document header
Listing 9.2	editodoc.cpp	Document code
Listing 9.3	editovw.h	View header
Listing 9.4	editovw.cpp	View code
Listing 9.5	editor.h	Document template
Listing 9.6	editor.cpp	Application code
Listing 9.7	edsplitf.h	Splitter header
Listing 9.8	edsplitf.cpp	Splitter code

Listing 9.1. Editodoc.H

```
// editodoc.h : interface of the CEditorDoc class
//
/////////////////////////////////////////////////////////////////////////////
const MAX_LINES = 100;
class CEditorDoc : public CDocument
{
protected: // create from serialization only
        CEditorDoc();
        DECLARE_DYNCREATE(CEditorDoc)
        CSize m_sizeDoc;
// Attributes
public:
    CSize GetDocSize() {return m_sizeDoc;}
// Operations
public:
   CString data_string[MAX_LINES];
    long line_number;
// Implementation
public:
        virtual ~CEditorDoc();
        virtual void Serialize(CArchive& ar);
                        // overridden for document i/o
```

continues

Listing 9.1. continued

```
#ifdef _DEBUG
        virtual     void AssertValid() const;
        virtual     void Dump(CDumpContext& dc) const;
#endif
protected:
        virtual     BOOL     OnNewDocument();
// Generated message map functions protected:
        //{{AFX_MSG(CEditorDoc)
            // NOTE - the ClassWizard will add and remove member functions here.
            //   DO NOT EDIT what you see in these blocks of generated code !
        //}}AFX_MSG
        DECLARE_MESSAGE_MAP()
};
```

Listing 9.2. Editodoc.Cpp

```
/////////////////////////////////////////////////////////////////////////////
// editodoc.cpp : implementation of the CEditorDoc class
//
#include "stdafx.h"
#include "editor.h"
#include "editodoc.h"
#ifdef _DEBUG
#undef THIS_FILE
static char BASED_CODE THIS_FILE[] = __FILE__;
#endif
/////////////////////////////////////////////////////////////////////////////
// CEditorDoc
IMPLEMENT_DYNCREATE(CEditorDoc, CDocument)
BEGIN_MESSAGE_MAP(CEditorDoc, CDocument)
        //{{AFX_MSG_MAP(CEditorDoc)
            // NOTE - the ClassWizard will add and remove mapping macros here.
            //   DO NOT EDIT what you see in these blocks of generated code !
        //}}AFX_MSG_MAP
END_MESSAGE_MAP()
/////////////////////////////////////////////////////////////////////////////
// CEditorDoc construction/destruction
CEditorDoc::CEditorDoc()
```

```cpp
{
    line_number = 0;
    m_sizeDoc = CSize(800, 1000);
}
CEditorDoc::~CEditorDoc()
{
}
BOOL CEditorDoc::OnNewDocument()
{
    if (!CDocument::OnNewDocument())
        return FALSE;
    return TRUE;
}
/////////////////////////////////////////////////////////////////////////////
// CEditorDoc serialization
void CEditorDoc::Serialize(CArchive& ar)
{
    if (ar.IsStoring())
    {
        ar << line_number;
        for (int loop_index = 0; loop_index <
        line_number; loop_index++){ ar <<
        data_string[loop_index];
        }
    }
    else
    {
        ar >> line_number;
        for (int loop_index = 0; loop_index <
        line_number; loop_index++){ ar >>
        data_string[loop_index];
        }
    }
}
/////////////////////////////////////////////////////////////////////////////
// CEditorDoc diagnostics
#ifdef _DEBUG
void CEditorDoc::AssertValid() const
{
    CDocument::AssertValid();
}
```

continues

425

Listing 9.2. continued

```
void CEditorDoc::Dump(CDumpContext& dc) const
{
    CDocument::Dump(dc);
}
#endif //_DEBUG
///////////////////////////////////////////////////////////////////////////
// CEditorDoc commands
```

Listing 9.3. Editovw.h

```
// editovw.h : interface of the CEditorView class
// ///////////////////////////////////////////////////////////////////////////
class CEditorView : public CScrollView
{
protected: // create from serialization only
    CEditorView();
    DECLARE_DYNCREATE(CEditorView)
// Attributes
public:
    CEditorDoc* GetDocument();
    void OnInitialUpdate();
    virtual void OnUpdate(CView* pSender, LPARAM lHint = 0L,
        CObject* pHint = NULL);
// Operations
public:
// Implementation
public:
    virtual ~CEditorView();
    virtual void OnDraw(CDC* pDC);  // overridden to draw this view
#ifdef _DEBUG
    virtual void AssertValid() const;
    virtual void Dump(CDumpContext& dc) const;
#endif
    // Printing support
protected:
    virtual BOOL OnPreparePrinting(CPrintInfo* pInfo);
    virtual void OnBeginPrinting(CDC* pDC, CPrintInfo* pInfo);
```

```
      virtual void OnEndPrinting(CDC* pDC, CPrintInfo* pInfo);
// Generated message map functions
protected:
    //{{AFX_MSG(CEditorView)
    afx_msg void OnChar(UINT nChar, UINT nRepCnt, UINT nFlags);
    //}}AFX_MSG
    DECLARE_MESSAGE_MAP()
};
#ifndef _DEBUG     // debug version in editovw.cpp
inline CEditorDoc* CEditorView::GetDocument()
    { return (CEditorDoc*) m_pDocument; }
#endif
```

Listing 9.4. Editovw.Cpp

```
// editovw.cpp : implementation of the CEditorView class
//
#include "stdafx.h"
#include "editor.h"
#include "editodoc.h"
#include "editovw.h"
#ifdef _DEBUG
#undef THIS_FILE
static char BASED_CODE THIS_FILE[] = __FILE__;
#endif
/////////////////////////////////////////////////////////////////////////////
// CEditorView
IMPLEMENT_DYNCREATE(CEditorView, CView)
//IMPLEMENT_DYNCREATE(CEditorView, CScrollView)
BEGIN_MESSAGE_MAP(CEditorView, CView)
//BEGIN_MESSAGE_MAP(CEditorView, CScrollView)
    //{{AFX_MSG_MAP(CEditorView)
    ON_WM_CHAR()
    //}}AFX_MSG_MAP
    // Standard printing commands
    ON_COMMAND(ID_FILE_PRINT, CView::OnFilePrint)
        ON_COMMAND(ID_FILE_PRINT_PREVIEW, CView::OnFilePrintPreview)
END_MESSAGE_MAP()
```

continues

Listing 9.4. continued

```
/////////////////////////////////////////////////////////////////////////////
// CEditorView construction/destruction
CEditorView::CEditorView()
{
}
CEditorView::~CEditorView()
{
}
/////////////////////////////////////////////////////////////////////////////
// CEditorView drawing
void CEditorView::OnDraw(CDC* pDC)
{
    CEditorDoc* pDoc = GetDocument();
    TEXTMETRIC tm;
    pDC->GetTextMetrics(&tm);
    int yval = 0;
        for(int loop_index = 0; loop_index <= pDoc->line_number; loop_index++){
        pDC->TextOut(0, yval, pDoc- >data_string[loop_index],
          pDoc->data_string[loop_index].GetLength());
        yval += tm.tmHeight;
    }
}
/////////////////////////////////////////////////////////////////////////////
CEditorView printing
BOOL CEditorView::OnPreparePrinting(CPrintInfo* pInfo)
{
    // default preparation
    return DoPreparePrinting(pInfo);
}
void CEditorView::OnBeginPrinting(CDC* /*pDC*/, CPrintInfo* /*pInfo*/)
        {
            // TODO: add extra initialization before printing
        }
void CEditorView::OnEndPrinting(CDC* /*pDC*/, CPrintInfo* /*pInfo*/)
{
    // TODO: add cleanup after printing
}
void CEditorView::OnInitialUpdate()
{
    SetScrollSizes(MM_TEXT, GetDocument()->GetDocSize());
}
```

```
/////////////////////////////////////////////////////////////////////////////
// CEditorView diagnostics
#ifdef _DEBUG
void CEditorView::AssertValid() const
{
    CView::AssertValid();
}
void CEditorView::Dump(CDumpContext& dc) const
{
    CView::Dump(dc);
}
CEditorDoc* CEditorView::GetDocument() // non-debug version is inline
{
    ASSERT(m_pDocument->IsKindOf(RUNTIME_CLASS(CEditorDoc)));
    return (CEditorDoc*) m_pDocument;
}
#endif //_DEBUG
/////////////////////////////////////////////////////////////////////////////
// CEditorView message handlers
void CEditorView::OnChar(UINT nChar, UINT nRepCnt, UINT nFlags)
{
    CEditorDoc* pDoc = GetDocument();
    CClientDC dc(this);
    OnPrepareDC(&dc);
    if(nChar == '\r'){
        pDoc->line_number++;
    }
    else{
        pDoc->data_string[pDoc->line_number] +=nChar;
        TEXTMETRIC tm;
        dc.GetTextMetrics(&tm);
        dc.TextOut(0, (int) pDoc->line_number * tm.tmHeight,
            pDoc->data_string[pDoc->line_number],
            pDoc->data_string[pDoc >line_number].GetLength());
    }
    pDoc->UpdateAllViews(this, 0L, NULL);
    pDoc->SetModifiedFlag();
    CView::OnChar(nChar, nRepCnt, nFlags);
}
void CEditorView::OnUpdate(CView*, LPARAM, CObject*)
{
                    Invalidate();
}
```

Listing 9.5. Editor.H

```
}// editor.h : main header file for the EDITOR application
//
#ifndef __AFXWIN_H__
    #error include 'stdafx.h' before including this file for PCH #endif
#include "resource.h"          // main symbols
/////////////////////////////////////////////////////////////////////////
// CEditorApp:
// See editor.cpp for the implementation of this class
//
class CEditorApp : public CWinApp
{
public:
    CEditorApp();
// Overrides
    virtual BOOL InitInstance();
// Implementation
    //{{AFX_MSG(CEditorApp)
    afx_msg void OnAppAbout();
        // NOTE - the ClassWizard will add and remove member functions here.
        //   DO NOT EDIT what you see in these blocks of generated code!
    //}}AFX_MSG
    DECLARE_MESSAGE_MAP()
};
```

Listing 9.6. Editor.Cpp

```
/////////////////////////////////////////////////////////////////////////
// editor.cpp : Defines the class behaviors for the application.
//
#include "stdafx.h"
#include "editor.h"
#include "edsplitf.h"
#include "mainfrm.h"
#include "editodoc.h"
#include "editovw.h"
#ifdef _DEBUG
```

```
#undef THIS_FILE
static char BASED_CODE THIS_FILE[] = __FILE__;
#endif
///////////////////////////////////////////////////////////////////////////// //
CEditorApp
BEGIN_MESSAGE_MAP(CEditorApp, CWinApp)
    //{{AFX_MSG_MAP(CEditorApp)
    ON_COMMAND(ID_APP_ABOUT, OnAppAbout)
        // NOTE - the ClassWizard will add and remove mapping macros here.
        //      DO NOT EDIT what you see in these blocks of generated code !
    //}}AFX_MSG_MAP
    // Standard file based document commands
    ON_COMMAND(ID_FILE_NEW, CWinApp::OnFileNew)
        ON_COMMAND(ID_FILE_OPEN, CWinApp::OnFileOpen)
    // Standard print setup command
        ON_COMMAND(ID_FILE_PRINT_SETUP, CWinApp::OnFilePrintSetup)
END_MESSAGE_MAP()
/////////////////////////////////////////////////////////////////////////////
// CEditorApp construction
CEditorApp::CEditorApp()
{
    // TODO: add construction code here,
    // Place all significant initialization in InitInstance
}
/////////////////////////////////////////////////////////////////////////////
// The one and only CEditorApp object
CEditorApp NEAR theApp;
/////////////////////////////////////////////////////////////////////////////
// CEditorApp initialization
BOOL CEditorApp::InitInstance()
{
    // Standard initialization
    // If you are not using these features and wish to reduce the size
    //  of your final executable, you should remove from the following
    //  the specific initialization routines you do not need.
    SetDialogBkColor();         // set dialog background color to gray
    LoadStdProfileSettings();   // Load standard INI options (including MRU)
    // Register the application's document templates. Document templates
    //  serve as the connection between documents, frame windows and views.
```

continues

Listing 9.6. continued

```
        AddDocTemplate(new CMultiDocTemplate(IDR_EDITORTYPE,
            RUNTIME_CLASS(CEditorDoc),
            RUNTIME_CLASS(CMDIChildWnd),        // standard MDI child frame
            RUNTIME_CLASS(CEditorView)));
    // create main MDI Frame window
    CMainFrame* pMainFrame = new CMainFrame;
    if (!pMainFrame->LoadFrame(IDR_MAINFRAME))
        return FALSE;
    pMainFrame->ShowWindow(m_nCmdShow);
    pMainFrame->UpdateWindow();
    m_pMainWnd = pMainFrame;
    // create a new (empty) document
    OnFileNew();
    if (m_lpCmdLine[0] != '\0')
    {
        // TODO: add command line processing here
    }
    return TRUE;
}
/////////////////////////////////////////////////////////////////////////////
// CAboutDlg dialog used for App About
class CAboutDlg : public CDialog
{
public:
    CAboutDlg();
// Dialog Data
    //{{AFX_DATA(CAboutDlg)
    enum { IDD = IDD_ABOUTBOX };
    //}}AFX_DATA
// Implementation
protected:
virtual void DoDataExchange(CDataExchange* pDX);      // DDX/DDV support
//{{AFX_MSG(CAboutDlg)
        // No message handlers
    //}}AFX_MSG
    DECLARE_MESSAGE_MAP()
};
CAboutDlg::CAboutDlg() : CDialog(CAboutDlg::IDD)
{
    //{{AFX_DATA_INIT(CAboutDlg)
```

```
    //}}AFX_DATA_INIT
}
void CAboutDlg::DoDataExchange(CDataExchange* pDX)
{
    CDialog::DoDataExchange(pDX);
    //{{AFX_DATA_MAP(CAboutDlg)
    //}}AFX_DATA_MAP
}
BEGIN_MESSAGE_MAP(CAboutDlg, CDialog)
    //{{AFX_MSG_MAP(CAboutDlg)
        // No message handlers
    //}}AFX_MSG_MAP
END_MESSAGE_MAP()
// App command to run the dialog
void CEditorApp::OnAppAbout()
{
    CAboutDlg aboutDlg;
    aboutDlg.DoModal();
}
/////////////////////////////////////////////////////////////////////////////
// CEditorApp commands
```

Listing 9.7. Edsplitf.H

```
// edsplitf.h : header file
//
/////////////////////////////////////////////////////////////////////////////
// CEdSplitFrame frame with splitter
#ifndef __AFXEXT_H__
#include <afxext.h>
#endif
class CEdSplitFrame : public CMDIChildWnd
{
    DECLARE_DYNCREATE(CEdSplitFrame)
protected:
    CEdSplitFrame();    // protected constructor used by dynamic creation
// Attributes
protected:
    CSplitterWnd    m_wndSplitter;
```

continues

Listing 9.7. continued

```
public:
// Operations
public:
// Implementation
public:
    virtual ~CEdSplitFrame();
    virtual BOOL OnCreateClient(LPCREATESTRUCT lpcs, CCreateContext* pContext);
    // Generated message map functions
    //{{AFX_MSG(CEdSplitFrame)
        // NOTE - the ClassWizard will add and remove member functions here.
//}}AFX_MSG
    DECLARE_MESSAGE_MAP()
};
```

Listing 9.8. Edsplitf.Cpp

```
/////////////////////////////////////////////////////////////////////////////
// edsplitf.cpp : implementation file
//
#include "stdafx.h"
#include "editor.h"
#include "edsplitf.h"
#ifdef _DEBUG
#undef THIS_FILE
static char BASED_CODE THIS_FILE[] = __FILE__;
#endif
/////////////////////////////////////////////////////////////////////////////
// CEdSplitFrame
IMPLEMENT_DYNCREATE(CEdSplitFrame, CMDIChildWnd)
CEdSplitFrame::CEdSplitFrame()
{
}
CEdSplitFrame::~CEdSplitFrame()
{
}
BOOL CEdSplitFrame::OnCreateClient(LPCREATESTRUCT /*lpcs*/,
    CCreateContext* pContext)
{
```

```
    return m_wndSplitter.Create(this,
        2, 2,       // TODO: adjust the number of rows, columns
        CSize(10, 10),    // TODO: adjust the minimum pane size
        pContext);
}
BEGIN_MESSAGE_MAP(CEdSplitFrame, CMDIChildWnd)
    //{{AFX_MSG_MAP(CEdSplitFrame)
        // NOTE - the ClassWizard will add and remove mapping macros here.
        //}}AFX_MSG_MAP
END_MESSAGE_MAP()
/////////////////////////////////////////////////////////////////////////
// CEdSplitFrame message handlers
```

That wraps up your exploration of multiple documents and multiple views. You have come far in this chapter—from SDI to MDI, from single views to multiple views and splitter windows. You have seen how to let multiple views communicate with each other and learned to create scrollable views. Chapter 10 helps you investigate debugging and learn how to handle C++ exceptions.

Exception Handling and Debugging

E rrors occur even for the best programmers. In fact, the longer the program, and the more complex the code, the more likely errors are to appear. Errors come in several different types—those that cause design-time errors, those that cause run-time errors, and those that make your programs produce incorrect or unexpected results (bugs).

Visual C++ handles the first type, design-time errors, by refusing to run programs until they are fixed, and it usually offers some assistance in the form of help and help messages. The second two types are up to you to fix, and they are what this chapter is about: run-time errors and bugs.

A run-time error is what Visual C++ refers to as a *trappable error;* that is, Visual C++ recognizes that there was an error and generates an exception. You can then handle the exception with the TRY and CATCH macros, as the examples in this chapter show. This enables you to take some corrective action if errors do occur.

Bugs are different—and sometimes more difficult—to solve. When your program has a bug, Visual C++ usually doesn't recognize that there is a problem, but the code doesn't operate as intended. In this case, you solve the problem by examining the program's operation line by line.

This chapter starts with an examination of exception handling used to process run-time errors. Then you learn about the actual process of debugging and find out how to remove logic errors from your programs.

Exception Handling

In many languages, library functions return error codes that you can examine. For example, in C, the fopen() function returns a NULL file pointer if it cannot open a file, in the following way:

```c
#include <stdio.h>
void main()
{
    FILE *file_pointer;
    if((file_pointer = fopen("hello.txt", "w")) != NULL){
        fwrite("Hello, world.", strlen("Hello, world."), 0, \
        file_pointer);
        fclose(file_pointer);
    }
    else printf("Error writing hello.txt\n");
}
```

In Visual C++, however, errors like this are handled with exceptions. That is, if you can't open a file in Visual C++, an exception of type CFileException is generated (this is because it is not standard to check return values from constructors). Programs often include sensitive code that can cause run-time errors—exceptions—and notoriously, this includes file-handling code. In Visual C++, you enclose such code in a TRY macro block, as follows:

```
TRY
{
    [*** Sensitive code ***]
}
:
```

If any of the code in the TRY block causes an exception, you can handle that exception in a CATCH block, as follows:

```
TRY
{
    [*** Sensitive code ***]
}
CATCH(CException, e)
{
    [*** Exception-handling code ***]
}
END_CATCH
```

Here, "e" is the name of the exception generated, and CException is the type of exception. In particular, Visual C++ offers these exception classes to handle various run-time errors, as follows:

Exception Class	Description
CMemoryException	Memory exceptions
CNotSupportedException	Service not supported
CArchiveException	Archive exceptions
CFileException	File exceptions
OsErrorToException	Convert DOS error to exception
ErrnoToException	Convert error number to exception
CResourceException	Resource exceptions
COleException	OLE exceptions

The actual cause of the exception is stored in the exception object's m_cause data member. For example, the possible values of CArchiveException::m_cause appear in table 10.1.

Table 10.1. CArchiveException::m_cause

CArchiveException::badClass	Cannot read object into new object type

continues

439

Table 10.1. continued

CArchiveException::badIndex	File is invalid
CArchiveException::badSchema	Cannot read object of different version
CArchiveException::endOfFile	End of file reached
CArchiveException::generic	General error
CArchiveException::none	No error
CArchiveException::readOnly	Cannot write into a read-only archive
CArchiveException::writeOnly	Cannot read from a write-only archive

This example takes a look at CFileException handling, because file handling can cause many run-time errors. The possible values for CFileException::m_cause appear in table 10.2.

Table 10.2. CFileException::m_cause Values

CFileException::accessDenied	File access denied
CFileException::badPath	Path is invalid
CFileException::badSeek	Error setting file pointer
CFileException::directoryFull	Directory is full
CFileException::diskFull	Disk is full
CFileException::endOfFile	End of file reached
CFileException::fileNotFound	File could not be found
CFileException::generic	General error
CFileException::hardIO	Hardware error
CFileException::invalidFile	File is invalid
CFileException::lockViolation	Attempt to lock region already locked

`CFileException::none`	No error
`CFileException::removeCurrentDir`	Cannot remove current directory
`CFileException::sharingViolation`	Sharing violation—load share.exe
`CFileException::tooManyOpenFiles`	Exceeded allowed number of open files

When you use the Serialize() function already built into your Visual C++ applications, Visual C++ handles the run-time file errors for you. For example, if the user tells the program to read a file from drive A and no disk is in the drive, Visual C++ places an error box on the screen as shown in figure 10.1.

Figure 10.1. Visual C++ handling a file error.

If you handle file operations yourself (as you did in Chapter 8), you are responsible for handling file exceptions as well. You may recall that in Chapter 8, you wrote a file named hello.txt to the disk in the following way:

```
void CFileView::OnFilewrite()
{
    CString hello_string = "Hello, world.";

    CFile file("hello.txt", CFile::modeCreate | CFile::modeWrite);

    file.Write(hello_string,
    hello_string.GetLength());
    file.Close();
}
```

Now you might try to write the file to drive A—even though no disk is in the drive—as follows:

```
void CFileView::OnFilewrite()
{
    CString hello_string = "Hello, world.";
    CFile file("a:hello.txt", CFile::modeCreate | CFile::modeWrite);
    file.Write(hello_string,
    hello_string.GetLength());
    file.Close();
}
```

This segment generates a file exception. You can recognize the sensitive nature of the file-handling commands like this if you put them into a TRY block in the following way:

```
void CFileView::OnFilewrite()
{
    CString hello_string = "Hello, world.";
    TRY
    {
        CFile file("a:hello.txt", CFile::modeCreate | CFile::modeWrite);
        file.Write(hello_string, hello_string.GetLength());
        file.Close();
    }
}
```

Now you are ready to handle the file exceptions that might arise. Do that in a CATCH block, as follows:

```
void CFileView::OnFilewrite()
{
    CString hello_string = "Hello, world.";
    TRY
    {
        CFile file("a:hello.txt", CFile::modeCreate | CFile::modeWrite);
        file.Write(hello_string, hello_string.GetLength());
        file.Close();
    }
    CATCH(CFileException, e)
    {
        MessageBox("File could not be opened");
    }
    END_CATCH
}
```

Note that you include the END_CATCH macro at the end of the CATCH block; this allows you to set up multiple CATCH blocks (explained later in this chapter). END_CATCH indicates that there are no more such blocks to come.

You can execute the new code as modified. In this case, you are putting a message box on the screen that displays the message File could not be opened, as shown in figure 10.2.

Figure 10.2. Handling a file exception.

Now you have handled your first file exception. If a file operation problem occurs, the code in the CATCH block is executed. In fact, you can be more specific with your error message if you check the m_cause data member (as given in table 10.2). That might appear as follows in the code:

```
void CFileView::OnFilewrite()
{
    CString hello_string = "Hello, world.";
    TRY
    {
        CFile file("a:hello.txt", CFile::modeCreate | CFile::modeWrite);
        file.Write(hello_string,
        hello_string.GetLength());
        file.Close();
    }
    CATCH(CFileException, e)
    {
    switch(e->m_cause)
    {
        case CFileException::accessDenied:
            MessageBox("File access denied");
            break;
        case CFileException::badPath:
            MessageBox("Path is invalid");
            break;
```

```
        case CFileException::diskFull:
            MessageBox("Disk is full");
            break;
        case CFileException::fileNotFound:
            MessageBox("File could not be found");
            break;
        case CFileException::hardIO:
            MessageBox("Hardware error");
            break;
        case CFileException::lockViolation:
            MessageBox("Attempt to lock region already locked");
            break;
        case CFileException::sharingViolation:
            MessageBox("Sharing violation—load share.exe");
            break;
        case CFileException::tooManyOpenFiles:
            MessageBox("Exceeded allowed number of open files");
            break;
        }
    }
    END_CATCH
}
```

You also can handle such messages without message boxes. If you prefer, you can send this kind of message to the debug window. The *debug window* is a window that stays open on the screen while you are developing a program, ready to display the messages sent to it. Because the debug window is a powerful debugging tool, it is examined next.

The Debug Window

Instead of using the MessageBox() function, you can send output to the debug window by using the TRACE() macro, as follows:

```
void CFileView::OnFilewrite()
{
    CString hello_string = "Hello, world.";
    TRY
    {
        CFile file("a:hello.txt", CFile::modeCreate | CFile::modeWrite);
        file.Write(hello_string, hello_string.GetLength());
        file.Close();
    }
```

```
CATCH(CFileException, e)
{
        TRACE("File could not be opened");
}
END_CATCH
}
```

In this case, the text File could not be opened appears in the debug window. To see that, you first must open that window. Find the icon for the MFC Trace Options application in the Visual C++ program group. Click this icon now to open the corresponding program, as shown in figure 10.3.

Figure 10.3. The MFC Trace options window.

Make sure that the Enable Tracing item is selected, as figure 10.3 shows. You also can set other tracing options here; for example, you can display all Windows commands your program gets this way. Now click OK to enable tracing.

Another application that comes with Visual C++ is the debug window itself; this icon is labeled DebugWin. Open that application now, as shown in figure 10.4.

Now that the debug window is ready, run the program. After you try to write to the nonexistent disk, you see the display in the debug window shown in figure 10.5. Note that the warning says that a file exception is being thrown. In addition, you see the text sent there: File could not be opened.

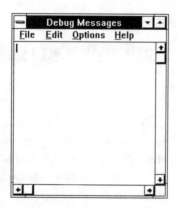

Figure 10.4. The Visual C++ Debug Messages window.

Figure 10.5. The Visual C++ Debug Messages window displaying a warning.

The TRACE() macro gives you one way of sending text to the debug window. As you can see, the debug window can come in very handy: it is an independent window that can display information about and from the program you are running. This can give you a quick way of debugging a program if you want to watch the progress of a few variables; you only have to send them to the debug window.

TRACE() will send only text to the debug window; if you want to send numerical values, you must do that yourself by sending them to the program's (predefined) afxDump variable, as follows:

```
void CFileView::OnFilewrite()
{
    CString hello_string = "Hello, world.";
    TRY
    {
        CFile file("a:hello.txt", CFile::modeCreate | CFile::modeWrite);
        file.Write(hello_string, hello_string.GetLength());
        file.Close();
    }
    CATCH(CFileException, e)
    {
        afxDump << "File could not be opened " << e->m_cause << "\n";
    }
    END_CATCH
}
```

This is the standard method of dumping an object's contents in Visual C++. The output goes to the debug window, so make sure that your program is being run in debug mode.

Two such build modes exist: Debug and Release mode. The Debug build mode enables all the debug options (including line-by-line execution of the code), and Release mode disables those options. Generally, you develop an application in Debug mode and release it after it has been built in Release mode (Release mode programs are smaller and run faster). You select the build mode with the Project... item in Visual C++'s Options menu, opening the dialog box shown in figure 10.6.

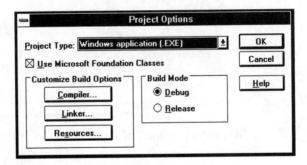

Figure 10.6. Selecting Debug Build mode.

You can determine whether you are in Debug mode by checking the way the _DEBUG variable is defined, as follows:

```
void CFileView::OnFilewrite()
{
    CString hello_string = "Hello, world.";
    TRY
    {
        CFile file("a:hello.txt", CFile::modeCreate | CFile::modeWrite);
        file.Write(hello_string, hello_string.GetLength());
        file.Close();
    }
    CATCH(CFileException, e)
    {
        #ifdef _DEBUG
            afxDump << "File could not be opened " << e->m_cause << "\n";
        #endif
    }
    END_CATCH
}
```

With this code, you can send text and numerical values (here e->m_cause) to the debug window, as shown in figure 10.7.

Figure 10.7. Numerical values in the Debug Messages window.

Catching Multiple Exceptions

As the program stands, you can handle only file exceptions. But you will deal with other kinds of exceptions: memory exceptions, archive exceptions, and so on. The next question is "How do I handle two or more types of exceptions?" You can do that with an AND_CATCH() macro block. In general, you can catch multiple exceptions in the following way:

```
TRY
{
    [*** Sensitive code ***]
}
CATCH(CException1, e)
{
    [*** Exception1-handling code ***]
}
AND_CATCH(CException2, e)
{
    [*** Exception2-handling code ***]
}
AND_CATCH(CException3, e)
{
    [*** Exception3-handling code ***]
}
END_CATCH
```

You can check for both file and memory exceptions in the code as follows:

```
void CFileView::OnFilewrite()
{
    CString hello_string = "Hello, world.";
    TRY
    {
        CFile file("a:hello.txt", CFile::modeCreate | CFile::modeWrite);
        file.Write(hello_string, hello_string.GetLength());
        file.Close();
    }
    CATCH(CFileException, e)
    {
        #ifdef _DEBUG
            afxDump << "File could not be opened " << e->m_cause << "\n";
        #endif
    }
```

```
AND_CATCH(CMemoryException, e)
{
    #ifdef _DEBUG
        afxDump << "Memory could not be allocated "<< e->m_cause << "\n";
    #endif
}
END_CATCH
}
```

In this way, you can handle exceptions of different types. Now it's clear why you need an END_CATCH macro: you need something to indicate that there are no more CATCH blocks to follow.

Note also that you may not want to handle all possible exceptions in a particular CATCH block; rather, you may want to handle some exceptions but pass the rest on to a more general CATCH block. If that general CATCH block encloses the particular one, you can pass the exception on to the outer block with the THROW_LAST() macro. This passes the exception on to the next level of CATCH block as follows:

```
TRY{
    TRY{
        [*** Sensitive code ***]
    }
    CATCH(CException, e){
        if(e->m_cause == HANDLED_EXCEPTION){
            [*** Handle exception ***]
        }
        else{
            THROW_LAST();
        }
    }
    END_CATCH
}
CATCH(CException, e){
    [*** Additional exception-handling code ***]
}
END_CATCH
```

This segment allows you to handle specific exceptions in a local CATCH block but pass other exceptions up to the next level. In the file application, that might appear as follows:

```
void CFileView::OnFilewrite()
{
    CString hello_string = "Hello, world.";
    TRY{
        TRY{
            CFile file("a:hello.txt", CFile::modeCreate | CFile::modeWrite);
            file.Write(hello_string, hello_string.GetLength());
                file.Close();
        }

            CATCH(CFileException, e){
                if(e->m_cause == CFileException::fileNotFound){
                    MessageBox("File not found");
                }

            else{
                    THROW_LAST();
            }
        }

        END_CATCH
    }
    CATCH{
        MessageBox("File error");     //General file error.
    }
    END_CATCH
}
```

The complete listing of fileview.cpp—including exception handling—appears in listing 10.1.

Listing 10.1. Fileview.Cpp with Exception Handling

```
// fileview.cpp : implementation of the CFileView class
//
#include "stdafx.h"
#include "file.h"
```

continues

Listing 10.1. continued

```
. #include <string.h>
  #include "filedoc.h"
  #include "fileview.h"
  #ifdef _DEBUG
  #undef THIS_FILE
  static char BASED_CODE THIS_FILE[] = __FILE__;
  #endif
  //////////////////////////////////////////////////////////////////////////
  // CFileView
  IMPLEMENT_DYNCREATE(CFileView, CView)
  BEGIN_MESSAGE_MAP(CFileView, CView)
      //{{AFX_MSG_MAP(CFileView)
      ON_COMMAND(IDM_FILEWRITE, OnFilewrite)
      ON_COMMAND(IDM_FILEREAD, OnFileread)
      //}}AFX_MSG_MAP
      // Standard printing commands
       ON_COMMAND(ID_FILE_PRINT, CView::OnFilePrint)
           ON_COMMAND(ID_FILE_PRINT_PREVIEW,
                 CView::OnFilePrintPreview)
  END_MESSAGE_MAP()
  //////////////////////////////////////////////////////////////////////////
  // CFileView construction/destruction
  CFileView::CFileView()
  {
      // TODO: add construction code here
  }
  CFileView::~CFileView()
  {
  }
  //////////////////////////////////////////////////////////////////////////
  // CFileView drawing
  void CFileView::OnDraw(CDC* pDC)
  {
      CFileDoc* pDoc = GetDocument();
      // TODO: add draw code here
  }
  //////////////////////////////////////////////////////////////////////////
  // CFileView printing
  BOOL CFileView::OnPreparePrinting(CPrintInfo* pInfo)
```

```
{
    // default preparation
    return DoPreparePrinting(pInfo);
}
void CFileView::OnBeginPrinting(CDC* /*pDC*/, CPrintInfo* /*pInfo*/)
{
    // TODO: add extra initialization before printing
}
void CFileView::OnEndPrinting(CDC* /*pDC*/, CPrintInfo* /*pInfo*/)
{
    // TODO: add cleanup after printing
}
/////////////////////////////////////////////////////////////////////////
// CFileView diagnostics
#ifdef _DEBUG
void CFileView::AssertValid() const
{
    CView::AssertValid();
}
void CFileView::Dump(CDumpContext& dc) const
{
    CView::Dump(dc);
}
CFileDoc* CFileView::GetDocument() // non-debug version is inline
{
    ASSERT(m_pDocument->IsKindOf(RUNTIME_CLASS (CFileDoc)));
    return (CFileDoc*) m_pDocument;
}
#endif //_DEBUG
/////////////////////////////////////////////////////////////////////////
// CFileView message handlers
void CFileView::OnFilewrite()
{
    const MAX_LEN = 20;
    const MAX_ITEMS = 4;
    CString hello_string = "Hello, world.";
    TRY
    {
        CFile file("a:hello.txt", CFile::modeCreate | CFile::modeWrite);
        file.Write(hello_string, hello_string.GetLength());
        file.Close();
    }
```

continues

Listing 10.1. continued

```
CATCH(CFileException, e)
{
        switch(e->m_cause)
        {
            case CFileException::accessDenied:
                MessageBox("File access denied");
                break;
            case CFileException::badPath:
                MessageBox("Path is invalid");
                break;
            case CFileException::diskFull:
                MessageBox("Disk is full");
                break;
            case CFileException::fileNotFound:
                MessageBox("File could not be found");
                break;
            case CFileException::hardIO:
                MessageBox("Hardware error");
                break;
            case CFileException::lockViolation:
                MessageBox("Attempt to lock region already locked");
                break;
            case CFileException::sharingViolation:
                MessageBox("Sharing violation—load share.exe");
                break;
            case CFileException::tooManyOpenFiles:
                MessageBox("Exceeded allowed number of open files");
                break;
        }
    }
    AND_CATCH(CMemoryException, e)
    {
        #ifdef _DEBUG
            afxDump << "Memory could not be allocated " << e->m_cause << "\n";
        #endif
    }
    END_CATCH
    char output_string[MAX_ITEMS][MAX_LEN];
    strcpy(output_string[0], "This");
    strcpy(output_string[1], "is");
```

```
    strcpy(output_string[2], "a");
    strcpy(output_string[3], "test.");
    CFile random_file("data.dat", CFile::modeCreate |
    CFile::modeWrite);
    for (int loop_index = 0;loop_index < MAX_ITEMS;
        loop_index++)
    {
    random_file.Write(output_string[loop_index], MAX_LEN);
    }
    random_file.Close();
}
void CFileView::OnFileread()
{
    const MAX_LEN = 20;
    char data_string[MAX_LEN];
    CFile file("hello.txt", CFile::modeRead);
    UINT number_read = file.Read(data_string, MAX_LEN);
    CClientDC dc(this);
    dc.TextOut(0, 0, data_string, number_read);
    char input_string[MAX_LEN];
    CFile random_file("data.dat", CFile::modeRead);
    random_file.Seek(MAX_LEN, CFile::begin);
    number_read = random_file.Read(input_string, 2);
    dc.TextOut(0, 0, input_string, number_read);
    random_file.Close();
}
```

That's all for exception handling; next, you learn about debugging.

Debugging

The types of errors you explore next—program logic errors—are often not as easy to handle as trappable exceptions. Logic errors (bugs) do not show up when you build the .exe file, but they do appear when your program produces unexpected results. Fortunately, Visual C++ provides you with some good tools for debugging.

Testing Programs

When programs run, they usually operate on ranges of data; for example, a program may read the value of an integer from the user, and that value can range from -32,768 to 32,767 (if the value couldn't vary, there would be no point in reading it in). The limits of that value, -32,768 and 32,767, are called the value's *bounds*. When you are trying to check your programs for potential problems, you must cover the whole range of such values. That doesn't normally mean checking every value between -32,768 and 32,767, but it does mean checking values at the bounds of this range, as well as checking some mid-range values and any other values that are likely to give you problems.

For example, this value may represent the number of students in a class. Suppose that you have summed all their test scores and now want to divide by it to find the class average. Fifteen or twenty students may be no problem, but what if the user enters a value of zero? Even though zero is in the allowed range for unsigned integers, dividing by it will result in a problem. Or what if you store the students' test scores in another unsigned integer and find that as the number of students increases, the division does not give you the accuracy you want? Checking your program's bounding values like this is vitally important; in general, every crucial variable has bounds, and you should check all combinations of these values when you run your program to see how they interact (this is particularly important when it comes to array indices).

Of course, you should check mid-range values as well. Some combinations of such values may give you unexpected errors. The longer you test your program under usual and unusual operating circumstances, the more confidence you will have in it. As programs get more complex, the testing period normally gets longer and longer, which is why major software companies often send out hundreds of preliminary versions of their software (called *beta* versions) for testing by programmers (the final software package is usually the *gamma* version).

In addition, you should attempt to duplicate every run-time problem that may occur to see how your program will react. File operations are great at generating such errors—for example, what if the disk is full and you try to write to it? What if the specified input file doesn't exist? What if the specified file to write is already read-only? What happens if the disk has been removed? What if the user asks you to write record -15 in a file? Generating every conceivable set of problematic circumstances, of course, is difficult; but the closer you come, the more polished your application will be.

Debugging at Work

When you build programs using the Debug build option (see figure 10.6), you can use the debugging tools in Visual C++'s Debug menu, as shown in figure 10.8.

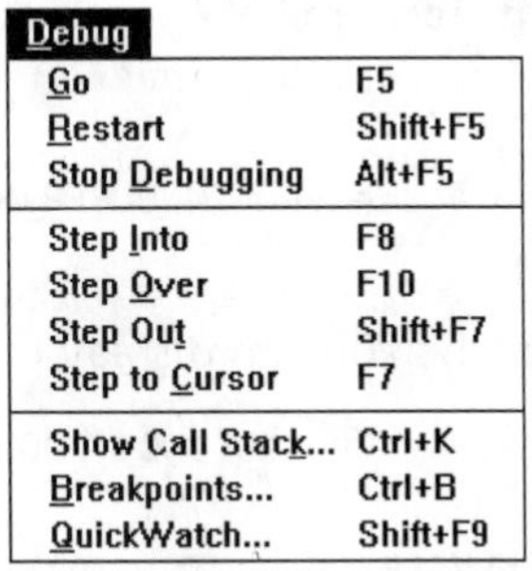

Debug	
Go	F5
Restart	Shift+F5
Stop Debugging	Alt+F5
Step Into	F8
Step Over	F10
Step Out	Shift+F7
Step to Cursor	F7
Show Call Stack...	Ctrl+K
Breakpoints...	Ctrl+B
QuickWatch...	Shift+F9

Figure 10.8. Visual C++'s Debug menu.

You can put this to work with an example. Suppose that you want to develop the program to average students' scores. As a test, you might simply load each element of the test score array with a value of 50, giving an average score of 50. This example uses the OnDraw() function so the result of the program is displayed as soon as the program runs, as the following segment shows:

```
void CDbugView::OnDraw(CDC* pDC)
{
    const NUMBER_STUDENTS = 5;
    int scores[NUMBER_STUDENTS];
    scores[0] = 50;
    scores[1] = 50;
    scores[2] = 50;
    scores[3] = 50;
    scores[4] = 50;
        :
```

Then, you find the average score this way:

```
void CDbugView::OnDraw(CDC* pDC)
{
    const NUMBER_STUDENTS = 5;
    int scores[NUMBER_STUDENTS];
    scores[0] = 50;
    scores[1] = 50;
    scores[2] = 50;
    scores[3] = 50;
    scores[4] = 50;
    int sum;
    for(int loop_index = 1; loop_index < NUMBER_STUDENTS; loop_index++){
    sum += scores[loop_index];
    }
    int average = sum / NUMBER_STUDENTS;
        :
```

Finally, you can display the following results:

```
void CDbugView::OnDraw(CDC* pDC)
{
    const NUMBER_STUDENTS = 5;
    int scores[NUMBER_STUDENTS];
    scores[0] = 50;
    scores[1] = 50;
    scores[2] = 50;
    scores[3] = 50;
    scores[4] = 50;
    int sum;
    for(int loop_index = 1; loop_index < NUMBER_STUDENTS; loop_index++){
    sum += scores[loop_index];
    }
    int average = sum / NUMBER_STUDENTS;
    char out_string[30];
    wsprintf(out_string, "The average is: %d", average);
    pDC->TextOut(0, 0, out_string, strlen(out_string));
}
```

Here, you need to print out the average as an integer because not everyone will have floating-point support loaded in Visual C++. You might place this code into the view object of an SDI project named dbug.mak. When you run the program, however, you get the result shown in figure 10.9—The average is 3044—when you expected a value of 50. Clearly, there's a problem, and it is time to debug.

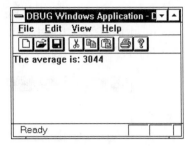

Figure 10.9. Debugging the project—first try.

Breakpoints

You might start with a breakpoint. Setting a *breakpoint* at a particular line in the code halts program execution at that point. For example, you might want to check whether the program is having difficulty printing the value correctly. To test this, you can set a breakpoint at the end of your program, as follows:

```
void CDbugView::OnDraw(CDC* pDC)
{
    const NUMBER_STUDENTS = 5;
    int scores[NUMBER_STUDENTS];
        :
        :
    int average = sum / NUMBER_STUDENTS;
    char out_string[30];
    wsprintf(out_string, "The average is: %d", average);
    pDC->TextOut(0, 0, out_string, strlen(out_string));
}
```

Then when you get to that location, you can check the value in the variable average. If the value is 50, you know that the program is having trouble printing it out.

To set a breakpoint here, move the insertion point to this line and press F9, highlighting that line as shown in figure 10.10. Now program execution will halt here automatically.

If you select the Breakpoints... item in the Debug menu, the Breakpoint dialog box opens, as shown in figure 10.11; this dialog box provides an

459

easy way of handling and locating your breakpoints, line by line. In addition, the F9 key toggles breakpoints. To turn the breakpoint off, place the insertion point there and press F9 again.

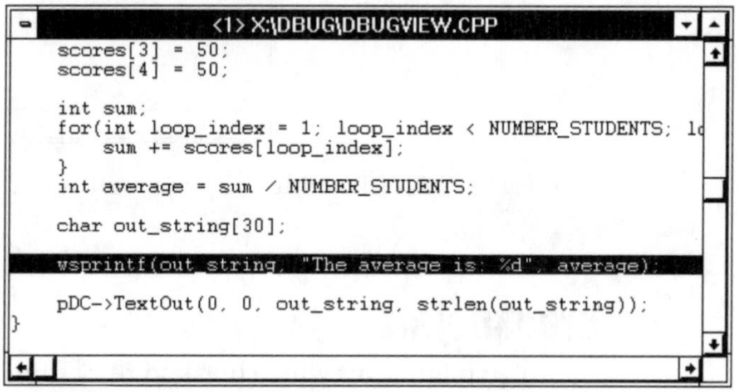

Figure 10.10. Setting a breakpoint.

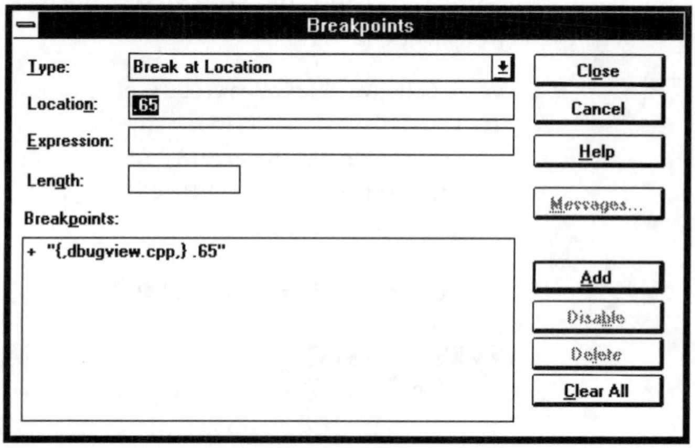

Figure 10.11. The Breakpoint dialog box.

If you execute the program by using the Execute line in the Project menu, the breakpoint is ignored. To debug the program, you must use the Go item in the Debug menu to start execution (see figure 10.8). When you do, the program is run up to (but not including) the code in the breakpoint line.

Do that now. The program is now halted at this point, as follows:

```
void CDbugView::OnDraw(CDC* pDC)
{
    const NUMBER_STUDENTS = 5;
    int scores[NUMBER_STUDENTS];
        :
        :
    int average = sum / NUMBER_STUDENTS;
    char out_string[30];
    wsprintf(out_string, "The average is: %d", average);
    pDC->TextOut(0, 0, out_string, strlen(out_string));
}
```

The value in average should equal 50. To check it, place the insertion point on the word *average* and press Shift-F9 or select the QuickWatch item in the Debug menu. This opens the QuickWatch window, as shown in figure 10.12. This window allows you to examine variables as you debug; here you see that the value in average is indeed 3044, which means that you have a math error, not a printing error.

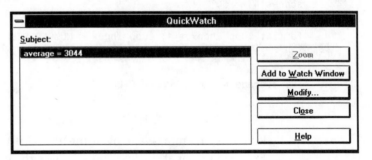

Figure 10.12. The QuickWatch window.

Notice the Modify... button in the QuickWatch window; this allows you to modify the value of a variable as your program is running. If you click it, the Modify Variable dialog box opens, as shown in figure 10.13. You can use this box to change the value of the average if you want to—even while the program is running.

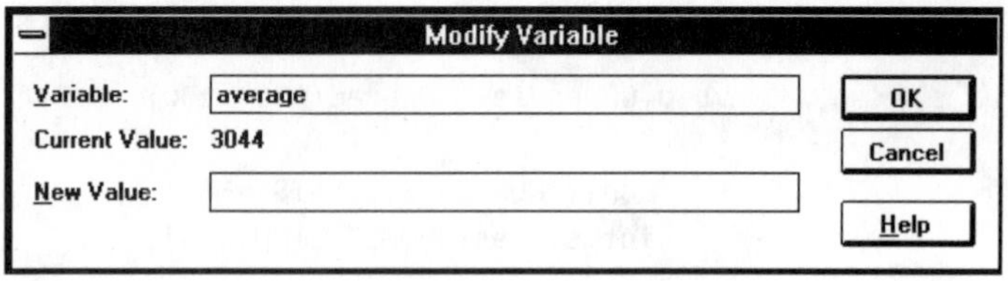

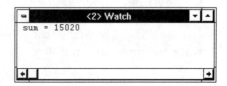

Figure 10.13. The Modify Variable box.

End the program now by selecting the Stop Debugging item in the Debug menu. You need to set the breakpoint earlier to catch the bug; for example, you might set the breakpoint when you build up the sum of all the test scores, as follows:

```
void CDbugView::OnDraw(CDC* pDC)
{
    const NUMBER_STUDENTS = 5;
    int scores[NUMBER_STUDENTS];
    scores[0] = 50;
        :
    scores[4] = 50;
    int sum;
    for(int loop_index = 1; loop_index < NUMBER_STUDENTS; loop_index++){
    sum += scores[loop_index];
    }
    int average = sum / NUMBER_STUDENTS;
        :
}
```

Run the program again by using the Go item in the Debug menu. Execution stops at the line you set. Place the insertion point on the sum variable and press Shift-F9 to open the QuickWatch window; next, click the button marked Add to Watch Window, adding sum to the Watch window, as shown in figure 10.14.

<2> Watch

sum = 15020

Figure 10.14. The Watch window.

Loading variables this way into the watch window gives you a way of keeping continual track of their values. As you move through a program, you are able to watch how selected variables change.

Here, however, you see that the value in sum is 15020 when it should be 0 (the program has not executed the line sum += scores[loop_index] even once at this point). The problem is clear—sum was never initialized to 0. Stop the program and fix that problem like in the following way:

```
void CDbugView::OnDraw(CDC* pDC)
{
    const NUMBER_STUDENTS = 5;
    int scores[NUMBER_STUDENTS];
    scores[0] = 50;
        :
    scores[4] = 50;
    int sum = 0;
    for(int loop_index = 1; loop_index < NUMBER_STUDENTS; loop_index++){
    sum += scores[loop_index];
    }
    int average = sum / NUMBER_STUDENTS;
        :
}
```

Start the program again; execution continues until it reaches the breakpoint. Now you see that sum is equal to 0 in the Watch window, as shown in figure 10.15.

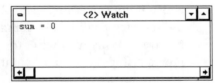

Figure 10.15. Watch window—second try.

Single Stepping

At this point, you can execute the program line by line. You can use the debug Step commands several ways:

Step Command	Shortcut	Means
Step Into	F8	Step into function
Step Over	F10	Step over function
Step Out	Shift-F7	Step to end of function
Step to Cursor	F7	Step to insertion point

Each of these commands causes program execution to progress by one line; if you use Step Into (by pressing F8), the program steps through each line of code, including function calls. That can be awkward if you come to a line in the following way:

```
void CDbugView::OnDraw(CDC* pDC)
{
    const NUMBER_STUDENTS = 5;
    int scores[NUMBER_STUDENTS];
        :
        :
    int average = sum / NUMBER_STUDENTS;
    char out_string[30];
    wsprintf(out_string, "The average is: %d", average);
    pDC->TextOut(0, 0, out_string, strlen(out_string));
}
```

Here Step Into takes you through the code of the TextOut() function, which is not something that will prove very useful. Instead, you should use the Step Over (F10) command here to avoid stepping into called functions. When you select the Go command in the Debug menu, the program stops at the breakpoint, as follows:

```
void CDbugView::OnDraw(CDC* pDC)
{
    const NUMBER_STUDENTS = 5;
    int scores[NUMBER_STUDENTS];
    scores[0] = 50;
        :
    scores[4] = 50;
    int sum = 0;
```

```
    for(int loop_index = 1; loop_index < NUMBER_STUDENTS; loop_index++){
    sum += scores[loop_index];
    }
    int average = sum / NUMBER_STUDENTS;
        :
}
```

Continue stepping through the loop with the Step Over (F10) command. If you get tired of following the loop interactions, you can place the insertion point in the line following the loop and use the Step to Cursor command (F7) to get to this point, as follows:

```
void CDbugView::OnDraw(CDC* pDC)
{
    const NUMBER_STUDENTS = 5;
    int scores[NUMBER_STUDENTS];
    scores[0] = 50;
        :
    scores[4] = 50;
    int sum = 0;
    for(int loop_index = 1; loop_index < NUMBER_STUDENTS; loop_index++){
    sum += scores[loop_index];
    }
    int average = sum / NUMBER_STUDENTS;
        :
}
```

At this point, the program has completed the loop and should have added 50 five times to give a value of 250 in sum. As you can see in the Watch window in figure 10.16, however, sum holds only 200.

Figure 10.16. Watch window—third try.

This is a problem, but the solution is easy to find. As you can see by checking the previous code, the variable loop_index starts off with a value of 1, not 0.

```
for(int loop_index = 1; loop_index < NUMBER_STUDENTS; loop_index++){
sum += scores[loop_index];
}
```

This is a common C++ problem. Fix that now and rerun the new program.

```
void CDbugView::OnDraw(CDC* pDC)
{
    const NUMBER_STUDENTS = 5;
    int scores[NUMBER_STUDENTS];
    scores[0] = 50;
         :
    scores[4] = 50;
    int sum = 0;
    for(int loop_index = 0; loop_index < NUMBER_STUDENTS; loop_index++){
    sum += scores[loop_index];
    }
    int average = sum / NUMBER_STUDENTS;
    char out_string[30];
    wsprintf(out_string, "The average is: %d", average);
    pDC->TextOut(0, 0, out_string, strlen(out_string));
}
```

This time you get the desired result—The average is: 50—as shown in figure 10.17. That's the correct answer: you have debugged your program. The fixed code appears in listing 10.2—dbugview.h—and listing 10.3—dbugview.cpp.

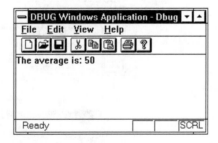

Figure 10.17. The debugged program at work.

Listing 10.2. Dbugview.H Debugged

```cpp
// dbugview.h : interface of the CDbugView class
//
/////////////////////////////////////////////////////////
///////////////////
class CDbugView : public CView
{
protected: // create from serialization only
    CDbugView();
    DECLARE_DYNCREATE(CDbugView)
// Attributes
public:
    CDbugDoc* GetDocument();
// Operations
public:
// Implementation
public:
    virtual ~CDbugView();
    virtual void OnDraw(CDC* pDC);   // overridden to draw this view
#ifdef _DEBUG
    virtual void AssertValid() const;
    virtual void Dump(CDumpContext& dc) const;
#endif
    // Printing support
protected:
    virtual BOOL OnPreparePrinting(CPrintInfo* pInfo);
    virtual void OnBeginPrinting(CDC* pDC, CPrintInfo* pInfo);
    virtual void OnEndPrinting(CDC* pDC, CPrintInfo* pInfo);
// Generated message map functions
protected:
    //{{AFX_MSG(CDbugView)
        // NOTE - the ClassWizard will add and remove  member functions here.
        // DO NOT EDIT what you see in these blocks of generated code
!
    //}}AFX_MSG
    DECLARE_MESSAGE_MAP()
};
#ifndef _DEBUG     // debug version in dbugview.cpp
inline CDbugDoc* CDbugView::GetDocument()
    { return (CDbugDoc*) m_pDocument; }
#endif
```

Listing 10.3. Dbugview.Cpp Debugged

```cpp
////////////////////////////////////////////////////////////////////////
// dbugview.cpp : implementation of the CDbugView class
//
#include "stdafx.h"
#include "dbug.h"
#include <stdio.h>
#include "dbugdoc.h"
#include "dbugview.h"
#ifdef _DEBUG
#undef THIS_FILE
static char BASED_CODE THIS_FILE[] = __FILE__;
#endif
////////////////////////////////////////////////////////////////////////
// CDbugView
IMPLEMENT_DYNCREATE(CDbugView, CView)
BEGIN_MESSAGE_MAP(CDbugView, CView)
    //{{AFX_MSG_MAP(CDbugView)
        // NOTE - the ClassWizard will add and remove mapping macros here.
        // DO NOT EDIT what you  see in these blocks of generated code !
    //}}AFX_MSG_MAP
    // Standard printing commands
    ON_COMMAND(ID_FILE_PRINT, CView::OnFilePrint)
        ON_COMMAND(ID_FILE_PRINT_PREVIEW, CView::OnFilePrintPreview)
END_MESSAGE_MAP()
////////////////////////////////////////////////////////////////////////
// CDbugView construction/destruction
CDbugView::CDbugView()
{
    // TODO: add construction code here
}
CDbugView::~CDbugView()
{
}
////////////////////////////////////////////////////////////////////////
// CDbugView drawing
void CDbugView::OnDraw(CDC* pDC)
{
    const NUMBER_STUDENTS = 5;
    int scores[NUMBER_STUDENTS];
    scores[0] = 50;
    scores[1] = 50;
```

```
        scores[2] = 50;
        scores[3] = 50;
        scores[4] = 50;
        int sum = 0;
        for(int loop_index = 0; loop_index < NUMBER_STUDENTS; loop_index++){
            sum += scores[loop_index];
        }
        int average = sum / NUMBER_STUDENTS;
        char out_string[30];
        wsprintf(out_string, "The average is: %d", average);
        pDC->TextOut(0, 0, out_string, strlen(out_string));
}
/////////////////////////////////////////////////////////////////////////
// CDbugView printing
BOOL CDbugView::OnPreparePrinting(CPrintInfo* pInfo)
{
        // default preparation
        return DoPreparePrinting(pInfo);
}
void CDbugView::OnBeginPrinting(CDC* /*pDC*/, CPrintInfo* /*pInfo*/)
{
        // TODO: add extra initialization before printing
}
void CDbugView::OnEndPrinting(CDC* /*pDC*/, CPrintInfo* /*pInfo*/)
{
        // TODO: add cleanup after printing
}
/////////////////////////////////////////////////////////////////////////
// CDbugView diagnostics
#ifdef _DEBUG
void CDbugView::AssertValid() const
{
        CView::AssertValid();
}
void CDbugView::Dump(CDumpContext& dc) const
{
        CView::Dump(dc);
}
CDbugDoc* CDbugView::GetDocument() // non-debug version is inline
```

continues

469

Listing 10.3. continued

```
{
    ASSERT(m_pDocument->IsKindOf(RUNTIME_CLASS(CDbugDoc)));
    return (CDbugDoc*) m_pDocument;
}
#endif //_DEBUG
/////////////////////////////////////////////////////////////////////////////
// CDbugView message handlers
```

As you can see, Visual C++ has some powerful tools available for debugging. You have been able to set breakpoints, halting the program's execution at selected points. Additionally, you have examined variables in the QuickWatch window, tracked them in the Watch window itself, and single-stepped through your code. As you can imagine, these debugging features help program development significantly.

That Is It

That concludes your investigation of debugging and exception handling—and your exploration of Visual C++. You have come far in this book—from seeing the rudiments of C++ to seeing it in action, from understanding what a class is to learning how to override functions, from examining the parts of a window to creating them yourself.

You have seen dialog boxes, menus, buttons, text boxes, graphics functions, insertion point handling, file handling, mouse handling, and much more. You also have seen how to support multiple documents and multiple views—and now you even know how to debug your programs. As you now know, Visual C++ provides you with a package of exceptional power for Windows programming. All you have to do now is put it to work for yourself.

Windows Program Design

This appendix is all about the conventions to which other Windows programmers will expect your programs to adhere. If you are going to develop products for sale or distribution on a large scale, this appendix is for you. Windows programs are different from DOS programs in many ways, and one of the primary differences is consistency—that is, supporting a common user interface. You will learn more about that in this appendix.

Windows Programming Philosophy

If you are a developer working in Windows, you should first of all be a Windows user as well as a Windows application user. The people who use your program will have a set of standard expectations that they expect you to fulfill. This is part of the attraction of Windows; if you know how to use a particular type of application (for example, a word processor), you can often use other ones without additional instruction. In fact, Windows developers should try to make their programs as intuitive as possible so that almost no instruction is required. Ideally, a simple set of Windows skills (such as clicking the mouse buttons, selecting text, and using menus) should be enough to let the user use your program, although that is not usually possible with larger, specialized applications.

In addition, your program should strive to be robust—as in the opposite of fragile—in the sense that users feel they have a useful tool that will perform in expected ways and not crash when they try something new. To be robust means that a program can operate under a wide variety of conditions and inputs and not fail; a robust program is one that the user comes to regard as trustworthy. This is important: If some kind of trappable error occurs, your program should handle it with recovery code of some sort, not simply halt. Minimize or eliminate any commonly encountered conditions that your application cannot handle.

Realize that the user needs to be the one controlling the program and the program flow in Windows, not the other way around. A Windows developer should try to give the user as much utility as possible and make that utility present in an easy-to-understand way. Windows customarily uses graphical objects to provide a set of tools for the user, and you should make as many of these tools available at once as possible (that is, give users as many options as possible). Don't overwhelm users, however; if your window is becoming crowded with buttons, put some options into menus (you should continually display only those options that will be in continual use).

Also, a Windows program should provide feedback to users about what is going on when they use the options that are available. For example, do not let your program freeze when undertaking a long operation—at least switch the mouse cursor to the hourglass symbol or use a gauge control to show the status of the operation.

A Windows program operates in an environment where other programs are operating too, so it should not hog resources. One other point here is that no matter how minimal your program, it should meet at least one Windows expectation: Provide the user with a way to quit. That is usually done with the File menu's Exit item (shortcut key Ctrl-X).

Now you can examine the accepted mouse and keyboard Windows standards.

Mouse Actions

The mouse actions that have become standard are probably already familiar to you—clicking, double-clicking, and so on. Clicking is usually done with the left mouse button (left-handed users can use the Windows control panel to switch the buttons if they wish). As yet, there is no standard use for the right mouse button. In addition to the single click (which makes a selection or activates a control) and double-click (which opens applications and selections), you can also use the mouse with the Shift and Ctrl keys. These two operations are primarily used in making selections, and the way they work—along with the other mouse operations—is presented in table A.1.

Table A.1. Windows Mouse Conventions

Action	Mode	Means
Click	Control:	Activates
	Selection:	Selects
	Text:	Positions insertion point
Ctrl-click	Selection:	Toggles current selection only
Double-click	Control:	Activates
	Selection:	Opens
Drag	Control:	Moves control if draggable
	Selection:	Encloses area for selection
	Navigation:	Moves selection
Shift-click	Selection:	Extends selection

Keyboard Actions

Many standard operations for the keyboard are used in Windows because all mouse actions are supposed to be possible with the keyboard alone (a fact you should always keep in mind). If users type a simple letter or number, they are supplying your program with data input. On the other hand, Ctrl-letter key combinations are usually reserved for (menu) short-cut commands, and Alt-letter combinations are reserved for (menu and button) access key commands. A number of the function keys, F1 through F12, have pre-defined meanings (for example, F1 displays Help), and you'll find them—along with other standard keyboard operations—in table A.2. Many of these you will probably be familiar with—such as using the Tab key to move from control to control in a dialog box (and Shift-Tab to go backwards), but some of the keys may take you by surprise. For example, Alt-F4 is supposed to close the application, while Alt-F6 moves to an MDI window's next open document.

Table A.2. Windows Keyboard Conventions

Key	Mode	Means
Alt		Used with letters to create access keys
Alt-Esc		Switches to next application window in Windows
Alt-F4		Closes application
Alt-F6	MDI:	Moves to next open window
Alt-Shift-Esc		Switches to previous application window in Windows
Alt-Shift-F6	MDI:	Moves backwards to next open window
Alt-Shift-Tab		Reverses order of Alt-Tab
Alt-Tab		Shows application stack, activates top application
Backspace	Selection:	Deletes entire selection
	Text:	Deletes character to the left
Ctrl		Used with letters to create shortcut keys
Ctrl-B	Text:	Bold
Ctrl-D	Text:	Double underline
Ctrl-Down	Text:	Next paragraph

Key	Mode	Means
Ctrl-End	Navigation:	Moves to bottom right of document
Ctrl-Esc		Shows all running applications, lets you choose
Ctrl-F4		Closes window
Ctrl-F6	MDI:	Moves top document to bottom of stack
Ctrl-Home	Navigation:	Moves to top left of document
Ctrl-I	Text:	Italic
Ctrl-PgUp	Navigation:	Moves to top of window
Ctrl-PgDown	Navigation:	Moves to bottom of window
Ctrl-Shift-F6	MDI:	Reverses operation of Ctrl-F6
Ctrl-Space	Text:	Stops character formatting
Ctrl-U	Text:	Underline
Ctrl-Up	Text:	Previous paragraph
Ctrl-W	Text:	Word-by-word underline
Ctrl-X		Quits an application
Del	Selection:	Deletes entire selection
	Text:	Deletes character to the right
Down arrow	Controls:	Next choice
	Text:	Down one line
End	Navigation:	Moves to rightmost position of row
Enter	Controls:	Presses selected button
Esc	Dialogs:	Closes dialog
	Modes:	Exits current mode
	Selection:	Cancels current selection

continues

Table A.2. continued

Key	Mode	Means
F1		Help
F6		Moves clockwise to next pane
F8	Mode:	Toggles extend mode
F10	Mode:	Toggles menu bar
Home	Navigation:	Moves to leftmost position of row
Insert	Mode:	Toggles between overstrike and insert
Left arrow	Text:	One position to the left
	Controls:	Next choice to left
PgDown	Navigation:	Next screenful of data
PgUp	Navigation:	Previous screenful of data
Right arrow	Text:	One position to the right
	Controls:	Next choice to right
Scroll Lock	Navigation:	Scrolls data, does not move cursor
Shift		Changes function keys and Tab to opposite
Shift-F6		Moves counter-clockwise to next MDI pane
Shift-Tab		Reverses operation of Tab
Space	Controls:	Clicks buttons with focus
Tab	Dialogs:	Next field or control
	Text:	Inserts a tab
Up arrow	Controls:	Previous choice
	Text:	Up one line

Standard menus also include some generally accepted entries. The next section takes a look at the Edit, File, and Help menus. In general, the accepted order of menu names in the menu bar is as follows: File, Edit, View, Tools, Window, and Help (Help is always last).

The Edit Menu

The Edit menu—if present—usually includes the items in the following list (note that these items are shown in the order in which they usually appear in an Edit menu):

Menu Item	Description
Undo	Undoes the last operation
Cut	Cuts selected text
Copy	Copies selected text (usually to clipboard)
Paste	Pastes (usually from clipboard) to selection
Paste Link	Pastes a DDE link
Find...	Finds text (opens Find dialog box)
Replace...	Replaces text (opens Replace dialog box)

NOTE

Users find it helpful if you use separator bars to divide menu items into logical groups.

The File Menu

The File menu usually has the following standard entries (in the order shown here):

Menu Item	Description
New	Creates a new document
Open...	Opens a document (displays Open dialog box)
Save	Saves a document
Save As...	Saves a document (opens a dialog box allowing path, file type, etc.)
Print...	Prints a document (displays Print dialog box)
Exit	Exits the application (almost always present)

The Help Menu

The Help menu usually has the following standard items (in the order shown):

Menu Item	Description
Contents	Displays list of help topics available
Search	Searches for a help topic
Index	Displays an index of help topics
About	Provides information about application

For the interested developer: More Windows standards exist than the ones covered here. In fact, entire books on this topic alone are available. If you are unsure about a Windows standard, make sure you do the necessary research before releasing your product.

B

About the Diskette

The diskette contains programs from the Visual C++ book. To install those projects on your hard disk, use the installa.bat or the installb.bat program on the diskette. Installa.bat will install the programs from your A: drive, and installb.bat will install the programs from your B: drive. It is important that these programs be installed in the directory c:\vcbook—for example, the .mak project files refer to the .cpp, .h, .def, and .rc files in that directory. The following projects are on the diskette.

Project	How To Use It
calc.mak	A pop-up calculator. Select the Calculator... item in the File menu. Place an integer in the top text box, another in the next lower text box, and click the = button to see the sum of the two appear in the lowest text box.
caret.mak	A character and mouse input example. Type characters and see them appear at the caret; click a new location to move the caret and type again to see the new text appear there.

continues

Project	How To Use It
db.mak	A listbox example. In this database program, type an item with at least one space in it, such as `Apples 25 in stock`. Select Add Item in the Database to add this to the database. Type another item, such as `Oranges 25 in stock` and add it to the database the same way. Now select Find Item in the database to open the database dialog box. The listbox will have two items: `Apples` and `Oranges`; select the record you want to look up—double-click it or highlight it and click OK—to see that record retrieved in the main window.
editor.mak	A rudimentary multi-window editor showing how to use multiple documents and views. Type in the window that appears—including the `<Enter>` key. To open another document, use New. To open another view on the same document, select New Window in the Window menu. As you type in one view, characters will appear in all of the views connected to that document. You can also save, retrieve, and print text, but note that in this example program, only lines that were followed by the `<Enter>` key are saved in a file or printed—for example, typing `<Enter>` stores the current line in the document—and this program uses its own exclusive file format.
file.mak	A file writing and reading example. Select Write File in the File menu to write the file hello.txt with the text `Hello, world.` in it. To read the file back in and display its contents, select the Read File menu item.
hello.mak	An example showing how to display the text `Hello, world.` in a window.
notepad.mak	A pop-up notepad example showing how to use text boxes. Select the Notepad... item in the Notepad menu, opening that dialog box. Click the text box to give it the focus and type text in it. You can also mark text with the mouse, and use the Cut and Paste buttons.

Project	How To Use It
paint.mak	A graphics example—this is a mouse-driven paint program. Select the drawing tool you want from the Tools menu: Point, Draw, Line, Rectangle, Ellipse, or Fill. Use the mouse to draw with these tools.
spread.mak	A grid control spreadsheet example—make sure the grid control has been loaded into Visual C++ before using this project. Select Spreadsheet in the Spreadsheet menu. Type integers in the box labeled Data:. Next, click on a cell in the spreadsheet's A column, placing the integer in that cell. The spreadsheet is written to add the values in cells A1 to A4 and place the result in cell A5.

Index

Symbols

& (shortcut keys), 161
+ operator, 111
-> arrow operator, 59
. dot operator, 12
// comments symbol, 12
::. operator, 22
<< left-shift operator, 11
<< operator
 versus printf ( ), 12
>> right-shift operator, 12
?: operator, 12
[ ] index operator, 57
\t (tab code), 162

~ tildes, 30
0 return values (function), 22
386-enhanced mode, 3

A

accelerator keys
 adding to programs, 162
 connecting to menu, 163-165
 key combination options, 162
 naming, precautions, 162
 saving, 165
accelerator resource
 icon, 163
accelerator table, 163
Accelerator Table Editor, 163
active windows, 100
Add Name (Phonbook menu) command, 178
AddHead (CObList class) member function, 386, 389
adding
 buttons, dialog box, 209
 cell values, spreadsheets, 291-292

data members to
classes, 218
data strings to list
boxes, 271
member functions, 212
menu items,
177-202, 267
window, 293
scroll bars, MDI child
windows, 407-415
splitter windows, editor
application, 419, 422
AddTail (CObList class)
member function, 386
advancing, carets, 127-128,
141-142
afxDump variable, sending
numbers to debug
window, 446
allocating memory with
constructors, 29-34
Alt-letter combinations,
Windows programming
standards, 474
ampersand (&), creating
shortcut keys, 161
AND_CATCH( )
macro, 449
ANSI_FIXED_FONT stock
objects, 322
ANSI_VAR_FONT stock
objects, 322
App Studio, 53
App Studio (Tools menu)
command, 152
App Studio Type box, 152
App Wizard, 53
creating classes, 54
file creation, 54-56

Options dialog box, 54
phonebooks, 179
appending, 178-192
AppendMenu ( ) function,
180-182
parameters, 181-182
values
MF_CHECKED, 181
MF_DISABLED, 181
MF_ENABLED, 181
MF_GRAYED, 181
MF_MENUBARBREAK,
181
MF_MENUBREAK, 182
MF_OWNERDRAW,
182
MF_POPUP, 182
MF_SEPARATOR, 182
MF_STRING, 182
MF_UNCHECKED, 182
Applicable Section of
Dbdoc.H, listing 6.3,
282-283
applications
designing, keyboard
considerations, 101
exiting, 4
see also programs
AppWizard, 101
Multiple Document
Interface check box, 101
AppWizard (Project menu)
command, 53
Archive exceptions,
exception class, 439
arrays
adding indexes, 186-187
creating, 186
in stacks, 30-31

arrow operator (->), 59
AssertValid (CObject class)
member function, 383
atof( ) function, 233

B

backround color, restoring,
187-188
base classes, 34
within derived classes, 35
beta version software, 456
BLACK_BRUSH stock
object, 322
BN_CLICKED edit notifica-
tion message, 217
BN_DOUBLECLICKED edit
notification message, 217
Boolean flags, setting, 308
bounding color, 331
bounds, 456
boxes
combo, 283-284
dialog, 203-259
message, 204-207
Breakpoint dialog box, 460
breakpoints, 459-463
Breakpoints... item (Debug
menu), 459
Browse menu, Class
Wizard command, 108
browsing, 108
brush patterns,
creating, 329
brushes,
designing, paint
program, 322
stock see stock objects

Build (Project menu)
  command, 9
build modes
  checking, _DEBUG
    variable, 448
  debug, 447
  release, 447
buttons, 203
  adding to dialog box, 209
  cancel, 206
  clicking, from code, 276
  controls, 204

C

C, C++ advantages over,
  9-14
C++
  // comments symbol, 12
  advantages over C, 9-14
  base classes, 34
  class inheritance, 34-38
  classes, 14-18
    overloading functions,
      41-45
    overriding functions,
      38-40
  data type checking, 41
  delete keyword, 31
  derived classes, 34
  functions
    need of prototypes, 15
    overloading, 41-45
    overriding, 38-40
  malloc ( ), 30
  modularity, 10
  new keyword, 30
  objects, 13-18

initializing, 29-34
one-line comments, //
  symbol, 12
operator overloading, 12
  restrictions, 12
operators, 11-12
predefined streams, 11-13
  applying, 11
  cin, 12
  cout, 11-12
  printing, 41-42
  sample programs, 13
calc.mak program (sup-
  plied with book), 479
Calc.rc, listing 5.7,
  238-243
Calcdlg.cpp, listing 5.6,
  237-238
calculator example,
  229-243
Calcview.cpp, listing 5.5,
  234-237
cancel buttons, 206
caption bar, highlighted,
  100
Caption box, 162
caption text, highlighted,
  100
~CArchive (CArchive class)
  member function, 388
CArchive (CArchive class)
  member function, 388
CArchive class, 387
  ~CArchive member
    function, 388
  CArchive member
    function, 388
  Close member
    function, 388

Flush member
  function, 388
GetFile member
  function, 388
IsLoading member
  function, 388
IsStoring member
  function, 388
operator >> member
  function, 388
operator<< member
  function, 388
Read member
  function, 388
ReadObject member
  function, 388
Write member
  function, 388
WriteObject member
  function, 388
CArchiveException
  exception class, 439
    possible return values,
      439-440
caret.mak programs, 479
carets, 100
  adding, 123
    adding to view
      class, 124
    adding to windows,
      122-134
    creating, 126
  advancing, 123, 127-128,
    141-142
  displaying, 126-127,
    140-141
  functions, 123
  hiding, 128-129, 140-141

moving precautions, 141
setting to mouse
location, 140
CASE, 53
CATCH macro, 437-439
CB_ADDSTRING combo
box control message, 284
CB_DELETESTRINGcombo
box control message, 284
CB_DIR combo box
control message, 284
CB_FINDSTRING combo
box control message, 284
CB_GETCOUNT combo
box control message, 284
CB_GETCURSEL combo
box control message, 284
CB_GETEDITSEL combo
box control message, 284
CB_GETITEMDATA combo
box control message, 284
CB_GETLBTEXT combo
box control message, 284
CB_GETLBTEXTLEN
combo box control
message, 284
CB_INSERTSTRING combo
box control message, 284
CB_LIMITTEXT combo
box control message, 284
CB_RESETCONTENT
combo box control
message, 284
CB_SELECTSTRING combo
box control message, 284
CB_SETCURSEL combo
box control message, 284
CB_SETEDITSEL combo
box control message, 284

CB_SETITEMDATA combo
box control message, 284
CB_SHOWDROPDOWN
combo box control
message, 284
CBN_DBLCLK combo box
message, 218, 283
CBN_DROPDOWN combo
box message, 218, 283
CBN_EDITCHANGE
combo box message,
218, 283
CBN_EDITUPDATE combo
box message, 218, 283
CBN_ERRSPACE combo
box message, 218, 283
CBN_KILLFOCUS combo
box message, 218, 283
CBN_SELCHANGE combo
box message, 218, 283
CBN_SETFOCUS combo
box message, 218, 283
CBrush member functions
CreatHatchBrush( ), 328
CreatSolidBrush( ), 328
CClientDC class, device
context objects, 112
CDbDoc class
implementation, 379
interface, 282
CDbView class
interface, 278
CDC class functions, 58-59
CDC class objects, 58
CEditorDoc class
implementation, 424-426
interface, 423
CEditorDoc construction/
destruction, 404

CEditorView class
interface, 426-427
cells (spreadsheet)
labeling, 288
values, adding, 291-292
~CFile (CFile class)
member function, 357
CFile (CFile class) member
function, 356-357
CFile class, 356-362
~CFile member
function, 357
CFile member function,
356-357
Close member
function, 356
Duplicate member
function, 356
Flush member
function, 357
GetPosition member
function, 357
GetStatus member
function, 357
LockRange member
function, 357
member functions, 356
Open member
function, 357
options, 359
Read member function,
357, 361
Remove member
function, 357
Rename member
function, 357
Seek member
function, 357

SeekToBegin member function, 357

SeekToEnd member function, 357

SetLength member function, 357

SetStatus member function, 357

UnlockRange member function, 357

Write member function, 357

writing a file, 358-361

CFileException, exception class, 438-439
possible return values, 440-441

CFileView class implementation, 367, 451

CFirstApp, 61

CFirstApp object, 69-78

CFirstView, 56

CFirstView::OnDraw( ) function, 56

CFrameWnd, 189

characteristics, of views, 125-126

characters
adding to strings, 111
reading, 179
storing, 180

CheckMenuItem( ) function, 172

CHelloDlg class, 211-214

child windows, 67

children, MDI (multiple document interface), 400-402

cin (keyboard input stream), 12

circles, parameters, 47

class behaviors, defining, 301, 430

class definitions, 35

Class Device Context, see CDC

class inheritance (C++), 34-38

Class Library Reference, 92

Class Wizard, 53, 110
connecting functions, 402
creating new classes, 420
menus, 157-160
user-interface messages, intercepting, 176-177

Class Wizard (Browse menu) command, 108

classes, 14-18
adding data members to, 218
base, 34
CArchive, 387
CDbDoc, implementation, 379
CFile, 356-362
CHelloDlg (dialog), 211-214
CMDIFrameWnd, multiple document application, 400
CPadDoc, 374
creating, 15-18
CScrollView, 409-410
CVBControl, 288
CView, 409

declarations, header files, 69

defining, 35-36

derived, 34

device context, 57-59

exception see exception class

including data, 17

inheritance, 18

listed, 109

overloading functions, 41-45

overriding functions, 38-40

predefined, 57

relation to objects, 15

clearing strings, 140

clicking buttons from code, 276

client area
mouse messages, 134
windows, 4

client-area device context, 112

Close
CArchive class member function, 388
CFile class member function, 356
File menu command, 9
Output window/System menu command, 9

closed figures, drawing, 323

closing files, 360

CMainFrame, 189
class, implementation, 220
object, 61, 78-84

CMDIFrameWnd class, multiple document application, 400

CMemoryException exception class, 439

CNotSupportedException exception class, 439

~CObject (CObject class) member function, 383

CObject (CObject class) member function, 382-383

CObject class
AddHead member function, 386, 389
AddTail member function, 386
AssertValid member function, 383
~CObject member function, 383
CObject member function, 382-383
~CObList member function, 386
CObList member function, 386
DECLARE_DYNAMIC member function, 383
DECLARE_SERIAL member function, 383-385
Dump member function, 383
Find member function, 386
FindIndex member function, 386

GetAt member function, 386

GetCount member function, 386

GetHead member function, 386

GetHeadPosition member function, 386, 392

GetNext member function, 386, 392

GetPrev member function, 386

GetRuntimeClass member function, 383

GetTail member function, 386

GetTailPosition member function, 386

IMPLEMENT_DYNAMIC member function, 383

IMPLEMENT_SERIAL member function, 388

InsertAfter member function, 386

InsertBefore member function, 386

IsEmpty member function, 386

IsKindOf member function, 383

IsSerializable member function, 383

operator delete member function, 383

operator new member function, 383

operator= member function, 383

RemoveAll member function, 386

RemoveAt member function, 386

RemoveHead member function, 386

RemoveTail member function, 386

RUNTIME_CLASS, 383

Serialize member function, 383

SetAt member function, 386

~CObList (CObList class) member function, 386

CObList (CObList class) member function, 386

code (programming)
mouse in, 136-142
with menus, 157-160

codes, error, library functions, 438

Col grid property, 289

COleException exception class, 439

color
bounding, 331
filling figures with, 331-333
selecting paint program, 322-325
values, RGB( ), 315

columns (spreadsheet) labeling, 289

combo box (CB) control messages, 284

combo box notification (CBN) errors, 283

combo boxes, 283-284

commands
  Add Name (Phonebook
    menu), 178
  App Studio (Tools
    menu), 152
  AppWizard (Project
    menu), 53
  Build (Project menu), 9
  Class Wizard (Browse
    menu), 108
  Close
    File menu, 9
    System menu, 9
  Execute (Project menu), 9
  New (Project menu), 8
  New item (File menu), 7
  Open (File menu), 56
  Save As (File menu), 7
  Step Into, 464
  Step Out, 464
  Step Over, 464-465
  Step to Cursor, 464-465
  Tools menu
computer-aided software
  design, see CASE, 53
connecting functions,
  Class Wizard, 402
constructors, 29
  allocating memory with,
    29-34
context, multiple Views
  device, 415-419
context code, 104
controls, 4, 100, 203-204
  buttons, 204
  dialog box,
    reshaping, 211
  main window, 298
  scroll bars, 204

selecting, 100
text boxes, 204
VBX, 288-298
windows notification
  codes, 217
conventions, Windows
  Edit Menu, 477
  keyboard, 474-477
  mouse, 473
  programmers, 471-478
coordinate systems,
  tracking, 408
correcting program errors,
  see debugging
cout (predefined C++
  stream), 11-12
CPadDoc class
  implementation, 374
  interface, 258
CPadView class
  implementation, 249
CPaintView class
  implementation, 340-346
  interface, 309, 318, 346
CPen member
  function, 323
CPhone View, 179
CreateCaret( ) function, 123
CreatePen( ) member
  function (CPen), 323
CreateSolidCaret( )
  function, 123
CreatHatchBrush( ),
  CBrush member
  functions, 328
creating
  brush patterns, 329
  carets, 126
  classes, 15-18, 54

destructors, 30
device context, 112
dialog boxes, 263
documents, 101-103
graphics images, 305
menus, 150-160
  paint programs,
    306-308
new classes, Class
  Wizard, 420
notepad, 245
phonebooks, 177-202
pop-up calculator, 229
programs, 9
shortcut keys, 161
stack classes, 19-22
stacks, 11
views, 103-122
CreatSolidBrush( ), CBrush
  member functions, 328
CResourceException
  exception class, 439
CScrollView class, 409-410
CSpreadView class,
  implementation, 296
CString, 57
  objects, storing data, 86
CTestView class
  implementation, 395
  interface, 394
Ctrl-letter key combina-
  tions, programming
  standards, 474
cursor (mouse), 100
cutting text, 246
CVBControl class, 288
CView class, 409
CWnd class objects,
  carets, 123

D

data
  associating with
    objects, 17
  checking types in C++, 41
  encapsulating, 11
  including classes, 17
  initializing, 30
  private, 17-18
  protected, 17-18
  public, 17
  pushing, 21
  spreadsheet,
    entering, 291
  transferring, data string
    to dig object, 269
  updating
    with member
      functions, 213-216
    with member
      variables, 216
data members, adding to
  classes, 218
  documents, 86
  line_number, MDI
    use, 403
data strings
  adding to list boxes, 271
  transferring to dig
    objects, 269
data_string[ ], storing data
  for display, 403
database program,
  updating to handle files,
  376-381
Datadlg.Cpp, listing 6.1,
  277-278

db.mak program,
  263-283, 480
Dbdoc.Cpp, listing 8.3,
  379-381
Dbugview.Cpp Debugged,
  listing 10.3, 468-470
Dbugview.H Debugged,
  listing 10.2, 467
Dbview.H, listing 6.2,
  278-282
deallocating memory with
  destructors, 31-34
debug build mode, 447
Debug build option, 457
Debug menu, 457
  Breakpoints... item, 459
  Go item, 462
  QuickWatch item, 461
  Stop Debugging
    item, 462
Debug Messages
  window, 446
_DEBUG variable, build
  mode, 448
debug window, 444-448
  numeric values, sending
    to window, 446- 448
  text
    sending to debug
      window, 446
    sending to window,
    448
  TRACE( ) macro, 444-446
debugging programs, 455
  Step commands, 463
DebugWin icon, 445
DECLARE_DYNAMIC
  (CObject class) member
  function, 383

DECLARE_DYNCREATE( )
  macro, 80, 85
DECLARE_SERIAL
  (CObject class) member
  function, 383-385
declaring objects, 21
default focus, 101
DEFAULT_PALETTE stock
  objects, 322
defining
  class behaviors, 301, 430
  member functions, 22,
    36-37
delete keyword, 31
deleting text in
  windows, 327
derived classes, 34
  definitions, 35
design-time errors, 437
designing
  dialog boxes, 203-259
  form views, 299-300
  paint program
    brushes, 322
    pens, 322
  resources, 151
DestroyCaret( )
  function, 123
destructors, 29
  creating, 30
  deallocating memory
    with, 31-34
device context, 112
  CDC class objects, 58
  client area, 112
  creating, 112
    CCLientDC class, 112
  reorienting, 414
device context class, 57-59

device context origin,
  setting to document
  origin, 413
device coordinates, 408
DEVICE_DEFAULT_FONT
  stock objects, 322
dialog box controls
  Grid control, 284
  reshaping, 211
dialog boxes
  adding buttons, 209
  creating, 263
  default focus, 101
  designing, 203-259
  Edit, 9
disabling menu items,
  176-177
displaying carets, 126-127,
  140-141
document data, 406
  strings, 92, 191
  text, 141
    in resized window, 406
DKGRAY_BRUSH stock
  object, 322
dlg.mak file, 208
Dlgwin.Cpp, listing 6.7.,
  301-304
document scrolling
  boundaries, 410
document object, 85
document origin, 414
document size,
  acquiring, 411
document templates,
  71-72
document view,
  updating, 412

documents
  adding data members, 86
  creating, 101-103
  viewing, 67-68
DoModal( ) function
  (CDialog), 214-215
DOS
  differences with
    Windows, 2
  programming, 50
dot operator (.), 12, 16
drawing
  closed figures, 323
  ellipses, 329-353
  in white, 324
  lines, 320-321, 324
  rectangles, 325-329
drawing code, adding, 115
drawing mode, 334
drawing tools, program-
  ming, 311-314
drop-down menus, 149
Dump (CObject class)
  member function, 383
Duplicate (CFile class)
  member function, 356
DWORD (doubleword)
  value, 187

Editodoc.Cpp, listing 9.2.,
  424-426
Editodoc.H, listing 9.1,
  423-424
Editor.Cpp, listing 9.6.,
  430-433
Editor.H, listing 9.5, 430
editor.mak program,
  400, 480
editovw.cpp, 410
Editovw.Cpp, listing 9.4,
  427-429
Editovw.h, listing 9.3., 426
Edsplitf.Cpp, listing 9.8,
  434-435
Edsplitf.H, listing 9.7,
  433-434
Ellipse tool, 329
Ellipse( ) function, 329
ellipses, 150
  drawing, 329-353
  parameters, 47
embedded objects, 103
Empty ( ) function, 140
empty stacks, 23
EN_CHANGE edit notifica-
  tion message, 218
EN_ERRSPACE edit notifi-
  cation message, 218
EN_HSCROLL edit notifi-
  cation message, 218
EN_KILLFOCUS edit
  notification message, 218
EN_MAXTEXT edit notifi-
  cation message, 218
EN_SETFOCUS edit
  notification message, 218
EN_UPDATE edit notifica-
  tion message, 218

E

edit controls, 203
Edit dialog box, 9
Edit menu, programming
  standards, 477
edit notification (EN)
  messages, 217

EN_VSCROLL edit notification message, 218
Enable Tracing item, MFC Trace Options window, 445
Enable( ) function, 177
EnableMenuItem( ) function, 174
enabling menu items, 176-177
encapsulating, 11
END_CATCH macro, 443, 450
error codes, library functions, 438
error conditions, checking for in stacks, 24-25
error handling, Serialize( ) function, 441
errors
    (CBN) combo box notification, 283
    design-time, 437
    logic, *see* bugs
    result (bugs), 437
    run-time, 437
        exception handling, 438-455
event-driven programming, 50-51
exception class
    CArchiveException, 439
        possible return values, 439-440
    CFileException, 438-439
        possible return values, 440-441
    CMemoryException, 439

CNotSupportedException, 439
COleException, 439
CResourceException, 439
OsErrorToException, 439
exception handling, file exceptions, 441-443
    multiple exceptions, 448-455
    run-time errors, 438-455
Execute (Project menu) command, 9
Exit item, 4
exiting
    applications, 4
    Exit item, 4
    programs, 4
expectations, Windows programs, 471
extended flags, 104
extractor operators, 12

F

figures
    drawing, 323
    filling with color, 331-333
    graphics, stretching, 333-353
file access, 363
file errors, *see* exception handling, file exceptions
file exceptions
    exception class, 439
    see also exception handling
file items, grayed, 175

File menu, 4, 150
    Close command, 9
    New item command, 7
    Open command, 56
    Save As command, 7
file-handling capabilities, Visual C++, 355
file.mak program, 480
files
    App Wizard created, 54-56
    choosing, 6
    closing, 360
    opening, 358
    project, 7
    random access files, 363
    reading, 361-373
    resource, 151
    selecting, 6
    sequential, 363
    writing to, 360
fileview.cpp, implementation of the CFileView class, 451
Fileview.Cpp, listing 8.1, 367-370
filling figures with color, 331-333
Find ( ) function, 182
Find (CObList class) member function, 386
Find( ) function, 57
FindIndex (CObList class) member function, 386
First.Cpp and First.H, listing 2.1, 73-78
FirstDoc object, 84-90
Firstdoc.cpp and Firstdoc.h, listing 2.3, 87-90

FirstView object, 90-97
Firstvw.cpp and Firstvw.h, listing 2.4, 92-97
flags, Boolean, setting, 308, 373
floating point values, 43, 233
FloodFill( ) member function, 331
Flush member function
  CArchive class, 388
  CFile class, 357
fopen( ) function
  error code returned, 438
  exception handling, 438
form views, 299
  designing, 299-300
frame windows, 78
framework (programs), 84
freehand drawing program, 316-331
ftoa( ) function, 233
function member
  GetNumProperty( ), 289
  GetStrProperty( ), 289
  SetNumProperty( ), 289
  SetStrProperty( ), 289
function keys, programming standards, Windows, 474
functions, 17, 37
  0 return values, 22
  AppendMenu ( ), 180-182
  associating with objects, 17
  CDC class, 58-59
  defining, 22, 36-37
  dummy, 183-185, 189
  finding MFC classes, 92

from object pointer, 59
member, 17
  adding, 212
  defining, 36-37
need of prototypes, 15
overloading, 41-45
  examples, 42-43, 46-47
  precautions, 43
  stacks, 44-46
  with different parameters, 46-47
overriding, 38-40
  in derived classes, 39
private, 17-19
protected, 17
prototypes
  declaring, 46
public, 17
virtual, 70
Function-Overloading Stack Example, listing 1.3, 44-45

GetDlgItemText( ) function, 232
GetDocSize( ) function, 411-412
GetDocument ( ) function, 140
GetDocument( ) function, 86, 91
GetFile (CArchive class) member function, 388
GetHead (CObList class) member function, 386
GetHeadPosition (CObList class) member function, 386, 392
GetKeyState ( ) function, 106-107
GetLength( ) function, 57, 103
GetNext (CObList class) member function, 386, 392
GetNumProperty( ) member function, 289
GetParent ( ) function, 173
GetPosition (CFile class) member function, 357
GetPrev (CObList class) member function, 386
GetRuntimeClass (CObject class) member function, 383
GetStatus (CFile class) member function, 357
GetStrProperty( ) member function, 289
GetSubMenu( ) function, 176

G

gamma version software, 456
GetActiveDocument( ) function, 190
GetActiveView( ) function, 190
GetAt (CObList class) member function, 386
GetBkColor( ) function, 187
GetCount (CObList class) member function, 386
GetDlgItemInt( ) function, 232

GetTail (CObList class)
member function, 386
GetTailPosition (CObList
class) member function,
386
GetTextExtent( )
function, 128
GetTextMetrics( ) function,
125-126
height of line, 405
Go item (Debug
menu), 462
Graphical User Interfaces,
see GUIs
graphics images
creating, 305
stretching, 333-353
GRAY_BRUSH stock
object, 322
grayed items, 150, 175
graying menu items,
174-176
Grid control, dialog box
control, 284
grid properties, 289
grid.vbx file, 286
grids, 261-304
IDC_GRID1 variable, 288
GUIs (Graphical User
Interfaces), 2

H

handlers, 177
handling files, database
program, 376-381
header files, 22
class declarations in, 69

height of line,
GetTextMetrics( ), 405
hello.mak program, 480
Hellodlg.cpp, listing 5.4,
228-229
Hellodlg.h, listing 5.3, 227
Help menu, Windows
programming
standards, 478
HideCaret( ) function, 123
hiding carets, 128-129,
140-141
HOLLOW_BRUSH stock
object, 322
horizontal scroll bar, 5
Hungarian notation, 51-53

I-J

iconic state, 4
icons
accelerator resource, 163
highlighted caption
text, 100
ID numbers
dummy, 183-185
new menu items,
183-185
IDABORT return value
DoModal function, 215
MessageBox( )
function, 207
IDC_GRID1 variable
control grid, 288
IDCANCEL return value
DoModal function, 215
MessageBox( )
function, 207

IDD_DIALOG1 dialog
box, 286
IDIGNORE return value
DoModal function, 215
MessageBox( )
function, 207
IDM (menu ID) prefix, 152
IDM constants, 157
IDNO return value
DoModal function, 215
MessageBox( )
function, 207
IDOK return value
DoModal function, 215
MessageBox( )
function, 207
IDR (resource ID)
prefix, 152
IDRETRY return value
DoModal function, 215
MessageBox( )
function, 207
IDYES return value
DoModal function, 215
MessageBox( )
function, 207
image, saving/restoring,
paint program, 353
IMPLEMENT_DYNAMIC
(CObject class) member
function, 383
IMPLEMENT_SERIAL
(CObject class) member
function, 388
implementation
CDbDoc class, 379
CEditorDoc class,
424-426
CFileView class, 367

CMainFrame class, 220
CPadDoc class, 374
CPadView class, 249
CPaintView class,
340-346
CSpreadView class, 296
CTestView class, 395
implementation file,
datadlg.cpp, 277
inactive menus, 183
index operator [ ], 57
indexes, adding to arrays,
186-187
inheritance, 18
defining classes, 36
initial conditions (menu
items), 171
initializing
data, 30
objects, in C++, 29-34
stacks, 25, 30-31
variables, 110-111
InitInstance( ) function,
70-72
InsertAfter (CObList class)
member function, 386
InsertBefore (CObList
class) member
function, 386
insertion point see caret
insertor operators, 12
installing programs
supplied with book
(installb.bat), 479
instances, 70
intercepting messages, 189
user-interface messages,
176-177

interface
CDbDoc class, 282
CDbView class, 278
CEditorDoc class, 423
CEditorView class, 426
CPadDoc class, 258
CPaintView class, 309,
318, 346
CTestView class, 394
IsEmpty (CObList class)
member function, 386
IsKindOf (CObject class)
member function, 383
IsLoading (CArchive class)
member function, 388
IsSerializable (CObject
class) member
function, 383
IsStoring (CArchive class)
member function, 388

K

key conventions, see
keyboard shortcuts
key state, 104
key-reading program
(Key.Mak, on the disk),
listing 3.1, 115-122
key-reading program with
Caret, listing 3.2, 129-134
keyboard
designing applications,
101
Windows, 100-101
keyboard actions, pro-
gramming standards,
473-477

keyboard input streams,
cin, 12
keyboard port, 105
keyboard shortcuts,
101, 104
see also accelerator keys;
shortcut keys
keystroke messages, 103
WM_CHAR, 103
WM_KEYDOWN, 103
WM_KEYUP, 103
WM_SYSKEYDOWN, 103
WM_SYSKEYUP, 103
keystrokes, 105
noprinting, 107
scan code, 105
system, 104
typematic, 105
keywords
protected, 79-80
this, 112-122

L

labeling (spreadsheet)
cells, 288
columns, 289
rows, 290
LB_ADDSTRING list box
message, 270
LB_DELETESTRING list
box message, 270
LB_DIR list box message,
270
LB_FINDSTRING list box
message, 271
LB_GETCOUNT list box
message, 270

LB_GETCURSEL list box message, 270

LB_GETHORIZONTALEXTENT list box message, 271

LB_GETITEMDATA list box message, 271

LB_GETITEMRECT list box message, 271

LB_GETSEL list box message, 270

LB_GETSELCOUNT list box message, 271

LB_GETSELITEMS list box message, 271

LB_GETTEXT list box message, 270

LB_GETTEXTLEN list box message, 270

LB_GETTOPINDEX list box message, 271

LB_INSERTSTRING list box message, 270

LB_RESETCONTENT list box message, 270

LB_SELECTSTRING list box message, 270

LB_SELITEMRANGE list box message, 271

LB_SETCOLUMNWIDTH list box message, 271

LB_SETCURSEL list box message, 270

LB_SETHORIZONTALEXTENT list box message, 271

LB_SETITEMDATA list box message, 271

LB_SETSEL list box message, 270

LB_SETTABSTOPS list box message, 271

LB_SETTOPINDEX list box message, 271

LBN_DBLCLK edit notification message, 218

LBN_DBLCLK list box notification code, 265

LBN_ERRSPACE edit notification message, 218

LBN_ERRSPACE list box notification code, 265

LBN_KILLFOCUS edit notification message, 218

LBN_KILLFOCUS list box notification code, 265

LBN_SELCANCEL list box notification code, 265

LBN_SELCHANGE edit notification message, 218

LBN_SELCHANGE list box notification code, 265

LBN_SETFOCUS edit notification message, 218

LBN_SETFOCUS list box notification code, 265

Left( ) function, 57, 182

libraries, Microsoft Foundation Class (MFC), 57

library functions, error codes, 438

line_number data member, MDI use, 403

lines, drawing
   paint program, 320-321
   solid, 324

LineTo( ) function, 318

list box control messages, 270

list box notification (LBN) codes, 265

list boxes, 204, 261-304
   database example, 262-263

listings
   1.1. The Stack Object, 28-29
   1.2. Stack with Constructor and Destructor, 32-33
   1.3. Function-Overloading Stack Example, 44-45
   2.1. First.Cpp and First.H, 73-78
   2.2. Mainfrm.Cpp and Mainfrm.h, 80-84
   2.3. Firstdoc.cpp and Firstdoc.h, 87-90
   2.4. Firstvw.cpp and Firstvw.h, 92-97
   3.1. A Key-reading Program (Key.Mak, on the disk), 115-122
   3.2. Key-reading Program With Caret, 129-134
   3.3. Mouse-enabled CCaretView Class, 142-147
   4.1. Menuview.cpp, 165-168
   4.2. Menu Section of Menu.rc, 168-171
   4.3. Phonevw.pp, 192-196
   4.4. Mainframe.cpp, 196-199

4.5. Phonedoc.cpp, 199-201

5.1. Mainfrm.cpp, 220-223

5.2. Pertinent Sections of Dlg.rc, 223-227

5.3. Hellodlg.h, 227

5.4. Hellodlg.cpp, 228-229

5.5. Calcview.cpp, 234-237

5.6. Calcdlg.cpp, 237-238

5.7. Calc.rc, 238-243

5.8. Padview.cpp, 249-252

5.9. Pertinent Sections of Pad.rc, 252-256

5.10. Paddlg.cpp, 257-258

5.11. Paddoc.h, 258-259

6.1. Datadlg.Cpp, 277-278

6.2. Dbview.H, 278-282

6.3. Applicable Section of Dbdoc.H, 282-283

6.4. Spreaddl.H, 294

6.5. Spreaddl.Cpp, 294-296

6.6. Spreavw.Cpp, 296-298

6.7. Dlgwin.Cpp, 301-304

7.1. Paintvw.Cpp, 340-346

7.2. Paintvw.H, 346-347

7.3. Paint.Rc, 348-353

8.1. Fileview.Cpp, 367-370

8.2. Paddoc.Cpp, 374-376

8.3 Dbdoc.Cpp, 379

8.4. Testview.H, 394-395

8.5. Testview.Cpp, 395-398

9.1. Editodoc.H, 423-424

9.2. Editodoc.Cpp, 424

9.3. Editovw.h, 426

9.4. Editovw.Cpp, 427-429

9.5. Editor.H, 430

9.6. Editor.Cpp, 430-433

9.7. Edsplitf.H, 433-434

9.8. Edsplitf.Cpp, 434-435

10.1. Fileview.Cpp with Exception Handling, 451-455

10.2. Dbugview.H Debugged, 467

10.3. Dbugview.Cpp Debugged, 468-470

LockRange (CFile class) member function, 357

logic errors, *see* bugs

logical coordinate, 414

logical coordinates, 408

looping, stacks, 25-26

LTGRAY_BRUSH stock object, 322

M

m_cause data member exception handling, file exceptions, 443-444 possible return values, 439-440

m_GridControl member variable, 288

macros
   AND_CATCH( ), 449
   CATCH, 437-439
   DECLARE_DYNCREATE( ), 80, 85
   END_CATCH, 443, 450
   THROW_LAST( ), 450
   TRACE( ), 444-446
   TRY, 437-438

main menu, 149

main window
   accessing, 173
   controls, 298
   menu object, accessing, 173-174

Mainframe.cpp, listing 4.4, 196-199

Mainfrm.cpp, 5.1 listing, 220-223

Mainfrm.Cpp and Mainfrm.h, listing 2.2, 80-84

malloc ( ), 30

Mapping Mode options, 412

Maximize box, 4

maximizing windows, 4

MB_ABORTRETRYIGNORE message box types, 206

MB_APPLMODAL message box types, 205-206

MB_DEFBUTTON1 message box types, 206

MB_DEFBUTTON2 message box types, 206

MB_DEFBUTTON3 message box types, 206

MB_ICONASTERISK message box types, 206

MB_ICONEXCLAMATION message box types, 206
MB_ICONHAND message box types, 206
MB_ICONINFORMATION message box types, 207
MB_ICONQUESTION message box types, 207
MB_ICONSTOP message box types, 207
MB_OK message box types, 207
MB_OKCANCEL message box types, 207
MB_RETRYCANCEL message box types, 207
MB_SYSTEMMODAL message box types, 205
MB_SYSTEMMODEL message box types, 207
MB_YESNO message box types, 207
MB_YESNOCANCEL message box types, 207
MDI *see* Multiple Document Interface
MDI child windows, adding scroll bars, 407-415
MDI children *see* children, MDI
member functions
    adding, 212
    CArchive class, 388
    CBrush
    CFile class, 356
    CObject class, 382-385
    CObList class, 386-389
    CPen, 323

FloodFill( ), 331
GetLength ( ), 103
    updating data with, 213
member variables, data, updating with, 216
memory,
    allocating, with constructors, 29-34
    deallocating, with destructors, 31-34
Memory exceptions, exception class, 439
menu bars, 4, 149
    file items, grayed, 175
Menu Item Properties box, 171
menu items
    adding, 267
        window, 293
    enabling, 183-185
    paint program tools, 311
Menu Items Properties box, 153
Menu Section of Menu.rc, listing 4.2, 168-171
menu system,
    opening, 152
menus
    adding items, 177-202
    adding shortcut keys, 160
    check marks, adding, 172
    check marks in, 150
    checking items, 171-174
    connecting accelerator keys, 163-165
    conventions, 149-150
    creating, 150-160

Debug, 457, 462
drop-down, 149
dummy, 183-184
grayed items, 150, 174-176
inactive, 183
initial conditions, 171
item status, enabling/disabling, 176-177
main menu, 149
making objects of, 176
menu bar, 149
new items
    connecting to programs, 188-189
    ID numbers, 183-185
opening, 154
paint programs, creating, 306-308
pop-up, 149
saving, 154
separator lines, 171
setting conditions, 171
submenus, 149
with code, 157-160
Menuview.cpp, listing 4.1, 165-168
message box (MB) types, 205-206
message boxes, 204
MessageBox( ) function, return values, 207
messages
    combo box (CB) control, 284
    edit notification (EN), 217
    intercepting, 189
    keystroke, 103

list box control, 270
mouse
  client area, 134
  nonclient area, 135
Windows, 61-63
MF_BYCOMMAND nFlag,
  172
MF_BYPOSITION nFlag,
  172
MF_CHECKED, 181
MF_CHECKED nFlag, 173
MF_DISABLED, 181
MF_DISABLED nFlag, 175
MF_ENABLED, 181
MF_ENABLED nFlag, 175
MF_GRAYED, 181
MF_GRAYED nFlag, 175
MF_MENUBARBREAK, 181
MF_MENUBREAK, 182
MF_OWNERDRAW, 182
MF_POPUP, 182
MF_SEPARATOR, 182
MF_STRING, 182
MF_UNCHECKED, 182
MF_UNCHECKED nFlag,
  173
MFC classes, finding
  functions, 92
MFC CString object, 102
MFC file handling,
  356-357
MFC objects, serialization,
  381
MFC Trace Options
  application, Visual C++
  program group, 445
MFC Trace Options
  window, Enable Tracing
  item, 445

Microsoft Foundation
  Class (MFC) library, 57
Microsoft Windows, *see*
  Windows
Mid( ) function, 57
minimizing windows, 4
MK_CONTROL value, 139
MK_LBUTTON value, 139
MK_MBUTTON value, 139
MK_RBUTTON value, 139
MK_SHIFT value, 139
MM_HIENGLISH mapping
  mode, 412
MM_HIMETRIC mapping
  mode, 412
MM_LOENGLISH mapping
  mode, 412
MM_LOMETRIC mapping
  mode, 412
MM_TEXT mapping
  mode, 412
MM_TWIPS mapping
  mode, 412
modes, 51
  drawing, 334
  mapping, 412
modified flag, setting, 373
Modify Variable dialog box
  (QuickWatch window),
  461
modularity (C++), 10
Most Recently Used (MRU)
  list of files, 373
mouse, 134-147
  actions, 134-147
  cursor, 100
  in code, 136-142
  key codes, 105-107

messages
  client area, 134
  nonclient area, 135
  out of windows, 135
mouse action program-
  ming standards,
  Windows, 473
Mouse-enabled
  CCaretView Class, listing
  3.3, 142-147
MoveTo( ) function, 318
MRU, *see* Most Recently
  Used
msg.mak file, 205
Multiple Document
  Interface (MDI)
  applications, 400-407
  displaying document
  data, 406
Multiple Document
  Interface check box,
  101, 151
multiple documents,
  399-435
multiple meanings,
  operators, 12
multiple views, 399-435
multiple Viewsdevice
  context, 415-419
multiple-window
  editor, 419

N

naming
  accelerator keys,
  precautions, 162
  shortcut keys, 161

New (Project menu)
command, 8
new classes, creating, 420
New item (File menu)
command, 7
new keyword (C++), 30
New Project window, 8
Project Type box, 8
nFlags parameter, 139,
172-173
nonclient area (windows),
5
mouse messages, 135
nonprinting keystrokes,
107
notepad
creating, 245
example, 243-259
updating to handle files,
370-376
notification codes, win-
dows controls, 217
nRepCnt parameter, 105
virtual key code, 105
NULL_BRUSH stock object,
322
numeric values, sending to
the debug window,
446-448

O

Object IDs box, class
listings, 109
object pointers, accessing
functions from, 59
object-oriented program-
ming, 51

objects, 10-18
associating data with, 17
associating functions
with, 17
CFirstApp, 61, 69-78
CMainFrame, 61, 78-84
communicating be-
tween, 85
constructors, 29
CString, storing data, 86
CWnd class, carets, 123
declaring, 21
destructors, 29
device context, 112
CDC class, 58
embedded, 103
FirstDoc, 84-90
FirstView, 90-97
initializing in C++, 29-34
menus as, 176
MFC, serialization, 381
MFC CString, 102
private functions, 14
public functions, 14
relation to classes, 15
returning pointers to,
190-191
stacking, 18-29
stacks, 11
stock, 322
Objects IDs box, 158
OEM scan field, 105
OEM_FIXED_FONT stock
objects, 322
offset, 366
OLE exceptions, exception
class, 439
OnAddname ( ) function,
179

OnChar ( ) function, 107
OnClickedButton1( )
function, 232
OnCommand ( ) function,
189
OnDraw( ) function, 59,
68, 92, 457-458
displaying text in resized
window, 406
one-line comments, //
symbol, 12
OnFileNew( ) function, 72
OnFileRead( ) function,
361
writing a file, 358
OnFileWrite( ) function,
358
OnKeyDown ( ) functions,
104
OnKeyUp ( ) function, 104
OnMessage functions,
64-65
OnMouseMove( ) function,
91, 316
OnPaint( ) function, 63
OnUpdate( ) function, 412
Onxxx ( ) function, 183
Open (CFile class) member
function, 357
options, 359
Open (File menu) com-
mand, 56
opening
files, 358-360
menu system, 152
menus, 154
operator, overloading, 12
operator << (CArchive
class) member function,
388

operator >> (CArchive class) member function, 388

operator delete (CObject class) member function, 383

operator new (CObject class) member function, 383

operator= (CObject class) member function, 383

operators
+ (plus key), 111
::., 22
<< (left-shift), 11
versus printf ( ), 12
>> (right shift), 12
?:, 12
dot operator (.), 12
extractors, 12
insertor, 12
multiple meanings, 12
overloading, 12, 111-112
restrictions, 12

options
check marks, 150
Debug build, 457

Options dialog box (App Wizard), 54

original equipment manufacturers, *see* OEM

origins
context to document, 413
new, 138
setting to mouse location, 140

OsErrorToException, exception class, 439

Output window, 9

overloading, operators, 111-112

overloading, (functions), 41-45
examples, 42-43, 46-47
precautions, 43
stacks, 44-46
with different parameters, 46-47

overriding (functions), 38-40
in derived classes, 39

P

pad.mak file, 243

Paddlg.cpp, listing 5.10, 257-258

Paddoc.Cpp, listing 8.2, 374-376

Paddoc.h, listing 5.11, 258-259

Padview.cpp, listing 5.8, 249-252

paint program
brushes, designing, 322
colors, selecting, 322-325
creating menus, 306-308
freehand drawing, 316-331
images
restoring, 353
saving, 353
lines, drawing, 320-321
pens
designing, 322
selecting, 322-325

rectangles, drawing, 325-329
writing, 308-353

paint program tools, menu items, 311

paint.mak program (supplied with book), 481

Paint.Rc, listing 7.3, 348-353

paint.rc files, 306

Paintvw.Cpp, listing 7.1, 340-346

Paintvw.H, listing 7.2, 346-347

paintvw.h object, 309

parameters, 172-173
AppendMenu ( ) function, 181-182
for circles, 47
for ellipses, 47
multiple numbers, overloading functions, 46-47
nFlags, 139
nRepCnt, 105
point, 140
TextOut( ), 60

pasting text, 246

pens, paint program
designing, 322
selecting, 322-325
styles, 323

Pertinent Sections of Dlg.rc, listing 5.2, 223-227

Pertinent Sections of Pad.rc, listing 5.9, 252-256

philosophy, Windows
    programming, 471-472
Phonebook menu, Add
    'Name command, 178
phonebooks
    adding names, 180
    appending, 178
    creating, 177-202
    selecting names, 178
Phonedoc.cpp, listing 4.5,
    199-201
Phonevw.pp, listing 4.3,
    192-196
pixels, setting in windows,
    314-316
Point drawing tool,
    selecting, 310
point parameter, 140
pointers, returning to
    objects, 190-191
pop-up
    calculator, creating, 229
    menus, 149
popping, see retrieving
ports, keyboard, 105
predefined classes, CString,
    57
prefixes
    IDM (menu ID), 152
    IDR (resource ID), 152
printf ( ), 12
    tab code, 162
printing
    ASCII codes, 41-42
    screen, 11-12
    string objects in win-
        dows, 57
    strings, 41-42
        to windows, 190-191

TextOut ( ) function, 113
private data, 14
private functions, 14
program logic errors, see
    bugs
programming
    CASE, 53
    CFirstApp object, 69-78
    classes, 69
    CMainFrame object,
        78-84
    conventions, Windows,
        471-478
    DOS, 50
    drawing tools, 311-314
    event-driven, 50-51
    FirstDoc object, 84-90
    FirstView object, 90-97
    in Windows, 50-53
    object-oriented, 51
    On events, 51
    philosophy, Windows,
        471-472
    skeleton code, 53
    standards, Windows
        Edit menu, 477
        File menu, 477-478
        Help menu, 478
        keyboard actions,
            473-477
        mouse action, 473
    view classes, 56
    Windows, 50
    with Visual C++
        in Windows, 5-6
programs
    adding accelerator keys,
        162
    as objects, 13-18

as projects, 7
calc.mak, 479
caret.mak, 479
connecting menu items,
    188-189
creating, 9
db.mak, 480
debugging, 455-470
drawing code in, 115
editor.mak, 480
ending, 9
exiting, 4
file.mak, 480
framework, 84
hello.mak, 480
instances, 70-73
key-reading, 115-122
Key-reading Program
    With Caret, 129-134
menus, creating, 150-160
mouse, 136-142
    clicking, 138-139
    cursor movement,
        136-138
paint, 305
    freehand drawing,
        316-331
    writing, 308-353,
        309-353
paint.mak, 481
provided with this book,
    479-481
running, 9
    multiple copies
        (instances), 70
spread.mak, 481
testing procedures,
    456- 457
    checking bounds

values, 456-457
setting breakpoints, 459-463
see also applications
project files, 7
Project menu
  AppWizard command, 53
  Build command, 9
  Execute command, 9
  New command, 8
Project Type box, 8
projects, 7
  SDI, 179
protected keywords, 79-80
prototypes, 15
  declaring functions, 46
PS_DASH pen style, 323
PS_DASHDOT pen styles, 323
PS_DOT pen styles, 323
PS_INSIDEFRAME pen styles, 323
PS_NULL pen styles, 323
PS_SOLID pen style, 323
public data, 14
public functions, 14
push ( ) function, 112
pushing
  data, 21
  values, 19-20

Q

QuickWatch (Debug menu), 461
QuickWatch window, 461
QuickWin Application, 8

R

R2_BLACK windows drawing mode, 334
R2_COPYPEN windows drawing mode, 335
R2_MASKNOTPEN windows drawing mode, 334
R2_MASKPEN windows drawing mode, 334
R2_MASKPENNOT windows drawing mode, 334
R2_MERGENOTPEN windows drawing mode, 334
R2_MERGEPEN windows drawing mode, 335
R2_MERGEPENNOT windows drawing mode, 335
R2_NOP windows drawing mode, 334
R2_NOT windows drawing mode, 334
R2_NOTMASKPEN windows drawing mode, 334
R2_NOTMERGEPEN windows drawing mode, 334
R2_NOTXORPEN windows drawing mode, 334
R2_WHITE windows drawing mode, 335
R2_XORPEN windows drawing mode, 334
random access files, 363
Read member function
  CArchive class, 388
  CFile class, 357, 361

reading
  characters, 179
  files, 361-373
  floating point numbers from text boxes, 233
  records, 364
  values, 12
    text boxes, 232
ReadObject (CArchive class) member function, 388
records
  reading, 364
  writing, 364
Rectangle tool, 325
rectangles, drawing, paint program, 325-329
redrawn windows, 51
release build mode, 447
Remove (CFile class) member function, 357
RemoveAll (CObList class) member function, 386
RemoveAt (CObList class) member function, 386
RemoveHead (CObList class) member function, 386
RemoveTail (CObList class) member function, 386
Rename (CFile class) member function, 357
reorienting device context, 414
repeat count, 105
reshaping dialog box controls, 211
Resource exceptions, exception class, 439

resource files, 151
resources
    designing, 151
    see also accelerator keys;
        dialog boxes; icons;
        menus
Resources box, 152
restoring paint program
    images, 353
result errors (bugs), 437
retrieving values, 19, 21-22
    with loops, 26-27
return values,
    MessageBox( ) functions,
    207
RGB( ) color values, 315
Right( ) function, 57
Row grid property, 289
rows, spreadsheet, label-
    ing, 290
run-time errors, 437
    exception handling,
        438-455
running programs, 9
RUNTIME_CLASS (CObject
    class) member function,
    383

S

Save As (File menu)
    command, 7
saving
    accelerator keys, 165
    images, paint program,
        353
    new menus, 154
    shortcut keys, 161

scan code, 105
screens, printing, 11-12
screen-area coordinates,
    135
scroll bars, 203-204
    MDI child windows,
        adding, 407-415
    vertical, 5
scrolling boundaries,
    documents, 410
SDI (Single Document
    Interface), 179
SDI application, db.mak,
    263-283
Seek (CFile class) member
    function, 357
Seek( ) member function,
    363
SeekToBegin (CFile class)
    member function, 357
SeekToEnd (CFile class)
    member function, 357
selecting
    colors, paint program,
        322-325
    files, 6
    pens, paint program,
        322-325
    Point drawing tool, 310
SelectObject( ) function,
    324
SendDlgItemMessage( )
    function, 272, 283
sending numbers or text to
    the debug window,
    446-448
Separator check box, 171
separator lines, 171
sequential files, 363

serialization, 355, 370
    customizing, 381-398
Serialize (CObject class)
    member function, 383
Serialize( ) function,
    370-372, 406
    error handling, 441
Service not supported,
    exception class, 439
SetAt (CObList class)
    member function, 386
SetCaretPos( ) function,
    123
SetDlgItemInt( ) function,
    232
SetDlgItemText( ) func-
    tion, 232
SetFlagsFalse( ) function,
    311
SetLength (CFile class)
    member function, 357
SetNumProperty( ) mem-
    ber function, 289
SetPixel( ) function, 317
SetStatus (CFile class)
    member function, 357
SetStrProperty( ) member
    function, 289
SetTextColor( ) function,
    187
setting
    Boolean flags, 308
    breakpoints, testing
        procedures, 459, 462
    modified flag, 373
    new origins, 138
    pixels in windows,
        314-316
    values in text boxes, 232

shortcut keys
  adding to menu, 160
  creating, 161
  custom, 160-162
  naming, 161
  precautions, 161
  saving, 161
ShowCaret( ) function, 123
Single Document Interface, (SDI), 179 *See* SDI
sizing handles, 211
skeleton code, writing, 53
solid lines, drawing, 324
splitter windows, 400, 420
  adding to editor application, 419, 422
spread.mak program (supplied with book), 481
Spreadl.cpp, listing 6.5, 294-296
Spreaddl.H, listing 6.4, 294
spreadsheets
  cells
    labeling, 288
    values, adding, 291-292
  columns, labeling, 289
  data, entering, 291
  example, 284-288
  rows, labeling, 290
Spreavw.Cpp, listing 6.6., 296-298
stack classes, creating, 19-22
stack pointer, 18
  decrementing, 23-24
Stack Object, listing 1.1, 28-29
Stack with Constructor

and Destructor, listing 1.2, 32-33
stacking objects, 18-29
stacks, 11, 18-29
  arrays in, 30-31
  creating, 11
  decrementing stack pointer, 23-24
  empty, 23
  error conditions, checking for, 24-25
  function overloading, 44-46
  initializing, 25, 30-31
  looping, 25-26
  operations, 20
  pushing values, 19
  retrieveing values, 19
standards, programming
  Edit menu, 477
  File menu, 477-478
  Help menu, 478
  keyboard actions, 473-477
  mouse action, 473
Step commands, debugging programs, 463
Step Into command, 464
Step Out commands, 464
Step Over command, 464-465
Step to Cursor commands, 464-465
stock brushes, 327
  See Stock objects
stock objects (device context), 322
Stop Debugging item (Debug menu), 462

storing
  characters, 180
  data, 186-187
    CString objects, 86
    for display, data_string[ ], 403
  number of lines in the document, 406
streams, predefined, 11-13
  applying, 11
  cin, 12
  cout, 11-12
stretching graphics figures, 333-353
string objects, printing in windows, 57
strings
  adding characters, 111
  clearing, 140
  displaying, 92, 191
  printing to windows, 190-191
submenus, 149
system keystrokes, 104
System menu (Output window), Close command, 9
system menu box, 4
SYSTEM_FIXED_FONT stock objects, 322
SYSTEM_FONT stock objects, 322

T

tab codes
  \t, 162
  printf ( ), 162

Tab key
  navigating windows with, 100
  programming standards, Windows, 474
tab order (windows), 100
templates, document, 71-72
testing procedures, programs, 456-457
  checking bounds values, 456-457
  setting break points, 459-463
Testview.Cpp, listing 8.5, 395-398
Testview.H, listing 8.4., 394-395
text
  adding to windows, 66
  cutting, 246
  deleting from windows, 327
  displaying, 141
  erasing, Windows, 187
  pasting, 246
  restoring, Windows, 187-188
  sending to the debug window, 446-448
text boxes, 203
  controls, 204
  reading values, 232
  setting values in, 232
Text grid property, 289
TEXTMETRIC structure, height of one line, 405
TextOut ( ) function, 57, 66, 92, 113, 464
  parameters, 60

this keyword, 112-122
  passing functions, 113
THROW_LAST( ) macro, 450
thumbs, 5
tildes (~), 30
title bar, 4
toolbar, 208
tools
  Ellipses, 329
  Rectangle, 325
Tools menu, App Studio command, 152
TRACE( ) macro, debug window, 444-446
tracking coordinate systems, 408
transferring data from data string to dig object, 269
transition state, 104
trappable error, 437
TRY macro, 437-438
typematic keystrokes, 105

U

Unlock (CFile class) member function, 357
update messages, user-interface, 176-177
UpdateAllViews ( ) function, 114-115, 416-419
updating
  data
    with member functions, 213-216
    with member variables, 216

document view, 412
notepad to handle files, 370-376
user-interface messages
  intercepting, 176-177
  location, 176

V

values
  DWORD (doubleword), 187
  for IDM constants, 157
  in text boxes
    reading, 232
    setting, 232
  pushing, 20
    onto stacks, 19
  reading, 12
  retrieving, 19, 21-22
    with loops, 26-27
variables
  declaring, 15-18
  initializing, 110-111
  Windows, Hungarian notation, 51
VBX controls, 288-298
vertical scroll bar, 5
view classes, 56
  adding carets to, 124
  CFirstView, 56
view object, 85
viewing documents, 67-68
views
  creating, 103-122
  determining characteristics, 125-126
virtual functions, 70

virtual key codes, 105-106
  mouse, 105-107
virtual memory capacity, 3
Visual C++
  sample programs, 6-9
  Workbench, 6
Visual C++ program group,
  MFC Trace Options
  application, 445

W-Z

white, drawing in, 324
WHITE_BRUSH stock
  object, 322
Windows
  386-enhanced mode, 3
  caret, 100
  controls, 100
  cursor, 100
  differences with DOS, 2
  drawing modes, 334
  erasing text, 187
  extended memory, 3
  File Manager, 3
  handling file capabilities,
    356
  history of, 2-3
  Hungarian notation,
    51-53
  keyboard shortcuts
    accelerator keys,
      162-165
    shortcut keys, 160-162
  keyboard with, 100-101
  messages, 61-63
  mouse messages, 134
  Program Manager, 3

programming, 50-53
  conventions, 471-478
  philosophy, 471-472
  with Visual C++, 5-6
programming interface,
  surface area, 49
restoring text, 187-188
Task List, 3
version 1.01, 2
version 2.0, 3
version 3.0, 3
version 3.1, 3
virtual memory capacity,
  3
windows, 3-5
  system menu box, 4
without mouse, 6
windows, 3-5
  active, 100
  adding
    carets, 122-134
    menu items, 293
    text, 66
  backround color, 187
    restoring, 187-188
  caption bar, highlighted,
    100
  child, 67
  client area, 4
  controls, 4
  debug, 444-448
  Debug Messages, 446
  deleting text, 327
  File menu, 4
  focus, 100
  frame, 78
    highlighted, 100
  horizontal scroll bar, 5
  Maximize box, 4

maximizing, 4
menu bar, 4
Minimize box, 4
minimizing, 4
mouse, 135
navigating with Tab key,
  100
New Project, 8
nonclient area, 5
Output, 9
printing string objects
  in, 57
redrawn, 51
setting pixels, 314-316
system menu box, 4
tab order, 100
title bar, 4
vertical scroll bar, 5
windows controls, notification codes, 217
Windows developer
  programming philoso-
  phy, 471
Windows MessageBox( )
  function, 204-207
WinMain( ) function, 63
wizards, 53
WM_CHAR message, 103,
  402
WM_COMMAND message,
  158
WM_CREATE message, 157
WM_KEYDOWN message,
  103
WM_KEYUP message, 103
WM_LBUTTONDBLCLK
  message, 134
WM_LBUTTONDOWN
  message, 134-136

WM_LBUTTONUP mes-
sage, 134-136
WM_MBUTTONDBLCLK
message, 134
WM_MBUTTONDOWN
message, 134
WM_MBUTTONUP
message, 134
WM_MOUSEMOVE
message, 134, 402
WM_PAINT message, 419
WM_RBUTTONDBLCLK
message, 134
WM_RBUTTONDOWN
message, 134-136
WM_RBUTTONUP mes-
sage, 134-136
WM_SYSKEYDOWN
message, 103
WM_SYSKEYUP message,
103
Workbench, 6
Write member function
CArchive class, 388
CFile class, 357
WriteObject (CArchive
class) member function,
388
writing
files, CFile class example,
358-361
paint program, 308-353
records, 364
to files, 360

DISK REPLACEMENT ORDER FORM

In the event that the disk bound into this book is defective, Prentice Hall Computer Publishing will send you a replacement disk free of charge.

Please fill out the information below and return this card to the address listed below with your original disk. Please print clearly.

BOOK TITLE _____ ISBN _____

NAME _____ PHONE _____

COMPANY _____ TITLE _____

ADDRESS _____

CITY _____ STATE _____ ZIP _____

Prentice Hall Computer Publishing, 11711 North College Avenue, Carmel IN 46032.
ATTN: Customer Service Department

LIMITED WARRANTY REGISTRATION CARD

In order to preserve your rights as provided in the limited warranty, this card must be on file with PHCP within thirty days of purchase.

Please fill in the information requested:

BOOK TITLE _____ ISBN _____

NAME _____ PHONE NUMBER ( ) _____

ADDRESS _____

CITY _____ STATE _____ ZIP _____

COMPUTER BRAND & MODEL _____ DOS VERSION _____ MEMORY _____ K

Where did you purchase this product?

DEALER NAME _____ PHONE NUMBER ( ) _____

ADDRESS _____

CITY _____ STATE _____ ZIP _____

PURCHASE DATE _____ PURCHASE PRICE _____

How did you learn about this product? (Check as many as applicable.)

STORE DISPLAY ____ SALESPERSON _____ MAGAZINE ARTICLE _____ ADVERTISEMENT _____ OTHER (Please explain) _____

How long have you owned or used this computer?

LESS THAN 30 DAYS _____ LESS THAN 6 MONTHS _____ 6 MONTHS TO A YEAR _____ OVER 1 YEAR _____

What is your primary use for the computer?

BUSINESS _____ PERSONAL _____ EDUCATION _____ OTHER (Please explain) _____

Where is your computer located?

HOME _____ OFFICE _____ SCHOOL _____ OTHER (Please explain) _____

If your computer uses 5 1/4-inch disks...

Although most personal computers use 3 1/2-inch disks to store information, some computers use 5 1/4-inch disks for information storage. If your computer uses 5 1/4-inch disks, you can return this form to Brady to obtain a 5 1/4-inch disk to use with this book. Fill out the remainder of this form and mail to:

Visual C++ Programming

 Disk Exchange
Brady
11711 N. College Ave., Suite 140
Carmel, IN 46032

We will then send you, free of charge, the 5 1/4-inch version of the book software.

Name _____   Phone _____

Company _____   Title _____

Address _____

City _____   State _____   ZIP _____